The Ultimate Adventure Sourcebook

THE COMPLETE RESOURCE FOR ADVENTURE SPORTS AND TRAVEL

DATE DUE

PRINTED IN U.S.A.

PAUL MCMENAMIN: AUTHOR, EDITOR, PHOTO DIRECTOR
RONNA NELSON: DESIGNER, PHOTO EDITOR
SUSAN WATROUS: ASSOCIATE EDITOR
COORDINATING EDITOR: LARRY LARSON

DESIGN ASSISTANTS: JILL FINCH, DEKA MOORE, MASON YAFFEE
ASSISTANT PROOFREADER: ALEXANDRA HALSEY
PRODUCTION ASSISTANT: JAMES MCMENAMIN
RESEARCHERS: DEVON BATES, SUSAN MCINTIRE, JAMES MCMENAMIN
TYPOGRAPHY: INDIAN ROCK IMAGESETTING
COVER DESIGN: KAREN E. SMITH
GRAPHICS COORDINATOR: MICHAEL J. WALSH

Turner Publishing, Inc.

Adventure is a human need. We recognize it as the daring thing which makes us bigger than our usual selves. Adventure is the curiosity of man to see the other side of the mountain, the impulse in him that makes him break his bonds with lesser things and frees him for greater possibility.
-Walt Burnett, *The Spirit of Adventure*

CONTENTS

PHOTO: Humpback whale, southeast Alaska/ART WOLFE

Introduction

Granite Falls Rapid, Grand Canyon/WILEY/WALES, PROFILES WEST

Tomorrow's life is too late. Live today.
-Martial

▼

I F YOU'VE EVER TRIED TO ORGANIZE AN ADVENTURE TRIP to a remote destination, or even just tried to find a good ski resort in a foreign country, you know how difficult it can be to get the information you need quickly and efficiently. You can spend days hunting down the vital phone numbers or addresses you need. And, when you do run across a list of resorts or tour companies, there's usually no easy way to pick the one which is best for you. Most magazines aren't particularly helpful in this regard, because they're reluctant to recommend one potential advertiser over another.

This is where the Ultimate Adventure Sourcebook comes into play. This resource will tell you the best places to go, the best trips to take, and the best outfitters or guides to employ. When you can organize an adventure by yourself, we encourage you to do so. When it makes sense to have a fully outfitted trip, we give you a list of the top-ranked outfitters, and let you know how much you'll have to pay, and what kind of services you can expect.

We hope you use this book frequently, and that it will be the first resource you consult when planning an adventure trip in North America or abroad. If you like the book, let your friends know. With your active support, the next edition of the Ultimate Adventure Sourcebook will be even bigger and better.

Guide to Using The Adventure Sourcebook

Unlike some other adventure guides, this book is organized by activity, not location. We've learned through experience that when you're interested in a particular adventure sport, you want to get the pertinent facts quickly, and not have to wade through unrelated topics. You'll find that our service listings are quite comprehensive compared to other vacation guides. We give you more because our listings are not limited to trips offered by advertisers or commercial sponsors. We are free to choose the finest adventures offered by the best outfitters, tour companies and resorts worldwide. And, when we think you don't need the services of a commercial tour operator at all, we'll tell you.

Outfitter/Resort Ratings

No company bought its way into this book. We accept no outfitter or resort advertising, and charge no listing fees. We have included only those operators with solid reputations and quality activities. Often, however, you will find a number of outfitters going to the same place, or offering similar services. To help you select the best operations, we rate outfitters ★ to ★★★★★, based on their expertise and experience, the overall quality of their trips, the service they give, the level of customer satisfaction, and to some extent the variety of trips they offer, although a small outfitter can be, and often is, rated higher than a big company.

All outfitters in this book are solid companies offering good vacation value for the money. This earns a minimum of one star. Two stars denotes a very good outfitter, whose trips are much better than average. A three-star outfitter is superior, offering highly recommended trips. A four-star outfitter is one of the very best in its class, in all respects. In a given category, four stars ordinarily connotes the highest levels of competence, skill, experience and customer satisfaction. In most fields this is the highest rating given. Five stars is a "none better" classification reserved for outfitters that are truly the best in the world.

Outfitter Rating Summary

★–Good, able and competent.
★★–Very good, much better than average.
★★★–Superior, highly recommended.
★★★★–Truly outstanding, among the very best of its kind.
★★★★★–Absolutely the best. None better.

Trip/Tour Ratings

The Ultimate Adventure Sourcebook contains a number of large comparison charts which describe particular categories of adventure trips, or resort services. For example, one chart covers 40 great white-water rafting runs, while another describes 20 top windsurfing resorts worldwide. In these charts, as well as in reviews of particular tours or trips, we rate specific vacation experiences for quality and value.

One star means a good trip which is enjoyable and worthwhile. Two stars denotes a very good trip, recommended to be of high quality. Three stars indicates a superior trip that is highly recommended. Four stars denotes an outstanding trip, excellent in all respects, that is clearly one of the best of its kind offered to the public. Five stars is our top rating, and is reserved for "lifetime experiences"--adventures so exciting, enriching and rewarding as to be truly unforgettable.

We also use a value rating. A good value is designated by one dollar sign, an exceptional value by two.

Trip Rating Summary

★–A good trip, enjoyable and worthwhile.
★★–Very good, recommended.
★★★–Superior, highly recommended.
★★★★–Truly outstanding, the very best of its kind.
★★★★★–Extraordinary adventure of lasting value--"an experience of a lifetime."
$–Good Value $$–Great Value

Selecting the Right Trip

Don't shy away from the one and two-star trips or outfitters. Remember that each of these listings has been pre-selected from dozens of alternative offerings. In other words, everyone is good. Don't use the rankings as a final arbiter either. Each trip is a little bit different; you should choose the one that suits your particular interests and needs best, even if it has fewer stars than something else. And remember that you don't need a guide at all for many of the best adventure vacations--all it takes is courage, imagination, and a willingness to try new things. Going without a guide is often the best way to experience a foreign land, as this brings you in closer contact with the culture you came to see.

If you reject the food, ignore the customs,
fear the religions and avoid the people,
you might better stay home.
-James Michener

Choosing an Outfitter

Once you have a good idea of what you want to do and where you want to go, contact the outfitters or agencies we've listed. Many have toll-free numbers that make it easy to request information. Go through the catalogs or brochures carefully. Learn when the trips depart and exactly how much they cost. Prices or itineraries may have changed since this book was printed. Find out any hidden costs--ground transport, food and park fees are often extra. Be sure to ask for recommendations from past customers.

The Adventure Passport
Cutting the Cost of Your Vacation

Purchasers of the Ultimate Adventure Sourcebook qualify for our exclusive Adventure Passport program. This provides substantial discounts on trips and tours from participating outfitters and resorts. To exercise your discount privileges, you must first register your name in our directory.

When you register you will be entitled to cost savings when booking your trip directly with participating outfitters. Discounts will usually be a minimum of $25 or 5 percent, and may go as high as 15 percent of the total trip cost. This discount privilege, valid for 12 months, could easily save you hundreds of dollars annually. If your traveling companions wish similar discounts, they must purchase their own copies of the Ultimate Adventure Sourcebook.

To obtain Adventure Passport discounts, send your registration card to: **BOKEN, Passport Department**, *P.O. Box 360, Santa Barbara, CA 93102.*

Live Your Dream

The Ultimate Adventure Sourcebook was crafted to help people make their dreams a reality. Hopefully it will inspire you, and ease doubts you may have had about traveling to faraway lands. Remember that adventure, by definition, involves the unexpected. Don't try to plan every detail, or anticipate every contingency--you'll go crazy. Be enthusiastic and let your momentum carry you away. Just commit yourself, pack your bags, and go.

Don't worry about everything turning out exactly as planned. If you forget your camera, just get another. If you can't find a travel partner, go alone. The key is to keep reaching for what you really want, and not fall victim to excuses. Remember, life is not a dress rehearsal.

W hatever you can do, or dream you can,
begin it. Boldness has genius, power,
and magic in it.   -Johann von Goethe

Alpine Mountaineering

Ascent of Mt. Aspiring, New Zealand/ACE KVALE, CLAMBIN PRODUCTIONS

We do not live to eat and make money.
We eat and make money in order to be able to enjoy
life. This is what life means and what life is for.
-Mountaineer George Leigh Mallory

▼

Mountaineering defines high adventure. To reach the top of a major summit, you must transcend fear, conquer gravity and push yourself to the limit. There is nothing equivocal about a successful climb. When you've made it, you've made it, and the accomplishment is unconditional. That is perhaps why climbing has always appealed to those who want to put themselves to the ultimate test.

Mountaineering encompasses three basic activities--alpine expeditions, rock-climbing and ice-climbing. For alpinists, we review the best climbing schools around the country, as well as dozens of guided summit climbs worldwide. Rock-hounds will find a list of 10 great places to practice their moves, and reviews of the top rock-climbing guides around the country. If nothing but the most vertical adventures will do, we describe winter programs which will help you master the gravity-defying art of climbing ice.

CHAPTER

1

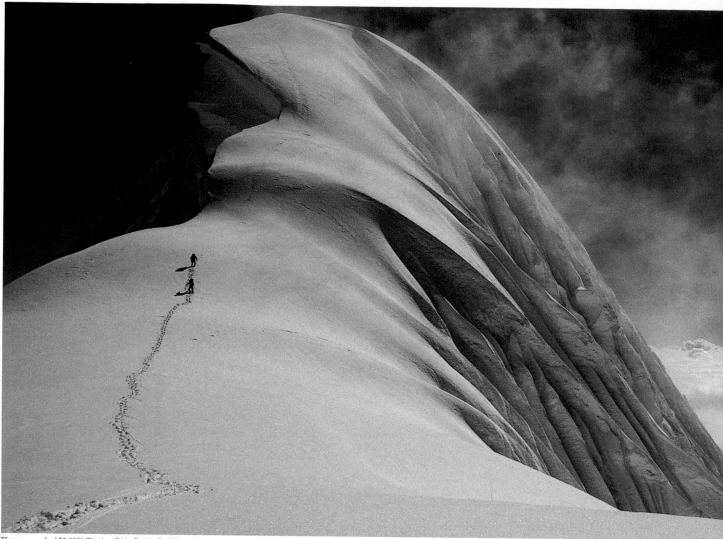

The snow peak of 21,000' Chopiqualki in Peru's Cordillera Blanca/CHARLIE FOWLER

CERTAIN SUMMITS ARE CONSIDERED CLASSICS--EITHER BECAUSE THEY ARE THE highest peaks on a continent or because they hold a special place in the heritage of mountaineering. Below, we feature a number of these ultimate climbs, including the Matterhorn, Mt. McKinley and Aconcagua. You'll also learn about the world's best training expeditions, such as a climb of Mexico's three volcanoes, which will provide you with the skills needed to tackle a major summit on your next vacation.

THE ALPS

The Matterhorn, Mt. Blanc and the Eiger

Looking for something really worth bragging about at the next class reunion--how about climbing the Alps' three most famous peaks: the Matterhorn, Mt. Blanc and the Eiger? Every summer, Alaska's Genet Expeditions offers a European Grand Slam expedition that gives even novice climbers the opportunity to bag all three classic peaks in a single 20-day vacation. Under the leadership of expert Welsh climber John Evans, participants will learn the fundamentals of alpine climbing and then test their newfound abilities on 1 or 2-day roped ascents of all three summits.

During the program, participants stay in valley tent camps or alpine climbers' huts, while they are readying for each of the major climbs. The first few days will be spent around the glaciers of Mt. Blanc practicing alpine mountaineering skills, including use of ropes and anchors, crevasse rescue, and both French and German ice ax and crampon technique.

Once all participants are secure in their alpine skills, the group will undertake a 2-day ascent of Mt. Blanc, western Europe's tallest summit. Though the highest of the Grand Slam's three peaks, Mt. Blanc is not difficult technically, and is a good break-in climb for those without much experience with a roped ascent. Next, the group moves to Grindewald to ascend the Eiger's West Flank, a moderate snow ramp leading to the summit. Before the summit attempt, the group will spend a few days polishing their technical skills. Despite the Eiger's formidable reputation, the West Flank route is non- technical and can be mastered by most climbers without too much difficulty. The last goal of the Grand Slam tour is the Matterhorn. This famous peak can be very challenging, but the group should be able to reach the top in a single day.

Although completing the Grand Slam is no mean feat, Genet's program is suitable for most anyone with some alpine camping experience who can carry a 40-pound pack five to six hours a day. Previous technical climbing experience will be valuable, but is not a prerequisite. Cost for the 3-week adventure will be roughly $3,200, plus airfare

Six Great Alpine Adventures

to Geneva. Climbers must bring all their own personal gear, including crampons and ice ax. Genet provides tents, ropes, all collective equipment, most food, and all transport within Europe. Contact Genet Expeditions, 4602 Business Park Blvd., Anchorage, AK 99503, (800) 334-3638.

For intermediate level climbers looking for a considerably less expensive three-summit adventure, American Alpine Institute (AAI) offers combo Mt. Blanc, Eiger and Matterhorn climbing tours in July, August and September. The 10-day programs cost about $2,000, including huts but not hotels. Participants should have experience in both glacier climbing and Class V rock-climbing. Contact AAI, 1212 24th, Bellingham, WA 98225, (206) 671-1505. You can also hire your own guide, who must be UIAGM certified. We recommend John Hogg, a Canadian based in Andermatt, Switzerland, (011 44) 6 8353. If this is your first major climb, Mountain Travel/Sobek offers 10-day basic climbing seminars at Mt. Blanc and the Matterhorn in July and August for $2,550. Call (800) 227-2384.

NEW ZEALAND

Southern Alps Mountaineering

If scaling a mountain peak is your idea of an ultimate winter holiday, look no further than New Zealand. (Our winter is summer in the Southern Hemisphere.) A vast range of snow-capped peaks runs almost the entire length of New Zealand's South Island, encompassing an area greater in size than the Alps of Europe.

The best mountaineering program in New Zealand is run by Alpine Guides, which operates out of Mt. Cook on the South Island. Alpine Guides boasts an international roster of guides and instructors, including veterans of major expeditions and first ascents. Alpine Guides offers a full range of activities: major summit climbs, technical rock-climbing, ski mountaineering, mountain rescue, even paragliding.

For novice mountaineers, we recommend Alpine Guides' basic Mountain Experience course. This weeklong program

will teach you all the important skills you will need on a summit expedition, such as an ascent of Mt. McKinley. You'll feel like a Boy Scout on the first day, learning the basic knots and rope skills. Next you'll be introduced to rapelling, or abseilling as they call it Down Under. You'll be strapped into a harness, with a doubled climbing rope rigged into special rapelling hardware. With a final word of reassurance from your instructor, you take that first step--over the edge of an eight-story sheer wall and straight out into space.

After the abseilling clinic, the group heads up the slopes of Mt. Cook to practice the essential techniques for snow and ice travel. You'll be shown how to arrest a fall on a 60-degree slope using just your ax and crampons, and how to set snow belays. Construction of emergency shelters and igloos is also covered. After a couple of days in the Southern Alps, it's back to the rocks for the technical climbing class. Here you'll learn how to place "protection"-- pitons, nuts and jammers--into rock cracks to secure your climbing rope. All the major

Michael Graber ascending Mt. Fitzroy, Patagonia/GALEN ROWELL

belaying techniques will be demonstrated, and the students will climb some pretty serious rock faces (5.6 to 5.9 under the American rating system).

The course concludes with instruction in glacier travel and crevasse rescue, carried out on massive ice fields a few miles from Alpine Guides' Mt. Cook basecamp. This is the most physically demanding part of the course--grueling but vital training. On high-altitude expeditions, more climbers are lost to crevasses than any other hazard.

Cost for Alpine Guides' 8-day basic alpine course, is $1,500 New Zealand (about $950 US), including bunkhouse accommodation and most gear (you must supply boots and suitable clothing). A successful graduate of the course is eligible to join one of Alpine Guides' major climbs. Contact Alpine Guides (Mt. Cook), P.O. Box 20, Mt. Cook, New Zealand, (011 64) 3 435-1834.

ARGENTINA

Ascent of Aconcagua

Located in the Argentine Andes, 23,085' Aconcagua is the highest mountain in the Western Hemisphere, a peak so tall that it can be seen from the Chilean coast on a clear day. As one of the classic seven summits (the tallest peaks on each continent), it is one of the most sought-after goals in the world of mountaineering.

Numerous guide services from around the world run climbing expeditions to Aconcagua every year. Most take the Normal Route, a ridge trail that can be negotiated by most reasonably fit persons, after acclimatization. Unfortunately, the lower sections of the Normal Route are often littered with debris from the many expeditions that have passed along the way. We recommend that you take an alternate path, such as the Polish Route, up Aconcagua's lower flanks. Unless you have strong technical and glacier climbing skills, however, don't plan on finishing the climb via the Polish Route--it is just too tough. The best plan for most climbers is to traverse back to the Normal Route to finish the last 4,000' to Aconcagua's summit. Although this route does not present much of a technical challenge, the extreme altitude, lack of oxygen, and the danger of sudden, violent storms

(the mountain creates its own climate) make experienced mountaineering judgment and leadership essential.

The American Alpine Institute (AAI) would be our first choice for an Aconcagua expedition. No American guide service has more experience on Aconcagua, or more skilled guides. All AAI trips take the Polish Route through the lower elevations. After preparatory climbs of lesser peaks in the area, novice and intermediate climbers will attempt the summit via the Normal Route. Those with previous alpine climbing experience, and the ability to follow a mid-fifth

Alps ice-climbing/COURTESY AUSTRIAN NATIONAL TOURIST OFFICE

class route with heavy packs, will attempt a Polish Route ascent to the top. AAI's Aconcagua expeditions run for 24 days in January and February and cost about $2,600 in 1992.

Experienced climbers with some technical experience may prefer the Aconcagua trip run by Alpine Skills International (ASI). From Punta del Inca, the climbers travel by mules 27 miles up the Horcones River to make the basecamp at 14,000' Plaza de Mulas, where there is a hut. ASI doesn't do any warm-up climbs, so extra time is spent on the way up for acclimatization. The summit will be attempted via the Polish Route, and some fairly serious technical

pitches will be encountered. Participants should be very fit, with the ability to carry heavy packs for extended periods. The January expedition will cost about $2,200 in 1993. Contact ASI, P.O. Box 8, Norden, CA 95724, (916) 426-9108; FAX: (916) 426-3063. Each year, Michael Covington's Fantasy Ridge Guide Service also offers an outstanding Polish Ridge expedition suited for seasoned climbers. Contact Fantasy Ridge, P.O. Box 1679, Telluride, CO, (303) 728-3546. Price will be about $3,000.

If you've never tackled a big peak before, Mountain Travel offers a 17-day Normal Route program that avoids the tough technical sections. The hike in could be more scenic, but pack animals carry the heavy gear. Participants will climb surrounding peaks to hone skills and acclimatize before attempting Aconcagua itself. The price was $2,300 in January 1992. Contact Mountain Travel/Sobek, (800) 227-2384.

ALASKA

Denali (Mt. McKinley) Expedition

Fittingly called Denali, "the Great One," 20,320' Mt. McKinley is the highest peak in North America. It is a major summit which requires stamina, a solid grounding in alpine skills, and a bit of luck (weatherwise) to conquer. The greatest challenges are the extreme and unpredictable weather conditions that can cause white-out for days, or drop temperatures from comfortable to dangerously cold in a few hours.

Sadly, each season some climbers don't make it back from Denali. With rare exceptions, these were mountaineers who chose to make the climb in a self-guided group. The safety records of the best McKinley guide services are exemplary. The message is clear--if you're smart, and want to reach the top of McKinley, go with a pro. Alaska-Denali Guiding (ADG) enjoys the best reputation among Mt. McKinley concessionaires. ADG is directed by Brian Okonek, who has guided in Alaska for 15 years, and has made some 20 trips to the summit.

While Denali can be climbed via three different routes, each with a different degree of difficulty, if this is your first big peak, we recommend the West Buttress

Camp II, Mt. Everest, Nepal/CHRIS NOBLE

approach. This can be done by most fit climbers who have completed a basic mountaineering course, and have some high-altitude camping experience. However, you will have to haul lots of gear--50 pounds or more on your back, plus a sled.

The West Buttress Route is the most popular and least difficult path to the summit. This does not mean, however, that it is an easy climb. Climbers must walk 18 miles and ascend 13,000' to reach the top, coping with unpredictable weather, changing snow conditions, threatening crevasses and steep, icy slopes.

ADG enjoys a high success rate on McKinley--more than 60 percent of its customers reach the summit. Groups are limited to nine climbers, with three guides. Participants must be in excellent physical condition, have extensive backpacking experience and some familiarity with the use of ice ax and crampons. An ADG McKinley expedition ranges from $2,400 to $2,500. For more information, contact Alaska-Denali Guiding, Inc., P.O. Box 566, Talkeetna, AK 99676, (907) 733-2649.

Other highly recommended guide services for McKinley are Mountain Trip and Fantasy Ridge Guiding. Mountain Trip concentrates on the West Buttress, while Fantasy Ridge usually does more difficult routes. Like ADG, Mountain Trip and Fantasy Ridge run small groups with low cli-

ent to guide ratios. Both firms use progressive techniques--i.e. they travel light--yet have excellent safety records. Call Fantasy Ridge at (303) 728-3546 (see p. 15), or contact Mountain Trip, P.O. Box 91161, Anchorage, AK 99509, (907) 345-6499.

MEXICO

The Volcanic Trilogy

Rising from the highland valleys east of Mexico City, Pico de Orizaba (18,851'), Popocatépetl (17,761') and Iztaccihuatl (17,343') are the third, fifth and seventh highest peaks in North America. Mexico's three highest summits are not technically demanding, but the routes can be extremely strenuous, traversing slopes of scree and talus, snowfields and glaciers. This trio of volcanic peaks is an excellent introduction to mountain climbing--a great practice exercise for a major climb such as Mt. McKinley. Virtually all participants will shatter their own personal altitude records, and the price is right--under $1,000 total land cost.

Alpine Skills Interna-

tional (ASI) is the logical choice for a three-volcano expedition. ASI's Mexican Volcanoes trip has been one of its most popular offerings for many years. Participants travel by bus to the Vincente Guerro lodge at 13,000', where they will acclimatize and brush up on basic skills. The lodge serves as a base camp for ascents of Iztaccihuatl and Popocatépetl before the group moves on to a 200-year-old casa in Tlachi-chuca to stage the ascent of Orizaba. The cost for the 9-day November trip should be approximately $1,000. Call (916) 426-9108.

Another excellent Mexican trilogy expedition is run by the Colorado Mountain School (CMS), P.O. Box 2062, Estes Park, CO 80517, (800) 444-0730. CMS' mountain skills training is thorough, and its schedule allows plenty of time to enjoy the local culture. Land cost for the 10-day, three-summit expeditions will be around $1,000, with four departures between mid-November and mid-January. If two summits will suffice and you'd like to spend an extra day or two sightseeing, you will probably prefer Mountain Travel's Mexican Volcanoes trip. On the 12-day journey participants will climb Orizaba and Popocatépetl. Cost ranges from $1,100 to $1,300, depending on the group's size. The trips depart in February, March, October and November. For more information on these trips, contact Mountain Travel, (800) 226-2384.

Erika and Peter Whittaker, Mt. Rainier/CHRIS NOBLE

ECUADOR

High Andes Adventure

Ecuador's major summits (Cotopaxi and Chimborazo) are far more scenic and considerably more challenging than the Mexican volcanoes. This is the perfect trip for someone who wants to learn serious mountaineering skills and put them to use on mountains that are worth writing home about. For novice mountaineers who want to climb some big, impressive mountains in a 2-week vacation, Ecuador is the place.

The most experienced American guide service in Ecuador is the American Alpine Institute (AAI). AAI offers 14-day climbing programs November through February every year, utilizing two different formats. The basic AAI program, aimed at those who have some formal alpine training and previous high-altitude experience, climbs three superb peaks, 18,997' Cayambe, 19,348' Cotopaxi, and 20,703' Chimborazo. The second program, set up for novice climbers, is an instructional itinerary that climbs the two highest peaks, but substitutes a mountain skills seminar for the Cayambe ascent.

Ecuador's third highest peak, Cayambe, has glaciers that are large and varied, providing both challenge for advanced climbers and great training conditions for novices. The summit climbers must leave well before dawn to make it to the top and back again in a day. There is an easy glacier climb to a saddle and then the group must rope up to ascend the 35-degree slopes to the crater. It is then an easy but scenic walk above the clouds to the summit.

Cotopaxi, the world's highest active volcano, comes next on AAI's agenda. The push to the summit again begins in darkness, as the group climbs 30- to 35-degree snow and ice ramps to reach a 17,000' glacial platform at dawn's light. The remaining 2,000' to the top puts the climbers' technical skills to the test. The group must belay across snow bridges, skirt crevasses and then ascend the 40-degree slopes of Cotopaxi's upper glacier. At the summit, the group is rewarded with spectacular views of nine major peaks and Cotopaxi's 1,000' deep summit crater.

The third summit is Chimborazo, Ecuador's highest peak, a massive dormant volcano rising nearly 11,000' above Ecuador's central valley. Far more challenging than most volcanic summits, Chimborazo has complex faces and glaciers that require careful application of alpine skills. AAI attacks the West Face, a moderately steep and varied approach with 25- to 40-degree slopes and some glacier ice.

AAI's Ecuador programs, both standard and instructional, cost $1,640 in 1992, including all meals, equipment and ground transportation in Ecuador.

If AAI's trips are booked, both the Colorado Mountain School (CMS) and Mountain Travel Sobek offer 2-week trips to the Ecuadorian Andes. Both companies will take you up Cotopaxi and Chimborazo; CMS also adds a canoe trip down the Amazon. Call CMS at (800) 444-0730, or Mountain Travel at (800) 227-2384.

Glacier climbing in the Alps/DIDIER GIVOIS

Eight Great Mountaineering Schools

THE BEST PLACES TO GET UPWARDLY MOBILE

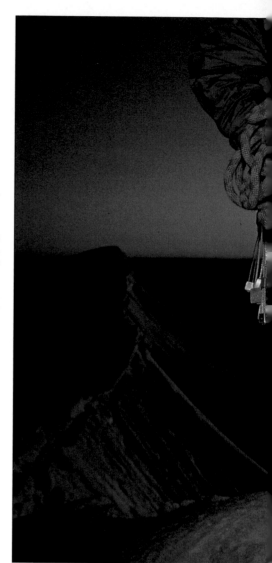

■ AMERICAN ALPINE INSTITUTE (AAI)

1212 24th, Bellingham, WA 98225, (206) 671-1505. Programs: mountaineering, rock, ice, winter skills, guided climbs, ski mountaineering, mountain rescue. AMGA Accredited.

AAI conducts a fine basic climbing course of 6, 12 or 18 days which covers ice- and rock-climbing skills and glacier travel technique. The program operates in the Cascades and is suitable for all skill levels. AAI also leads ascents of major peaks and offers both climbing and ski mountaineering expeditions to Mt. McKinley and other Alaskan destinations. We strongly recommend AAI's programs in Mexico and South America. Rock-climbing is taught in Baja, and AAI leads groups each year to climb the three Mexican volcanoes. A number of summit expeditions, suitable for novice mountaineers, are run to 20,000'+ peaks in Ecuador, Peru and Bolivia. AAI is a very well-established operation that offers the complete spectrum of mountaineering services at moderate prices. Rating: ★★★★

Eichorn's Pinnacle, Cathedral Peak, Yosemite/GORDON WILTSIE

■ ALPINE SKILLS INTERNATIONAL

P.O. Box 8, Norden, CA 95724, (916) 426-9108; FAX: (916) 426-3063. Programs: ski mountaineering, mountaineering, ice, rock, treks, guided climbs, winter skills. AMGA Accredited.

Based in the Sierras near Lake Tahoe, Alpine Skills International (ASI) runs a very popular and comprehensive year-round alpine program. ASI's strong suits are classic alpine climbs and ski mountaineering. Skiers will enjoy ASI's unique programs which combine summit climbs with alpine and telemark ski descents. While many of ASI's programs are designed for those with good rock- and snow-climbing skills, ASI also offers a variety of expeditions (Ecuadorian Andes, and Mexican volcanoes e.g.) that are suitable for those with a limited amount of previous alpine experience. ASI conducts what are probably the best haute route ski tours in the Sierras. Rating: ★★★★

■ COLORADO MOUNTAIN SCHOOL (CMS)

P.O. Box 2062, Estes Park, CO 80517, (800) 444-0730, (303) 567-5758. Programs: mountaineering, rock, ice, guided climbs, treks, ski mountaineering. AMGA Accredited.

Colorado Mountain School earns our endorsement as one of the nation's very best. It does a great job with novices, yet it also offers challenging multi-pitch climbs for intermediates looking to become advanced climbers with the ability to lead. In addition to its rock courses, CMS conducts expeditions to major peaks around the world, including Mt. McKinley and Mooses Tooth in Alaska, Mt. Logan in the Yukon, the Mexican volcanoes, Huascaran and Aconcagua in Latin America, and Kilimanjaro in Africa. At $925–$995, CMS's three volcanoes trip is a bargain-priced introduction to high-altitude climbing. CMS has drawn high praise from past participants, particularly for its attention to individual student needs and its great Rocky Mountain climbing sites. Rating: ★★★★

■ EXUM MOUNTAIN GUIDES

Grand Teton National Park, Box 56, Moose, WY 83012, (307) 733-2297. Programs: mountaineering, rock, ice, mountain rescue. AMGA Accredited.

Exum provides the most experienced and versatile alpine guide service in the northern Rockies. Exum is one of the oldest climbing schools in North America, having operated in the Tetons since 1935. Exum's former and current guides include many of America's most famous climbers. Customized training programs for all levels can be arranged, and Exum can put together a guided ascent to Grand Teton as well as dozens of local peaks. The rock program is outstanding, with some of the best instructors anywhere. Exum also offers a full range of winter programs, from ice-climbing to ski touring. Rating: ★★★★

Dawn in the Austrian Alps/TIROL TOURIST BOARD

"Jackson Hole Mountain Guides is one of the few really serious mountain guide services in the States. They not only offer excellent instruction for the beginning climber but their guides are qualified to take you on any level climb, whether rock, ice or ski mountaineering."

For beginners, we suggest the 4-day Grand Teton Climber Course ($500) which features an ascent of Grand Teton summit on the final day. Experts will enjoy the 8-day Advanced Climbing Course ($1,000). Jackson Hole Mountain Guides also features outstanding ice seminars, as well as custom guided climbs. Prices are subject to change. Rating: ★★★★

■ NATIONAL OUTDOOR LEADERSHIP SCHOOL (NOLS)

P.O. Box AA, Lander, WY 82520, (307) 332-6973. Programs: mountaineering, rock, ice, expeditions, mountain rescue, outdoor survival, ski mountaineering. AMGA Accredited.

NOLS is much more than a climbing school, offering a broad range of outdoor activities including trekking and sea kayaking. Its mountaineering programs tend to be longer in duration (3 to 5 weeks) and more intensive than other schools listed here. The climbing skills instruction is very thorough and safety oriented, though NOLS doesn't always use the latest equipment or state-of-the-art techniques. As a result, NOLS climbers may be burdened with heavier packs than one might carry with a more progressive guide service. For more information on NOLS, see Chapter 24, Survival Schools and Wilderness Training. Rating: ★★★

■ THE INTERNATIONAL ALPINE SCHOOL/ BOULDER MOUNTAIN GUIDES (IAS)

P.O. Box 3037, Eldorado Springs, CO 80025, (303) 494-4904. Programs: mountaineering, rock, ice, guided climbs, expeditions, ski mountaineering.

Founded in 1968 by noted climber Jeff Lowe, the International Alpine School/ Boulder Mountain Guides (IAS) has developed into one of the best full-service climbing schools in the country. In the alpine arena, IAS offers a dozen major summit trips, among them a highly recommended 24-day Polish Route ascent of Aconcagua in January 1993, and a terrific 15-day alpine seminar in the French Alps. This program, which runs in July, combines rigorous snow and glacier skills training with five classic ascents including Mt. Blanc. Cost is about $2,100. For rockhounds, 3 and 5-day rock-climbing seminars are offered spring through fall with special women's classes every month. In winter, IAS conducts one of America's finest ice-climbing courses on the frozen waterfalls of Ouray, Colorado. Rating: ★★★

■ JACKSON HOLE MOUNTAIN GUIDES & CLIMBING SCHOOL

P.O. Box 7477, 165 N. Glenwood, Jackson, WY 83001, (307) 733-4979. Programs: mountaineering, rock, ice, guided climbs, winter skills, ski mountaineering. AMGA Accredited.

The Jackson Hole Mountain Guides & Climbing school, the only year-round climbing service in the Tetons, is widely acknowledged as one of the very best in the business. The school offers a wide variety of programs, with small classes and very skilled guides. Patagonia's company founder, Yvon Chouinard, has stated that

■ RAINIER MOUNTAINEERING INC.

535 Dock Street, Tacoma, WA 98402, (206) 627-6242; Summer Address: Mount Rainier National Park, Paradise, WA 98397. Programs: mountaineering, winter skills, mountain rescue, ice, guided climbs. AMGA Accredited.

Rainier Mountaineering is the only guide service on 14,410' Mt. Rainier, the highest peak on the West Coast. Rainier Mountaineering is best known for its ice and snow training and Rainier summit work. Among the 1-day programs offered are the snow and ice school, crevasse rescue program, basic rock-climbing school, and Rainier summit climb. Longer programs include a 6-day mountain medicine seminar, a 5-day expedition seminar featuring trip planning, logistics and glacier camping along with a summit climb, and an annual Mt. McKinley expedition. Rating: ★★★

WORLDWIDE CLIMBING EXPEDITIONS

THIS IS JUST A SAMPLE OF THE MAJOR GUIDED EXPEDITIONS. WHERE MORE THAN ONE GUIDE SERVICE goes to a destination, we feature those offering the best value and lowest client/guide ratios. Climbing trips are classified Grades 1-5, with 5 being the most difficult (equivalent to Mt. Everest). A Grade 3 summit can be reached by most strong persons with some high-altitude experience and basic mountaineering skills (ice ax and crampons, ropes, belays). We also use the Yosemite Decimal System ratings, e.g. 5.7, to describe technical climbing difficulty. Abbreviations: previous mountaineering experience required (PME); previous technical climbing experience required (TCE); Alaska-Denali Guiding (ADG); Alpine Skills International (ASI); American Alpine Institute (AAI); Colorado Mountain School (CMS), Eastern Mountain Sports (EMS), International Alpine School/Boulder Mountain Guide (IAS/BMG), International Mountain Climbing School (IMCS).

Sunrise on Mt. Rainier/KEITH GUNNAR/REI Adventures

SUMMIT(S)	HEIGHT	FEATURES	DIFFICULTY	GUIDE SERVICES
BOLIVIA				
Cordillera Real Summits	21,200'	Five major 20K' peaks incl. Condoriri and Huayana Potosi. Glaciers. Illimani option.	Grade 3-4	AAI, ASI
Illimani	21,201'	Bolivia's highest. Superb ridge views. 19,000' high camp. Some technical climbing. This is a beautiful peak that can be done separately or added to Cordillera Real.	Grade 3.5	AAI, CMS, Summits (AAI 5 day $680 option)
CANADA				
Mt. Robson	12,972'	Canada's top challenge. Difficult & steep. Success is weather dependent. PME.	Grade 4	ASI; AAI
Mt. Waddington	13,177'	Highest peak in Coast Range. Multiple climbs of lesser peaks. Mountain seminar.	Grade 3.5	NOLS
ARGENTINA				
Aconcagua (Polish Route)	22,834'	S. America's highest peak. Tech. Polish Route, challenging glacial ascent, long haul. PME.	Grade 4	AAI, IAS/BMG, Fan. Ridge
Aconcagua (Normal Route)	22,834'	ASI takes easy route, much less scenic. IMCS uses Polish Route, then moderate traverse.	Grade 3	Mtn. Trav., IMCS (combo rt
CHILE				
Ojos del Salado	21,932'	World's highest active volcano. 17,000' start. An excellent intro high-altitude climb.	Grade 2	Mountain Travel
ECUADOR				
Cotopaxi, Chimborazo, Cayambe (Three Summits)	20,561'	Ecuador's highest peaks. Very scenic and rewarding. Outstanding intermediate mtg. trip. Cotopaxi, Chimborazo and 19,000' Cayambe or 18,000' Tungurahura. Acclimatization ascent.	Grade 3	AAI, CMS, ASI, Mtn.
FRANCE				
Mont Blanc Region	15,777'	15 days, 5 ascents, ice skills training. Excellent preparation for big climbs.	Grade 3	IAS/BMG, AAI
Mt. Bl., Matterhorn, Eiger	15,777'	14 days, mtg. training, PME-intermediate level. Serious alpine climbing. Expert guides.	Grade 3.5	AAI, Genet Expeditions
MEXICO				
Three Volcanoes	18,851'	Orizaba and two next highest Mexican peaks, 17,761' Popocatépetl & 17,343' Iztaccihuatl.	Grade 2	ASI, CMS, Summits
NEPAL				
Khumbu Himal (Island Peak)	20,304'	Non-tech. ascent of Kala Patar (18,000'); Island Peak, views of Everest.	Grade 3	Karakoram Experience
Mt. Mera	21,247'	Non-tech. climb near 4 of 5 highest peaks in world, incl. Everest and Kanchenjunga.	Grade 2.5	Mtn. Madness, Karakoran
NEW ZEALAND				
Mt. Cook	12,349'	NZ's tallest peak; 1:1 guide/student ratio. Strong PME. Weather can be very difficult.	Grade 3.5	Alpine Guides, Mt. Cook
Mt. Tasman	11,475'	Strong snow and ice skills needed. 1:1 student/guide ratio. Heli-lift included. PME.	Grade 3.5	Alpine Guides, Mt. Cook
PERU				
Pisco, Huascaran, Alpamayo	22,225'	3 superb snow peaks. PME and some technical skills required. Politically sensitive area, so you should go with an organized expedition. (Alpamayo only is a 6-day option.)	Grade 3.5	IAS/BMG, ASI
USA				
Devil's Thumb (AK)	12,500'	One of 50 classic N. American climbs. Ability to follow 5.9 climb, & high fitness required.	Grade 3.5	IAS/BMG
Grand Teton	13,770'	3-day course & climb is popular. 5.4 easy route or 5.7 complete ridge (extra 800' pitch).	Grade 3	Exum Mtn. Guides
Mt. Baker	10,778'	Highest in Cascades. Three routes from easy to very difficult (e.g. headwall ascent requires very strong snow and ice skills).	Grade 2.5-4	AAI, Mtn. Madness
Mt. Elias (AK)	18,008'	N. America's 3rd highest peak—climbed only 15 times. Rugged weather. 3-mile high face.	Grade 4.5	Mt. Elias Guides (907) 277-6867
Mt. McKinley (Denali)	20,320'	Serious, major expedition. 4 routes, 2 non-technical. Very high fitness required. PME.	Grade 4-4.5	ADG, Fan. Ridge, NOLS
Mt. Shuksan	9,127'	One of prettiest peaks in US. Moderate (glacier) or intermediate ascent, with 5.0 climb up final chimney. Excellent basic climb with superb views.	Grade 2.5-3	AAI
Rockies Summits	14,000'	Sangre de Christo Needle tech. ascent, two other challenging peaks. Ice travel. TCE.	Grade 3.5	IAS/BMG
USSR				
Mt. Elbrus	18,841'	Highest peak in Europe. Non-technical snow climb. Lift to 11,000'. Ski descent option. REI climb is well organized and a bargain. A great peak for a personal altitude record.	Grade 2	Mtn. Travel, Summits, REI Adv. (800) 622-2236
Pic Kommunisma	24,595'	Highest summit in USSR (Central Asia); serious, difficult climb. Heli-lift to 13,800' basecamp. REI combines with 23,304' Korzhenevskaya, another tough, technical climb.	Grade 4	REI Adventures (800) 622-2236

MOUNTAIN MADNESS

Expedition Dates	Trip Days	Cost	Rating
Apr-Aug	13	$1700	★★★★
July	14	$1850+	★★★
Aug-Sept	5-8	$600-1000	★★★
July-Aug	14-30	$2500	★★★
Dec, Jan	24	$2600 (1992)	★★★★
Jan-Feb	17	$1800 (1992)	★★★
Nov	15	$2300 Est.	★★
Feb, Mar, Nov	14-16	$1540-2040	★★★★★
Travel (2 peaks only)			
July-Aug	12-15	$2350 Est.	★★★
July-Aug	14	$2000-3200	★★★★
Nov-Jan	9-11	$950-1200	★★
Call	20	$2200 Est.	★★★
Apr, Oct-Nov	29	$2700-3100	★★★
Nov-Mar	6-7	$2600 NZ	★★★★
Nov-Mar	6-7	$2600 NZ	★★★
June-July	24	$3000 Est.	★★★★
Spring	21	$3200	★★★★
Summer	2-3	$260-380	★★★
Summer	2-3	$260-390	★★★
Summer	25	Call	★★★★
April-Jul	18-24	$2400-2800	★★★★
Summer	2	$250	★★★★
Year-round	5	$600	★★★
Jul, Aug	14-16	$1100-2300 (REI lowest)	★★
August	30	$1900	★★★

CLIMBING EXPEDITION GUIDES

In addition to the mountaineering schools featured on pages 18-19, the following organizations lead guided expeditions to a multitude of summits worldwide.

■ **ALPINE GUIDES**

P.O. Box 20, Mt. Cook, New Zealand, (011 64) 3 435-1834; FAX: (011 64) 3 435-1898. UIAGM Accredited.

Alpine Guides is probably the Southern Hemisphere's finest mountaineering concern, offering summit climbs, training seminars, winter glacier skiing and even paragliding. Each year Alpine Guides leads major expeditions, including a McKinley trip, but it specializes in guided ascents of major peaks in New Zealand's Southern Alps, including Mt. Cook and Mt. Tasman. Alpine Guides' own helicopters are used to access remote peaks. Rating: ★★★

■ **HIMALAYAN KINGDOMS**

20 The Mall, Clifton, Bristol, BS8 4DR, Great Britain, (011 44) 272 237163; FAX: (011 44) 272 744993 outside UK.

Himalayan Kingdoms is a world leader in big mountain expeditions, having successfully organized many first ascents of the highest peaks in the world. The major expedition will be a 51–day June ascent of Pakistan's 26,402' Broad Peak, the world's 12th highest mountain. Cost will be £4,750, and previous high-altitude climbing experience is required. Expeditions to lesser peaks suitable for novices include 18,510' Mt. Elbrus (USSR, August, 20 days, £1,200), 20,938' Parchemo (Nepal, September, 28 days, £2,100), and 20,082' Stok Kangri (Nepal, August, 22 days, £2,000). (Prices are quoted round-trip from London.) Rating: ★★★

■ **INTERNATIONAL SCHOOL OF MOUNTAINEERING (ISM)**

Club Vagabond, CH-1854 Leysin, Switzerland, (011 41) 25 34 1321. UIAGM Accredited.

ISM offers acclaimed 1 to 3-week seminars in alpine climbing and trekking, and ski mountaineering. This is a good place to combine a climbing course with a few days of off-piste skiing. ISM's talented guides also lead guided climbs to both lesser and major peaks in the European Alps, as well as summits in Latin America. All instructors are fluent in English. Rating: ★★★★

■ **KARAKORAM EXPERIENCE**

Trekkers Lodge, 32 Lake Road, Keswick, CA12 5DQ, Great Britain, (011 44) 7687 73966, or 7687 72267.

Karakoram is one of England's leading adventure companies. It specializes in tours to Himalayan trekking peaks in the 16,500' to 21,000' range. Its 1991 destinations include Gondoro Peak in Pakistan (18,356'), Menthosa (21,138') in India, and Mera (21,246'), Island Peak (20,304'), and Ramdung (19,320') in Nepal. Karakorum has a wealth of experience in the Himalayas, and its trips offer good value. Most trips average three weeks and cost about £2,100 with round-trip air from London. Rating: ★★★

■ **MOUNTAIN MADNESS**

4128 SW Alaska, Suite 206, Seattle, WA 98136, (206) 937-8389; FAX: (206) 937-1772.

An adventure travel agency, Mountain Madness offers alpine expeditions throughout the world. Featured trips include Mt. Baker and the Ruth Glacier in Alaska, and Africa's three highest summits, Kilimanjaro (Tanzania), Mt. Stanley (Uganda) and Mt. Kenya (Kenya). Mountain Madness also organizes ice-climbing, rock-climbing, and alpine skills seminars in the Pacific Northwest. It is not a full-time mountaineering school, however. Rating: ★★★

■ **SUMMITS**

P.O. Box 214, Mt. Rainier, WA 98304, (206) 569-2992; FAX: (206) 569-2993.

Summits offers guided climbs to many of the world's most noted peaks including Aconcagua, Kilimanjaro, Elbrus (USSR), Illimani (Bolivia), McKinley, and the Ecuadorian and Mexican volcanoes. The volcano trips and Kilimanjaro are suitable for novices, while other summits will test even seasoned climbers. Summits is operated by noted climber Peter Whittaker. Prices range from $1,200 for Mexico to $2,500+ for a major peak such as McKinley. Rating: ★★★

5.9 route outside Salt Lake, Utah/SCOTT MARKEWITZ

TOP GUIDE SERVICES

Among the general mountaineering schools listed above, three stand out from the pack for the quality of their rock-climbing programs, and for the expertise of their rock instructors:

Exum Mountain Guides (Rock Rating: ★★★★), **The Int'l Alpine School/Boulder Mtn. Guides** (Rock Rating: ★★★★), **Jackson Hole Mtn. Guides & Climbing School** (Rock Rating: ★★★★).

In addition to these well-established programs, we have selected 10 other outstanding rock-climbing schools/guiding services. In most cases their primary focus is technical climbing, although many also offer programs in alpine expedition skills.

■ ADIRONDACK ALPINE ADVENTURES
P.O. Box 179, Keene, NY 12942, (518) 576-9881.

Adirondack Alpine Adventures (AAA), now in its seventh year, offers a very broad range of training programs in rock and ice-climbing--over 100 different courses conducted year-round. The popular 2-day Intro to the Vertical World features rapelling, belaying and top-roped climbs for $160, a good value. Weeklong beginning, intermediate and advanced rock seminars are also offered from May through October for $480. For strong climbers (those who can follow a 5.7 pitch), AAA conducts a 5-day seminar on leading. Specialty classes in double rope technique and "hard rock" (5.8+ difficulty) are also a challenge. Small class sizes are guaranteed. Rating: ★★★

■ EASTERN MOUNTAIN SPORTS CLIMBING SCHOOL
Main Street, P.O. Box 514, North Conway, NH 03860, (603) 356-5433.

In business for over 20 years, the EMS Climbing School in North Conway, New Hampshire, offers reasonably priced courses for those looking to master the fundamentals of rock-climbing. It shares the superb Cathedral and White Horse Ledges with rival climbing school IMCS. Visit both companies and pick a guide who suits your style--both schools have very skilled instructors. We recommend the 4-day basic program, which costs $365 for a group of two, and $580 for one-on-one instruction--the best way to learn. Novices can take the 1-day beginner or intermediate course for $110, but once you get past the knot-tying and safety lessons, this doesn't allow much time on the rock. Rating: ★★★

■ FANTASY RIDGE GUIDE SERVICE

c/o Michael Covington, P.O. Box 1679, Telluride, CO 81435, (303) 728-3546.

Michael Covington's Fantasy Ridge Guide Service is one of the most respected rock schools in the business. His operation offers superb rock-climbing seminars in Telluride, as well as ice-climbing courses each winter in Ouray, Colorado. Both winter and summer courses run $500–$750 for 5 days, and custom guiding is also available on an hourly basis. These technical programs are truly superior, with low student/guide ratios, and customized instruction closely matched to the student's abilities. The instructors are all superb climbers. Fantasy Ridge also offers alpine expeditions to Denali ($2,700–$6,000) and Aconcagua ($2,900). Rating: ★★★★★

■ HIGH ANGLE ADVENTURES, INC.

5 River Rd., New Paltz, New York 12561, (800) 777-2456, or (914) 658-9811. AMGA Accredited.

High Angle Adventures is one of the most professional operations on the East Coast, boasting 18 years of experience in the Shawangunks. It has top-notch guides, many of whom are 5.13-rated climbers, capable of leading even the most difficult pitches. The climbing site is superb, a major rock wall two and one-half miles long. High-friction quartzite rock and abundant horizontal striations offer good holds that allow even novices to climb with confidence. A 1-day course (three students maximum) costs $100, including all equipment, even climbing shoes. One-on-one training, particularly popular with intermediates, costs $150 per day. High Angle's base at New Paltz is less than two hours from New York City. Rating: ★★★

■ THE INTERNATIONAL MOUNTAIN CLIMBING SCHOOL (IMCS)

Main Street, North Conway, NH 03860, (603) 356-7013. AMGA Accredited.

We can recommend IMCS without reservation as one of the best operations in the country. Chief guide Rich Wilcox and his assistants are ace climbers and equally skilled teachers. Most courses have a 3:1 maximum student/guide ratio, and IMCS uses progressive techniques and state-of-the-art equipment. Train on weekdays if you can--you'll find the most popular training routes at North Conway's Cathedral Ledge much less crowded then. A daylong rock class runs $110, while a 4-day basic course costs $365, with group discounts available. Rating: ★★★★

■ MOUNTAIN GUIDES ALLIANCE

P.O. Box 266, North Conway, NH 03860, (603) 356-5310, or (603) 447-3086.

Mountain Guides Alliance runs a small operation, but it is outstanding in every respect. The guides have very strong technical skills, use the latest techniques, and are good teachers, especially George Hurley. This isn't one of those schools where you'll be dragged behind a guide who is more interested in demonstrating his own abilities than in sharing his knowledge and fostering real enthusiasm. Programs are run on a custom basis, with no more than two students assigned to a single guide in most situations. In addition to summer rock programs, the Mountain Guides Alliance runs excellent winter ice-climbing programs. Most classes range from $80–$125 per day. Rating: ★★★★

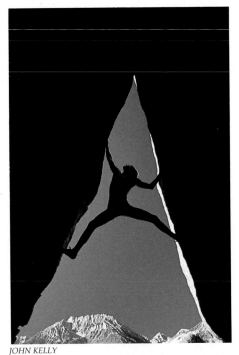

JOHN KELLY

■ SENECA ROCKS CLIMBING SCHOOL

P.O. Box 53, Seneca Rocks, West Virginia 26884, (304) 567-2600, or (304) 567-2254. AMGA Accredited.

The Seneca Rocks in West Virginia's Allegheny Mountains of West Virginia are renowned for their dramatic sandstone pinnacles. With very grippy rock surfaces blessed with an abundance of handholds, this is a great place to learn the basics. This school has a reputation as one of the best small climbing schools in the East. The strength of the program is its commitment "to produce climbers, not just customers."

Instruction is tailored to each student's abilities, with an emphasis on safety. The 3-day basic and intermediate programs cost $75-$85 per day. Rating: ★★★★

■ SKY'S THE LIMIT GUIDE SERVICE & CLIMBING SCHOOL

HCR 33, Box 1, Calico Basin--Red Rock, NV 89124-9204, (702) 363-4533. AMGA and UIAGM Accredited.

Red Rock, Nevada, features a wide variety of rock formations, good for rank novices to experts, although most routes are best for intermediates and above. For the past 10 years, under the direction of UIAGM guide Randall Grandstaff, Sky's the Limit has taught rock technique at this superior, yet little-known climbing site. The basic 1-day rock-craft course costs $135, while intermediate and advanced classes cost $125. Advanced weekend seminars in leading, big-wall technique and self-rescue run $195. Rating: ★★★

■ VERTICAL ADVENTURES CLIMBING SCHOOL & GUIDING SERVICE (VA)

P.O. Box 7548, Newport Beach, CA 92658, (714) 854-6250.

In the summer, VA operates out of Idyllwild, climbing granite in the Sierra. In the winter, it moves to Joshua Tree, one of America's best winter climbing areas. Joshua Tree offers an incredible diversity of rock formations, making it ideally suited for all levels of climbers. Introductory 1-day courses cost $58, while intermediate classes range from $70–$75. Two-day seminars begin at $125, while the Big Wall Seminar, featuring Yosemite-style techniques, costs about $180. Rating: ★★★

■ YOSEMITE MOUNTAINEERING SCHOOL AND GUIDE SERVICE

Yosemite National Park, CA 95389, (209) 372-1335 (June–August), or (209) 372-1244 (Sept–May). AMGA Accredited.

Yosemite is *the* place to learn big-wall climbing. The Yosemite Mountaineering School (YMS) conducts a full range of classes on some of the world's finest granite. The 1-day basic or intermediate seminars cost about $75 for two persons per guide. The intermediate Level II program highlights jamcrack skills, direct aid and self-rescue, and is a prerequisite for YM's guided climbs. For strong climbers, YM offers 2-day Advanced Free-Climbing and Direct Aid seminars for $150. Even experts can benefit from the Direct Aid course if they are planning their first long climb. Rating: ★★★★

Ten Rock Training Areas

COLORADO
▲
Boulder Area

With a name like Boulder, you would expect the climbing to be good in this college town, and you'd be right. While experts will head farther north into Estes Park, close to downtown Boulder are a number of good training sites, including Flatirons and Eldorado Canyon. The Wind Tower in Eldorado Canyon is one of the best beginners' pinnacles around. Contact the International Alpine School/Boulder Mountain Guides in Eldorado Springs, (303) 494-4904.

CALIFORNIA
▲
Joshua Tree

Just three hours by car from Los Angeles, Joshua Tree is considered by many to be America's leading winter climbing site. The crystal quartz monzonite offers a superb climbing surface, with sharp edges, abundant cracks and a very high friction factor. With over 3,000 recorded climbs, there is an endless variety of routes from ultra-easy to 5.10+. Beginners will enjoy Echo Rock, while Headstone Rock and Saddle Rock have good routes in the 5.7-5.8 range, including the classic Walk on the Wild Side (5.8). Vertical Adventures is the leading guide service here. Call (714) 854-6250.

Tuolumne Meadows

Yosemite is where John Muir learned to climb, and it remains the heartland of American rock-climbing. You'll find a host of well-scouted 5.3 to 5.6 routes which most novices can master after an introductory weekend of training. The sky's the limit as far as advanced routes are concerned; Yosemite is where they wrote the book on big-wall climbing. Call the Yosemite School of Mountaineering, (209) 372-1355 (Jun-Aug), or (209) 372-1244 (Sept-May).

IDAHO
▲
City of the Rocks, Burley

While the City of the Rocks offers everything from gentle scrambling to experts-only climbs, the vast majority of routes are suitable for climbers-in-training. The wind-scoured desert granite provides solid holds, and many of the routes have bolted protection for added safety. Novices can quickly negotiate 5.4 Elephant Rock, and within a few days follow on the challenging Rye Crisp or Wheat Thins routes, both 5.7s. Other popular moderate climbs are the Lost Arrow Spire, and Morning Glory (5.6+). Contact Sawtooth Mountain Guides, P.O. Box 18, Stanley, ID 83278, (208) 774-3324.

NEW HAMPSHIRE
▲
North Conway

Many elite climbers started on North Conway's famed Cathedral and White Horse Ledges, two New England classics. With granite faces of 500' and 900', respectively, Cathedral and White Horse offer endless climbing options, many with fixed protection. There are over 200 recorded routes on each ledge, starting at 5.3. Popular multi-pitch graduation climbs include Thin Air (5.6) on White Horse, and Sliding Board

Cochiti Mesa, New Mexico/CHRIS NOBLE

(5.7) on Cathedral. North Conway has some of the best climbing guides in the country, including George Hurley of Mountain Guides Alliance, (603) 356-5310, and Rich Wilcox of the International Mountain Climbing School, (603) 356-7064.

NEW YORK
▲
The Shawangunks, New Paltz

The Shawangunks can be a busy place on weekends, but there's still no better training site close to New York. The "Gunks" offer very sound, high-friction rock, and the largest concentration of high-quality moderate climbs in the country. Many novices can follow 5.6-5.7 routes such as High Exposure on the first day. After a few days, try setting your sights on popular intermediate climbs such as Wild Horses (5.9) and Arrow (5.8). Contact High Angle Adventures from April through November. For further information, call (914) 658-9811.

NORTH CAROLINA
▲
Table Mountain, Linville

South of the Mason-Dixon Line, you won't find many better places to learn the ropes than North Carolina's Table Mountain. The quartzite rock offers a variety of routes, mostly multi-pitch, and many up to 400'. Popular novice climbs include the Cave Route and Jim Dandy on the East Face, both 5.5s. If you want to climb in solitude, hike about 45 minutes to the amphitheater, where you'll find good edges, few crowds and fine exposure, almost 1,000' above the Linville Gorge. To book guides for Table Mountain and nearby Looking Glass Rock (mostly 5.7+), contact Black Dome Mtn. Shop, (704) 274-4280, or Looking Glass Outfitters, (704) 884-5854.

OREGON
▲
Smith Rock, Terrebone

If you're located in the Pacific Northwest, and would like to learn rock-climbing in a dry, sunny environment, Smith Rock is hard to beat. While it's peppered with a variety of easy training routes which can be scouted from the ground, it also has some extremely difficult world-class pitches, which attract many of climbing's noted "rock stars." The Smith Rock Climbing School runs beginning through advanced courses on the Rock daily, March through November. Call Mike Volk at (503) 548-1888.

WASHINGTON
▲
Castle Rock, Leavenworth

Leavenworth is the premier rock-climbing area in the Cascades, with eight major crags within a 10-mile radius of town. Castle Rock itself boasts over 60 routes, from 5.3 to a daunting 5.12. Situated on the east slope of the Cascades, Leavenworth is dry and warm, spring through fall. The good weather, combined with short approaches and a wide variety of routes, make Leavenworth a great choice for all classes of climbers. Contact the American Alpine Institute, (206) 671-1505, for classes and guided climbs.

WYOMING
▲
Grand Teton area

Any list of classic American climbs would have to include the Tetons, home to Exum Mountain Guides, the nation's oldest climbing school. Most novices take Exum's basic course which will, after a couple of days' training, put them atop Grand Teton summit via a 5.7 ridge route. Contact Exum at (307) 733-2297.

GREAT ICE-CLIMBING PROGRAMS

John Reed, Bridal Veil Falls, Provo Canyon, Utah/CHRIS NOBLE

C LASSIC ICE-CLIMBING TECHNIQUE evolved as part of the general repertoire of alpine skills used on summit climbs. In the past 15 years, however, improved techniques and more advanced equipment have revolutionized ice-climbing, allowing vertical ascents of frozen waterfalls--the ultimate stairways of ice. If you have dreamed of conquering gravity in a winter wonderland, here are the best places to go throughout North America.

ADIRONDACKS

If you're new to the world of ice screws and crampons, try Adirondack Alpine Adventure's (AAA) 2-day Water Ice intro course for $240. You will be taught all the basics and follow a guided climb with no more than two students per instructor. For a more intensive experience, we can strongly recommend AAA's ice-climbing seminars, either Level I for Novices, or Level II for intermediates. The climbing sites are well-selected and the ice itself is excellent and reliable, yet plenty challenging. If that's still not enough ice for you, AAA offers a $240 2–day specialty Walls & Waterfalls course that will teach you advanced techniques for moving on ice gullies, frozen walls and waterfalls. For details, call AAA at (518) 576-9881.

CASCADES

One of Rainier Mountaineering's most highly regarded programs over the years has been its 5-day snow and ice-climbing seminar taught at 10,000' Camp Muir on Mt. Rainier. The curriculum is customized to match the particular skills of participants, from novices to experts. All courses feature training in snow shelters, glacier travel and crevasse rescue, as well as ice-climbing technique. The high point of the program is the summit climb at course's end. This is a solid course, though the student/guide ratio is relatively high. Cost for 5 days is about $480. Call (206) 627-6242.

NEW HAMPSHIRE

North Conway's International Mountain Climbing School (IMCS) enjoys a worldwide reputation for its specialty ice-climbing programs. Winter conditions in New Hampshire create superb climbing ice, something hard to find West of the Rockies. If you're serious about learning to climb ice from first-rate instructors, this program is one of the best available anywhere in North America. Excellent equipment is provided, although the student/guide ratio could be better. Cost for a 4-day basic ice-climbing seminar is $365, while a 3-day intermediate program runs $290. IMCS' advanced 2-day ice-climbing course, offering more waterfalls, steeper ascents and a 3:1 student/guide ratio costs $185. Call IMCS at (603) 356-7013.

ROCKIES

With its many frozen waterfalls, Ouray, Colorado, the "Ice Capital" of the Rockies, offers some of the best climbing ice in the world, against a spectacular natural backdrop. The Int'l. Alpine School/Boulder Mountain Guides (IAS) conducts a superb Ice Experience course in Ouray every winter. (You should note that both Outward Bound and NOLS have sent instructors to International Alpine School to learn state-of-the-art ice technique.) The 5-day class covers basic French techniques for low-angle ice as well as skills for climbing, protecting and belaying on vertical ice. Call IAS at (303) 494-4904. Michael Covington's Fantasy Ridge Guiding, (303) 728-3546, also runs outstanding ice-climbing courses at Ouray each winter. Cost for 5 days with lodging ranges from $550-$750 depending on grade level-- beginning, intermediate or advanced. The student/guide ratios are commendably low, and the guides are among America's most expert icemen.

SAWTOOTHS

Every fall, Sawtooth Mountain Guides conducts a 4-day Alpine Ice seminar on the slope of 12,655' Mt. Borah, Idaho's only glacier. The first two days are spent learning basic

and intermediate techniques, and practicing with the hardware--crampons, ice hammers, ice screws and other aids. Then participants ascend to the summit along the challenging 2,000' North Face route. Cost for 4 days, including food and equipment but not lodging, is $380. Contact Sawtooth Mountain Guides, (208) 774-3324.

Merrill Bitter, Finger of Fate, Provo Canyon, Utah/CHRIS NOBLE

SIERRAS

Alpine Skills International (ASI) conducts weekend ice-climbing courses on frozen waterfalls at California's June Lake and Lee Vining Canyon. This is one of the best locations for vertical ice on the West Coast offering sections suitable for beginners, as well as for experienced climbers seeking more challenging top-roped ascents. Courses run each January and February at a cost of $185, and ASI provides a full selection of equipment, including the latest high-tech hardware. For details, call ASI at (916) 426-9108.

TETONS

Jackson Hole Mountain Guides' 8-day Alpine Ice-Climber Course may be the best of its kind offered by an American climbing school, providing all the challenge you could want. This advanced course features three classic Teton ascents: Middle Teton Glacier, the Enclosure Couloir and the Black Couloir. Cost for the program, which runs in late August (when conditions are best), will be about $1,000. Four-day winter ice-climbing seminars are also offered each January in Wyoming and Utah for about $500. Call Jackson Hole Mountain Guides at (307) 733-4979.

FRENCH ALPS

British-based Mountain Experience leads ice-climbing seminars to Chamonix, France, each summer. There, along the flanks of Mt. Blanc and nearby summits are numerous vertical icefalls and glaciers ideal for learning ice-climbing technique. While most climbers have some previous technical climbing experience, novice instruction is also available. Seminars cost roughly $130 per day, depending on size of group. Contact Mountain Experience, The Cottage, Whitehough Head, Chinley, Stockport SK12 6BX, England, (011 44) 663 7 50160. The Int'l Alpine School/Boulder Mtn. Guides also offers a 15-day French Alps program which combines ice-climbing on the Boissons Glacier with five summit ascents in the Mt. Blanc range. Call (303) 494-4904.

ALPINE MOUNTAINEERING

INSURANCE

Things can happen while climbing. Common injuries include fractures, frostbite and concussions. Even altitude sickness can be debilitating for some. We urge you not to undertake any climbing program without good personal medical insurance. Most accredited climbing schools are bonded and insured, but the type and amount of coverage varies considerably, so you should still have your own insurance. Read your policy carefully. Make sure there is no exclusion for high risk activities, such as climbing. If you need to acquire new medical insurance, carriers specializing in coverage for foreign trips are listed in Chapter 29.

You will also want trip cancellation and evacuation insurance. Trip cancellation insurance will cover non-refundable air and land costs forfeited when you cancel a climbing course because of family or personal illness or disability. Evacuation insurance will cover the cost of emergency medical evacuation from wilderness areas. This coverage is essential. An emergency helicopter evacuation from a remote summit can easily cost $1,000 or more. Ask your guide service if it can place trip cancellation and evacuation insurance for you. Alpine Skills International, for example, provides such insurance to its climbers for approximately $6 per $100 of trip cost.

Climbing rack/JOEL ROGERS

MAGAZINES

Climbing magazine, P.O. Box 339, 502 Main Street, Carbondale, CO 81623, (303) 963-9449, is a great bimonthly journal. The emphasis is on rock-climbing, with many features on alpine ascents.

Mountain magazine, P.O. Box 184, Sheffield, S11 9Dl, England, is the UK's leading mountaineering and rock-climbing journal. Published six times yearly, it offers excellent reports on climbing sites in the European Alps, and is a good source of information on commercial Himalayan expeditions.

BOOKS

How to Rock-Climb, by John Long, is one of the best introductory rock-climbing guidebooks. Available for $9.95 from Chockstone Press, Inc., P.O. Box 3505, Evergreen, CO 80439.

Mountaineering--the Freedom of the Hills, 4th ed., 542 pages, $19.95 from the Mountaineers, (800) 553-HIKE. This is it: the most complete guide to alpine mountaineering available in English. From rope technique to avalanche rescue, it is the bible of climbing, and a necessary resource for any serious mountaineer.

Rock Climbs in the White Mountains of New Hampshire, $22.95, Mountain Imagery, P.O. Box 210, Eldorado Springs, CO 80025, is the definitive guide to rock-hopping in the East Coast's top climbing area.

Snow and Ice Climbing, by John Barry, $16.95, from Alpenbooks, P.O. Box 761, Snohomish, WA 98260, (206) 568-4181. Barry's 160-page guide is a must read for anyone getting started in this most technical of all climbing disciplines. Authoritative and well-written.

Sources: Michael Chessler Books, P.O. Box 4267--Dept. 58, Evergreen, CO 80439, (800) 654-8502 or (303) 670-0039 in CO, is America's largest bookstore specializing in climbing and expeditions. Call for a free catalog.

VIDEOS

Basic Rock-climbing shows you the fundamentals needed to challenge a big wall. Filmed on location in Yosemite. Send $39.95 plus $2.50 shipping to Vertical Adventures Prod., P.O. Box 8188, Calabasas, CA 91372. Californians, add sales tax.

Moving Over Stone is a classic rock-climbing video available for $39.95 plus $3.00 shipping from Range of Light Productions, P.O. Box 2906, Mammoth Lakes, CA 93546, (619) 935-4648. Range of Light also features excellent skiing and mountain-biking videos.

On the Rocks and **Over the Edge** are truly outstanding rock-climbing videos, both winners of international awards. *Over the Edge* features mind-boggling big-wall climbs, while *On the Rocks* captures 5.13 climbs--the ultimate--on film. Both are available from OTR, Box 93974, Los Angeles, CA 90093, (213) 466-4921.

To the Summit is a quality video of Genet Expeditions' 1986 climb of Mt. McKinley. Shot by a professional cinematographer, this is a great way to preview a major climb. You can obtain a copy from Genet Expeditions, 4602 Business Park Blvd., Anchorage, AK 99503, (800) 334-3638.

ALPINE CLUBS AND ORGANIZATIONS

Commercial mountaineering programs in the United States are regulated by the **American Mountain Guides Association,** P.O. Box 2128, Estes Park, CO 80517, (303) 586-0571. If you're thinking of hiring a guide service not recommended in this chapter, contact the AMGA to check out the company's professional standing and safety record. Another source of information on amateur guides and climbing programs is the **Appalachian Mountain Club,** (603) 466-2727.

Canadian climbing guide services are regulated by the **Canadian Mountain Guides Association,** P.O. Box 1537, Banff, ALB, Canada TOL OCO. This organization can provide you with a list of qualified guides in most provinces. In many respects, certification standards for individual guides are more rigorous in Canada than in the United States, so you can generally be assured that an accredited guide is highly qualified.

Outside of North America, mountain guiding services are controlled by the **UIAGM,** which accredits individual guides as opposed to schools. The UIAGM certification standards are very high, requiring extensive formal training and testing. In selecting a foreign guide, insist that he or she hold a valid UIAGM certification.

Dawn on Mt. St. Elias, Wrangell-St. Elias National Park/BOB JACOBS, ST. ELIAS GUIDES

Dogsledding

The wild places are where we began.
When they end, so do we.
-David Brower

▼

The Arctic and Antarctic, the loneliest, most forbidding regions on earth, are the last great frontiers. As habitats for both land and aquatic species, the Arctic and Antarctic regions are unique resources. Here you will find the largest concentrations of sea birds on the planet, vast herds of caribou and other migratory species, and countless other forms of wildlife.

Not so long ago, the distant reaches of the Arctic and Antarctic were accessible only to native Eskimos and intrepid explorers. In recent decades, however, the adventure travel industry has made it possible for ordinary people to visit these areas by air, land and sea. The range of available polar adventures is limited only by your imagination. In this chapter we review the full spectrum of Arctic and Antarctic travel opportunities--dogsledding, wildlife cruises, ski tours, sea kayak tours, snowmobile treks, and even expeditions to the North and South Poles. If this sounds like your idea of adventure, read on.

CHAPTER
2

Adelie Penguin, Antarctica / ART WOLFE

A TRIP TO THE ARCTIC OR ANTARCTIC IS A VERY SPECIAL EXPERIENCE--QUITE literally an odyssey to the ends of the earth. These are regions where, given the extremes of the climate and the vast distances between settlements, everyday life is an adventure. And nowhere else can you escape into a world so untouched by humans, where the great creatures of the wild still thrive. For those who seek a land untamed, where true exploration and discovery are still possible, the Arctic and Antarctic are unsurpassed.

NORTH POLE

Journeys to the Top of the World

Been everywhere, done everything? In that case, why not hop a flight to the North Pole? Or if you prefer to take your time, cruise to the pole on a nuclear-powered, 75,000-horsepower Soviet ice-breaker.

All kidding aside, for true adventure, few things can rival a trip to the North Pole. Just getting there is the challenge. Most visitors to the pole arrive by air, but the 500' icebreaker, Sovetskiy Soyuz, now of-fers a unique alternative for those who prefer the brute force approach. This 21,000-ton giant can penetrate ice 16 feet thick. It is the only type of surface craft to have made the full Northeast Passage, steaming all the way to the geographic pole, right through the polar icecap. The Soyuz completed her maiden commercial voyage in 1991, and passengers agreed it was memorable--particularly watching from the bow as the ship blasted through solid pack ice at 10 knots. Though no luxury yacht, the Soyuz is well-appointed and carries western physicians and science lecturers. The ship boasts two helicopters and Zodiac inflatables for exploring the ice floes. The 3-week voyage departs in July and costs $18,000. Book passage through Quark Expeditions of Stamford, CT, (800) 223-5688.

For a mere $10,000, you can get to the North Pole on an aerial expedition. The polar flight is done in stages--hopscotching over some of the most spectacular scenery in the Arctic. Trip participants gather at Resolute, Canada, the northernmost point served by regularly scheduled flights. From there, the expedition Twin Otter flies to Eureka, a weather station on Ellesmere Island. Along the way, the aircraft will fly low over massive glaciers and icebergs, or head inland to observe herds of musk ox.

After Eureka, the next stop is Lake Hazen, the final staging ground for the polar odyssey. Up to three days will be spent on standby, awaiting weather clearance. Everything must be right, as there is only enough cached fuel for one polar assault. When conditions are safe, the Otter will take off at dawn. A few hours later it will set down at the top of the world.

Seven Ultimate Polar Adventures

Unfortunately, the stay will be brief, as the aircraft must return the same day. Cost for the 8-day April expedition is about $9,900 from Resolute. Contact Special Odysseys, 3430 Evergreen Point Road, P.O. Box 37A, Medina, WA 98039, (206) 455-1960.

If you want to add whimsy to your North Pole flight, try Adventure Canada's annual North Pole Golf Tournament. Weather permitting, participants will play holes in each of the four national zones at

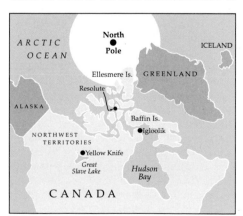

the geographic North Pole--Canada, USSR, USA and Greenland. Contact Adventure Canada, 1159 W. Broadway, Vancouver, BC, Canada V6H 1G1, (604) 736-7447. The April journey will cost about $10,200.

SOUTH POLE

Overland by Ski and Ski-Doo

In 1988 the first commercial South Pole expedition reached the pole after skiing across 750 miles of Antarctic wilderness. The entire starting group of nine men and two women made the 50-day journey under their own power. No major mishaps befell the group, and all the skiers came home in good shape, except for some minor frostbite. The expedition was organized by Mountain Travel and supported by Adventure Network International (ANI).

In the wake of this success, ANI has announced two new overland trips from the South Pole. On both tours you fly to the geographic South Pole, then ride out on snowmobiles. (The Ski-Doos are air-lifted to the pole along with cached food and fuel

supplies.) The first tour returns directly to the Patriot Hills basecamp. The second, longer expedition crosses the Ross Ice Shelf to Cape Evans where the group will be picked up by a waiting expedition vessel. Both tours will run in late November or December, the warmest season at the bottom of the world. The Patriot Hills expedition runs about 3 weeks, and costs roughly $50,000. The Cape Evans journey may last a month or longer (including time at the basecamp), and costs a full $100,000 per person, making this first-ever expedition the most expensive vacation on the planet.

For those wishing a more reasonably-priced adventure, ANI offers a 2-week, $9,500 Heart of Antarctica trip. Participants stay at the Patriot Hills basecamp, visit nearby glaciers and harbors using skis or snowmobiles, and board ANI's expedition aircraft for overflights of Mt. Vinson and the Ellesworth Mountains. There is also a shorter 6-day $6,500 Patriot Hills program featuring flight-seeing and a single day of skiing. ANI's most challenging trip is the 2-week Ellesworth Mountain Ski Safari.

Climbing on Weinke Island, Antarctic Peninsula/RICK RIDGEWAY, ADVENTURE PHOTO

This $9,500 overland tour is designed for fit skiers with previous winter camping experience. Contact ANI, 200-1676 Duranleau Street, Vancouver, BC, Canada V6H 3S5, (604) 683-8033; FAX: (604) 689-7646.

ANTARCTICA

Mountaineering

Antarctica's highest peak, the Vinson Massif (Mt. Vinson), remains one of the world's ultimate climbing destinations. It is estimated that fewer than 130 persons have reached the top of Mt. Vinson, the most remote of the Seven Summits.

Climbing Mt. Vinson is an arduous and expensive quest. Even though the mountain is not terribly steep--there is a moderate glacier ramp most of the way up--many top climbers consider Mt. Vinson to be a tougher summit than Mt. McKinley, due to the rugged Antarctic environment. The weather is unpredictable and incredibly harsh when it turns bad--100 mph winds and 40 below zero temperatures are possible even in the Antarctic's "good" season.

The vast expense of transporting a climbing team to the heart of Antarctica make Mt. Vinson one of the costliest propositions in mountaineering. Adventure Network International (ANI), which has supported more than a dozen expeditions to Mt. Vinson, charges $19,500 person for

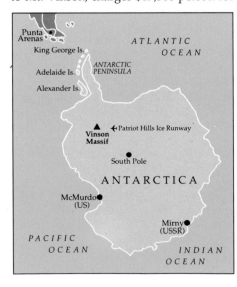

its 2-week expeditions, scheduled for December 1992 and January 1993. Call ANI at (604) 683-8033 for details.

If bagging Mt. Vinson is not glory enough, there are still virgin (and near virgin) peaks left in Antarctica. Many of the summits surrounding Mt. Vinson in the Ellesworth Range have never been scaled. And 13,000' Mt. Jackson, the highest peak on the Antarctic Peninsula, has never been climbed by a commercial group, despite being relatively non-technical. (Access is very difficult, and the weather is notoriously unstable.) The second highest peak in Antarctica, 15,895' Mt. Tyree, has only been conquered twice. Only 165' lower than Mt. Vinson, Tyree is much steeper and much more dangerous. With the ascent requiring an 8,000' technical attack of the West Face, and then a traverse across razor-edged ridges exposed to high winds, Mt. Tyree is for experts only. However, ANI founder Pat Morrow believes the northeast ridge offers a far less technical approach, but no team has yet attempted this route. You could be among the first.

ELLESMERE ISLAND

Sea Kayaking

If you go on one Arctic kayak expedition in your life, make it this one. Ecosummer Expeditions is the premier sea kayak outfitter in the Arctic, and its Ellesmere Island Arctic Dreams trip is by far the company's most rewarding northern kayak itinerary. On this journey paddlers will visit the fjords of Ellesmere's Kane Basin. Using folding kayaks airlifted from Resolute (the northernmost settlement in Canada), you explore inlets and iceberg-filled waterways, camping on shore as well as on ice floes.

Ellesmere is so far north (about 80 degrees latitude) that there is continuous sunlight in summer. Far removed from civilization, the utter silence of the environment is at first startling. Ecosummer founder Jim Allan, who leads the Ellesmere trip, has observed that most visitors are "blown away" by Ellesmere at first. "It's such a surreal environment. Everything is so totally different.... Everything is sculpted--by the water, by the tide, by the wind."

There are a few polar bears about, but primarily you'll observe walrus, and bearded and ring seals. When camping on ice floes, seals may bask only a few yards from your tent. Musk ox and migratory snow geese are also abundant. But Allan's favorite animals are the wolves. "The wolves are beautiful. They're the most beautiful creatures you can see up there. They're big--[and] always on the move."

Though the environment can be harsh (the travel window this far north is a short four weeks in July and August), this trip is suitable for any person with some wilderness camping experience. The group paddles an easy five to 20 miles per day, covering 10 miles on average. Eighty percent of Allan's charges have no previous sea kayaking experience. Cost will be roughly $3,500 US, not including the flight to Resolute from Montreal. Contact Ecosummer Expeditions, 1516 Duranleau Street, Granville Island, Vancouver, BC, Canada V6H 3S4, (604) 669-7741.

GATES OF THE ARCTIC

Dogsled and Ski Trip

The Gates of the Arctic National Park and Preserve is one of the largest wilderness areas (8.4 million acres) in North America. Being the most remote and northern national park, it remains truly wild, almost completely untouched by civilization. Alaska's Brooks Range runs through the park, with two peaks, Frigid Crags and Boreal Mountain, forming the "Gates" from the central Brooks Range into the high Arctic. In these latitudes above the Arctic Circle, round-the-clock sunlight affords perfect conditions for viewing the moose, caribou, dall sheep, bears, wolves and fox that inhabit the park.

Alaska's Sourdough Outfitters runs challenging combination dogsled-ski trips each April through the Gates of the Arctic Preserve. The trip begins with a ski plane flight from Bettles, Alaska to a wilderness outpost at Eroded Mountain. For the next 9 days, the group travels north through the dramatic Koyukuk River Valley. Dog teams carry all communal gear and heavy personal items while tour members take turns skiing and mushing. The longest day's run is 15 miles, and daytime temperatures average 20 degrees.

Arctic hunter/DAN GURAVICH, ALLSTOCK

Camps are made in heated-wall tents along a dogsled trail. On the sixth day, you'll actually ski through the Gates, and make camp just north, with fantastic views of the Gates, Hanging Glacier Mountain, and nearby frozen waterfalls. Day eight takes the group to the confluence of the Koyukuk River and Ernie Creek where you'll be met by a ski plane for the flight back to Bettles.

This trip is a true wilderness adventure--one of the most unique commercially guided ski tours in the world. It is demanding, but any intermediate skier with some wilderness experience should be able to handle the conditions. No mountaineering skills are required, though you must bring your own expedition-grade equipment. The price is $1,995 for 10 days (8 in the wild). For further details, contact Sourdough Outfitters, P.O. Box 90, Bettles, AK 99726, (907) 692-5252.

ANTARCTICA

Cruise & Zodiac Adventure

Antarctica is a place of otherworldly beauty. Here you will find giant glaciers stretching to the horizon, blue-hued icebergs as tall as 10-story buildings, and rocky harbors that shelter an incredible variety of wildlife. On the northern-most end of the Antarctic Peninsula, across Drake's Passage from Cape Horn, you can observe seals, petrels, cormorants, albatross, and colonies of penguins numbering in the tens of thousands. In the Antarctic summer, humpback, fin, right and sei whales ply the cobalt waters near shore.

Unless you are prepared to under-take an enormously expensive overland expedition (with a price tag starting at $15,000 per person), the best way to see Antarctica is by cruise ship, preferably one outfitted with small launches or Zodiac inflatables. These small maneuverable craft are essential for exploring the lesser

inlets and ice floes that make this most remote of continents so unique.

Every year, Society Expeditions organizes 15 to 30-day cruises to the shores of the Antarctic Peninsula. Society Expedition's large, ice-strengthened cruise ships navigate close to the massive glaciers and giant bergs that mark Antarctica's coastline. While in Hope Bay, Paradise Bay and smaller inlets, passengers will board 15-person Zodiac inflatables to venture shoreward, passing almost within arm's reach of molting glaciers and floating ice. Zodiacs are also used to land on Deception Island, an active volcano, and to visit King George Island, site of research stations for eight countries.

Society Expeditions' cruises operate every year between November and March. As you might expect, these deluxe trips are not for those on a tight budget. Cruises start at about $5,500 for 15 days with a small inside cabin. You can pay as much as $18,000 for a deluxe cabin on a 4-week cruise. Contact Society Expeditions, 3131 Elliott Avenue, Suite 700, Seattle, WA 98121, (800) 426-7794; FAX: (206) 285-7917.

Lindblad's Special Expeditions and Mountain Travel also offer Antarctic cruises

Antarctic Peninsula/JOEL SIMON, COURTESY SOCIETY EXPEDITIONS

that visit the Antarctic Peninsula and explore small inlets by Zodiac. Both companies run good trips, with excellent guides, and have traditionally offered more attractive prices than Society Expeditions, particularly for those wanting a large, private cabin. Contact Mountain Travel/Sobek,

6420 Fairmont Ave., El Cerrito, CA, 94530, (800) 227-2384, or Lindblad's Special Expeditions, 720 Fifth Avenue, New York, NY 10019, (800) 762-2003.

YUKON

Arctic Ocean River Run

Even though this book contains a whole chapter on rafting, no guide to Arctic adventure would be complete without a Yukon river trip above the Arctic Circle. Our pick is Ecosummer Expeditions' Firth River trip, which takes you through Canada's Barrenlands National Park all the way to the Arctic Ocean. During your run you'll witness the full panoply of Arctic topography--alpine meadows, open tundra, ancient glaciers and deep canyons.

The Firth snakes through scenic valleys rich with wildlife. Expect to see moose, wolves, musk ox, and, when you reach the sea, beluga whales, walrus and seals. A special highlight of the 11-day trip is the caribou migration. Ecosummer has arranged the trip to coincide with the annual July migration of the Porcupine caribou herd--numbering over 180,000 animals.

For a trip combining outstanding wild-life, extremely remote wilderness scenery, and the pleasure of a river float (this is not a whitewater run), the Firth trip is one of the very best. You will also find that the $2,600 US price compares favorably with other trips that offer only caribou viewing from a land basecamp. Call Ecosummer Expeditions, (address above), (604) 669-7741.

If you prefer to travel in June, you can view the Porcupine herd on a raft trip through Alaska's Arctic National Wildlife Refuge. In recent years, raft expeditions on both the Kongakut and Hulahula rivers have floated right through the middle of thousands of swimming caribou. Trips cost about $1,900 per week. Contact Alaskan outfitters ABEC, or Arctic Treks, both reviewed on the opposite page.

Top Arctic/ Subarctic Outfitters

Digging out, Ruth Glacier, Alaska/CHRIS NOBLE

*I*F OUR RECOMMENDED ARCTIC AND SUBARCTIC TRIPS HAVE INSPIRED YOUR APPE-tite for adventure, here's a list of some of the best guide services and outfitters operating in the polar and subarctic regions. The programs they offer run the gamut from full-on polar expeditions, to sled-team supported ski tours, or Arctic river journeys.

ALASKA

■ ALASKA DISCOVERY WILDERNESS EXPEDITIONS
369 South Franklin St., Juneau, AK 99801, (907) 586-1911.

You can look, but you won't find any better wilderness guide service than Alaska Discovery, now in its 19th year. Alaska Discovery offers both land and sea treks to many of Alaska's most scenic areas, including the Tongass National Forest, the Russell Fjord Wilderness Area, and the Tatshenshini River area. It is also the only guide service allowed to operate in Glacier Bay. Alaska Discovery's wilderness raft and canoe expeditions are some of the best in the world. Rating: ★★★★

■ ABEC
1304 Westwick Drive, Fairbanks, AK 99712, (907) 457-8907.

ABEC is one of Alaska's oldest and most established wilderness guide services. It specializes in rafting, kayaking, canoeing and backpacking trips in the Brooks Range and Lake Clark. Trips range from 7-22 days, start at about $120 per day, and are offered year-round. ABEC can also book trips with Ron Yarnell's excellent backcountry guide service, Wilderness: Alaska/Mexico, 1231

Sundance Loop, Fairbanks, AK 99709, (907) 479-8203. Rating: ★★★

■ ARCTIC TREKS
P.O. Box 73452, Fairbanks, AK 99707, (907) 455-6502.

A family operation, Jim Campbell's Arctic Treks has offered outstanding summer hiking and rafting programs in the Brooks Range since 1979. Strongly recommended is a float down the Hulahula River in the heart of the Arctic National Wildlife Refuge. Few trips offer a better combination of big mountains, wilderness solitude and wildlife. The 10-day $2,400 June trip coincides with the migration of the 180,000-strong Porcupine caribou herd. Arctic Treks also runs float trips down the Koyakuk, Noatak and Kongakut rivers. Custom trips are a specialty. Hikers can choose from challenging alpine routes, or day-hikes from a high arctic basecamp. Rating: ★★★

■ SOURDOUGH OUTFITTERS
P.O. Box 90, Bettles, AK 99726, (907) 692-5252.

Sourdough is the oldest and best known outfitter/guide service in the Brooks Range. Along with summer backpacking and river trips, Sourdough offers dogsledding and sled-supported cross-country ski trips each winter. (See featured trip on page 33.) Rating: ★★★

CANADA

Yukon and Northwest Territories

■ ARCTIC WATERWAYS
RR2, Stevensville, ONT, Canada L0S 1S0, (416) 382-3882; FAX: (416) 382-3020.

For over 18 years, Arctic Waterways has conducted wilderness float trips on the NWT's Coppermine and Horton Rivers. These 12-day leisurely expeditions take you into remote tundra areas above the Arctic Circle. Drifting along the river and camping at night, you'll have opportunities to observe eagles, falcons, musk ox, and caribou during their annual migrations. Special emphasis fishing trips can be arranged as well. This is a family operation, directed by folks who really love the backcountry. Cost will be about $2,600 CDN with air taxi from Yellowknife. Rating: ★★★

■ BLACK FEATHER WILDERNESS ADVENTURES
40 Wellington Street, East Toronto, ONT, Canada M5E 1C7, (416) 862-1555.

For the past 20 years, Black Feather has been one of the very best canoe and trekking outfitters in Canada. Black Feather runs a host of northern rivers in the Yukon and NWTs, including the Wind, Bonnet Plume, Mountain, Natla-Keele, Hess, Hood, Burnside and Nahanni. (A trip down the Nahanni, a river of legendary beauty, is profiled in our Canoe & Kayaking Chapter.) These canoe trips range from mild (Class I) to wild (Class III+), so you will find something to suit you, no matter what your skill level. Black Feather's canoe trips run 1 to 3 weeks and range in price from about $700 to about $3,200. In addition to its river programs,

Black Feather offers 8 to 14-day summer treks in North Yukon Nat'l Park, Kluane Park and other scenic areas. Rating: ★★★★

■ CANADA NORTH OUTFITTING, INC.

P.O. Box 3100, 87 Mill Street, Almonte, ONT, Canada K0A 1A0, (613) 256-4057; FAX: (613) 256-4512.

Canada North Outfitting (CNO) has a broad range of tours in the Canadian Arctic and subarctic. One of the most popular programs is CNO's Igloolik dogsled trip (8 days from Montreal, $3,400). CNO also offers tours to Inuit villages at Pond Inlet and Cape Dorset on Baffin Island (9 days, about $2,900), hiking trips in Auyuittuq Park on Baffin Island (11 days, about $1,750), polar bear- and walrus-watching trips to Coats Island at the north end of Hudson Bay (9 days, about $3,800), and polar bear expeditions to Cape Churchill, (5 days, about $1,500). All prices are subject to change. Rating: ★★

YUKON

The Canadian Arctic
■ ECOSUMMER EXPEDITIONS

1516 Duranleau Street, Granville Island, Vancouver, BC, Canada V6H 3S4, (604) 669-7741.

Ecosummer Expeditions (ESE) is one of the most respected wilderness outfitters in Canada. It offers many fine tours to the eastern Canadian Arctic, ranging from yacht cruises to rugged overland trips. ESE has pioneered 95 percent of its trip itineraries, and it is the clear choice for most of its destinations. We highly recommend ESE's 2-week summer sea kayak trips to Digges Sound and Ellesmere Island. (See featured trip on page 33.)

Ecosummer also offers 11-day raft expeditions on Alaska's Tatshenshini, and Canada's Firth and Nahanni Rivers. The Tatshenshini trip costs approximately $2,300, while the Firth River odyssey runs about $2,400, and the Nahanni $2,300. Land-based options include a backpack trek across Ellesmere Island (14 days, about $3,700), and a Northern Yukon National Park trek through the British Mountains to the edge of the Arctic Ocean (10 days, about $1,800). Rating: ★★★★

Wilderness rafting on Alaska's Tatshenshini River/CHRIS NOBLE

■ BAFFIN ISLAND AREA OUTFITTERS

If a package tour is not your style, you can arrange your own Arctic itinerary by contacting one of Baffin Island's many native or resident outfitters. Expect to save 20 to 30 percent over the cost of an agency-booked trip. All the following guide services arrange spring dog-team trips or Ski-doo trips. For updated listings, contact NWT Tourism, (800) 661-0788.

Broughton Island (Auyuittuq National Park/ Cumberland Peninsula): Laymeekee Qimmilik Outfitter, Broughton Island, NWT X0A 0B0, (819) 927-8932. Igloolik (Melville Peninsula): Tuputaq Enterprises (Emile Immaroitok), Igloolik, NWT X0A 0L0, (819) 934-8876. Iqaluit: Madelaine Lake Enterprises Outfitter, Box 1238, Iqaluit, NWT X0A 0H0; Nuna-Kuuk Outfitting, Box 123, Iqaluit, NWT X0A 0H0, (819) 979-6027. No rating.

■ SPECIAL ODYSSEYS

3430 Evergreen Point Road, P.O. Box 37A, Medina, WA 98039, (206) 455-1960.

Special Odysseys offers an 8-day North Pole trip out of Resolute Bay for $9,900 in April. Weeklong snowmobile or dogsled wilderness treks on Baffin and Ellesmere Islands depart in April, May and June at a cost of about $3,300 from Ottowa, Canada. Strongly recommended is the June Marine Mammals trip--7 days of travel over the pack ice of Baffin Bay by snowmobile, at a cost of about $4,200. Special Odysseys is most proud of its March Aurora trip which offers a bit of everything--high Arctic exploring, wildlife watching and Inuit village tours. The $3,500 itinerary includes Arctic wildlife parks, Queen Elizabeth Island and Northern Greenland. Rating: ★★★

GREENLAND

■ ARCTIC ADVENTURE ApS

Aaboulevarden 37, DK-1960 Frederiksberg Copenhagen, Denmark, (011 45) 1 37 12 33.

This Danish agency books everything from hiking trips to deluxe hotel-stays in South Greenland, Disko Bay and Ammasilik. (Greenland is a self-governing Danish protectorate.) Trips are offered year-round at competitive prices. Rating: ★★

■ GREENLAND TRAVEL AGENCY (GTA)

P.O. Box 330, DK-3900 Nuuk (Godthab), Greenland, (011 299) 2 24 55; Telex: 90668.

Greenland is a spectacular destination, with the biggest mountains and fjords in the Arctic. From luxury flightseeing and cruising tours to overland dogsledding, Greenland Travel Agency provides a wide variety of Arctic adventures. Don't miss the Jakobson (Illulissat) Ice Fjord. It is truly one of the most spectacular sights in the entire Arctic. You can view from aircraft or special expedition vessels. A domestic agent for GTA is Borton Overseas, (800) 843-0602. You can request brochures from the Danish Tourist Board, (212) 949-2333; FAX: (212) 983-5260. Rating: ★★

WORLDWIDE

■ LINDBLAD'S SPECIAL EXPEDITIONS
New York, NY, (800) 762-0003.

■ MOUNTAIN TRAVEL/SOBEK
El Cerrito, CA, (800) 227-2384.

■ QUARK EXPEDITIONS/ SALEN LINDBLAD CRUISING
Stamford, CT, (800) 223-5688.

■ SOCIETY EXPEDITIONS
Seattle, WA, (800) 426-7794.

These agencies offer cruises to Alaskan waters, and to the Antarctic Peninsula and nearby islands. Antarctic itineraries are quite similar, so shop for the best price. Quark offers unique Soviet cruises, including a Soviet icebreaker trip to the North Pole (see p. 30). Mountain Travel offers hiking and rafting trips in Alaska's Arctic National Wildlife Refuge, and schedules a Mt. Vinson expedition each winter. Of these companies, Mountain Travel offers the most variety and challenge, Society Expeditions the most luxury. Ratings: ★★★ (all cruises)

South Pole Ski Expedition, windy camp at 83 degrees south latitude/GORDON WILTSIE

POLAR EXPEDITIONS & ARCTIC SUMMIT CLIMBS

POLAR OVERLAND EXPEDITIONS ARE SERIOUS, DIFFICULT UNDERTAKINGS. Even with today's technology, getting to a pole, or just venturing overland above the Arctic Circle, remains an ultimate test of human stamina, courage and preparation. Climbing expeditions in Arctic regions can be just as challenging as overland polar trips. The mountains of Alaska and Antarctica are remote, high and tough to conquer, both due to the technical skills required, and the extremes of climate and weather. The companies listed below can organize an expedition, provide the equipment and guides, and arrange the support services you will need (air taxis, food caches, etc.) to make your adventure a successful one.

■ **ADVENTURE NETWORK INTERNATIONAL**
200-1676 Duranleau Street, Vancouver, BC, Canada V6H 3S5, (604) 683-8033; FAX: (604) 683-6892.

Founded in 1985 by a multinational group of expedition guides, Adventure Network International (ANI) is recognized as the top Antarctic expedition support service. ANI has assembled a team of guides, pilots and suppliers who can handle all phases of polar trips, airborne or overland. ANI operates the only private basecamp in Antarctica. ANI is also the only company to lead expeditions to both the North and South Pole--including the 1988 South Pole Skiing Expedition. Though ANI built its reputation on serious expeditions, it also offers less rugged adventures, such as

Antarctic wildlife cruises. Rating: ★★★★

■ **ALASKA-DENALI GUIDING, INC.**
P.O. Box 566, Talkeetna, AK 99676, (907) 733-2649.

Alaska-Denali Guiding offers a full range of wilderness adventures (ski touring, trekking, kayaking) year-round. Its staff has the capacity to lead high Arctic expeditions to remote areas, or to organize climbs of major peaks. It has the most experienced guides and most enviable safety record on Mt. McKinley. This is a world-class operation. Rating: ★★★★

■ **MOUNTAIN TRIP**
P.O. Box 91161, Anchorage, AK 99509, (907) 345-6499.

Gary Bocarde's Mountain Trip is another

outstanding mountaineering guide service for Mt. McKinley and other high peaks in the Alaska and Wrangell Ranges. Highly recommended. Rating: ★★★

■ **ST. ELIAS ALPINE GUIDES**
P.O. Box 111241, Anchorage, AK 99511, (907) 277-6867.

St. Elias Alpine Guides, owned and operated by veteran polar explorer Bob Jacobs, offers wilderness expeditions throughout Alaska, specializing in Wrangell-St. Elias National Park. Jacobs' company has earned quite a reputation for guided climbs of Mt. St. Elias, North America's third highest peak, and numerous first ascents of high peaks in the Alaska and Brooks Ranges. Jacobs' trips offer real adventure--high-altitude mountaineering, glacier treks, and guided explorations of remote Arctic regions. Rating: ★★★

■ **DOUG GEETING AVIATION**
P. O. Box 42, Talkeetna, AK 99676, (907) 733-2366.

Just about anybody who is anybody in the mountaineering world uses Doug Geeting's company for air charters and expedition support. A legend in Alaska, his customers includes such superstar alpinists as Galen Rowell, Rick Ridgeway, Jeff Lowe and Jim Bridwell. Using fixed-wing craft, he will transport climbing teams to remote basecamps, and make regular overflights to check the group's status. Rating: ★★★★

The Top Dogsled Tour Operators

Iditarod dog, bred to race / RONNA NELSON

Mushing All-stars

*F*OR HUNDREDS, PERHAPS THOUSANDS OF YEARS, THE DOGSLED WAS THE PRIMARY mode of land travel in the far north. Even today, with bushplanes and snowmobiles, the dogsled remains a vital mode of transportation in the most remote reaches of the Arctic.

A good musher with a strong team can travel up to 70 miles per day over flat country on a long Arctic day. Driving a team is not easy. The dogs tire too fast if the driver rides the sled runners all the time. So, to keep things moving, one must alternate between running and riding. On steep hills, or in the deep snow, the musher will have to get out and push. This requires plenty of stamina and strength, but mushing is by no means just for he-men.

The ultimate challenge in dogsledding is the Iditarod Trail Race, a 1,049-mile test of skill and endurance that runs from Anchorage to Nome, Alaska. The reigning Iditarod champion, and three-time past winner, is a woman, Susan Butcher. Since the late '70s, Butcher has bred her own huskies, and she is recognized worldwide as the very best in the business. Her success has proven to the world that women are more than tough enough to meet any challenge the Arctic can present.

Susan Butcher's remarkable achievements demonstrate that skill, heart and determination are more important than pure muscle when it comes to dogsledding. So even if you're no Olympic athlete, you can enjoy a wilderness dogsled tour if you've got enthusiasm, and a well-developed

Susan Butcher / RONNA NELSON

appreciation for nature. Outfitters tell us that the most satisfied dogsledding customers are those with a strong love for animals. Those who really enjoy the dogs get the most out of the experience.

Among our recommended Arctic adventures above, you'll find quite a few dogsled trips, some to far-flung destinations such as the South Pole. If these trip descriptions have stirred your interest, you should contact one of the dogsled outfitters listed here. These companies offer a wide range of services, from half-day dogsled rides to wilderness expeditions of a week or more. Prices for wilderness trips average $150 per day per person, including guide. Most of these outfitters run their own kennels, and employ guides with five to 20 years of mushing experience.

Sourdough has a wealth of experience in the far north, but it contracts with two or three different mushers, so expect some variation in quality. Rating: ★★★

CANADA

Yukon and Northwest Territories

■ ADVENTURE NORTHWEST

P.O. Box 2435, Yellowknife, NWT, Canada X1A 2P8, (403) 920-2196.

Adventure Northwest runs a variety of mushing tours, from day-trips to 11-day wilderness dogteam safaris to the Northern Frontier zone of Canada's NWT. Trips depart from Great Slave Lake. The longer tours cost about $300 per day. Rating: ★★

■ GREAT SLAVE SLEDGING CO. LTD

P.O. Box 2882, Yellowknife, NWT, Canada X1A 2R2, (403) 920-4542, or (403) 873-8249.

This outfitter runs custom dogsled tours from Yellowknife on Great Slave Lake to nearby wilderness areas in the Northern Frontier/Big River zone. Rating: ★★★

Baffin Zone/Ellesmere Island

■ SPECIAL ODYSSEYS

(206) 455-1960. See outfitter review on page 36. Sled trips on Baffin and Ellesmere Islands between April and May. Rating: ★★

Boundary Country Area
(Minnesota/Canada Border)

■ BOUNDARY COUNTRY TREKKING

Gunflint Trail HC64, Box 590, Grand Marais, MN 55604, (800) 322-8327, or (218) 388-4487.

If you'd like to find out what a dogsled tour is like, but can't handle the expense of

Mushing in Alaska/COURTESY ALASKA DIVISION TOURISM

a true high Arctic trip, there are options worth exploring. Our suggestion? Head for northern Minnesota's Boundary Waters Wilderness Area, along the Canadian border. There, in "Boundary Country" as it is called, you can drive your own dogteam over frozen lakes and forest trails, spending the evenings in remote wilderness cabins or shelters. Experienced guides will lead the way and teach you the fine points of backcountry mushing.

The leading Boundary Country dogsled outfitter is Boundary Country Trekking (BCT), based in Grand Marais, Minnesota. BCT takes small groups on 3 to 4-day journeys through the Boundary Wilderness and nearby Superior National Forest. Evenings on the trail are spent in heated yurts or log cabins. BCT's trips are lead by Arleigh Jorgenson, one of the most respected and experienced mushers in the business. Jorgenson runs his own 50-dog kennel, and has competed in most of North America's leading dogsled races, including the Iditarod.

The price is $550 for 3 days, and about $725 for 4 days. Ski-only programs cost approximately $100 per day. Make reservations well in advance. Contact Barbara or Ted Young. Rating: ★★★★

■ WINTERGREEN LODGE

1101 Ring Rock Rd., White Iron Lake, Ely, MN 55731, Phone and FAX: (218) 365-6022.

From a comfortable wilderness lodge, Wintergreen offers guided sled tours from 2 to 7 days, with optional ski touring. Trips are led by expert guide, Paul Schurke, co-leader of the 1988 North Pole dogsled expedition. Club and collegiate groups are a specialty. Cost is roughly $500 for 4 days and 3 nights, including food. Rating: ★★★

GREENLAND

■ BORTON OVERSEAS

5516 Lyndale Ave. South, Minneapolis, MN 55419, (800) 843-0602; FAX: (612) 827-1544.

In March and April, Borton Overseas runs 8-day Greenland tours featuring two days of dogsledding out of Ammasalik. Participants tour Ammasalik Fjord and Sarfagajik Fjord and cross frozen lakes to visit a remote Eskimo hunting village. Cost is about $2,895 from Copenhagen, and longer programs are available. Rating: ★★

JOHN PLUMMER, F-STOCK PHOTOGRAPHY

Automotive Sport

Approaching the apex/JEFFREY R. ZWART

You completely ignore everything and just concentrate.
You forget about the whole world and you just...are part
of the car and the track.... It's a very special feeling.
You're completely out of this world.
There is nothing like it.
-Jochen Rindt, Formula 1 Champion

▼

*L*et's face it, fast is fun. In these days of speed traps and radar, however, your license won't last long if you're pushing the performance envelope on the street. The place to learn and improve high-speed driving skills is on a track, under controlled conditions, with expert instruction. In this chapter you'll learn where to go to master high-performance driving, and how to get started in amateur racing, if that's your ultimate goal.

We review the leading high-performance driving schools in North America, where you can learn to drive almost anything from go-karts to formula cars, or even learn specialty techniques such as ice driving or drag racing. You'll find out about innovative training technology, such as outrigger-equipped sedans that you can push to the edge of control and beyond. You'll also learn the easiest and fastest way to obtain an SCCA Novice Racing License, your ticket to life in the fast lane.

CHAPTER
3

North America's Best Driving Schools

Choosing a Driving School

DRIVING SCHOOLS ARE NOT ALL ALIKE. EACH HAS ITS PARTICULAR STRENGTHS and weaknesses. Picking the right driving school is not simply a matter of choosing the "best." You want to pick the best for you, based on your particular needs, whether that is learning how to respond to emergencies on the street, or bringing down your lap times on the track.

Most of the larger driving schools offer both types of programs-- advanced street driving, as well as actual race training. Whichever you favor, look for the right equipment when choosing a program. For street driving, pick a school with training vehicles that can safely simulate the most extreme situations. The Bondurant School, for example, uses outrigger-equipped skid cars, while the Bertil Roos School has a specially designed slide car that can alter its handling characteristics with the flick of a switch by the instructor (and no advance warning for the student).

If your main objective is to become a weekend racer, pick a school that offers wheel to wheel competition as a regular part of the curriculum. The SCCA Enterprises School, the Jim Hall Kart Racing School, and the Jim Russell School all offer programs that let you cut your racing teeth in on-track competition. At these schools, you will have a chance to drive the very same vehicles that you may eventually use in amateur competition.

DODGE GTU Racer/RICH CHENET

■ Skip Barber Racing School (East)
Route 7, Canaan, CT 06018, (203) 824-0771.

Skip Barber, past three-time SCCA champion, presides over one of the most complete driving programs to be found anywhere. His school offers performance driving courses for the street, as well as competition training for the track. The Barber race programs start with a 3-hour $250 Introduction to Racing. Next are 3-day and 5-day Competition Courses, for $1,850 and $2,700 respectively. If you're really serious, go for the 8-day Racing Program ($3,800). This is one of the finest advanced competition programs in the country. All competition classes are SCCA and IMSA-approved, and utilize Formula Ford and BMW 3-Series race cars.

Barber's street program, the BMW/Advanced Driving School, offers 1 and 2-day sessions in BMW M3 and 325i sedans. The classes feature high-speed handling and emergency safety instruction. Cost is $450 for 1 day, $880 for two days. This BMW program is offered at Lime Rocks (CT),

Formula 1, the pinnacle of auto racing/JEFFREY R. ZWART

The Bondurant program at Firebird includes a wide variety of SCCA and IMSA-approved courses for racers and non-racers alike: 1-Day Advanced Highway Driving Course ($450 using your own car, $600 with a specially prepared Bondurant car); 2 or 3-day High-Performance Driving Course (2 days $895, 3 days $1,325); and the 4-day Grand Prix Course in both Formula Fords and Bondurant Mustang GTs ($2,495). New for 1992 is a special 2-day course for teen-age drivers. The price will be $895. Last but not least, the Bondurant School offers a unique 4-day, anti-terrorist executive protection course. It'll cost you $2,495 to drive like James Bond. All Bondurant courses feature innovative techniques, including an outrigger-equipped Mustang skid car. (Prices are subject to change without notice.)

Instruction★★★★ Street Skills★★★★ Equipment★★★
Race Training★★★ Value★★★ Facilities★★★★

■ FRAN-AM RACING SCHOOL

(Elf-Winfield School of France), 1409 S. Wilshire Drive, Minnetonka, MN 55343, (612) 541-9461; FAX: (612) 541-1380.

The Fran-Am Racing School operates intensive race-training programs at the Paul Ricard circuit, home of the French GP, and at the Magny-Cours track, also in France. Some of the world's best drivers trained with Fran-Am, including former World Champion Alain Prost and Francois Cevert. This is not a school for yuppies learning to speed-shift their BMWs. Fran-Am provides serious formula racing instruction, and novices may find themselves a little outgunned. The 4-Day SCCA-approved Racing Course is run with Martini Formula Renault Turbos, and ranges between $2,395-$2,755 including instruction, use of a Formula Renault, and hotel accommodations in Paris for 6 nights. The program runs from the end of February through the first of September. A truly heroic performance at the school may attract the attention of sponsors Elf and Renault,

Sebring (FL), Road America (Elkhart Lake, WI), and Sears Point and Willow Springs (CA). Competition classes run at all those locations, plus 15 other tracks nationwide including Watkins Glen (NY), Mid-Ohio (OH), and Pocono (PA).

Instruction★★★★ Street Skills★★★ Equipment★★★
Race Training★★★★ Value★★ Facilities★★★

■ SKIP BARBER RACING SCHOOL (WEST)

Sears Point Int'l Raceway, 29355 Arnold Drive, Sonoma, CA 95476, (707) 939-8000.

The Skip Barber West Racing School operates year-round at Laguna Seca, Sears Point and Willow Springs raceways in California. It also conducts special programs in Seattle each summer. The Sears Point program was introduced in 1990, and with the Bondurant School's move to Phoenix, the Barber School is now the only driving school at this fine track, only 50 minutes from downtown San Francisco. Skip Barber West conducts the same programs, at the same prices, as Skip Barber's national driving school. However, the West Coast school is independently owned and operated. For rating, see above.

■ BOB BONDURANT SCHOOL OF HIGH PERFORMANCE DRIVING

Firebird Raceway, P.O. Box 60968, Phoenix, AZ 85082-0968, (800) 842-7223, or (602) 961-1111.

The Bondurant School, established in 1978, is America's most experienced driving school. Notable alumni include Al Unser, Jr., and Rick Mears. Formerly based at Sears Point Raceway in California, the school now operates at the Firebird track in Phoenix. Bondurant's brand new Phoenix facility was especially designed from the ground up for high-performance driving instruction. The track itself is one of the safest around, with wide run-outs, and few obstructions. As a dedicated training facility, the Firebird center can operate seven days a week, all year long. (Many other schools have to give up their track for weekend SCCA races.)

Trackside conference/COURTESY SKIP BARBER RACING SCHOOL

who offer the top student in the school a full, sponsored season of racing with the factory Formula Renault team.

Instruction★★★ Street Skills★ Equipment★★★★
Race Training★★★★ Value★★ Facilities★★★★

■ PITARESSI MOTOR SPORTS RACING SCHOOL

1940 N. Victory Boulevard, Portland, OR 97217, (503) 285-4449.

If you want a serious, no-frills program that will put you on an SCCA or IMSA grid as quickly as possible, the Pitaressi Racing School (PRS) is a good choice. The basic 2-day racing/high-performance course costs $600 if the student provides his own car, $1,000 if Pitaressi's race-prepped Toyotas are used. Further individualized advanced racing seminars are offered for $300 per day ($500 using the school's car). Pitaressi also offers a half-day skid control course for $150. All race-training programs are SCCA- and IMSA-approved. While PRS is first and foremost a training ground for budding racers, Pitaressi also pays the rent with a very successful corporate driving program. Up to 30 corporate staffers can learn the secrets of driving at speed for $6,500 in school cars, or $4,595 in their own vehicles. Pitaressi uses a skid car in all his programs, and provides sector timing and videotaping for his advanced racing seminars.

Instruction★★★ Street Skills★★ Equipment★★
Race Training★★★ Value★★★ Facilities★★

■ PORSCHE PRECISION DRIVING SCHOOL WITH DEREK BELL

P.O. Box 11912, Fort Lauderdale, FL 33339, (305) 561-2881.

Derek Bell has won the 24 hours of Le Mans five times; he knows how to make a Porsche perform, and how to do it safely. His 1 and 2-day courses teach Porsche owners to cope with their vehicles' unique handling properties, and drive safely at high speeds.

JEFFREY R. ZWART

This course is a must for any 911 Turbo driver, who should learn about trailing throttle oversteer from an expert. Students provide their own vehicles for programs conducted at Blackhawk Farms, Bryar, Bridgehampton, Firebird, Laguna Seca, Morosco, Pocono, Road America, Roebling Road, Texas World Speedway, Watkins Glen and Willow Springs.

Instruction★★★ Street Skills★★★★ Equipment★
Race Training★★ Value★★ Facilities★★ to★★★★

■ POWELL MOTORSPORT ADVANCED DRIVING SCHOOL

R.R. 1, Blackstock, ONT, Canada, L0B 1B0, (416) 985-9741; FAX: (416) 985-0679.

You'll have fun at the Powell School. All classes feature skid training, and the top-level course will teach you 180- and 360-degree spins and handbrake turns--wild moves you usually only see in the movies. The 1-day Advanced Driving Course costs $325 for Level 1, $360 for Level 2. The emphasis is on braking, skid control and emergency handling. Both courses utilize special skid cars pioneered by the Powell School, and feature over 300 miles of actual driving, far more than any other 1-day school.

For those looking for more excitement, the Powell School offers a 3-day advanced program in 150 mph ZR-1 Corvettes. During the $1,495 3-day Level I session you'll practice emergency braking and skid control, and then go out on the Mosport track to practice high-speed driving skills, communicating with your instructor via radio. The $2,995 Level III ZR-1 class offers all this, plus 500 miles of track time over the course of 3 days. In addition, both 3-day classes cover advanced skills such as handbrake turns and 360-degree full-power spins. The Powell School operates spring through fall at Mosport Park in Oshawa, Ontario. (Note: All stated prices are in Canadian dollars, worth approximately $.85 US.)

Instruction★★★★
Street Skills★★★★
Equipment★★★
Race Training★
Value★★★
Facilities★★

■ ROAD ATLANTA DRIVER TRAINING CENTER

Route 1, Braselton, GA 30517, (404) 881-8233.

The Road Atlanta Driver Training Center conducts a variety of SCCA- and IMSA-approved driving courses at the Road

Atlanta Track year-round. Street-oriented programs include 1 and 2-day Performance Handling courses in modified Nissan 240ZX and 300ZX cars ($325 for 1 day, $525 for 2 days). These are basically advanced defensive driving courses, offering one-on-one training with an instructor in the car. Racers in training can choose from 1, 2 and 3-day Road Racing courses at a cost of $495, $1,195, and $1,500 respectively. Modified 300ZXs are used for all the road racing courses, and instructors ride with students around the track. School graduates can also schedule advanced lapping days for $395 per day. (Note: prices are subject to change.)

Instruction★★★ Street Skills★★★ Equipment★★★
Race Training★★★ Value★★to★★★ Facilities★★★

■ BERTIL ROOS DRIVING SCHOOL

P.O. Box 221, Blakeslee, PA 18610, (800) 722-3669; or (717) 646-7227.

The Bertil Roos Driving School may not

Flat-out in the rain, 1989 Canadian Grand Prix/JEFFREY R. ZWART

be the most well-known driving academy in the country, but it is definitely one of the best, and it is the only program offering a money-back guarantee. If you attend, or have attended, an equivalent course that is better overall than the Roos 1-day Introduction to Racing, or 3-day Grand Prix Racing Program within 12 months of graduating, the Roos School will refund the full amount of your tuition.

In addition to being the only guaranteed program, the Bertil Roos School is one of the few schools where you can really compete on the track. Passing is allowed, students are not liable for crash damage, and the Roos School doesn't impose rev limits on its formula cars. Classes are limited to no more than 15 students, with a 1:3 teacher-student ratio.

The Bertil Roos School teaches emergency handling with specially engineered

slide cars. The cars can change handling characteristics at the instructor's command, forcing the student to cope with completely unanticipated conditions. This vehicle is used in all basic classes at Roos' SCCA- and IMSA-approved driving academy. Programs offered include the 1-day $300 Introduction to Racing Course in sedans and formula cars; the $1,300 2-day Preparation for Racing Course covering passing, car set-up, and racing strategies; and the $1,950 3-day Grand Prix Racing Course which utilizes both sedans and Formula Ford 2000 race cars. You can combine the Super-Advanced and Grand Prix courses as a 5-day race week for $2,900--a $350 savings

over the separate classes. (Race week graduates will be eligible to receive their SCCA novice license.) Lap practice is also offered for $450 per day at Pocono Int'l Raceway, where the Bertil Roos Driving School operates year-round.

Instruction★★★★   Street Skills★★★★   Equipment★★★★
Race Training★★★★   Value★★★   Facilities★★★

■ JIM RUSSELL RACING DRIVER'S SCHOOL

1023 Monterey-Salinas Highway, Salinas, CA 93908, (408) 372-7223, (800) 821-8755.
P.O. Box 119, Mt. Tremblant, QUE, Canada J0T IZ0, (819) 425-2739.

British racer Jim Russell pioneered the world's first performance driving schools 30 years ago in Britain and Italy. That heritage is carried on by programs now operating at Laguna Seca in California, the Mont Tremblant circuit in Canada, and Donington Park in England. A serious program for future racers, the Russell School is highly regarded among professionals in the sport. 1989 Indy winner Emerson Fittipaldi calls the Russell School "the best in North America." SCCA and IMSA-approved courses are conducted in Formula Fords and Mazda-powered Formula Russells. A half-day introductory course costs $299, while the 3-day Russell Techniques of Driving program in Formula Fords costs $1,895. It will cost you $2,495 for the Advanced Driving Course, 3 days of training in Formula Russells. Longer programs and customized instruction are also available for those with the money. (Note: prices may be increased later in 1992.)

Instruction★★★★   Street Skills★★★   Equipment★★★★
Race Training★★★★   Value★★★   Facilities★★★

■ SCCA ENTERPRISES NATIONAL RACING SCHOOL

7476 South Eagle Street, No. 5, Englewood, CO 80112, (303) 693-2111.

This innovative program may be the most efficient way to acquire a Sports Car Club of America (SCCA) novice racing license. After

Student racers/COURTESY SKIP BARBER RACING SCHOOL

just two weekends you can be competing in a real race car, the SCCA's one-design Spec Racer. The program, conducted by SCCA Enterprises' own staff, works as follows. During the first 2 days, usually Wednesday and Thursday, you'll join a class of a dozen novices for intensive racing instruction at one of a number of selected race tracks located throughout the US. On Saturday, you'll take the SCCA regional driver's school, and then run a short novice race in the afternoon. If you pass muster, you'll be signed off to run in the regional race on Sunday. Upon completing the full 4-day program, you can return home with your SCCA novice racing permit.

The SCCA Racing School takes care of all the details. The 2-day basic course fee of $1,300-$1,700, depending on location, covers instruction, 7 hours of track time, rental of the Spec Racer, helmet, gloves and driving suit. The full 4-day course fee of $2,500-$3,000 covers all this, plus your SCCA membership, race entry fee and all related paperwork. You'll get approximately 10 hours of track time over the 4 days, including your Sunday race. Completing the 4-day course is the quickest and easiest way to obtain your racing license, and the price is quite reasonable when you compare it against the costs of mounting your own campaign.

Instruction★★★   Street Skills★   Equipment★★★★
Race Training★★★★   Value★★★   Facilities★★★

■ SOUTHARD'S SCHOOL OF RACING
P.O. Box 1810, New Smyrna Beach, FL 32069, (904) 428-3307, or (800) 422-9449.

All true racers got their start on dirt, or so the legend goes. You can see if you've got what it takes to race on dirt at Southard's School of Racing. The training program features a 5-day racing course run on asphalt or dirt for $850 with your own car, $1,600 using the school's own race-prepped stock cars. (This is a school for serious oval racers, and most students bring their own late-model stockers.) There is also a 4-day classroom program for $640. Frankly, we'll pay the extra $200 to get out of the classroom and on to the track. All instructors are former racers, including dirt-track ace Larry Moore, and stock-car pilot Will Cagle. Southard's doesn't cut corners when it comes to equipment. All eight training cars are full-blooded racers, just like you find at Daytona. In fact, one of Southard's stockers was featured in Tom Cruise's movie, *Days of Thunder.*

Instruction★★   Street Skills★★   Equipment★★★
Race Training★★★   Value★★★★   Facilities★★

■ SPENARD-DAVID RACING SCHOOL
Rural Rte. 2, Shannonville, ONT, Canada K0K 3A0, (613) 969-0334; FAX: (613) 969-0458.

The Spenard-David Driving School provides SCCA-approved training in both stock and formula cars. Stock-car fans can sign up for a 3-day IROC-Z Camaro course for $1,595. At additional cost, you can participate in an informal Camaro race series at the school. Formula car classes, under the direction of racer Richard Spenard, include the following: $595 1-day Introductory Course in Formula 2000 cars; $1,895 3-day Level 1 Racing Course in Formula 2000 cars; 1 or 2-day Level II, Advanced Techniques course for Level I graduates and/or competition license holders, also in Formula 2000 racers. The Advanced course costs $595-$795 for one day, $1,295 for both. All courses are taught on the Fabi and Nelson tracks at Canada's Shannonville Motorsport Park. (Note: all stated prices are in Canadian dollars, worth approximately $.85 US.)

Instruction★★   Street Skills★★   Equipment★★★
Race Training★★★   Value★★★   Facilities★★

■ WILLOW SPRINGS INTERNATIONAL DRIVING SCHOOL
The Driver's Connection, Willow Springs International Raceway, P.O. Box X, Rosamond, CA 93560, (805) 256-2471.

The Driver's Connection was originally organized to teach celebrities how to go around corners in the Long Beach Grand Prix Celebrity Challenge Race. Now the same race-prepped Toyotas piloted by celebrities are used for three SCCA-approved high-performance driving courses conducted at the Willow Springs Raceway in Southern California. Plunk down $400 for the 1-day Car Control Course. For $800 you can enroll in the 2-day Car Control and Racing Basics class. Or, you can go whole

RICH CHENET

Al Unser, Jr., Indy Car champion/JOHN ASHLEY

hog, and take the 4-day Road Racing Techniques and Strategies Course for $1,500. Individualized training is also available at $400 per day, all-inclusive.

Instruction★★	Street Skills★★★	Equipment★★
Race Training★★	Value★★★	Facilities★★

SPECIALTY SCHOOLS

Drag Racing

■ THE DRAG RACING SCHOOL
P.O. Box 140369, Gainesville, FL 32614, (904) 373-7223.

The Drag Racing School is the only full-time program of its kind in the country. Here you'll learn the secrets of the top straight-line racers, and you'll get the opportunity to practice what you learn behind the wheels of some very hot quarter-mile machines. The Drag Racing School's 2-day basic drag racing course costs $1,150 and uses 700hp Super Gas and Gas dragsters. The 4-day Top Alcohol drag racing seminar puts you in the cockpit of a Top Alcohol dragster or alcohol Funny Car for $2,500. This is an excellent, well-established program, run by a very professional staff. Just remember there's a $2,500 deductible if you get sloppy and miss a shift.

Instruction★★	Street Skills★	Equipment★★★★
Race Training★★★	Value★★	Facilities★★

Kart Racing

■ THE JIM HALL KART RACING SCHOOL
1555-G Morse Avenue, Ventura, CA 93003, (805) 654-1329.

The Jim Hall School is the only driving instruction program in the country conducted exclusively in karts. Though the karts are small, don't consider this kid stuff. Modern racing karts can top 130 mph, run from zero to 60 mph in five seconds, and pull a gut-wrenching 1.5 Gs in a turn. A number of the world's top drivers, including Indy car aces Emerson Fittipaldi, Al Unser, Jr. and Mario

Andretti, cut their teeth on karts, so you'll be in good company. Kart training is an excellent way to master basic competition techniques and learn whether you want to continue on with racing. A weekend in karts can be done for a fraction of the cost of a similar program in a formula car.

A wide range of training options are available, but novices should opt for Hall's 2-day $400 Triple Crown package, consisting of an intro class followed by advanced on-track sessions emphasizing racing lines, braking skills and passing strategies. For those with some previous karting experience, Hall recommends his 2-day Race School. This $550 program covers vehicle dynamics, safety, racing lines, braking drills and inter-class competition.

Instruction★★★	Street Skills★★	Equipment★★
Race Training★★★★	Value★★★★	Facilities★★

Stock Car Racing

■ BUCK BAKER RACING SCHOOL
5000 Currituck Drive, Charlotte, NC 28210, (704) 527-2763, or (704) 596-8930.

If you liked *Days of Thunder*, you'll love the Buck Baker Racing School. Here, you can learn oval track technique with former NAS-CAR driver Buck Baker in real Winston Cup stock cars. Baker's 3-day $1,800 Winston Cup Driving Course takes you around the North Carolina (Rockingham) Motor Speedway or the Atlanta International Raceway in Chevrolet, Pontiac and Ford Winston Cup stockers. For would-be racers who have successfully completed the basic course, Baker offers a one-on-one advanced Winston Cup Course for $1,500 per day. This course is conducted completely on the track under real-life race conditions. Students run wheel to wheel, and nose to tail at over 100 mph just like the big boys. For those looking for something a little more down-to-earth, Baker also runs a 2-day high-performance driving weekend. Cost is $1,000 per person for groups under 10, $800 for groups over 10.

Instruction★★	Street Skills★★	Equipment★★★
Race Training★★★	Value★★★	Facilities★★

Winter Driving

■ FORD-MICHELIN ICE DRIVING SCHOOL
P.O. Box 774167, Steamboat Springs, CO 80477, (303) 879-6104.

If you're tired of slipping and sliding every time winter rolls around, this school may be for you. The school opens its doors each winter near the end of November, and offers both group and private instruction in Fords and Lincoln Mercurys. The basic program is a half-day Ice Driving Immersion Course, offering sit-down instruction followed by 2 hours on the ice track for about $80. For $180 you can do the 1-day Formula 1 Course, which provides an afternoon of ice driving followed by a video review session. Add another afternoon of ice driving, and you've completed the $300 1 and 1/2-day Grand Prix Course. (Note: prices are subject to change.)

Instruction★★	Street Skills★★★★	Equipment★★
Race Training★	Value★★★	Facilities★★

Karts are inexpensive, yet surprisingly fast/COURTESY JIM HALL KART RACING SCHOOL

The Racing School Experience

RACING SCHOOL IS NOT A PLAYGROUND FOR ADULTS. AT $250-$500 PER DAY, HIGH-performance training is a major investment that demands serious commitment. If you just want to spin a few laps on a track, go to the Malibu Grand Prix and save your money. To get the most out of the driving school experience you should be prepared to study hard, and progress methodically, building one skill upon another. There is no magic to becoming a fast driver. If you master the fundamental techniques, learning to drive with precision and control, you will see the results in your lap times. Just don't expect to become a champion overnight.

TEXTBOOK TO TRACK

What to Expect

While the curricula at the many driving schools varies enormously, virtually all schools combine some classroom instruction with actual on-track training. In the lecture segment of driving school, the instructors will explain the physics of cornering, the right way to apex a turn, the principles of skid recovery, and the basic rules of racing.

After the classroom sessions, you'll put theory into practice on the track and the skidpad. Many programs begin with a slalom session--running the cones is the best way to get the feel of the car at its handling limits. Graduating to the track, you will practice specific high-performance skills such as use of braking markers, drafting and throttle-steering. In street-oriented programs, you will be taught how to deal with lock-up during braking, and how to initiate and recover from both front-end and back-end skids. You may also be taught specialty skills such as handbrake turns and driving on ice.

BEYOND THE BASICS

Your goal on the track is to become a precision driver, not to break lap records. Skill is more important than bravado. Many schools impose rev limits on the students (you get fined if you break the rules), so you shouldn't attempt to push the car to its limits. The key objectives are: driving the correct line through the turn; braking at the markers on every lap; keeping your momentum through the turns; and executing all driver inputs (braking, shifting, turning and throttle control) smoothly and precisely.

It is this last point--achieving consistency and smoothness--that separates the most successful students from the also-rans. The best drivers don't scrub off speed in the turns unnecessarily, don't patch their tires under hard braking, and never pick the wrong gear. At the highest levels of competition, aggressiveness can win races, but if you carry anything home from your driving school, it should be the ability to drive with precision and smoothness, lap after lap, mile after mile.

YOUR SCCA LICENSE

Without a formalized training program, earning your SCCA competition license can be confusing, time-consuming and expensive. That's why the SCCA National Racing School was created--to help a novice get a racing license quickly, easily and at reasonable cost. If you have some previous racing experience, the SCCA General Competition Rules prescribe a number of ways you can obtain your license. However, if you are a complete novice, you will need to take the following steps:

1. Join the SCCA. (This is included in the SCCA Enterprises National Racing School 4-day competition program listed above.)

2. Get a novice permit, commonly known as a logbook. This allows you to enter SCCA

F Sports-racing is one of the many SCCA amateur classes/JOHN ASHLEY

Jackie Stewart's Principles of Performance Driving is an information-packed handbook for those looking to get started in amateur racing. $29.95 from Classic Motorbooks, P.O. Box 1, Osciola, WI 54020, (800) 826-6600; FAX: (715) 294-4448.

Bob Bondurant On High Performance Driving, 2nd Ed., offers a good, basic overview of Bondurant's driving school curriculum. $12.95 from Classic Motorbooks.

Competition Driving, by Alain Prost (1990). This is the newest and most detailed guide to race driving currently available. It covers all types of competition driving, including formula cars, rally cars and go-karts. $19.95 from Classic Motorbooks.

Going Faster is an excellent 90-minute video compiled by the Skip Barber Racing School in cooperation with ESPN. Shot mostly behind-the-wheel of a Formula Ford, this is probably the best race training video available. $79.95 from Rock Orchard Productions, P.O. Box 3399, Wallingford, CT, 06494, (800) 458-2257, or Classic Motorbooks.

Drive to Win with Mario Andretti teaches the essential skills for competition driving on the track. It's aimed at budding racers, but is also useful for those who want to improve their street skills. $49.95 for two separate 60-minute tapes from Classic Motorbooks.

Drivers' Schools around the country, and, then to enter regional races, provided you have met entry requirements.

3. Fulfill the SCCA novice permit requirements. To qualify, most novices must complete two regional SCCA driver's training school sessions. However, the National Racing School's 2 days of intensive instruction will satisfy one of the two required driver's schools. (Regional schools do not supply cars, mechanics or driving equipment as part of the instructional package, unlike the National Racing School.)

4. Complete one Sunday Regional SCCA Race. After you complete two regional races, you can earn your regional license. A total of six regional races must be completed in order to obtain the next classification, a National License.

As explained above, enrollment in the SCCA 4-day National Racing School includes everything you need to get your novice racing license, from your wheels to your racing gloves. All you need to bring is your shoes. At many tracks around the country, SCCA Enterprises also rents Spec Racers for new licensees competing at regional races.

The Cost to Compete—The Bottom Line

So you want to go racing? Well, it doesn't come cheap. We've compiled a list of what you'll have to pay for a competitive machine in many of the popular amateur racing classes. If the cost of the car doesn't leave you too discouraged, just remember that you'll have to transport it, maintain it, and keep it in engines and tires during the season. Racing is not a poor man's sport.

Car	Engine	Chassis	Complete
Basic Racing Kart	$1,300	$1,400	$2,700
Unlimited Super Kart			$6,000
Formula 440			$8,500
Formula Vee	$4,000	$8,500	$12,500
Spec Racer (Sports Renault)			$15,000
Formula Ford	$5,500	$21,900	$27,400
Sports 2000	$6,500	$35,000	$41,500
		Lola T-90	
Super Vee	$18,000	$45,000	$63,000
		Ralt RT-5	
Formula Atlantic	$15,000	$58,000	$73,000

Ballooning

RON BEHRMANN

It's the journey that counts, not the arrival.
-Montaigne

▼

Whether drifting over the quiet fields of Burgundy, or cresting the Rockies at dawn's light, ballooning possesses a certain singular magic. Ballooning has been with us for centuries, but only in recent years has the growth of the commercial balloon industry allowed the average person to make recreational flights throughout North America and the world. Balloon operators can be located near most major metropolitan areas in the United States, and a number of specialty operators offer tours throughout the world, including East Africa and even Egypt.

Many novices get hooked on ballooning after an initial flight or two, and decide to take up the sport seriously, buying their own balloons, or joining a ballooning club. We tell you how this can be done, and what it will cost to operate your own balloon.

We've listed dozens of commercial balloon operations worldwide, and described the best ballooning vacation packages. You'll also find a comprehensive calendar of ballooning events in the United States. For many, going up in a hot-air balloon represents a lifetime dream. Read on and you'll learn how to make that dream come true.

CHAPTER

4

Chateau Rocheport, France/COURTESY BOMBARD BALLOON ADVENTURES

ALLOONING OFFERS BOTH SPECTACLE AND SERENITY, A CELEBRATION OF color and an escape from the humdrum of everyday life. The late Malcolm Forbes cherished the tranquil magic of ballooning, popularizing the sport among princes and potentates. But ballooning is not just for the rich and famous. A deluxe champagne flight almost anywhere in America runs $100-$150. And for those seeking the ultimate lighter-than-air experience, we feature some of the world's greatest ballooning adventures, from the Alps to the plains of Africa.

BURGUNDY
Castles and Vineyards

Nothing epitomizes luxury ballooning better than a flying tour of the famed vineyards and chateaux of Burgundy. Such a trip is the showcase offering of Bombard Balloon Adventures, an American company specializing in high-end package balloon holidays in Europe. From Paris, you will be whisked on the TGV (Tres Grande Vitesse) to Le Creusot in Burgundy, first class of

course. On arrival, after visiting world-class vineyards, you ascend in your balloon above Burgundy, flying over medieval castles and patchwork vineyards. In the evening, pilots and passengers dine like royalty in the 14th-century vaulted chambers of Chateau Savigny-les-Beaune. If you haven't got the picture yet, this trip defines first-class adventure travel.

On your second day, you visit the Patriarche family cellar, home to 10 million bottles, representing five centuries' vin-

tage. There's wine tasting before lunch at Chateau Rochepot, a stunning cliff-top fortress. After touring the chateau, fire up your balloon to soar over the intricately patterned tile roof and the nearby Cote d'Or vineyards. The next day, you'll explore the 12th-century fortified city of Chateauneuf, then visit more vineyards, including Chateau Commarin (complete with 13th-century castle and moat), and Clos de Vougeot, your departure point for your final balloon flight over Burgundy. Your fourth day is free for further exploration of Beaune, a 14th-century walled city and ancient capital of Burgundy.

If you're prone to worrying about the conditions of the third world, don't take this trip, which runs about $3,150 per person; you can't help but feel a little guilty drinking the world's best wines and having the run of a half-dozen French castles. But if nothing but the ultimate ballooning experience will do, this is the adventure for you. Contact Bombard Balloon Adventures, 6727 Curran Street, McLean, VA 22101, (800) 862-8537, or (703) 448-9407; FAX: (703) 883-0985.

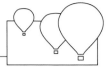

Seven Superb Ballooning Holidays

AUSTRIA

Salzburg Sojourn

As European cities go, few are more picturesque than Salzburg. Situated on the banks of the Salzach River, Salzburg is tucked between two large mountains, only a few kilometers from the Austrian Alps.

Bombard Balloon Adventures conducts a 5-day balloon tour of the Salzburg region, which has to rank among the finest European balloon experiences available. On the first day, you'll fly over nearby farmlands and forest. The next day, you visit the Hohensalzburg Fortress, a massive castle which served as the seat of power for the Hapsburg empire. From this vantage point, 400' above the city, you can look out over baroque villas, churches and monasteries, ringed by formal gardens.

Salzburg, in its Old World style, is like a fairy-tale land, a world apart from the hustle and bustle of the 20th century. After the visit to Hohensalzburg, you'll fly along Salzburg's scenic foothills, floating over some of Austria's most impressive palaces.

The next day, visit Mondsee, a small, lakeside village at the foot of the Drachenwald and Schafberg Ranges. From there you'll balloon close to the Alps, skimming alpine meadows beneath massive glaciers.

Bombard Balloon Adventures pulls out the stops on the fourth day. First there is a boat ride across St. Wolfgang Lake to the small village of St. Gilgen. After debarking, you'll be the guest of Austrian Princess Manni Wittgenstein at her country home. After a final luncheon, the group will board balloons for a flight over nearby valleys, lakes and villages. After a sumptuous brunch on the fifth day you depart for America where you can attempt to recover from all this luxury. Cost for the trip is about $4,350 per person.

Great as this trip is, it would be a shame to leave Austria after only five days. While you're there, we recommend that you take a few days to hike in the countryside, particularly in the Tirol. Contact the Austrian National Tourist Office at (212) 944-6880, or (213) 477-3332 for complete information.

SWITZERLAND

Winter Balloon Festival

Imagine 50 balloons rising simultaneously from the glistening snow of the Swiss Alps, soaring above valleys and 10,000' peaks. This spectacle takes place every January at the Chateau D'Oex Winter Alpine Balloon Festival in Gstaad, Switzerland, an event that draws balloonists from over 15 countries. The festival lasts 10 days, with special events including a dirigible demonstration, mountain hangglider flying, and long-distance flights over the Alps, weather permitting. You can visit the event as a spec-

COURTESY BOMBARD BALLOON ADVENTURES

tator, or if you want to fly, Bombard Balloon Adventures offers a 9-day ballooning holiday coordinated with the festivities. Flights are made every day, with mass ascensions held five times during the festival. As you might expect, Bombard's customers stay in deluxe hotels, and dine at the finest restaurants in the region.

Bombard Balloon Adventures has participated in the festival for six years running, and its giant 180,000-cubic-foot tulip balloons have become a familiar sight over the Alps. If money is no object, stay the full 9 days for $7,990 per person. When you're not flying, you can ski at nearby resorts. If the price of a Hyundai seems a bit much for a week and a half's vacation, Bombard Balloon Adventures also offers a 6-day, 5-night program in the Gstaad region for $4,990. You will fly over the same region, but not in conjuction with the festival.

The Chateau d'Oex Festival is truly one of the most exclusive events in the world. If you want to try winter ballooning at its best, contact Bombard Balloon Adventures, (800) 862-8537.

COLORADO

Rocky Mountain High

The Rockies region is one of the top spots for ballooning in North America. The scenery is superb, and the choice of ballooning sites is extensive. You can sample a variety of

BRIAN LAWLER

ballooning adventures from day-flights at six different resorts to high-altitude balloon expeditions across the Continental Divide. There are a number of ballooning events each year in the Rockies which draw balloonists from across the country. Colorado Springs, for example, hosts a huge Labor Day gathering which attracts over 100 balloons. You can arrange with one of the nearby balloon services to join in the fun.

It's easy to organize your own Rockies balloon odyssey, making day-flights at all the major resort towns: Fort Collins, Boulder, Arvada, Aspen, Vail, Colorado Springs, Englewood and Denver. (Consult our listings on page 60 for recommended commercial balloon operators in these areas.) And, if you want to take a break from flying for a day or two, hit the ski slopes; many Colorado balloon companies offer winter flights, so you can go down the mountain one day, and up in the air the next.

If you want to try an extended mountain flight over the Rockies, contact Aviation Adventures Aloft of Fort Collins, CO, (800) 537-8842. One of America's leaders in alpine ballooning, Aviation Adventures Aloft can arrange a customized Rockies flight of any duration, if you're able to foot the bill, which will be substantial. Expect a mountain flight to run $1,000 per day, more if a gas balloon is used. Crossing the Rockies by balloon is truly a once-in-a-lifetime experience. This is the only part of the United States where a mountain flight can be arranged through a regular commercial operator.

AUSTRALIA

Down Under Dawn Flight

Imagine floating above the outskirts of Sydney, looking out at the Harbor Bridge, the Opera House and other famous landmarks. Or, consider passing silently over herds of kangaroos and other native wildlife in the South Australian backcountry. You can book balloon flights at many locations in Australia, both near the larger cities of Sydney and Melbourne, and in nearby valleys in New South Wales and Victoria. In the Sydney area, Adventures Australia can fly you from any of six locations near Australia's largest city. Single flight sessions are most popular, but an itinerary can be customized according to your wishes, if your pocketbook permits it. Contact Balloon Adventures Australia, 16 Lyte Place, Prospect, NSW 2149, Australia, (01161) 2 622 5267; FAX: 2 622 6414.

For flights in New South Wales and Victoria, we recommend Chris Dewhirst's Balloon Sunrise, 39 Smith

JENNY HAGER, ADVENTURE PHOTO

Street, Richmond, Victoria 3121, Australia, (011 61) 3 4277 596. A few years back, Dewhirst established a world record flying his balloon over Mt. Everest. No, you won't do anything so daring, but you can rest assured that you will be in expert hands. Single-day flights are offered in the Camden and Hunter Valleys, Sydney, or from Melbourne and Rutherglen in Victoria. Melbourne is one of the few cities in the world where you can enjoy the beauty of an urban dawn flight as you pass effortlessly over the town, watching the flickering city lights below.

If you've got more time, we highly recommend Dewhirst's ballooning weekends in Victoria's wine growing regions. You'll spend 2 days floating gently over the patchwork of Victorian vineyards in the dawn, and visiting wineries in the afternoons. Total cost for food, flights and lodging, is about $300 US per person. You could easily pay as much for just two one-hour flights, so this represents good value.

If you're heading into Australia's heartland to visit Ayers Rock, continue on to Alice Springs for a balloon flight over Australia's dramatic Red Centre. In the still dawn, Red Centre Balloon Flights will take you aloft over the vast central desert of Alice Springs. You'll view kangaroos, wild horses and wallabees on the ground below, and see the first light on the ancient red rocks of the McDonald Range. Flights, including a deluxe champagne breakfast, cost about $135 US and can be booked through Australia's World Expeditions, c/o Worldwide Adventures, Suite 727, 920 Yonge Street, Toronto, ONT, Canada M4W 3C7, (800) 387-1483.

AFRICA

Kenya Balloon Safari

One of the greatest thrills in ballooning is ascending over Kenya's Maasai Mara Game Reserve at dawn's light. Suspended in stillness, you watch the night mist clearing on the plains below, as herds of antelope and zebras rise to greet the new day. As you pass over watering holes crammed with all variety of creatures, flocks of birds lift in flight, spooked by the balloon's slow-moving shadow. On the open veldt below, lions stalk their prey while baboons and wild dogs stare up curiously at your silent craft. The sensation is remarkable.

The Maasai Mara in Kenya is the most popular ballooning site in Africa, and balloon flights are available from many loca-

BRIAN LAWLER

tions within the Game Reserve including the Mara Sorova Camp, the Mara Serena Camp, Governor's Camp and the Keekorok Lodge. At present no commercial operator runs point-to-point balloon safaris in Africa. You'll have to settle for 30- to 90-minute dawn flights which typically cost from $175 to $350 per person.

Most African specialty travel agencies can add a Kenyan balloon trip to a regular East African safari itinerary. We recommend the companies listed in our Safari Chapter, in particular Wildlife Safari, 346 Rheem Boulevard, Moraga, CA 94556, (800) 221-8118, or (800) 526-3637 in CA. Wildlife Safari offers ballooning over the Maasai Mara as a regular part of its Wings Over Kenya tour.

When booking an African balloon excursion, go with an established, bonded operator. The following companies have US-trained pilots and carry $1 million in liability insurance: Trans-World Safaris, P.O.

Box 44690, Nairobi, Kenya (launch sites Mara Sorova and Mara Serena); Balloon Adventures, P.O. Box 47557, Nairobi, Kenya (launch site--Keekorok Lodge); Musiara, P.O. Box 48217, Nairobi, Kenya (launch site--Governor's Camp).

NEW MEXICO

Albuquerque Balloon Fiesta

This is it, the ultimate balloon festival. Every October, the Albuquerque Balloon Fiesta plays host to 625 balloons, viewed by more than 800,000 spectators. The Fiesta is a photographer's dream, with legions of balloons filling the sky with color. You'll see every kind of balloon made, from small solo balloons to huge replicas of cartoon characters, UFOs and other fantasy creations. Hundreds of balloons lift off in mass dawn ascensions, filling the New Mexico sky. Equally spectacular, on Sunday evenings during the 9-day Fiesta over 300 balloons will lift off at sunset, glowing like

RON BEHRMANN

giant candles in the night sky.

At Albuquerque, ballooning is just part of the spectacle. Past events have featured the US Navy Skydiving Team, plus an all-female team of skydivers, the Misty Blues. The six-time world champion US Army Golden Knights parachute team traditionally performs during the Fiesta's final weekend, demonstrating wild freefalls and intricate aerial maneuvers. High school marching bands and air shows further add to the festivities. Those in attendance will

rub elbows with a truly international crowd. This event attracts balloon pilots and support crews from dozens of countries worldwide, including Germany, Luxembourg, France, England, Japan and Switzerland.

The Balloon Fiesta is by far the biggest, most dramatic, and most popular event of its kind in the world. Even if you don't want to fly, you should consider attending the Fiesta to see the colors, night-glow ascensions, balloon races, and the circus-like magic that takes over Albuquerque for a week and a half each fall. For information, contact the Albuquerque International Balloon Fiesta, 8309 Washington Place N.E., Albuquerque, NM 87113, (505) 821-1000. To book accommodations, write the Albuquerque Convention & Visitors Bureau, P.O. Box 26866, Albuquerque, NM 87125, (800) 243-3696, or (505) 243-3696 in NM. To arrange for a balloon flight, contact the World Balloon Corporation, 4800 Eubank Boulevard N.E., Albuquerque, NM 87122, (505) 293-6800.

Mass ascension at Albuquerque Balloon Fiesta/RON BEHRMANN

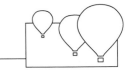

Night glows, Albuquerque/RON BEHRMANN

Specialty Balloon Tour Operators

WHILE MOST COMMERCIAL BALLOON SERVICES JUST OFFER SHORT RIDES, THERE are a few companies that specialize in balloon vacation packages. These companies typically combine a land tour with a series of ascensions, or arrange a hotel-flight package in conjunction with a major ballooning event. If you want a serious balloon holiday, here are the folks to call.

■ ADVENTURE BALLOONS

3 Queens Terrace, Hanwell, London, England W7 3TS, (011 44) 81 840 0108.

One of Britain's leading commercial ballooning operations, Adventure Balloons offers ballooning weekends in Somerset from July through October, which can be combined with horseback riding, caving, sailing and other activities. Adventure Balloons also offers package ballooning holidays in France and Ireland starting at about $700. Rating: ★★★

■ AIR ESCARGOT

Remigny 71150, France, (011 33) 8587 1230; or Travel Anywhere, 88 Purchase Street, Rye, NY 10580, (914) 967-5330; FAX: (914) 921-0521.

Air Escargot conducts 1-day to 1-week luxury trips in Burgundy featuring daily balloon rides, gourmet dining and deluxe lodging in fine hotels and chateaux. Prices start at about $300 per day, per person. Tours operate from April through November. We recommend Air Escargot as a less expensive alternative to Bombard Balloon Adventures' rather costly tours. Rating: ★★

■ BOMBARD BALLOON ADVENTURES

6727 Curran Street, McLean, VA 22101-3804, (800) 862-8537, or (703) 883-0985.

Created by America's Cup yachtsman and record-holding balloonist Buddy Bombard, Bombard Balloon Adventures is the largest and most successful balloon tour operator in the world, having served over 14,000 customers in the past 15 years. Bombard's company has the most balloons, the best pilots, the finest accommodations, and, as you might expect, the highest prices. What can you say, living well has never been cheap. Bombard's balloon tours of Britain, France, Italy, Switzerland and Austria are clearly the class of the field--ultimate vacations for those with the financial wherewithal. Rating: ★★★★

■ CLUB ADVENTURE

P.O. Box 549, Carpinteria, CA 93014, (805) 684-7903.

This is a new organization that offers 4 to 8-day package ballooning holidays in Albuquerque, Las Vegas, Phoenix, Boise, Grand Junction (CO), London (Ontario), and the Pacific Northwest. These multi-activity trips combine ballooning with biking, wine tasting, rafting or hiking. The wildest option is an annual pilgrimage to carnival in Rio De Janeiro in Brazil--you party in the city and balloon in the countryside. The Rio trip costs about $2,800, while other balloon tours range in price from $1,300 to $2,500. Depending on location, the balloons will either be operated by Club Adventure, or flown under contract by well-established commercial balloon operators. Rating: ★

■ TIME BALLOONS

P.O. Box 45691, Atlanta, GA 30320, (800) 635-8741, or (404) 997-1444.

Time Balloons arranges weekend balloon trips and customized balloon vacations throughout North America. Destinations include New Mexico, Colorado, New York, Canada, Tennessee, Florida and Georgia. Time Balloons can package a vacation to include the Albuquerque Balloon Fiesta, the Festival du Montgolfier in Quebec, or one of many other major North American balloon events. If you've been dreaming of a great balloon holiday getaway, this is one of the best enterprises to contact. Time Balloons is set up to provide a complete package, including luxury accommodations, gourmet dining, and additional recreation such as wine tasting, horseback riding and snow skiing. Time Balloons specializes in customized itineraries--just tell them what you want and they will make it happen. Rating: ★★★

SCOTT SPIKER

Becoming a Balloonist

*A*FTER AN INITIAL SHORT FLIGHT OR TWO, MANY PEOPLE FALL IN LOVE WITH THE sport of ballooning, and want to learn to pilot their own ship. In the sections which follow, we explain the basics of the sport, and how you can obtain your balloon pilot's license.

BALLOON BASICS

Almost all recreational balloons use hot air supplied by a propane burner. The bag, or envelope, is 50-80' tall, and constructed of polyester or nylon fabric coated with polyurethane to reduce porosity. The basket, or gondola, is made of wicker, aluminum, or heavy-duty synthetic material. With a ground crew of up to eight helpers, the balloon is inflated on the ground by a blower and then the trapped air is heated by the propane burner until the envelope is upright.

During flight, the burner is used to control the balloon's altitude by warming the air in the envelope. (To ascend, you must increase the envelope temperature.

BRIAN LAWLER

You must also burn periodically just to maintain altitude, as the envelope is constantly cooling. Rapid descents require spilling hot air from a vent at the top of the envelope.) Fifteen to 20 gallons of propane are used on a typical one to two-hour flight.

A balloon's only means of propulsion is the wind, but it must be gentle. A 10-mph breeze is the maximum allowable for regular sport flying. During a two-hour flight, a balloon may fly up to 10 miles overland and ascend to 2,000' or so. Higher flights are possible, but there is no real reason to exceed 2,000' unless there is a mountain to cross. There is no direct way to steer or guide a balloon--it drifts with the wind. However, as the wind blows in different directions at different altitudes, an expert balloonist has some control over his path by changing altitude and finding a wind blowing where he wants to go.

GETTING YOUR LICENSE

Balloons, like fixed-wing aircraft and helicopters, are regulated by the Federal Aviation Administration (FAA). You must therefore complete a formal certification program before you're allowed to fly. FAA licensing requirements include a minimum of 10 hours of flight training with at least one hour of solo flight. Fifteen hours of actual air time are required by the average private student before he is ready for certification. He then must also pass a written exam, and successfully complete a check flight. The written exam covers federal aviation requirements, meteorology and general rules of ballooning. Every two years, pilots must renew their ratings by passing a Biennial Flight Review, administered by a commercial pilot.

The cost of a good flight training program, with all equipment provided by the balloon school, ranges from $1,800-$3,500. If the student supplies his own balloon, chase vehicle, etc., this cost goes down to $600-$1,000. Below we list numerous balloon centers which operate flight training programs. Before you sign up for any program, it pays to comparison shop in your local area. Prices can vary greatly. It's also advisable to go with a school that has full-time instructors, and an FAA examiner on staff.

BUYING A BALLOON

If you want to fly more than a few times each year, you should seriously consider purchasing your own equipment. You'll need a balloon, basket, burner, fuel tank(s),

RON BEHRMANN

instruments, inflator fan, and trailer. You can pick up the entire rig, used, for less than $10,000. For a new outfit, figure on at least $15,000 (without trailer) but you could easily spend $50,000 or more if you want the latest instrumentation and a deluxe, custom envelope. When buying a balloon, look for these features: Nomex (fireproof) skirt and throat, Kevlar cables, polyurethane and UV coating on fabric, parachute-top or spring-top deflation valve, and leather-trimmed basket. Necessary instruments are an envelope temperature gauge, vertical speed indicator (variometer), altimeter, and fuel pressure and fuel quantity gauges.

A basic sport balloon should have flat-felled, load-taped seams for the gores (panels), and a capacity of at least 70,000 cubic feet. The most popular size balloon, the AX-7, has a capacity of 77,500 cubic feet, which will safely carry one pilot plus two passengers. Larger balloons (production envelopes come in sizes up to 150,000 cubic feet) cost more, but will allow you to carry more passengers, and use the burner less

often. The leading balloon manufacturers are Aerostar, The Balloon Works, Cameron, and Thunder & Colt. Check your yellow pages for local dealers, or contact the manufacturers at the addresses below.

When buying a balloon, comparison shop. Resist the temptation to buy the first one you see. Most dealers will offer a demo ride if you're seriously interested. Talk to owners of other balloons to get a sense of the features you may want--the capacity and number of gores (8-32), for example. If you are thinking about buying a used envelope, make sure it has received an official annual inspection. To get a sense of the reliability of various brands, call a balloon insurance underwriter--in general, the balloons with the best safety records are the cheapest to insure.

Aerostar International, Inc., 1813 "E" Ave., P.O. Box 5057, Sioux Falls, SD 57117, (605) 331-3500; FAX: (605) 331-3520.

Cameron Balloons, P.O. Box 3672, Ann Arbor, MI 48106, (313) 426-5525.

The Balloon Works, P.O. Box 827,

Statesville, NC 28677, (704) 878-9501.

Thunder & Colt, 4017 E. Baldwin Road, Holly, MI 48442, (313) 695-5115.

PRICE OF ADMISSION

Ballooning is not cheap, but you don't have to be a millionaire to enjoy the sport. Your main costs are fuel, insurance, depreciation of the envelope and annual inspections. Fuel (propane) will cost from $.60 to $1.30 per gallon, and you'll burn 12-15 gallons per hour. Insurance will vary according to your flying area and experience, but count on a minimum of $600 per year. A well-maintained envelope will provide 300-400 flight hours. If you fly 50 hours per year (the national average), this gives a useful envelope life of about seven years. If you paid $10,000 for the envelope your depreciation therefore averages about $1,700 per year. Add another $200-$300 for annual inspections. Thus, if you fly 50 hours per year, your direct costs will run $3,500-$4,000 annually. There are also chase-vehicle expenses and transportation costs. It is a good idea to have some refresher training each year as well from a top-level pilot/ trainer. This will cost $50 per hour. With everything included, then, an active balloonist will probably spend $4,500-$5,000 per year on the sport.

One way to cover those expenses is to win prize money in a balloon competition. With ballooning becoming ever more popular and therefore attractive to commercial sponsors, purses have been going up each year for the major balloon festivals. The top balloon festivals now offer prize money in the $25,000 range, and it is common for purses of $10,000 to be handed out even in smaller events.

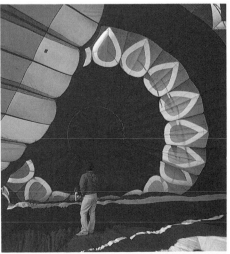

BRIAN LAWLER

59

BRIAN LAWLER

HOT-AIR BALLOON SERVICES OPERATE IN MOST AREAS OF THE UNITED STATES AND Canada. Most of these companies give short, 1 to 2-hour balloon rides with brunch or a picnic. Balloon trips cost an average of $70 per person per half hour. The average champagne flight costs $135 per person, for a 3-hour experience with 60-90 minutes in the air. Some companies offer longer balloon tours, but this will cost an average of $500-$1,000 per day. If you do not see a listing for your area, consult your yellow pages.

UNITED STATES

ARIZONA

Unicorn Balloon Co., 15001 N. 74th St., Ste. F, Scottsdale, AZ 85260, (800) 468-2478. A very solid company. Morning or evening rides start at $125.

Cirrus Airship, 2407 E. Shea Blvd., Phoenix, AZ 85027, (602) 971-4853. Very professional, 7 years experience, flights offered 7 days per week, year-round.

CALIFORNIA

Adventures Aloft of Napa Valley, P.O. Box 2500, Yountville, CA 94599, (707) 255-8688. Very professional, with a dozen balloons and 15 years in the Napa Valley--great wine-country trip.

Balloon Aviation of Napa Valley, 6525 Washington St., Ste. 7, Yountville, CA 94559, (800) FOR-NAPA in CA, or (707) 252-7067. 17 years experience; excellent balloon school. Can organize custom flight tours as well as rides.

Big Sky Balloons, Box 5665, Auburn, CA 95604, (916) 885-6717, or (800) BIG-SKYE in Northern California. Rides over the Sierra foothills, $155 per person. 10 years experience.

Skysurfer Balloon Co., 1221 Camino Del Mar, Del Mar, CA 92014, (619) 481-6800. One of America's very best since 1978. 7 balloons, 5 full-time pilots. 1-hour flights with buffet, $135-$145.

COLORADO

Aviation Adventures Aloft, 2200 Airway Ave., Fort Collins, CO, (800) 537-8842, or (303) 493-4959. 10 years experience. FAA-approved accelerated training program. Mountain flights.

Camelot Balloons, Inc., P.O. Box 1896, Vail, CO 81658, (303) 476-4743. Outstanding year-round programs, great scenery. $195 per person.

Life Cycle Balloon School, 2540 S. Steele St., Denver, CO 80210, (303) 759-3907. Excellent operation with new balloons and experienced pilots. Flight training and rides ($325 for two people).

Unicorn Balloon Co., 300B Aspen Airport Business Ctr., Aspen, CO 81611, (800) HOT-AIR7, or (303) 925-5752. Aspen's most experienced balloon center; excellent champagne flights.

FLORIDA

Sport Balloons, 1540 N. Franklin, Tampa, FL 33602, (813) 223-5787. $125 per person. Florida's top operator since 1973. Pilots Disneyworld balloons.

GEORGIA

Time Balloons, P.O. Box 45691, Atlanta, GA 30320, (800) 635-8741, or (404) 497-9987. Also custom balloon holidays worldwide.

KENTUCKY

Balloon Odyssey, 13005 Middletown Indus. Blvd., Ste. J, Louisville, KY 40223, (502) 245-1588. Excellent operation since 1974. Many balloons, flights 7 days/ week, year-round. $135 per person.

MAINE

Balloon Rides, 17 Freeman Street, Portland, ME 04103, (207) 761-8373, or (207) 772-4730. Flights on custom basis year-round. $135 per person.

MASSACHUSETTS

Balloon School of Massachusetts, Dingley Dell, RFD #1, Palmer (Brimfield), MA 01069, (413) 245-7013. Country flights for 3 or more persons; pilot/instructor Clayton Thomas is superb.

MICHIGAN

Upper Wind Balloon Port, 1308 Emerald, Niles, MI 49120, (616) 683-3036. 7 days per week, $150-$175 per person. (Close to Chicago.)

Michigan Balloon Corp., P.O. Box 20113, Lansing, MI 48901, (800) 537-1616. Excellent reputation, very active program.

NEW HAMPSHIRE

The Ballooning Center of New Hampshire, 10 Martha Drive, Derry NH 03038, (603) 434-1910. Balloon rides and training year-round.

NEW MEXICO

World Balloon Corporation, 4800 Eubank Blvd. NE, Albuquerque, NM 87111, (505) 293-6800. New Mexico's oldest and most respected balloon operation. Great rides and outstanding instruction. $135 per person champagne flight.

NEW YORK

Adirondack Balloon Flights, P.O. Box 65, Glens Falls, NY 12801, (518) 793-6342. Champagne flights over scenic mountain valleys and lakes. April through November, $175 per person.

NEVADA

Aerovision Balloons, Inc., P.O. Box 1998, Gardenerville, NV 89410, (800) HOT-AIR6. Year-round training and rides ($145 champagne flight). Group specials.

Zephyr Balloons, 120 Mary St., Reno, NV 89509, (702) 329-1700. North Nevada's most experienced operator. Rides in Reno, Sparks, Truckee (CA), year-round starting at $115 per person. Hotel/casino shuttle service.

NORTH CAROLINA

Aerial Ascensions Ltd., 4613 Grayling Dr., Apex, NC 27502, (919) 387-1088 (Raleigh suburb). Sales, training, champagne flights.

Balloons Over Charlotte, 3709 Sweetgrass Lane, Charlotte, NC 28226, (704) 541-7058. 16 years of experience. Excellent champagne flights.

OHIO

Clear Sky Balloon Port, 6929 Tylersville Road, W. Chester, OH 45069, (800) 733-2053, (513) 779-1427. Near Cincinnati. $130-$145 (kids half-price.)

Balloon Tours of America, P.O. Box 723, Kent, OH 44240, (216) 673-6777. Ohio's leading balloon operator with 18 years of experience. 7 days per week, champagne flight costs $275 per couple.

Ad Ventures Aloft, Inc., 2695 Cypress Way, Cincinnati, OH 45212, (513) 351-5656. Sales, rides, flight training. $110-$135 per person.

PENNSYLVANIA

Dillon Hot-Air Balloon Service, 850 Meadow Lane, Camp Hill, PA 17011, (717) 761-6895. $150 per person. 6 days per week, weather permitting.

RHODE ISLAND

Stumpf's Balloons, P.O. Box 913, Bristol, RI 02809, (401) 253-0111. Very scenic coastal champagne flights, May-Oct., $200-$225 per person. Sales, balloon accessories and instruction.

SOUTH CAROLINA

Eagle Balloons, P.O. Box 60744, Charleston, SC 29419, (803) 552-3782. Five years experience. $125 per person.

TENNESSEE

AeroStation Ltd., 119 Featherstone, Franklin, TN 37064, (615) 794-8655. High-quality program with skilled pilots. $225, 2 people. Nashville area.

Memphis Hot Air Balloons, Inc., 8145 Creekside Circle North, Cordova, TN 38018, (901) 755-6820. $250 for two people, one hour.

TEXAS

Austin Aeronauts, 1700 Elmhurst Dr., Austin, TX 78741, (800) 444-3267. Superior program since 1981. Champagne flights $150. Lake flights, night flights for $300. Worldwide on custom basis.

Rainbow's End, 7826 Fairview, Houston, TX 77041, (713) 466-1927. Houston's best since 1984. Rides year-round with 3 balloons. $250 for two persons. Sales and instruction.

Above It All Ballooning, 7902 Picador, Houston, TX 77083, (713) 277-1788. 20 years experience. 1-hour flight, $220 for two persons.

AirVenture Balloons, 1791 Millard, Suite D, Plano, (Dallas), TX 75074, (214) 422-0212. Rides, sales, flight training. $150 per person, 90 minutes.

UTAH

Balloon Adventures, 2040 Sunnyside Ave., Salt Lake City, UT 84108, (flying site is Park City), (801) 645-8787. FAA flight instruction and rides. Lovely Rocky Mountain setting. $75-$135 per person.

Moon's Balloons, P.O. Box 4192, Park City, UT 84060, (801) 645-9092. Excellent company, since 1974, 8 balloons. $75/half hour, $135/hour. Highly recommended.

Maasai Mara Balloon Safari/RONNA NELSON

VIRGINIA (D.C. AREA)

Balloons Unlimited, P.O. Box 3190, Oakton, VA 22124, (703) 281-2300. 7 days per week. $135 per person per hour.

WASHINGTON

Airial Balloon Company, 10123 Airport Way, Snohomish, WA 98290, (206) 568-3025. Rides and instruction in beautiful valley. Guaranteed 60-90 minutes air-time, great morning brunch, $145 per person. $115 sunset flight.

Balloon Depot, 16138 NE 87th, Redmond, WA 98052, (206) 881-9699. Seattle-area flights have been rated the prettiest in the US by Ballooning magazine. Evening flights are recommended, $110-$150.

Great Northwest Aerial Navigation Company, 7616 79th SE, Mercer Island, WA 98040, (206) 232-2023. Beautiful Snohomish Valley champagne flights, $110-$150. 7 days per week.

AFRICA

No cross-country flights are offered currently in Kenya, but day-flights can be booked through your travel agent, either separately, or as part of a safari itinerary. Use one of the following operators: Trans-World Safaris, P.O. Box 44690, Nairobi, Kenya (Mara Sorova and Mara Serena); Balloon Adventures, P.O. Box 47557, Nairobi, Kenya (Keekorok Lodge); Musiara (Governor's Camp), P.O. Box 48217, Nairobi, Kenya.

AUSTRALIA

Balloon Adventures Australia, 16 Lyte Place, Prospect, NSW 2149, Australia, (011 61) 2 622 5267; FAX: 622 6414. Camden (Sydney), Mudgee, all of New South Wales.

Balloon Sunrise, 39 Smith St., Richmond, Victoria 3121, Australia, (011 61) 3 4277 596. Rides and flight training with world record holder Chris Dewhirst. Locations: Hunter Valley, Camden Valley, Rutherglen, Canowindra, Melbourne.

CANADA

Balloon Dimensions, Bay A, 6908 6th St. S.E., Calgary, ALB, T2H 2K4, (403) 243-3200; FAX: (403) 252-0359. $150 CDN champagne flights, Mountain flight expeditions (12,000' balloon crossing of the Rockies), $2,500-$10,000 CDN.

Pegasus Ballooning, R.R. 11, 17370 23rd Ave., White Rock, BC V4B 5E7, (604) 531-3400; FAX: (604) 531-3408. March-Oct., 6 days/week. Champagne flight, $175 CDN per person. Group discounts.

Windship Aviation Ltd., 5615 103rd St., Edmonton, ALB, T6H 2H3, (403) 438-0111; FAX: (403) 438-6756. Edmonton's leading balloon company. Champagne flights, $150 CDN per person.

EGYPT

Airship & Balloon Company Ltd., Unit 19, Stafford Park 12, Telford, Shropshire, England TF3 3BJ, (011 44) 952 292 945; FAX: (011 44) 952 292 930. This British firm offers balloon rides in Shropshire and Luxor, Egypt where you can soar over temples and the Nile. Flights in India may be available also.

GREAT BRITAIN

Adventure Balloons, 3 Queens Terrace, Hanwell, London, England W7 3TS, (011 44) 81 840 0108. Instructional flights and ballooning weekends in Somerset from July through October. Also balloon holidays in Normandy, France from about $750.

The Balloon Base, Air 2 Air Ltd., Vauxhall House, Coronation Road, Bristol, England BS3 1RN, (011 44) 272 633 333; FAX: 272 632 263. Trips booked throughout all of United Kingdom: Lake District, London, Midlands, Yorkshire Dales, Stratford.

SCANDINAVIA

Scandinavian Adventures, c/o Worldwide Nordic, USA, P.O. Box 1129, Maplewood, NJ 07040, (201) 736-8488. Dawn and afternoon balloon flights over the Stockholm archipelago. Cost, with champagne breakfast or dinner, is about $260 per person. May through August.

BALLOONING

BUNGEE JUMPING

The Newest Craze

Bungee jumping, once the exclusive province of daredevils, is now being marketed to the public as the ultimate weekend adventure. For about $100, Bungee Adventures of Mountain View, California will take you up in a balloon, strap you into a waist and chest harness, and let you plunge 150 feet into space. The price includes a video of your first jump.

Why do it? As one first-timer said, "It's all about conquering fear--tackling something wild and frightening for the first time." Freefall lasts only a few seconds, but the rush is incredible as you plunge headfirst toward the ground, stopping just 50 feet short of impact. When the bungees grow taut, you instantly recoil 75 feet back up towards the balloon, your body cartwheeling in all directions. You'll sweat through a half-dozen yo-yos before the bungees stabilize, and you can make peace again with your stomach. When all movement finally stops, the balloon lowers you gently to the ground.

Bungee Adventures is the brainchild of two brothers, John and Peter Kockelman. These bungee pioneers achieved national fame for their Reebok sneaker commercial. They have coordinated over 10,000 jumps, and launch 100 jumpers each weekend. Contact Bungee Adventures at 2218 Old Middlefield Way, Suite G, Mountain View, CA 94043, (415) 903-3546.

BRIAN LAWLER

Balloon bungee jumping/MARK SHAPIRO

ORGANIZATIONS

Balloon Federation of America (BFA)
P.O. Box 400, Indianola, IA 50125, (515) 961-8809.

Australian Ballooning Federation Ltd.
P.O. Box 21, Diggers Rest, Victoria, 3427, Australia, (011 61) 3 740 1868.

British Balloon and Airship Club
c/o Travelgas Ltd., Fazeley St, Birmingham BS, England.

Federation Francais d' Aerostation
6 Rue Galilee, 75016 Paris, France, (011 33) 1 46 33 56 82.

Aero Club of Austria
Section Ballooning, Prinz Eugen Strasse 12, A-1040, Wien, Austria, (011 43) 1 505 1028.

Deutscher Aero Club Frei Ballon Kommission
c/o Walter Muller, Fahrenkotten 9, 4300 Essen A-5, Germany, (011 49) 201 46 2496.

Ballooning Commity ACCS
c/o Mr. Gerold Signer, Espenstrasse, 22 CH 9630 Wattwil, Switzerland, (011 41) 74 72196.

Real Aeroclub de España
Attn: Dolores Feliu, Carrera de San Jerinomo, 15 28014 Madrid, Spain, (011 34) 91 429 85 34.

BOOKS

Ballooning, the Complete Guide to Riding the Winds, by Dick Wirth. This is the biggest and most readable introduction to the sport. Good tips on learning to fly and ballooning abroad. Available from Random House, New York, NY.

Taming the Gentle Giant, by Imogen Norwood. This is the most complete ballooning textbook, and is used by students and commercial and private pilots nationwide. FARs and airspace charts included. $15.95 plus $2.00 shipping from Land O'Sky Aeronautics, P.O. Box 636, Skyland, NC 28776, (704) 684-2092.

The Art of Hot-Air Ballooning, by Roger Bansemer. A big, colorful book with great illustrations, this was Malcolm Forbes' favorite. $34.95 plus $2.50 for shipping from Gollum Press, 2351 Alligator Creek Rd., Clearwater, FL 34625.

MAGAZINES

Ballooning, the Journal of the Balloon Federation of America, P.O. Box 51, Post Mills, VT 05058, (802) 333-4883.

Skylines, Bob Dawson Ed., P.O. Box 1703, Portales, NM 88130, (505) 562-2412. This Balloon Federation newsletter lists scheduled ballooning events nationwide.

MAJOR NATIONAL BALLOONING EVENTS

(Call for exact dates and locations)

Albuquerque (NM) Balloon Fiesta--First week of October, 625 balloons, cars and cash prizes. Fiesta office, (505) 821-1000.

Battle Creek (MI) Int'l Balloon Championship--July 4th weekend, 150 balloons, $24,000 prize. (616) 962-4076, or (616) 962-0592.

Canadian Balloon Championships (Festivale de Montgolfier), St. Jean (Quebec)--August, 100+ balloons. (514) 346-6000.

Cincinnati (OH) Annual Balloonfest--May (Memorial Day), 60 balloons, $10,000 prize. John Kanis, (513) 752-6700.

Colorado Springs (CO) Balloon Classic--Labor Day, 100+ balloons. (719) 635-7506, ext. 22, or Dewey Rheinhard, (719) 473- 2120.

Glens Falls (NY) Balloonfest, last weekend of September. (518) 761-6366.

Greeley (CO) Annual Halloween Balloon Rally--October, 50 balloons. Joyce Bundgaard, (303) 759-3907.

Greenville (SC) Freedom Weekend Aloft--July 4th weekend, 150 balloons, $45,000 prize. Keri Hall, (803) 282-8501.

Jackson (MI) Hot Air Jubilee--Third week in July, 50 balloons, $15,000 prize. (517) 782-8221.

Kent (WA) Balloon Classic--Third weekend in July, 35 balloons. Kent Parks Dept., (206) 859-3991.

Mississippi Int'l Balloon Classsic--last weekend in June, at Greenwood, 75 balloons, $7,500 prize. Linda Rutherford, (601) 455-6397.

Montrose (Telluride, CO) Balloon Affair. July 4th week. Joyce Bundgaard, (303) 759-3907.

Nashville (TN) Dr. Pepper Balloon Classic--Third weekend in June, 70 balloons, $20,000 prize. (615) 794-8655, or (615) 373-4575.

National Hot-Air Balloon Championships, (Middletown, OH in 1992)--August, 200 balloons, $64,000 prize. BFA, (515) 961-8809.

National Balloon Classic--Late July-August, (Indianola, IA), 150 balloons, $30,000 prize. Marlene Wall, (515) 961-8415.

North Amer. Balloon Championships--June, Baton Rouge (LA). BFA (515) 961-8809

Portland Rose Festival Balloon Classic (Beaverton, OR)--June, 45 balloons, $10,000 prize. Shannon Parker, (503) 227-2681.

Reno (NV) Great Balloon Race--Labor Day, 100+ balloons. (800) FOR-RENO.

St. Paul (MN) Winter Carnival and Balloon Festival--Late January, 30 balloons. Carnival information, (612) 297-6953.

Sunday River (Maine) Annual Winter Balloon Festival--February, 30 balloons. (800) 543-2SKI, or (207) 824-3000.

Thunderbird Balloon Classic (Glendale, AZ)--November, 150 balloons. Judy Contraras, (602) 978-7208.

VIDEOS

Bombard Balloon Adventures offers a 40-minute video featuring flights in Burgundy, the Loire Valley and Austria. Follow the balloons over castles, famous chateaux and picturesque villages. $20 from Bombard Balloon Adventures, 6727 Curran Street, McLean, VA 22101-3804, (800) 862-8537.

The Balloon Works in North Carolina makes some of the most beautiful, artistic envelopes in the world. See how they are crafted in this 22-minute video. $29.95 from the Balloon Works, Firefly Video, P.O. Box 827, Statesville, NC 28677, (704) 878-9501.

Red Rocks Rally, Gallup, New Mexico/RON BEHRMANN

Bicycle Touring

Owens Valley, California/GORDON WILTSIE

*The bicycle is the last machine
simple enough to be understood by its owner.*
-Spokesong (Broadway play)

▼

*B*icycle touring is booming. Dozens of tour companies offer hundreds of guided trips, with options ranging from sailing cruises to rafting adventures. With the increasing popularity of mountain bikes, many outfitters now offer mountain bike tours in the US and abroad. Generally, the quality of commercial tours is quite high, and most customers seem to be very satisfied with the package tour experience. Costs are creeping upward, as guided tours, particularly those in Europe, become more deluxe, catering to an older and more affluent group of cyclists.

If you've started to think about a bicycle tour, you'll know how difficult it can be to select the right trip. This chapter will steer you to the best outfitters, and help you choose the best tour to fit your budget and interests. We also give you advice on how to organize your own self-guided tour, and list some of the best mountain biking destinations in North America.

CHAPTER
5

DENNIS COELLO

*T*HE MOST EFFICIENT MEANS OF TRANSPORTATION EVER INVENTED, RIDING A bicycle is also the perfect way to experience a new destination for the first time. You ramble slowly, interacting with your environment, rather than passing it by in a blur. From mild to exotic, we have selected some of the very best tours and destinations below. Any one of them can be the trip of a lifetime.

SAN JUAN ISLANDS

Northwest Odyssey

The San Juans, located west of Seattle, may well be the premier coastal touring destination in North America. The San Juans offer just about everything you could ask for: moderate scenic terrain, plentiful parks and campgrounds, charming country inns, boat rides, and easy access to major cities and tourist centers. Whether you're planning on touring for two days or 20, the San Juans and nearby

Gulf Islands won't disappoint even the most demanding cycle tourist.

A good starting point is Port Townsend, about an hour's drive west from Seattle by car. From Port Townsend, cross Admiral Inlet by ferry to Whidbey Island. There are many resorts on Whidbey where you can book lodging, as well as excellent campgrounds at Fort Casey, Fort Ebey, Oak Harbor and Deception Pass State Parks. It can be crowded in the summertime, so you'll probably want to move on after a day or two. Cross the bridge at the north end to Fidalgo Island, and head north along Burrows Bay to the camp-

ground at Washington Park. An island loop, including the town of Anacortes, makes a nice day-trip.

If you're planning to include Canada's Gulf Islands in your trip, take the ferry across Puget Sound to Sidney. From there it's an easy ride to Victoria to the south, or you can catch another boat to Salt Spring, Galiano, and other Gulf Islands to the north. If you stay on the American side, hop off the ferry at Shaw Island in the middle of the Sound. There's a nice campground here, but mainly it's a good base to explore nearby San Juan, Lopez and Orcas Islands. Orcas probably has the nicest scenery, Lopez the easiest peddling, and San Juan the best restaurants and facilities. On Orcas, don't miss Mt. Constitution. From its 2,400' peak, you get a great view of the entire area. San Juan's Friday Harbor has many interesting little shops, and the west-side road offers nice, open views most of the way (elsewhere in the San Juans you will ride between thick stands of trees most of the time).

Because the San Juans are so popular,

Seven Ultimate Bicycle Vacations

we strongly advise that you make reservations well in advance. If you can travel in May, September or October, do so. The weather is pleasant, roads and campgrounds will be much less crowded, and you may find prices in the inns and resorts to be a bit lower. Before you go, pick up a copy of *Touring the Islands*, by Peter Powers and Renee Travis. This great little book, with its 3D maps of all the Gulf and San Juan Islands, and up-to-date listings of lodgings and campgrounds, is exactly what a bike touring guide should be--handy, easy to use, modern and accurate.

It's a snap to organize your own San Juans trip, but if you want a support van and planned itineraries, a number of excellent organized trips are available. Bicycle Adventures, (206) 786-0989, offers an outstanding 8-day trip that takes you to the San Juans, Vancouver Island (Victoria), and Hurricane Ridge on the nearby Olympic Peninsula. You can customize the itinerary with diving, sailing or sea kayaking excursions. Cost is $1,266 including inn lodging and most meals. A shorter 6-day San Juans tour runs $936. Backroads Bicycle Touring also offers a good 6-day Puget Sound trip. Cost is $1,030 if you stay at inns, or $595 if you camp. Call (800) 245-3874.

MAINE

Sail and Cycling Adventure

With its quiet roads, gentle terrain and picturesque fishing villages, the Maine coast is an ideal two-wheel touring destination. However, there's more to Maine than can be seen from the saddle of a touring bike. No Maine coast holiday would be complete without a visit to out-of-the-way islands that can only be reached by boat. An ideal trip, in our view, would combine both land and sea segments. This summer, Vermont Bicycle Touring will offer such a trip combining leisurely coastal cycling with 3 days of island-hopping aboard the schooner Roseway, one of Maine's most popular sailing vessels.

The trip begins in Camden, home port for much of the Maine windjammer fleet. After sailing to Islesboro Island, the riders and their bikes will be rowed ashore to explore the island's 30 miles of country roads. The next morning the Roseway will sail to North Haven Island, home to abundant wildlife and classic 19th-century mansions. After reboarding the schooner, the group returns through Penobscot Bay to Camden Harbor.

From a quiet country inn on Clark Island, a pristine hideaway, participants will spend the next 3 days exploring the nearby coast. Highlights are visits to the Rockport lighthouse, the charming village of Port Clyde, and Monhegan Island. Overall, this is an easy trip, suited to young and old alike. Cost for the 6-day holiday is $799 per person, with departures July through September. If you want a longer vacation, you can easily cycle on your own for a week, and then book a sailing segment through the Maine Windjammer Association, (800) 624-6380. Cruises last from 3 to 8 days, at an average cost of $100 per day. (See Chapter 18 for more details.)

DENNIS COELLO

FRANCE

The Great Wine Regions

If you want to combine the good life with your cycling, there's nothing quite like France. Here you can peddle leisurely from one world-class vineyard to the next, pausing for a luxurious picnic along the Rhone, Loire or Dordogne Rivers. You can dine in top Michelin Guide eateries, and spend your evenings in fine chateaux, living the life of the rich and famous.

One of the most popular touring venues in France is the Dordogne River Valley. A typical itinerary will take you from Beaulieu or Argentat to Rocamadour, La Tryne, Sarlat, Les Eyzies de Tayac with its famous Font-de-Gaume cave, and finishing up at Bergerac or Tremolat. The Dordogne boasts some of France's most beautiful scenery, and more castles (1,000 within 100 square miles) than any other destination in France. The hotels and restaurants in the Dordogne are of a very high standard, making this region the first pick of many deluxe commercial tours. Progressive Travels, (800) 245-2229, offers a 9-day luxury Dordogne tour for approximately $2,500 that features an optional ($150) hot-air balloon ride over

Rocamadour and the surrounding countryside. For those on a budget, Euro-Bike Tours, (815) 758-8851, runs a fine 10-day, $1,600 trip that takes you the full length of the Dordogne from Argentat to Bordeaux. Vermont Bicycle Touring, (802) 453-4811, also offers an 8-day tour of the Bordeaux region for $1,399 plus $140 bike rental.

For adventurous types, consider Europeds' River Gorges trip. You ride from the Dordogne to Provence, passing through the remote hills of the Massif Central. Highlight of the trip is a day's canoe run down the

Ardeche River Gorge. Price for the 8-day journey is $2,125. Call Europeds at (800) 321-9552. Another itinerary of choice takes you through the Champagne region. Here you'll find three principal viticultural areas, the Cote des Blancs, La Vallee de la Marne and La Montagne de Reims. You can visit them all on an easy 6-day loop out of Reims. On your journey be sure to include stops at Epernay, Vertus and Chateau-Thierry along the Marne River. At each of these destinations, you can sample world-class bubbly and sleep in superb country inns. You can easily do this Champagne tour independently, particularly if you speak some French.

To experience two cultures in one trip, explore the Alsace region, along the Franco-German border. If you follow the historic Route Du Vin, you can visit Strasbourg, the Black Forest, Mont Sainte-Odile, and many small villages, while sampling vineyards on both sides of the Rhine. Continuing south, you can stop in picturesque Riquewhir and Münster, where the food, culture and beverages are decidedly un-French. For gastronomic diversity, this is a good pick. Chateaux Bike Tours offers a 6-day deluxe Alsace tour for about $1,495. Call (800) 678-BIKE, or (303) 393-6910 inside Colorado.

CANADIAN ROCKIES

Scenic Wonderland

If you haven't been to the Canadian Rockies yet, go. Don't worry about the expense; there is an extensive network of youth hostels, and you'll find campgrounds and lodges galore. The scenery is unequalled in all of North America. With four great national parks to ride through (Kootenay, Banff, Yoho and Jasper), there are any number of options for a tour of a few days or a few weeks.

If you want to cover a lot of ground in a short period on relatively flat roads, cycle the Icefields Parkway from Jasper south to Banff. Along the way you'll pass Sunwapta Falls, the Columbia Icefields and Lake Louise. There are excellent campgrounds along the route, and numerous great day-hiking trails right off the main road.

A more challenging ride will take you from Banff over Vermillion and Sinclair Passes, then south through Kootenay National Park. The road can be steep, but the scenery is fantastic. Stop at Radium Hot Springs for some R&R before heading north through the Columbia River Valley to Golden, a whitewater rafting hotspot. From there, you'll experience the best of Rockies scenery in Yoho National Park. Be sure to stop and hike up into the nearby mountains to see one of Yoho Park's many aquamarine alpine lakes. There are many trails in this area which are also open to mountain bikes. When you come down out of Yoho, head on to Lake Louise and back to Banff. There's a good youth hostel in Banff, but it's often full, so call ahead.

If you're really adventurous, you can start a Rockies trip in the United States, passing through Glacier National Park in

Canadian Rockies/DENNIS COELLO

Montana, before turning north through the Waterton Lakes National Park on your way up to Alberta. The scenery on both sides of the border is magnificent, and there are first-rate lodges inside both parks. The peddling can be tough, however; you'll have to use your lowest gears on Glacier Park's spectacular Going-to-the-Sun Highway, and there can be fierce westerly winds while you're in the border region.

Because there is so much to see and do in Canada's Rockies, and because good accommodations of all kinds are easy to find, we would not hesitate to do this trip by ourselves, as long as we were prepared to climb some serious mountain passes without sag-wagon assistance. There are many good touring books that can help you plan the best itinerary. *The Canadian Rockies Bicycling Guide,* by Gail Helgasson and John Dodd, is one of the best.

If you want to go with a guided tour, Backcountry Bicycle Tours offers a fine 6-day trip for roughly $900 which combines Glacier and Waterton Lakes National Parks. Hotels are first class all the way. Call Backcountry at (406) 586-3556. For serious cyclers, Bikecentennial offers a challenging Great Parks 22-day camping tour that takes you all the way from Glacier National Park to Jasper at the north end of the Icefields Parkway. Cost is $740, including most food. Call (406) 721-1776 for details. Rocky Mountain Cycle Tours of Alberta runs a variety of tours in the Rockies costing $850-$950 for 6 days, including lodging in deluxe inns and all meals. Call (403) 678-4451. (For outfitter addresses, see pages 74-76.)

IRELAND

Biking the Emerald Isle

Ireland is a cyclist's dream--a place of verdant countryside, picturesque villages and dramatic coastline. Throughout this island country you'll find small bed and breakfasts offering clean and cozy accommodations for very modest rates, usually under $20 a night. There are no great mountain ranges to cross, and no heavy traffic with which to contend. On this quiet island, the pace of a cyclist suits the land well.

Ireland is unquestionably one of the best cycle touring destinations in the world. It's small scale makes it possible to see much of the countryside in a week or two. Conveniently, a good share of the prettiest scenery is packed together in County Kerry, Ireland's magical southwestern corner. Most tours of this region begin in Shannon, a pretty city that can be reached by direct flights from America.

From Shannon, ride south to Tralee and Killarney, charming towns with many colorful pubs. Taste the local brew (Ireland has hundreds of regional beers), and meet the locals. Tell them your grandfather was Irish and you'll be welcomed like a returning hero. After Killarney, explore the Ring of Kerry, a beautiful area of high, rocky headlands, quaint harbors and peaceful villages. Don't miss the Dingle Peninsula; here the road snakes along sheer hillsides high above the Atlantic.

If you have the time, once you've completed the Ring of Kerry put your bike on a train and head north to County Donegal, land of Keats. From Donegal Town, head north to Letterkenny, then follow the southern shore of Lough Swilly to Land's End at Fanad. This region has a timeless quality, with few settlements and nary a tourist in sight. From Fanad, follow coastal roads south. You'll pass isolated bays and harbors, and cross through the rugged, forbidding terrain of the Bloody Forelands, where Gaelic is still the mother tongue. This is the one stretch of Ireland where you may have trouble getting a room without reservations.

Continue south along the coast to Sligo, and then west through County Mayo. They say the sun never shines in County Mayo, but when it does, it is one of the prettiest places you'll ever see. Explore the remote west coast of County Mayo, perhaps taking a day-trip by boat to one of the offshore islands. Then work your way south, passing by dramatic Killery Harbor that separates Mayo to the north and County Galway to the south.

Once you reach County Galway, it's time to turn east and head back towards Shannon. You can either follow the coast, or swing inland past Ballynahinch and Lough Corrib. Here you'll find some of Ireland's best trout fishing. It's possible to cross from the west coast to Galway City in a day, and then it's only another day's ride to Shannon airport, and your flight home.

In three weeks, you could see virtually all of western Ireland. In two weeks, you can see most of the highlights of the southwest and far north, if you cross between Kerry

and Donegal by train or bus. Either way you will have a memorable trip that need not cost more than $50 per day, if done independently. If you want to take a package trip, Travent Int'l, Euro-Bike Tours, and Vermont Bicycle Touring (VBT) all offer fine Irish tours. Euro-Bike Tours runs a 14-day loop out of Shannon for about $2,000 all-inclusive, while Travent and VBT offer deluxe 8-

Otter Rock area, Oregon/PAUL McMENAMIN

day Ring of Kerry trips for $2,175 and $1,700 respectively. Airfare will be another $650 to $850 round-trip from the East Coast. (See pages 74-76 for full outfitter listings.)

OREGON & CALIFORNIA

The Pacific Coast Highway

A trip down the Pacific Coast Highway is truly one of America's ultimate cycling

adventures. Unfortunately traffic is increasing along the coastal roadway every year, but there is still plenty of stunning scenery once you get away from the big cities. Virtually all cyclers run the route north to south to have the prevailing winds at their backs. You can start as far north as Vancouver if you're ambitious, but a more reasonable starting point is Portland, Oregon. Take Highway 6 through the coastal range to Tillamook and then turn left to begin your journey south. The first sections can be disappointing, with too much seaside development. After a hundred miles or so, it's time to break out the camera. Try to pass through the Otter Rock area, just north of Newport, in the afternoon when the fog has lifted. This is the most dramatic, and, we think, the most beautiful stretch of the Oregon coast.

Farther south, the Gold Beach area, just below Port Orford, is a great spot for camping and beach walks. If you plan to camp in the state parks in the summertime, however, be sure to make advance reservations. After crossing the Oregon-California border, you'll pass through scenic Redwood National Park which stretches for 40 miles along the main route, Highway 101. South of the park you'll have to climb through the Coastal Range to connect with Highway 1 at Ft. Bragg. The next couple of days' riding will take you along the Mendocino coast, one of the highlights of the trip. Twenty miles south of Mendocino, cross the Russian River and continue on to the little town of Elk. Some think this quiet outpost has the best ocean views on the West Coast.

From here on, the road continues to snake its way along rugged headlands as you wind your way toward San Francisco. When you reach Bodega Bay, check out the local eateries for great oysters, and make a day-trip to nearby Pt. Reyes if you've got the time. As you approach San Francisco, don't blast across the bridge, but stop just short and explore the Marin Headlands National Rec-

reation Area--a perfect place for a mid-day picnic, with views that will leave you amazed. South of San Francisco be sure to explore Monterey, Carmel and the Point Lobos Nature Preserve. You'll probably be anxious to get to Big Sur, but frankly points farther north are more impressive. Once you've gotten to San Simeon, you've hit all the highlights, and you may want to wrap up the tour.

Each summer, Bikecentennial operates a 28-day Pacific Coast camping tour from Seattle to San Francisco that we can recommend for strong cyclists. Price is $890. Call (406) 721-1776. Vermont Bicycle Touring, (802) 453-4811, markets a good 8-day California trip for roughly $1,300 that will take you along the coast route between the California wine country and San Francisco. (Addresses on pages 74-76.)

NEW ZEALAND

Southern Hemisphere Getaway

For hardy bicycle travelers, who don't mind changeable weather and a fair share of hills, New Zealand is an enormously rewarding destination. There are few places on earth where the scenery is more beautiful, or the locals more friendly. While budget motels can be hard to find, New Zealand does have an extensive network of youth hostels where travelers can bed down in relative comfort for under $15 per night. The hostels, which are open to all ages, are conveniently situated near all of New Zealand's major tourist areas. Camping--the best way to make Kiwi friends--is another good alternative for budget-minded travelers.

While the North Island generally offers better weather and flatter roads, the South Island boasts the finest scenery. Those with a limited amount of time should probably spend most of it in the south. The preferred South Island itinerary begins at Picton, the debarking point for the

BRIAN BAILEY

ferry from Wellington, New Zealand's capital city. From Picton, you can ride west through the Marlborough Sounds area, stopping for a boat ride at the town of Havelock before reaching Nelson, a sunny community on the Tasman Bay. Many riders then proceed down the lush western coast, but be forewarned--it is typically very gray and wet here, so you should have a support vehicle to rescue you from downpours. After passing Franz Josef and Fox Glaciers, hardy cyclists can cross the spectacular Haast Pass through New Zealand's 12,000' Southern Alps. The road conditions can be horrendous, so van support is again essential. The pass road will take you to Wanaka and then Queenstown, a lovely resort town and sports center which caters to the adventurous. After a few days in Queenstown, you can ride back up the eastern side of the Alps, or take a

coastal route--either way ending up in Christchurch where you can catch a direct flight back to the States.

A number of outfitters offer New Zealand bike tours. Backroads Bicycle Touring offers an excellent 17-day tour that hits virtually all the scenic highlights of the South Island. Trips depart December through March at a cost of roughly $2,450. Call (800) 245-3874. New Zealand Pedaltours, the leading Kiwi bike touring company, offers a wide variety of 6 to 18-day road bike tours throughout both islands. Tours range in price from about $700 to $2,200 and can be booked through Forum Travel International in the US, (510) 671-2900.

If you're looking for a real adventure on two wheels, consider Outer Edge Expedition's unique 16-day mountain bike adventure. After crossing the Southern Alps from east to west by van, you'll ride through tropical rainforest in Paparoa National Park, and then hike up the Fox Glacier, passing numerous large waterfalls. The highlight of the trip is a helicopter-assisted mountain bike descent from 7,000' Mt. Lochnagar in Mt. Aspiring National Park followed by a serious session of whitewater rafting.

After the heli-lift to the summit, riders will descend 5,000' through the Shotover River Valley, traversing snowfields and rushing streams. The group trades pedals for paddles as they board rafts to challenge the Class IV-V Shotover River, one of the finest whitewater runs in the world. Two more days are spent near Queenstown, where participants can sample (on their own nickel) a wide variety of activities, ranging from bungee-jumping to jet-boating. Outer Edge's heli-bike tours are scheduled for December and February, and will cost about $2,400 including lodging, all equipment and most meals. For more information, contact Outer Edge Expeditions, 4500 Pontiac Trail, Walled Lake, MI, 48390, (800) 322-5235.

GREAT BICYCLE TOURS AROUND THE WORLD

F OR THOSE WITH A LIMITED AMOUNT OF TIME AND SUFFICIENT FINANCES, AN ORGANIZED TOUR WILL probably give you the best vacation experience, primarily because your lodging is prearranged and a sag-wagon provides support along the way. This chart contains the essential information for 40 of the most interesting and best-run bicycle tours worldwide. Prices were confirmed at the time we went to press, but may be changed without notice. This is particularly true for foreign tours which are subject to fluctuating exchange rates.

Trips are rated ★ to ★★★★★ for quality; 1-5 for difficulty, 5 being the hardest. Codes as follows: WA (includes airfare); MB (mountain bike); BYO (bike rental costs extra); $ (special value); BT (boat trip); RFT (raft trip); WS (water sports, i.e. snorkeling, sailing); DLX (top-class food & lodging); EST (estimated price).

KENNETH REDDING/BIG DOGS

LOCATION	DESCRIPTION	DIFFICULTY	TOUR DAYS
NORTH AMERICA			
ALASKA			
Alaska Range MB	Denali Highway, Alaska Range camping, Wrangell-St. Elias Park, Mt. Blackburn.	3–5	13
CANADA			
BC Heli-bike MB	Heli-lift to Selkirk and Purcell Mtns., descend mining trails and snowfields. Radical.	3–5	5
Great Parks North	Montana, Glacier Nat'l Park, Logan Pass, Waterton Lakes, Kootenay Valley. Beautiful.	4	22
Icefields Alpiner	Banff, Cont'l Divide, Kootenay & Columb. Rivers, Lake Louise, Columb. Icefields, Jasper.	3.5	7
Nova Scotia	Halifax, fishing villages, Mahone Bay, Lunenburg, Windsor. Moderate terrain.	2.5	9
NEW ENGLAND			
New Englander	Bar Harbor, Acadia Nat'l Park, Rockland, White Mtns., Green Mtns., end Burlington, VT.	3	14
PACIFIC COAST			
North Cascades	Columbia River, Mt. Rainier, Mt. St. Helens, forests, lakes, North Cascades Nat'l Park.	4.5	15
Oregon South Coast	Newport to Cal. border, Rogue River Valley, sea caves, Otter Crest Lodge, Gold Coast.	3.5	8
Puget Sound	Pt. Townsend, Whidbey, Fidalgo, Orcas, San Juan & Vancouver Islands, ferry rides.	3	8
ROCKIES			
Holy Cross 100 MB	Rockies Wilderness inn to inn, 11,000' ridges, mining towns, fishing. Tough ride.	4.5	6
Yellowstone Ride	Yellowstone Park and Paradise Valley. Wildlife trails, hot springs, the best rooms in the park.	3	6
Rocky Mtn. Rambler	Denver-Boulder, Estes Park, 12,000' ridge road, Grand Lake, Niwot Range, Cont'l Divide.	4	5
American Safari	Grand Teton MB trails, rafting excursion, llama trekking, luxury tent camping.	3	7
SOUTHEAST			
Horse & Wine Country	Virginia hunt country--horse farms, vineyards, mansion accommodations. Balloon option.	3	3
Shenandoah Valley	Blue Ridge Parkway, fall foliage, forests, historical sites, waterfalls, farmlands.	2.5	5
SOUTHWEST			
Bryce/Zion/Gr. Canyon	Cedar Breaks Mnmt., Bryce Cyn., Kaibab Plateau, Grand Cyn., Zion Nat'l Pk. Inn or camp.	3.5	9
Canyonlands MB	White Rim Trail, and Needles and Maze District in Canyonlands Nat'l Park. Indian ruins.	3.5	3-5
AFRICA			
Kenya Rift Valley	Nairobi-Rift Valley, Nakuru, Lake Baringo, Maasai Mara Nat'l Park, Lake Victoria, villages.	2	18
Zimbabwe	Matebeleland, Hwange & Matopos Nat'l Parks, RFT Zambezi River, Victoria Falls, wildlife.	2	16
ASIA			
Bali MB Inn Tour	Bali Hyatt, Lake Bratan, Bedugal, Lake Batur, Balina Beach, Tirtagangga Palace, Ubud.	3.5	12
Japan Explorer	Osaka, Noto Peninsula, Takoaka plains, Toyama Mtns., Kyoto, Osaka.	3	16
Nepal MB Odyssey	Remote areas new to bikes, short foot-treks, RFT, riverside roads. Moderate terrain.	3.5	18 (3, 7 avail.)
Silk Road MB	From Tashkent USSR to Western China on ancient trade route. High passes. Pine forests.	3.5	25
EUROPE			
FRANCE			
Dordogne	Castle to castle, Rocamadour, balloon option, Sarlat, Les Eyzies (cave art). Superb food.	1	9
Loire Valley	Paris, Loire Valley--Amboise, Chinon, Angers, vineyards, small villages, good scenery.	1	9
Provence-Riviera	Rhone River to Rochegude, Avignon, St. Remy, Medit. coast, Michelin cuisine & accom.	3	9
GERMANY/FRANCE			
Alsace	Superb wines & food, Strasbourg, Mt. St. Odile, Rhine River, 15th-century towns, castles.	2	6
GREAT BRITAIN			
Scottish Borders	Edinburgh, River Tweed, Thirlestane Castle, Eildon Hills, Scott's View, Floors Castle.	3	6
GREECE			
Classical Greece	Athens, Delphi, Corinth, Mycenae, Greek coast, Zakinthos Island, Olympia, Acropolis.	3	14
IRELAND			
Western Coast	Limerick, Killarney, Dingle Peninsula/Bay, Dromoland Castle. Flat & rolling hills.	3	10
PORTUGAL			
Valleys & Vineyards	Oporto, Peneda-Geres Nat'l Park, Rio Lima, Arcos de Valdevez, Viana Do Castello.	2	9–11
SCANDINAVIA			
Denmark & Sweden	Copenhagen, Svendborg, Funen Island, Jutland Peninsula., BT to Sweden, Isle of Zealand.	2	14
SWITZERLAND			
Pedal & Pole	Verbier (Matterhorn, Mt. Blanc), 4-star hotel, 4 days Alps MB, 2 days glacier skiing.	4	8
MEXICO/SOUTH AMERICA			
Andes to Amazon MB Tour	Machu Picchu, ride through Vilcanota Valley, descend 12,000' to Amazon Manu Park. Canoe trip.	4	14
Baja La Paz MB	Desert trails, Sea of Cortez, beach camp, Valle Perdido, Todos Santos, 15-mile descent.	4	8
Chile/Argentina MB	Santiago, Nahuel Huapi and Huechulafquen Nat'l Parks, volcanos, lakes, Bariloche, Puerto Varas.	4	18
Costa Rica Adventure Week	MB in Santa Rosa Nat'l Park, also horseback riding, rafting, canoeing and snorkeling.	2	8 (1 biking)
SOUTH PACIFIC			
French Polynesia	Five islands: Tahiti, Bora Bora, Tahaa, Huahine, Raiatea, sailing trips, WS.	2	10
New Zealand	Marlborough Sounds, Nelson Lakes Nat'l Park, Haast Pass, BT Milford Sound, Queenstown.	4	17
Papua New Guinea	MB, Wahgi Valley (Stone Age Wigmen tribes), Highlands and Tagari River, rafting.	3	14

COURTESY VERMONT BICYCLE TOURING   ROD WALKER/COLORADO TOURIST BOARD   ROBERT WHITE/BUTTERFIELD AND ROBINSON

Company	Support Van	Guide	Cost	Miles/Day	Lodging	Dates	Rating
REI Adventures	Yes	Yes	$1300+BYO	40	Camp	Aug	★★★
Kootenay MB Tours	Unnec.	Yes	$1600 EST	NA	Lodge	Jul, Aug	★★
Bikecentennial	No	Yes	$740 EST+BYO	30–60	Camp	Summer	★★★$
Timberline	Yes	Yes	$700EST	50	Inns	Summer	★★$
VT Bicy. Touring	Yes	Yes	$1199	38	Fine Inns	Summer	★★
Bikecentennial	No	Yes	$570 EST+BYO	45	Camp	July-Aug	★★
Bicycle Adventures	Yes	Yes	$2100+BYO	40–90	Good Inns	Summer	★★★★
Bicycle Adventures	Yes	Yes	$1250+BYO	75	DLX Inns	Summer	★★★
Bicycle Adventures	Yes	Yes	$1270+BYO	40	DLX Inns	Summer	★★★
Paragon Guides	Yes	Yes	$900+BYO	15–20	B&Bs, and 1 Hut	Summer	★★★
Backcountry Bicy. Tours	Yes	Yes	$870	25–45	DLX lodge	June, July, Sept	★★★
Timberline	Yes	Yes	$790 EST+BYO	50	DLX lodge	Summer	★★
Off the Deep End	Yes	Yes	$750	25–30	Tent Camping	June-Aug	★★★$
VCC/Four Seasons	Yes	Yes	$279–$399 EST	20–40	DLX Inn	May-Oct	★★
VCC/Four Seasons	Yes	Yes	$759 EST	20–50	DLX Inn	May-Oct	★★
Backroads	Yes	Yes	$1295/795+BYO	20–60	Inn or Camp	July-Sept	★★
Rim Tours	Yes	Yes	$265-$500+BYO	20–40	Camp	Spring, Fall	★★★
Bicycle Africa	No	Yes	$1290+BYO	40	Tent Camp/Inns	June/July	★★
Bicycle Africa	No	Yes	$1290+BYO	25	Inns	July	★★
Backroads	Yes	Yes	$1790+BYO	20	DLX Inns	May	★★
Asian Pacific	Yes	Yes	$3198+BYO	25–50	Tourist Inns, Zen Temples	Apr, July, Oct	★★
Above the Clouds	Yes	Yes	$1650	25–40	Modest Inns	Nov, July, March	★★★
REI Adventures	Yes	Yes	$3500+BYO	60–70	Tent Camping	Aug	★★★
Progressive Travels	Yes	Yes	$2500	30	DLX Chateaux	May-Oct	★★★
Butterfield & Robinson	Yes	Yes	$2800	30	DLX Chateaux	Summer	★★★
Chateaux Tours	Yes	Yes	$2350 EST	30–35	DLX Chateaux	May-Oct	★★
Chateaux Tours	Yes	Yes	$1495 EST	30–35	Grand Hotels	July-Oct	★★
Peter Costello	Yes	Yes	$750 EST	25–35	Inns, B&B	May-Sept	★★$
Classic Tours	Yes	Yes	$1450	35	Inns, Hotels	June, Sept	★★★$
VT Bicy. Touring	Yes	Yes	$1700+BYO	28 average	Inn, Small Hotels	July, Aug	★★★★
Cycle Portugal, (800) 245-4226	Yes	Yes	$1400 EST+BYO	20–35	Rustic Inns	July-Oct	★★★$
Euro-Bike	Yes	Yes	$2300 EST	25–35	Hotels	Summer	★★
Europeds	Unnec.	Yes	$1650 EST	15–20	DLX Hotel	Summer	★★
A.W.E., (800) 444-0099	Yes	Yes	$1500	10–30	Hotels/Camp	May, Sept.	★★★★
Baja Expeditions	Yes	Yes	$975, Air incl.+BYO	25	Camping/Motels	Nov-Apr	★★★$
Condor Adven. (303) 331-9977	Yes	Yes	$1800	20	Inns/Camping	Jan-March	★★★
Forum Travel Int'l	No	Yes	$1000	20–40	Rustic Inns	Year-round	★★
Off the Deep End	Unnec.	Yes	$2330+BYO	25	Resort Hotels, Yachts	April-Oct	★★★
Backroads	Yes	Yes	$2450+BYO	25–70	DLX lodges	Dec-Mar	★★★★
Off the Deep End	Yes	Yes	$2565+BYO	20	Resorts, Hotels	June, July	★★★

The Leading Bike Tour Operators

DENNIS COELLO

From more than 100 candidates, we've selected 18 of the best domestic bicycle tour companies. Some run tours worldwide, while others specialize in a limited region. They are all well established, come recommended by past customers, and offer a high level of service. You should feel confident to book a tour with any one of them, recognizing that, as a general rule, the more you pay, the more deluxe the trip will be.

■ ASIAN PACIFIC ADVENTURES
826 So. Sierra Bonita Ave., Los Angeles, CA 90036, (213) 935-3156.

Not just a bike touring company, Asian Pacific offers a wide range of adventure trips to some of the world's most exotic destinations. Bike tours are offered to China, the USSR, India, Thailand and Japan. The China trips (two road bike tours in the south, and one mountain bike excursion in Sichuan) have been popular with past customers, and are available from few, if any, other outfitters. This is a solid operator with one-of-a-kind trips. Rating: ★★

■ BACKCOUNTRY BICYCLE TOURS
P.O. Box 4029, Bozeman, MT 59772, (406) 586-3556.

Backcountry is a small, family-run business, but nearly every trip in its catalog is a clear winner. Top tours include the San Juans (see p. 66) and Glacier National Park/Canadian Rockies (see p. 69), Yellowstone, Bryce Canyon/Zion National Parks, and a Montana Rockies trip featuring biking, horseback riding and rafting--all in 6 days. All trips are van supported, and every night is spent in a superb country inn or B & B--usually the very best to be had. Trips run $800 to $980 for 5 to 6 days, covering 35-60 miles daily. Rating: ★★★

■ BICYCLE ADVENTURES
P.O. Box 7875, Olympia, WA 98507, (206) 786-0989.

Bicycle Adventures concentrates on the Pacific Northwest, offering more itineraries there than any other company. (Trips are also available in California and Kona, Hawaii.) Prices are 10 to 20 percent lower than the big outfitters, the trip leaders are terrific, the itineraries well planned, and special activities such as diving, kayaking and sailing can be added to most tours. Fat-tire fans should check out the 6-day, $860 North Cascades/Methow Valley, and $896 Mt. St. Helens mountain bike trips. Rating: ★★★

■ BIKECENTENNIAL
P.O. Box 8308, Missoula, MT 59807, (406) 721-1776; FAX: (406) 721-8754.

Bikecentennial offers no-frills trips for hardy cyclists. Bikecentennial's trips tend to go more miles, cross more mountain ranges, and offer more challenge than other tours. Many trips do not offer van support, but then you won't pay premium prices. Bikecentennial is a large company with greater cycling expertise, and more domestic itineraries than just about anybody. It is a good choice if you want a professionally planned trip at modest cost. Rating: ★★$

■ BACKROADS BICYCLE TOURING
1516 5th Street, Berkeley, CA 94710-1713, (800) 245-3874, or (510) 527-1555 in CA.

Backroads is the IBM of bicycle touring. It has the nicest catalog, the shiniest vans and one of the largest selections of tours. If we were looking for a premium trip offering high-quality accommodations, easy peddling and top-notch van shuttle service, Backroads would be our choice. However, Backroads runs very large groups (20+) on some tours--something we don't particularly like. Prices are steep as well, particularly on some of the shorter domestic inn tours. We still recommend Backroads very highly, but be aware that you're paying a premium price for some destinations. Rating: ★★★; ★★★★ if price did not count.

■ BUTTERFIELD & ROBINSON
70 Bond Street, Toronto, ONT, Canada M5B 1X3, (800) 387-1147 USA, or (800) 268-8415 in Canada.

Butterfield & Robinson (B&R) is a major player in the bike touring industry offering an incredible variety of deluxe tours throughout North America and Europe. B&R has built its reputation on great European trips featuring the very best hotels, superb cuisine and excellent tour guides, however, most of B&R's tours are quite expensive. A typical 9-day tour in France will run over $2,800 per person this year--$300 to $600 more than you would pay B&R's competitors. For those with less financial clout, B&R offers more reasonably priced family and student holidays. (B&R started as a student bike touring company.) Rating: ★★★; ★★★★ if price did not count.

■ CHATEAUX BIKE TOURS
P.O. Box 5706, Denver, CO 80217, (800) 678-BIKE, or (303) 393-6910.

Chateaux Tours specializes in moderate rides through the wine regions of France. Many outfitters offer the same type of trip, but Chateaux features Michelin star restaurants and superb accommodations in beautiful chateaux. The trips aren't cheap, averaging $1,400 to $2,400 for 5 to 9 days including food, but you're really traveling first class, along well-chosen routes with excellent tour leaders. You shouldn't book a deluxe French tour without reviewing what Chateaux has to offer. Rating: ★★★

■ CLASSIC BICYCLE TOURS
P.O. Box 668, Clarkson, NY 14430, (800) 777-8090.

Classic Bicycle Tours is a small, lower profile company that offers fine small-group trips to some less trendy destinations including Greece, Quebec, Prince Edward Island (Canada), Ireland, Great Britain, France (Dordogne Valley) and Tennessee. Prices are good: 7-day trips start at $750, and 2 weeks in Greece is available for under $1,450. This is a good 20 percent less than some of the big companies. With 10 years of experience, Classic is a proven performer, and we wouldn't hesitate to go with them if we liked a particular itinerary. Rating: ★★$

■ PETER COSTELLO LTD.
P.O. Box 23490, Baltimore, MD 21203, (410) 783-1229.

Peter Costello runs the best road bike tours in Scotland, one of the nicest touring destinations in the world. The roads are relatively gentle and the scenery is lovely. Just be prepared for dampness and a chill, even in August. We have to say, however, that you should seriously consider touring Scotland on your own. There is an abundance of charming, modestly priced B&Bs, you can cover longer distances by train, and the Scots are helpful and very hospitable. Rating: ★★★$.

■ EURO-BIKE TOURS
P.O. Box 40, Dekalb, IL 60115, (815) 758-8851.

Euro-Bike Tours is a bit like a bicycle supermarket. Pick just about any place in Europe, and Euro-Bike can take you there. This well-established operator goes to some of the great, out-of-the-way spots that other companies miss. All guides are multilingual, and they really know their way around. With 19 years of experience, Euro-Bike Tours has one of the strongest track

records in Europe, well-chosen itineraries, and reasonable prices (a 2-week tour runs about $2,250). Accommodations are very good, but not super luxurious. The cuisine never disappoints. Rating: ★★★$.

■ EUROPEDS TOURS
883 Sinex Ave., Pacific Grove, CA 93950, (800) 321-9552.

While many commercial bike tours in Europe feature more eating than riding, Europeds offers luxury tours as well as faster-paced, more challenging rides in both France and Switzerland. You can select a relatively flat, easy journey through the Dordogne or Provence (a bargain starting at $999 for 5 days), or more intense rides through the Pyrenees and the Alps. Compared with the competition, Europeds' tours generally cover more

DENNIS COELLO

ground, and spend more time in hilly country where the scenery is best. Prices are reasonable, yet lodging and food are of a high standard. Rating: ★★

■ FORUM TRAVEL INTERNATIONAL
91 Gregory Lane, Suite 21, Pleasant Hill, CA 94523, (510) 671-2900.

Forum Travel International (FTI) books tours for a variety of tour companies worldwide, offering trips to many remote and exotic locations. With hundreds of different tour options, FTI is a good bet if you're looking for something truly unusual. Before you book, make sure a solid foreign outfitter such as New Zealand Pedaltours will be

used. FTI's strong suits are its trips to Latin America, Asia and the South Pacific. Typically, FTI's tours combine modest accommodations with very reasonable pricing. Rating: ★★$.

■ PROGRESSIVE TRAVELS
1932 First Avenue, Suite 1100, Seattle, WA 98101, (800) 245-2229, or (206) 443-4225.

Progressive Travels offers luxury trips for those who want the very best. Progressive has carved out a niche in the premium end of the market with superior European tours featuring great hotels and superb dining. Typical cost is $2,500 for 8 to 9 days. Progressive is now introducing less costly domestic tours to cater to travelers on a budget. Progressive is a good choice if you're really looking for something special, with many interesting diversions included in the basic tour price. Destinations will include France, Italy, Ireland, New Zealand and the Pacific Northwest. Rating: ★★★

■ REI ADVENTURES
P.O. Box 88126, Seattle, WA 98138-0126, (800) 622-2236.

REI Adventures offers a wide variety of road and mountain bike tours to destinations worldwide including Alaska, Canyonlands, Nepal, the USSR and China. REI is a recognized leader in Soviet touring, and its mountain bike tours in Alaska, led by ace guide Steve Casper, are unique and reasonably priced--about $100 per day. Most tours are moderate in difficulty, and the foreign trips feature a strong emphasis on local culture. REI's guides are extremely knowledgeable, and its customer service is outstanding. Rating: ★★★$

■ ROCKY MOUNTAIN CYCLE TOURS
P.O. Box 1978, Canmore, ALB, Canada T0L 0M0, (800) 661-2453, or (403) 678-6770.

With over 13 years of experience, Rocky Mountain Cycle Tours (RMCT) is one of Canada's premier bike touring companies. RMCT specializes in weeklong inn tours in the Canadian Rockies, but also leads tours to six European countries, California, Hawaii and New Zealand. The routes through Canada are superb, support services are top-notch, and the accommodations are luxurious. If you have the money, this is probably your best choice for a Canadian Rockies cycling vacation. Consider Timberline or Bikecentennial if you're willing to rough it a little in order to keep costs down. Rating: ★★★

■ TIMBERLINE BICYCLE TOURS

7975 E. Harvard, Unit J, Denver, CO 80231, (303) 759-3804.

This is a down-to-earth touring company for real riders--those who want to travel the best roads, regardless of elevation, at a brisk pace. If you're a good rider who will enjoy the challenge of 45-55 miles per day climbing mountain passes, Timberline is your company. Timberline also offers some of the most interesting and reasonably priced mountain bike tours around. If you don't need luxury and are looking for a good deal, call Timberline first. Most weeklong trips are priced under $850. Rating: ★★$.

■ VERMONT BICYCLE TOURING

P.O. Box 711, Bristol, VT 05443, (802) 453-4811; FAX: (802) 453-4806.

Vermont Bicycle Touring (VBT) was a pioneer in the bike touring industry, and few companies can match its overall excellence. VBT offers numerous well-planned trips nationwide that have earned high praise from customers. VBT doesn't seem to be spoiled by success, and its prices haven't gotten completely out-of-hand. (Most trips run about $125 per day.) In 1990 VBT merged with Open Roads Bicycle Touring and will continue to offer many of Open Roads' popular foreign trips, including Ireland and Nova Scotia. VBT is a very solid outfit that does everything a good touring company should. VBT would be our first choice for many destinations. Rating: ★★★★

■ VERMONT COUNTRY CYCLERS (VCC)/ FOUR SEASONS CYCLING/TRAVENT INT'L

P.O. Box 145, Waterbury Center, VT 05677, (802) 244-5215; FAX: (802) 244-6126.

Vermont Country Cyclers (VCC) and Four Seasons Cycling, two of America's leading tour companies, merged in 1990. Each continues to offer its own hallmark tours, but all bookings are handled by VCC's Waterbury Center office. VCC offers the same kinds of tours as Vermont Bicycle Touring with a similar level of quality and price. Five-day New England tours typically cost about $700 with outstanding accommodations in country inns and B&Bs.

VCC's foreign trips are run by its sister company, Travent International. Travent's luxury tours in France, Italy, Denmark, Ireland and Great Britain are mostly slow-paced, catering to an older crowd with plenty of money. Lodging is first class all the way, and the tours are very well run. Travent's British and Italian trips are among the best. Rating: ★★★★ (Domestic); ★★★ (Foreign)

MOUNTAIN BIKING

Autumn colors in Utah/CHRIS NOBLE

12 TOP MOUNTAIN BIKE SPOTS

CALIFORNIA

■

Mt. Tamalpais, Marin County

Getting there: Follow signs from Mill Valley, CA.

Terrain: Steep grade with rolling hills at top and great views, lower sections of single track through redwoods.

Best routes: Bear Valley Trail; Coast Trail to Stinson Beach or Muir Beach; Olema to Pt. Reyes National Seashore.

Contact: *Trail Head Rentals in Olema, CA, (415) 663-1958.* Resource: **The Marin Mountain Bike Guide** by Armor Todd.

COLORADO

■

Crested Butte Area

Getting there: Start trail at Aspen, CO.

Terrain: Steep ascents and descents, forested and rocky, high-altitude passes, great vistas.

Best routes: Taylor Canyon, Ohio Pass (Gunnison Nat'l Forest), descend to Marble along Crystal River.

Contact: *Timberline Tours, (303)759-3804.*

HAWAII

■

The Big Island

Getting there: Start from Kilauea Crater Park.

Terrain: Steep hills, ridge trails, solidified lava flows, soft dirt trails in valleys.

Best Routes: Kilauea Crater Rim Drive, Chain of Craters Road, Waipio Valley Trail, Kumukahi Lighthouse Trail.

Contact: *Bicycle Adventures, (206) 786-0989; Red Sail Sports, (808) 885-2876.*

MINNESOTA

■

Maplewood State Park

Getting there: 50 miles southeast of Moorehead, MN.

Terrain: All kinds--grasslands, forests, rolling hills, deep valleys. Many lakes and streams. Abundant wildlife.

Best Routes: 25-mile loop trail.

Contact: *Maplewood State Park, Box 422, Pelican Rapids, MN 56572, (218) 863-8383.*

NORTH CAROLINA

■

Pisgah and Nantahala National Forests

Getting there: Head to mountains from Asheville, NC.

Terrain: Unlimited single-tracking through dense forest. All types of trails--rolling or steep and challenging.

Best Routes: Tsali Trail to Fontana Lake--switchbacks, rolling climbs, banked turns; Little Tennessee River Trail.

Contact: *Blue Ridge Bicycle Club, Box 309, Asheville, NC 28802.*

TENNESSEE

■

Great Smoky Mountains National Park

Getting there: Access park from roads on TN/NC border.

Terrain: Jeep trails, forestry roads, rolling hills and steep switchbacks. Wilderness permits required in some areas.

Best Routes: Ridge trails from Calderwood, TN and Crestmont, NC.

Contact: *Cherokee Nat'l Forest Office, 2321 Ocoee Street, Cleveland, TN 37311.*

TEXAS

■

Big Bend National Park

Getting there: Enter Park from Lajitas, TX, in the Rio Grande Valley.

Terrain: Desert jeep trails, moderate climbs and descents.

Best Routes: Rio Grande River Road; Old Oar Road; Chisos Mountains and hot springs near Rio Grande Village.

Contact: *National Park Service, Big Bend Nat'l Park, TX 79834, (915) 477-2251.*

VERMONT

■

Northeast Kingdom Area

Getting there: Start from Craftsbury Common, VT.

Terrain: Rolling hills through wooded forests, mostly dirt roads.

Best Routes: Over 240 miles of trails centered in Craftsbury.

Contact: *Craftsbury Sports Center, Box 31, Craftsbury Common, VT 05827, (802) 586-7767 (guided trips available).*

VIRGINIA
■
New River Trail State Park

Getting there: Access Park from Austinville, VA.

Terrain: Abandoned railroad bed--steady, mild grade, smooth. Blue Ridge mountain and river scenery. Fall foliage.

Best Routes: Combine cycling with canoeing from Galax, VA.

Contact: *New River State Park, Route 1, Austinville, VA 24312, (703) 699-6778.*

WISCONSIN
■
The Birkie Trail

Getting there: Start at Hayward, WI.

Terrain: Thick hardwood forest with lots of climbs and descents, through glaciated terrain. Tough and beautiful.

Best Routes: Point 00 to Telemark; 50 km overall.

Contact: *Chequamegon Fat Tire Festival, (715) 798-3811.*

UTAH
■
Canyonlands National Park

Getting there: Drive from Moab, Utah to trailheads.

Terrain: Mostly flat, but uphills are steep; sand, gravel and rock trail surfaces. Jeep trails and some single-track.

Best Routes: Arches Nat'l Park loop, Kane Creek Canyon, White Rim Trail (Canyonlands), Slickrock Trail. Head upcountry to the La Sal Mountains. Warner Lake is a good starting point, and Batchelor Basin has scenic trails.

Contact: *Supt., Arches Nat'l Park, (801) 259-7164; US Forest Service, Moab, (801) 259-7155; Rim Tours, (800) 626-7335.*

WYOMING
■
Red Desert

Getting there: Off Highway 28, northeast of Rock Springs, WY, or southeast of Lander (45 minutes' drive).

Terrain: Mostly hard-packed jeep trails, game tracks and graded gravel roads. Very scenic.

Best Routes: Old Freight Road, Honeycomb Buttes, ghost town loop.

Contact: *Jeff Davis, Desert Cycles, 211 Red Canyon, Lander, WY 82520; Great Divide Tours, 336 Focht Road, Lander, WY 82520, (800) 458-1915.*

OFF-ROAD OUTFITTERS

CHRIS NOBLE

*T*HERE ARE A NUMBER OF TOUR OPERATORS WHO SPECIALIZE IN BACKCOUNTRY BIKING holidays. Some, such as Off the Deep End Travels, feature point-to-point trips in exotic locales. Others, such as the Otter Bar Lodge, offer day-trips from a fully equipped lodge. KMB Tours even offers heli-biking in the Rockies.

■ **ABOVE THE CLOUDS TREKKING**
P.O. Box 398, Worcester, MA 01602, (800) 233-4499, or (508) 799-4499 in MA.
Destinations: Nepal, Pakistan, Tibet.

■ **BACKCOUNTRY BICYCLE TOURS**
P.O. Box 4029, Bozeman, MT 59772, (406) 586-3556.
Destinations: Montana Rockies, Yellowstone, Bryce Canyon/Zion Nat'l Parks.
Programs: Guided deluxe MB tours, 3-7 days.

■ **BICYCLE AFRICA**
4887 Columbia Drive South, Seattle, WA 98108, (206) 767-3927.
Destinations: All Africa south of the Sahara.
Programs: 2 to 4-week tours with emphasis on local culture, wildlife and scenic areas.

■ **BAJA EXPEDITIONS**
2625 Garnet Avenue, San Diego, CA 92109, (800) 843-6967.
Destinations: Northern Baja, and La Paz area, Mexico.
Programs: 1 to 2-week overland trips. Baja trips feature swimming, snorkeling, etc.

■ **BOREALIS BACKCOUNTRY CYCLING**
2900 Boniface Parkway, #656, Anchorage, AK 99504, (907) 562-4493.
Destinations: Kenai Peninsula, Matanuska Valley, Denali Nat'l Park area.
Programs: Wilderness MB Tours 3-5 days. Spectacular scenery.

■ **ELK RIVER TOURING CENTER**
Highway 219, Slatyfork, WV 26291, (304) 572-3771.
Destinations: West Virginia backcountry.
Programs: Weekend to 6-day, inn to inn MB tours $210-$475; combo raft/bike adventure.

■ **KOOTENAY MOUNTAIN BIKE TOURS**
P.O. Box 867, Nelson, BC, Canada V1L 6A5, (604) 354-4371.
Destinations: Alberta and British Columbia, Canada, Baja.
Programs: Wilderness MB Tours, including heli-biking.

■ **THE MOUNTAIN BIKE SCHOOL**
800 Mountain Road, Mount Snow, VT 05356, (800) 451-4211, or (802) 464-3333, ext. 328.
Destinations: Vermont and New Hampshire.
Programs: Weekend tours and race training.

■ **OFF THE DEEP END TRAVELS**
P.O. Box 7511, Jackson, WY 83001, (800) 223-6833, or (307) 733-8707 in Wyoming.
Destinations: Australia, Papua New Guinea, Thailand, French Polynesia, Nepal, Wyoming (Wind River, Tetons, Snowy Range).
Programs: Fully outfitted adventure tours.

■ **OTTER BAR LODGE**
P.O. Box 210, Forks of Salmon, CA 96031, (916) 462-4772.
Destinations: Trinity Wilderness.
Programs: America's premier MB destination resort. Great food, lodging, trails and kayaking.

■ **PARAGON GUIDES**
P.O. Box 130, Vail, CO 81658, (303) 949-4272.
Destinations: Colorado Rockies.
Programs: Hut to hut MB tours through wilderness backcountry.

■ **RIM TOURS**
94 West First North, Moab, UT 84532, (800) 626-7335, or (801) 259-5333 for bike rentals.
Destinations: Canyon Country, Utah.
Programs: Bike rentals and 2-6 day tours.

BICYCLE TOURING

SELF-GUIDED TOURS

If some of the prices for deluxe guided tours put you off, take heart. It is easier to put together your own van-supported tour than you may think, and it doesn't have to be an ordeal. If we were contemplating a 3-week North American tour, we would arrange the whole thing ourselves. Using the following guidelines, you can plan a trouble-free bicycle tour that can easily save you $50-$75 per day.

1. Select the general destination you wish to tour. Then, pick up a regional biking tour guidebook and map out an itinerary. Tour company catalogs can be very useful for route planning as well.

2. Once you've settled on a route, order a specialized bicycle tour map from Bikecentennial. Customized for each route, these handy references include elevation charts and suggested daily itineraries.

3. Assemble the equipment you'll need: roof rack, tire-changing kit, heavy-duty bicycle pump, first-aid kit, cooking kit, stove, and sleeping bags, pads and tents if you will be camping. Get a youth hostel card. (Contrary to popular belief, youth hostels are open to persons of all ages.)

4. If you plan to camp out in popular areas such as national parks, make advance reservations with the park offices to ensure you'll have a spot.

5. If you'll be traveling by air, comparison shop for the best price, and book your tickets well ahead of time to get the best value. Call your air carrier to find out packing requirements and shipping charges for the bikes. For help in air ticketing and ground connections, Bikecentennial offers a travel service for members. Call (800) 735-7109.

6. A week before you depart, call the inns and hostels you plan to visit to confirm your reservations. Buy those little extras you'll need on the trip--spare inner tubes, spoke wrench, handlebar padding, extra water bottles, good bicycle shoes. Do a 50-mile test ride with your group to make sure everything is in order.

DENNIS COELLO

DOLLARS AND SENSE

We've figured what two couples would pay for a 14-day, vehicle-supported tour assuming the group will camp one day in three, stay at a hostel one day in three, and book a hotel on the third day. Even including the cost of a roof rack and airline shipping fees (some airlines will take the bikes for free), a 2-week tour for four persons costs only $2,562, complete. That works out to $640 per person, or $46 per day. Compare this to commercial tours which average $1,750-$2,200 per person for 2 weeks.

Sag-wagon rental and gas ($40/day incl. mileage):	$560
Hostel & Camping, 9 nights ($7/day per person):	$252
Deluxe Inn, 4 nights ($35/night per person):	$560
Food ($15/day per person):	$840
Airline Baggage Fees ($25/bike each way):	$200
Roof Racks, Spare Wheel:	$150
Total Cost for 4 riders for 14 days:	$2,562
Cost per person for 14 days:	$640

In Europe you can expect to save even more, as clean rooms in modest inns can be obtained for under $20 per night in Spain, Portugal, Italy, Ireland and Scotland.

BOOKS

The Best Bike Rides in New England, by Paul Thomas. The title says it all. $9.95 from Bikecentennial.

Bicycling the Pacific Coast, by Tom Kirkendall and Vicky Spring. This 224-page guide covers 2,000 miles from British Columbia to the Mexican border. Good maps and hill profiles. This is the bible of West Coast touring. $10.95.

The Canadian Rockies Bicycling Guide, by Gail Helgasson and John Dodd, is the book we would take along on a Canadian road trip. Sixty different tours are covered in detail, with fine maps and a handy list of hostels. $10.95.

Cycle Touring in New Zealand, by Bruce Ringer. This 320-page guide, with detailed maps and tour descriptions, is by far the best resource for both North and South Islands. $14.95 from the Mountaineers, (800) 553-HIKE.

Europe by Bike, by Ken and Terry Whitehall, features 18 great European bike tours from 100 to 800 miles in length. $10.95 from Alpenbooks, (206) 568-4181.

Miles From Nowhere--A Round the World Bicycle Adventure. Barbara Savage and her husband biked 23,000 miles in 25 countries over two years, and this is her journal of the adventure. You'll find it fascinating and inspirational.

Touring the Islands, by Peter Powers, is a must for any Pacific Northwest cycle tourist. This little gem fits in your pocket and has wonderful 3D maps that show you where the hills are.

VIDEOS

Bicycle Repair Video. Are you all thumbs when it comes to adjusting a derailleur, or truing a wheel? This video is the most painless way to learn basic maintenance that will keep you rolling. You'll be guided by Tom Cuthbertson, author of the zillion-selling classic, **Anybody's Bike Book.** $19.95 from Bikecentennial.

ALL THE FACTS

Bikecentennial has compiled a resource guide covering weather, road conditions, prices, food, lodging and recommended routes for hundreds of destinations in the US and abroad. This is an invaluable source of detailed, first-hand information from those who have been there. Call (406) 721-1776.

Canoes & Kayaks

KEVIN O'BRIEN

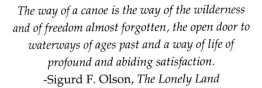

The way of a canoe is the way of the wilderness and of freedom almost forgotten, the open door to waterways of ages past and a way of life of profound and abiding satisfaction.
-Sigurd F. Olson, *The Lonely Land*

▼

*R*ivers are pathways to adventure. Whether exploring a remote waterway by canoe, or navigating a kayak through raging rapids, river-running offers both escape and challenge. Shallow in draft and light in weight, canoes and kayaks can pass over the smallest tributaries, and be portaged between lakes and around difficult rapids. This allows a canoeist or kayaker to venture into unspoiled territories, where refuge from the modern world can be found.

This chapter covers the full spectrum of inland paddling, from smoothwater canoe-tripping to Class V whitewater kayaking. We feature nine ultimate paddling vacations worldwide, and for those looking for fun close to home, we review 30 of North America's best rivers for self-guided excursions. For thrill-seekers, we describe some *very* serious whitewater trips and review the top paddling schools in North America--the best places to learn Eskimo rolls and other advanced whitewater techniques from the experts.

CHAPTER
6

DIDIER GIVOIS

F ROM A PEACEFUL CANOE TREK THROUGH THE CANADIAN INTERIOR, TO A
thrilling kayak descent of jungle whitewater, just about any
thing is possible for a paddler looking for adventure. And though expeditions to remote foreign rivers can be costly, you'll find that most
guided paddling trips are relatively inexpensive. Even fully outfitted trips
typically cost less than $100 per day, including food, rental and guide.

GRAND CANYON

Small Boats, Big Water

Traditionally, the Colorado has been a big-raft destination only. However, thanks to changes in the National Park Service river regulations, it is now possible for advanced paddlers to run this greatest of American rivers on a raft-supported kayak trip.

Though most of the river is fairly smooth and quiet, in spots the Colorado features the most outrageous hydraulics and standing waves that you'll find anywhere in North America. These can be negotiated with relative ease in a large raft, but in something as small as a kayak, you have to be awfully good to make it through in one piece. For this reason, any kayak expedition should be accompanied by a support raft which can carry the kayaks and their crews through the most hazardous sections.

Although the Park Service does allow properly qualified private kayak groups to run the Colorado, access to the river has been tightly controlled, and the waiting period for kayak permits is now well over two years. Thus, for practical purposes, the only way to run the river anytime soon is with a regularly scheduled commercial trip. Most kayakers and whitewater canoeists who run the Colorado now do so in conjunction with a commercial rafting trip.

At present, Dvorak's Expeditions, Nantahala Outdoor Center, and Otter Bar Kayaks conduct raft-supported kayak trips down the Colorado, designed for advanced paddlers. Dvorak runs 225 miles of the Grand Canyon, on 5, 8 and 12-day adventures. Bill Dvorak cautions that even though his guides will direct kayakers to the safest sections, the Colorado is a powerful river, and kayakers must have a strong roll and very competent boat-handling skills. Trips run from May through October and cost about $170 per day including food and raft support, but not kayak rental. Contact Dvorak's Expeditions, 17921-AT, US Highway 285, Nathrop, CO 81236, (800) 824-3795, or (719) 539-6851.

Nantahala will take you down the whole length of the Colorado in 12 days, providing raft support for advanced kayakers and expert decked canoeists. Nantahala offers two 13-day trips in September, each costing $1,725, including all equipment and food. Contact Nantahala Outdoor Center, 41 US

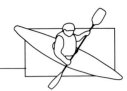

Nine Great Paddling Adventures

19W, Bryson City, NC 28713, (800) 232-7238. Otter Bar runs a 13-day full river trip for experienced kayakers with a strong roll. This raft-supported trip costs $1,250 including food, but not kayak rental. Contact Otter Bar, P.O. Box 210, Forks of Salmon, CA 96031, (916) 462-4772.

TEXAS

Rio Grande Canoe Running

Forming the border between the US and Mexico, the Rio Grande passes through classic canyon country as it flows southeast through Big Bend National Park. While the Class IV upper stretch of the Rio Grande near the New Mexico border (the Taos Box area) demands advanced skills, most of the Rio Grande is a relatively gentle float ideal for first-time canoe-trippers. Overall, a journey down the Rio Grande through Big Bend and the lower canyons is one of the best novice canoe adventures in America.

On a weeklong Rio Grande trip, you will spend most of your time within the confines of Big Bend Park. The scenery here is rug-

ged and colorful. And though there is a fair amount of tourist activity in Big Bend Park, particularly in Mariscall and Boquillas Canyons, the lower canyons are little-traveled. As a rule, you will have few encounters on the river with other boaters, except in the busiest of holiday periods.

The best time of year to canoe the Rio Grande is May and June; paddlers should avoid the low water period in February. The water is a comfortable 65-70 degrees, and air temperatures are 70-90 during the day. Almost all of the river is suitable for novice paddlers. After a couple days of practice on the quieter sections, even first-timers should be able to handle all the rapids you'll find from Big Bend southward. And most commercial trips offer raft support, so you can elect to skirt any sections that are too tough.

A number of fine outfitters offer raft-supported canoe trips on the Rio Grande. Dvorak's Expeditions runs 90 miles of the Rio Grande's lower canyons in March, May, June and October. The pace is slow, allowing paddlers time to perfect boating skills and to enjoy the many hot springs. Along the way,

paddlers have the option of switching between rafts, canoes and kayaks. The 7-day trips will cost roughly $815. Contact Dvorak's Expeditions at (800) 824-3795, or (719) 539-6851 (address above). Nantahala

ALAN FORTUNE

83

Outdoor Center, (800) 232-7238, (address on pp. 82-83), also offers 9-day raft-supported trips in October and November for $760.

For those on a budget, the Rio Grande is a fine self-guided trip, if you have some previous canoe-camping experience. Contact the National Park Service, Big Bend Nat'l Park, Alpine, TX 79834, (915) 477-2251, for a list of Big Bend concessionaires who rent canoes and can help you plan an itinerary.

WEST VIRGINIA

Class V Expert Odyssey

The Allegheny mountains of West Virginia contain the greatest single concentration of Class IV-V runs in North America. World-class rivers such as the Cheat, the Gauley, the Tygart, and the Upper Youghiogheny offer continuous whitewater with more thrills per mile than you'll find just about anywhere. For example, the upper section of the Gauley is a solid Class V, with huge waves and very high water volume. The Tygart boasts Glens Falls, the most powerful, runnable rapid in the Appalachians. The very technical Upper Yough, once thought unrunnable, is the steepest waterway east of the Rockies. The Cheat features tight passages over steep drops, with many rapids upgraded to Class V after changes wrought by floods in 1985.

As a whole, the West Virginia river system is noted for very fast water flow, steep drops, and narrow, technical passages. Unlike many western rivers which feature long, smooth passages followed by pockets of rapids, the rivers of West Virginia are marked by back-to-back rapids--continuous thundering whitewater. The runs are relatively short, but yield a high-adrenaline excitement hard to duplicate anywhere else.

Total novices can sample West Virginia's wildest rivers on a raft excursion with any

WILEY/WALES, PROFILES WEST

SCOTT SPIKER

number of competent outfitters. (Contact USA Whitewater, (800) USA-RAFT, and consult Chapter 16 for other recommended outfitters.) To do these runs in a kayak or decked canoe, however, you had better have solid Class IV paddling skills. And even if you're an expert, we'd recommend going with a knowledgeable local river guide. Nantahala Outdoor Center has organized a unique West Virginia River Week program which will take expert paddlers to five of the best runs in the state. The program runs in May for expert-level canoeists and in October for advanced kayakers. The cost is $630 for 5 days including meals, local transportation, boat and river gear. Contact Nantahala Outdoor Center, (address above), (800) 232-7238.

If you're new to the sport, Class VI River Runners conducts 2 to 6-day clinics for novice/intermediate kayakers on the New, Gauley and Greenbrier Rivers. The classes cover all the essentials: paddle strokes, eskimo rolls, wet exits, and eddy turns. Clinics run May though October and start at $95 per day, including food and transport. Contact Class VI, Box 78, Ames Heights Rd., Lansing, WV 25862, (800) 252-7784.

CANADA

NWT Nahanni Nirvana

The Nahanni is a dream river, one of the most scenic waterways on the planet. Situated in a remote corner of the Northwest Territories, it flows through a wild landscape of legendary scale and beauty. The Nahanni has been called Canada's Grand Canyon, but that is a bit deceptive. The

terrain is more like Yosemite Valley, with forested hills and massive granite rock faces. There is also far less activity on the Nahanni than on the Colorado, and never any competition for a campsite.

It takes three weeks to navigate the full length of the Nahanni, which flows southeast from the Continental Divide, cutting its way through the 150-mile long Nahanni National Park. Even within the park's boundaries, the Nahanni is truly wild. You are always very far from civilization, at least 100 miles from the nearest real town. The upper half of the river, outside the park, is the whitewater section, best suited for experienced paddlers. Starting at Moose Ponds, the Nahanni's source, the river runs approximately 100 miles to the park boundary. Over this stretch, paddlers pass through the Rock Gardens, a long section of continuous Class II and III whitewater.

As it nears the northern end of the National Park, the Nahanni flattens out, and the voyage becomes a peaceful float through impressive granite canyons, home to moose, elk, and many large bird species. The section of the Nahanni within the park offers riverside hot springs and good fishing, although the scenery is certainly the main attraction, particularly Virginia Falls. At twice the height of Niagara, Virginia Falls is the most spectacular cascade in North America.

One of the best outfitters for the Nahanni is Black Feather Wilderness Adventures, 1341 Wellington West, Ottawa, ONT, Canada K1Y 3B8, (613) 722-9717. Black Feather's trips can also be booked through Vancouver's Ecosummer Expeditions, (604) 669-7741. Price for a full 3-week Nahanni adventure is $3,500 CDN. A shorter 2-week voyage through the parklands only is $2,750 CDN. Another recommended Canadian outfitter is Nahanni River Adventures, Ltd., Neil Hartling, P.O. Box 8368, Station F, Edmonton, ALB, Canada T6H 4W6, (403) 439-1316.

NEPAL

Duckies on the Sun Khosi

Nepal is more than mountains and monasteries. Both in spring, when the Himalayan snowpack begins to melt, and in fall after the rainy season, Nepal's rivers run high and fast, creating enjoyable whitewater conditions. Most of the river-running in Nepal is done in rafts, most commonly on the Trisuli River, but for those who want to pilot their own craft there are alternatives. Hardcore kayakers have been known to ship their craft from the States, but this is a logistical nightmare. A far easier way to go is to join Off the Deep End Travels (ODET) on a duckie (inflatable kayak) trip down the Sun Khosi, Nepal's River of Gold.

Though lightweight and comfortable, duckies are not just children's toys. Even first-timers will find these buoyant and forgiving craft ideal for navigating the alternating stretches of flatwater and Class II rapids on the Sun Khosi. (Novices will be carried through the Class III-IV sections on the upper Sun Khosi in support rafts.)

A voyage down the Sun Khosi showcases Nepal's diverse landscape. From its headwaters at the base of the Himalayas, the river runs through turbulent, rock-filled canyons and then winds its way into the verdant subtropical valleys of the Terai plains, Nepal's breadbasket. Navigating through sheer-walled gorges, you will pass under rope suspension bridges strung high above the river. It is not unusual for villagers to climb out on these bridges en masse, waving to the paddlers below.

Sun Khosi duckie trips are offered February through May, and October through November by ODET in conjunction with Regal Duckie River Journeys. ODET's 13-day river journeys run at a gentle pace, allowing plenty of time to explore riverside villages, or hike the surrounding countryside. Price will be $1,735 without airfare. Contact Off the Deep End Travels, P.O. Box 7511, Jackson, WY 83001, (800) 223-6833, or (307) 733-8707 in WY.

OREGON

Rogue River Kayak Clinics

There may be no better place west of the Rockies to learn whitewater kayaking skills than Oregon's Rogue River. The Rogue offers great variety, from stillwater pools to Class IV rapids which can challenge even experts. Just as importantly, the Rogue is the home of Sundance Expeditions, one of America's finest river training centers. While Sundance offers something for everyone, its 9-day basic seminar is by far its most popular program. Paddlers in training stay at a comfortable backcountry lodge, enjoying home-cooked meals served by a friendly staff. To be truthful, the riverfront location and relaxing ambience of the lodge has been as important to Sundance's success as the quality of the kayaking.

GARY BRETTNACHER

85

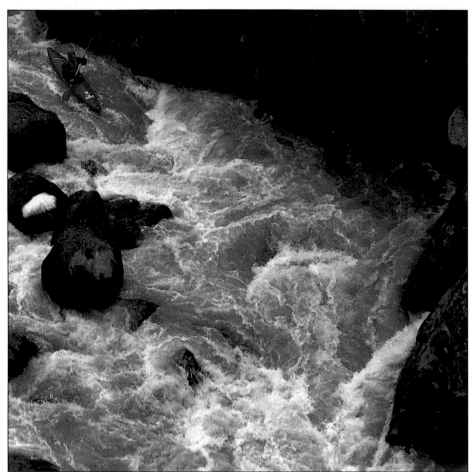

STEVE GILROY

The first 5 days of the program are devoted to acquiring the basic skills required to pilot a kayak safely through Class III rapids. You'll practice basic strokes, perfect the infamous eskimo roll, and learn how to maneuver through eddies and currents. The staff at Sundance is patient, and each kayaker receives individualized attention.

After completing the skills training, the training group will make a 4-day, 40-mile run down the Rogue River Gorge. The students will perfect their whitewater technique in Class II-III rapids under the watchful eyes of instructors. All food and personal gear is carried in support rafts. Water levels have varied considerably in recent years, but ordinarily there is good volume all summer. The lower water at summer's end can actually be better for novices, although spring high-water offers the most excitement. Sundance's 9-day intro program will cost about $1,250, including meals, lodging and all gear. Sundance offers a wide variety of other programs for more advanced kayakers. Contact Sundance at 14894 Galice Road, Merlin, OR 97532, (503) 479-8508.

MINNESOTA

Boundary Waters Wilderness Voyage

The Boundary Waters Canoe Area (BWCA) along the Minnesota-Canada border can rightly be called the mecca of North American canoeing. The BWCA and Ontario's adjoining Quetico Provincial Park comprise a combined 2.2 million acres of wilderness ideal for canoe exploration. More than 5,000 lakes and 3,000 islands dot the BWCA's interior, affording limitless possibilities for paddling adventures.

If you're seeking the greatest solitude and the prettiest scenery, head for the Canadian side. Popular Quetico destinations include Lake Kahshahpiwi, Sarah Lake and Agnes Lake. Great fishing is to be found at Basswood Lake, which straddles the border. On the American side, if you've got 10 days or so you can do a great loop trip starting at Lake One and returning by way of Snowbank Lake or Moose Lake.

Commencing a Boundary Country trip is not as simple as driving up to a waterway and setting off; the BWCA is a strictly controlled wilderness, and no motorized transport is allowed within its perimeters. Hence, most of the better destinations require a portage for a day or more before you can plunk your canoe in the water. For those with limited time, we recommend a fly-in trip. This will save you many hours of toil, and permit you to visit remote hideaways where you're almost assured of having an entire lake to yourself. A weeklong fly-in trip will cost about $600 per person. The Quetico side has the most pristine fly-in destinations, including Three-Mile Lake, Wolseley Lake and Lake La Croix.

Because of the BWCA's popularity, you must reserve a spot early to be assured of a wilderness permit. Last year all the summer permits for Quetico were spoken for by the end of February. However, the leading outfitters usually manage to get permits well into the spring, at least for the American side. Wise travelers should still start their planning early, however.

There are more than a dozen canoe outfitters operating in the BWCA. Canadian Waters Inc., 111 East Sheridan, Ely, MN 55731, (800) 255-2922, is one of our favorites. Owners Dan and Jon Waters are friendly and knowledgeable, and they can outfit any kind of trip from basic to a deluxe fly-in, on both sides of the border. Other recommended outfitters include Tom & Woods' Moose Lake Wilderness Trips, P.O. Box 358, Ely, MN 55731, (312) 777-3400; Gunflint Northwoods Outfitters, (Bruce Kerfoot), HC64-Box 750, Grand Marais, MN 55604, (800) 328-3325; and Sawbill Canoe Outfitters, Box 2127, Tofte, MN 55615, (218) 387-1360. With all these companies, canoe rental runs $15-$35 per day, while an outfitted trip (without guide) is about $60-$75 per day. Air charters run about $100-$150 person.

MEXICO

Jungle Whitewater Adventure

In the jungles of southern Mexico, ancient home of the Mayas, lie two of the world's most exotic and beautiful rivers, the Jatate and the Usumacinta (Usu). The turquoise waters of the Jatate drop along miles of staircase rapids quite unlike anything else in the world. The Usu snakes through a lush, original-growth jungle, home to Mayan ruins and teeming wildlife.

Unless you want to cart your own kayak down to Mexico, the best way to explore these unique waterways is on a guided trip. Each spring, Utah's Slickrock Adventures leads 15-day Jatate trips and

10-day Usumacinta tours (January through March for the Jatate and January through April for the Usu). The Jatate, located in the Chiapas region, "Land of the Turquoise Waters," is the most spectacular of the two rivers. Dissolved limestone in suspension colors the water a striking aquamarine--a condition normally associated with glacier melt. But unlike the turquoise pools beneath glaciers, the waters of the Jatate are invitingly warm--in the high 70s.

Along with its incredible waters, the Jatate is renowned for its travertine rock formations--a series of steep limestone drop-offs which create a virtual staircase of rapids. Nearby Agua Azul National Park, which Slickrock visits during the tour, boasts the most extensive travertine formations on the planet--a dozen or more major falls in a span of a half-mile. Advanced kayakers can run many of these falls, a feat that ranks as one of the ultimate experiences in the world of sport kayaking.

One of Mexico's biggest rivers, the Usumacinta, flows through the world's second largest rainforest, passing remote Indian villages and three ancient Mayan cities. While the river offers some Class II-III rapids, the Usu is mostly slow and easy. However, with its archaeological highlights, and many waterfalls, springs, caves and sandy beaches, the Usu still makes for a world-class river trip.

Slickrock charges $925 for 10 days on the Usumacinta and $1,195 for 15 days on the Jatate, or $995 for 9 days without Agua Azul. Intermediate (strong Class III) kayak skills are required for the Jatate, while the Usu is suitable for beginners; paddle raft options are available for both rivers. Contact Slickrock Adventures, P.O. Box 1400, Moab, UT 84532, (801) 259-6996. If Slickrock's Usu trip is booked, Nantahala Outdoor Center, (800) 232-7238, offers a similar 12-day trip in January and February.

NEW ZEALAND

Seven River Sampler

A land of powerful rivers fed by abundant rainfall and snowmelt, New Zealand is a whitewater paradise. And since seasons are reversed in the Southern Hemisphere, New Zealand makes a great winter getaway. On both the North and South Islands, world-class rivers run fast and strong, flowing reliably most of the year. Their waters drop quickly through steep gorges and canyons, offering continuous Class III-V rapids.

Since most of New Zealand's best whitewater runs are short, daylong affairs, you should sample a number of rivers during a holiday Down Under. American outfitter Dvorak Expeditions has put together a great 17–day river tour that takes experienced kayakers down seven of New Zealand's best rivers on both islands. After flying in to Auckland, New Zealand's capital, the paddlers will run the North Island's three top rivers in succession: the Motu, the Rangitaiki and the Mohaka. Then the group will cross by ferry to the South Island. From a base in Queenstown in the Southern Alps, Dvorak's kayakers will sample four of the wildest rivers in Australasia: the Kawarau, the Landsborough, the Rangitata, and of course, the legendary Shotover.

The fabled Shotover is without a doubt one of the most exciting day runs in the Southern Hemisphere. Plunging through steep-walled Skipper's Canyon, the Shotover explodes with back-to-back Class IV-V rapids. At the end of the run, paddlers encounter the infamous Oxenbridge tunnel, which cuts right through the canyon wall. When water levels are right, paddlers can run the tunnel--a hair-raising experience unique in the world of paddling.

This seven-river odyssey is not for neophytes. A very strong river roll and technical whitewater experience is essential. If you're not sure of your skills, Dvorak offers a rafting option. Dvorak runs New Zealand trips in December and January. Price for the 17–day trip will be roughly $2,000, but this can change with exchange rates. Round-trip airfare is $900-$1,100. While the price includes ground transport, kayaks, meals and lodging, kayakers should bring all their own personal gear--helmets, life vests, spray skirts and wetsuits.

If 17 full days of river-running sounds like overkill, you can arrange daily kayak rentals and guiding with local Kiwi river outfitters. On the North Island, we recommend River Rats Rafting Co., 205 Hobson St., Auckland, NZ, FAX: (011 64) 9 307-1073. For the South Island, contact Kawarau Raft Expeditions, P.O. Box 266, Queenstown, NZ, (011 64) 3 442-9792; FAX: 3 442-7867. Brochures can be obtained from the New Zealand Tourism Office, (800) 388-5494.

DIDIER GIVOIS

JOHN KELLY

THIRTY GREAT WATERWAYS

Here are some of North America's very best rivers for self-guided canoe or kayak trips. Many are officially designated Wild and Scenic Rivers--the nation's most treasured waterways. Featuring predominantly flat water or gentle rapids, most of these rivers can be run confidently without a guide, if you do your homework ahead of time. Before you set off, you should talk to local river guides, obtain maps from official agencies, pre-plan your portages, and scout the most difficult stretches.

NORTHEAST
▼

Allagash River, Maine

A north-flowing river with few rapids, the Allagash is one of the best long-distance canoe rivers in the East. In a week, you can do a great 90-mile trip from Telos Lake to Allagash Falls.

St. Croix River, Maine

The St. Croix is a New England classic, a waterway with a long heritage of recreational canoeing. A good starter river for building your skills, the St. Croix offers continuous Class I and II whitewater--fun, but never overwhelming.

St. John River, Maine

The St. John offers long stretches of Class I-II waters, with many fine camping areas along the way. You will find the St. John less crowded than most New England rivers in the summertime.

Connecticut River, New Hampshire

The upper (New Hampshire border) section of this classic New England canoe river is best, with alternating gentle rapids and fast water. A good starting point is just below Canaan, VT.

Hudson River, New York

More scenic than you might expect, the Hudson is often overlooked as a recreational river, though it is one of the best rivers in the Northeast for the average paddler. It is mostly Class I-II, but it gets rougher north of Glens Falls. Spring offers the best water conditions.

SOUTHEAST
▼

Green River, Kentucky

You can select a variety of easy trips along the Green River, which flows for 370 miles through Kentucky's heartland. The flatwater sections within Mammoth Cave National Park are a good choice.

Chattooga, North & South Carolina

The Chattooga, the river in the movie *Deliverance*, is easily one of America's finest waterways--very wild and very beautiful. The lower stretches are for experts only, but Section Two near the Georgia border is an easy Class II run at most water levels. Section Three can be run by intermediates, except at high water.

New River, NC, VA, WV

As it runs through North Carolina and Virginia, the New is mild enough for beginners. Things get interesting in West Virginia, below Bluestone Lake, with increasing whitewater. Below Thurmond, West Virginia, lie the East's biggest rapids, suitable for experts only.

Obed-Emory, Tennessee

The Obed-Emory river system, Tennessee's only Wild and Scenic River, is one of America's prettiest waterways. The upper stretches are for experts only, but novices can handle the Clear Creek tributary--27 miles of Class II water through unspoiled wilderness.

Shenandoah, Virginia

The South Fork of the Shenandoah cuts through a scenic valley between the Blue Ridge and Lesser Masanuttens mountains. The 100 miles of smooth but fast water between Port Republic and Front Royal make for a great 5-day trip.

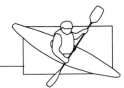

CENTRAL

▼

Buffalo, Arkansas

The Buffalo offers fine Class I-II river-running along the 150 miles between Boxley and Buffalo, with many caves and pools to explore. In the early season the upper 30 miles can be hazardous during peak flood, while in late summer water levels can be very low over the same stretch.

Current River, Missouri

The 100 miles of the Current River within the Ozark National Scenic Riverways Park make for a great 5 to 6-day trip that can be done year-round. Campsites are numerous, the water is relatively flat but fast flowing, and the river takes you through pretty stretches with hardwood groves atop limestone bluffs.

GREAT LAKES

▼

Au Sable River, Michigan

Gentle waters, very scenic country, and great fishing make the Au Sable one of Michigan's favorite waterways.

Boundary Waters, Minnesota

Covering thousands of square miles of unspoiled wilderness, the Boundary Waters Canoe area is a paddler's paradise. There are so many places to go that it never seems crowded even with 150,000 canoeists annually. Permits should be reserved months in advance.

St. Louis River, Minnesota

One of Minnesota's most scenic rivers, the St. Louis is a fine venue for day-trippers, with many good playspots and varied river dynamics. Most of the river is Class I, but some Class III rapids may have to be portaged by beginners.

SOUTHWEST

▼

Middle Colorado River, Utah

No, the Colorado is not just for experts. If you stick to Ruby and Horsethief Canyons, you can enjoy 27 miles of Class I and II sections suitable for open canoes and rookie kayakers. This makes a great 2 to 4-day trip. Skilled paddlers with permits may continue on to Class IV Westwater Canyon.

San Juan River, Utah

The San Juan River, running through Utah's colorful Canyonlands, offers one of the most dramatic Class I-II trips in the world. The steep rock canyons are second only in scale to the Grand Canyon of the Colorado. April is the time to run this river; avoid dangerous high-water conditions.

Rio Grande, New Mexico-Texas

Intermediates can navigate the Pilar section of the Rio Grande which ranges from flat to Class III, followed by many miles of gentle water. Great desert scenery--see our featured trip on p. 83.

ROCKIES

▼

Rio Chama, Colorado

The Rio Chama is one of Colorado's best destinations for novices and intermediates, offering pleasant Class II stretches suitable for 2 to 4-day trips.

Yellowstone River, Montana

The moderate section of the Yellowstone between Livingston and Billings affords a great 6-day trip for novices/intermediates. Avoid the dangerous sections in Yellowstone Park.

Upper Missouri River, Montana

Featuring passages through breathtaking

JOHN KELLY

canyons, the upper Missouri can be run by canoeists with a modicum of experience. The stretch from Fort Benton to US Highway 191 is a designated Wild and Scenic River.

Main Payette River, Idaho

The Main Payette near Boise, with Class I-II conditions on warm, dam-controlled waters makes a fine 1 or 2-day trip for novices. The river is easily accessible, and most rapids can be scouted from nearby roads.

WEST

▼

American River, California

The lower section of the American River is a good training ground for beginning paddlers, though water levels drop dramatically late in the season.

Deschutes River, Oregon

Although it is also a prime whitewater river, the Deschutes runs through very pretty country, and is not too demanding in the 100 miles north of Bend, Oregon.

The Klamath River, Oregon

One of the West's best learning rivers, the Klamath has many Class I and II sections ideal for practicing whitewater skills in relative safety. However, because the Klamath also contains many Class IV-V rapids, you should consult with a local guide before selecting your route.

CANADA EAST

▼

Ottawa River, Quebec

Flowing west for over 300 miles between a group of large lakes, the Ottawa is a prime choice for a wilderness tour. Paddling is fairly easy, except for the first 40 miles which contain some tough rapids.

Moisie River, Quebec

The Moisie runs over 260 miles from the mountains to the St. Lawrence, through some of Canada's most beautiful river valleys with spectacular gorges and waterfalls. The Moisie makes a great 2-week trip, but the Class III-IV rapids in the upper section should be portaged.

CANADA WEST

▼

Okanagan Region, British Columbia

The Okanagan Valley has long been the focus of BC canoeing. Paddle Lake Okanagan, or canoe-camp along any of 10 nearby rivers. This area offers a great variety of recreational opportunities and classically beautiful, easy-running waterways. Canoes can be rented in Kelowna, BC from Lee's Outfitters, (604) 762-8156, or Okanagan Canoe Holidays, (604) 762-8156.

Big Salmon River, Yukon Territories

Situated deep in the heart of the Yukon territories, the Big Salmon is hard to get to, but worth it. The river begins as a chain of three lakes, then runs for 115 miles. Wildlife galore and nothing above Class II makes this an ideal wilderness trip for novices.

MacKenzie River, Northwest Territories

Very wide, very long, but mostly gentle, the MacKenzie is the major river of the Canadian Northwest. It winds through a vast, remote wilderness--you can paddle for days without seeing a trace of civilization. Pick a route on the 300-mile stretch between Fort Simpson and Fort Norman.

North America's Top Training Centers

WHILE FLATWATER CANOEING ISN'T DIFFICULT, WE'D RECOMMEND SOME BASIC paddling training if you're heading off on your first long-distance canoe trek. If you want to be able to negotiate serious rapids (Class III and above), either in a canoe or kayak, top-quality, professional instruction is essential. Here is our list of the top paddling centers in North America. Most feature a wide variety of programs, from half-day clinics to multi-day instructional expeditions. Most of the Eastern schools offer both canoe and kayak training, while the Western schools focus primarily on whitewater kayaking.

EAST

■ OUTDOOR CENTRE OF NEW ENGLAND
10 Pleasant Street, Millers Falls, MA 01349, (413) 659-3926.

In operation since 1980, the nonprofit Outdoor Centre is arguably the best river school in the Northeast. The Outdoor Centre has outstanding instructors, good prices, and a wide range of canoe and kayak courses. One to 5-day classes in open canoe, decked canoe, tandem canoe and kayak are offered year-round for $75-$100 per day. Specialty clinics in canoe poling, slalom, river rescue, squirt boating and kayak racing are offered for the same price. Bed & Breakfast lodging costs $35 per night. The Outdoor Centre also boasts the largest American Canoe Association (ACA) instructor certification program in the Northeast with 4 and 5-day resident courses. If we lived in New England, the Outdoor Centre would be our first choice, without hesitation. Rating: ★★★★

■ SACO BOUND
P.O. Box 119, Center Conway, NH 03813, (603) 447-2177.

Now in its 19th year, Saco Bound is New England's oldest paddling center. Saco Bound's whitewater school in Errol, NH conducts canoe and kayak training seminars for novices and intermediates on the Class II and III Androscoggin, New England's only continually running, summer whitewater river. More intensive training is offered on Class III sections of the Kennebec River near Saco Bound's West Forks, Maine, basecamp. Two to 5-day programs operate from June 15 to Labor Day, at an average cost of $75 per day. Saco Bound boasts a complete riverside complex with campground, restaurant and motel. Rating: ★★★

■ W.I.L.D./W.A.T.E.R.S.
Box 197-A, Route 28 at The Glen, Warrensburg, NY 12885, (518) 494-7478.

Located on the banks of the Hudson River, W.I.L.D./W.A.T.E.R.S. (WW) offers quality training in both kayaks and canoes (open, C-1, and C-2). Many companies claim to offer personalized instruction, but WW really does. There are four levels of classes, each tailored for specific skill and experience levels. WW's ACA-certified instructors are very good--much better than you'll find in most schools. Highly recommended are WW's specialty clinics (e.g. squirt boat and women-only classes) taught by world-class paddlers. Clinics start at $230 for 2 days, including instruction, meals, lodging and all equipment. WW has a full retail shop, and students can stay at WW's comfortable Glen House Lodge for $28 per night including meals. Rating: ★★★

SOUTHEAST

■ NANTAHALA OUTDOOR CENTER
US 19W, P.O. Box 41, Bryson City, NC 28713, (704) 488-2175, or (704) 488-6737; FAX: (704) 488-2498.

Nantahala is the paddling school by which the rest are judged. It has been around as long as anyone, and offers the most comprehensive training program in North America. A partial list of the river skills classes available includes: Basic Canoe, C-1 (decked canoe), 5-day Basic or Intermediate Kayak, 7-day Fast Track Kayak, Racers Workshop, Raft Guide Training, and Rowing Technique. Nantahala also offers 4 and 5-day intensive river weeks which take you down a variety of rivers within a particular region. Instruction is available on many of the major destination trips (Rio Grande, Costa Rica and Scotland,

kayaks. MKC is based on the Madawaska River, a dam-controlled waterway located within scenic Algonquin Park. The controlled release assures good water flow all summer long. MKC also operates on the fast-moving Petawawa and Ottawa Rivers. Classes are small, and are taught by some of Canada's most experienced instructors. Beginner to advanced courses run 2 to 5 days, starting at $174 CDN for a weekend. (Lodging is extra and these rates are subject to currency fluctuation.) This is a great place to learn whitewater skills in a pristine environment. Rating: ★★★

■ WHITEWATER SPECIALTY

N3894, Hwy. 55, White Lake, WI 54491, (715) 882-5400.

Now in its 15th year, Whitewater Specialty is Wisconsin's leading river training center. Seminars are offered for all levels of paddlers in both kayaks and canoes (solo, C-1 and tandem). Training is designed to progress logically from one skill to the next. You won't be pushed ahead until you've mastered each essential technique. Classes are small, and are conducted on ponds and nearby Class II-IV rivers. The majority of programs are for novices, but the advanced paddling classes also attract river runners from throughout the Great Lakes area. The 3-day basic course costs about $275 including boat, equipment and food, but not lodging. Rating: ★★★

ROCKIES

■ BOULDER OUTDOOR CENTER

2510 North 47th Street, Boulder, CO 80301, (303) 444-8420.

The Boulder Outdoor Center (BOC) is a real hot-bed for paddle sports. BOC's ranks of instructors include some of the most talented kayakers in the sport, real all-stars with numerous first descents of rivers in Central America and Mexico to their credit. If you are looking for a school that can push you up to the Class III+ level quickly, BOC is a good choice. In addition to its on-river training seminar, BOC offers guided trips to the Cache La Poudre River near Ft. Collins, and to the Rio Grande. BOC's main emphasis is on kayaking, but canoe programs are offered as well. Rating: ★★★

■ BILL DVORAK'S KAYAK AND RAFTING EXPEDITIONS

17921-AT US Highway 285, Nathrop, CO 81236, (800) 824-3795, or (719) 539-6851.

for example). Nantahala's instructors are patient and skilled, and many other paddling centers send personnel to Nantahala for instructor workshops and certification. Nantahala has its own on-site cabin and bunkhouse lodging. Rating: ★★★★★

CENTRAL/GREAT LAKES

■ KAYAK AND CANOE INSTITUTE

U. OF MINN. (Duluth), 108 Kirby Student Center, 10 University Drive, Duluth, MN 55812, (218) 726-6533.

The Kayak and Canoe Institute (KCI) is a major national training center that handles over 7,000 students annually. Instruction in every type of paddling is offered, at bargain basement prices. For example, a 3-day weekend kayaking course is $125 for beginners, $95 for intermediates. Both whitewater and flatwater decked and open canoe courses cost $85-$95 for a weekend, while a 3-day kayak touring class on Lake Superior costs $155.

Being state-funded in part, KCI is able to offer instruction and destination trips at prices most private outfitters can't touch. Seven days in the Boundary Waters Canoe Area costs only $214, while an 11-day, combined raft/kayak trip on Idaho's Salmon River is only $555. This is less than half the cost of some Idaho outfitters. Other bargains are the 10-day multi-river West Virginia tour for $489, and expedition canoeing in Canada (various itineraries). Rating: ★★★

■ MADAWASKA KANU CENTER

39 First Ave., Ottawa, ONT, Canada K1S 2G1, (613) 594-KANU.

Madawaska Kanu Camp (MKC) offers whitewater training in canoes as well as

Bill Dvorak's school, one of America's very best, offers 1 to 12-day instructional seminars on Class II-III rivers such as the Green, Dolores and Arkansas. Dvorak recommends a 5 to 7-day seminar for the serious paddler, while a 3-day program will give you a good solid introduction to whitewater technique. On-river seminars begin at about $300 for 3 days including food and equipment. We recommend the 6-day program on the Green River for $900.

The Dvorak catalog reads like the ultimate river wish-book--his operation runs 29 separate canyons on 10 different rivers, and you can combine kayak/canoe training with hair-raising rafting on the same trip. Dvorak also offers a wide array of foreign trips. Rating: ★★★★

WEST

■ NORTHWEST OUTDOOR CENTER
2100 Westlake Avenue N., Seattle, WA 98109, (206) 281-9694.

The Seattle area is not known as a haven for whitewater sports, but the Northwest Outdoor Center (NWOC) runs a strong introductory kayak training program from the spring through fall. Basic training (eskimo rolls) is conducted in heated pools in Seattle, and then classes head for the Class II-III Skykomish and Wenatchee Rivers in the Cascades for on-the-water training. Weekend programs cost $115 (plus $45 for kayak rental), while the 5-day Total Immersion school costs $450 including meals, lodging, transport, boats and all gear. Rating: ★★

■ OTTER BAR KAYAK SCHOOL
P.O. Box 210, Forks of Salmon, CA 96031, (916) 462-4772.

The Otter Bar Kayak School may be America's only high-end whitewater destination resort. With a superb lodge, excellent mountain biking nearby and challenging rapids at your doorstep, this is a great spot to spend a holiday while learning whitewater technique. Classes are small (3:1 student/teacher ratio), serious and effective. The Lodge amenities and quality of the river have earned Otter Bar many repeat customers. The only down-side is that river levels can run low during the late summer. Otter Bar offers 7-day clinics for beginners June through August, 7-day intermediate programs April through June, and 5-day intermediate or advanced courses in April. Five-day sessions cost $780, while weeklong courses run $1,095. Lodging, meals and equipment are included. The advanced courses, some of the best on the West Coast, teach you surfing, pirouettes, eddy hopping and other expert maneuvers. Rating: ★★★★; ★★★ in low-water years.

■ SUNDANCE EXPEDITIONS, INC.
14894 Galice Road, Merlin, OR 97532, (503) 479-8508.

With the exception of Otter Bar, Sundance is probably head and shoulders above the rest of the West Coast kayak schools. It's clear that Sundance aims to produce skilled and enthusiastic kayakers who will continue with the sport, not just run customers through a training regimen. The facilities are not as deluxe as Otter Bar, but water levels can be more reliable, and Sundance transports its students to a number of rivers in the area. Rapport between students and instructors is excellent, and you'll hear nothing but praise for the program from alumni. The basic program runs for 9 days at a cost of approximately $1,225, including permits, lodging and meals, plus a 4-day raft-supported trip down one of Oregon's rivers such as the Deschutes or the Rogue. No canoe training is offered. Rating: ★★★★

CANOEING & KAYAKING

OUTFITTING A TRIP

In choosing a canoe outfitter, above all look for experience and top-quality equipment. If you are going to an area requiring portaging, you will want the latest in lightweight gear, such as Kevlar canoes and ultralight tents. The more well-established outfitters will know the best destinations within a particular region.

Many of the paddling schools reviewed above lead river trips to destinations throughout North America. Some of our other favorite river runners have been identified in the Best Trips section at the beginning of this chapter. However, these represent only a small sample of the qualified river guides and outfitters in North America. For example, there are probably at least 50 canoe outfitters worthy of mention in Canada alone. To find listings for other qualified river guides and outfitters, consult **Canoe** magazine, *P.O. Box 3146, Kirkland, WA 98083, (206) 827-6363*, or contact the following organizations:

America Outdoors, *(Nat'l River Guides Assoc.), P.O. Box 1348, Knoxville, TN 37901, (615) 524-4814; FAX: (615) 525-4765.*

National Association of Canoe Liveries and Outfitters, *Route 27 and Catro Route 2, Box 2119, Butler, KY 41006, (606) 654-4111.*

NWT Tourism, *Box 1320, Yellowknife, NWT, Canada X1A 2L9, (800) 661-0788.*

Eastern Canadian River Outfitters Association, *c/o New World Expeditions, Rouge River Road, Calumet, Quebec, (819) 242-2168.*

Yukon Outfitters Assoc., *Bag Service, 2762 Whitehorse, Yukon, Canada Y1A 5B9.*

ORGANIZATIONS

American Canoe Association, 8550 Cinderbed Road, Suite 1900, P.O. Box 1190, Newington, VA 22122-1190. Publishes American Canoeist newsletter; source for canoe route guides and local club listings.

Canadian Recreational Canoeing Association, P.O. Box 500, Hyde Park, Ont. NOM 1ZO. Source for river recommendations and local canoeing clubs.

DAVID STOECKLEIN

KAYAK EXPEDITIONS

Because of its limited carrying capacity, a river kayak is not a particularly good cruising vehicle. However, multi-day kayak trips are feasible if you arrange for a support raft to carry your gear. Nantahala Outdoor Center, Dvorak River Expeditions, Slickrock Adventures, and the Kayak and Canoe Institute are among the leaders in raft-supported kayak river trips (see addresses above). You'll find a number of other companies that offer raft-supported trips in the Rafting section of this book, Chapter 16.

ARTICLES

"Juiced Up and Ready to Roll," by Michael McRae (Outside magazine, March 1984), is a vivid and entertaining account of whitewater kayaking on Class III-IV rivers in Northern California. If you're wondering what the thrill of advanced whitewater paddling is really about, read this piece. Check your library, or contact the Otter Bar Lodge, Forks of Salmon, CA 96031 for a reprint.

BOOKS

The Canoer's Bible (1989 ed.), by Robert Douglas Mead, gives you just about all you need to know about canoe selection, paddling technique and canoe camping. Good discussion of canoe destinations and excellent appendices listing sources for regional maps and guidebooks. $7.95 from Doubleday Books.

Song of the Paddle, by Bill Mason, is a beautiful, photo-illustrated guide to wilderness canoe-camping. Read this book before you head out on any long canoe trip. $21.95 from Canoe magazine, (800) MY-CANOE.

The Complete Whitewater Sourcebook packs all the information you need for river-running nationwide: phone numbers, water levels, regional guidebooks, access points and permit requirements. If you are planning your own wilderness river trip, buy this book. $12.95 from the Boat People, (408) 258-7971.

Idaho Whitewater, by Moore and McLaren, covers 80 runs for all skill levels. Each river is described and mapped in great detail in what has become the bible for Idaho river-running. About 220 pages with many color photos. $19.95 from the Boat People.

Makens' Guide to U.S. Canoe Trails, by James Makens, features brief but useful descriptions of virtually all the most popular canoe lakes and rivers in the United States. Le Voyageur Publishing Co., 1319 Wentwood, Irving, TX.

The New England White Water River Guide, by Ray Gabler, is the best single where-to-go book for the Northeastern canoeist. Available from the Appalachian Mountain Club, 5 Joy Street, Boston, MA 02108.

Western Whitewater, From the Rockies to the Pacific, by Cassady, Calhoun and Cross, is the most useful advanced river guidebook in print. Fifty top rivers are reviewed and mapped in great detail, while you'll find the basics on more than 100 other popular runs. This volume has the best maps and river logs of any current publication. Highly recommended. $22.50 from the Boat People.

The White Water Handbook, by John Urban, shows you the latest techniques for getting down those tricky sections in a canoe. Available from the Appalachian Mountain Club, (address above).

White Water Trips for Kayakers, Canoers, & Rafters on Vancouver Island; White Water Trips. . . in British Columbia, by Betty Pratt-Johnson, are two excellent sourcebooks for the Canadian West.

Scuba Diving

*Los Islotes, Sea of Cortez, Baja/*TOM CAMPBELL

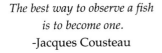

*The best way to observe a fish
is to become one.*
-Jacques Cousteau

▼

*D*iving allows us to explore a new world, a weightless environment unlike anything above the surface. Unbounded by gravity, the diver enjoys a special freedom which must be experienced to be understood. The underwater realm teems with life--brilliantly colored fish, exotic flora and fascinating marine mammals--providing an endless resource for learning and discovery.

With most of the planet covered by water, the variety of possible diving destinations is infinite. However, it is in the tropics where most divers will experience the ultimate in underwater enjoyment. In the warm, clear waters of the Caribbean, the Indian Ocean and the South Pacific, fish school by the thousands, and radiant corals are everywhere. In this chapter we provide a comprehensive guide to the top dive destinations around the globe, from the busy dive havens of Cozumel to the remote islands of Micronesia. We explain how to find the best deals in the most popular dive venues, as well as how to travel to the world's remaining underwater frontiers.

CHAPTER
7

MARTY SNYDERMAN

*T*HE CONDITIONS THAT MAKE FOR GREAT DIVING--WARM TRANSLUCENT WATER, good weather and tropical locales--also make for a terrific getaway vacation. You'll find great bargains at the big Caribbean resorts, while exotic destinations, such as Borneo and Micronesia, promise true underwater adventure.

FIJI

South Pacific Paradise

Ask divers who have sampled most of the world's leading dive spots where they would go for a perfect dive vacation, and more often than not, Fiji is the answer. Topside, Fiji is Polynesia at its best-- unspoiled and uncrowded. The water is warm and clear, and there is every imaginable shape and variety of coral in all colors of the rainbow. The variety of dive sites is staggering--from the air, Fiji appears as a vast patchwork of coral, covering hundreds of square miles.

Fiji is one destination where there is no clear choice between live-aboard and land-based options. Both offer advantages and disadvantages. On a live-aboard you will be able to explore the more remote dive sites, and log the most dives per day. On the other hand, you will miss the experience of living on a tropical island, which is one of the best reasons to visit Fiji in the first place. The outer islands are quiet, idyllic retreats where civilization truly slips from your consciousness. The Fijians are a wonderful people, fun-loving and warm-hearted.

The hotbed of Fijian diving is the northern group of islands including Vanua Levu, Matagi and Taveuni. The Fijian dive resort of choice, the best for experienced divers is Dive Taveuni. The diving is among the best in Fiji (though currents can be strong), and the lodge has been recently upgraded. If you want a little more luxury, you should consider the Namale Plantation, a perfect honeymoon getaway spot. Na Koro on Vanua Levu is another beautiful resort with superb beaches.The Kontiki resort is more rustic, but offers plenty of topside activities, and is the only Fijian resort offering three-tank boat dives. The two leading live-aboard boats are the 60' Matagi Princess and the 115' Pacific Nomad. The Nomad is the better dive platform, but the dive sites are less than ideal. The Matagi Princess features better cabins and dives the best northern reefs. It is also less expensive--$1,050 for 5 nights versus $1,725 per week for the Nomad.

Those with limited time may wish to dive the main island of Viti Levu. Despite strong currents, the Beqa Lagoon is easily the best dive area on Viti Levu, boasting fascinating cuts, passages and overhangs, and vividly colored soft coral walls. Lagoon dive trips can be arranged with Beqa Divers on arrival in Fiji and cost about $70 per day (two tanks). You can book Fijian dive vacations directly, or contact an agency such as Tropical Adventures, (800) 247-3483.

Eight Great Diving Adventures

BAHAMAS

Swimming with Dolphins

If we had a limited amount of vacation time and were looking for a truly unique underwater experience, we would head straight for the Bahamas. There, in the waters off Grand Bahama Island, divers can experience the special thrill of open-ocean diving with dolphins.

The Bahamas' leading dive-with-dolphins program is offered by the Underwater Explorer's Society (UNEXSO) based in Freeport. Since 1979, UNEXSO has offered a two-part program utilizing dolphins captured from nearby waters. For about $60, both divers and non-divers can swim with dolphins in saltwater pens maintained at the UNEXSO Freeport dive center. Much more exciting, however, are the open-ocean dives. After being released into the ocean, the animals rendezvous with the dive boats a mile offshore. Under the supervision of the dolphin handlers, the divers interact with the dolphins--feeding them, stroking them, and

riding their dorsals for short distances. It is all fairly businesslike (the dolphins perform their duties in response to hand signals), but it is still the experience of a life-

time for most divers. UNEXSO has been criticized for keeping dolphins in captivity, but it is to be remembered that once the dolphins are released into the sea, nothing compels them to return. Contact UNEXSO, (800) 992-DIVE, or (809) 373-1244 in the Bahamas.

If UNEXSO's program seems too artificial, it is also possible to dive with wild dolphins off Grand Bahama, although contact with the creatures is not such a sure thing. One of the Bahamas' leading liveaboards, the 80' catamaran Bottom Time II, makes regular trips to the shallow turquoise banks north of Grand Bahama--the favored playground of schools of wild spotted dolphins. On a good day, dolphins surround the boat by the time the anchor is secure. Familiar with the operation, the wild mammals circle around the dive ladders, and swim close to the divers during the entire session. The Bottom Time II is fast, stable and very comfortable. It has 15 private cabins, and all the amenities, even an onboard film lab. Contact Bottom Time Adventures, (800) 234-8464.

STEPHEN FRINK

CAYMAN ISLANDS

Diving Disneyland

The Caymans are the most popular dive destination in the Caribbean, and despite the heavy use, there are few better dive locales in the Northern Hemisphere. The water is warm, the wall-diving is world class, and the visibility is consistently excellent--the best in the central Caribbean.

While the Caymans have countless good dive sites, Grand Cayman can be crowded, and those in the know prefer Cayman Brac and Little Cayman. The coral is less chewed up, and there are more fish. Little Cayman's Bloody Bay Wall is spectacular, while favorites on Cayman Brac include Sea Fan Wall and Butterfly Reef.

No trip to the Caymans would be complete without a chance to dive with stingrays in the shallows of Grand Cayman's North Sound. Treasure Island Divers, (800) 872-7552, visits the sound three times a week. Here, at Stingray City and Sand Bar, divers can hand-feed the rays in crystal clear 10- to 15-foot waters. While on Grand Cayman, don't miss its famed North Wall. It starts fairly deep, at 70 feet, so you must monitor your dive times carefully.

The quality of the dive shops in the Caymans is high--a result of the intense competition. You won't go wrong with any of the top operators including Ron Kipp's Bob Soto's Diving, Ltd., (800) 262-7686; Quabbin Divers, (809) 949-5597; and Red Sail Sports, (800) 255-6425, all based on Grand Cayman. If you want to log the most dives each day, we recommend a live-aboard. Brac Aquatic's Little Cayman Diver, (800) 458-2722, has been called the Caribbean's best boat, while the Cayman Aggressor, (800) 348-2628, is also excellent. It is less luxurious, but far more stable.

AMOS NACHOUM

MICRONESIA

Wreck-Diving Adventures

Micronesia, which includes the islands of Truk, Palau, Pohnpei and Yap, is on everyone's list of top 10 dive locales. Here you will find unequaled wreck-diving, great visibility, large sea creatures and thick schools of tropical fish.

Truk, the site of one of WW II's great air and sea battles, is a wreck-diving site without peer. In all there are over 80 diveable wrecks--you could spend a month here and not see it all. Truk's underwater world is not just rusting hulks. With time the wrecks have become artificial reefs alive with corals and sea life. Scuba Times magazine has written: "Truk Lagoon is the absolute ultimate.... Dive it and be spoiled forever." Unfortunately, most wrecks are fairly deep, between 60 and 90 feet, so the lagoon is not the best destination for novices.

Those looking to explore the most interesting wrecks and log the most dives should seriously consider a live-aboard. Your choices are the 170' Thorfinn, or the 120' Truk Aggressor. Both are comfortable, well-equipped vessels with quality crews. While the Thorfinn stays in the lagoon, the Aggressor visits the outer atolls and reef walls every week, providing a needed break from wreck-diving. The Aggressor also features double staterooms with private heads--a nice touch. An 8-day Aggressor live-aboard trip runs about $1,900, while the Thorfinn runs about $1,500.

After Truk, Palau is Micronesia's leading attraction. Indeed, Palau has been ranked as one of the best all-around dive sites in the world. A large atoll with over 200 islands, Palau offers diversity found nowhere else. The variety of dive sites in a small area is staggering, with 60 great drop-offs starting at surface levels and

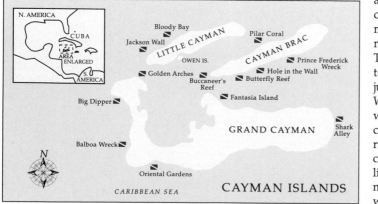

AUSTRALIA
Coral Sea Adventure

For many divers, Australia, with its famed Great Barrier Reef and legendary Coral Sea, represents the ultimate dive destination. The water is a warm 75 to 85 degrees, visibility ranges from good to spectacular, and there are enough outstanding dive sites to last a lifetime.

Diving is extremely competitive in Australia, so you can find any type of trip you want, at surprisingly low prices. Cairns (pronounced "cans") in Northern Queensland is Australia's dive mecca, and here you will find superb vacation values. A half-dozen excellent dive shops, such as Down Under Dive and Pro Dive, are headquartered along the Cairns waterfront, making comparison-shopping easy and productive. The most popular offerings are 3 to 4-day Barrier Reef live-aboard trips, typically priced at under $450, a good 20 percent less than similar trips advertised by US dive agencies. Day-trips out of Port Douglas are available, but so much time is spent getting to the reef that the diving itself is too rushed to be truly enjoyable.

For serious divers, a live-aboard trip is the only logical way to go. During 3 to 4 days offshore, you can sample a host of Barrier Reef sites, making a half-dozen dives a day, more if you add night dives. First-time divers can also enroll in a certification course in Cairns which concludes with a 3-day offshore trip to the reef.

While the Barrier Reef is excellent by any measure, if you are looking for the maximum quantity and variety of sea creatures, you should head much farther offshore out to the Coral Sea. The water is very warm, and during the best seasons visibility can exceed 200 feet. The sea mounts of Marion Reef are magnets for aquatic life, attracting everything from schooling tropicals to whale sharks. Many believe that the Yongala wreck is the single best dive in the world. It is virtually guaranteed that you will see vast numbers of fish and large pelagics, and visibility is regularly 200' or better between August and November. Visit the Yongala in June to observe schools of 25-foot mickey whales.

For those seeking an extended dive trip aboard a first-class vessel, we recommend the Si Bon in Port Douglas, and Mike Ball Watersports in Port Townsend. Renowned for its deluxe amenities and superb crew, the Si Bon must be reserved months in advance. Mike Ball offers excellent multi-day trips aboard luxurious twin-hulled dive craft. His large catamarans are fast, comfortable, stable and have many special features ideal for diving. The new 100' Spoilsport is probably the best dive boat in operation anywhere.

Australian dive trips can be booked through agencies such as See & Sea, (800) 348-9778, and Tropical Adventures, (800) 247-3483. However, you can save plenty if you bargain directly with the Aussie dive shops. (See pp. 104-05 for phone listings.)

dropping to 300 meters. Water is 82 degrees, with visibility regularly 125 to 200 feet. Palau boasts a dozen blue holes, and a famed five-chambered cave system. The sea life is superb--1,000-pound clams, thick schools of reef fish, and large pelagics.

The classiest hotel in Palau is the Palau Pacific--a good choice if you have non-diving companions. Otherwise the rustic Nikko Palau is quite adequate. The best land-based dive operation in Palau is Fish n' Fins. Its divemasters know all the top sites, and it employs fast, modern dive boats. If you have time left after Truk and Palau, we recommend a 2 or 3-day visit to Yap. Yap's Mil Channel is perhaps the best place in the world for giant mantas--close encounters are virtually guaranteed.

While you can make your own arrangements with a number of Micronesian dive operations (Micronesia Aquatics, Fish n' Fins, and Yap Divers are among the best), it is easier, and not much more costly, to book a package vacation through a US-based dive agency. Innerspace Adventures, (800) 333-SEAS, and Tropical Adventures, (800) 247-3483, are two good choices.

GETTING CERTIFIED ON YOUR VACATION

Even if you've never dived before or your certification has lapsed, you can still enjoy a rewarding dive vacation. Most good dive centers around the world offer certification courses for first-time or out-of-practice divers.

PADI or NAUI certifications are the most widely recognized, so select a PADI or NAUI training facility if possible. Before you choose a course, comparison shop with these points in mind. How much does the complete course cost, including the ocean dives? How many hours are spent in the pool versus the open water? Is the training pool deep enough to permit proper equalization? (It should be at least eight feet.) What dive gear are you required to buy, and does the shop offer discounts on these items? How many years has the facility been in business, and how experienced are the instructors? Can you get a partial refund if you cannot complete the course? How many students are in each class? (The fewer the better, and never more than 10 per instructor.) If the course involves boat dives, how many per day are you allowed? How much does it cost to add extra dive days once the course is complete?

The better dive shops will give reassuring answers to all these questions. When booking a foreign dive training program, however, try to avoid full payment in advance, and make sure that your spot is guaranteed. You don't need to purchase lots of costly gear before you go. Do obtain a top-quality mask that fits perfectly. But until you've decided how serious a diver you want to become, you probably should not invest in a custom wetsuit, or expensive gauges and dive computers.

TOM CAMPBELL

BAJA

Big Time Diving Close to Home

Baja's Sea of Cortez is close to home, relatively inexpensive, and there are few better places to see large marine animals. The water is neither as clear nor as warm as in the Caribbean, but conditions are still superior to what you'll find north of the border. Big sea creatures are what Baja diving is all about--sea lions, mantas, schooling hammerheads, and even whales.

The two major dive hubs in Baja are Cabo San Lucas and La Paz. In Cabo, the oldest and by far the best dive shop is Amigos Del Mar, which coordinates the diving at most of the major resorts. In La Paz, a half-day to the northeast, the diving is done from beach resorts, such as the Hotel Las Arenas and Hotel Los Arcos. Although the shoreside resorts are appealing, for serious divers a live-aboard is the best way to go. Many of the better dive sites, such as the Salvatierra wreck, El Bajo sea mounts (mantas and hammerheads) and Los Islotes Island (sea lions), are quite a distance from the beach resorts. With a live-aboard you avoid time wasted in transit, permitting you four or five dives per day, rather than just two. Baja Expeditions, (800) 843-6967, runs 7-day live-aboard trips on the 80' Don Jose July through November. The crew is excellent, but don't expect luxuries like air conditioning. The cost is about $1,600 per person, including airfare from Los Angeles, Tucson or Tijuana.

Sea Safaris, (800) 262-6670, the leading agency for Baja, can book both live-aboard trips and land-based diving at a half-dozen resorts in Los Cabos and La Paz. Resort holidays start at under $300 for 4 days/3-nights with 2 days of diving.

BORNEO

Sipadan Island--Aquatic Eden

The hottest new dive destination in the world is Borneo's Sipadan Island. The praise for Sipadan is unparalleled. The World Wildlife Fund observes, "No other spot on the face of this planet has more marine life than this island." Jacques Cousteau adds, "I have seen other places like Sipadan--45 years ago--but now we have found again an untouched piece of art."

In objective terms, Sipadan offers more attractions per dive than just about anywhere--more fish, more turtles, more coral, and more diversity. You can expect to see 10 turtles per dive, and schools of 300 or more barracuda. The variety and numbers of large pelagics is astonishing. With 2,000' drop-offs just yards from the beach, all the action is close by. Ninety percent of the footage of a recent Cousteau television special on Sipadan was shot right in front of the dive shop. You can literally don your gear at the resort, and swim out 50 yards for the best diving of your life.

The dive operation on Sipadan is run by Borneo Divers. The resort is rustic but comfortable, with hot showers and good food. A maximum of 30 guests stay in cozy thatch huts. Divers should bring all their own gear except weight belts as the rental inventory is very limited. No special health risks are present (you won't need malaria medicine), but dives are limited to three per day since there is no decompression chamber nearby. Note: visibility, which normally exceeded 80 feet, declined to 40 feet or less in summer 1991 for reasons unknown. An 11-day Sipadan holiday costs about $2,400 with airfare. Call Sea Safaris, (800) 821-6670, or Tropical Adventures, (800) 247-3483.

GALAPAGOS

South American Spectacle

The water can be chilly, the visibility less than ideal, but the Galapagos Islands offer aquatic attractions that can't be found anywhere else. It was in these remote islands, 600 miles west of Ecuador, that Charles Darwin found inspiration for his theory of evolution.

This locale is a fantasy world for divers accustomed to nothing but small fish. Along with thick schools of tropicals, there are numerous sea turtles, sea lions and large pelagics. Various dive sites have their own special attractions--sharks, penguins or even the marine iguanas, remarkable creatures found nowhere else on earth. Nothing can prepare you for your first underwater encounter with an iguana. With their human-like limbs, they look like small green frogmen. Unafraid and largely uninterested in humans, they permit divers to approach very closely as they bottom-feed. It's tough diving, however, as the iguanas stick to shallow waters with lots of surge.

Since the Galapagos are maintained as a wilderness preserve, there are no beach resorts. Therefore, all diving is done on a live-aboard basis. There are a number of good live-aboard vessels, (the Encantada is probably the best), most with trained naturalists on board. Dive trips can be booked through See & Sea Travel, (800) 348-9778, and other agencies.

Pufferfish/TOM CAMPBELL

CHOOSING A DIVE TOUR

A T THE MOST POPULAR DIVE SPOTS SUCH AS THE CAYMANS AND COZUMEL, YOU'LL find as many as two dozen dive companies eagerly competing for your business. Choosing the best dive operation isn't always easy. Here are some factors that separate the great dive trips from the disappointing ones.

Land-based vs. Live-aboard

In many of the world's top dive spots, such as the Coral Sea, Micronesia and the Solomon Islands, a live-aboard trip beats a land-based dive vacation hands down. On a live-aboard, you spend the maximum amount of time in the water. If you get up early, and dive shallow, it's quite possible to do six dives a day from a well-equipped dive boat. At a land resort, by contrast, you're lucky to get three dives per day, since so much time is lost in transit. Even the best live-aboards get claustrophobic, however, so plan to take some shore leave after five to six days.

Dive Boat and Divemaster

Not all dive boats are created equal. A premium vessel should have an onboard compressor, and be able to carry at least 40 reserve tanks. Boats with large reserve air chambers are the best; they allow the speediest refills, and you don't have to lug so many tanks aboard. Select an easy-to-board vessel with a large, open gear-donning area. Stability and deck space are also important--and here, a big catamaran can't be beat. At sea, comfort counts; hot showers and private cabins are worth the extra cost.

Divemasters come in all varieties, from superb to downright dangerous. If possible, choose a dive program that uses western divemasters--especially in places like Mexico, Thailand and the Red Sea. Western divemasters, as a rule, are much more safety conscious and professional.

Variety in the Dive Sites

No matter how spectacular, any dive site becomes old hat quickly. Select a dive trip that visits a variety of locations, preferably at least two sites per day. Try to mix reef-diving with wall-diving, and add something of special interest, such as a lobster hole or shipwreck. Choose a locale where there's plenty to see above 45 feet. In general, shallow dives offer more clarity, color and sea life. Your air supply will also last longer near the surface.

Recreational Options

Even in the best locations, you may grow tired of diving after three or four days. On a live-aboard, you'll want to return to shore for a respite. At a land-based resort, you may want to try another sport, or simply do nothing for a spell. Many tours offer a discount for days that you don't dive. Or, it may be possible to combine diving with sailing, fishing or windsurfing, all for a single price. Look for these features when comparing itineraries.

30 GREAT DIVE SITES WORLDWIDE

COURTESY LANDFALL PRODUCTIONS

MOST OF THE WORLD'S BEST DIVE SPOTS, IF JUDGED BY THE ABUNDANCE AND VARIETY OF SEA LIFE, clarity of water and quality of coral, are found in the tropics. For this reason, the vast majority of the recommended dive destinations in this chart are located far from the mainland US. However, you'll find plenty of world-class diving in the Carribean, which is but a few hours away for those who live on the East Coast. Still, if you seek nothing less than the ultimate in underwater experiences, you'll want to experience far-flung destinations such as Malaysia, Papua New Guinea and the South Coral Sea. Usually the best way to explore these diving frontiers is by live-aboard. While you will sacrifice the comforts of a land-based resort, a live-aboard will generally give you more actual diving--expect five to seven dives per day, instead of the two or three offered by most land resorts. CODES: LB (land-based tours); LA (live-aboard trip); AIR (includes round-trip airfare).

Location	Site Description	Water Temp. & Visibility	Best Dive Season	Recommended Dive Shops
AUSTRALIA (GREAT BARRIER REEF)	Lots of fish despite the heavy dive traffic & incredible diversity of coral. Top spots: Cod Hole, Osprey, Bougainville and Flynn Reefs. Marine life: giant clams, turtles, sharks, and hundreds of small tropicals.	73-85 50'-120'	Aug-Dec	Pro Dive, Deep Sea Div Den, Down Under Dive
(SOUTH CORAL SEA)	Lihou Reef, Yongala wreck rank among world's top 10 dive sites. Unreal visibility on the far offshore sites, with amazing numbers of fish. Marion Reef has 220' pinnacles.	75-80 70'-200'	Aug-Dec	Mike Ball Dive Exped.
BAHAMAS	With 890 islands, the Bahamas offer incredible diversity--deep and shallow reefs, countless wrecks, blue holes, caves. Long Island is popular for wall and wreck-diving.	68-85 70'-125'	All (Summer best)	Stella Maris Resort, Peter Hughes, UNEXSO
BAJA (SEA OF CORTEZ)	Baja offers the best diving in the northern Pacific. Lots of mantas, dolphins, whales and sea lions. The Salvatierra is a fantastic wreck dive. Los Islotes has scores of sea lions. El Bajo sea mount is famed for schooling hammerheads.	68-78 30'-70'	All (Summer best)	Amigos Del Mar
BELIZE	Lighthouse Reef is world class. Great site variety. Try Southwest Cut, Long Cay Wall, Blue Hole, Half Moon Cay wall. Huge fish by Caribbean standards.	80 90'-125'	All (Summer best)	Manta Reef Resort
BONAIRE	Northwestern end of island near Washington Park is best. Great numbers of fish, sharks, mantas, lovely corals. Nearby Klein Curuçao also has fine, unspoiled reefs.	80 90'-125'	All	Dive Bonaire (Divi), Habitat Dive
CALIFORNIA (CHANNEL ISLANDS)	Anacapa, San Miguel, San Nicholas have seals, otters, abalone, lobster. Numerous day and overnight trips year-round. Kelp forests. Winter water is cold, but very clear.	52-64 30'-100'	All	Diver's Den, SB Aquatics
CAYMAN ISLANDS (GRAND CAYMAN, LITTLE CAYMAN, CAYMAN BRAC)	Bloody Bay Wall on Little Cayman is ranked by many among the world's top 10 sites. Sea Fan Wall, Garden Eel Wall and Butterfly Reef are superior venues on Cayman Brac. Many dive sites are crowded. Don't miss Stingray City.	80+ 80'-200'	All	Quabbin Dives, Bob Soto's Diving, Red Sail Sports
COCOS ISLAND (COSTA RICA)	Open water with strong currents. Countless big animals--turtles, mantas, whale sharks, huge pelagics. Very deep shelf; suited for experienced deep-water divers only.	80 50'-100'	Nov-Aug	Diving Safaris, Tropical Adven.
COZUMEL	Would you believe 80,000 divers a year? This level of activity (though still less than the Caymans) has reduced the numbers of fish, but you'll still find great wall-diving at Santa Rosa and Palancar, and excellent coral mounts at Columbia Shallows.	75-82 50'-100'	All	Carribean Divers, Dive Paradise, Fantasia, Caribbean Argonauts
EGYPT (HURGHADA, SHARM EL SHEIK)	Ras Mohammed and nearby sites are busy, and the closest reefs are somewhat chewed up. However, Trian Straits and the Dunraven wreck are still super. Summer is best.	68-85 40'-100'	All	Sinai Divers, Aquamarine Diving
FIJI	The northern islands (Taveuni, Matagi, Qamea) are truly world class with superb coral, profuse marine life, and amazing visibility. Beqa Lagoon is tops on the main island.	73-76 100'-200'	All (Rain Jan-Feb)	Dive Taveuni, Beqa Dive Qamea Beach Club
FLORIDA KEYS	The Keys offer the best diving in the mainland US. The top dive shops offer world-class instruction, and the dive options are almost endless. Many great wrecks, such as Duane, Bibb and Eagle.	72-88 30'-100'	All	Admiral Dive Acad., Ke West Divers, Ocean Dive
GALAPAGOS	Marine mammal mecca. Darwin Island offers sharks, whale sharks, turtles, rays, huge schools of fish, numerous sea lions, iguanas, penguins. April, May are warmest.	68-78 60'-100'	Oct-May	See & Sea (agency), Trop. Adven. (agency)
HAWAII (MAUI)	Fish life is somewhat depleted, but there are a multitude of interesting sites near shore, including Lanai underwater park. A fine choice for dive training.	74-80 50'-100'	All	Cen. Pac. Divers, Lahain Divers, Maui Dive Shop
(KONA)	100 excellent dive sites with lava tubes, caves, abundant fish. All dive sites are close to shore. Puffers, eels and octopus are common.	75-81 50'-100'	All	King Kamehameha, Dive Makai, Kona Coast
INDONESIA (BORNEO) (SIPADAN)	According to the World Wildlife Fund, "No other spot on the face of the planet has more marine life than this island." There's every imaginable variety--turtles, tropical fish, schooling barracuda, sharks and superb coral.	80+ 40'-150'	All (Low visibility Aug-Sept)	Borneo Divers (contact agencies)
KENYA	Watamu Bay and Kisite-Mpunguti Marine Parks offer quality diving with fish everywhere. Top spots: Big 3 Caves (Watumu), Shimoni Reef (Kisite), Pemba Island.	75-80 50'-100'	All	Turtle Bay Divers at Hemingway's
PALAU	Spectacular walls and limestone formations. Top spots: Blue Holes, Chandelier Cave. Lots of color, and many fish, sharks and turtles. Yap extension offers rays.	80-83 90'-150'	Sept-May	Fish n' Fins NECO Marine
PAPUA NEW GUINEA	Walindi and Banana Reefs and Rabaul wrecks are world class. Prolific sea life, and huge fish, manta rays, whale sharks, killer whales. Richly colored, large coral masses.	75-82 70'-150'	All (Rain Nov-Jan)	Walindi Plantation
PHILIPPINES (TUBBATAHA REEF)	Tubbataha, accessible only by live-aboard, is amazing--500' vertical walls, schools of giant mantas, tropical fish by the thousands. Great abundance of life--large and small.	85 100'-200'	March-June	Poseiden Ven., See & Sea (Live-aboard agents)

TOM CAMPBELL

MARTY SNYDERMAN

COURTESY CARL ROESSLER, SEE & SEA TRAVEL

Recommended Live-Aboards	Accommodations	Package Per Week	Comments	Rating
Coralita Si Bon	Many budget hotels on Cairns waterfront, Live-aboard Recom.	$275 3 days, $1100 to $1800/wk (both LA)	The Reef is far enough offshore that you should go for at least 3 days at a time. Avoid the 1-day programs which are too rushed.	★★★
Pacific Thunder, Spoilsport (best)	Live-aboard Only	$2600 deluxe LA (10 days)	Yongala wreck is a virtually guaranteed superb dive for clarity, sea life, and number of animals. The Coral Sea is truly world class.	★★★★★
Bottom Time, Crown Diver	Stella Maris, Divi Bahamas Resort	$800+ LB	Enjoy diving sites from the Bond films, and the Shark Reef off Long Island. Fish tend to be small. Winter can be too cold.	★★★
Don Jose (Baja Expeditions), Baja Explorador	Hotel Palmilla (Cabo), Hotel Rancho Leonoro, Hotel Punta Pescadero	$1650 LA, AIR $600+ LB	Stick with a US-based dive tour for safety. Live-aboard is best, but major East Cape hotels have good gear and decent divemasters. June to November is best for large schooling species.	★★★
Belize Aggressor, Belize Explorer	Turneffe Lodge, Lighthouse Reef Resort	$1295 LA $750+ LB	Massive drop-offs. Richest fish diving in Caribbean. Excellent coral and good numbers of large pelagics. Remote islands are best.	★★★★
Antilles Aggressor	Capt. Don's Habitat, Sand Dollar Condos	$650 LB $1295 LA	One of the better Caribbean areas for visibility and a wide variety of fish, good drop-offs. Stay away from the reefs near the major hotels.	★★★
Truth Aquatics, Scuba Lover	Live-aboard Only	$350 LA 4-day	This is probably the best dive area on the West Coast of the US. Weekends can be crowded. For lobster and abalone, look no further.	★★
Little Cayman Diver, Cayman Aggressor, Gulfstream	Hyatt Regency (Grand), Tiara Beach Hotel (Brac), Pirate's Point (Little Cayman)	$1100+ AIR	Little Cayman has the best diving by far, other than by live-aboard, but the other islands have the nicest resorts. Not many fish, but the Caymans remain Carib's best destination. Great nightlife.	★★★★
Okeanos Aggressor Undersea Hunter	Coro Bici, San Jose	$1995 (10 days)	Ultimate big-animal adventure for experienced deep-water divers. Don't expect much near surface. Featured in Cousteau TV specials.	★★★★
NA	Casa Del Mar La Ceiba	$270+	Over-dived but still fun, and a major bargain, if you go with a package. Almost all drift diving--the current does all the work. Choose a shop such as Caribbean Divers that has fast boats to the reefs.	★★★
Fantasea II, Ghazala	Sharm El Sheik hotels	$750 LB $1600 LA	Sharm El Sheik remains the focus of Red Sea diving. Visibility and the sea life are great in the summer, but winter can be quite poor.	★★★
Pacific Nomad, Matagi Princess	Dive Taveuni, Namale Plant., Na Koro Resort	$1800 LB, AIR $1400 LA	Fiji is still an unspoiled paradise. The people are wonderful. Consider a live-aboard to explore smaller islands and outer reefs.	★★★★★
Admiral Dive	Casa Marina, Quality Inn	$650-$1100LB	Wreck diving is superb throughout the Keys, and corals are surprisingly good. Visibility and fish populations aren't great. Good reefs include Crocker, Alligator, Molasses and Sombrero.	★★★
Encantada (Best), Lammer Law	Live-aboard Only	$1750	Extraordinary mass and variety of sea creatures. Where else can you swim with iguanas and penguins? Don't expect vivid coral though.	★★★★
Not Recommended	Old Lahaina Pl. Inn	$650 incl. car	Maui is a multi-sport paradise. Dive one day and windsurf the next. Coral is abundant, and the package prices can't be beat.	★★
Kona Aggressor	King Kamehameha, Kona Reef	$550 incl. car, $1500 LB	Dive mornings to avoid the tradewinds. Kaiwi Point offers caverns and arches. Dive Makai is superb--very skilled and conscientious.	★★★
NA	Bungalow lodging	$2300 (11 days incl. airfare)	Sipadan may be the last great diving frontier. Consisting of a massive 2,800' seamount, expanding at the top, it is a marine life magnet. Superb diving right off the beach. Summer visibility has declined.	★★★★★
Ghanima (Call Trop. Adv. 800-247-3483)	Hemingway's (Malindi), Shimoni Reef Hotel	$850 LB	Dolphins, mantas, whale sharks and other big sea creatures abound. Clouds of reef fish at Penba Island. Still undiscovered.	★★
Sun Tamarin	Palau Pacific, Marina Hotel	$1500 LB $1695 LA	Incoming tide brings clear water and truly spectacular wall diving. Large schools of fish, sharks and rays. Great diversity of dive sites.	★★★★
Telita (best)--book 18 months ahead, Taleo, Tambu	Walindi Plantation	$900, $2750 LA (11 days)	A true diving frontier. Action-packed with more sea life, more coral per dive than almost anywhere. PNG topside is also a great cultural experience, but land resorts are unreliable--things go wrong.	★★★★
Lady of the Sea Tristar (See & Sea)	Live-aboard Only	$900+ LA	Tubbataha is on many top 10 lists. The coral is stunning, while the volume of fish, especially at night, is phenomenal.	★★★★

LOCATION	SITE DESCRIPTION	WATER TEMP. & VISIBILITY	BEST DIVE SEASON	RECOMMENDED DIVE SHOPS
ROATAN & GUANAJA (BAY ISLANDS)	Noted for wall-diving, plus spur and grove system. Top spots: Mary's Place, Valley of Kings (Coco Resort), and Prince Albert wreck. Great sea fans and sponges.	78-82 55'-90'	All	Posada Del Sol (Resort base)
SABA	The best of the Dutch Antilles. Large fish for the Caribbean; pristine reefs, with good pinnacles and drops. You always need a boat, as reefs are deep and Saba has no beaches.	75-85 70'-125'	All	Sea Saba Dive Ctr.
SEYCHELLES	Fantastic white sand beaches--a tropical paradise. 100 varieties of coral, 900 species of fish. The granite geology offers arches, pinnacles and sheer walls, all covered with brilliant coral. Outer islands (Aldabra) are rich, virgin coral atolls.	70-80 70'-200'	All	Coral Strand Hotel, Desroche Resort
SOLOMON ISLANDS	Everything you could want. Great wall and drift dives, neon coral, many undived WWII wrecks. Large numbers of mantas, sharks and large schooling fish. Outstanding invertebrate life makes for great night dives.	75-80 70'-150'	All	Only remote villages
ST. VINCENT & GRENADINES	Thirty-three islands and cays. Vertical walls, caves and big reefs, most virtually untouched by divers. St. Vincent has black sand beaches, waterfalls, nightlife.	70-80 30'-80'		Dive St. Vincent (809) 457-4714
SUDAN (RED SEA)	Big walls, covered with soft corals, hammerheads, mantas, incredibly profuse reef fish. One of the top three places in the world in all categories--color, clarity, big animals, steep walls, numbers of fish. Live-aboards depart from Sharm El Sheik, Egypt.	73-83 90-150'	May-Oct	None recommended
THAILAND	The Similan Islands and Angthong Marine Park are undiscovered gems. Crystal water, abundant coral, and wild granite and limestone formations. No crowds ever.	70-82 70'-150'	Mar-Oct	Andaman Sea Diving, Koh Samui Divers
TRUK	Truk Lagoon offers spectacular wreck diving. Feb, Mar, Sept and Oct have best visibility, but June through Sept is the calmest period. 90 divable wrecks.	80 80'-150'	All	Blue Lagoon, Micronesia Aquatics
TURKS & CAICOS	General Caribbean reef life, good drop-offs, nice shallows, fine beaches, great place to combine beachcombing/sun worshiping with diving.	75-80 90'-125'	Mar-Nov	Divi Resorts (Peter Hughes)

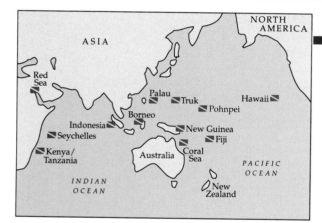

WORLD DI

Australia

Pro Dive, Marlin Parade, P.O. Box 5551, Cairns, QLD, Australia 4870, phone and FAX: (011 61) 70 519915.
Deep Sea Divers Den, Cairns, QLD, Australia, (011 61) 70 312223; FAX: (011 61) 70 311210. PADI 5-Star.
Down Under Dive, Cairns, QLD, Australia, (011 61) 70 311288; FAX: (011 61) 70 311373, or call Sea Safaris (800) 821-6670, in US.
Coralita, Cairns, QLD, Australia, (011 61) 70 546398 (Live-aboard). Very popular. Advance booking required.
Si Bon, Port Douglas, QLD, Australia, (011 61) 70 985195 (Live-aboard). Outstanding. Book well in advance.
Mike Ball's Dive Exped., 252 Walker Street, Townsville, QLD, Australia 4810, (011 61) 77 723022; FAX: (011 61) 77 212152. Superb dive boats, but fairly expensive.

Bahamas

Bottom Time Adventures (Live-aboard catamaran), P.O. Box 11919, Ft. Lauderdale, FL 33339, (800) 234-8464.
Crown Diver/Crown Islander (Live-aboard), (800) 841-7447.
Divi Bahamas Resort (Peter Hughes Diving Center), 54 Gunderman Road, Ithaca, NY 14850, (800) 333-3484.
Neal Watson's Undersea Adven., Bimini, (800) 327-8150.
UNEXSO (Underwater Explorers Society), P.O. Box F2433, Freeport, Bahamas, (800) 992-3483, or (809) 373-1244.

Baja, Mexico

Amigos Del Mar, P.O. Box 43, Cabo San Lucas, Baja, Mexico, (800) 447-8999, (011 684) 30505. Oldest Cabo dive shop.
Baja Expeditions (Live-aboard), 2625 Garnet Avenue, San Diego, CA 92109, (800) 843-6967. Baja's best diving--based in La Paz.
Hotel Rancho Leonoro (Buena Vista), write to P.O. Box 2573, Canoga Park, CA 91306, (818) 703-2049.

Belize

Aggressor Fleet Ltd. (Live-aboard), Drawer K, Morgan City, LA 70831, (800) 348-2628.
Aquanaut Explorer, (305) 491-0333 (Live-aboard).
Journey's End Caribbean Club, P.O. Box 13, Ambergris Caye, Belize, C.A., (800) 541-6796; FAX: (011 501) 26 2028.
Turneffe Island Lodge, (800) 338-8149.
Lighthouse Reef Resort, P.O. Box 40915, Houston, TX 77240, (800) 423-3114.

California (Channel Islands)

Divers' Den, 22 Anacapa Street, Santa Barbara, CA 93101, (805) 963-8917.
Truth Aquatics (Live-aboard), Sea Landing, Breakwater, Santa Barbara, CA 93109, (805) 962-1137.
Sport Chalet Divers, University Towne Center, La Jolla, CA, (619) 552-0712, (800) 722-7166, and 9 other locations.

Cancun/Cozumel

Scuba Cancun, P.O. Box 517, Q. Roo 77500, Mex. (011 988) 3 10 11. (Only PADI 5-Star in Cancun).
Caribbean Divers, P.O. Box 191, Cozumel, Q. Roo, Mexico, (011 52) 987 21080; FAX: (011 52) 987 21426.
Dive Paradise, c/o Trop. Advent., 111 2nd North, Seattle, WA 98109, (800) 247-3483. American-run, quality shop, but older boats.
Fantasia Destinations, (800) 336-3483. Large, roomy boats; good divemasters.
Scuba Shack (Dive Cozumel), 241 Ave. Melgar, Cozumel, Q. Roo, Mexico, (800) 231-9707, in Texas (713) 772-4500.

Cayman Islands

Don Foster's Dive Grand Cayman, P.O. Box 151, Grand Cayman, Cayman Islands BWI, (809) 949-7025; FAX: (809) 949-8651.

Peter Hughes Dive Tiara, Divi Resort, Steak Bay, P.O. Box 238, Cayman Brac Island, BWI, (800) 367-3484.
Little Cayman Diver (Live-aboard), Brac Aquatics, P.O. Box 28008, Tampa, FL 33682, (800) 458-2722; FAX: (813) 935-2250.
Quabbin Dives, P.O. Box 157 George Town, Grand Cayman, BWI, (809) 949-5597.
Ron Kipp's/Bob Soto's Diving Ltd., P.O. Box 1801, Grand Cayman, (800) 262-7686. (Bargain package tours.)

Costa Rica

El Ocotal Resort, c/o Pioneer Tours, P.O. Box 22063, Carmel, CA 93922, (800) 388-2107; FAX: (408) 626-9013.
Okeanos Aggressor, (Live-aboard), (504) 384-0817.

Egypt

Sinai Divers, See & Sea Travels, (800) 348-9778, or Tropical Adventures, (800) 247-3483.

Fiji

Beqa Divers, G.P.O. Box 777, Suva, Fiji, (011 679) 361 088, FAX: (011 679) 301 717.
Dive Taveuni, P.O. Matie, Taveuni, Fiji, (011 679) 680 441.
Matagi Island Diving, Box 83, Waiyevo, Taveuni, (800) 247-3483.
Matagi Princess, (Live-aboard), (011 679) 880 260.
Pacific Nomad, (Live-aboard), (800) GO-2FIJI.

Florida Keys

Divers Unlimited, 6023 Hollywood Boulevard, Hollywood, FL 33024, (305) 981-0156. PADI 5-Star; prize-winning training.
Key West Divers, US1 Stock Island, Key West, FL 33040, (800) 87-DIVER. Generally considered the best in Key West.
Divers Den Key Largo, 110 Ocean Drive, Key Largo, FL 33037, (800) 527-DIVE, (305) 451-DIVE. PADI 5-Star.
Lady Cyana Divers, P.O. Box 1157, Islamorada, FL 33036, (800) 221-8717. Great boat, friendly staff.
Capt. Chambers Charters, P.O. Box 16633, Key Largo, FL 33037, (305) 451-1805. Excellent service; great skipper/divemaster.

Galapagos

Encantada (Live-aboard) and **Beagle III** (Live-aboard)--Consult See & Sea Travel, or Tropical Adventures.
Lammer Law (95' Live-aboard sailboat), Trimarine, P.O. Box 4065, St. Thomas, VI 00803.

Hawaii

Bubbles Below, 6251 Hauaala Road, Kapaa, HI 96746, (808) 822-3343. A superb small program; dive computers supplied.
Central Pacific Divers, 780 Front Street, Lahaina, Maui, HI 96761, (800) 551-6767, PADI 5-Star. Complete packages from $579.
Dive Makai, P.O. Box 2955, Kailua-Kona, HI 96740, (808) 329-2025.

COURTESY CARL ROESSLER, SEE & SEA TRAVEL

Recommended Live-aboards	Accommodations	Package Cost Per Week	Comments	Rating
Bay Isl. Aggressor, Reef Runner	Posada Del Sol, CoCo View, Romeo's Reef Resort	$700 LB $1200 LA	White sand beaches and lush jungles; all Carib corals abound. Great for novices with crevices, caves and drop-offs close to surface (30').	★★★
Antil. Aggressor, Sea Dancer, Carib. Expl.	Juliana's Apartments, Captain's Quarters	$1000 LB $1250 LA	Saba is one of the great undiscovered Caribbean dive areas. On a live-aboard, you can also visit the Lesser Antilles and BVI.	★★★★
My Way, Privilege, Fantasea II	Coral Strand Hotel, Des Roche Resort, La Digue	$800 LB $950 LA	No more beautiful islands in the world. Visibility is superb, and you'll see more kinds of fish than you can imagine. Don't miss Amirantes and Aldabra outer isles.	★★★★
Bilikiki	Live-aboard Recommended	$1800 LA $2950 (11 days AIR)	Go here soon before the word is out. Vast numbers of fish. Many virgin reefs and scores of wrecks to explore. The best of Fiji and Truk in one place. Malaria risk is real here. Not for beginners.	★★★★
Landfall Productions	Umbrella Beach Hotel	$799+	St. Vincent and the Grenadines are not the best in the Caribbean, but the diving is still very good and dive sites are not crowded.	★★★
Colona IV (See & Sea Travel)	Live-aboard Only	$2900 (12 days)	The Sudan is truly an ultimate dive destination--and is still an unexplored frontier. Everything's great--the visibility, the fish, the large marine animals and the corals.	★★★★
Andaman Explorer	Any of numerous local bungalows	$350-$700	Southern Thailand is cheap and diving is still relatively rare. Going with a local dive shop is probably the best dive value in the world.	★★★
Thorfinn, Truk Aggressor	Hotel Continental, Christopher Inn, Maramar	$800+ LB $1400+ LA	You'll want to get off Moen Island, where all the hotels are located. Try a 3-island tour with Pohnpei and Palau, or visit Yap for mantas.	★★★★★
Aquanaut, Dancer	Ramada Inn (Caicos), Divi Resort	$1255	Perfect place for couples or familiy to enjoy a vacation in paradise.	★★★

DIRECTORY

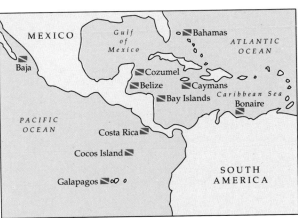

Elite Dives, 67239 B Kahaone Loop, Waialua, Oahu, HI (808) 637-9331. (Oahu and Molokai--luxury dive boat.)
King Kamehameha Divers, 75-5660 Palani Rd., Kailua-Kona, HI 96740, (800) 525-PADI. PADI 5-Star.
Kona Aggressor (Live-aboard), P.O. Box 2097, Kailua-Kona, HI, (800) 344-KONA, or (808) 329-8182. Luxury 85' dive vessel.
Kona Coast Divers, 75-5614 Palani Rd., Kailua-Kona, HI 96740, (800) 562-DIVE. PADI 5-Star.
Maui Dive Shop, P.O. Box 1018, Kihei, Maui, HI 96753, (808) 879-3388; FAX: (808) 871-5179. 6 Locations. PADI 5-Star.

Indonesia
Borneo Divers, (Sipadan Island)--See featured trip.
Dive Indonesia, 3rd Floor, Hotel Borobudur Inter-Continental, Jl. Lapancan Banteng Selatan 1, Jakarta 10110, Indonesia, (011) 62 21 370108 x 76024; FAX: 3803567.
Indonesian Diving Adventures, Bali Mandira Cottages, Kuta, Bali, Indonesia, c/o DIVE Travel, 6151 Orchard Lake Road, Suite 204, West Bloomfield, MI 48322, (313) 851-4008. (Agency)
Tropical Princess (Live-aboard), c/o Poseiden Tours, 359 San Miguel Drive, Newport Beach, CA 92660, (800) 854-9334.

Micronesia
Guam Divers, P.O. Box 3361, Agana, Guam 96910, (011 671) 477-1161; FAX: (671) 477-2775.
Fish n' Fins, (Palau's most established dive shop.) Call US agents (800) 833-SEAS, or (800) 854-9334.
NECO Marine, P.O. Box 129, Koror, Republic of Palau 96940, (011) 6809 1755; FAX: (011) 6809 880.
Yap Divers, P.O. Box 177, Yap, W.C.I. 96943, (011 691) 350 2301, or call Tropical Adventures, (800) 247-3483
Note: You should consult a dive travel agency for a full review of the dive options in Micronesia. Call Trip n' Tour Micronesia, (800) 348-0842, or (800) 843-8956, Innerspace Adventures (800) 833-SEAS, or Tropical Adventures, (800) 247-3483.

Netherlands Antilles (Aruba, Bonaire, Curaçao)
Antilles Aggressor, (Live-aboard), P.O. Drawer K, Morgan City, LA 70381, (800) 348-2628; FAX: (504) 384-0817.
Habitat Dive & Photo (Bonaire), c/o 1080 Port Boulevard, Suite 100, Miami, FL 33132, (800) 327-6709.
Dive Bonaire (Peter Hughes), Divi Flamingo Beach Hotel, (800) 367-3484.
Red Sail Sports, P.O. Box 218, Oranjestad, Aruba, N.A., (011 29) 78 31228; FAX: (011 29) 78 32655; package tours: (800) 255-6425.
Saba Deep Dive Center, P.O. Box 22, Fort Bay, Saba, Netherlands Antilles, (011 599) 4 63347.
Underwater Curaçao, c/o Lions Dive Hotel, Bapor Kibra z/n Curacao, N.A., (800) 451-9376; FAX: (011 599) 9 618200.

Papua New Guinea
Dive Bougainville Pty., Ltd., P.O. Box 661, Arawa, NSP, Papu'a New Guinea, (011 675) 952 595.
Telita (Live-aboard), (011 675) 611186, and Melanesian Explorer (Live-aboard), call Tropical Adventures, (800) 247-2483.

Philippines
Lady of the Sea (Live-aboard), Poseidon Ventures (800) 854-9334 or (714) 644-5344.
Tristar (Live-aboard), call See & Sea Travel, (800) DIV-XPRT.
El Nido Resort (Palawan Island), Ten Knots MR Mezzanine, Makati, Metro Manila, Philippines, (011 632) 810 4101.
Bonito Island Resort, Dive Center, Inc., 2172-B Pasong Tamo Street, Makati, Metro Manila Philippines, (011 632) 819 1158.
Philippine Dive Versions, Gretchen Hutchinson or Edgar Ventura, 1383 Campanilla, Dasmarinas Village, Makati, Metro Manila, Philippines, (011 632) 810 9233.

Puerto Rico
Caribe Aquatic Adventures, San Juan Bay Marina, P.O. Box 2470, San Juan, P.R. 00902, (809) 724-1882. NAUI facility award.
Parguera Divers Training Center, P.O. Box 514, Tr. 304 KM 3.2, Lajas, P.R. 00667, (800) 234-7282, (809) 899-4171. Secluded resort; best wall-diving in Puerto Rico.

Roatan and Bay Islands
Anthony's Key Resort, (800) 227-3483, or (305) 858-3483.
Coco View Resort, Roatan, Bay Islands, (800) 282-8932.
Posada Del Sol Resort, Guanaja, (800) 642-DIVE, (excellent).
Reef Runner (Live-aboard), and resort options, Roatan Charter, Inc., P.O. Box 877, San Antonio, FL 33576-0877.

MEXICO · Gulf of Mexico · Bahamas · ATLANTIC OCEAN · Baja · Cozumel · Belize · Caymans · Bay Islands · Caribbean Sea · Bonaire · PACIFIC OCEAN · Costa Rica · Cocos Island · Galapagos · SOUTH AMERICA

Seychelles
My Way (70' Live-aboard), call (800) 443-0799.
Coral Strand Hotel and Desroche Resort--contact Seychelles Tourist Office, P.O. Box 33018, St. Petersburg, FL 33733.
Ultramarina, 4 Pl. Dumoustier 44000, Nantes, France, FAX: (800) 284-5871. (Agency for all Indian Ocean dive sites.)

Thailand
Fantasea Divers, Box 74, Phuket 83000, Thailand, phone and FAX: (011 66) 76 321 309. US Agent, (800) 443-0799.
Phuket Int'l Diving Center, Coral Beach Hotel, Paton Beach, Phuket, Thailand 83121, (011 66) 76 321, 106 13.
Siam Diving (Phuket), call (800) 821-6670 or (800) 262-6670 in CA.

Truk
Aggressor Fleet Ltd., P.O. Drawer K, Morgan City, LA 70381, (800) 348-2628.
Blue Lagoon Dive Shop, (011) 691 330 2796, (800) 348-0842 in US.
Micronesia Aquatics, (011) 691 330 2204, or contact Tropical Adventures, (800) 247-3483.
Thorfinn, (Live-aboard), (800) 462-9739, or contact See & Sea Travel, (800) 348-9778.

Virgin Islands
Baskin in the Sun, P.O. Box 108, Tortola, B.V.I., (800) 233-7938; FAX: (809) 494-5853. PADI 5-Star. Very good divemasters.
DIVE B.V.I., P.O. Box 1040, Virgin Gorda, B.V.I., (809) 495-5513; FAX: (809) 495-5347. Three shops. PADI 5-Star.
Dive Experience Inc., P.O. Box 4254, Christiansted, St. Croix, USVI 00820, (809) 773-3307. PADI 5-Star.
V.I. Divers, Ltd., Pan Am Pavilion, Christiansted, St. Croix, USVI 00820, (800) 544-5911, (809) 773-6045. PADI 5-Star; since 1971.

TOM CAMPBELL

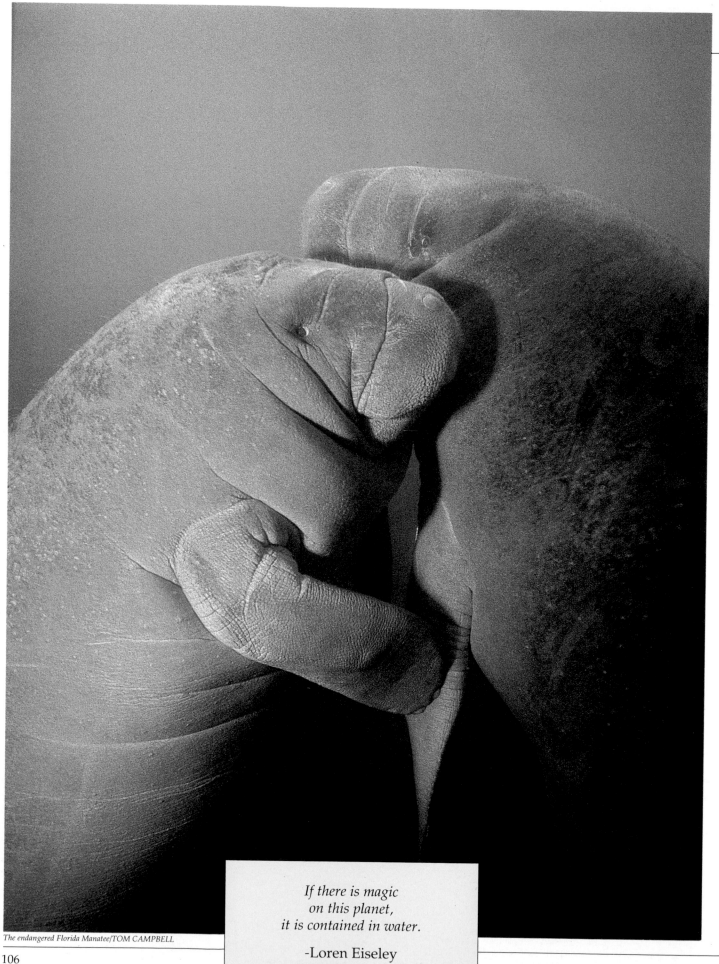

The endangered Florida Manatee/TOM CAMPBELL

*If there is magic
on this planet,
it is contained in water.*

-Loren Eiseley

TOOLS OF THE TRADE

IN GENERAL, DIVE TECHNOLOGY HAS EVOLVED slowly, and the equipment used today is not all that different from the gear employed 15, or even 20 years ago. However, in the past few seasons products have hit the market which promise significant improvements in the quality of sport diving, allowing longer dives, with increased safety margins and reduced waiting periods (surface intervals) between dives.

The Wheel

For decades the PADI dive charts, which calculate the maximum time you can safely spend at a given depth, have been based on US Navy dive tables. These tables assume that the diver reaches his or her maximum depth at the onset of the dive, and then stays there until surfacing. Sport divers, by contrast, typically go to maximum depth, ascend to a lesser depth for a period, then ascend once or twice more before ultimately surfacing. During such a multi-step dive, a diver actually sheds some of the nitrogen he or she absorbed at maximum depth--gradually decompressing during the course of the dive. This permits the diver to stay underwater safely for a longer period of time than had he or she remained at maximum depth the entire dive.

The new PADI Wheel incorporates this principle in its dive tables. To use the Wheel you plan out your dive, selecting the maximum depth (always first), then second deepest, and so on. The Wheel will tell you when to surface, and what surface interval you will require before you can dive again. Using the multi-level dive concept, the Wheel is a breakthrough, allowing longer dives with shorter surface intervals, and more dives in a given day. This can make a real difference in your dive holiday. You can get the Wheel at any PADI dive center.

COURTESY SHERWOOD, INC.

Dive Computers

Submersible Dive Computers (SDCs) use a microprocessor and depth sensor to gauge how long a diver can safely remain at a given depth. After he surfaces, the computer calculates surface intervals to assist dive planning. Use of an SDC will permit the sport diver the maximum safe dive times underwater, and will reduce surface intervals dramatically. On tropical dive trips where most diving is done between the surface and 40 feet, a diver using an SDC may be able to do six or seven dives a day. Using the older PADI tables, he might be limited to four or five. Use of the SDC simplifies dive planning; however, you should always work out your dive profiles manually, and never rely on the SDC exclusively.

Good dive computers remain expensive ($400 and up), but if you do more than 20 dives per year you *should* purchase one. Below we list the popular dive computers and their important features. We recommend models that will log at least seven dives, and fit in a standard console.

High-Capacity Air Tanks

Virtually all scuba tanks in use today, both steel and aluminum, are filled to a safe level of 3,000 psi. Depending on overall size, 65 and 80 cubic inches being the most common, such tanks will allow the average diver 45 to 60 minutes on one fill. With the advent of the Sherwood Genesis 3,500 psi scuba tank, divers can now carry roughly 15 percent more air for a given tank volume. Moreover, since Genesis tanks are smaller and lighter than conventional designs-- a Genesis 100 is no larger than a standard 80--a diver can go up one tank size in volume with no increase in weight or bulk. All this means that a diver who gets 60 minutes from an aluminum 80 could stay down 85 minutes using a Genesis tank of the same physical size and heft.

The other big benefit of the Genesis system is that all but the largest (120) size tanks are neutral or negatively bouyant. By contrast, an aluminum 80 has 3.3 pounds of positive bouyancy, which must be countered with additional lead on your weight belt. The Genesis system thus allows you to dive longer, and carry significantly less lead--a real boon when you're hauling yourself back on board. What are the drawbacks of the Genesis? First, many domestic and most foreign dive shops cannot yet fill to 3,500 psi. Second, you must buy Sherwood's Genesis first stage to handle the higher pressure, so the bottle is not your only expense.

DIVE COMPUTER COMPARISON CHART

Model and Price	Mounting	Elapsed time/depth/ No Decom. Time Remaining	Dive Memory	Water Activated	Ascent Alarm	Air Supply	Safe Fly	Batt. Life	Max Depth	Decom. Dives
Beuchat Aladdin Pro $625	wrist or console	Yes/Yes/Yes	9 dives no limit	Yes	Yes	No	Yes	5 yrs.	330	Yes
Dacor Micro Brain Pro Plus, $610	wrist or console	Yes/Yes/Yes	6 dives 48 hours	Yes	No	No	No	Rech.	130	Yes
Sherwood Source $450	wrist or console	Yes/Yes/Yes	7 dives no limit	No	Yes	No	Yes	3 yrs.	249	Yes
Orca Edge $715	separate unit	Yes/Yes/Yes	no log	No	No	No	No	NA	160	Yes
Orca Skinny Dipper Mark II, $425	separate unit	Yes/Yes/Yes	no log	No	Yes	No	Yes	600 hrs.	130	Yes
Orca Delphi $649	console with air pressure	Yes/Yes/Yes	3 dives	Air start	Yes	Yes	Yes	NA	130 or 300	Yes
Sunto SME-EL $500	wrist or console	Yes/Yes/Yes	10 dives no limit	Yes	Yes	No	Yes	1,000 hrs.	190	Yes
Tekna Computek $650	console with air pressure	Yes/Yes/Yes	10 dives no limit	Air start	Yes	Yes	Yes	4 yrs.	250	Yes
U.S. Divers' Monitor II, $630	wrist or console	Yes/Yes/Yes EBT	9 dives no limit	Yes	Yes	No	Yes	5 yrs.	300	Yes
U.S. Divers' Datascan III, $725	console with air pressure	Yes/Yes/Yes EBT	no log	Air start	Yes	Yes	Yes	6,000 hrs.	165	Yes

Note: The prices are suggested retail. Where both wrist and console models are offered, the lower price was given. (Console models cost $100-$125 more on average.) Many of these computers offer other features such as water temperature, graphic readouts of nitrogen content, and dive profiles. The most significant extra feature in day-to-day diving is the extended bottom time (EBT) offered by the U.S. Divers. By using Rogers and Powells' six-tissue tables, rather than the standard Navy three-tissue tables, these computers are less conservative when calculating bottom-time limits for multi-level dives.

Dive Travel Agencies

THE FOLLOWING AGENCIES CAN BOOK LAND-BASED OR LIVE-ABOARD DIVE vacations worldwide, handling everything from air transport to lodging. They offer a valuable service, particularly for the most far-flung dive venues. Some, such as See & Sea, specialize in live-aboards, while others, such as Island Dreams, focus on major land resorts. Don't assume that even the best agencies have in-depth knowledge of foreign dive operations, and remember that agencies are middlemen--you can often save money by contacting foreign dive shops directly. For example, a 4-day Barrier Reef trip booked in Cairns, Australia, was 20 percent cheaper than similar trips offered by US agencies.

■ **INNERSPACE ADVENTURES,** *13393 Sorrento Drive, Key Largo, FL 34644, (800) 833-SEAS; FAX: (813) 596-3891. Destinations: Bahamas, Bay Islands, Belize, Cancun, Caymans, Cozumel, Dry Tortugas, Roatan, Truk, Palau, Yap.*

Innerspace is a serious dive agency, with a 20-year track record. Micronesia and the Caribbean are its specialties. Every staff member is a diver, and Innerspace arranges many custom tours for dive shops and clubs. Innerspace offers good values, as it favors smaller resorts over the big-name luxury resorts. Its prices, often 5 percent less than the competition, are particularly good for Micronesia. Innerspace's trips are almost exclusively land-based.

Destinations ★★★	Dive Expertise ★★★
Live-aboard (Only Tortugas)	Value ★★★★
Land-based ★★★	Service ★★

■ **ISLAND DREAMS TRAVEL,** *7887 Katy Freeway, Suite 105, Houston, TX 77024, (800) 346-6116. Destinations: Belize, Bonaire, Caymans, Cozumel, Roatan/Bay Islands.*

Island Dreams sends divers by the thousands to the major dive meccas of the western Caribbean. Representing a host of resorts, they offer some very low-priced packages if you're looking for a land-based resort vacation, and don't mind seeing lots of other divers. Choose another agency if you want to dive an exotic, remote destination.

Destinations ★★★	Dive Expertise ★★★
Live-aboard ★★	Value ★★★★
Land-based ★★★	Service ★★★

■ **LANDFALL PRODUCTIONS,** *1055 Monroe St., Santa Clara, CA 95050, (800) 525-3833, (408) 246-4710 in CA; FAX: (408) 983-0677. Destinations: Baja, Bay Islands, Belize, Bonaire, BVI, Caymans, Cozumel, Fiji, Galapagos, Micronesia, St. Vincent, Grenadines, St. Lucia.*

Landfall Productions is a newer specialty agency offering value-oriented, land-based and live-aboard trips to most of the world's leading dive sites. Being new, Landfall doesn't have the site knowledge of the older agencies, but it offers some very good deals, and has exclusives on certain Caribbean locations.

Destinations ★★★	Dive Expertise ★★★
Live-aboard ★★	Value ★★★
Land-based ★★★	Service ★★

■ **SEA SAFARIS TRAVEL, INC.,** *3770 Highland Avenue, Suite 102, Manhattan Beach, CA 90266, (800) 821-6670, or (800) 262-6670 in CA. Destinations: Australia, Baja, Bay Islands, Belize, Bonaire, Caymans, Cozumel, Curaçao, Fiji, Indonesia, Micronesia, Philippines, New Guinea, Red Sea, Thailand.*

Sea Safaris, one of the largest dive travel agencies, books international dive trips for individuals, dive shops and travel agents. This is a good place to start if you want all the options worldwide. All staffers are divers, and most are fairly knowledgeable. However, the service could be improved--you sometimes have to call two or three times to get what you need.

Destinations ★★★★★	Dive Expertise ★★★
Live-aboard ★★★	Value ★★★
Land-based ★★★	Service ★★

■ **SEE & SEA TRAVEL SERVICE, INC.,** *50 Francisco Street, Ste. 205, San Francisco, CA 94133, (800) 348-9778, or (415) 434-3400. Destinations: Australia, Bay Islands, Belize, Bonaire, BVI, Caymans, Cozumel, Curaçao, Fiji, Galapagos, Indonesia, Micronesia, Philippines, New Guinea, Thailand.*

Carl Roessler's See & Sea is a full-service agency devoted exclusively to divers. It specializes in first-class live-aboards in the world's best dive sites. See & Sea is probably the best choice for Micronesia and Red Sea live-aboard trips. This is one agency we would use ourselves, particularly for a remote dive venue, such as the Sudan or the Solomons. See & Sea tours are aimed at active, serious divers, not those looking for a Club Med-type holiday.

Destinations ★★★★	Dive Expertise ★★★★
Live-aboard ★★★★	Value ★★★
Land-based ★★★	Service ★★★

■ **TROPICAL ADVENTURES,** *111 Second Avenue North, Seattle, WA 98109, (800) 247-3483, (206) 441-3483 in WA. Destinations: Africa, Australia, Baja, Belize, Bonaire, Borneo, Caymans, Costa Rica, Cozumel, Fiji, Galapagos, Hawaii, Indonesia, Micronesia, New Guinea, Red Sea, Seychelles, Solomons.*

With two decades of experience, Tropical Adventures (TA) is one of the first agencies we would call. TA has pioneered tours to many exotic dive venues, and is the only agency offering regularly scheduled trips to East Africa. Tropical Adventures consistently uses the best resorts and live-aboards. You'll find president Bob Goddess knowledgeable and helpful, but there have been complaints about unresponsive office staff.

Destinations ★★★★★	Dive Expertise ★★★★
Live-aboard ★★★★	Value ★★★
Land-based ★★★★	Service ★★

SCUBA DIVING

WHAT TO BRING

The biggest problem facing globe-trotting divers is choosing how much of their own gear to bring along. Dive equipment is bulky, heavy, and difficult to stow in hard luggage capable of withstanding rough treatment by airline baggage handlers. If you're planning a trip to a remote destination, you should really make an effort to limit the amount of gear you bring, even if it breaks your heart not to pack that new hot-pink weight belt you just bought.

Essential Equipment

Mask and Snorkel. Keep them in plastic boxes for protection, and bring a spare mask if you're a hard fit.

Dive Watch and Compass. Keep a cheap, plastic 50m waterproof watch as a back-up timer. Tape your compass to protect the crystal in transit.

Lycra Skinsuit. When diving in the tropics, a skinsuit is all that most people need. Skinsuits offer a bit of warmth, and vital protection when swimming around coral. You can mail-order one for under $60.

Bouyancy Compensator/Backpack (BC). Most dive shops or boats supply BCs but they are often worn-out, don't fit well and sometimes leak. BCs aren't cheap, but you won't regret the investment.

Dive Computer. After your air pressure gauge, this is your most vital piece of gear. Few dive shops in distant locales will have rentals available, so bring your own.

Lights. Always carry a high-quality lamp, even on day dives. It will help illuminate your gauges in murky water. Chemical light sticks serve as useful running lights on night dives.

Gloves. Though gloves are essential when diving around coral, most dive boats don't carry spares. Bring both a neoprene set, and a lighter cloth pair for the tropics.

Optional Equipment

Regulator. Almost all dive operators can provide regulators, equipped with octopuses in most cases. If your rental regulator doesn't breath easy and reliably,

MARTY SNYDERMAN

insist on a better one until you are satisfied.

Fins. Premium hard fins are heavy and bulky. For most boat dives, rental fins are fine, since you enter the water where you want to be and don't need the extra kicking power. For shallow dives, we even prefer the cheap, slip-on rubber fins which are comfortable, and protect your heel.

Gauges (depth, air pressure). A faulty air pressure gauge is very rare. However, we have seen many depth gauges that were unreliable. You may want to bring your own if you don't have a dive computer.

Things to Leave Home

Weight Belts. It is pointless to bring weights with you. You can always get them at your destination.

Full Wetsuits. A skinsuit is all you need in the tropics; and you can always borrow a top if you need one.

Air Tanks. Bringing your own bottle has little value since you will be using as many as seven tanks a day on a good trip.

Bulky Camera Equipment and Spearguns. Rent what you need near the end of your holiday. The hardware will only complicate things at first.

AIR TRAVEL

If you are taking your own tanks to your dive site, they should be carried empty, and some airlines will insist that all valving be removed. You should hand-carry all gauges and other fragile items on board. A broken mask or busted camera can ruin your whole vacation.

From a safety standpoint, it's undesireable to dive after flying; jetlag can leave you at less than peak performance. On the other hand, never take an airplane flight within 24 hours after your last dive. Flying at altitude in a low-pressure environment can cause decompression sickness if you have excess residual nitrogen in your blood. Always wait a day before you fly.

BOOKS & VIDEOS

Pisces Books' **Diving and Snorkeling Guides** are the leading dive sports resources for Hawaii, the Cayman Islands, the Virgin Islands, the Florida Keys, Bonaire and Curaçao. Available at dive shops and larger bookstores.

The **Encyclopedia of Recreational Diving**, from PADI, tells you all you need to know about the technical side of the sport and reviews top dive sites worldwide. Order from PADI, 1251 East Dyer Road, #100, Santa Ana, CA 92705.

Sea Fans Video Magazine provides 90-minute video reviews of dive sites around the world including Bonaire, Kauai, Maui, Saba, Honduras, Puerto Rico, Marianas, Palau, the Caymans, Truk, Belize, BVI, Cozumel, Red Sea, Bahamas, Guam and USVI. Resorts as well as underwater sites are featured. The tapes are out of production but copies should still be available at many local dive shops.

INSURANCE

Specialized Divers' accident insurance covering decompression sickness, ear problems, emergency evacuation, and miscellaneous diving-related injuries is available from Diver's Alert Network (DAN), (800) 446-2671, or Diver's Security Insurance, (800) 288-4810. We recommend such coverage whenever you are diving in a remote area far from the nearest hospital.

Fishing

DAVID STOECKLEIN

Many men go fishing all their lives without knowing that it is not fish they are after.
--Henry David Thoreau

▼

*A*merica's estimated 45 million anglers spend billions each year on their sport. However, it has long been observed that 10 percent of the fishermen catch 80 percent of the fish. Skill and the right equipment are vital to success, but the key to a rewarding fishing trip is the right fishing hole. Unless you go where the fish are biting, you can spend a small fortune on tackle and still get skunked, no matter what your angling skills. This won't happen if you head to any of the world-class fishing destinations we feature in this chapter.

We have reviewed dozens of fishing publications, and considered the recommendations of some of the world's leading sport fishermen. From this information we've identified more than 50 of the finest river, lake and ocean fishing sites around the world--enough for a lifetime of angling. You'll also find recommended lodges, guides and outfitters. All of the fisheries we've selected are proven winners that should offer some of the best fishing you have ever had.

CHAPTER
8

On the Deschutes, Oregon/ANDY ANDERSON

Y OU DON'T HAVE TO TRAVEL TO THE FOUR CORNERS OF THE GLOBE TO CATCH FISH. However, if you're thinking of devoting your precious annual vacation to angling, you want a destination that delivers the fish reliably, year in and year out. Here are seven such truly superior fisheries--places where you're virtually guaranteed to hook up quality fish in big numbers, even if you're new to the sport.

ALASKA

Where Size Counts

When most city folks head to Alaska on a fishing vacation, they want to catch salmon, preferable very big salmon--Alaskan kings. While there are literally scores of great king salmon fisheries in Alaska, the most accessible, and still one of the most productive destinations is the Kenai River. The Kenai meets the sea at Soldotna, which can be reached easily by car or coach from Anchorage. Despite its notoriety, the Kenai remains Alaska's number one trophy river. Each year the world's largest kings (up to 90 pounds) and hosts of sockeyes return to the Kenai in May, June and July. Call Kenai Peninsula Fishing, (907) 283-2665, to book charter trips and local guides.

Another great destination for salmon fishing is Lake Iliamna. Sockeyes, kings and humpbacks run in great numbers from June through August, the kings ranging up to 50 pounds. Although cheaper options are available, most visitors to Iliamna go the deluxe lodge route, which runs a whopping $2,500 to $3,500 per week. This does usually cover fly-out wilderness fishing and guides. From a fly-out base at Lake Iliamna you can also fish the Lake Clark Wilderness Preserve, as well as Katmai National Park, both superior destinations for salmon, as well as rainbow trout. The leading Iliamna area lodge is the Valhalla,

(907) 276-3569, but there are many other fine, less costly lodges. Call Alaskan Experience at (800) 777-7055, or (907) 276-5425.

If you want trout *and* salmon, head farther north to Lake Creek, famed for its rainbows, as well as its runs of June kings and August silver salmon. Lake Creek is a beautiful, remote waterway running from the slopes of Mt. McKinley 65 miles to the confluence with the Yentna. Salmon often pause for days at the entrance to the creek before heading upstream, or continuing up the glacial Yentna. Ed and Judy Sharpe maintain a simple but lovely lodge, the Wilderness Place. Cost is $1,995 for a week, solid value by Alaska standards. A float trip is a great option here. You can float Lake Creek below the lodge, or run the nearby Good News River. A 7-day float on the Good News is considered one of the best wilderness trips in Alaska. Contact Alaska River Adventures, (907) 276-3418.

If trophy silver salmon is your calling, the Karluk River on windswept Kodiak Island is the place to go. The Karluk has the biggest silver run in Alaska, and it has

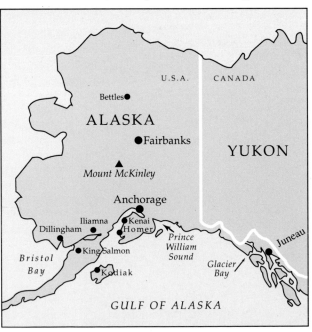

Seven
Ultimate
Fishing
Adventures

yielded virtually every world record silver salmon. The salmon run all summer long, but the biggest silvers often come late, in September, joining the steelhead when the seasons begin to change.

Alaska is far more than a salmon destination, however. For fans of big fish, really big fish, Alaska means halibut. In Alaska, a halibut doesn't get a second glance unless it tips the scales in the hundreds of pounds. How big are they? A 200-pounder can easily measure six feet from side to side. When you first see a large one, it looks as if you have hooked a small submarine. And seasoned halibut fishermen really do take firearms on board to deliver the coup de grace to the giant fish. While you can fish halibut from a

number of ports, Homer is the prime fishery. Day-trips on larger vessels run about $125, while private charters begin at about $200 and can go much higher. If you're lucky, however, you can sell your prize to local canneries. To reserve a spot or arrange a charter, contact Central Charter bookings in Homer, (800) 478-7847, or (907) 235-7847.

CHRISTMAS ISLAND

Bonefishing Mecca

When fishermen agree on anything, it is a noteworthy event. However, anglers acknowledge that the single most prolific bonefishing destination in the world is Christmas Island, a tiny atoll 90 miles north of the Equator and 1,300 miles south of Hawaii. Noted angler Lefty Kreh, writing in the Baltimore Sun comments: "The flats are huge, composed of hard sand and provide good wading. On these flats roam probably the most bonefish you'll see in a lifetime. A good saltwater angler should be able to average at least 20 bonefish a day."

Because of its proximity to the Equator, Christmas Island offers excellent angling year-round. Reflecting tidal conditions, two weeks of each month are noticeably better than the other two, so you should time your arrival accordingly. If you get tired of the flats, try your hand at the off-shore light-tackle fishing. Taking 10 wahoo a day is common, and the good-eating yellowfins are abundant as well.

Trips can be booked with a variety of agencies, including the Fly Shop (800) 669-FISH, and Fishing Int'l, (800) 950-4242.

Package trips start at $1,900 per week including round-trip airfare from Honolulu.

MONTANA

Classic American Streams

Montana is the heartland of American trout fishing. Here you will find more excellent streams and first-rate outfitters than in the rest of the Rockies combined.

Among Montana's many blue-ribbon trout rivers, the Big Horn may be the class of the field. With a population of 5,200 fish per mile, in less than 10 years it has earned a reputation as one of the most productive fly-fishing destinations in the Lower 48. The Big Horn is accessible to the general public, though you may want to hire a guide, both to help you choose the best flies, and lead you to the river's most productive sections. Contact the Big Horn Trout Shop, (406) 666-2375, or Quill Gordon Fly Fishers, (406) 666-2253, both in Ft. Smith. For riverside lodging, nothing tops the Royal Bighorn Lodge. A 3-day package, including guided float trips, costs about $700. Book through the Fly Shop, (800) 669-FISH.

Another legendary Montana trout destination is the Big Hole River area. Here you can fish the Big Hole itself, as well as a half-dozen other top streams including the Beaverhead, the Upper Clark Fork and the Wise. Craig Fellin's Big Hole Outfitters, based 45 minutes south of Butte, runs one of the best operations around. A recent customer said, "Excellent fishing in magnificent country, with topnotch guides and first-rate accommodations." Cost is about $1,400 per head for 6 days and 5 nights. Late June to July is generally the best time, although the trout bite all summer. Book through Frontiers, (800) 245-1950. Another top spot is the Madison River, which is best fished in June. The first few miles below Earthquake Lake are particularly productive. An outstanding guide on the Madison is Mike Lawson of Henry's Fork Anglers, (208) 624-3595.

Before you head off to Big Sky country, pick up a copy of the *Montana Angling Guide* by Chuck Fothergill and Bob Sterling. It provides detailed maps of all the classic fishing holes, and many little-known spots as well. A companion book for Wyoming is available. We also recommend *The Fabulous Bighorn with Gary Borger*, a 60-minute float trip video. In this $40 travelogue, Borger demonstrates both basic and expert fly preparation and casting techniques.

DAVID STOECKLEIN

New Zealand's South Island/NATHAN BILOW

NEW ZEALAND

Wild Trout of the Southern Alps

For many trout fishermen, New Zealand represents the pinnacle of fly-fishing. New Zealand boasts scores of great rivers and crystalline spring creeks teeming with wild trout. Despite its many attractions, however, New Zealand is less than ideal for novices. Kiwi trout are notoriously shy, and a novice fly-fisherman, even one who has paid thousands to fish at a top lodge, can come away frustrated. Still, few places combine trophy angling with unspoiled natural beauty as well as New Zealand.

The South Island is recognized as the country's angling mecca, though fewer than 6,000 foreign fishermen make the journey each year to the trophy-laden streams of the Southern Alps. Among the many great South Island lodges, the Lake Rotorua Lodge is hard to beat. Here, in scenic Nelson Lakes National Park, you can catch truly big fish on 42 different streams. (The average trout caught last year weighed 4.49 pounds.) Another superior South Island haunt is the Lake Brunner Lodge which boasts many world-class spring creeks. If only the ultimate will do, head to Dick Fraser's Cedar Lodge. Located on the banks of the Makarora River near Mt. Aspiring National Park, the lodge caters to just eight anglers a week, and employs bush planes, helicopters, jeeps and even jetboats to ac-cess some of New Zealand's most pristine trout waters. Cost is a mind-numbing $3,000 per week, including fly-outs.

If you have time to visit the North Island, head to Lake Taupo. There you can either hire a local guide, or fish on your own. (Ask the local shops for recommended trout streams and flies.) If you prefer a deluxe lodge try Tony Hayes' Tongariro Lodge, which has rights to the major outlet from Lake Taupo. Another top North Island lodge is the Poronui Ranch, near the Rangitiki, the North Island's major wilderness river. With private access to the Mohaka River, guests can count on some of the most prolific brown trout fishing in the country. To book any of the lodges listed, call Frontiers, (800) 245-1950,

DAVID STOECKLEIN

or the Fly Shop, (800) 669-FISH.

We feel compelled to add that the fishing scene in New Zealand is not only for the rich. Don't be put off by the prices of the high-end lodges. The locals can't afford such places either, but they still manage to catch plenty of trout. Many great trout streams can be reached by 4WD vehicle, or on foot over New Zealand's extensive network of wilderness trails. You'll find the ever-friendly Kiwis more than willing to direct you to the best spots.

COSTA RICA

Billfishing Paradise

For many, big game fishing means one thing--billfish. For years Kona was known as a top destination, only to be supplanted by Baja. The bad news is that the marlin are thin in Cabo too these days. However, if you head south to Costa Rica's Pacific Coast you will find a sail and marlin fishery far better

than Hawaii or Mexico even in their heydays.

Nothing is ever guaranteed in the world of angling. Or is it? At Costa Rica's Golfito Sailfish Rancho, owners Jon and Ginny Kollman are so sure that you'll catch a billfish if you fish at least three days, that they offer free lodging on a return trip within the next 12 months for those who missed out the first time. Although the Golfito Lodge is relatively new, the waters around Golfito have long been recognized as one of the world's richest billfishing areas. Seven major rivers and 25 smaller streams empty into the Golfo Dolce providing a natural hatchery for small baitfish which attract the billfish in great numbers. Along with blue marlin, sailfish, roosterfish and amberjack are plentiful. A week's stay, with 5 days fishing, starts at about $1,600.

An equally good billfishery is the Gulf of Papagayo to the north. Blue and black marlin are abundant and the sailfishing is considered by many to be the world's best. Anglers can expect 10 to 30 billfish shots a day with multiple hook-ups a regular occurrence. A recent visitor reports: "This is a great place for sailfish--we caught 19 sailfish in three days, nine our first day. We raised about 40 sailfish and two marlin, landing one blue that was about 250 pounds. There is also great light-tackle fishing for dorado, wahoo and yellowfin."

The leading resort in the Papagayo Gulf is Mark Tupper's Bahia Pez Vela, (800) 327-2880. It offers serious anglers a high-tech fishing program with deluxe onshore facilities. We also recommend Flamingo Bay Pacific Charters, 1112 E. Las Olas Boule-

vard, Ft. Lauderdale, FL 33301, (800) 654-8006, or (305) 765-1993. Flamingo Bay operates fast, modern 35- to 45-footers. The nearby Flamingo Beach hotel is a lovely, first-class facility. A 7-day package with 4 days of fishing runs about $2,300. Boat charter only costs $450 to $750 per day. Costa Rican holidays can be booked by Fishing International, (800) 950-4242, and PanAngling, (800) 533-4353.

VENEZUELA

The Atlantic's Ultimate

If you're really serious about hooking billfish, look no further than Venezuela. Outstanding catches of white and blue marlin and sailfish have established Venezuela as one of the ultimate destinations for Atlantic billfish. An hour's cruise from shore on the La Guaria Bank, hordes of baitfish and a series of offshore plateaus attract all four of the major Atlantic billfish species. During the fall white marlin season, catches of 10 or more billfish are common, and the coveted Grand Slam--white marlin, blue marlin and sailfish is an everyday possibility. February through March blue marlin predominate, typically weighing in at 300 to 800 pounds. Sailfish and swordfish run year-round.

Along with the great billfishing, expect to take your share of yellowfin tuna, wahoo and dolphinfish. There are a number of local sportfishing boats that can take you out for $350 to $650 per day, or you can book a package trip with the La Guaria Gamefish Club. The Club has speedy twin-diesel sportfish, tournament-rigged with full electronics and the best tackle. The Club can arrrange side trips to Angel Falls, Caracas, or other nearby points of interest. A 5-day

DARRELL JONES

trip with 3 days fishing costs $800 to $1,500 per person, including round-trip air from Miami. (Generally, the bigger the boat, the higher the price.) South Fishing, (800) 333-3347, offers some of the best package deals, but you should also check with Fishing International, Frontiers, and PanAngling as prices can fluctuate. Because La Guaria is so popular, both with foreigners and Caracas' elite, advance reservations are a must. While in Venezuela, you can sample world-class tarpon fishing at Rio Chico, and bone-fishing at Los Roques. (See page 124.)

ARGENTINA
Trout Fishing's Best-kept Secret

During the course of researching this book, we have often been asked where we would go, if we had to choose just one trout-fishing destination. New Zealand was a candidate, but it's best for skilled anglers, and we wanted a place where just about anyone could catch lots of jumbo-sized trout. Montana and Alaska have their merits, but on careful reflection, Argentina gets the nod. One recent visitor said: "The trout fishing in Argentina consists of the best trout water I've ever seen. I'm comparing this to Iceland, Canada, Alaska, Idaho and Montana. I caught 22 rainbows and browns in two pools in three hours. Only six of them were under 15 inches."

Argentine trout fishing is centered along the eastern flank of the Andes near the Chilean border. A good starting point is San Carlos de Bariloche, which can be reached by air from Buenos Aires. The best fishing is found between the city of Esquel, in the province of Chubut, and Junin de los Andes in the province of Neuquen, which is probably the finest venue of all. The best angling is from February to mid-April. You'll find browns, rainbows, brook trout, and a smattering of landlocked salmon. The average size runs about two pounds, with some fish going to eight pounds. Many rivers have lots of action but limited size, similar to Montana, and some are catch and release only. If you do some research and learn some Spanish before you go, there is no reason not to do the trip independently. The best trout fisheries, including

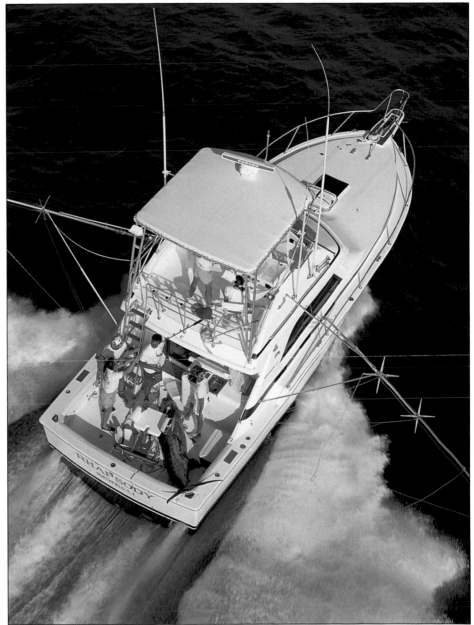

the Caleufu, Correntoso, Limay and Chubut are so productive that you won't come home empty-handed. Of course, you'll catch more fish with a seasoned guide such as Laddy Buchanan. He can be reached at Las Heras 2948 4H, 1425 Buenos Aires, Argentina, (011 54) 1 802 3362.

The Frontiers agency now books a number of superior Argentine itineraries. November through March, renowned guide Kent Schoenauer, who has lived in Argentina for the past two decades, leads 4, 7 and 10-day excursions in the beautiful Los Alcerces Park area. Last season his clients landed brown trout as large as eight pounds, and brooks up to six pounds.

Catch and release tallies of two dozen per day were common. In the San Martin de Los Andes region, Frontiers uses Patagonia Outfitters. This is a full-time professional operation which maintains its own 25,000-acre ranch with 30 kilometers of private beats on the Malleo River. Fishing a half-dozen prolific streams from the ranch base, Patagonia's customers regularly bring 20 or more trout to a rod in a single day.

Frontiers' trips are limited to small groups of anglers, so it's essential to book early. The prices range from about $2,900 to $3,600 with four different itineraries. Contact Frontiers, P.O. Box 161, Wexford, PA 15090, (800) 245-1950.

FRESHWATER DESTINATIONS

DAVID STOECKLEIN

THERE SIMPLY ISN'T ROOM IN THIS BOOK TO LIST ALL THE AREAS WHERE YOU CAN spend an enjoyable weekend and catch your limit. However, for those planning a special fishing vacation, who want to experience the richest, least-spoiled fishing grounds in the world, we have assembled a list of 20 world-class freshwater destinations, places where you'll find an abundance of fish, great scenery, and very little competition from other anglers.

UNITED STATES

ALASKA

▼

Location: Lake Iliamna

Access: Fly-in from Anchorage, AK.

Game Fish and Seasons: Sockeye, king, and humpback salmon (June to Aug), rainbow, 5+ lbs common (June, Sept best).

Lodges and Guides: Alaskan Experience, (800) 777-7055, or (907) 276-5425 (central booking); Valhalla Lodge, P.O. Box 6583, Anchorage, AK 99502, (907) 276-3569; Iliamna River Lodge, 8536 Hartzell Rd., Anchorage, AK 99507, (907) 349-9111.

Fishing Highlights: This is prime salmon country--even novices will hook up. The summer sockeye run brings 50-lb kings. Fly-outs and float trips are included in many lodge deals.

Cost: $2,600-$3,700 per week, all-inclusive; guide only is $200+ per day for two anglers.

Rating: ★★★★

Location: Katmai Wilderness (Brooks, Kulik, King Salmon, & Ukak Rivers, Grosvenor Lake, Lake Nanek)

Access: Fly-in from Anchorage to King Salmon.

Game Fish and Seasons: Sockeye, king salmon (July-Sept), grayling, Dolly Varden, rainbow trout (May-June, Sept-Oct).

Lodges and Guides: Brooks Lodge, Grosvenor Lodge, Kulik Lodge, all c/o Katmailand, Inc., 4700 Aircraft Dr., Anchorage, AK 99502, (800) 544-0551, or (907) 243-5448.

Fishing Highlights: The Katmai region boasts some of Alaska's most renowned lodges.

The guides are first rate. Count on a massive sockeye run every year, and fierce rainbows. The wilderness scenery is fantastic.

Cost: $1,500-$3,000 per week (low price basic cabins, no fly-outs).

Rating: ★★★★

CALIFORNIA

▼

Location: Fall River

Access: Fall River Mills, CA.

Game Fish and Seasons: Rainbow, some browns (Apr-Nov).

Lodges and Guides: The Fly Shop, 4140 Churn Creek Road, Redding, CA 96002, (916) 222-3355, or (800) 669-3474.

Fishing Highlights: Wild trophy trout up to 5 lbs, barbless & artificial lure only; excellent fishing on nearby Hat Creek and McCloud River.

Cost: $1,200 per week--consult the Fly Shop; guide and boat $225 per day for two anglers.

Rating: ★★

COLORADO

▼

Location: Roaring Fork River

Access: Drive from Basalt, CO.

Game Fish and Seasons: Rainbow, brown,

and brook trout (July-Aug).

Lodges and Guides: Frying Pan Anglers, 6692 Frying Pan Road, Basalt, CO 81621, (303) 927-3441.

Fishing Highlights: Probably most productive trout stream in Colorado. Good fishing in nearby Frying Pan River and alpine streams.

Cost: $275 per day float, $180 per day wade trip with guide, two anglers.

Rating: ★★★

FLORIDA
▼

Location: Lake Okeechobee

Access: Okeechobee and Moore Haven, FL.

Game Fish and Seasons: Largemouth bass (Feb-Apr best).

Lodges and Guides: 24 local fishing camps, incl. Calusa Lodge, Rt. 2, Hwy. 78, Moore Haven, FL 33471, (813) 946-0544; Griffin Guides, 26 Canal Way, Okeechobee, FL 34974, (813) 467-4314.

Fishing Highlights: Many 10-lb bass taken on plastic worms. This is America's second largest lake--450,000 acres.

Cost: $1,300 per week with lodging, boat; $150 per day with boat, guide, two anglers.

Rating: ★★

GEORGIA
▼

Location: Lake Seminole

Access: At Bainbridge, GA.

Game Fish and Seasons: Trophy largemouth, striped, hybrid and white bass (Feb-June).

Lodges and Guides: Jack Wingate, Lunker Lodge, Box 3311, Bainbridge, GA 31717, (912) 246-0658.

Fishing Highlights: Striped bass to 50 lbs, bigmouth 10-12 lbs; whites and hybrids on nearby Flint River.

Cost: $250 per week lodging; about $950 with guide & boat; guide $130 per day with two clients.

Rating: ★★

IDAHO
▼

Location: Selway River

Access: Explore the 18 miles from Lowell, ID to Selway Falls campground.

Game Fish and Seasons: Rainbow trout, cutthroat trout, July; best flies are dry Humpy and wet Royal Coachman.

Lodges and Guides: Contact Idaho Outfitters and Guides Assoc., P.O. Box 95, Boise, ID 83701, (208) 342-1438, or (208) 342-1919 (directory).

Fishing Highlights: River access is tightly controlled, preventing over-fishing. The scenery and wildlife are outstanding.

Cost: Guide $125 per day with two anglers; more for overnights.

Rating: ★★★

MICHIGAN
▼

Location: Au Sable River

Access: Drive from Grayling, MI.

Game Fish and Seasons: Rainbow and brown trout, (Apr, May, June). Use dry Dark Cahill and wet Slate Coachman.

Lodges and Guides: Gates Au Sable Lodge and Pro Shop, 471 Stephan Bridge Rd., Grayling, MI 49738, (517) 348-8462.

Fishing Highlights: Michigan's best trout fishing especially from Grayling to Lake Tecon.

Cost: About $1,200 per week all-inclusive with guide; guide only $200 per day for two anglers.

Rating: ★★

MONTANA
▼

Location: Bighorn River

Access: Drive from Fort Smith, MT.

Game Fish and Seasons: Brown and rainbow trout (Apr-May, July-Sep).

Lodges and Guides: Big Horn Trout Shop, P.O. Box 477, Ft. Smith, MT 59035, (406) 666-2375; Quill Gordon Fly Fishers, P.O. Box 597, Fort Smith, MT 59035, (406) 666-2253;

DAVID STOECKLEIN

George Anderson's Yellowstone Angler, 124 N. Main Street, Livingston, MT 59047, (406) 222-7130. Royal Big Horn Lodge, (800) 669-FISH.

Fishing Highlights: 2,700 browns/mile, 7-10 lbs not uncommon. Day floats from Afterbay Dam, or Hardin, MT are recommended.

Cost: Big Horn Lodge, $695 for 3 days; guide $200 per day for two anglers.

Rating: ★★★

NEW MEXICO
▼

Location: San Juan River

Access: 20-mile stretch near Navajo Dam, NM.

Game Fish and Seasons: Rainbow & brown trout, 4-7 lb, and 19" average (Aug-Nov best).

Lodges and Guides: San Juan Troutfitters (Harry Lane), P.O. Box 243, Farmington, NM 87499, (505) 327-9550; Abe's Fly Shop, P.O. Box 6428, Navajo Dam, NM 87419, (505) 632-2194.

Fishing Highlights: Abundant, big trout. San Juan is considered by some to be the best trout stream in the western US--catching 10 five-pounders a day is not uncommon. There are three miles of expert trophy water--barbless hooks, artificial lures, keep only one large (20+") fish per day.

Cost : $35-$60 per night, motel only; $235 per day for float trip, with two anglers and guide.

Rating: ★★

OREGON
▼

Location: Deschutes River

Access: Warm Springs to Maupin, OR.

Game Fish and Seasons: Rainbows on upper (May to June); steelheads on lower river (Aug-Sept, Dec-Jan).

Lodges and Guides: Rick Killingsworth, (503) 389-0607; Dick Rice, (509) 773-4999; Oregon Guides & Packers Assoc., Box 10841, Eugene, OR 97440, (503) 683-9552 (request directory).

Fishing Highlights: Trophy rainbows, but artificials and barbless hooks only.

Cost: Guide and boat $200 per day for two anglers.

Rating: ★★★

PENNSYLVANIA
▼

Location: Fishing Creek

Access: Start at Benton and work up to Grassmere Park.

Game Fish and Seasons: Brown and rainbow trout, (late May-June); best flies are dry Light Cahill, wet Hare's Ear.

Lodges and Guides: Fishing Creek Outfitters, Barry and Cathy Beck, R.D. #1, Box 310-1, Benton, PA 17814, (717) 925-2225.

Cost: $75-$135 guide only.

Fishing Highlights: Fishing Creek wasn't named by accident. This is easily one of the Northeast's most productive trout streams. The Becks also operate an outstanding fly-fishing school here.

Rating: ★★

WASHINGTON
▼

Location: Quinault River

Access: Go upstream from the Graves Creek Campground along the Quinalt and tributaries.

Game Fish and Seasons: Rainbow trout and salmon, (June, July, Sept). Use dry Royal Coachman and wet White Maribou.

Lodges and Guides: A drive-to destination, there are no lodges. Washington Guides Assoc., (206) 472-5558, can suggest local guides.

Fishing Highlights: Catch salmon and trout in the same day.

Cost: Typical guide charges are $150-$200 for two anglers.

Rating: ★★★

WYOMING

▼

Location: Green River

Access: Drive from Pinedale (upper), or Green River (lower), WY.

Game Fish and Seasons: Rainbow and brown trout (Apr-May, Aug-Sept).

Lodges and Guides: Contact High Country Flys, 75 E. Broadway, P.O. Box 3432, Jackson, WY 83001, (307) 733-7210.

Fishing Highlights: The Green is probably the best trout stream in Wyoming. Fish Pinedale to La Barge and below Fontenelle Reservoir. There is also good fishing on the nearby Salt, Snake South Fork, Black Fork and Hams Fork.

Cost: Guides charge $190-$250 per day for two anglers, more for float trips.

Rating: ★★

CANADA

ALBERTA

▼

Location: Bow River

Access: Drive from Calgary.

Game Fish and Seasons: Rainbows and brown trout, (May, July, Sept). Late October is good for browns.

Lodges and Guides: Alberta Drift, 222 Midridge Crescent, Calgary, ALB, Canada T2X 1 C6, (403) 256-9172; Great Waters Alberta (John Andreasen), Box 9071, Station F, Calgary, ALB, Canada T2J 5S7, (403) 271-5460.

Fishing Highlights: Orvis' President Leigh Perkins says the Bow offers the finest dry fly-fishing for rising rainbows in North America; 16-18 inches are abundant, but catch and release applies. The Bow is placid and easily floated in 14' John boats.

Cost: $575 all-inclusive for 4 nights, 3 days; day-trips run $170 per person with boat and guide.

Rating: ★★★★

Location: Amethyst Lake, Tonquin Valley, Jasper Nat'l Park

Access: 250 miles from Calgary, drive to Jasper, then pack in by horse 14 miles.

Game Fish and Seasons: Rainbow and brown trout (July-Sept).

Lodges and Guides: Jasper Wilderness, Tonquin Valley Pack and Ski Trips Ltd., Gordon and Dorothy Dixon, Box 550, Jasper, AB, Canada T0E IE0, (403) 852-3909. (Excellent food; instruction available.)

Fishing Highlights: A little-known secret spot, Amethyst boasts some of the best alpine fly fishing in Canada--rainbows run to 10 lbs, brook trout to 3-4 lbs. Raising 50 catch and release in an afternoon is not uncommon. Nearby Lake Moat offers good dry fly fishing.

Cost: 5 days runs about $450 including food, and horsepack in and out.

Rating: ★★★

QUEBEC

▼

Location: George River/Helen's Falls

Access: Fly from Montreal to Schefferville, Quebec. Helen's Falls is 40 miles upriver.

Game Fish and Seasons: Brook and lake trout (July-Sept), char, Atlantic salmon (Aug-Sept).

Lodges and Guides: Ungava Adventures, 29 Morgan Road, Baie D-Urfe, Quebec, H9X 383, Canada; George River Lodge, P.O. Box 1238, Shafferville, QUE, Canada, (418) 585-3477.

Fishing Highlights: Fantastic August Atlantic salmon runs--15 to 20-lb. fish in great numbers. The remote site means little competition. Bring spinning tackle in July. Herds of caribou migrate across the George River each year.

Cost: $1,600-$3,500 per week.

Rating: ★★★

CHILE

Location: Chilean Andes

Access: South from Santiago to Valdivia

Game Fish and Seasons: Brown & rainbow trout, 3 lbs average (Nov-Apr).

Lodges and Guides: Futaleufu Lodge, and Bloom's Camp--book both through the Fly Shop,

Releasing brown trout on 16-mile Creek, Moudlow, Montana/WILL BREWSTER

(800) 669-FISH; Sportstour, P.O. Box 3300, Santiago, Chile, FAX: (011 56) 2 6982981; Cimalahue Fishing Lodge (Adrian Dufflocq), P.O. Box 2, Lliffen, Chile.

Fishing Highlights: Chile offers great scenery and world-class fishing--30 trout per day is not uncommon. There are many fine streams and lakes within a small radius, and you can easily cross over to fish nearby Argentine hotspots. Futaleufu is a new, American-run lodge limited to four anglers per week. It has miles of private water, serviced by jeeps, horses and drift boats. Cimalahue is an ultra-private retreat with superb fishing.

Cost: $2,500 per week at Futaleufu; Sportstour about $1,500 per week; Cimalahue is about $370 per day for food and lodging only.

Rating: ★★★★

EUROPE

Location: Broadlands (Test Valley), Hampshire, England

Access: Train from London to Romsey.

Lodges and Guides: Lee Park Lodge (formerly estate of Lord Mountbatten). Services provided: Lodging, food, private beats, guides. Contact Frontiers, (800) 245-1950.

Fishing Highlights: England's premier chalk streams, the rivers Test and Itchen, run through Broadlands, a 6,000-acre private estate. Crystalline waters feature free-rising rainbows and browns averaging 16 inches. Experienced anglers can expect to hook 10 to 20 fish per day on dry fly, although the rainbows can be selective.

Cost: $2,975 per week all-inclusive.

Special Attractions: This is an elite, even fabled fishery, frequented by Britain's nobility. The grounds are stunning, and located close to many tourist attractions, including Stonehenge.

Rating: ★★ (fish), ★★★★ (ambience)

Location: Ponoi River, USSR

Access: Ground transport from Murmansk.

Game Fish and Seasons: Atlantic Salmon, late June through September.

Lodges and Guides: Trips are arranged by Frontiers, (800) 245-1950.

Fishing Highlights: This may be the best new Atlantic salmon fishery on the planet. In 1990, 16 anglers landed 1,190 fish during the first two weeks of the season. There are huge numbers of fish, averaging 8 lbs in June, ranging into the 20s in the fall. The action is wild--the salmon attack flies aggressively and fight ferociously when hooked.

Cost: $5,700-$6,000 per week with round-trip air to Murmansk.

Rating: ★★★★

NOTE: Most Americans underestimate the quality of European fishing. France boasts chalk streams equal to Britain's, there is good trout fishing in Austria, the Pyrenees and the Julian Alps, and the salmon fishing in Iceland, Norway and Russia is world class. All these destinations, plus Ireland and Scotland (salmon, sea-trout, trout), are served by agencies such as Fishing International or Frontiers.

ANDY ANDERSON

GREAT AMERICAN FLY FISHING SCHOOLS

FLY-FISHING IS AS MUCH ART AS SPORT, AND IS BEST LEARNED FROM A MASTER. AT THE top schools listed below you can learn basic skills, or refine your technique and correct bad habits you may have picked up learning on your own. Each school offers customized instruction from novice to expert, and most also offer guide services. Typical cost is $100-$125 per person per day without lodging. Codes: Fly-Fishing School (FFS); Casting Instruction (CI); Fly-tying classes (FT); Guiding Services (GS).

NORTHEAST

■ **L.L. BEAN FLYFISHING SCHOOL**, *Casco Street, Freeport, ME 04033, (800) 341-4341, ext. 3100*. FFS, CI, FT. 3-day classes on New England rivers, $375 including equipment, also 4-day intermediate program in Maine, $995 all-inclusive.

■ **THE ORVIS COMPANY, INC.**, *Historic Route 7A, Manchester, VT 05254, (800) 548-9548, or (802) 362-3750*. FFS, CI. 1 to 3-day basic school and specialty classes April through August each year, in four locations in New England, $125-$390.

■ **FISHING CREEK OUTFITTERS**, *R.D. #1, Box 310-1, Benton, PA 17814, (717) 925-2225*. FFS, CI, FT. Weekend clinics, plus classroom sessions, $250 without lodging. Custom instruction--$125 per day.

■ **THE JOAN AND LEE WULFF FISHING SCHOOL**, *HCR 1, Box 70, Main Street, Lew Beach, NY 12758, (914) 439-4060*. FFS, CI. 2-day weekend trout school, and flycasting clinic. Private lessons: (914) 439-3798.

SOUTH

■ **ORVIS ROANOKE INC.**, *Market Square, 19 E. Campbell Ave., Roanoke, VA 24011, (703) 345-3635*. FFS, CI, GS. 2-day clinics on private streams, $300 including tackle; also private lessons, and guide services.

■ **MURRAY'S FLY SHOP**, *Box 156, 121 Main Street, Edinburg, VA 22824, (703) 984-4212*. FFS, CI, FT. 2-day weekend fly-fishing clinics: small-mouth bass, spring creek trout, or mountain trout--$200 with all tackle.

MIDWEST

■ **A.J. BURROWS TROUT & GROUSE**, *300 Happ Road, Northfield, IL 60093, (708) 501-3111*. FFS, CI, FT. 1 and 2-day schools and hourly instruction.

■ **PINE LAKE FLY SHOP**, *17021 Chillicothe Rd., Chagrin Falls, OH 44022, (216) 247-6480*. FFS, CI, FT. 1 and 2-day streamside FFS, $125-$200, lodging extra.

■ **THORNAPPLE ORVIS SHOP**, *P.O. Box 133, Thornapple Village, Ada, MI 49301, (616) 676-0177*. FFS, CI, FT, GS. 2-day, $225 program on the Rogue, richest trout stream east of the Mississippi; 1:1 evening class $100.

ROCKIES

■ **ANDERSON'S YELLOWSTONE ANGLER**, *P.O. Box 660, Highway, 89 South, Livingston, MT 59047, (406) 222-7130*. FFS, CI, GS. 2-day weekend schools, $200 with all tackle, June through August. Guided river trips $225-$240 per day for two anglers.

■ **THE FLYFISHER LTD.**, *252 Clayton Street, Denver, CO 80206, (303) 322-5014*. FFS, CI, FT, GS. 2-day evening class $55, or $55 on-stream Saturday class. Guided river trips $190 per day for two anglers.

■ **HIGH COUNTRY FLYS**, *P.O. Box 3432, 75 East Broadway, Jackson, WY 83001, (307) 733-7210*. FFS, CI, FT, GS. 1-day class $220 for one to four persons. Guided float trips $220-$290 for two anglers.

■ **BOB JACKLIN'S FLY SHOP**, *P.O. Box 310, West Yellowstone, MT 59758, (406) 646-7336*. FFS, CI, FT, GS. 1 and 2-day classes and guided float trips starting at roughly $115 per day per person (two anglers).

■ **MONTANA TROUTFITTERS ORVIS SHOP**, *1716 W. Main St., Bozeman, MT 59715, (406) 587-4707*. FFS, CI, FT, GS. 2-day weekend schools $100 (1 day on-stream). Deluxe 4-day school with float trip, roughly $995 per person, all-inclusive.

■ **SILVER CREEK OUTFITTERS**, *P.O. Box 418, 507 N. Main, Ketchum, ID 83340, (208) 726-5282*. CI, FT, GS. Personalized casting class, $200 per day, $165 half-day, for two anglers.

WEST

■ **THE FLY SHOP**, *4140 Churn Creek Road, Redding, CA 96002, (916) 222-3555, or (800) 669-3474*. FFS, CI, FT, GS. 1-day class $100, 3-day clinic with 2 days on river, $575 with room and board.

■ **KAUFMANN'S STREAMBORN FLY SHOP**, *8861 S.W. Commercial, Tigard, OR 97223, (800) 442-4359, or (503) 639-7004*. FFS, CI, FT, GS. 3-day school on Deschutes River, $390 all-inclusive. 4-day guided float trip, $775 per person. Also Seattle and Bellevue, WA locations, call (206) 448-0601.

■ **MAMMOTH ADVENTURE CONNECTION**, *P.O. Box 353, Mammoth Lakes, CA 93546, (800) 228-4947, or (619) 934-0606*. FFS, CI, GS. 3-day Sierra trout school, May-October, $425 per person with lodging and tackle. Guided trips from $165 per day with lodging.

SALTWATER DESTINATIONS

Bonefishing on the flats, Christmas Island/DAVID STOECKLEIN

HERE IS OUR LIST OF 20 OF THE BEST SALTWATER FISHING DESTINATIONS AROUND the globe. There's a strong foreign emphasis because the best big game fishing is found in the tropics--where warm waters and abundant bait fish attract the big species. In foreign waters, there are also simply fewer anglers competing for the fish. Codes: PA (PanAngling), (800) 533-4353; FI (Fishing International), (800) 950-4242; FRT (Frontiers), (800) 245-1950; WW (World Wide Sportsman), (800) 327-2880.

UNITED STATES

ALASKA

❖

Destination: Cook Inlet/Deep Creek

Game Fish & Season: Jumbo king salmon (mid-May to July); giant halibut to 200 lbs.

Top Lodges & Charters: Chihuly's Charters, P.O. Box 39294, Ninilchik, AK 99639, (907) 567-3374; Will's Copper King Charters, (907) 567-3479.

Cost: $100-$115 per person per day.

Fishing Highlights: King salmon and halibut fishing on the same trip. Kenai kings to 80 lbs.

Rating: ★★★★ (Fish), ★★★ (Charters)

CALIFORNIA

❖

Destination: San Diego

Game Fish & Season: April through September for albacore, yellowtail, yellowfin tuna, bluefin tuna, dorado. The spring is best for yellowtail, while tuna peaks in late summer.

Top Lodges & Charters: Pt. Loma Sportfishing, 1403 Scott Street, San Diego, CA 92106, (619) 223-1627; Fisherman's Landing, 2838 Garrison Street, San Diego, CA 92106, (619) 222-0391; H & M Landing, (619) 222-1144.

Cost: $150-$200 per day for overnights, with tackle; $60-$120 per person for day boats.

Fishing Highlights: Most of the fishing is done in Mexican waters. Very productive 10 to 20-day long-range trips to Mexico's southern islands. The big boats are excellent.

Rating: ★★ (Fish), ★★ (Charters)

FLORIDA

❖

Destination: Key West

Game Fish & Season: Blue and black marlin, sailfish (Sept-Nov); kingfish, yellowtail, grouper (Dec-Jan); dolphin, snapper (spring).

Top Charters: Oceanside Marina, 5050 Maloney Avenue, Key West, FL 33040, (305) 294-4676 (ask for Ralph Delph, Bubba Gaston, Ken Harris); First Key West Marina, US Highway 1, Stock Island, FL 33040, (305) 296-8504 (ask for Jack Kelley, or Jose Wejebe).

Cost: $350-$800 per day; e.g. Bubba Gaston charges $600 for four anglers on 55' sportfisher.

Fishing Highlights: Good black marlin mid-September to early November. Winter kingfish range up to 70 lbs. Crews and boats are first rate.

Rating: ★★★ (Fish), ★★★ (Charters)

HAWAII

❖

Destination: Kona Coast (Big Island)

Game Fish & Season: Pacific blue and striped marlin, yellowfin tuna, wahoo, mahi-mahi, amberjack, dorado--summer is best for nearly all.

Top Charters: Kona Charter Skippers Assoc., 755663 Palani Road, Kailua-Kona, HI 96740, (800) 762-7546, or (808) 329-3600. Ask for specific skippers including Peter Hoggs, Tom Rodgers, Jeff Faye, Chip Fischer, Rick Rose.

Cost: $2,000+ per week; $325-$650 per boat full day, $350 half-day (40' Bertram or Hatteras).

Fishing Highlights: Blue marlin average 150-300 lbs; yellowfin tuna and mahi-mahi are strong at South Point. Kona hosts an International Billfish Tournament each August.

Rating: ★★ (Fish), ★★★ (Charters)

NORTH CAROLINA
❖

Destination: Hatteras/Continental Shelf
Game Fish & Season: Mahi-mahi (Apr-Nov), white and blue marlin (June and July), yellowfin tuna (Apr-May), wahoo, dolphin (Apr-Oct), king mackerel (Mar-June, late Sept to Christmas).

Top Charters: Capt. Jerry Shepard, Tuna Duck, (919) 986-2257; Capt. James Loebesack, Outlaw; Capt. Alex Wood, Miss Jenny--contact both via Hatteras marina phone: (919) 986-2166.

Cost: $750 per day for boat with six anglers.

Fishing Highlights: Very productive fishing grounds for the best eating fish: mahi-mahi, dolphin, wahoo and tuna. On a good day you can raise 20 tuna and 60+ dolphin, and 20 dolphin even on a bad day. Marlin are unpredictable, but a grand slam is possible in late June and July. Only an hour from the Continental Shelf, Hatteras offers a much shorter passage to big game grounds than other North Carolina ports such as Nags Head.

Rating: ★★★ (Fish), ★★★ (Charters)

VIRGIN ISLANDS
❖

Destination: St. Thomas, U.S.V.I.
Game Fish & Season: Strong blue marlin July through October; full or black moons are the best. Some white marlin, also dolphin in the summers as well. Bonefish run inside.

Top Charters: Cruise and Gold 36' Hatteras, and other American sportfishers; Guide Ed Wynns is recommended for bonefish and tarpon. Accommodations at Sapphire Beach Marina. Contact FI, (800) 950-4242.

Cost: $875 per day for boat and skipper. $1,200-$2,000 per week for fishing/lodging package. Skippers will also meet cruise boats, and take passengers on day-trips for $250 per head.

Fishing Highlights: The Virgins are suprisingly productive billfish grounds, possibly the best in the world for Atlantic blue marlin. Good boats average 4-10 billfish shots per day--better than Cabo and Kona. The fishing grounds are a mere 45 minutes from port, and the shoreside amenities will keep your non-angling travel partners happy.

Rating: ★★★ (Fish), ★★★ (Charters)

AUSTRALIA

Destination: Cairns, Queensland
Game Fish & Season: Marlin & sailfish (Aug-Jan); wahoo, tuna, dolphinfish, mackerel (year-round); trevally, barracuda, queenfish (inshore).

Top Charters: Captain Calvin Tilly--contact FRT, (800) 245-1950; Captains Bobby Jones, Frank Thompson--contact FI, (800) 950-4242.

Cost: $1,600+ per day for deluxe 4-person live-aboard; light-tackle fishing for smaller billfish and other species close to shore averages $750 per day for land-based boat and skipper.

Fishing Highlights: Small black marlin in the 40- to 250-lb class are found inshore most of the season. But if you want to catch 1,000-lb trophy blacks, go late September through early December, and count on spending some time at sea. As the big fish move down the Ribbon Reefs, migrating south, they cannot be reached from any land-based lodge, except Lizard Island. Anglers must use live-aboard boats, or combo of gameboat and mothership. The land-based boats leave daily from either Cairns or Townsville.

Rating: ★★★ (Fish), ★★★ (Charters)

BAHAMAS

Destination: Andros Island
Game Fish & Season: Bonefish (Nov-July), tarpon, permit, barracuda, shark. Late spring and summer is best as winter cold fronts can take fish

DARRELL JONES

off the flats and obscure water visibility.

Top Lodges: Andros Island Bonefish Club (best fishing), contact WW, (800) 327-2880; Kemps Bay Club (best lodging). Contact PA or FI.

Cost: $1,400-$1,600 per week with shared guide; $1,000 for 5 days; $150 per day for guide.

Fishing Highlights: Andros is the best spot in Eastern Caribbean for large bonefish. There are also 50- to 100-lb tarpon. Both major clubs feature excellent rooms, guides and equipment.

Rating: ★★★ (Fish), ★★★ (Lodges)

BELIZE

Destination: Manta Reef, Barrier Reef
Game Fish & Season: Bonefish and permit in 80 square mile lagoon (Nov-July); barracuda, snapper on reefs; tuna, marlin and sailfish offshore. Tarpon at Barrier Reef.

Top Lodges: Manta Reef Resort, (800) 342-0053, and Turneffe Flats for bonefish, (800) 338-2880 (WW); El Pescador on Ambergris Caye for bonefish and tarpon (PA & FRT).

Cost: El Pescador--$1,200 per week; Manta or Turneffe about $1,500 per week, or $800 without fishing.

Fishing Highlights: Belize has some of the best bonefishing in the Caribbean--both at Manta Reef and Turneffe. Manta's vast shallow lagoon is a casting delight, and 20 strikes in an afternoon is common. The shallow-water tarpon fishing at Ambergris Cay is also excellent. Offshore big game fishing is improving; this is one of the best locations to fish both flats and bluewater.

Special Attractions: Both Manta Reef and Turneffe Island offer world-class scuba diving.

Rating: ★★★ (Fish), ★★ (Lodges)

COSTA RICA

Destination: Gulf of Papagayo
Game Fish & Season: Blue and black marlin (April-Nov); dorado, yellowfin, roosterfish, snapper (year-round).

Top Lodges: Bahia Pez Vela, contact World Wide Sportsman, (800) 327-2880; El Ocotal, Pioneer Tours, (800) 288-2107 or FI; Tamarindo, contact FI or Papagayo Excursions, Apartado Postal #35, Santa Cruz Guanacaste, Costa Rica, (011) (506) 680859; FAX: (011) (506) 220568.

Cost: Pez Vela--$2,000-$2,500 per week, $1,700 5 days; El Ocotal--$2,400 (6 days, fishing); Charter $250-$550 daily depending on boat size.

Fishing Highlights: The Gulf is considered by many to offer the best billfishing in the world. 10-30 billfish shots per day and multiple hookups happen regularly. Crack crews operate large, high-performance sportfishers. The resorts are Costa Rica's most deluxe.

Rating: ★★★★★ (Fish), ★★★ (Lodges)

Destination: Quepos
Game Fish & Season: Sailfish, dorado, wahoo, mackerel, tuna and roosterfish (Jan-May).

Top Lodges & Charters: La Mariposa is best hotel. FI and PA use twin-engine sportfishers with American crews. World Wide Sportsman, P.O. Drawer 787, Islamorada, FL 33036, (800) 327-2880; FAX: (305) 664-3692, acts as agent for a number of boats in Puerto Quepos.

Cost: $1,300 for 4 days, 3 days' fishing with 3 anglers. $625-$700 per day for top boat and skipper. (Tom Bradwell is recommended.)

Fishing Highlights: Quepos offers prime sailfishing--raising 10-15 sails per day per boat is common. Dorado are plentiful as well, but Americans come for the billfish, which never disappoint. Quepos' prices are rising, but remain on the low end of Costa Rica's top fishing areas.

Rating: ★★★★ (Fish), ★★★ (Charters)

FIJI

Destination: Viti Levu, Vanua Levu Islands
Game Fish & Season: Blue and black marlin, wahoo, dolphin, yellowfin tuna, some sailfish. December through May is best.
Top Lodges: Ocean Pacific Club, Na Koro Resort. Contact FI, (800) 950-4242.
Cost: $1,400-$1,800 per week with 5 days fishing. 30 percent less without fishing.
Fishing Highlights: Fiji is basically a yellowfin destination; don't count on catching many billfish. This new angling frontier offers unfished waters and Polynesian paradise onshore.

Rating: ★★ (Fish), ★★★ (Lodges)

MAURITIUS

Destination: Mauritius is a tropical island about 1,800 miles from the east coast of Africa.
Game Fish & Season: Blue and black marlin (Oct-April), yellowfin tuna, (Mar/April and year-round), skipjack tuna (March-May and year-round), wahoo (Sept-Jan), dorado (year-round), mako, hammerhead and blue sharks (Aug-Sept).
Top Lodges: La Pirogue Hotel; Club Santre de Peche (package tours); Meridien Paradis hotels book fishing charters. Contact Abercrombie & Kent, (800) 323-7308, or Travcoa, (800) 992-2003.
Cost: 10 days $4,000-$6,000 with 4 days fishing, all-inclusive; 1-day charter $750 for 45-footer.
Fishing Highlights: Mauritius has large populations of marlin, swordfish and tuna, and many world-record catches were made in these waters. A 50-minute run gets you to deep water and big game fish.

Rating: ★★★★ (Fish), ★★★ (Lodges)

MEXICO

Destination: Loreto
Game Fish & Season: Dorado (mahi-mahi), spanish mackerel, many other species. Good fishing year-round.
Top Lodges & Charters: El Presidente, (800) 472-2427; Baja Fishing Adventures, (800) 451-6997; Baja Safari, (800) 248-9900, or (408) 375-2252.
Cost: Hotel/air packages start at $500 per week from Los Angeles. Boat, guide, hotel runs $600+ per week. Boat-only starts at $50 per day.

Fishing Highlights: Best fishing value around--30 percent cheaper than Cabo San Lucas. Wild dorado runs in July. Nearby islands are rich fisheries.

Rating: ★★ to ★★★ (Fish), ★★ (Charters)

Destination: Ascension Bay, Yucatan
Game Fish & Season: Bonefish and barracuda year-round; permit (if you're lucky); tarpon at Casa Blanca.
Top Lodges: Ascension Bay Bonefish Club (ABBC); Casa Blanca Lodge; contact FI, (800) 950-4242, or the Fly Shop (800) 669-FISH.
Cost: ABBC $1,650 per week, Casa Blanca $2,500 per week, with air from Cancun.
Fishing Highlights: The new ABBC, in a once inaccessible area near Cancun, is a superb bonefish and permit destination rivaling any fishery in the world. Guide Jan Isley is terrific. Head to the Casa Blanca if you want more luxury and deluxe cuisine. Both are quality American-run lodges for serious anglers. Try nearby Boca Paila or Pez Maya for outstanding saltwater fly-fishing for bonefish and tarpon.

Rating: ★★★★ (Fish), ★★ (Lodges)

KENYA

Destination: Malindi (north of Mombasa)
Game Fish & Season: Blue, striped and black marlin, sailfish (fall) bonefish, tarpon.
Top Lodges & Charters: Hemingway's Re-

Heading out at dawn's light, Caribbean/DARRELL JONES

sort, Malindi, Kenya. Book through Safariworld, NY, (800) 336-5500.
Cost: $700-$1,500 per week land only; $400 per day for 30' boat with four anglers.
Fishing Highlights: In terms of billfish size and numbers, Kenya rivals Hawaii and Cairns. All the deep-sea fishing is done out of Hemingway's, a first-class, modern beachfront resort with excellent service and amenities.

Rating: ★★★ (Fish), ★★★★ (Lodge)

NEW ZEALAND

Destination: Bay of Islands/Whitianga/Whangaroa, North Island
Game Fish & Season: Striped, black and blue marlin (Jan-Apr), shark, yellowtail (Oct-May) and yellowfin tuna (Dec-May).
Top Charters: Major Tom Sportfishing Safaris, P.O. Box 203, Russell, NZ, (011 64) 9 403-7200; FAX: (011 64) 9 403-7537 (See Islands magazine feature, Nov. 1990); Gamefishing Charters, P.O. Box 263, Paihia, NZ, (01164) 9 402-7311.
Cost: $60-$100 per angler per day when available. $400-$600 US per day for full boat charter of 40' Sportfisher.
Fishing Highlights: New Zealand's large gamefish grounds encompass 300 miles of the northeast coastline of the North Island--an unspoiled area of great beauty. Charter bases include Russell, Paihia (Bay of Islands), Whangaroa, Whitianga and Whakatane.

Rating: ★★★ (Fish), ★★★ (Charters)

VENEZUELA

Destination: Rio Chico
Game Fish & Season: Tarpon (Aug-Dec), snook, white marlin (fall).
Top Lodges: Rio Chico Lodge (FI, PA); South Fishing, (800) 333-3347.
Cost: $1,500+ per week; $850 for 4 nights.

Fishing Highlights: Spectacular tarpon fishing—expect 20-50 small strikes per day, 10 percent 10-30 lbs in size. Fish tarpon in the mangroves one day and then try your hand at the fall white marlin fishing offshore (though this is not a world-class offshore fishery). Quite good accommodations and food. For superior peacock bass fishing, drive three hours to Lake Tamanaco.

Rating: ★★★ (Fish), ★★ (Lodge)

Destination: Los Roques Archipelago
Game Fish & Season: Bonefish, tarpon, barracuda, pompano, mackerel. Avoid November to March (high winds and unpredictable water levels).
Top Lodges: Frances Caye Lodge (FRT) (best service); Live-aboard (FI); Macabi Lodge, (800) 669-FISH, (Fly Shop).
Cost: $2,000 8 days; $1,500 6 nights; $2,395 for 8 days with airfare from Houston, Miami or NY.
Fishing Highlights: Los Roques may well offer the Caribbean's best flats fishing. 48 islands create a huge area of flats harboring 3- to 7-lb bonefish which school by the hundreds.

Rating: ★★★★ (Fish), ★★ (Lodges)

FISHING

TOUR AGENCIES

The following agencies all offer package holidays to North America's major fishing centers, as well as exotic angling destinations around the world.

Angler Adventures, P.O. Box 872, Lyme, CT 06371, (203) 434-9624. (Caribbean and South America) Rating: ★★

Fishing International, P.O. Box 2132, Santa Rosa, CA 95405, (800) 950-4242. (Freshwater: Central and South America, Canada, Europe, New Zealand; Saltwater: Australia, Bahamas, Baja, Belize, Christmas Isl., Costa Rica, Venezuela.) Rating: ★★★

Frontiers, P.O. Box 161, Pierce Mill Road, Wesford, PA 15090, (800) 245-1950, (412) 935-1577. (Freshwater: New Zealand, Australia, England, Yugoslavia, USSR, Chile, Argentina; Saltwater: Australia, Mexico, Brazil, Puerto Rico, Venezuela, Iceland, Christmas Island.) Rating: ★★★

Kaufmann's Streamborn Fly Shop, P.O. Box 23032, Portland, OR 97223, (503) 639-6400. (Freshwater: New Zealand, Chile, Argentina, Alaska, Canada; Saltwater: Andros Island, Bahamas, Belize, Christmas Isl., Venezuela) Rating: ★★★

PanAngling Travel Service, 180 N. Michigan Avenue, Chicago, IL 60601, (800) 533-4353. (Caribbean, Central and South America) Rating: ★★

WILDERNESS GUIDES

As an ultimate fishing escape, a wilderness trip is hard to top. Typically you'll use floatplanes, rafts or drift boats for access. Deluxe fly-in lodge trips can cost upwards of $3,000 per week, while basic camping trips start at about $150 per day per person for three anglers and a guide.

Alaska Wilderness Travel, 715 Fireweed Lane, Suite E, Anchorage, AK 99503, (907) 277-7671, can book any type of backcountry fishing vacation, from deluxe fly-in lodges to wilderness float trips on a dozen different rivers. For great fishing, we recommend a 7-day float trip down the serene Goodnews River or Lake Creek with outfitter Alaska River Adventures,

JOHN KELLY

(907) 276-3418. Rating: ★★★

Brestler Outfitters, P.O. Box 766, Wilson, WY 83014, (800) 654-0676. Trout-fishing float trips on six different rivers near the Tetons and Yellowstone. Fully outfitted trips from June through October, $300 per day. Rating: ★★

Glacier Wilderness Guides, Box 535, W. Glacier, MT 59936, (406) 888-5333 summer, (406) 862-4802 winter, or (800) 521-7238. Float fishing trips on North and Middle Forks of the Flathead River. From $150 per day per person. Rating: ★★

Helfrich River Outfitters, 47555 McKenzie Highway, Vida, OR 97488, (503) 896-3786. This third-generation outfitter runs 1 to 6-day drift boat trips on the Rogue, Owyhee, McKenzie and Salmon Rivers. Costing $175-$1,900 per person, these trips are great for anglers looking to hook rainbows, cutthroats and steelheads on dry flys. Rating: ★★★★

Paul Roos Outfitters, 1630 Leslie Avenue, Helena, MT 59601, (406) 442-5489. Guided backcountry float trips to remote Montana rivers and lakes. Itineraries customized for your interests and abilities. $250 for 1 day; 5 days from $1,850 per person. Rating: ★★

ANGLING BOOKS

The American Fisherman's Fresh and Saltwater Guide is a collection of in-depth reports on great fishing sites worldwide. Very useful lists of fishing holes and bait choices. Winchester Press (1976).

Fly-Fishing, a Beginners' Guide, by David Lee, is the best basic how-to book we've found. With great illustrations, this book can benefit almost any angler, not just novices. Prentice Hall, Englewood Cliffs, NJ (1982).

Light-Tackle Fishing Guides of North America, by Richard Swan, is the leading "Who's Who" directory for fishing guides in the US and Canada. From Clearwater Press, Reno, NV.

Fly-Fishing in Salt Water, by Lefty Kreh, outlines the skills you need to catch the major saltwater fish on fly. Good treatment of recommended tackle and flies. $19.95 from Kaufmann's Streamborn.

World Guide to Fly-Fishing, by Jim Chapralis. This definitive 420-page resource covers New Zealand, Alaska, Canada, Central America, Iceland, Norway and Mexico. $24.95 from PanAngling.

VIDEOS

Video previews of major foreign fishing destinations are available from Fishing Int'l, (address above), (800) 950-4242.

Christmas Island Video. Before you fly halfway around the globe, invest $15.00 in this video to see what to expect. From Kaufmann's Streamborn, (800) 442-4239.

Venezuela Tarpon and Bonefish. This new video features tarpon fishing in Tacarigua National Park and a visit to Los Roques, a bonefish hotspot. $19.95 from Fly Fishing magazine.

Fly Casting with Mel Krieger. Good video showing skills for both novices and experts. Fine live fishing sequences for bass, trout and salmon. 60 minutes. $29.95.

South Island Sampler. Experience the best of wilderness fishing in New Zealand's South Island. Great footage of remote areas. $39.95 from Kaufmann's Streamborn.

Hanggliding & Soaring

The Oregon Coast/JOHN HEINEY

*Once you fly, you will walk with your eyes skyward.
For there you have been, and there you will go again.*
-Leonardo DaVinci

▼

*P*owered flight is largely utilitarian-- getting from point A to point B. "Freeflight," or gliding, is the antithesis--the means *is* the end. It is the very challenge associated with non-powered flight that captures our imagination and stirs our sense of adventure.

Boosted by new technology, allowing lighter, faster, better-flying craft, the popularity of hanggliding and soaring grows steadily every year. These are elite sports that require considerable training and skill, but which offer a degree of challenge and freedom few other activities can match.

In this chapter we review and rank the top hanggliding and soaring training centers, list great freeflight holidays, and describe how to earn your hanggliding or soaring pilot ratings.

HELMUT MULLER

CHAPTER
9

Hanggliding

SINCE ITS ORIGINS MORE THAN TWO DECADES AGO, THE SPORT OF HANGGLIDING has progressed enormously. The equipment is stronger, safer, and offers dramatically improved performance. Today's advanced hanggliders rival the performance of regular fixed-wing gliders of just a few decades past. Using new, high-performance double-surface gliders, advanced pilots can easily climb to 10,000' or higher in the right conditions, soaring for hours on end. Hand- and ballistic-launched parachutes have added an increased element of safety, and the development of tandem training has cut the time needed to achieve your intermediate pilot rating by an impressive 30 percent.

GETTING STARTED

The First Flight

A tandem flight is the best way to experience hanggliding for the first time. A specially certified instructor will take you up for 15 to 30 minutes, flying at altitudes of 2,000' or more. Under the pilot's guidance, you will help steer the craft through 360s and other advanced maneuvers. Depending on location, the price of an initial tandem ride will range from $50 to $100.

If that first flight stirs your sense of adventure, the next step is to sign up for a formal training program. This is not a do-it-yourself sport. As with any form of aviation, hanggliding is serious business, and you must learn from professionals. You should choose a training center with instructors certified by the United States Hang Gliding Association, (USHGA), P.O. Box 8300, Colorado Springs, CO 80933, (719) 632-8300. (All the American schools listed in this chapter have USHGA-certified teachers.)

Choosing a School

Choosing the right flight school can make the difference between becoming a skilled pilot and abandoning the sport at an early stage. (Ninety percent of hanggliding students never make it past the novice stage.) When selecting a school, if possible, choose one from our list of top training centers. By all means, be sure that whatever school you select has experienced, certified instructors. Good physical facilities are also essential. The best schools have gentle training hills that are flyable in a variety of wind conditions. Class size is very important. With more than seven people flying the same bunny hill, you may spend more time waiting than learning. Price is a valid consideration, but more important than the hourly rate is whether the school offers some kind of maximum price for any given rating--guaranteeing all the lessons it may take to reach that particular level.

Good equipment is vital. Training gliders should be of recent vintage, ideally with wheels to ease the task of hauling them back up the hill. The most progressive schools have flight simulators that let you get the feel of maneuvering the glider before you ever leave the ground. Tandem training will also be offered by the best schools, although this is more impor-tant for intermediate instruction. If the school features tandem towing, make sure it uses Air Time of Lubbock (ATOL) equipment, which is the only system approved by all US glider suppliers.

Lastly, a good training center will provide a thorough ground school curriculum covering flight theory, site discipline (deciding when and where to fly), weather conditions, and equipment assembly and care. Printed flight manuals should be supplied as part of ground school, and the fee for a novice course should include USHGA membership

DOING IT

From Novice to Hang II

Before we go much further, we should explain some important hanggliding terminology--the "Hang" rating system. The USHGA classifies flying sites and pilots according to a rating system: Student; Hang I (Beginner); Hang II (Novice); Hang III (Intermediate); Hang IV (Advanced); and Hang V (Master).

Any serious training program will be aimed at getting the student to the Hang I level, which allows low level flights over gentle slopes. Hang I programs typically cost $300 to $400. For practical purposes, the more important threshold is getting your Hang II rating. At this level, you are qualified for high-altitude solo flights. Hang II flight programs vary in length according to the flight conditions and the ability of the student pilot, but you can expect to pay $500 to $800 for a program of 10 to 20 lessons. Some flight centers offer unlimited lessons until you achieve your Hang II rating.

The actual learning process is not complicated. After a few hours of ground school you'll make your first runs on level ground to become familiar with the feel of the glider. Then it's time to attempt your first flight. On the first day, expect to make five to 15 trial takeoffs, each lasting from 10 to 20 seconds, depending on the wind conditions and terrain. You'll experience very little glory in your first few hours of hanggliding--managing a 30-foot wing isn't easy, even for experts. The glider will seem heavy and awkward, your harness restrictive. Even with a patient and understanding instructor, it will be hard to make smooth and positive movements of the control bar. But don't be discouraged--everyone goes through this stage.

After a few more afternoons of training, each time building to longer, higher flights, you'll have earned your Hang I rating, once you've passed the obligatory written exam. As a Hang I pilot, you are certified for flights up to 150' maximum altitude, on gradual, open slopes. This may not sound like much, but remind your friends that 150' is the height of a 15-story building.

You should not delay making the jump from Hang I to Hang II status. Your flying skills can get rusty if you wait too long before getting back in the harness. Most students can progress from Hang I to Hang II with another 10-15 hours of instruction. To achieve Hang II you must be able to make smooth 90-degree S-turns over preselected points, land within 40' of a designated target, demonstrate controlled flight 40' above ground level (AGL), and pass another written exam. With the Hang II rating you're allowed to fly up to 300' AGL, and in smooth winds up to 18 mph. Once you've gotten the Hang II rating, you can consider yourself a real flyer, capable of leaving the bunny hills behind.

TANDEM INSTRUCTION

From Hang II to Hang III

Traditionally, new pilots struggled to progress from novice to intermediate (Hang II to Hang III) because the more difficult skills had to be self-taught while in the air. Trying to do things one had never done before was a frustrating process of trial and error. Without the

Tandem flying with a friend/JOHN HEINEY

hands-on guidance of an experienced instructor, novices experienced a long learning curve which discouraged many from continuing with the sport. Tandem training has changed all this.

With tandem training, students can progress much more quickly to higher altitudes and more advanced turns and landings than if they were to learn on their own. During tandem training, also known as accelerated training, student and instructor are harnessed to an oversized glider. The hangglider is launched or towed to an altitude 2,000' or more above ground level--seven times as high as the Hang II pilot is allowed to fly on his own. Flying side-by-side for 15 minutes or longer, the instructor demonstrates maneuvers (e.g. 360s, riding thermals, making landing approaches) which the student then practices.

After four or five tandem sessions, most novice pilots will have mastered Hang III flying skills, although another 20 hours or so of air time is required to actually attain the Hang III certification. This means that a typical Hang II flyer will achieve his intermediate rating in two-thirds the time it would take with conventional flight training.

BUYING A HANGGLIDER

After you have obtained your Hang II rating, usually after 15 to 20 lessons, you should consider buying your own hangglider if you want to continue with the sport. A basic single-surface design, good for novices, can be purchased new for under $1,200. If you are a strong Hang II flyer, however, you will probably want to move into a double-surface glider. A very high quality, double-surface kite can be purchased for under $2,500 new, and for $2,000 or less used. We've selected the best of the latest designs below, as recommended by top pilots around the country. Before you make any purchase, arrange for a test flight from a local dealer, and try to use the glider at a launch site with which you are familiar.

Novices (Hang I to Hang II): UP Lite Dream (single surface); Wills Wing Skyhawk (single surface) and Spectrum (double surface).

Intermediate (up to two years experience and Hang III): Wills Wing Spectrum, Pacific Airwave Vision Mark IV, Delta Wing Super Dream, Moyes Mission.

Advanced Intermediate (solid Hang III): Wills Wing Sport, Delta Wing Mystic, UP Comet III, Pacific Airwave Formula.

Advanced (experienced Hang III to Hang IV): Seed Wing Soft Sensor & Easy Racer, Wills Wing HP, Pacific Airwave Magic Kiss.

Very Advanced/Racer (Hang IV): Seed Wing Sensor & Racer, UP Axis, Moyes XS, Wills Wing HP AT.

Manufacturers

For detailed information on the top new hanggliders on the market, visit your nearest flight center, or contact the following manufacturers:

Moyes California, *752 B Casiano Drive, Santa Barbara, CA 93105, (818) 887-3361; FAX: (818) 702-0612;* **Pacific Airwave,** *P.O. Box 4384, Salinas, CA 93912, (408) 422-2299; FAX: (408) 758-3270;* **Seedwings,** *41 Aero Camino, Goleta, CA 93117, (805) 968-7070; FAX: (805) 968-0079;* **UP Int'l,** *4054 W. 2825 North, Mountain Green, UT 84050, (801) 876-2211; FAX: (801) 876-3003;* **Torrey Pines Gliders** *(Delta Wing), 10343 Roselle, Ste. 9, San Diego, CA 92121, (619) 457-4454;* **Wills Wing,** *1208 H East Walnut, Santa Ana, CA 92701, (714) 547-1344; FAX: (714) 547-0972.*

HANGGLIDING HOLIDAYS WORLDWIDE

THE LIGHT WEIGHT AND PORTABILITY OF MODERN HANGGLIDING EQUIPMENT make it possible to fly just about anywhere there is a hill and a bit of breeze. Just to give you an idea of the hanggliding travel options that exist out there, we've selected three special hanggliding adventures that offer some of the most exciting flying to be found anywhere.

SWITZERLAND

Swiss Alps Hanggliding Trek

Hanggliding and paragliding are wildly popular in Switzerland. There are an estimated 14,000 pilots by latest count--all in a country the size of New Hampshire. Along with spectacular scenery, you'll find easily accessible launch sites, a wide range of inexpensive accommodations, and good transportation wherever you choose to fly.

While it's possible to organize your own flying tour to the Alps, the easiest way to go is to rent a glider on the other side of the Atlantic. For American pilots, Ron Hurst's Hang Gliding Safaris can arrange every aspect of a Swiss flying trip, from renting equipment to booking hotels. Hurst can also secure liability insurance through the Swiss Hang Gliding Association, which you're required to have before you launch. You will also need a USHGA Advanced rating to fly on your own in Switzerland. Intermediates (Hang III) must be accompanied by a certified Swiss hanggliding flight instructor. Hurst can locate an instructor or you can get the names of Swiss certified teachers and flight schools by writing to **Swiss Hanggliding Federation (SHV/FSVL)** at *Postfach 1301, CH-8620, Wetzikon, Switzerland.*

Hurst rents single-surface gliders for $35-$45 per day, double-surface gliders for $45-$80. Harness and parachute will run another $15-$30. For approximately $120 per day plus expenses, Hurst provides full guide services and retrieval. A wide range of accommodations is available, from hostels at about $20 per night, to nice hotels starting at $50 per person. To be assured of having the equipment you want when you arrive, contact Hurst at least three weeks in advance. Hurst does not rent instruments, so bring your own. Contact **Ron Hurst Hang Gliding Safaris**, *Jostenstrasse 21, Ch-8854, Galgenen, Switzerland, (011 41) 55 64 5229; FAX: (011 41) 55 64 5223.* All prices are subject to change.

High above Maui/TOM SANDERS

MEXICO

Winter Hanggliding Safari

Baja Mexico's warm, sunny skies provide a great escape for flyers grounded by winter rain, ice or snow at home. The Hang Gliding Center of San Diego offers combination tours that take you to some of Southern California's best flying sites (e.g. Lake Elsinore, Torrey Pines) and to exceptional flying areas across the border in northern Mexico. Launch sites range from 1,400' to 2,700' above ground level, allowing hour-long flights, once to twice daily. The winter tours are probably the most popular, but summer trips can also be arranged with 30 days' advance notice.

Because land transport is used all the way (HGC's special hanggliding "limo"), these trips, which start at $500 for 8-9 days (6-7 flying days), are much less expensive than a full-on safari to the Mexican interior. The price covers all transportation via 4WD vehicle, site guides and radios. Most participants bring their own equipment, but gliders can be rented for an additional $60 per day. This program is designed principally for experienced pilots, but special itineraries can be tailored for beginners as well. Tour participants spend evenings in San Diego area hotels. For further information, call the **Hang Gliding Center,** *4206-K Sorrento Valley Boulevard, San Diego, CA 92121, (619) 450-9008.*

HAWAII

Island Adventure

Looking for the ultimate hanggliding experience? How about flying over Maui's 10,000' Haleakala volcano, one of the most spectacular places on earth? Hang III-IV pilots can launch from the summit while Hang I and II flyers can soar from 4,000' and 6,000' sites. David Darling's Soar Maui offers hangglider rentals and guiding services for pilots who want to soar the volcano or other scenic sites on Maui. Customers come from around the world, drawn by Maui's reliable lift and beautiful scenery. Cost to rent a kite is $50 for 1 day, $80 for 2 days, $100 for 3. Darling, who has flown Maui since 1978, will also guide you to a site and recover your craft for $35. Soar Maui operates 6 days a week, March through January. Flyers should bring their own harness, radio and gear. Gliders available for rental include: Pacific Airwave Mark IV and Magic Kiss, and the Wills Wing Sport. Rentals and beginner classes are offered, ranging from $50 for the first day to $250 for a 6-day Hang II Program. Contact **Maui Soaring Supplies,** *R.R. 2, Box 780, Kula, Maui, HI 96790, (808) 878-1271.*

Top Hanggliding Schools

WE RECOMMEND THAT YOU LEARN THE SPORT AT A WELL-ESTABLISHED HANG-gliding center with professional, USHGA-certified instructors. All of the 20 schools listed below offer certified instruction under the USHGA rating system. While the leading schools in each region have been listed, some worthy programs in the more active areas, such as California, have been omitted to ensure nationwide coverage. If none of the listed schools is located near you, contact the USHGA for a complete listing of certified instruction programs. Before committing to an expensive training program, it's wise to comparison shop, and talk to a few different instructors. Try to find a patient teacher with whom you can develop rapport. (Note: "PG" indicates that paragliding training is also available.)

ARIZONA

■ DESERT HANGGLIDERS
4319 W. Larkspur, Glendale, AZ 85304, (602) 938-9550.

Bob Thompson runs one-on-one flight training for all levels of pilots, but he specializes in helping Hang II flyers make their way to Hang III status. The emphasis is on thermal technique and cross-country skills. Thompson flies from a number of outstanding sites in Arizona including the Sheba and Merriam Craters--open hills with 360-degree launches. Cost is $100 per day for first-timers, with advanced instruction priced according to the pilot and flying site. Thompson does not operate a storefront, but he is one of the most respected instructors in the Southwest. Rating: ★★

CALIFORNIA

California has a greater concentration of high-quality freeflight schools than almost anywhere in the world. All of the following hanggliding flight centers are excellent.

■ CHANDELLE HANG GLIDING CENTER
488 Manor Plaza, Pacifica, CA 94044, (415) 359-6800.

Chandelle is one of America's most experienced hanggliding centers, with over 17 years in the business. It uses excellent beach and inland flying sites, with very reliable lift. Weekend trips are offered to Big Sur, Elk Mountain and other scenic flying sites. Chandelle's training program features highly indi-vidualized attention, with a strong emphasis on safety. A full-day intro hanggliding class costs $85, while tandem lessons run $175 per day. Rating: ★★★ PG

■ THE HANGGLIDING CENTER
4206-K Sorrento Valley Boulevard, San Diego, CA 92121, (619) 450-9008.

The Hanggliding Center is a full-service facility offering USHGA-certified instruction, flight simulators, equipment rentals, as well as organized flying tours in Southern California and Mexico. Chief instructor John Ryan is superb. With five certified tandem instructors, the Hanggliding Center offers one of the most extensive tandem programs in the country. Training courses cost $75 for all-day, $270 for 3 full days (15-20 flights--guaranteed Hang I). Tandem training runs about $110 per day. Rating: ★★★

■ HANGGLIDER & PARAGLIDER EMPORIUM
613 N. Milpas Street, Santa Barbara, CA 93103, (805) 965-3733.

Santa Barbara offers reliable sea-breeze lift, one of the best training hills on the West Coast, and outstanding advanced sites in the nearby foothills. The Hangglider Emporium provides very high quality individualized instruction, and Director Ken DeRussey is widely regarded as one of the best teachers in the country. An intro class costs $75, while a 3-day program to Hang I runs about $350. Hanggliding vacation packages can also be arranged. Rating: ★★★ PG

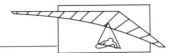

MISSION SOARING CENTER
1116 Wrigley Way, Milpitas, CA 95035, (408) 262-1055.

Mission Soaring Center is the largest and oldest full-service flight center in Northern California, offering year-round training, 7 days a week. Classes are conducted on gently sloped sand dunes at Scott Creek Beach, 12 miles north of Santa Cruz. Mission uses special ultralight gliders for novice training along with flight simulators--equipment that really improves the learning process. An intro class costs $90, a tandem lesson runs $125, while the complete pilot course is priced at $995. This is a superior facility, one of the best in the country. Rating: ★★★★ PG

TORREY FLIGHT PARK
2800 Pines Scenic Drive, San Diego, CA 92037, (619) 452-3202; FAX: (619) 452-3203.

Torrey Flight Park's coastal breezes combine with mountain thermals to offer year-round great flying. Torrey offers a complete range of certified instruction from novice to advanced. Special training in aerobatics, cross-country flight, and paragliding is also offered. With a restaurant, ample parking and great ocean views, the Torrey Flight Park is considered by many to be the best all-round freeflight facility on the West Coast. Rating: ★★★ PG

WESTERN HANG GLIDERS
P.O. Box 828, Marina, CA 93933, (408) 384-2622.

Western Hang Gliders conducts year-round classes on the forgiving sands of Marina Beach near Monterey Bay--a superb novice site. All levels of instruction are offered, from novice training (including tandem flights) to specialized week-long mountain and cross-country clinics for advanced pilots. Basic classes start at $75, and advanced clinics run about $400. Rating: ★★★

WINDSPORTS SOARING CENTER
16145 Victory Boulevard, Van Nuys, CA 91406, (818) 988-0111; FAX: (818) 988-1862.

Joe Greblo's Windsports operation is renowned in the hanggliding industry for its progressive, high-quality training with tremendous attention to detail. Windsports is the largest freeflight school in Southern California, and has trained over 4,000 pilots in its 15-year history. Tandem instruction is a Greblo specialty. Flying

side-by-side with the instructor, a student can achieve intermediate flying skills in two-thirds the normal time. Simulators and videos are also used to speed progress. An intro class is $99, while a combo novice hill and tandem program costs $199. Rating: ★★★★

COLORADO

EAGLE'S NEST SCHOOL OF HANG GLIDING/PARAGLIDING
P.O. Box 25985, Colorado Springs, CO 80936, (719) 594-0498.

In business since 1985, Eagle's Nest is a small operation, but it adheres to high standards of training and certification. An intro class costs $50, while a 2-day package is offered for $100. (Four or five lessons are typically required to obtain the Hang I rating.) Purchasers of new

Telluride, Colorado/JOHN HEINEY

hanggliders receive free lessons from Beginner to Hang II level. Rating: ★★ PG

GOLDEN WINGS
1103 Washington Ave., Golden, CO 80401, (303) 278-7181, or 279-7951.

Golden Wings is a full-service, storefront operation that offers instruction for all levels, tandem flying, and towing over the flatlands of eastern Colorado. Mountain flying clinics are conducted for skilled flyers. Regular instruction is $90 per day. An introductory (Hang I) program is

$375, while a guaranteed Hang II program with tandem flights and 10 days of instruction costs $775. Rating: ★★

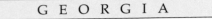

GEORGIA

LOOKOUT MOUNTAIN FLIGHT PARK
Rt. 2, Box 215-H, Rising Fawn, GA 30738, (404) 398-3541; FAX: (404) 398-2906.

Lookout Mountain is the largest and most popular hanggliding center in the southern United States. It offers excellent ramp-launch novice hills with a large, 32-acre landing field, and many good intermediate sights within a few minutes of the flight park. Both conventional and tandem instruction are available, starting at about $90 for an introductory class. We recommend the $500 Mountain Package program, which takes novices from their first class through the high-altitude flight and Hang II rating. This is *the* place to go in the Southeast. Rating: ★★★

MICHIGAN

PRO HANG GLIDERS
569 W. Annabelle, Hazel Park, MI 48030, (313) 399-9433.

With 12 years of experience, Pro Hang Gliders (PHG) is Michigan's leading (and only USHGA-certified) freeflight training center. PHG employs a good beginners' hill with launch options from 40'-120'. PHG also runs a fine step-towing program, using a stationary winch. With the tow option, you can fly year-round, even without a breeze. The introductory class costs $75, while the 3-day Hang I program runs $170. Instruction is individualized for each student. Rating: ★

NEVADA

ADVENTURE SPORTS
3680 Research Way, No. 6, Carson City, NV 89706, (702) 883-7070.

Adventure Sports provides certified lessons (both solo and tandem), sales, service and repair. A 1-day intro class costs $85, and the $350 5-10 lesson package (20 hours) takes most students to the Hang II level. Mountain tours to sites in the nearby Sierras (Slide Mountain, McClelland Peak, Red Rock--selected to match pilot ability), are offered for $75 per day including glider. Rating: ★★ PG

Flying over the dunes of the Kalahari Desert, Africa/COURTESY FIREBIRD HANGGLIDERS

NEW YORK

■ MOUNTAIN WINGS, INC.
150 Canal Street, Ellenville, NY 12428, (914) 647-3377.

Mountain Wings is New England's oldest and most experienced hanggliding school. The school offers a full flight park, repair service and certified instruction for all levels. Classes employ stationary simulators and videotape reviews. Cost is $85 for an intro class, $160 for a 2-day Hang I program, $450 for 6 days (close to Hang II). Mountain Wings operates year-round, with classes 6 days a week in summer. Rating: ★★ PG

NORTH CAROLINA

■ COROLLA FLIGHT
P.O. Box 1021, Kitty Hawk, NC 27949, (919) 261-6166.

Greg DeWolf, with over 10,000 solo flights and 2,000 hours of tandem flying, is one of the top tandem pilots in America, if not the world. He runs a very progressive tandem training program in the Outer Banks region of North Carolina. Using the ATOL system, DeWolf offers tandem tows to 1,500'-2,000', allowing lengthy flights in smooth ocean air. One tandem flight costs about $65, while a 3-lesson program runs $145. In contrast to Kitty Hawk Kites' program, DeWolf's major focus is on producing skilled pilots, rather than giving short rides to the maximum number of customers. Rating: ★★★

■ KITTY HAWK KITES
P.O. Box 1839, Nags Head, NC 27959, (800) 334-4777, or (919) 441-4124.

Kitty Hawk is the East Coast's leading hanggliding school; in the past 15 years, it has trained over 100,000 students. All lev-

HANGGLIDING WORLDWIDE

Excellent instruction at reasonable rates is available in the British Isles, France, Austria and Switzerland. Austria is the value leader if you want to fly the Alps. Contact the organizations or hanggliding schools listed below for more information on flying in Europe.

AUSTRIA

A complete list of licensed Austrian hanggliding schools is available from the **Austrian National Tourist Office,** *11601 Wilshire Boulevard, Suite 2480, Los Angeles, CA 90025, (310) 477-3332.* Or, contact the **Osterreichischer Aero-Club,** *Dept. Hanggliding, Prinz Eugen Strasse 12, A-1040, Vienna, Austria, (011 43) 222 65 1128, or 1129.*

GREAT BRITAIN

Cairnwell Hang Gliding and Par-agliding School, *Cairnwell Mountain, Braimar, Aberdeenshire, Scotland AB3 5XS, (011 44) 3397 41331.*

High Adventure, *Tapnell Farm, Isle of Wight, England P041 0YJ, (011 44) 983 754042.* Britain's largest hanggliding school offers a $400 1-week flying holi-

day, including equipment, instruction and island transportation. Farmhouse accommodation is also available.

FRANCE

A directory of French hanggliding schools and clubs is available from the **Federation Francaise de Vol Libre,** *54 Bis, Rue De La Buffa 0-6000, Nice, France, (011 33) 93 88 6289.*

SWITZERLAND

There are 23 hanggliding schools in Switzerland. For addresses, contact **Schweizerischer Hangegleiterverband,** *Postfach, 8620 Wetzikon, Switzerland, (011 41) 1 932 43 53,* or **Aero Club of Switzerland,** *Department of Hanggliding, Lidostrasse 5, 6006 Lucerne, Switzerland, (011 41) 41 31 21 21.*

---

els of certified instruction are offered, with the major emphasis on beginner/novice training. Flights are made over scenic coastal dunes, using the latest training methods, including tandem flights and ATOL towing. A half-day, $60 beginner lesson includes ground school, video review and a guaranteed five short flights. Three lessons cost $149, while an 8-lesson package, usually sufficient for the Hang I rating, costs $375. The $395 winter package offers unlimited training flights November through March. Although Kitty Hawk runs a quality program, to satisfy its high volume, it does employ some relatively

inexperienced instructors. It is also devoting much of its efforts to paragliding instruction. Rating: ★★★ PG

NEW HAMPSHIRE

■ MORNINGSIDE FLIGHT PARK
RFD 2, Box 109, Claremont, NH 03743, (603) 542-4416.

Morningside, New England's oldest freeflight center, offers 4-hour introductory hanggliding lessons for $85. Three launch sites of varying altitude are used for training, and an ATV is used to retrieve the kites from the bottom of the hills. A 4-day Hang I program runs $360. This is New England's leading training center. Rating: ★★ PG

TENNESSEE

■ SEQUATCHIE VALLEY SOARING
Rt. 2, Box 80, Dunlap, TN 37327, (615) 949-2301.

Sequatchie Valley is an excellent train-

ing venue with a forgiving radial launch ramp and an active local hanggliding club. Training classes are small. Costs are $59 for an intro flight, $499 for a full Mountain Solo flight program. With 100 miles of ridges and reliable thermals, the valley is also very popular with advanced cross-country pilots. Rating: ★★

UTAH

■ WASATCH WINGS
2534 East Murray Holladay Rd., Holladay, UT 84117, (801) 254-7455.

Now in its 15th year, Wasatch Wings utilizes the splendid Point of the Mountain training site which combines a 300' beginner hill with a 1,000' Hang II launch. A 1-day intro class costs $75, while a 5-lesson Hang II program runs $350. Novices will appreciate Wasatch Wings' Dream ultralight gliders which are much easier to carry up the hill. Tandem training is available. Rating: ★★ PG

Soaring

THE ULTIMATE FLIGHT EXPERIENCE

MANY OF US HAVE DREAMED OF SOARING LIKE EAGLES, RIDING THE INvisible currents of the wind. Both thrilling and serene, soaring is a treat for the senses, freeflight in its ultimate form. With soaring centers located in many of America's most scenic destinations, you can fly the spectacular Hana coast of Maui, soar over the Colorado Rockies, or circle above the vineyards of California's wine country. Modern sailplanes have been called "the most beautiful machines ever crafted by man." And their performance matches their looks. In the hands of an expert, a modern sailplane can fly hundreds of miles, and stay aloft for hours on end.

WHERE TO GO
■

There are hundreds of gliderports located throughout North America. Most are listed in the yellow pages under "gliding" or "aviation." To help you choose among them, we have selected 17 of the top flight training centers nationwide. For a complete list of soaring sites in North America, write to the Soaring Society of America (SSA), P.O. Box E, Hobbs, NM 88241-1308, (505) 392-1177. Request the Soaring Site Directory, a booklet available for $3.00. The SSA also has selected information on foreign soaring centers which is available to SSA members upon request.

WHAT IT COSTS
■

A half-hour scenic ride in a training-class glider will cost from $35-$75. A 30 to 40-minute ride in a high-performance fiberglass glider will run from $65 to $100. Flight training costs approximately $45-$65 per hour for plane and instructor. Aerial tows will average about $15-$20 per flight.

To be able to fly on your own, you must enter a formal flight training program with an FAA-certified instructor. It will typically cost $700-$1,100 to reach the solo point, and that much again to obtain your pilot's license. In the next section we describe the process for earning your wings.

TYPES OF LIFT
■

Thermal, Ridge and Wave

The essence of soaring is the quest for lift. To stay in the air, all gliders, from basic trainers to the most sophisticated open-classers, must have lift. Without it, no matter how good the pilot, gravity will prevail and the ship must land.

There are three basic kinds of lift: thermal, ridge and wave. Thermal lift is produced when the sun warms the ground, causing the surface air to rise. Thermals take many forms, from large masses of rising air to narrow turbulent shafts, no more than 100' across. Ridge lift is produced by winds blowing against a mountain range. As the wind hits the ridge, it bounces upwards. On the opposite side of the crest, the wind veers down. Accordingly, ridges can be soared on the windward side only.

Wave lift arises when a large mass of air spills over a mountain range just like a waterfall. When the wave of air hits the valley floor, it bounces upwards, sometimes ascending for miles. Waves, the strongest form of lift, permit spectacular ascents of 2,000' per minute to altitudes beyond 35,000'. Flying a wave is the ultimate soaring experience. Once past the rotor, an area of turbulence at the bottom of the wave, the air is incredibly smooth and stable, allowing the glider to cruise as if it's on rails.

LEARNING TO SOAR

■

Your First Ride--What to Expect

The first time you climb into a glider, it may seem like an oversized toy, cramped and ungainly. However, as soon as you are released from the tow-plane, a half-mile or so above the ground, your perceptions will change. The glider is at home in the air, a creature in its element.

On your first flight, the craft will likely be a two or three-place Schweizer glider, an American design that has been the mainstay of commercial soaring for decades. At some of the larger facilities, you can fly in a high-performance two-seater such as the Grob 103, which is capable of 120 mph speeds, and aerobatics that will have your head swimming.

On to Solo and License

During the initial phase of training, qualifying to solo, you will practice with an instructor in a dual-control glider. The process will typically take 8-12 days of flying and 20-35 flights. Learning to solo at a commercial flight school will cost $800-$1,500, while learning with a club will cost about half that amount.

Choosing the right school begins with selecting the right type of glider--high performance versus low performance. Most flight schools and clubs train novice pilots in Schweizer 232s or 233s, low-performance, forgiving ships with a glide ratio of about 24:1. Though these do not soar as well as fiberglass sailplanes with glide ratios approaching 40:1, Schweizers are much easier for novices to fly.

On the other hand, most students take up soaring with the objective of flying high-performance gliders some day. Many top pilots advise that if you want to fly a high-performance sailplane eventually, then you might as well start in one. Schools that feature training in fiberglass gliders include: California City (CA); Soar Minden (NV); Chilhowee Gliderport (TN); and Chuckanut Soaring (WA).

The Last Hurdle--the Pilot's Rating

Seven hours of solo flight are required by the FAA to get your Private Pilot Glider license, followed by a written exam and an in-flight test. Achieving pilot status usually takes 20-25 flights--two weeks at a minimum for most students. Cost, at a commercial flight center, ranges from $700-$1,200, depending on aircraft and student ability.

Soaring over the Hawaiian coastline/TIMOTHY J. CISLO

*T*HERE ARE HUNDREDS OF LOCATIONS IN THE UNITED STATES WHERE YOU CAN learn to soar, and obtain your private pilot's license. However, we'd advise you to enroll with one of the leading flight schools listed below. All offer professional instruction, good equipment and superior soaring conditions. We have provided three kinds of ratings: "school" (quality of instruction, aircraft and facilities); "lift" (quality and reliability of lift); and "flying conditions" (percentage of good weather days, suitability of site for training and scenery).

ARIZONA

■ SOARING ESTRELLA SAILPORT
P.O. Box 858, Maricopa, AZ 85239, (602) 568-2318, or (602) 821-2903.

Estrella is simply one of the best schools on the continent. It has excellent aircraft, highly qualified instructors and a very professional training program. The Estrella staff will let you decide whether to train in a Schweizer or glass ship, depending on your interests. Lift is 80 percent thermal, with ridges two miles away. The flight school runs year-round, and there is soaring virtually every day from April to November. With its good flying conditions, and fine reputation, Estrella attracts pilot trainees from around the world. (For $10/night, convenient on-field bunkhouse lodging is available for trainees.) Training costs: $26/hr (pilot), $32/hr (S 233), $45/hr (Grob 103). Ratings: ★★★★ (school), ★★★ (lift), ★★★★ (flying conditions)

■ TURF SOARING SCHOOL
8700 West Caretree Highway, Peoria, AZ 85382, (602) 439-3621.

In operation since 1968, the Turf School is one of the largest soaring academies in the country. Instruction is offered year-round, 7 days a week. All basic training is done in Schweizer 233s. While we prefer the flight training at Estrella, the scenery is better at Turf, which is located about 45 minutes north of Phoenix. The weather is just about the best to be had anywhere. Basic lodgings and trailer spaces are available. An intro ride is $45 in a Schweizer, or $70 in a fiberglass ship. Training costs: $28/hr (pilot), $30/hr (S 233). Expect to pay about $1,300 to solo, and $1,200 more to obtain your license. Ratings: ★★★ (school), ★★★ (lift), ★★★★ (flying conditions)

CALIFORNIA

■ CALIFORNIA CITY SOARING
6301 Lindbergh Blvd., P.O. Box 2586, California City, CA 93504, (619) 373-2151, or 373-4341.

An area with world-class lift year-round, California City offers basic and advanced training in the high-performance ASK 21. The instruction program focuses heavily on quality air time--actually flying the aircraft in lift, rather than just repeating take-offs and landings. The two full-time instructors are very skilled and patient, and many top pilots come here for advanced wave and cross-country training. The rental fleet includes an ASW 20, Nimbus II, and other high-performance gliders. California City operates 7 days per week, year-round, with excellent wave flying in the winter. An introductory lesson is $50, while the cost to solo averages $900-$1,100, good value for a glass glider. Training costs: $25/hr (pilot), $45/hr (ASK 21). Ratings: ★★★ (school), ★★★★ (lift), ★★★ (flying conditions)

■ SKY SAILING AT WARNER SPRINGS SOARING CENTER
Highway 79, Warner Springs, CA 92086, (619) 782-0404.

Sky Sailing has offered quality soaring instruction for more than 30 years, first in Northern California, and now at Warner Springs, east of San Diego. Lift is mostly thermal, with some ridge and wave. The excellent Southern California weather allows true year-round flying. A 20-minute intro ride in a Schweizer costs $55, or $40 per person for two passengers. Owner Bret Willat is one of the most respected flight instructors in the business. Training costs: $24/hr (pilot), $24/hr (S 233), $39/hr (Grob 103). Ratings: ★★★★ (school), ★★ (lift), ★★★★ (flying conditions)

■ SKYLARK NORTH SOARING
Mountain Valley Airport, P.O. Box 918, Tehachapi, CA 93561, (805) 822-5267.

For the past 15 years, Skylark has operated a serious, full-time soaring school in Tehachapi, an outstanding site where many long-distance flights have originated. They don't cut corners here; the training program is thorough, and well organized. While a Grob 103 is available for rental by licensed pilots, all basic training is in Schweizers. An orientation flight costs $50. While this is a very professional flight school, the site is not ideal for beginners. The strong, turbulent afternoon winds often limit novice training to the mornings. Training costs: $24/hr (pilot), $24/hr (S 233), 3,000' tow is $27. Ratings: ★★★ (school), ★★★★ (lift), ★★ (flying conditions)

COLORADO

■ THE CLOUD BASE
5117 Independence Road, Boulder, CO 80301, (303) 530-2208.

The Cloud Base is the leading soaring center in the Rockies. Located close to the Continental Divide, the Cloud Base offers great scenery as well as good lift year-round. From May through August, look for good thermal conditions, while winter brings some of the best wave lift in the country, and there are always the Rockies for ridge-running. The school has a complete selection of gliders (Schweizer 233, 232, 1-36, and Grob 103 Acro), and operates year-round, 7 days a week, with two full-time instructors. The scenic intro rides over the Rockies, ranging from $40-$85, are spectacular. Training costs: $24/hr (pilot), $26/hr (S 233), $42/hr (Grob 103). Ratings: ★★★ (school), ★★★ (lift), ★★ (flying conditions)

FLORIDA

■ SEMINOLE FLYING AND SOARING
Seminole Lake Gliderport, Hwy 33 & 561, P.O. Box 120458, Claremont, FL 34712, (904) 394-5450.

Seminole, with the most flyable days of any site in the country, is a great choice for residential training programs from first flight to solo, or solo to private license.

COURTESY SOARING SOCIETY OF AMERICA

Low-cost lodgings are available for trainees, there is an FAA examiner on staff, and the good thermal lift permits cheaper, shorter tows. Most training is conducted in Schweizer 233s, but novices can also learn in glass gliders. An intro flight costs $35 in a 233, or $50 in a Grob (half-hour). Training conditions are excellent year-round. Training costs: $20/hr (pilot), $19-$35/hr (aircraft); approx. $800 to solo, $1,400-$1,600 to license (good value). Ratings: ★★★ (school), ★★ (lift), ★★★★ (flying conditions)

HAWAII

■ SOAR HAWAII, LTD.
266 Poipu Drive, Honolulu, HI 96825, (808) 637-3147, or (808) 395-9052 after hours.

Hawaii is a spectacular soaring destination. On one of Soar Hawaii's mile-high, 30-minute scenic flights, you can see Waimea Bay, Pearl Harbor, Diamond Head and most of Oahu for $50 per person. Compared to its competition, (the Honolulu Soaring Club, (808) 677-3404), Soar Hawaii offers a more serious, full-time flight training program-- 80 percent of its business is instruction, and many of its customers are airline pilots, which says a lot. Instruction is done in Schweizer 233s and Grob 103s. The trade winds provide excellent ridge lift most of the year, and in the winter time Kona winds often create wave conditions. Either way, it's possible to soar virtually every day of the year. Training costs: $30/hr (pilot), $20/hr (S 233), $50/hr (Grob 103); approx. $1,600-$2,000 from first flight to license. Ratings: ★★★ (school), ★★★ (lift), ★★★★ (flying conditions)

NEW YORK

■ HARRIS HILL SOARING CORP.
Harris Hill, R.D. #3, Elmira, NY 14903, (607) 734-0641.

Elmira, New York is where most of the American pioneers of the sport, including the Schweizer brothers, got their start. Harris Hill hosts many major soaring events each year and offers scenic rides in Schweizer 233s ($40), and in speedy, fiberglass ASK 21s ($50). The flight center operates year-round on weekends, 7 days a week in the summer. Formal flight training is conducted at the nearby Schweizer Soaring School, Elmira Corning Regional Airport, Box 147, 1 Airport Road, Elmira, NY 14902, (607) 739-3821. Ratings: ★★ (school), ★★★ (lift), ★★ (flying conditions)

NEVADA

■ HIGH COUNTRY SOARING
P.O. Box 70, Minden, NV 89423, (702) 782-4944; FAX: (702) 782-4384.

One of the best soaring sites in the world, Minden draws 60-70 percent of its clientele from abroad. High Country Soaring concentrates mostly on rentals for advanced sport flyers, but it also operates a quality flight school using high-performance glass gliders. (High Country is the only facility in North America to rent the Nimbus III, the world's most advanced sailplane.) The instructors are very experienced and extremely professional. Thermal and ridge lift can be a little unpredictable, but when the wave kicks in, even novices can fly for hours. High Country offers a superb 40-minute Tahoe scenic ride for $50, or a shorter Valley ride for $35. Training costs: $20/hr (pilot), $40/hr (Grob 103); $400-$600 for transition, $1,500-$2,000 for license. Ratings: ★★★★ (school), ★★★★★ (lift), ★★★ (flying conditions)

■ Soar Minden

P.O. Box 1764, Minden, NV 89423, (702) 782-7627, or (800) 345-7627.

Soar Minden is another upper-end operation that won't disappoint even the most advanced pilots. The training fleet is Nevada's largest, and while High Country may have the most expensive craft around, Soar Minden's aircraft, including a new self-launching DG 500, are far more sophisticated than you will find at most gliderports. A full training program is offered, from first flight to advanced aerobatics. Most training is done in Grob 103s, but a Schweizer 232 is also available. Owner Ellis Mickey runs a very professional operation, with highly qualified instructors and powerful tow-planes. All forms of lift are present, with more ridge flying than is done at High Country. Training costs: $1,200-$1,800 to solo. Ratings: ★★★ (school), ★★★★★ (lift), ★★★ (flying conditions)

PENNSYLVANIA

■ Keystone Gliderport, Knauff & Grove Inc.

RR 1, Box 414, Julian, PA 16844, (814) 355-2483.

A world-class soaring site, numerous cross-country records have been set from the gliderport at Julian (formerly Ridge Soaring). Pilots come from all over the world to fly here. In addition to basic instruction, Knauff & Grove offer specialty Instructor Revalidation Courses and advanced Cross Country Clinics. An introductory ride in a Grob 103 costs $45 for 2,000', while a mile-high flight is $85. The flight center is active March through November each year. The owners are champion pilots. Training costs: $28/hr (pilot), $42/hr (Grob 103). Ratings: ★★★ (school), ★★★★★ (lift), ★★ (flying conditions)

SOUTH CAROLINA

■ Bermuda High Soaring School

P.O. Drawer 809, Chester, SC 29706, (803) 385-6061.

One of the best run and most well-equipped training facilities in the country, Bermuda High is a top choice for those seeking a complete residential training program from first flight to pilot rating.

Unlike many facilities, instruction is the main focus at Bermuda High, which has operated a full-time flight school for 26 years. Bermuda High offers a unique fixed-priced policy that sets the maximum you will pay for any stage of training. Bunkhouse lodging is available for trainees at under $10 per day. Chester offers soarable conditions in thermals nine days out of 10 during the principal flying season, March through November. All basic training is conducted in Schweizers, though introductory rides are available

BERNARD DESESTRES, VANDYSTADT, ALLSPORT USA

for $40 in Grob 103s. Training costs: basic course to solo, 32 flights--$920; solo to private rating--$675; full pilot's license course--$1,800 (very good value). Ratings: ★★★★ (school), ★★ (lift), ★★ (flying conditions)

TEXAS

■ Southwest Soaring Enterprises, Inc.

P.O. Box 460, Caddo Mills, TX 75005, (903) 527-3124.

Located just 40 minutes from Dallas, Caddo Mills is generally regarded as the best soaring site in Texas. At Southwest Soaring, all flight training is done in high-performance Grob 103s, with skilled, full-time instructors. The school runs year-round with reliable 1,000' per minute thermal lift, spring through fall. There are no obstructions or power traffic near the twin 4,000' paved runways and two grass strips. Intro rides cost $35 for a 2,000' tow, $70 for 4,000'. Training costs: $18/hr (pilot), $40/hr (Grob 103). (First flight to solo averages $850 to $1,050, and most pilots can earn their private rating for under $1,500--excellent value for training in a Grob.) Ratings: ★★★★ (school), ★★★ (lift), ★★★★ (flying conditions)

VERMONT

■ Sugarbush Soaring

Box 123, Warren, VT 05674, (802) 496-2290.

Sugarbush, New England's leading soaring center for 23 years, is renowned for its spring and fall wave conditions. (When there's no wave, you fly ridge and thermal lift over Vermont's Green Mountains.) Each October, Sugarbush draws top pilots to its Fall Flight Competition and Wave Camp. Scenic rides are offered in the Schweizer 233, ASK 21 and Grob 103, starting at $55. Complete novice training is offered, and Sugarbush runs 3, 5 and 10-day wave and mountain flying workshops for licensed pilots. Sugarbush operates May through October, 7 days a week. Training costs: depends on program. Ratings: ★★★★ (school), ★★★ (lift), ★★ (flying conditions)

VIRGINIA

■ Skyline Soaring Club

Front Royal Airport, Front Royal, VA 22630, (703) 330-8655 (Club officer).

This club operation has replaced the popular Warrenton Soaring Center. Skyline offers a complete training program for members at reasonable rates. Introductory flights in Schweizer 233s cost $50, or $60 in a high-performance ASK 21. This region is noted for good ridge soaring over the nearby Blue Ridge Mountains. Programs run on weekends spring through fall. Training costs (subject to change): $35/hr (Schweizer 233 with pilot), $45/hr (ASK 21 with pilot). Ratings: ★★ (school), ★★★ (lift), ★★ (flying conditions)

WASHINGTON

■ Chuckanut Soaring

1328 Flightline Road, Burlington, WA 98233, (509) 757-0952.

In operation since 1981, Chuckanut is the only commercial soaring facility in western Washington. Set in the Chuckanut Range of the Cascades, this region is one of the most scenic in North America. Lift is good in the spring and summer, with Northwest cloud cover. Scenic flights and instruction are conducted in high-performance Grob 103s. An intro flight costs $35 for 20 minutes. Training costs: $22/hr (pilot), $30/hr (Grob 103), (good value). Ratings: ★★★ (school), ★★ (lift), ★★ (flying conditions)

ULTIMATE SOARING DESTINATIONS

IF YOU WANT TO EXPERIENCE THE ultimate in soaring--the highest altitudes and the longest flights--you'll need world-class lift. Here is our list of ultimate soaring sites, destinations offering peerless lift of each major type: wave, thermal and ridge. These are the best spots on the planet to soar like a champion.

WORLD-CLASS WAVES

▼

Minden, Nevada

The area around Minden, Nevada is generally considered to be the best wave flying destination in the country and perhaps the world. Here, powerful, high-velocity air masses spill over the 15,000' crest of the Sierra Nevada, and then bounce off the desert floor, creating the perfect wave. Expert pilots equipped with oxygen regularly fly Sierra waves to altitudes of 25,000' or higher.

The premier altitude award in soaring is a diamond pin, reserved for pilots achieving a 5,000-meter (16,404') elevation gain. The motto at Minden is "diamonds come cheap." Top pilots from around the world come to this corner of Nevada, just to see what it's like to strap on the oxygen, and climb at 2,500' per second. There are two excellent flight facilities in this area, High Country Soaring and Soar Minden. Both rent high-performance gliders set up for high-altitude flight. (See listings on pp. 139-40.)

WORLD-CLASS THERMALS

▼

New South Wales, Australia

The powerful and steady thermals which rise from the hot Australian interior yield some of the best soaring conditions to be found anywhere. For trained pilots wishing to experience gliding in the Southern Hemisphere, Alpha-Gliding Tours of Germany offers package soaring holidays at the excellent Narromine airfield in New South Wales, just a few hours from Sydney. Visiting pilots may charter ASH 25, ASW 22B and other high-performance sailplanes, and will receive specialized instruction from four-time world champion Ingo Renner. Australian gliding tours last 2 to 3 weeks and start at roughly 6,000 DM for 14

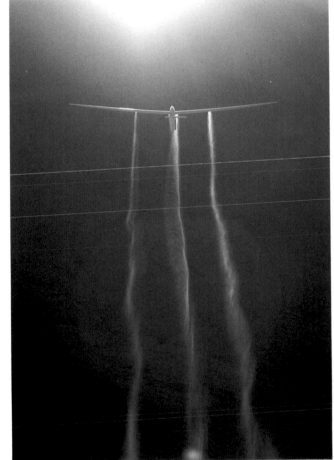

CHRISTOPHER WOODS

days, about $4,200, which covers round-trip airfare, all expenses in Australia, and 11 days of soaring. (Cut the price by about $1,200 if you get yourself to Sydney.) Contact **Alpha-Gliding-Tours,** *Im Herzenacker 12, D-6535 Gau-Algesheim, Germany, (011 49) 6725 3131; FAX: (011 49) 6725 2198.*

Nyeri, Kenya

Unique geography and Kenya's prevailing weather patterns make Nyeri a world-class soaring destination. Situated on a hot 6,000' desert plain, Nyeri experiences extreme night to day temperature differentials of 40 to 50 degrees--producing strong, fast-rising thermals. The high ridges of Mt. Kenya and the 13,000' Aberdare Range on either side of the airfield keep the wind direction almost constant, fostering solid and stable convection currents. All of this translates to superb lift year-round, except for the April and May rainy season.

Nyeri is an area for experienced pilots only. Launches are by winch only, and pilots must have at least 80 hours of solo experience, 30 of that in a fiberglass glider. Glider rental is about $40 per hour for two-seaters, and $45 per hour for high-performance solo gliders. Contact the **Kenya Soaring Club,** *c/o R. Pollard, P.O. Box 926, Nyeri, Kenya.*

WORLD-CLASS RIDGES

▼

Julian, Pennsylvania

Pilots come to Pennsylvania from around the world to fly the famed Bald Eagle Ridge stretching from eastern Pennsylvania to Knoxville, Tennessee. The current world distance record, a flight of more than 1,000 miles, was accomplished by a pilot flying the entire length of the ridge and back again. The best time for ridge soaring is in the spring and fall, while thermal soaring is also possible in the summer. Keystone Gliderport of Julian, (see opposite page), operates an excellent full-service flight center.

Austrian Alps

For the soaring pilot, the Austrian Alps offer more than just great scenery. The outstanding ridge lift in Austria's mountains permits experts to fly hundreds of kilometers, working the long valleys that stretch from the Swiss border all the way to Hungary. One very popular soaring site is the village of Wiener Neustadt, home of the 1989 World Gliding Championships. Contact the **Austrian National Tourist Office,** *11601 Wilshire Boulevard, Suite 2480, Los Angeles, CA 90025, (213) 477-3332.*

Horseback Riding

Wild horses in winter/DAVID STOECKLEIN

God forbid that I should go to any heaven
where there are no horses.
-R. B. Cunningham-Graham

▼

Over the centuries, the horse was man's primary beast of burden and mode of transport. Today, in developed countries, the horse no longer serves these functions, except on an ever dwindling number of working ranches. In the modern world, people ride for sport, and to experience the adventure of traveling as our ancestors did.

For both novice and expert riders, there is plenty of riding excitement to be had on virtually every continent. Imagine cantering through the surf in Montego Bay, fox-hunting in England, or crossing the Alps on horseback. Or, for the truly adventurous, how about galloping an Arabian in the shadows of Egypt's Great Pyramids, or exploring glaciers and volcanoes in Iceland? All these adventures and more are described in these pages. You'll also find a complete guide to the top western guest ranches, along with ratings of the best wilderness pack outfitters in North America.

CHAPTER
10

County Sligo, Ireland/MICHAEL KEVIN DALY

*I*N AN ERA OF JET TRAVEL AND SUPERHIGHWAYS, RIDING ON HORSEBACK IS admittedly old-fashioned. But it is still the best way to travel the wild backcountry, where roads are few and far between. And riding is one of the few forms of adventure that allows you to work with animals, not just watch them. Most riding tours are gentle, slow-paced outings suitable for the whole family, but if you're an experienced rider, you'll find a host of challenging adventures in these pages, from roping steers in Wyoming to galloping across the pampas of South America.

IRELAND

Connemara

The Connemara Peninsula, the setting of John Ford's classic film, *The Quiet Man*, is a near-legendary center for Irish horse-breeding. This part of Ireland's west-central coast rambles from Lough Corrib to the Atlantic, plunging from craggy mountains--the Twelve Bens and the Maumturks--into steep emerald valleys, past whitewashed cottages and stone castles on the shores of wooded lakes.

The rugged landscape, quick-change weather and a traditional Celtic culture add to the region's charm and mystique. To sample the best of Connemara riding, head to County Galway, home of the Loughrea riding center. Here, noted horseman Willie Leahy maintains a stable of a hundred horses, which he matches to the individual likes and abilities of his guests. Leahy's showcase offering, the Connemara Trail Ride, alternates inland and coastal routes, beginning each Monday at noon in front of Galway's Great Southern Hotel (a 90-minute

drive from Shannon Airport).

The 6-day trek follows bridle paths, beaches and mountain tracks at a moderate pace, with overnight stops at comfortable country inns. The horses are well trained and surefooted, but some riding skill is required as you spend up to 7 hours a day posting over moors, slogging through peat bogs, and clambering over rocky terrain. The highlight is a visit to Mweenish Island. Like most of southern Connemara, it's part of the Gaeltacht region, a national wilderness preserve. Seaside fields with stone walls invite jumping, and the broad beach at low tide inspires informal racing.

The Connemara Trail Ride is offered spring through fall each year at a cost of roughly $1,200 in May, June and September, and about $100 more in July and August. In the winter, Leahy runs an even more adventurous tour for skilled riders-- the Aille Cross Country Trail. The O'Deas Hotel will be your base for a week of cross-country jumping, with an optional 3 days of fox-hunting. The price will be about the same as the Connemara Trail Ride, with a

$100 fox-hunt surcharge.

The best time to visit is in August, when Connemara's largest town, Clifton, hosts the annual Connemara pony show, an event which draws equine enthusiasts from around the world. For more information, contact Connemara Trail, Loughrea, Co. Galway, Ireland, (011 353) 91 41246. Equitour and FITS Equestrian can also book Connemara tours and a wide variety of other Irish riding adventures. Contact Equitour, P.O. Box 807, Dubois, WY 82513, (800) 545-0019; FAX: (307) 455-2354; or FITS Equestrian, 2011 Alamo Pintado Road, Solvang, CA 93463, (800) 666-FITS, or (805) 688-9494; FAX: (805) 688-2943.

ICELAND

Land of Fire and Ice

For equestrians, Iceland may be the ultimate adventure destination. The rugged landscape is dotted with glaciers, volcanoes, lava flows and geysers--powerful evidence of the earth's continuing evolution. And Iceland's famous ponies are equally exotic--an ancient species found nowhere else.

The Icelandic ponies, direct descendents of horses brought by 9th-century Vikings, are small, tough, swift and surefooted. Iceland's ponies afford a practical means for visitors to travel through a land in a perpetual state of ecological change. The geological forces deep within the earth have created a wonderland of fire and ice. Geysers fume near glaciers. Snow-covered mountains feed crashing waterfalls. Black lava from 200 volcanoes flows next to green valleys awash in wild flowers.

If you decide to experience this wild domain from the back of a horse, you'll be expected to rough it a little. There are no fancy hotels in the island's hinterlands. Backcountry riders stay at rustic farms or in huts used in colder months by shepherds. In the most remote areas, you will bathe in natural hot springs rather than use showers. However, because a branch of the Gulf Stream meets the island's southwest coast, summer visitors will find the climate remarkably hospitable and temperate despite the sub-Arctic locale.

If you'd like to ride for just a day or two, simply visit any number of farms outside the capitol of Reykjavik. You can get a listing of farm-stay locations from the Iceland Tourist Board, 655 Third Avenue, New York, NY 10017, (212) 949-2333. To take a longer trip, contact the Ishestar agency at Baejarhraun #2, Hafnarfjord, Iceland, (011 354) 1 653044, or book through Equitour or FITS Equestrian in the United States.

For the average rider, we recommend the 10-day Hekla to Landmannalaugar Tour. This takes you through mountains, hot springs and lava fields near Mt. Hekla. You'll ride from 4 to 7 hours a day, staying at farms or rustic inns. The price, roughly $1,480, includes horse, tack, English-speaking guide, lodging and all meals. Another moderately paced journey available though Equitour--the Kjölur Ride--traverses the island from Laugarvatn in the south to Skagafjordur in the north. You will ride the historic King's Pass to Geysir (an active thermal area) and explore the spectacular icefields of the Hvitarnes Glacier.

Iceland riding trips are offered from late

Early spring, Austria/COURTESY AUSTRIAN NATIONAL TOURIST OFFICE

June through mid-August. Many tours are accompanied by 50 to 60 free-running horses, allowing riders to change mounts along the way. For more details, contact Equitour at (800) 545-0019, or FITS Equestrian at (800) 666-FITS.

SOUTH AMERICA

The Andes of Chile and Argentina

The horsemen of South America--the gauchos of Argentina and the huasos of Chile--carry on a heritage of Latin horsemanship dating back to the age of the Spanish conquistadors. On a riding tour of the great estancias (ranches) of Chile and Argentina, you can join these able riders on one of the truly great equestrian adventures: a trek from the pampas to Patagonia.

While you can make your own arrangements with private estancias in both Argentina and Chile, if you want to sample a wide variety of destinations in a short time, a package tour makes sense. FITS Equestrian has put together fine riding programs in both Chile and Argentina that don't cost an arm and a leg.

FITS' Argentinean tour, the Gaucho Trails Ride, begins in Buenos Aires. After a charter flight to the northern foothills of the Andes, you set off on a 3-day trek through dramatic Purmamarca Gorge. Next you head to the flatlands--the pampas of Entre Rios in east-central Argentina. Riders will stay at Estancia El Grabon, a large working ranch. For the next 4 days, the riders will join the gauchos in their daily duties-- roping, branding, moving cattle. The group then visits Victoria, a typical gaucho enclave, before heading south to Esquel in Patagonia. Once in Patagonia, the last leg of the tour follows Butch Cassidy's old trail through Bandits Canyon, along La Zeta Lagoon, and into Los Alerces National Park-- an unspoiled wilderness in the Andean foothills. Price for the 15-day tour (10 days of riding) will be approximately $1,700-- quite a good value.

A second South American adventure, the Cordilleras of the Andes Tour, skips up and down Chile's narrow backbone by train and horseback. The tour is led by Alex Braguine, an experienced, multilingual guide and riding instructor. The tour begins with a stay at Santiago's elegant Hotel Carrera. After a train ride to Curico and one night at an inn, the group heads out for 8 days and 7 nights of luxury camping. (Accommodations are at estancias or hotels for the balance of the 12-day tour.)

The mounts are Caballos Chileños, a breed noted for their cattle-working abilities as well as long-distance endurance. Riding is mostly at a moderate pace, with 8 days of actual riding. During the tour, riders pass through Chile's Andean forests and swamps, across rivers, past lakes, fumaroles and volcanoes, ending up in Curico. The price for the trip is approximately $1,880. Contact FITS Equestrian at (800) 666-FITS.

AUSTRIA

Riding the Alps

If we were forced to choose just one of the dozens of commercial riding tours available in Europe, chances are we would select a weeklong ride through the Austrian Alps. In our view, Austria offers the best of Europe in one place. The villages are small and charming, the people are industrious and incredibly hospitable to travelers, and the Alps offer a scenic playground the equal of any on earth.

Compared to neighboring France and Switzerland, Austria also offers excellent value for the traveling equestrian. A weeklong summer riding tour through the Alps costs less than $130 per day including food, guide, lodging in country inns and use of thoroughbred horses. Both FITS Equestrian and Equitour offer Austrian riding programs every summer. Their premier offering is the 8-day Grossglockner Tour. Starting at Neukirchen, guide Hannspeter Gantner will lead riders through the Alps to the slopes of the Grossglockner, Austria's tallest peak. The trip features fast gallops through valleys, and fantastic views from the upper elevations, as high as 8,200'.

For those who want to spend more time in the valleys, Gantner leads a second summer tour, the Alps of Kitzbühel. This trip spends a week traversing the beautiful Salzach Valley from Zell Am See to the base of the Grossglockner. After a first-day orientation ride, you venture through the valley and then climb past timberline to the Wildkogoel ski resort at 6,000'. You will overnight at an alpine chalet, then cross the valley to visit Höhen Tauern National Park. Along the way you will ride through wild flower-covered meadows, walk the horses through quaint postcard villages, and pass near medieval castles. The trip concludes with a gallop along the Salzach River to Stuhfelden, an ascent up narrow trails to the Sommertor, and a final ride through the Salzach meadows back to Neukirchen.

During these Austrian tours you'll stay at immaculate country inns and chalets. While these are not deluxe hotels, even the most modest country inns are maintained to exceptional standards--rivaling that of fine hotels in the States. The service is invariably efficient yet gracious.

We want to re-emphasize that both these trips are major bargains. The estimated cost of the Grossglockner ride is $1,000, while the Kitzbühel Alps ride is priced at about $950. This covers everything but lunches. For

information, contact Equitour at (800) 545-0019, or FITS Equestrian at (800) 666-FITS.

COLORADO

Rockies Wilderness Horsepacking

Although horsepacking adventures are offered throughout North America, some of our favorite trips run in Colorado. Here you will find abundant wildlife, beautiful alpine scenery and trails that are less heavily traveled than those in the Sierra or the Tetons.

The leading outfitter in southwest Colorado is the Rapp Guide Service, 47 Electra Lake Road, Durango, CO 81301, (303) 247-8923. Jerry and Anne Rapp take small groups (typically four to six riders) to a number of less-traveled destinations in the San Juan National Forest. Our favorite trip is a loop through Silver Mesa and the Needle Mountain Range. You depart from the Bear Ranch and travel for 5 to 6 days over rugged and dramatic mountains. The group crosses two 11,000' passes, spending 80 percent of the time above timberline. Cost is about $130 per day.

The Rapps' premier pack trip, an 8-day Best of the San Juans tour, begins with a train trip on the historic Durango to Silverton line. From the trailhead, you ride along the Continental Divide to a remote alpine valley, home to large herds of elk. Five days are spent at two different high camps before the group returns by rail to Durango. Cost is substantial--more than $1,300 last year--but past customers have raved about the scenery and the wildlife.

Another recommended horsepacking operation is the Bear Basin Ranch in south central Colorado. Guides Amy Finger and Gary Ziegler, trained naturalists and former Outward Bound instructors, lead 3 and 5-day pack trips into the rugged Sangre de Cristo range. Behind these razor-edged peaks lies a little-visited world of alpine meadows, shimmering lakes and countless miles of trails ideal for horsepacking. Amy and Gary specialize in custom trips on seldom-used routes. Their Ultimate Pack Trip follows game trails into incredibly remote areas. On all trips, Amy and Gary instruct customers on wilderness

skills, saddling technique and orienteering. To make reservations, contact A.W.E., P.O. Box 1486, Boulder, CO 80306, (800) 444-0099, the agent for Bear Basin.

EGYPT

The Ride of the Pharaohs

Everyone should visit Egypt at least once in his or her lifetime. The pyramids and tombs inspire awe unlike anything in the urban world. Even with throngs of tourists, there is something almost mystical about riding beside these ancient temples.

If you find yourself in Cairo on a regular sightseeing tour, you can take a taxi across the Nile to Giza on the West Bank. Offer your driver a few Egyptian pounds to find a reputable horse outfitter. (Camel rides are popular as well, but you will cover more ground, far more comfortably, on a horse.) Expect to pay less than $10 per hour to rent a good steed. Try to get one with some energy left in him--if you have a spirited horse and a cooperative guide, you will be allowed to gallop through the sands of the Sahara,

Makay, Idaho/DAVID STOECKLEIN

not more than a quarter-mile from the Great Pyramids. This has to rank as one of the greatest $10 adventures on the planet.

For those looking for more than a short day-ride, FITS Equestrian and Equitour offer organized Egyptian riding tours. The 11-day programs begin in Cairo with a transfer across the Nile to Giza. Riders rest up the first night at the fabled Mena House Oberoi Hotel, which has housed FDR, Agatha Christie and other luminaries. Here guests are wined and dined while enjoying superb views of Egypt's most famous sight-- the Great Pyramid of Cheops.

Two days' ride later, the caravan camps at the edge of Faijum Oasis. Daylight brings an optional ride along the banks of Lake Birket Quarun and a chance to visit the archaeological dig at Karamis, with the evening spent in the town of Faiyum. The Hotel Auberge Faiyum--a grand colonial hostelry--offers a pleasant interlude from camp life with huge rooms and beds, a full bar and food fit for visiting dignitaries.

The next few days are spent winding along ancient water canals, stopping to explore the remote pyramids at Dashur, Medu and Ellisht, and the tombs at Sakkara (a must-see on any Egyptian itinerary). The last day's ride leads back to Giza, leaving plenty of time to ponder the mysteries of Giza's mighty Sphinx and other ancient monuments.

The Ride of the Pharaohs is offered February through April and October through December--periods of moderate temperatures and blue skies. The cost from Cairo is approximately $2,130. As you will spend 4 to 7 hours per day in the saddle for 9 days running, this tour is best for experienced riders in good physical shape. For further information, contact Equitour at (800) 545-0019; or FITS Equestrian at (800) 666-FITS.

JOHN KELLY

WYOMING

Cattle Drive Vacations

Most recently popularized by Billy Crystal in *City Slickers*, the Wild West cattle drive is part of the American mythology. You rise at dawn's light, then mount your trusty quarter horse to guide the herd across the open prairie to new pastures. At night you relax around the campfire, enjoying the simple satisfaction of a job well done.

Today, at a number of working ranches throughout the West, you can relive the experience of the great American cattle drive, joining a trail boss and his cadre of cowboys on a 4 to 5-day trail drive, covering about 50 miles of ground. City slickers or not, guests will ride saddle to saddle with professional cowboys, roping, cutting and rounding up strays. Our favorite cattle drives are run by the High Island Ranch, located 60 miles southeast of Cody, Wyoming. What makes High Island's cattle drives so special is the scenery. Starting from an upper mountain lodge situated at 9,000', or the main ranch at 4,000', the drives move through the wild Wyoming high country, with great alpine vistas all along the route. You spend the first 3 days bunching up the herd at the ranch, before hitting the trail for 3 days and 2 nights. The main drives are scheduled for June and September, although the ranch hosts guests all summer. Adult prices are about $850 per week, and $550 for children age 12-16. Contact High Island, P.O. Box 71, Hamilton Dome, WY 82427, (307) 867-2374.

Another solid program is Cattle Drive America (CDA), based at the 47,000-acre Belvor Ranch along the Colorado-Wyoming border. Each year, CDA runs eight or nine different cattle drives between June and September.

CDA's premier cattle drive runs in late July, along the Good Night Loving Trail, the original trail from Texas to Cheyenne. The herd will be moved overland to market, with the drive culminating in the annual Cheyenne Rodeo. This route offers the complete western experience--frontier

towns, Indian reservations, and herds of buffalo and antelope. In Wyoming you will drive the herd through General Pershing's ranch, crossing high plateaus at more than 8,000'. This drive runs 9 days and costs about $1,500 per person. CDA's other drives last 5 days, and cost roughly $900. Contact Cattle Drive America (Belvor Ranch), 16776 Bernardo Center Drive, Ste. 215, San Diego, CA 92128, (619) 487-2125.

Farther west, Hondoo Rivers and Trails, based at Torrey, Utah, runs an excellent cattle drive through Capitol Reef National Park and the Dixie National Forest. The Canyonlands scenery on this drive is diverse and spectacular--from red rock buttes to cool aspen forests above 9,000'. A maximum of 10 guests accompany a half-dozen full-time cowboys on the 5 or 6-day journeys, offered in May and again in September. The price is a bargain--$600 to $675

Wild horse roundup, Shoshone/DAVID STOECKLEIN

A land of grass and wild flowers, endless vistas and clear water, this is ideal horse country. The trip is rigorous--you'll ride 25 miles a day on the average, spending up to 8 hours per day in the saddle. Lodging is in tents, communes and yurts. Food is local and basic--mutton, yak and noodles. The 10-day, 200-mile ride includes a visit to 21,650' Four Sisters Mountain and to the Wolong Panda Reserve. The remainder of the 23-day tour is spent in Beijing, Chengdu and Hong Kong.

On the Inner Mongolian journeys you will ride small, but hardy Mongolian horses fitted with Chinese army saddles. After flying to Beijing, you travel by train to Chengdu and then by bus to Zhenglan Qi, where the ride begins. Your mounts will carry you on a 200-mile loop north of Hohhot, capitol of Inner Mongolia. The route takes you through forests and along lakes and river banks. Near the Black Wind River you'll have a chance to explore the ruins of the former capitol of the Yuan Dynasty, circa 1250 A.D. Many parts of the itinerary are open only by special permission of the Chinese Army.

Again, this is no luxury trip. You stay in yurts, communes or camp out under the stars (the altitude is a moderate 4,000', so the nights aren't too cold). Baggage, food and camping gear are carried by a truck that meets the group at noon and day's end. City accommodations, however, are in first-class western-style hotels.

Boojum's Tibet and Inner Mongolia trips depart in late June and early August respectively. Advance bookings are important as groups are limited to 15. The Tibet trips cost $3,500, including all accommodation, meals and transportation within China. Mongolian trips run $3,250, all-inclusive. For further information, contact Boojum Expeditions, 14543 Kelly Canyon Road, Bozeman, MT 59715, (406) 587-0125.

including all gear and meals. Trust us, this is a great trip at a great price. Contact Hondoo's agent, A.W.E., P.O. Box 1486, Boulder, CO 80306, (800) 444-0099.

CHINA

Distant Lands, Ancient Cultures

One can hardly think of a more exotic destination than the high plateaus of Tibet and Mongolia, present-day provinces of China. A riding trip is the ideal way to experience these distant realms, where the horse has been the focus of the culture for centuries. Touring by horseback brings you closer to the local people--you travel as they do, experiencing their culture from the same vantage point, not as outsiders sealed off in a tourist bus.

As you might expect, there are no commercial outfitters in the far reaches of Tibet and Mongolia. However, for the past decade, Boojum Expeditions has offered challenging and rewarding 3-week riding expeditions to these remote areas of China. On Boojum Expeditions' trips you ride on local stock with traditional tack and saddle. Local herdsmen act as your guides, riding with you each day and tending the horses at night.

After visiting Chengdu, the capitol of Sichuan Province, Boojum's Tibetan ride begins in the Aba grasslands, on the eastern edge of the Tibetan Plateau. From here, the starting point of the Red Army's historic Long March, the Yellow River flows north and the Yangtze River flows south.

Kirghiz horseman, China/GALEN ROWELL

GREAT RIDING ADVENTURES WORLDWIDE

A T PRESENT, ONLY TWO MAJOR AMERICAN COMPANIES OFFER FOREIGN HORSE TRIPS: FITS EQUESTRIAN AND Equitour. These two companies actually go to many of the same destinations and even use the same foreign stables in many cases. In general, these tours are excellent. They visit premier riding destinations worldwide, at a fairly low cost. A full week of guided riding in the Austrian Alps, for example, is under $1,000 per person, including lodging in good inns.

CONTACT: **Equitour c/o Bitterroot Ranch,** *P.O. Box 807, Dubois, WY 82513, (800) 545-0019, (307) 455-2778;* and **FITS Equestrian,** *2011 Alamo Pintado Road, Solvang, CA 93463, (800) 666-FITS, (805) 688-9494; FAX: (805) 688-2943.* Note: Prices are subject to change in 1992. Expect 5-10 percent increases across the board. Trips are rated ★ to ★★★★★ for quality; $ for special value; skill levels are rated 1-5; 5 is the most advanced. Prices are per person, double occupancy. Codes used are: NP (National Park).

JOHN DENNY ASHLEY

LOCATION	TRIP	DESCRIPTION	OPERATOR(S)	TRIP DAYS	RIDING DAYS (HRS/DAY)
AFRICA	MAASAI MARA SAFARI (KENYA)	Maasai Mara Game Park, Siria Plateau, Lake Baringo Island, Samburu Game Reserve, Aberdare NP. All A+ wildlife.	Equitour FITS	16	7 (8 in 4WD)
	TANZANIA OVERLAND	Game parks between Mt. Kilimanjaro and Mt. Meru. Few tourists.	FITS	9	7 (3-6)
ARGENTINA	GAUCHO TRAILS	Private estancia in Pampas Humida, then Butch Cassidy Trail in Patagonia--Bandits Canyon, Los Alerces NP.	FITS	15	10 (4-6)
AUSTRALIA	SNOWY MOUNTAIN RIDE	High country wilderness trail ride--camping. Rivers, Kiandra Gold Fields, hot springs. 25 miles/day.	Equitour FITS	7 15	5 (7) 9 (4-6)
AUSTRIA	KITZBÜHEL ALPINE	High alpine trail, glaciers, meadows, alpine inns, Höhen Tauern NP, fast gallops.	Equitour FITS	8	6 (5-7)
	GROSSGLOCKNER TOUR	Ultimate alpine trail ride, glaciers, 8,000' trail, valley gallops, spectacular scenery, fine inns & chalets.	FITS Equitour	8	6 (4-7)
BELIZE	MAYAN JUNGLE EXPL.	Trail rides to caves, waterfalls, Mayan ruins, ride jungle streams, then 3 days on barrier reef beaches, deluxe hotel.	FITS Equitour	6 or 9	5 (4-5)
CANADA	QUEBEC FOLIAGE RIDE	Montreal, Gentilly River, gallops, sand dunes, maple forest.	Equitour	6	5 (5-6)
ENGLAND	EXMOOR	Stud farms, castles, Homer & Barle Valleys, manor house lodging. Many gallops across moors & heather.	FITS Equitour	8	6 (5-6)
	STONEHENGE TRAIL	A leisurely ride through the heartland of England. Visit Stonehenge via the Salisbury Plain. A good first tour.	FITS	8	6 (3-6)
FRANCE	LOIRE VALLEY	Saumur, Foret de Villandry, castle visits. Moderate rides. Country inn lodging.	Equitour FITS	11	9 (5-7)
	PERIGORD TRAIL	Through the Dordogne--rivers, chateaux lodging, vineyards, very scenic valleys, gourmet food.	FITS	8	6 (4-6)
	PROVENCE/CAMARGUE	Ardeche Mtns., Rhone River, Baronnies crest trail, St. Trini Eques. Ctr., Alpilles ridges, Durance Valley.	FITS	9	7 (4-7)
GERMANY	BLACK FOREST	Loeffingen, Rhine Valley, quaint villages, pine forests.	FITS	8	6 (4-6)
HUNGARY	MATRA-DANUBE TOUR	Ride through forests and along the Danube. Very scenic. Castle lodging. Fast ride on spirited mounts. Many gallops.	FITS	8	6 (4-6)
	ORSEG RIDE	Remote, beautiful region rarely visited, Lake Balaton, meadows, streams, near Austria--ideal riding territory. Fast and challenging.	FITS Equitour	8	6 (4-7)
IRELAND	DONEGAL FROM THE SADDLE	Moderate ride featuring gorgeous, diverse terrain--long beaches, mountains, lakes. Nice inns and excellent tour guide.	FITS Equitour	8	6 4-6)
	BEACH, DUNES & TRAILS	A lovely low-cost tour in Co. Sligo for independent riders. Beaches and green highlands. Riders must saddle, feed and groom horses.	Equitour FITS	8	6 (5-7)
ITALY	TUSCANY	Rendola, vineyards, Arno Valley, Mount St. Michele trails, manor houses, castles, Siena, forest gallops.	FITS Equitour	8	6 (4-5)
	SAINTS & WARRIORS	Fast-paced rides in Siena countryside on tall, strong horses: Anglo-Arabs, Tolfetanos, Maremmanos.	FITS	7	5 (4-7)
JAMAICA	MONTEGO BAY	Chukka Cove, beach to mountain ride, dressage/jumping lessons, visit villages, swim and run horses at beach.	FITS	8	Various
MOROCCO	ROYAL CITIES TOUR	Meknes, Volubilis, Fez, Rabat. Open country. Fast, strong horses.	Equitour, FITS	9	7 (4-7)
NEW ZEALAND	TWO ISLAND TOUR	Nature parks, rainforest, working ranches, alpine lakes, mile-long beaches, outstanding scenery and diversity.	FITS	14	11 (5-7)
PORTUGAL	LUSITANO RIDE	Alcainca, beach ride, calvary school, Mafra Nature Preserve.	Equitour, FITS	8	6 (4-6)
SCOTLAND	ARGYLL ADVENTURE	Heart of Scotland--Loch Fyne, Isle of Mull, Inveraray Castle, Duntrune Castle, wildlife park, gallops & jumping.	FITS	8	5 (4-6)
SPAIN	ANDALUSIA RIDE	Malaga, Almoraima preserve, long gallops, Costa De La Luz (Southern Route), beach gallops, Zahara, forest trails.	FITS	9	7 (6-8)
	EXTREMADURA (5 tours)	Options: Tietar Valley (farms & rivers); Guadalope (mtn. & forest); Corneja Valley (Avila, 6,000'); La Transhumanica (12 days); Route of Conquistadors (22 days).	FITS	8, 12, 22	6 (4-6)
UNITED STATES	CALIFORNIA COAST	Redwood Parks, Mendocino, beach gallops, xlnt. country inns.	FITS	8	7 (8)
	MONUMENT VALLEY	Awesome scenery. High desert, Indian ruins, Monument Valley loop trails from permanent basecamp (6 days camping).	Donnelly Stables (800) 346-4403	8	8 (6)
	PONY EXPRESS RIDE (Wyoming)	Oregon Trail, Sweetwater Canyon, old forts & mining towns, wild horse reserves, Pony Express stations, Cont'l Peak.	FITS Equitour	8	6 (5-6)

KEITH GUNNAR *COURTESY FRENCH TOURIST BOARD* *JOHN KELLY*

Horses	Tack	Skill Req'd.	Lodging Incl.	Food Incl.	Options	Cost	Season	Rating
Somali/Arab	French Trekking Australian	3	Yes	Yes	Full 14-day riding tour	$3600	Jan-Mar Jun-Oct	★★★★
Various	English	3	Yes	Yes	Ngorongoro safari	$1900	Jan-Oct	★★★
Various	Gaucho	3-4	Yes, 2 days camp	Yes	Gallops, work cattle	$1750	Spr, Fall	★★★
Various	Australian	3	Camp	Yes	10-day trip	$765 $2600 (15 days)	All	★★
Various	English	3	Yes	No	Town sightsee	$970	Summer	★★★★$
Various	English	4	Yes	No	Glacier walks	$970	Summer	★★★★★$
Various	Military	2	Some	Yes	3-day beach resort stay	$1000 $1350	All	★★★
Various	Eng./West.	1-3	Yes	Yes	Novice mounts	$585	Fall	★★
Hunters	English	4-5	Yes	Yes	Castle tours	$1700	Apr-Oct	★★★
Spanish breeds	English	2	Yes	Breakfast & lunch	Castle tours	$1550	May-Sep	★★★
Various	English	4	Yes	Yes	Castle tours	$1550	Jun-Sep	★★★★
Pelle Française	English	4	Yes	Yes	Wine tasting	$1150	May-Sep	★★★★$
Various	English	3-4	Yes	Yes	1-week option $650	$1550	Apr, May, Sep, Dec	★★★★
Hanover	English	3	Yes	Yes	Horse-drawn wagon	$950	May-Oct	★★
Kisber-Hungarian	English	5	Yes	Yes	Art museums	$1500	Apr-Oct	★★★★
Kisber-Hungarian	English	5	Yes	Yes	City visits	$1500	Apr, Aug	★★★
Irish Hunters Connemara Ponies	English	3	Yes	Yes	8-day hunt week for strong riders	$1500	Mar-Oct	★★★★
Hunters	English	4.5	Yes	Yes	2-week independent tour in Donegal	$750	All	★★★★
Various	English	2.5	Yes	Yes	Museum & castles	$1450	Apr-Oct	★★
See tour description	English	4	Yes	Yes	Palio Piazza historic race	$1985	May-Oct	★★★★
Various	English	2-3	Yes	No	Polo clinic	$1400 low $1750 high	All	★★★★
Arabians	English	4-5	Yes (4 days camp)	Yes	City shopping	$1200	Apr-Oct	★★★
Various	Eng./West./ Stock	3	Yes	Yes	1, 2 or 3 weeks	$1300/week average	Oct-Apr	★★★
Lusitano	English	3.5	Yes	Yes	Dressage display	$1525	Mar-Oct	★★★★
Hunters	English	4-5	Yes	Yes	Jumping, beach rides	$1800	Apr-Oct	★★★★
Andalusian	Portugese	3	Yes	Yes	14-day trip; northern itiner.	$1400	Mar-Nov	★★★
Spanish Arabian	Spanish	3-4	Yes	Yes	14 or 22 days	$1450 8 days $6123 22 days	All	★★★★★
Various	Eng./West.	3	Yes	Yes	2d week in SF $825	$1560	Summer	★★★
Quarter	Western	2	Yes (camp)	Yes		$1200	All	★★★
Quarter	Western	2	Yes	Yes	Fishing	$ 900	Summer	★★

151

Western Riding Vacations

FOR CITY DWELLERS, A WESTERN RIDING VACATION CAN BE THE PERFECT SUMMER escape for the whole family. You get away from the press of urban life to enjoy the best America has to offer: wide open spaces, clean air, unspoiled scenery. Many options are available. Organized trail rides or wagon trains take you across classic overland routes in Wild West style. On a working ranch or cattle drive you can learn horsemanship and ride the range alongside working cowboys. At western guest ranches you can ride easy trails, fish alpine trout streams, or just relax in a friendly country setting.

TRAIL RIDES AND WAGON TRIPS

If you *really* want to get away from it all, an organized trail ride or wagon trip may suit you better than a residential stay at a dude ranch. On a trail ride, you'll venture through the backcountry, often following an historic trail used by early homesteaders or Indians. A covered wagon trip lets you experience cross-country travel pioneer-style. Wagon trips tend to offer a bit more luxury than regular trail rides, as you can bed down on mattresses in the wagons, rather than sleep on the ground in tents. On most covered wagon trips, you have the option of shifting from wagon to horseback during the journey.

◼ DONNELLY STABLES AT GOLD CANYON
6010 South Kings Ranch Rd., Gold Canyon, AZ 85219, (800) 346-4403.

Donnelly Stables offers 5, 7 and 8-day horseback vacation packages in Arizona's most scenic locations including Monument Valley, the Superstition, White and Bradshaw Mountains, and Mogollon Rim (Zane Grey country). Monument Valley is a western dreamworld; the best way to experience it, by far, is on horseback. Get up early to witness the spectacular play of light on the valley's massive red rock formations. Valley tours run for 8 days in spring and fall for about $1,200. The other programs run about $650 for 5 days,

DAVID STOECKLEIN

with longer trips about $135 per day. On all trips you make daily rides from a comfortable basecamp with hot showers. Rating: ★★★

◼ BOX K RANCH
P.O. Box 110, Moran, WY 83013, (307) 543-2407.

The Box K's Jackson Hole Trail Ride celebrated its 21st anniversary last year, making it one of the most enduring adventure trips in Wyoming's high country. Much of the 5-day journey is spent above timberline on spectacular alpine routes in the Tetons. Although the trip is suitable for total greenhorns, the Trail Ride has long been popular with real horsemen. Most of the riders are horse-owners themselves, or have plenty of trail-riding experience. The trip runs for 7 days in August and September, and costs approximately $600-$650. Rating: ★★

◼ BAR T FIVE
P.O. Box 3415, Jackson, WY 83001, (307) 733-5386; FAX: (307) 733-3534.

For the past 19 years, the Bar T Five Ranch has offered covered wagon adventures in the scenic Targhee National Forest between Yellowstone and Grand Teton National Parks. Along the way you will be able to canoe on alpine lakes or take sidetrips to Calf Creek Falls in Yellowstone and the beautiful Fall River. While this is an authentic covered wagon trip (unlike some other operations, you won't see trucks at the campsites), comfort and convenience aren't forgotten. Both tents and wagons are supplied with foam pads, sheets and pillows. The food is excellent, prepared Dutch oven-style by talented cooks who double as wranglers. Trip participants can join in all wagon train activities--even harnessing and driving the teams. The 4-day trips run throughout the summer at a cost of $495 for adults, $450 for ages 9-14. This is a top quality program with many repeat customers. Rating: ★★★

◼ WAGONS WEST
Box 1156, Afton, WY 83110, (800) 447-4711, or (307) 886-9693.

Wagons West, celebrating its 21st season in 1992, offers authentic 2, 4 and 6-day covered wagon trips through the Grand Teton foothills in Wyoming. Guests can either ride in the wagons, or accompany the wagon train as outriders. The wagons move out early each day, allowing participants to make sidetrips on horseback during the afternoon and sunset hours. Anglers will find some great fly-fishing streams along the route.

In Wyoming, the wagon train travels through open ranges and high forests with great vistas of the Tetons. The food, served chuckwagon-style, is hearty, and there is western music each night. This is a time-tested program, great for families. Adult prices are $240, $465 and $635 for 2, 4 and 6 days respectively, $195, $365 and $510 for kids under 16. Groups discounts are available. Rating: ★★★

Bruneau roundup/DAVID STOECKLEIN

WORKING RANCH VACATIONS

If you want something more active than a conventional dude ranch vacation, consider spending a week at a working ranch. You'll share in the day-to-day operations of the ranch--rounding up strays, checking fences, and punching doggies. Visit during a seasonal roundup and you can join a real cattle drive--moving the herd by day, and camping out under the stars by night.

■ GRAPEVINE CANYON RANCH
P.O. Box 302, Pearce, AZ 85625, (602) 826-3185, or call A.W.E., (800) 444-0099.

Grapevine Canyon Ranch is an authentic working cattle ranch located high in the Dragoon Mountains, 85 miles southeast of Tucson. Skilled riders can work the range alongside real cowboys--riding herd and rounding up strays. Much of the terrain is steep and rugged, offering a real challenge for even experienced

trail riders. The Grapevine is open year-round; spring and fall are the best times to visit. Accommodations are first-class. You may ride like a real cowboy here, but you can still enjoy a little luxury at day's end. Cost is about $120 per person per day, including meals. Rating: ★★

■ HIGH ISLAND RANCH
P.O. Box 71, Hamilton Dome, WY 82427, (307) 867-2374.

If you want to experience real cowboy life, head up to Wyoming's High Island Ranch, a no-compromise working ranch where they'll put you in the saddle the first day you arrive and test your mettle until you leave. You'll help move the herd on a long-distance cattle drive from mountain pastures to Cottonwood Creek. This is the real thing, not a roundup staged solely for the guests. The spring drives run in

June and July, with a final trip from late August through mid-September. Price for one week is roughly $850 per person, double occupancy. Rating: ★★★★

■ SCHIVELY RANCH
1062 Road 15, Lovell, WY 82431, (307) 548-6688.

The Schively Ranch is another destination where you can join in actual ranch work in the company of real cowboys. Using the ranch's well-trained quarter horses, guests ride the range every day, assisting with ranch activities including roping, branding and cattle drives. In the spring and fall guests will help move the herd 60 miles to the ranch site located on the east slope of the Pryor Range on the Wyoming border. A small, family-run operation, the Schively Ranch handles no more than 14 guests at any time. The reputation of the Ranch has been spreading, so we recommend you book well in advance. The cost per week is about $650-$750. Rating: ★★★

GUEST RANCHES

If you want more comfort and convenience than you may get on a working ranch, an old-fashioned guest ranch stay may be the best choice. With dozens of fine ranches to choose from, you may wish to consult an agency before you pick your destination. **American Wilderness Experience (A.W.E.),** *P.O. Box 1486, Boulder, CO 80306, (800) 444-DUDE, or (303) 444-2622,* books vacations at more than 50 guest ranches in Colorado, Arizona, Wyoming and Montana. **Off the Beaten Path,** travel consultants located at *109 E. Main Street, Bozeman, MT 59715, (406) 586-1311, (800) 445-2995; FAX: (406) 587-4147,* will also help you select the best ranch for your interests. A $3 directory describing over 100 western ranches is published by the **Dude Ranchers' Association,** *P.O. Box 471, La Porte, CO 80535, (303) 223-8440.* Some of our favorite guest ranches are listed on the next page.

DAVID STOECKLEIN

153

Colorado

■ SKYLINE GUEST RANCH
Box 67, Telluride, CO 81435, (303) 728-3757.

The Skyline, one of the most beautiful ranches in North America, is hard to top as a western vacation destination. Guests can ride through green meadows in the lower elevations, or venture as high as 14,000' in the Rockies on a wilderness pack trip. Mountain biking, hiking and fly-fishing are also popular. (There is excellent fishing on nearby streams and lakes.) Accommodations and food are first class. In winter, Skyline offers nordic skiing at the ranch and downhilling at nearby resorts. Summer cost is $840 per person per week. Reservations for the summer are recommended one year in advance. Rating: ★★★★

■ WIND RIVER RANCH
P.O. Box 3410 AT, Estes Park, Colorado 80517, (303) 586-4212, or (800) 523-4212.

The Wind River Ranch offers deluxe facilities in a breathtaking setting just seven miles from Estes Park. You can ride through the National Park high country, returning home to excellent food and accommodations. Although there are better places for challenging riding (no overnight pack trips are offered), the Wind River Ranch offers all the extras. Special features include a stocked fish pond, live piano music and hayrides. Make reservations well in advance. Prices start at about $700 per person per week. Rating: ★★★

Idaho

■ WAIPITI MEADOW RANCH
Diana Haynes, H.C. 72, Cascade, ID 83611, (208) 382-4336 (radio-phone).

Located in Idaho's remote River of No Return Wilderness Area, the Waipiti Meadow Ranch offers an outstanding setting for high alpine horseback riding, as well as fishing, and rafting on the nearby Middle Fork of the Salmon River. The ridge-top pack trips are super, with great scenery and excellent fishing in a number of alpine streams and lakes. Near the ranch lodge are miles of day-riding trails, a stocked trout pond, a salmon stream, and plentiful wildlife. Daily rate is roughly $125 per person. Rating: ★★★

Montana

■ LONE MOUNTAIN RANCH
P.O. Box 69, Big Sky, MT 59716, (406) 995-4644; FAX: (406) 995-4670.

Lone Mountain operates in both summer and winter. June through October you can enjoy ranch activities and ride trails along the outskirts of Yellowstone Park, about 20 miles away. An Orvis-endorsed fly-fishing resort, Lone Mountain offers angling on the Madison and Gallatin Rivers, two of America's best trout streams. In the winter, you can cross-country ski from the ranch, or try telemarking in the nearby Spanish Peaks Wilderness. Prices start at $925 per week. Rating: ★★★

■ MOUNTAIN SKY GUEST RANCH
P.O. Box 1128, Bozeman, MT 59715, (800) 548-3392, or (406) 587-1244.

The Mountain Sky Guest Ranch, situated in Paradise Valley, is a deluxe, AAA four-diamond facility in a beautiful location. All the amenities are here: pool, tennis courts, gourmet dining and excellent fishing. The wranglers are very skilled and the horses are first rate. This is a high country ranch with top-flight amenities. Rating: ★★★

Wyoming

■ ABSAROKA RANCH
P.O. Box 929, Dubois, WY 82513, (307) 455-2275.

The Absaroka Ranch, nestled between the Absaroka Mountains and the headwaters of the Wind River, offers a scenic, isolated alpine experience. Guests stay in private cabins, with fine hiking, fishing and riding close at hand. The Absaroka Ranch's pack trips to the Washakie Wilderness east of the Tetons are among the best in the country. Owners Budd and Emi Betts take small groups through pristine river valleys and over 11,000' plateaus. Cost is about $115 per day for pack trips, or $650 per week at the ranch. Rating: ★★★★

■ BRIDGER MOUNTAIN RANCH
c/o Dave Warwood, 15100 Rocky Mountain Road, Belgrade, MT 59714, (406) 388-4463.

The Bridger Mountain Ranch is a good choice if you're looking for a rustic working ranch situated in the high country near Yellowstone Park. Learn wrangling skills at the ranch, or join guide Dave Warwood on a 4 to 8-day wilderness pack trip. These pack trips, which typically run between $150 and $200 per day, have been especially popular with fly-fishing enthusiasts. (Warwood's knowledge of the local fishing holes is without peer--his great-grandfather guided in these mountains over a century ago.) Rating: ★★★

Wagon string leaving camp/WILL BREWSTER

Packing horses into Lizard Lake, Taylor Hilgard Range, Montana/WILL BREWSTER

Wilderness Horse-packing Outfitters

WHILE PURIST BACKPACKERS MAY SCOFF AT THE USE OF PACK ANIMALS, HORSE-packing is a sensible and rewarding way to experience the wilderness. You can travel farther and faster into the mountains than on foot, and your horse can easily carry four times the load you could manage with a backpack. Don't fret about picking an outfitter. All those listed below are first rate; you won't go wrong with any of them.

Arizona

■ DOBBIN SHUPE
c/o A.W.E., P.O. Box 1486, Boulder, CO 80306, (800) 444-0099.

During the winter, when the snow covers the northern Rockies, outfitter Dobbin Shupe moves his outfit south from Colorado to Arizona's legendary Superstition Wilderness. Dobbin, a highly respected horse trader, trail boss and backcountry guide, has been in the horsepacking business for well over 40 years. His moving pack trips offer adventurous riding through Arizona's Indian country and the Sonoran high desert. Weeklong trips are scheduled February through April and range from $110 to $120 per day. This is a superior program in every respect; Shupe is considered by many to be one of the very best horsepackers anywhere. Rating: ★★★★

California

■ PINE CREEK PACK TRAINS
P.O. Box 968, Bishop, CA 93515, (619) 387-2797.

Brian and Dee Berner run fine low-impact pack trips on the eastern face of the Sierras. You can join a trans-Sierra crossing over high passes, or follow the John Muir trail along the Sierra Crest and through Kings Canyon National Park. In addition to horseback trips, the Berners offer daily trail rides, and guided pack trips. Prices range from $50 to $130 per day. Rating: ★★

■ SCHOBER'S PACK STATION
Route 2, Box 179, Bishop, CA 93514 , (619) 873-4785 summer, (619) 387-2343 winter.

Walter Shober, and his father before him, have outfitted pack trips in the eastern Sierras since 1930. While Shober's knowledge of the Sierras is without peer, he still runs a simple, low-cost operation without frills. From the base in North Lake near Bishop, Shober sends out mule and horse teams to a variety of destinations. Popular short pack trips take you to the Humphreys Basin and over the Piutte Pass to Hutchinson Meadows. A great longer trip takes you southwest via Muir Pass into Evolution Valley and Kings Canyon National Park. Count on Shober to get you to the top fishing holes in the area. Decades ago, Shober's father personally stocked most of the region's lakes. Cost for a horse or mule is $40 per day, and a packer is $80 per day. The longer trips are arranged on a custom basis, and riders must bring their own food and gear. Rating: ★★★

Colorado

■ RAPP GUIDE SERVICE
47 Electra Lake Road, Durango, CO 81301, (303) 247-8923.

Jerry and Anne Rapp's horse pack trips are among the best in Colorado (see featured trip on page 147). Trips run through the San Juan National Forest and Weminuche Wilderness and cost between $100 and $125 per day, including food and all gear. Groups are small, no more than five or six, and all trips are customized to the guests' interests and riding experience. Rating: ★★★★

Idaho

■ MYSTIC SADDLE RANCH
Stanley, ID 83278, (208) 774-3591.

You can venture into Idaho's rugged Sawtooth Mountains with Jeff and Deb Bitton's family horse pack trips. Itineraries of 1 to 10 days can be arranged for riders of all skill levels and ages, even little kids. Pack trips can be combined with rafting on the Payette River, or fishing at some of the Sawtooth's 180 wilderness lakes. The Spot-Pack program will drop hikers off at an isolated campsite, and then pick them up again on a prearranged date. Pack trips cost approximately $120 per person per day. The Bittons are extremely able and personable outfitters, with over 22 years of experience. Rating: ★★★

■ PIONEER MOUNTAIN OUTFITTERS
Route 2, 3321 Michigan Ave., Twin Falls, ID 83301, (208) 734-3679.

Tom and Debbie Proctor offer 3 to 5-day horse pack trips into Idaho's Pioneer and White Clouds mountain ranges. This region is home to cutthroat, rainbow and brook trout in 8,000' alpine lakes. Most itineraries are customized, small-group adventures which feature seven to 10 miles of riding each day, allowing plenty of time to enjoy the scenery. You can choose from easy family outings or rugged backcountry treks. Pack trips run about $115-$130 per day. Rating: ★★

Montana

■ CAYUSE OUTFITTERS
Box 1218, Livingston, MT 59047, (406) 222-3168.

Archaeologist Larry Lahren leads horse pack trips into the rugged Absaroka-Beartooth Wilderness Areas every summer. An extremely knowledgeable guide, Lahren runs small groups, and avoids the heavily traveled routes, so you won't have

the "Bob," prime habitats for moose, elk and bighorn sheep, are among the most dramatic on the continent. The Blixruds' pack trips run from 7 to 10 days and cost an average of $150 per day. Chuck is also an ace fishing guide who can lead anglers to some of Montana's prime alpine fishing spots. These trips are very popular; we recommend you book well in advance. Rating: ★★★

■ WILDERNESS OUTFITTERS
3800 Rattlesnake Drive, Missoula, MT 59802, (406) 549-2820.

Author of the definitive book on pack trips, *Packing In on Mules and Horses*, outfitter Smoke Elser is perhaps Montana's most renowned wilderness guide. For the past 27 years, he and his wife Thelma have

Oregon

■ OUTBACK RANCH OUTFITTERS
P.O. Box 384, Joseph, OR 97846, (503) 426-4037.

Ken Wick of the Outback Ranch is one of eastern Oregon's most knowledgeable outdoorsmen. He guides first-rate horse trips into Oregon's Wallowa Mountains and the Hell's Canyon region along the Oregon border. The Wallowas encompass a little known but beautiful region of high alpine lakes that has been called the Switzerland of America. In Hell's Canyon you can combine horse-packing with whitewater rafting and fishing on the Snake River. The basic horse pack trips cost about $120 per day, all-inclusive, and last from 3 to 10 days. Rating: ★★★

Utah

■ KEN SLEIGHT PACK TRIPS
Pack Creek Ranch, P.O. Box 1270, Moab, UT 84532, (801) 259-5505.

Ken Sleight offers wilderness trips from his ranch situated near Arches and Canyonlands National Parks. Overnight trips operate from the ranch to the South Mountain cabin from June through August, while horse-supported 3 to 6-day hiking tours are offered in Dark Canyon, the Grand Gulch Primitive Area, and Canyonlands National Park. (You walk while the horses carry the gear.) This region of Utah offers some of America's most dramatic scenery. First-time visitors will be astounded with the vistas. Trips cost about $125-$150 per day; the best time to travel is in the spring and fall. Rating: ★★

Breaking camp/WILL BREWSTER

other packers descending on your high country hideaways. Along with riding, fishing trips and float trips down the Yellowstone River can be arranged. Cayuse Outfitters' pack trips cost an average of $150 per day. Rating: ★★★

■ 7 LAZY P OUTFITTERS
Box 178, Choteau, MT 59422, (406) 466-2044.

For 32 years, Chuck and Sharon Blixrud have operated pack trips through the Bob Marshall Wilderness Area near Montana's Glacier National Park. The mountains of

run outstanding pack trips through the Bob Marshall Wilderness Area. He knows this area, a vast sanctuary where grizzlies and wolverines still roam, as well as any man alive. His pack trips are popular--90 percent of his riders are repeat customers. Elser runs a roving program each summer, covering the entire length of the "Bob" from north to south. Trips run 6 to 10 days at a cost of $160 per day. Specialty photography and fishing itineraries are also available. Rating: ★★★★

Washington

■ NORTH CASCADE SAFARIS
(Claude Miller), P.O. Box 250, Winthrop, WA, (509) 996-2350.

For the past 25 years, Claude Miller has run horsepacking excursions out of Winthrop, Washington into the verdant high country of the Okanogan National

Forest, midway between Seattle and Spokane. Miller knows the Cascades like the back of his hand, and he can put together just about any kind of trip you would want--from 3 days to 2 weeks. Two of the most popular routes are the Sawtooth Ridge Trail to Lake Chelan, and the Pacific Crest National Scenic Trail to the Canadian border, a spectacular trek through 8,000' passes. On most of the trips you cover less than 15 miles a day, so you won't have to spend all your time in the saddle. Miller tries to follow a day of hard riding with some R & R--allowing you time to fish and relax. Pack trips cost about $125 per day. Make reservations well in advance. Rating: ★★★

Wyoming

■ Paul Crittenden

Hidden Basin Outfitters (Jackson Hole), c/o A.W.E., P.O. Box 1486, Boulder, CO 80306, (800) 444-0099.

Paul Crittenden is a living legend in the Jackson Hole area--a true died-in-the-wool outdoorsman who has been around horses for the better part of four decades. Paul's domain is the Gros Ventre Wilderness and Granite Creek Valley, home of the some of the prettiest mountain scenery in Wyoming. His wilderness basecamp is comfortable, with amenities such as a heated mess tent and hot shower, not usually provided by backcountry outfitters. Three and 5-day trips are offered for approximately $125 per day, all-inclusive. Rating: ★★★

■ Dell Creek Ranch

Bondurant, WY 82922, (307) 733-4120.

The Dell Creek Ranch is ideally situated between major mountain ranges and wild rivers. Top guide Pete Cameron leads small, six-person pack trips into the scenic Gros Ventre Mountains and Wyoming Range, both blessed with abundant wildlife and great fishing. Cameron takes his groups to remote areas where you'll rarely encounter other campers. Pack trips run 3, 5 and 7 days; Cameron recommends the 5-day trips for first timers. The cost is about $110 per day per person, and a 10 percent discount is available for returning guests, children under 18 and groups of six. Horseback photo safaris are a popular specialty. Rating: ★★★

■ Lazy Boot Outfitters, Inc.

Greybull River Route, Box 49A, Greybull, WY 82426, (307) 765-2835.

Using a running pack string, Lazy Boot Outfitters goes deeper into the wild than many other horsepackers. From a wilderness basecamp, Lazy Boot's trips explore the distant corners of the Cloud Peak Wilderness Area and Big Horn National Forest. Led by expert naturalist guides with 20 years of experience, these outings offer excellent opportunities for wildlife photography (elk, deer and moose), and fly-fishing (brook, cutthroat and rainbow trout). The pack trips are all customized, with no more than six persons per group. Most trips run 4 to 7 days at a cost of about $135 per day per person. Rating: ★★

Canada

■ Horseback Adventures

P.O. Box 73, Brule, AB, Canada T0E 0C0, (403) 865-4777, or (403) 865-2641.

Horseback Adventures is a small family-run enterprise with over 45 years of experience in the Jasper National Park/ Willmore Wilderness Area, in northern Alberta. The trips run to pristine high alpine lakes--prime trout-fishing country. One and a half pound cutthroats and rainbows are plentiful. A guide plus two to four wranglers accompany each group of 8-14 riders, affording truly personalized attention. The price runs about $600 to $1,200 US for 6 to 12 days. If you've never visited the Canadian Rockies, be assured that these trips offer some of the finest scenery in the world. Rating: ★★★

■ Palliser River Guides & Outfitters

P.O. Box 238, Radium Hot Springs, BC, Canada V0A 1M0, (604) 347-9274.

Palliser Guides can take you to some of the most beautiful spots in the Royal Mountain Range in southeastern BC, the top of the Rockies Wilderness area. Guides are friendly and knowledgeable, and groups are limited to 12 persons. Along with trail rides, special fishing trips to three different regions and photo treks are offered. A typical 3-day trip costs about $300 US per person, all-inclusive. Pack support for extended camping trips is available. Rating: ★★

■ Warner & MacKensie

132 Banff Avenue, P.O. Box 2280, Banff, AB, Canada T0L 0C0, (800) 661-8352, or (403) 762-4551; FAX: (403) 762-8130.

Warner & MacKensie, the leading horse outfitter in Alberta, offers a broad range of wilderness pack trips and riding vacations in Banff National Park in central Alberta. Pack trips can be combined with lodge vacations, and special wildlife-viewing programs are available. The season

DAVID STOECKLEIN

runs from May through October and prices average about $150 US per day, all-inclusive. Rating: ★★ to ★★★ (depending on personnel)

Jungle Exploring

Huli Wigmen, Papua New Guinea/DR. PHIL RASORI

▼

The jungles of the world are our last great wildernesses. Here, despite all our technology, humans have not yet established dominance over nature. The inaccessibility of jungle regions has kept civilization at bay, allowing native cultures to survive relatively undisturbed by modernizing influences. While some areas such as the Amazon, have yielded to high-volume tourism, there still remain corners of the world where you can only travel by foot or dugout canoe. This chapter features these kind of special adventures--trips that take you into the verdant heart of the tropical jungle, to explore its untrammeled mysteries, and to meet the indigenous peoples face to face.

CHAPTER
11

FRANS LANTING/MINDEN PICTURES

A VISIT TO THE JUNGLE IS A VOYAGE BACK IN TIME, TO AN UNTAMED, PRIMEval world. However, the jungle world, as it has existed for millenia, is changing faster than most of us realize. The rivers are being dammed, the rainforests cut, and the creatures of the wild driven from their last sanctuaries. With every passing season, primitive tribes become more modernized, and the wilderness becomes less wild. The jungle is still there, but ours may be the last generation to experience it in all its mystery--so if you plan to go, go soon.

PAPUA NEW GUINEA

Back to the Roots of Man

The New Guinea tribesman, his face vividly painted, and his head ringed by an elaborate headdress, epitomizes the exotic appeal of jungle culture. Papua New Guinea, the last refuge of Stone Age tribes, remains a land of primitive traditions, of mysticism and of magic. For those seeking true adventure, there is no better destination than this land of razor-back mountains and hidden valleys.

In recent years, interest in Papua New Guinea (PNG) has increased dramatically, as Westerners seek out the ultimate in exotic travel. With the growth of tourism has come change. Few areas remain truly wild anymore, and few tribal cultures have not been altered by contact with the modern world. And yet, for those prepared to walk to the most remote settlements in Papua New Guinea's vast interior, there still remain opportunities to observe ancient tribal lifestyles and customs. Many tribal peoples remain isolated from the modern world, in villages accessible only on foot.

Most visits to primitive areas in New Guinea are organized by Trans-Niugini Tours, which is represented by Mountain Travel/Sobek and the Adventure Center in the United States, among other tour companies. The principal areas for tourism are the Sepik River, its tributary the Karawari River, and the high Tari Basin, home of the Huli people, so well known for their ceremonial face-painting and fantastic wig-hats. Sobek runs one of our favorite PNG tours, a 14-day sea/land journey that combines canoeing on the Sepik River with a 4-day trek to the Tari Basin. Trips depart nine months a year at a cost of approximately $2,800.

For hardy trekkers, Sobek will lead you across 84 miles of the infamous Kokoda Trail, site of bloody struggles in WWII. The trail is quite scenic, but you'd better be a strong hiker. Cost is approximately $1,350 for 12 days. If you can spare another week, and about $1,000, you can add the best river

Eight Great Jungle Adventures

run in the Pacific Rim to your vacation--a 6-day descent of the Watut River. This Class IV waterway drains from the rugged Stanley Range and boasts over 150 major rapids. For thrills, scenery and cultural value, the Watut expedition is a world-class adventure, one of the top trips in this book. Contact Sobek at 6420 Fairmont Ave., El Cerrito, CA 94530, (800) 227-2384.

A number of other adventure companies offer PNG tours, which typically combine coastal visits with short highland treks. Wilderness Travel, Overseas Adventure Travel, and Mountain Travel all offer some variation on this theme for $2,300 to $3,200. The Adventure Center offers a variety of PNG tours from 6 to 10 days, ranging in price from about $950 to $2,400. We encourage you to comparison shop among the many options available. Some people will want to sleep in bamboo huts in remote villages, while others will prefer more deluxe accommodations.

A trendy new PNG travel option is the mountain biking expedition. Off the Deep End Travels offers a 13-day mountain bike tour through the highlands. From a lodge basecamp, bikers will explore the hills around Tari for the first week. The group then heads to New Ireland, for a week of exploring coastal foothills and remote beaches. The pace will be fairly leisurely, so you need not be a fitness freak to enjoy yourself. The tour will of course hit the cultural highlights such as Huli villages in the Wahgi Valley, but Off the Deep End has thrown in some tropical R&R as well-- 2 days at the Madang Beach Resort. Price for the May and June tours will be approximately $2,500, excluding airfare. Contact Off the Deep End Travels, P.O. Box 7511, Jackson, WY 83001, (800) 223-6833, or (307) 733-8707 in Wyoming.

IRIAN JAYA

Trekking into the Stone Age

Irian Jaya, the western half of the island of New Guinea, is truly one of the last frontiers, a rugged, isolated land whose native inhabitants are only just now emerging from Stone Age living patterns. This section of the world's highest and second largest island remained largely unexplored until recent decades due to the difficult terrain and dense jungles. Passages through the

interior must be made on foot, over ancient trading routes between small villages. The trekking trails are rugged but beautiful, with many waterfalls and high passes overlooking blankets of clouds.

In recent years, Papua New Guinea has enjoyed a boom in tourism, but few Westerners have ventured to Irian Jaya. A trek through this region remains one of the world's great adventures, an opportunity to go back in time. However, an Irian Jaya trek is also serious business--some of the most primitive tribes are only 10 years removed from cannibalism, and unplanned encounters can mean trouble. No trip to the interior should be attempted without a knowledgeable and experienced guide.

Ecosummer Expeditions, the clear choice among outfitters, pioneered Irian Jaya trekking. Ecosummer offers a variety of 2 or 3-week land trips, ranging from moderate treks to tougher exploratory expeditions. Most trips begin with an exploration of the Baliem River Valley. You will visit the Dani tribespeople, known for their elaborate headgear and exotic ceremonies. Next, on the shorter treks, participants fly by charter aircraft to visit the Yali people of the east. From the Yali village, the group begins a 10-day overland trek along highland trade routes. The trail is scenic but rugged.

From Baliem, the longer exploratory expeditions depart by air to the Korrupun region to visit the Kim-Yal tribe. With the aid of Kim-Yal porters, the group descends to the Brazza River, a remote region first explored by outsiders within the last decade. Upon reaching the Brazza, contact will be made with the Momina tribes, and likely the Obina tribes, a group which receives virtually no other contact with Westerners. The tour concludes with a dugout canoe trip along the Asmat River.

If you haven't gotten the message yet, these Ecosummer trips are the real thing--serious expeditions offering a unique op-

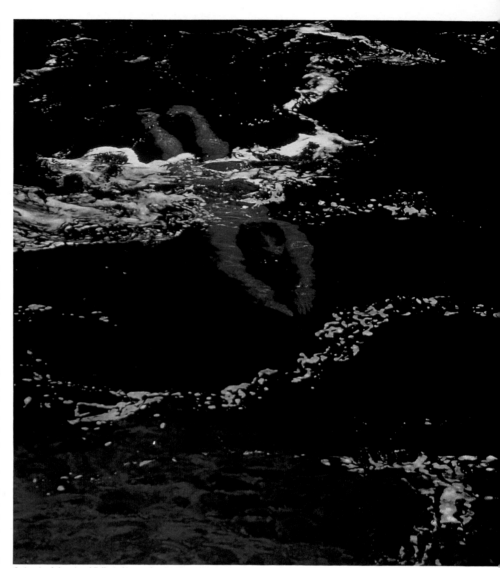

Swimming below Angel Falls, in Venezuela's Lost World/MICHAEL NICHOLS

portunity to observe some of the most primitive cultures on the planet. Both expeditions are reasonably priced. The 1991 price for the 15-day treks, including local charter flights, was about $1,800 US, while the 3-week exploratory expeditions ranged from $2,850 US. Ecosummer notes that "we utilize native porters, but it should be emphasized that the rugged topography makes it essential to be in good condition." Seven departures are offered between August and November, and prices are subject to change. Contact Ecosummer at 1516 Duranleau Street, Granville Island, Vancouver, BC, Canada V6H 3S4, (604) 669-7741. Mountain Travel/Sobek also offers a trip to Irian Jaya, featuring a trek through the Baliem Valley, and

a visit to the Dani tribe to observe native ceremonies. Only 4 days of the 10-day, $1,250 Sobek trip are actually spent on trek, so you'll see fewer remote villages than on the Ecosummer tours. For information, call Mountain Travel/Sobek at (800) 227-2384.

THE LOST WORLD

Angel Falls and Mt. Roraima

Known only to native Indians until 1935, when it was spotted by bush pilot Jimmy Angel, southern Venezuela's Angel Falls is the world's highest cascade. From a high plateau, the river overshoots a sheer sandstone edge and falls clear for over 3,200'. The water doesn't actually spill off the top. It drops into crevasses, then comes out of the mountain just below the rim. Thus, you can

On trek in Irian Jaya/MICHAEL NICHOLS

The adventurer has a number of Lost World itineraries from which to choose. The best value is offered by the Adventure Center, which offers a 21-day trip for $1,950. You begin with a 5-day canoe cruise up river to the Falls (if water levels are too low an overflight is substituted). This is followed by a 6-day trek to the summit of Mt. Roraima, where the group is rewarded with views of the Venezuelan rainforest from sheer 2,500' cliffs. The balance of the trip is spent visiting the gold rush region of El Dorado, and Venezuelan beaches in Vallecito and Caracas. Six days are spent camping, with 14 nights in rustic inns. The best time to go is May through November, when the water is high enough to allow the canoes to navigate all the way to the base of the Falls. Departures are year-round. Contact the Adventure Center, 1311 63rd Street, Suite 200, Emeryville, CA 94608, (800) 227-8747. For $800 more, Wilderness Travel offers a similar trip that has been very highly rated by past customers. In addition to the obligatory Mt. Roraima trek, and dugout canoe trips, you get an overflight of the Falls. Total price is about $2,600 for 20 days, exclusive of airfare to Caracas. Contact Wilderness Travel, 801 Allston Way, Berkeley, CA 94710, (800) 368-2794.

If you haven't got much time, you can join Sobek on an 11-day Lost World trek. After arriving in Caracas, two days are spent reaching the top of Mt. Roraima, a place Sobek describes as "an alternate universe of sculpted rock formations, odd-shaped crystal, bizarre carnivorous plants, and clear pools...It's like exploring a Japanese garden whose architect has pulled out all the stops in creating a zen environment of meditation and mystery." You camp overnight in a huge cave, then proceed to Canaima and Angel Falls. (A climb to the top is optional.) Trips depart in spring and fall at a cost of about $2,000. Call Mountain Travel/Sobek at (800) 227-2384.

COSTA RICA

Central America's Eden

Costa Rica may well be the most ecologically rich and geographically diverse region of its size on the planet. A land of towering volcanoes (it has over 40), high-altitude cloud forests, black sand beaches, raging whitewater rivers and dense tropical rainforest, Costa Rica is an ideal venue for jungle exploration. In this unique bridge between two major continents, plant and animal species from both northern and southern hemispheres thrive in an ecosystem still largely undisturbed by man. Costa Rica has set aside over 4 percent of its territory to wilderness preserves and a well-organized network of national parks. The abundance of animal life sustained in these protected zones has earned Costa Rica the reputation as the "wildlife sanctuary of the Americas."

Any proper Costa Rican jungle adventure should include Manuel Antonio National Park, Costa Rica's smallest and most beautiful park. This preserve is in a transition zone between northern dry forest and southern wet forest. The closed-canopy rainforest is interspersed with ceiba trees and filled with orchids. Monkeys, sloths, opossums and agouti are especially active in the cool mornings, as are more than 350 kinds of birds. Another recommended destination is the Carara Biological Preserve, a rich haven for both plant and animal life. While you're visiting the Costa Rican interior, don't miss an impressive geological sight, Poas, one of the deepest volcanoes in the world. Having last erupted only 12 years ago, billows of steam continue to vent from the main crater. A half-mile hike leads to a smaller crater. A clear water lake is surrounded by the dwarf trees of a cloud forest, where plants feed off the mist and every surface is alive with growth.

Among major outfitters, Wildland Adventures offers the most complete range of Costa Rica trips. Wildlife enthusiasts will

stand on dry land at the lip and look down. And the world's tallest waterfall is actually very quiet. The drop is so great that, except at the height of the wet season, very little of the water ever reaches the base of the falls. It becomes spray, carried off by the winds.

A few day's trek from Angel Falls is 9,094' Mt. Roraima, "Mother of Raging Torrents," a dramatic table mountain that served as the inspiration for the Arthur Conan Doyle science fiction work, *The Lost World*, about a land forgotten by time, where dinosaurs still roamed. This region is a uniquely isolated wilderness preserve, largely untouched by civilization. Here in this jungle heartland are found species that go back to the epoch when South America and Africa were one continent. Few who visit this region are disappointed. For most, the view of the Falls alone is worth the price of admission.

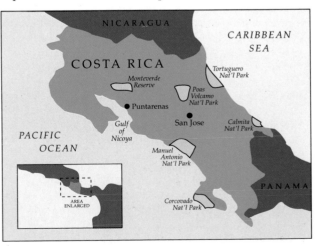

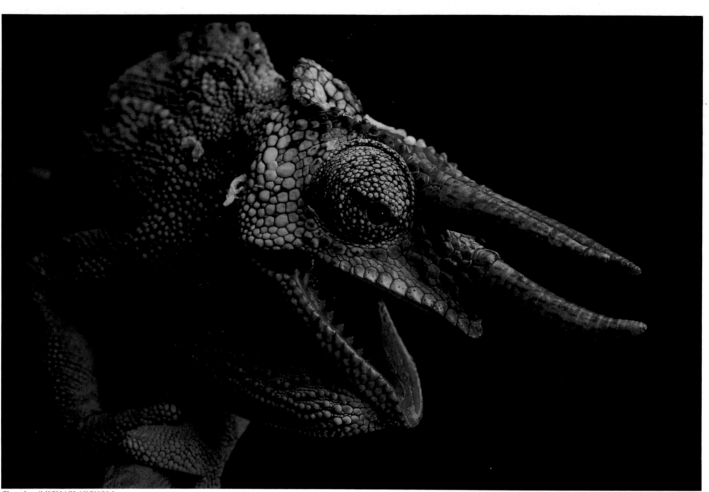

Chameleon/MICHAEL NICHOLS

enjoy the 11-day Tropical Odyssey which visits the Monteverde Cloud Forest, the Carara Biological Preserve, Manuel Antonio National Park and the Corcovado National Park where jaguar, ocelot and tapir survive in their last natural refuge. If you want to observe the natural spectacle of 300-pound sea turtles laying their eggs at Tortuguero National Park, choose Wildland's Jungle Odyssey, which offers, in addition to turtle-mania, jungle river trips and visits to Poas Volcano, Monteverde National Park, and the Carara Reserve.

Beach lovers should choose Wildland's 15-day Camping Safari which visits Costa Rica's biggest volcanos, and then heads to Cahuita National Park on the Caribbean coast. Here, local fisherman will take you by dugout to the remote Gandoca Wildlife Reserve and some of the most beautiful and isolated beaches in Central America. This tour as well as Wildland's other trips are guided by naturalists, and cost about $170 per day. You can add whitewater rafting ($85 per day) or a jungle cruise ($185 for 3 days) to any itinerary. Contact Wildland

Adventures, 3516 N.E. 155th, Seattle, WA 98155, (800) 345-4453.

International Expeditions leads an excellent 10-day tour through Costa Rica that visits volcanoes, the Monteverde Cloud Forest, the Gulf of Nicoya, the Carara Biological Preserve, and the Tortuguero National Park (nesting site of the Atlantic green sea turtle), as well as the capital city of San Jose--one of the first cities in the New World. The trip costs $1,998 including airfare from Miami. A 3-day pre-trip extension to Manuel Antonio National Park is about $525. Call International Expeditions at (800) 633-4734, or (205) 428-1700.

Although most Americans visiting Costa Rica for the first time may prefer to go with an organized tour, Costa Rica is a relatively good destination for the independent traveler. If you speak a little Spanish, and won't have a coronary if your bus arrives late, you'll find Costa Rica a great place to explore on your own. The people are friendly, the government is as stable as any in Latin America, and the country still hasn't been spoiled by tourism.

BELIZE

Wild Creatures, Lost Cities

"If the world had any ends, British Honduras would certainly be one of them," Aldous Huxley said. "It's not on the way from anywhere to anywhere." In 1981 this tiny country on the Caribbean, just south of the Yucatan Peninsula, gained independence as Belize. Unlike other Latin American nations, English is the official language. The dense rainforests, subtropical pine-covered mountains, grassy savannah and mangrove swamps are home to a great diversity of both temperate and tropical fauna. Belize also has the world's second largest barrier reef.

More than a thousand years ago Belize was the center of a vast Mayan empire; now only ruins testify to a time when the jungle was anything but still. Today, the country is a major archaeological center. New sites are still being rediscovered in the jungle. Xunantunich, near the border with Guatemala, is the most extensively excavated site. Located on a natural limestone ridge, the ancient city still offers a spectacular view down to the Mopan River and the surrounding forest. The 130-foot pyramid, El Castillo, is the tallest building in Belize even today. Another important site is Caracol, the Mayans' ceremonial center, a remote lost city located in the Chiquibil Forest Reserve, which can be reached only through guided treks. Lamani is another ceremonial center, which was in use for almost 3,500 years up until the 19th century.

Belize's natural resources make it an ideal jungle destination. Unlike many other tropical regions, the country still has extensive tracts of virgin rainforest. In 1986, Belize established the Cockscomb Basin Wildlife Sanctuary, the world's first jaguar preserve. Other cats protected in the preserve include the jaguarundi, margay and ocelot. Spider monkeys, fox, coatamundi, kinkajous, peccaries, tapir and white-tailed deer also live in the park.

For a moderately priced, diverse Belize adventure, consider Ecosummer Expeditions' 2-week Reef and Jungle Expedition. You spend the first week paddling sea kayaks through the cays of the barrier reef and camping on white sand beaches. Then you head inland to Cockscomb Basin for a week exploring the jaguar preserve and trekking between ancient Mayan temples. You'll be taken by native guides through the Mayan ceremonial cave system, and then conclude your Belize adventure with a jungle float trip down the famous River of Caves. This is a great combo trip, offering the best of land and sea. Cost for the 15-day program is roughly $2,195. Ecosummer also offers a 24-day Belize Explorer trip that gives you more of everything-- more time on the reef, more temples, more jungle exploring. On this $3,195 tour, you'll also enjoy a river kayak trip to the sea and a horseback trek to highland waterfalls. Contact Ecosummer Expeditions, 1516 Duranleau Street, Granville Island, Vancouver, BC, Canada V6H 3S4, (604) 669-7741.

International Expeditions has an 11-day natural history tour for about $2,000 and an 11-day Maya Heartland expedition for the same price, which includes airfare from Miami. The former spends several nights at Chaa Creek while exploring the Macal River and the Mountain Pine Region. The latter visits a number of archaeological sites. Both tours visit the progressive Belize Zoo. Four to 8-day add-on trips are available to Tikal (in Guatemala), and Copan (in Honduras), and Belize's barrier reef. Contact International Expeditions, One Environs Park, Helena, AL 35080, (800) 633-4734, or (205) 428-1700.

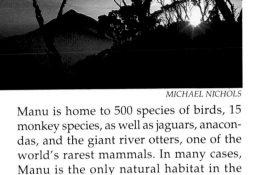
MICHAEL NICHOLS

MANU NATIONAL PARK

Nature's Own Zoo

No jungle destination in the world offers a greater abundance or variety of wildlife than Peru's Manu National Park. Manu, one of the largest nature preserves on earth, is an unlogged, old growth rainforest situated on the western rim of the Amazon River basin. Remote and untrammelled, Manu has no roads, no settlements, and no human residents save for a few primitive, nomadic Indian tribes.

In this undisturbed natural ecosystem, countless species of birds and mammals have found sanctuary. Designated a Biosphere Reserve by the United Nations, Manu is home to 500 species of birds, 15 monkey species, as well as jaguars, anacondas, and the giant river otters, one of the world's rarest mammals. In many cases, Manu is the only natural habitat in the world where these animals survive.

A trip to Manu is a unique opportunity to observe the richness of the jungle environment in its original state. In the treetops, macaws, toucans, parrots nest by the hundreds, joined by large numbers of capuchin and red howler monkeys. In the Park's undergrowth, peccary, tapir, ocelot and jaguar prowl in search of food. In the rivers swim turtles, caiman (South American alligators), and the giant river otters. These unique animals, which grow up to six feet in length, are endemic to Manu.

Wilderness Travel offers one of the best Manu Park tours. Its 19-day wildlife expedition begins with a visit to Machu Picchu

MICHAEL NICHOLS

Orangutans, Sumatra, Indonesia/MICHAEL NICHOLS

and Cuzco. You then descend from the Andes to Boca Manu, to board a 42' motorized dugout canoe, your river transport for the next 9 days. Between excursions up narrow tributaries and to riverine lakes, the group will make a number of day-hikes. You can even do nightwalks from jungle lodge basecamps. Exploring the jungle in Manu under a full moon is an experience not to be missed. One recent participant called this "the best trip I've ever been on, extremely professional." Wilderness Travel's Manu trip runs in July and August at a cost of roughly $2,600, without airfare. You can save about $500 by booking the "jungle only" portion of the trip, skipping the first 6 days in the Andes. Call Wilderness Travel at (800) 368-2794.

For much less money, Wildland Adventures runs 14-day Manu Camping Expeditions. The tour duplicates the Manu Park segment of Wilderness Travel's trip in most respects--including the nature walks and canoe excursions--although you sleep in tents, not a lodge. Sightings of jaguar, ocelot, tapir and other large mammals are common. Tours depart year-round and cost $1,490, a big savings over Wilderness Travel's equivalent "jungle only" tour. Call Wildland Adventures at (800) 345-4453.

If you prefer a more active Manu Park trip, Adventure Specialists offers a one-of-a-kind Andes to Amazon mountain bike odyssey in 1992. After exploring famed Machu Picchu, bikers will decend 12,000' from the Andes, passing through small villages on their way to Manu. There, the intrepid bikers will explore the park's interior by foot and canoe. The $1,650 tour runs in May and September. Contact Adventure Specialists, c/o A.W.E., P.O. Box 1486, Boulder, CO 80306, (800) 444-0099.

SUMATRA

The Land of the Red Ape

One of the largest and least populated of Indonesia's islands, Sumatra is a land of stunning contrasts and great mystery. Here you'll find high mountains, dense jungle rainforest and whitewater rivers. This is still nature's world, not man's. It has survived as one of the last natural preserves of many unique species including Asian tigers, rare Indonesian rhinos, and its most famous animal inhabitant, the orangutan--the "man of the forest."

The populated areas of Sumatra can be explored on your own without much difficulty, if you're reasonably intrepid and keep a copy of the Lonely Planet guide to Indonesia close at hand. Dirt-cheap accommodations can be found in almost all towns and villages, and if you learn some Indonesian you will find the people warm, interested and very receptive to travelers. If you are looking for a jungle experience rather than a cultural tour, however, you will need a professional guide. The interior of Sumatra is inaccessible, extremely undeveloped, and a great place to get lost.

For those who want to see Sumatra at its most wild and get the adrenalin pumping, Mountain Travel/Sobek offers jungle rafting trips down Sumatra's Alas River. Sobek pioneered the first descent of this major whitewater river a few years back, and now leads weeklong trips that combine a visit to the famed Bohorok Orangutan Preserve with a 4-day run of the Alas.

Navigating the Alas is an amazing experience. In its upper sections, you'll encounter serious Class III-IV rapids that will test your courage and your boatman's skills. You'll pass through sheer-walled rock gorges, then float through dense rainforest teeming with animal life. Monkeys and gibbons howl at the rafters from the riverbanks. The Alas is big-time adventure--it doesn't get any more wild and exotic than this. But don't just take our word for it. Get a copy of *The River of the Red Ape*, a superb one-hour documentary filmed during Sobek's first descent of the Alas. Land cost for the 8-day Sumatran expedition is about $975, but may increase later in 1992. Round-trip air passage to Jakarta, Indonesia will run another $900 or so, depending on the season. For further information, contact Mountain Travel/Sobek, (800) 227-2384.

If you want to see orangutans on a more luxurious tour, Overseas Adventure Travel (OAT) offers a 16-day Borneo wildlife safari that combines trekking and dugout canoeing, with a 3-day visit to the Sepilok Orangutan Preserve. You will also have a chance to observe sea turtles coming ashore to lay their eggs. Price is approximately $2,200, land only, March to October. Contact OAT, 349 Broadway, Cambridge, MA 02139, (800) 221-0814.

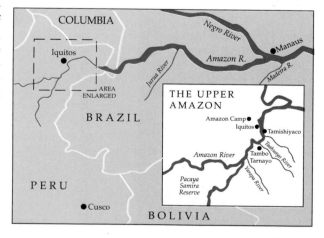

THE AMAZON
The Ultimate Jungle

The Amazon Basin is the world's largest river system, surpassing the flow of the next eight largest rivers combined. Its delta drains an area equivalent to the face of the moon, accounting for a full 20 percent of all the fresh water that reaches the world's oceans. The surrounding rainforest--the largest in the world--seems to be an impenetrable and hostile environment. In reality, the Amazon is a quiet place where a person could spend a lifetime studying the variety of life in one acre. To study the jungle's amazingly complex ecosystem, its cultures and their relationships to the jungle, you need a tour company that knows the rivers and is sensitive to your comfort level. Except for short hikes, tourist travel is by way of the rivers and creeks. The Amazon itself is so large that cruise ships regularly call at Manaus in Brazil, 1,000 miles up river. The best way to explore the upper Amazon and its tributaries is aboard a flat-bottomed delta cruiser, a smaller version of the Mississippi riverboats. Himalayan Travel markets economical cruises on two such vessels, the *Rio Amazonas* and *M/V Margarita*, which operate out of Iquitos, Peru. The price for an air-conditioned cabin starts at roughly $700 per week. Contact Himalayan Travel, P.O. Box 481, Greenwich, CT 06836, (800) 225-2380.

Every year Oceanic Society Expeditions (OCE) offers two unique tours which explore the upper Amazon and nearby Tahuyao and Ucayali Rivers aboard the 68' steamer, *Delphin*. The featured trip is a 15-day research expedition to observe and swim with Peru's unique pink freshwater dolphins in their natural habitat, Pacaya-Samiria National Park. This vast park, Peru's largest nature preserve, also harbors hundreds of bird species, as well as monkeys and other large mammals. The June and July expeditions will be led by dolphin experts Randall Reeves or Steve Leatherwood, co-authors of the Sierra Club Handbook on whales and dolphins. Forays up narrow tributaries will be made by small motor canoes. Cost for the 15-day program is $2,850, with airfare from Miami. Contact OCE, Fort Mason Center, Bldg. E, San Francisco, CA 94123, (415) 441-1106. A shorter 8-day cruise through Pacaya-Samiria is offered in June for $1,690, with air from Miami.

If you're looking to cruise in high style, Lindblads' Special Expeditions explores the Amazon in the 238' *M/S Polaris* from the Brazilian coast to Manaus. Zodiac inflatables are used to explore narrow tributaries, while trips to isolated Indian villages are led by knowledgeable guides. Cost for these 16-day voyages (6 days on the Amazon) is roughly $5,030 to $8,250, depending on cabin. Trips run in October and November and depart from Manaus. Contact Special Expeditions, 720 Fifth Avenue, New York, NY 10019, (800) 762-0003.

If you're willing to sacrifice luxury, Mountain Travel/Sobek will take you deep into the heart of the jungle from its Amazon Camp lodge on the river's bank near Iquitos. You'll visit Yugua Indian villages, track caiman from dugout canoes, and trek into the rainforest. A former wildlife research station, the Amazon Camp is ideally situated for observing animal life in the wild. Land cost for 6 days is about $980. Call Sobek at (800) 227-2384.

Having invested in airfare to Latin America, it makes sense to add other activities to a basic Amazon trip. Overseas Adventure Travel offers an 18-day tour that combines 2 days in the Tambopata Amazon Wildlife Reserve, 8 days of trekking to Machu Picchu, and a 7-day yacht cruise through the Galapagos Islands. Trips depart year-round and cost about $3,000, land only. Contact OAT at (800) 221-0814.

You can also arrange for smaller camping expeditions to Manaus, Peru through local English-speaking guides. Paul Zalis' *Who is the River* is an entertaining account of one such trip to the Amazon.

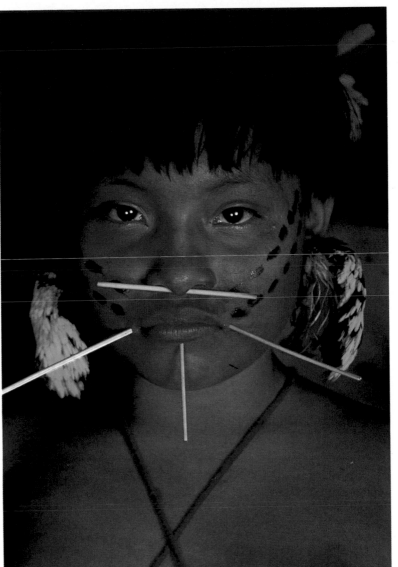

Young Amazonian girl/MICHAEL NICHOLS

*The Amazon is a tangle of life
fighting for a piece of the sky, a pressure of
green that forces you to react. It is a place that
with its bugs and its heat and sun and
animals and size and diseases is always at
you. It never lets up until it draws you out,
and when you become part of the tangle.*

-Paul Zalis, Who is the River

The Top Jungle Outfitters

Rafting group in Papua New Guinea/MOUNTAIN TRAVEL/SOBEK

THE ADVENTURE CENTER AND HIMALAYAN TRAVEL OFFER THE BEST SELECTION of low cost jungle trips, including a wide variety of Amazon journeys. Wildland Adventures has a very strong program in Central and South America, also at reasonable prices. For jungle river running, Mountain Travel/Sobek is the logical choice, while for Madagascar, Journeys is the clear pick. In Papua New Guinea, most outfitters use the same guide service, Trans-Niugini Tours, so choose your trip based on price and itinerary. Ecosummer pioneered Irian Jaya trekking, and would be our first pick if we were looking for a very challenging jungle adventure.

■ ADVENTURE CENTER

1311 63rd St., Suite 200, Emeryville, CA 94608, (800) 227-8747, or (510) 654-1879.

As agent for numerous tour companies worldwide, the Adventure Center offers a vast selection of itineraries. Prices are generally quite low, attracting a younger, more independent (and international) clientele than most other companies listed here. Be prepared to camp out, or stay in fairly spartan lodgings on many trips. Always ask which outfitter is actually running your trip. Best Jungle Destinations: Borneo, Venezuela/Lost World, Ecuador Amazon.

Value★★★★	Variety★★★★
Challenge★★★	Luxury★★
Guide Knowledge★★	Wildlife★★

■ ECOSUMMER EXPEDITIONS

1516 Duranleau St., Granville Island, Vancouver, BC, Canada V6H 3S4, (604) 669-7741.

Ecosummer specializes in sea kayaking, but its jungle programs are outstanding. It is the most experienced western operator in Irian Jaya, a place you really shouldn't visit on your own. The Belize program offers great diversity. Best Jungle Destinations: Belize, Irian Jaya (New Guinea).

Value★★★	Variety★
Challenge★★★	Luxury★★
Guide Knowledge★★★	Wildlife★★

■ HIMALAYAN TRAVEL

P.O. Box 481, Greenwich, CT 06836, (800) 225-2380.

Himalayan Travel has years of experience with Latin American trips, using a variety of local outfitters. It has an excellent selection of Amazon trips. It would be one of our first choices for a classic Amazon river cruise. Best Jungle Destinations: Amazon (river cruise), Chitwan Park (Nepal).

Value★★★★	Variety★★★
Challenge★★	Luxury★★
Guide Knowledge★★	Wildlife★★★

■ INTERNATIONAL EXPEDITIONS, INC.

One Environs Park, Helena, AL 35080, (800) 633-4734, or (205) 428-1700.

International Expeditions is a premium operator, specializing in jungle and wildlife tours. Its itineraries have been refined over many years, and it runs trips for a number of well-known groups, including the Nature Conservancy. Tour leaders are personable and customer satisfaction has been very high. Best Jungle Destinations: Belize, Costa Rica, Amazon.

Value★★	Variety★★★
Challenge★	Luxury★★★
Guide Knowledge★★★★	Wildlife★★★★

■ JOURNEYS/WILDLAND ADVENTURES

4011 Jackson Road, Ann Arbor, MI 48103, (800) 255-8735.

Journeys and sister company Wildland Adventures use able native guides, who know the flora and fauna of their homelands better than any outsider ever could. These well-organized tours really put you in touch with indigenous cultures. Most of the Latin American trips are run by Wildland, which, over the past two decades, has developed a strong network of local contacts in Costa Rica, Ecuador, Peru and Venezuela. Journeys is a top choice for Madagascar, with time-tested itineraries and reasonable prices. New this year is a trans-Brazil Wildlife Safari. Best Jungle Destinations: Costa Rica, Madagascar, Venezuela.

Value★★★★	Variety★★★
Challenge★★★★	Luxury★★
Guide Knowledge★★★★	Wildlife★★★★

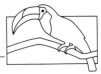

■ MOUNTAIN TRAVEL/SOBEK

6420 Fairmont Avenue, El Cerrito, CA 94530, (800) 227-2384, or (415) 527-8100.

Mountain Travel/Sobek is a large agency that offers trips to most of the major jungle destinations including the Amazon, Papua New Guinea and Costa Rica. In many cases trips are subcontracted to local outfitters. Sobek specializes in exotic river journeys. Best Jungle Destinations: Costa Rica, Papua New Guinea.

Value★★★	Variety★★
Challenge★★ to ★★★★	Luxury★★★
Guide Knowledge★★★	Wildlife★★★

■ OVERSEAS ADVENTURE TRAVEL

349 Broadway, Cambridge, MA 02139, (800) 221-0814; FAX: (617) 876-0455.

Overseas Adventure Travel (OAT), though best known for treks and safaris, offers a wide range of excellent, if pricey, jungle trips. Destinations include the Amazon, Borneo, Costa Rica, Thailand and Chitwan Park (Nepal). Best Jungle Destinations: Costa Rica, Borneo, Nepal.

Value★★	Variety★★★
Challenge★★	Luxury★★★
Guide Knowledge★★★	Wildlife★★★

■ SAFARICENTRE

3201 N. Sepulveda Boulevard, Manhattan Beach, CA 90266, (800) 624-5342 in CA, (800) 223-6046 nationwide.

The SafariCentre is another agency that books trips for a wide variety of smaller outfitters. This is a good choice if you wish to compare a number of itineraries covering the full price spectrum. Best Jungle Destinations: Amazon, Manu Nat'l Park, Papua New Guinea (Trans-Niugini Tours).

Value★★★	Variety★★★★
Challenge★ to ★★★★	Luxury★★★
Guide Knowledge-variable	Wildlife★★★

■ TRAVCOA

P.O. Box 2630, Newport Beach, CA 94530, (800) 992-2003, or (800 992-2004 in CA.

TRAVCOA is a high-end company that runs deluxe tours worldwide. The emphasis is on native culture and sightseeing, rather than adventurous activities. Most nights are spent at deluxe hotels or aboard cruise ships, although rustic lodges are used in New Guinea. Trips average about $5,000 for 3 weeks. Best Jungle Destinations: Amazon, Costa Rica, Papua New Guinea.

Value★★	Variety★★★
Challenge★★	Luxury★★★★
Guide Knowledge★★★	Wildlife★★★

■ WILDERNESS TRAVEL

801 Allston Way, Berkeley, CA 94710, (800) 368-2794, or (510) 548-0420 in CA.

Wilderness Travel offers a limited number of jungle trips, but they're very well run, and feature a variety of activities. Prices are fairly high, but customers have raved, particularly about the Manu trip. Best Jungle Destinations: Amazon Headwaters, Manu National Park, Lost World/Angel Falls.

Value★★	Variety★★
Challenge★★	Luxury★★★
Guide Knowledge★★★★	Wildlife★★★

THE VANISHING JUNGLE ENVIRONMENT

TROPICAL FORESTS COVER SEVEN PERCENT of the world's land surface and are home to half the known animal and plant species. However, on every continent and island in the tropics, the jungle is disappearing at an alarming rate, despite the preservation efforts of many international environmental groups. About 5.5 million square kilometers of rainforest remain in the world today, less than half the original amount. Most of the damage has been done in just the last 40 years.

We have already seen a dramatic reduction in the wildlife populations of Africa caused by even modest incursions of man into the wildlands. The effect on jungle regions, the richest wildlife habitats in the world, is bound to be the same. Within a few decades, or even years, many species will be lost, and areas once teeming with wildlife will be changed, probably forever. For the traveler seeking to experience the world's jungles in their natural states, the message is clear--go soon, before the great rainforests have yielded to man, and the exotic animals of the jungle are to be seen only in zoos and history books.

Amazon tribesmen in fire-ravaged rainforest/MICHAEL NICHOLS

JUNGLE EXPLORING

CHOOSING AN OUTFITTER

In the past, the world's great jungles were inaccessible to all but the most intrepid explorers. Today, however, the adventure travel industry has made it possible for anyone with sufficient funds to visit the most exotic jungle venues.

The very explosion in jungle travel however, has made it even more important to make the right outfitter selection when planning a jungle adventure. Many companies hire out their jungle trips to local outfitters of somewhat uneven quality. Some "jungle adventures" coddle participants in air-conditioned luxury and spend very little time in truly wild areas. Before you book a jungle trip, we advise that you consider the following:

How experienced is the outfitter in the locale?

Copycats abound in the adventure travel industry. One outfitter's success with a particular trip will spawn imitation. However, the pioneering companies will usually have hired the most talented guides, booked the best lodges, and chartered the most seaworthy vessels. It's therefore a sound strategy to stick with a well-established outfitter.

What company actually runs the tour?

Many big companies, including Mountain Travel/Sobek and SafariCentre, use smaller foreign outfitters to run their jungle trips. For example, SafariCentre and Sobek both use Trans-Niugini Tours in Papua New Guinea. You can often save money by booking directly with the smaller outfitter, or at least obtain a wider selection of itineraries and departures.

How many other tourist trips operate in the same area at the same time?

When you're visiting a remote tribe of Huli wigmen in the hinterlands of New Guinea, the last thing you want to see is 50 other tourists pointing cameras at anything that moves. Ask your outfitter for an honest assessment of the level of tourism in the area you want to visit. If you aren't happy with what you hear, check with other outfitters.

Are departures and group size limits guaranteed?

Outfitters are in business to make money like everyone else. However, this can cause problems when not enough people sign up for the trip you want to take. The outfitter may cancel your trip, or combine two trips, creating a tour group that is unmanageably large. A trekking group exploring remote villages should be no larger than 12 per-

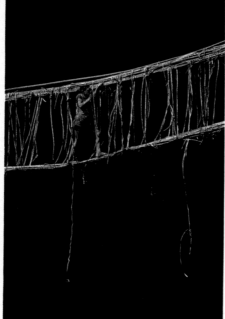

MICHAEL NICHOLS

sons, with six about ideal. Bigger groups tend to overwhelm small settlements, and your guide will be unable to offer you much personal attention. You can get around these problems by choosing an outfitter, such as Mountain Travel, that will guarantee your departure date and maximum group size.

HEALTH & MEDICINE

No matter what your condition, we strongly advise that you have a thorough physical exam before you head to the jungle. On some jungle treks you'll be expected to walk as much as 10 miles a day. Even if you're not carrying heavy equipment, or paddling a dugout canoe, the heat and humidity of the tropics will sap your energy quickly.

During your check-up, you should also get the shots and prescription drugs you will require. You will need anti-malarial medication, and this should be started at least four weeks before you depart. In addition, you should probably be vaccinated for cholera, typhoid, and in some cases yellow fever. Some experts advise an immunoglobulin injection, but you should discuss this with your physician. Be sure to have all your immunizations entered on an official International Health Certificate.

PHOTOGRAPHY

Tropical rainforests and expensive camera equipment don't mix. Wherever you go in the tropics you can expect your camera equipment to be exposed to a lot of moisture. If you're riding on a motorized canoe in the Amazon, for example, your camera can easily get soaked with spray. We recommend keeping your camera in a doubled zip-lock bag when not in use to protect the delicate electronic circuits. Keep some packs of silica gel inside to absorb moisture. Do the same with your film packs. (Film is very expensive in jungle areas, and slide film is virtually impossible to find, so bring plenty with you.)

PACKING & PERSONAL ITEMS

You don't need to bring much of anything to the jungle. A sturdy, comfortable pair of shoes, a sun hat, light cotton clothing, and reliable insect repellent and sunblock is all that you need. You don't want to carry heavy bags in 100 degree heat and 100 percent humidity. Try to stick to one small suitcase and a daypack.

On jungle hikes, shorts are tempting, but a pair of full-length lightweight cotton trousers will protect your legs from insects and thorns. When venturing into the bush, bring water bottles, and consider taking salt pills. Road-test insect repellent and sunblock before the trip to assure they don't irritate your skin.

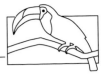
ENVIRONMENT

AMAZON

For the first-time visitor, the heat, humidity and insects in the Amazon can be overwhelming. Everywhere but the highland tributaries, you should expect steamy weather in the 90s. Rain falls year-round, but the winter brings the heaviest storms in most regions. Mosquitos are a major problem. If you are on a big jungle cruiser, keep your bug spray within arm's reach. The smaller motorized canoes move fast enough to keep insects at bay--until you reach your destination. Swimming is safe in much of the Amazon, though you should not drink river water at any point. The more popular lodges offer a fair degree of comfort, though nothing on a par with the best of East Africa. Though most tours utilize English-speaking guides, you should try to learn some of the local language before you go.

BELIZE

Located within the Tropic of Cancer, Belize is a warm, humid country, dominated by dense tropical rainforest and pine savannah. Daily temperatures average in the mid-80s year-round, dropping about 10 degrees in the evening. Evaporation from the jungle vegetation creates a very humid environment once you get more than a few miles inland. Water temperatures are ideal for swimming and diving, ranging between 75 and 82 degrees. Belize gets far less precipitation than other jungle areas such as the Amazon, and when it does rain, the showers are relatively light, falling for short spans in the afternoon.

No immunizations are required for travel to Belize, and malaria is not a serious problem, though taking anti-malarial medication is advisable. On most tours, you'll be staying in decent hotels or lodges with potable water. River water can be unhealthful, and should be avoided.

COSTA RICA

Costa Rica is an ecological wonderland. The terrain includes just about everything you can imagine, from volcanoes to coastal rainforests, and even inviting tropical beaches. In the highlands, expect mild days in the 70s and cool nights, especially in the Monteverde forests where temperatures can drop into the 50s at night.

In the lowlands, it will be humid, though not unpleasantly so, with temperatures to the 90s. Rain falls heaviest along the Pacific highlands, usually in the form of afternoon thundershowers. No immunizations are required to visit Costa Rica, and malaria is not a serious worry, although taking standard precautions is advised.

SUMATRA

An equatorial nation, Indonesia has hot, humid weather year-round, but cooling breezes along the coast make conditions comfortable most of the year. Malaria-carrying mosquitos are a real threat in many areas. Unfortunately, the bugs are now

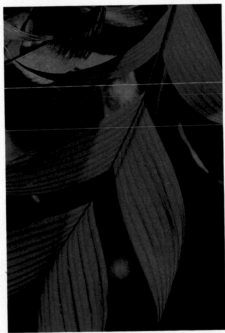

MICHAEL NICHOLS

highly resistant to most common anti-malarial medicines. Wear long clothing at night, use mosquito coils and insect repellents, and sleep under mosquito netting. Drink only boiled or bottled water whenever possible. Indonesian food is cheap and delicious, and you'll particularly enjoy the seafood and fresh fruit. No immunizations are required for travel to Indonesia, but it's wise to be vaccinated against cholera, typhoid and tetanus.

The rainy season in Indonesia, including Sumatra, runs between October and March every year. Although the rain typically falls in light tropical showers, getting hit by a real monsoon is a distinct possibility, particularly in January. When this hap-

pens, the skies open up, often for days, lowland areas flood, and your trip could be ruined, particularly if you're trying to hike jungle trails. The preferred time to travel is the relatively dry season from April to November, with May to August offering the best overall conditions.

PAPUA NEW GUINEA & IRIAN JAYA

There is no preferred time to travel in New Guinea. Like most equatorial regions, it has no dramatic seasonal changes. Conditions in the highlands, where most treks are run, is temperate year-round because of the 5,000'-6,000' altitudes. Expect warm days, with light rain most afternoons and cool nights. In the coastal and Sepik River areas, days are hot and humid while nights remain warm and steamy. January to March is the wet season, and mosquitos can be very bad, so bring long pants and shirts, and the best anti-malarial medicines you can find. Good sunblock is a necessity at all times.

In Irian Jaya and much of New Guinea, you will be traveling to extremely remote areas and visiting very primitive peoples. On some tours, you will be beyond the reach of western medicine for a number of days, and if you suffer a broken limb or other serious injury, you might have to wait days for evacuation. We strongly advise that you purchase comprehensive travelers' insurance before undertaking any wilderness trip in this area.

BOOKS

The Belize Guide, by Passport Press, $17.95 from the Travel Bookstore, 1514 N. Hillhurst, Hollywood, CA 90027, (213) 660-2101.

Costa Rica Traveler, Ellen Searby, Windham Bay Press. This is probably the best overall guide to the region. $11.95 from TravelBooks, 113 Corporation Road, Hyannis, MA 02601-2204, (800) 869-3535.

Life Above the Jungle Floor, by Don Perry. This is an entertaining journal of explorations and scientific discoveries in the Costa Rican rainforest. $8.95 from TravelBooks.

The South American Handbook, Prentice Hall, $29.95 (hardback), from TravelBooks. This is a big, comprehensive resource for Mexico, Central and South America.

Papua and New Guinea, A Travel Survival Kit, Lonely Planet Publications. This is the single best guide to independent travel in the region. Available at most bookstores for $14.95.

Indonesia, A Travel Survival Kit, Lonely Planet Publications, $14.95.

Motorcycle Touring

Two-up touring, Bryce Canyon National Park/COURTESY BMW OF NORTH AMERICA, INC.

172

Why do I ride motorcycles?
It's the freedom....
Once a child, always a child.
-Al McGuire, in CBS interview

▼

Motorcycling is an adventure--both as sport and as a form of exploration. Riding a motorcycle is much more than getting from point A to point B; it is an active, sensory experience. Unlike other modes of travel, the process of getting there is its own reward. There are risks, to be sure, but for most motorcyclists, they are far outweighed by the joys of riding.

For beginners as well as experienced motorcyclists, we offer a comprehensive guide to motorcycle travel worldwide. We describe a host of great tours around the globe, and review the top touring companies in the US and abroad. In addition, we present tips on planning your own two-wheeled adventures in North America and around the world.

CHAPTER
12

RICH COX

FOR A TRUE ADVENTURER, SUCH AS THE LATE MALCOLM FORBES, TWO WHEELS are often better than four. Though he could afford the best automobiles money could buy, Forbes preferred the freedom of his Harley touring motorcycle to the cloistered security of an automobile. Touring in a car, he maintained, was like "driving around in your living room." If you're a like-minded soul, one for whom the physical sensations of travel are as important as simply reaching your destination, touring by motorcycle is the ultimate escape.

THAILAND

Asia's Bargain Adventure

Mention Thailand and most people think of Buddhist temples, or maybe the flesh parlors of Bangkok. However, Thailand has much to offer the two-wheeled traveler. In fact, it is one of the best budget motorcycling destinations in the world. The food is great, the beaches are world class, you can find clean rooms for under $15 a night, and last but not least, you can rent a late model, 125cc dual-purpose bike for less than $10 US per day. Thus, you can have a great two-week touring holiday in Thailand for well under $600, including food, lodging and motorcycle rental.

All international flights to Thailand arrive in Bangkok. Thailand's capital city is noisy, hectic and crowded, but you'll want to spend a day or two just to find out if what they say about Bangkok is true. Spend 10 minutes at Club Lipstick on Patpong Road to get your answer. From Bangkok, head south if you want to sample heavenly beaches, head north if you want to visit scenic valleys and remote highlands. The weather may help you decide. The far north, near Chiang Mai, is cool even in the summertime. You can fly to Chiang Mai inexpensively on Thai Airways. On arrival, choose from many clean accommodations ranging from $7 to $30 per night.

In the center of Chiang Mai, you'll find a host of motorcycle rental agencies, all bidding for your business. You can rent a newish 50cc commuter bike for about $5 per day, or a 125cc dual-purpose bike for $8-$10. You can plan your trip with David Unkovich's fine English-language guidebook for motorcycling in Thailand, or David himself, an expatriate Aussie, can lead tours on request. Contact Chiang Mai Touring Club, P.O. Box 97, P.O. Mae Ping, Chiang Mai, Thailand, (011 66) 53-278518; FAX: (011 66) 53-212219.

Southern Thailand has suffered an explosion of tourism in the past decade, but it is still a cheaper, friendlier and more interesting version of Hawaii. The main tourist center is Phuket (pronounced poo-ket), and there you can find lodgings ranging

Eight Ultimate Motorcycle Tours

from $6-a-night bungalows to luxury hotels. We would take a bus from Bangkok to Phuket in the interest of economy, but direct flights are also available. Most of Phuket's tourist resorts are located along the west coast. Here you will find more motorcycle rental operations. Prices tend to be a little higher than Chiang Mai, but you can still get a good trailbike for about $10 a day. For about twice that, you can also rent some fairly exotic machinery, but a small dual-purpose bike is really the ideal mount for the often rough local roads.

In Phuket, you can easily venture to a dozen different beaches, all with warm, crystal clear water. The preferred activity is sitting at beachside restaurants, eating giant Siamese shrimp and quaffing fruit shakes enlivened with Thai whiskey.

If you're looking for a fun, cheap holiday in an exotic destination, where you'll be able to ride a motorcycle every day, Thailand is the ticket. Even with round-trip airfare of $1,000 or so, you can tour Thailand for less than you might spend on an ordinary vacation back home.

ARIZONA & UTAH

The Great Circle Tour

The Great Circle Tour through Arizona and southern Utah may be America's ultimate open-road odyssey. You can visit high deserts, tour a half-dozen national parks, and do it all in less than a week.

A good starting point for the tour is Flagstaff, Arizona. From there head north to the Highway 24 junction where you will turn east into Grand Canyon National Park. There are excellent hotels and campsites available, but you should book in advance between May and September.

Double back from the Grand Canyon, then take Highways 160 and 163 northeast towards Monument Valley, situated near the Utah-Arizona border. Monument Valley, site of countless westerns and television commercials, boasts scenery quite unlike anything else on earth. This is a great destination for a dual-purpose bike, but don't attempt to take a street bike into the

RICH COX

175

valley unless you want to be towed out.

Relatively cheap lodging can be had in the town of Mexican Hat, about 18 miles to the east on the banks of the San Juan River. Just out of town, take Highway 261 up through the Valley of the Gods. The route, which is partly unpaved, takes you up the face of a high mesa. From the top, you'll be treated to a breathtaking panorama of the Valley of the Gods and Monument Valley to the west.

After pausing on the crest, proceed north along 261 to connect with Highway 95. Go east and follow the sign to Moab and Arches National Park if you've got an extra day or two; otherwise, head west toward Glen Canyon and Lake Powell. The next 30 miles are motorcycling heaven--what could well be the best stretch of motorcycle asphalt in the States. The road surface is excellent, inspiring confidence even at high lean-angles. Each turn unlocks new vistas.

After Lake Powell, pick up Highway 24 towards Capitol Reef National Park. There is an excellent campground in the park, and you'll find two motels down the road in the little town of Torrey. For the final leg of the tour, pick up Utah Highway 12 south. Highway 12, regarded by many as the best sport-touring road in Utah, takes you way up to ridgeline--close to 9,000'--and the views are superb. Highway 12 then connects with Highway 10 to Bryce Canyon National Park and Mt. Zion National Park. Both are spectacular and shouldn't be missed. From Mt. Zion's west portal you can continue on to Las Vegas.

Many tour companies offer southwest trips, but riders must spend days trolling down the interstates. Only Pancho Villa Moto-Tours, (800) 233-0564, starts and finishes its program in Arizona, allowing you to spend all your entire holiday in the most scenic areas. Pancho Villa's 10-day, $2,000 tour utilizes new BMW GS80 machines, ideal for both on- and off-road exploration.

CALIFORNIA & OREGON

The Pacific Coast Odyssey

Famed Highway 1 along the California and Oregon coasts offers over 1,000 miles of verdant scenery and challenging curves.

If you start your trip in Los Angeles, as most riders do, the first 100 miles may be disappointing. However, if you cut over to Highway 264 at Santa Barbara, you'll be rewarded with great views as you cross over the coastal mountains. Just beyond the top of the pass is the Cold Springs Tavern, a legendary bikers' watering hole. After 25 more miles of two-lane asphalt, Highway 264 reconnects with 101 northbound. When you reach San Luis Obispo, follow the signs for Highway 1 and Big Sur.

North of Morro Bay (a good place for a seaside lunch) you'll head through open country toward San Simeon, home to the improbable Hearst Castle. Concentrate on your roadwork though, because some of the nicest bends are just north of town. Once you're past the Hearst Castle Park

Center, traffic thins out, and you'll feel like you're riding through the California of another era--before it discovered grid-lock and Burger Kings. After Big Sur, you'll hit civilization again--Carmel, Pacific Grove and Monterey. Take your time in Pacific Grove. There is a nice shoreline route, perfect for picnicking or exploring tidepools.

Once you reach San Francisco, be sure to explore the Marin Headlands at the north end of the Golden Gate Bridge. When you cross the bridge, turn to the right almost immediately, and cross back under the roadway. The Headlands road then climbs to the ridge, offering 180-degree views that are the equal of any in North America.

North of San Francisco, you're in for some serious riding. Pick up Highway 1 where it splits off for Stinson Beach. From Stinson, proceed north to Pt. Reyes Station. If you've got the time, head west out to the lighthouse, a 2-hour sidetrip. When you return to Highway 1, you've hit the big time--the next 100 miles north to Mendocino is probably America's best coastal motorcycle road.

Proceed north through Elk, Albion and Mendocino, but don't rush. Albion offers a cozy harbor where you can buy fresh salmon right off the boat, and Mendocino is home to many fine country inns, some with spectacular ocean views. North of Ft. Bragg, Highway 1 switchbacks through the redwoods until you rejoin Highway 101.

Just inside Oregon, you'll find great beaches between Brookings and Port Orford. North of Reedsport you'll encounter the most spectacular stretch. The road twists along sheer cliffs, high above the water. Stop for a photo opportunity and you can hear the surf pounding hundreds of feet below. Just north, Otter Rock (near Newport) boasts superb campgrounds. We

Sport-touring with friends/RICH COX

Highway 1 near Mendocino, California/RICH COX

advise continuing north as far as Tillamook and then heading inland on Highway 6 to finish your tour at Portland.

No commercial trip duplicates this itinerary, but you can ride the coast from San Francisco southward on tours with Von Thielmann, Edelweiss Bike Travel, or Desmond Adventures. (See pages 181-83.)

MONTANA & CANADA

Glacier Park & the Icefield Parkway

For spectacular high alpine scenery, Canada's Rockies rival anything you'll find in the European Alps. A tour along the great parkways of Alberta and British Columbia is a fantastic journey, a motorcycle trip of a lifetime.

The best place to start your Canadian odyssey is just south of the border, in Kalispell, Montana. From there, head east through Glacier National Park, operated jointly by the US and Canada. The route through the park on the famed Going to the Sun Highway is extraordinary. You climb thousands of feet up sheer rock walls to a 9,000' pass, with waterfalls and scenic viewpoints every few hundred yards. From the top you can see lakes, forests and the Montana plains 50 miles distant.

Once out of Glacier Park, head north on Highway 89 to Canada. As soon as you've crossed the border, be sure to visit Waterton Lakes Park and the Prince of Wales Hotel. At this point, you can blast straight up to Calgary, but you'll see more if you head west on Highway 3, crossing the Continental Divide into British Columbia. At Cranbrook, pick up Highway 93 north, which will take you into Kootenay National Park and the heart of the Rockies.

Continue on Highway 93 through the high passes to Lake Louise, the jumping-off point for the Icefields Parkway, a modern scenic highway that runs 145 miles north all the way to Jasper. Snow-capped peaks 12,000' high line the entire route, and the icefields run right down to the roadside in places. Everything is green, and all commercial development is hidden from view--hotels, stores, even gas stations. While you can easily do the length of the Icefields Parkway in a day, you'll want to take your time, exploring some of the nearby high-country foot trails. (Trailheads are posted every 10km or so along the Parkway.) Just park your bike at roadside and head for the hills. Within an hour or two you can be sitting on a mountainside full of wild flowers, looking down at an unbelievably aquamarine alpine lakes.

While Canada's parks have been shielded from overdevelopment, you needn't worry about finding a place to rest your head. Canada has an extensive system of campgrounds, and there are many quality lodges situated near the roads. There is also an excellent system of youth hostels that will accept travelers of all ages.

At present, there are few organized road tour options through the Canadian Rockies. Germany's mhs Motorradtouren offers a 15-day Southwest Canada tour in July, but it is expensive (about $3,700) because the bikes are shipped in from Europe. Rocky Mountain Moto Tours offers excellent 7 and 10-day alpine trips for $1,000 and $1,300 respectively, but these tours are done on dual-purpose bikes, and you wouldn't really want to bring a passenger. The best option is to ship your own machine to Washington or Montana, and start your tour from there.

EUROPE

Organized Tours through the Alps

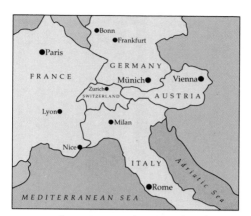

For many, the European Alps represent the ultimate motorcycle touring destination. With spectacular scenery, superb roads and countless charming villages to visit, the Alps offer everything you could want in a tour. And, because the boundaries of France, Switzerland, Austria and Italy all come together in the Alps, you can experience four different national cultures (and cuisines) in a few days.

While you can tour the Alps on your own motorcycle, the logistics of sending a bike over from the US, insuring it, and getting it back again can be overwhelming. Shipping will cost at least $1 per pound each way, and you'll have to have the bike crated before many shippers will touch it. Insurance will run you another $100 per week on the average. If you're going to stay three weeks or more, the most economical way to go is to purchase a motorcycle in Europe, and resell it when you leave. Germany's mhs Motorradtouren and some other tour operators have purchase/buy-back programs for American customers.

If you plan to travel for three weeks or less, an organized tour is the way to go. The best operations, such as Desmond's Alpentour and Edelweiss, have spent years developing itineraries that take you over spectacular passes, to the nicest hotels and most charming towns. Tour participants have praised these programs highly, and few complain about the price. If you're already looking at the cost of airfare to Europe and motorcycle rental, the extra cost of joining a complete tour is probably worth the money.

European weather dictates that you tour in the summer. Try to travel in June, July or September, as August is the busiest vacationing period for Europeans. There are many good routes to follow. We would start in Austria or Germany, work west to Switzerland, then head south to the French coast. After soaking up some sunshine, you can return northeast through Italy and Austria. You should visit Vienna if you've never done so. From Vienna, you can go on to visit Budapest for a day or two, but park your bike and take the train, because there can be a lot of red tape involved in crossing the border with a motorbike. Fly home from Vienna or southern Germany if you have to return the motorcycle.

What is the best part of the Alps? It all depends on your interests. Switzerland has the most spectacular roads, but Italy is friendlier, and France is more fun. Austria is a good choice if you're touring on your own. The roads are superbly maintained, everything works, and in the small villages you can get a spotless room or "zimmer" in a private home for under $20 per night, including breakfast.

A number of good op-

Goldwing on tour/RICH COX

erators offer Alps tours. All publish detailed itineraries worth reviewing. Beach's tours recently topped a customer satisfaction poll, and the Desmond Alpentour is consistently good. If you'd like to ride at a faster clip and save up to $70 per day, go with one of the major Austro/German tour companies such as Edelweiss, Motorrad Reisen, or mhs Motorradtouren.

NORTH CAROLINA

The Blue Ridge Parkway

North Carolina's Blue Ridge Parkway, running 470 miles from the Virginia border to Great Smoky Mountains National Park, is the longest designated scenic highway in North America. Shielded from all commercial development, the Parkway is like a wilderness trail for motorized travelers.

Snaking along mountain ridges, at an average altitude of 3,000', the Parkway offers nearly continuous views of forested hills and open meadows. At the 350-mile mark, the road climbs into the Black Mountains, passing through Mt. Mitchell State Park. (Mt. Mitchell, at 6,684', is the highest summit east of the Rockies.) Just a bit farther south, the Parkway winds through Craggy Gardens Recreation Area, where wild flowers bloom by the thousands on rugged hillsides.

The smoothness of the tarmac and the rhythm of the curves make the drive dream-like. It is not a route to speed through, rather one to savor. Many who have ridden throughout North America say that no other route, even the famed Pacific Coast Highway, is more ideally suited to two-wheeled exploration.

If you would like to ride the Blue Ridge Parkway and nearby Smoky Mountains with an expert local guide, we recommend North Carolina's Smoky Mountain Vacations. Smoky Mountain's director, Gary Dagiel, knows the Parkway intimately and is an authority on dozens of other great regional backroads. From June through September, his company runs weeklong guided tours through the region, departing from Asheville, North Carolina.

Riders bring their own bikes, and itineraries are tailored to the participants' riding styles and interests. Groups are limited to a maximum of 12. You'll visit small farms, and stay in quiet but elegant hotels and country inns. Cost is about $575, including accommodations, breakfast and

Blue Ridge Parkway, North Carolina/DAVID MUENCH

dinners. For further information, contact Smoky Mountain Motorcycle Vacations, 200 Upper Heron Cove Road, Weaverville, NC 28787, (704) 658-0239.

NEW ZEALAND

Unspoiled Paradise

New Zealand (NZ) is a perfect destination for motorcycle touring, at least in the summer--our winter--when the sun shines. The North Island is much like California (before it was overrun with people), while the South Island represents the best of the Pacific Northwest and Colorado combined. With only 3.5 million people in a land mass about the size of California, most places you go will be virtually undeveloped. At one point, we drove for 10 days without seeing a stoplight or a traffic cop.

You'll definitely want to visit both of New Zealand's islands. If you start in the north, your jumping-off point will be Auckland, NZ's largest city. From Auckland, we recommend you head north to visit the Bay of Islands. Keep to the smaller roads through farmlands along the coast. At the northernmost tip of the country is a great 100-mile beach that shouldn't be missed.

Looping back south, most people head straight for the geysers and sulphur pools near Rotorua. Instead, we would opt to explore the rugged and sparsely populated west coast, which offers long isolated beaches, verdant tropical vegetation, and even snow-capped volcanoes.

At the southern tip of the North Island is Wellington, New Zealand's capital. A city of hills, much like San Francisco, Wellington is your departure point for the ferry trip to Picton in the South Island. You will have to cross the Cook Straights, a notoriously rough stretch of water. Make sure that your touring rig is very well secured. It's not at all unusual to encounter 25' seas and 50 knot winds in this stretch of ocean. After debarking at Picton, you'll enjoy the winding road from South to Havelock, where you can board a small boat for a day tour of the nearby island farms. If you continue down the west coast, be prepared for serious downpours—some spots receive over 200 inches of rain every year. About halfway down the coast, cross inland along the scenic Haast Pass and head to the little town of Wanaka in the heart of the Southern Alps.

After Wanaka, you should continue south to Queenstown, NZ's outdoor recreation mecca. Sailing, rafting, jet-boating and even paragliding are just some of the recreational options available. Try to set aside a day to visit nearby Milford Sound. We strongly advise that you park the bike and go with a tour bus. Even in the summer, the Milford Highway is awash with water and gravel. Your last stop should be Christchurch. From there you can fly straight back to the States.

It will take a couple of weeks and about 1,800 miles of driving to do the circuit we've described. You can either rent a bike in Auckland or Christchurch, or go with an organized group. The leading NZ tour operator is John Rains' Te Waipounamu Motorcycle Tours, P.O. Box 673, Christchurch, New Zealand, (011 64) 3 794320; FAX: (011 64) 3 652155. A 2-week guided tour of both islands costs about $2,000, including motorcycle rental (750 to 1000cc BMWs and Yamahas), full accommodations, breakfasts and dinners, and ferry transfers. Te Waipounamu also rents

motorcycles separately for roughly $280 per week plus $.10 per km. On the North Island, Yamaha and Kawasaki bikes can be rented from Graeme Crosby Motorcycles, 299 Great North Road, P.O. Box 78-015, Grey Lynn, Auckland, NZ, (011 64) 9 763-320; FAX: (011 64) 9 765-033. The US agent is Von Thielmann Tours, or you can contact the NZ Tourism Office at (800) 388-5494.

American tour operators Beach's Motorcycle Adventures and Von Thielmann Tours also offer fine NZ motorcycling programs that hit the highlights of both North

In Moscow/COURTESY EDELWEISS BIKE TRAVEL

and South Islands. Book early, as the number of departures is quite limited. You'll find complete listings for both these companies later in this chapter.

RUSSIA

Touring in the Glasnost Era

Just a few years ago, the idea of touring in the Soviet Union would have seemed absurd. However, with glasnost and perestroika, just about anything is possible. A few years back, Austria's Edelweiss Bike

Travel pioneered the first commercial motorcycle tour to the Soviet Union, and Edelweiss now offers what is probably the best organized and most complete Soviet tour available, a 3-week journey through the heart of Russia.

The Edelweiss tour begins in Vienna, Austria. From there you ride along the Donau River to Budapest, Hungary. After crossing the Hungarian lowlands to the Russian border, you'll motor up challenging switchbacks, taking you over the Carpathian Mountains to Lvov. Then the riders cross the Ukraine to Brest, followed by a long passage through the woods of White Russia to Smolensk. After Smolensk the tour heads to Moscow and Leningrad.

In the Soviet cities, tour bikes attract considerable attention. Modern, large-displacement bikes are a rarity in Russia, and wherever the tour makes a stop, the riders are quickly surrounded by curious onlookers. Motor vehicles, whether cars or motorcycles, are still well beyond the means of the average Soviet worker. The positive side of this is that most Russian roads are virtually empty by North American standards. Even the streets of Moscow have very little traffic.

Though the Russian roadways are uncrowded, in many places they are rough and sorely in need of repair. For this reason, the preferred mount, at least for solo riders, is a large dual-purpose bike, like the Suzuki DR BIG750. Such a machine is included in the $4,395 price of the tour. If you plan to bring a passenger, 750cc to 1000cc BMW street bikes are available. Passengers pay $3,395. (Prices are subject to change.)

Edelweiss provides two guides (one in a support van), and an interpreter for each tour group. Although this trip does not offer spectacular scenery at every turn, as a cultural odyssey it is hard to top. Contact Edelweiss' US Agent, Armonk Travel, 146 Bedford Road, Armonk, NY 10504, (800) 255-7541, or (914) 273-8880. Von Thielmann Tours also offers a 21-day USSR trip in July and August. Last year's price was $3,700 for one rider, $7,250 for rider and passenger, with bike rental extra. Von Thielmann can ship your own bike from the States. Call (619) 433-7788.

Motorcycle Tour Operators Worldwide

In the Austrian Alps/COURTESY EDELWEISS BIKE TRAVEL

■ ALASKA MOTORCYCLE TOURS

*P.O. Box 622, Timothy McDonnell, Pres., Bothell, WA 98041-0622, (800) 642-6877, or (206) 487-3219. **Destination:** Alaska. **Equipment:** Honda Goldwings.*

June through August, Alaska Motorcycle Tours operates guided 7-day motorcycle tours from Anchorage, Alaska on new Honda Goldwings. Riders cover 1,600 miles through the Kenai Peninsula, Gold Rush country and Denali National Park. The $1,600 price includes motorcycle rental, fuel and lodging in luxury hotels. Riders pay for their own meals and transport their own luggage. Rating: ★★

■ AUSTRALIAN MOTORCYCLE TOURING

*(011 61) 3 233-8891; US Agent: Adventure Center Inc., 1311 63rd St., Emeryville, CA 94618, (800) 227-8747. **Destinations:** Southern Australia. **Equipment:** BMW R80.*

Run by the former president of the BMW Motorcycle Club of Victoria, Geoff Coat, Australian Motorcycle Touring conducts 8 and 10-day motorcycle trips from Melbourne aboard BMW R80s. The price ranges between $1,900 and $2,600, including motorcycle rental, gas and twin-share accommodations. (Passenger costs run $1,100-$1,900.) The Beemers are stone reliable and Coat is a qualified motor mechanic, so breakdowns should not be a worry, though the tours are not van-supported. Riders carry their own gear in hard saddlebags which are standard equipment on the bikes. This is probably Australia's best motorcycle tour company. Rating: ★★★

■ BAJA OFFROAD TOURS

*25108 Marguerite Parkway, Suite B-126, Mission Viejo, CA 92692, (714) 830-6569. **Destinations:** Baja, Mexico (Ensenada-Gulf of Baja). **Equipment:** Honda XR250 and XR600, Suzuki DR350 off-road.*

Baja Mexico is a premier off-road destination. Former Team Honda dirt-bike racer Chris Haines operates 4 and 7-day tours to southern Baja for $1,200 and $3,000 respectively. The shorter trip runs from the border to San Felipe, while the longer tour takes participants to La Paz along the Sea of Cortez. These trips are expensive, but everything is included--meals, hotels, even gas for the dual-purpose bikes is supplied by Haines. Rating: ★★

■ BEACH'S MOTORCYCLE ADVENTURES

*2763 West River Parkway, Grand Island, NY 14072, (716) 773-4960; FAX: (716) 773-5227. **Destinations:** Australia, Great Britain, European Alps, New Zealand. **Equipment:** BMW 800-1000cc road; Yamaha road in NZ.*

The Beach family has offered outstanding motorcycle tours since 1972, recently topping a Road Rider customer survey. Best known for their Alpine tours, they also run trips to Australia, Great Britain and New Zealand. The Beach tours feature high-quality BMW bikes, and a European buy-and-ride option is available. The Beaches can also ship your own bike to Europe, if you choose. The Alps and British tours cost $3,700 for 22 days, or $2,900 for 16 days, including airfare, hotels, food and van support. Motorcycle rental (BMW 800cc) is an additional $1,100 for 3 weeks, or about $800 for 16 days. Rating: ★★★

■ DESMOND ADVENTURES, INC.

*1280 S. Williams St., Denver, CO 80210, (303) 733-9248; FAX: (303) 733-9601. **Destinations:** European Alps, east and west, USA West. **Equipment:** Wide variety (see below).*

Desmond Adventures' 16-day Alpentour, operated continuously since 1979, has earned rave reviews from both the motorcycle press and past participants. The Desmonds now run two versions of the Alpentour: East (Switzerland, Italy, Austria), and West (Switzerland, Italy, Monaco, France), both priced at $3,995 for riders and $3,395 for passengers. This covers round-trip airfare from New York, hotels, most meals, motorcycle rental and insurance. New this year is a 15-day, $2,700 tour of the US Southwest and California. All tours are van-supported, with a wide variety of mounts including BMW K75S, K75C, K100RS, K100RT; Honda Trans-Alp 600, VFR 750, and CBR 600 and 1000, and ST 1100; Suzuki Katana 600, 750 and 1100; and Kawasaki Concours 1000. (The bigger bikes are surcharged.) Rating: ★★★★

■ EDELWEISS BIKE TRAVEL

*Steinreichweg 1, A-6414 Mieming, Austria; US Agent: Armonk Travel, 146 Bedford Road, Armonk, NY 10504, (800) 255-7451, or (914) 273-8880. **Destinations:** European Alps, Australia, Britain, Hungary, United States, USSR. **Equipment:** BMW and Suzuki 500-1000cc road, BMW 800cc dual-purpose.*

Edelweiss Bike Travel is a true global program, offering well-organized 2 and 3-week tours in Europe, the Mediterranean, Australia and the Western US. Edelweiss offers a bit more value on its Alps trips than the American competition, and its 12-day Affordable Alps trip is a bargain at $2,150, all-inclusive. Three-week European tours cost about $3,300 including accommodations, food and motorcycle rental (BMW K75). Edelweiss, the pioneer in Soviet touring, runs a remarkable central Russia tour (see page 180). Last year's cost was $4,395 for rider, $3,395 for passenger. Support vans are provided for all tours, and larger, 1000cc machines can be rented from Edelweiss for an extra $250–$550 per tour. The entire Edelweiss program is very professional and well managed. Rating: ★★★★$

stamina. If you're looking for real adventure, this is it. Rating: ★★

■ GREAT MOTORCYCLE ADVENTURES

8241 Heartfield Lane, Beaumont, TX 77706, (800) 642-3933, or (409) 866-7891. **Destinations:** *Mexico (Copper Canyon, Sierra Madre, Yucatan).* **Equipment:** *250-650cc dual-purpose and road.*

Great Motorcycle Adventures offers 1-week off-road tours and 18-day road trips to Mexico with departures from Texas. The popular 2-week trip to Mexico's Yucatan Peninsula costs $2,175 and includes all food and accommodations, fuel and insurance. The tour visits Mayan ruins, and allows time to enjoy diving and water sports along the Mexican coast. Road bike rental is an additional $1,175. We highly recommend the weeklong, off-road trips to Copper Canyon or the Sierra Madre mountains of northern Mexico. Both trips cost $875, with rental of a dual-purpose machine an additional $445. GMA's guides are fluent in Spanish, and are well versed in Mexican history and archaeology. Support vans follow all tours. Rating: ★★★

■ MHS MOTORRADTOUREN GMBH

Donnersbergerstrasse 32 D-8000, Munich 19, Germany, (011 49) 89 168 4888; FAX: (011 49) 89 1665 549. **Destinations:** *Canada, European Alps, Germany, Hungary, Kenya, Italy, South Africa, Tunisia, USA.* **Equipment:** *Suzuki 500-1100cc road; BMW road and dual-purpose.*

Mhs Motorradtouren, a relatively new German-based tour operator, offers a full range of motorcycle tours worldwide. The company's two Italian tours (Tuscany and Sicily/southern Italy) have been especially popular. The 2-week southern Italy adventure costs about $2,000, with motorcycle rental an additional $800 or so (a variety of late model Suzukis are available). The price includes first-class hotels and the finest Italian cuisine. Most tours do not have a support van, but all rental bikes (late model BMWs and Suzukis 500-1000cc) come with panniers. We recommend these tours highly. The route choices and rental equipment are consistently excellent. In addition to the organized tours, Motorradtouren offers independent rentals for $60–$100 per day, with 100 free miles per day. Bikes can be rented in Munich and Johannesburg, as well as New York, Miami, Los Angeles or San Diego. The "Drive USA" program permits one-way rentals from East Coast to West Coast, or vice versa. Rating: ★★★

Young riders, Cairo, Egypt/PAUL McMENAMIN

■ EXPLO-TOURS

Arnulfstrasse 134, 8000 Munich 19, Germany, (011 49) 89 160 789; FAX: 89 161 716. **Destinations:** *Tunisia, Algeria, Morocco, Central and South Africa.* **Equipment:** *Yamaha XT350.*

Explo-Tours offers excellent, challenging tours through central and northern Africa. Trips range from 1 to 8 weeks and cover thousands of kilometers, much of it off-road. Participants often provide their own machines, which Explo-Tours ships from Europe to Africa, although Yamaha dual-purpose bikes can be rented for about $290 per week. Prices vary for each trip, but about $1,900 for a 3-week trip is typical. This includes trans-Mediterranean transport, food in Africa, and camping equipment. A support van follows each trip. Most participants are German, but the guides are fluent in English. Explo-Tours' trips are serious, full-on desert adventures which require good physical fitness and

■ **MOTORRAD-REISEN**

Postfach 44 01 48, D-8000, Munich 44, Germany, (011 49) 89 39 57 68; FAX: (011 49) 89 34 48 32. US Agent: Jean Fish, P.O. Box 591, Oconomowoc, WI 53066, (414) 567-7548. Destinations: European Alps, France, Italy, Kenya, USSR. Equipment: Honda dual-purpose, BMW 600-1000cc road.

Motorrad-Reisen (MR), one of the leading German tour operators, provides a wide variety of trips throughout Europe, as well as the USSR and Kenya. MR can arrange for purchase of a BMW motorcycle in Europe, and can arrange to ship your bike to Europe from the United States. MR offers a fine 6-day alpine tour for roughly $1,450, with motorcycle rental an additional $920 or so. A 10-day tour through Southern France costs $1,900, exclusive of bike rental. MR's unique 10-day Kenya moto-safari aboard 600cc dual-purpose bikes costs about $2,700, including motorcycle rental, all food and accommodations. This is an excellent tour through one of Africa's most beautiful countries. Rating: ★★

■ **PANCHO VILLA MOTO-TOURS**

9437 E.B. Taulbee, El Paso, TX 79924, (800) 233-0564, or (915) 757-3032; FAX: (915) 562-1505. Destinations: Mexico (Baja, Sierra Madre, Central Coast, Yucatan), Costa Rica, Southwest US. Equipment: Most makes, incl. Harley, Honda and BMW 600-1200cc.

In operation since 1981, Pancho Villa Moto-Tours (PVMT) has long been the established leader in Mexico motorcycle touring, and it is now developing a variety of domestic itineraries. PVMT conducts a number of Mexican tours out of El Paso, ranging from 4 to 29 days in length. We strongly recommend PVMT's Colonial tour. Cost for 10 nights is $890 per person. On PVMT's remarkable 29-day Yucatan tour, you ride through jungle, deserts, rainforests and mountains, meet remote tribes and visit Mayan ruins. The $2,195 price includes full accommodations and most food. On most trips, motorcycle rental can be ar-

ranged by PVMT for an additional $45 to $85 per day. A wide variety of machines, including late model Harley-Davidsons, are available. Rating: ★★★

■ **ROCKY MOUNTAIN MOTO TOURS LTD.**

P.O. Box 7152, Stn. E, Calgary, ALB, T3C 3M1, Canada, (403) 244-6939; FAX: (403) 229-2788. Destinations: Canadian Rocky Mountains (BC and Alberta). Equipment: Honda 600cc dual-purpose.

Each summer, Rocky Mountain Moto Tours, Ltd. (RMMT), offers 7-day Bugaboo tours and 10-day Big Sky tours through the scenic and unspoiled backcountry of Alberta and British Columbia. Using 600cc dual-purpose bikes, RMMT makes full use of the bikes' off-road abilities on remote, but not difficult, backcountry routes. The price for the Bugaboo tour is roughly $1,100, which covers bike rental, hotel accommodation, fuel, breakfasts and dinners. The longer tour costs about $1,450, all-inclusive. We've ridden through these areas in summer, and can testify that the routes are superb. No special off-road experience is required. If you can swing the expense, a Canadian Rockies trip could be an experience of a lifetime. Rating: ★★

■ **VON THIELMANN TOURS**

P.O. Box 87764, San Diego, CA 92138, (619) 463-7788, or (619) 234-1558; FAX: (619) 234-1458. Destinations: US (Southwest), European Alps, Mexico, China, Thailand, Argentina, New Zealand. Equipment: 400-1200cc road, various makes.

Von Thielmann Tours is one of the oldest and most respected companies in the business, and has pioneered many new touring destinations, including mainland China and the USSR. Von Thielmann presently offers tours in Europe, China, Mexico, Argentina, Thailand, the US, Jamaica and New Zealand. Notable among Von Thielmann's many tour offerings are the 9-day Jamaica tour for about $1,400, including airfare, motorcycle and hotels; the 20-day Argentina tour for $2,750, including everything but motorcycle rental; and the 15-day Europe Grand Alpine tour for $2,300, including everything except bike rental.

In addition to guided tours, Von Thielmann offers motorcycle rentals, motorcycle shipping, and a European delivery program for new BMWs and used motorcycles of all makes. Von Thielmann's rental program rents 400cc to 1200cc bikes of all types from about $50 per day, with a 3-day minimum in Europe and a 2-week minimum in California. We can recommend Von Thielmann as a solid, reliable organization that can offer virtually any kind of motorcycle experience--whether you want to go it alone, or join an organized group tour. Rating: ★★★

Alpine touring/RICH COX

Independent Motorcycle Touring

RICH COX

COMMERCIAL TOURS ARE GREAT, BUT THEY CAN BE EXPENSIVE, AND YOU won't always be able to go exactly where you want, at your own pace. When you're on a self-guided tour you can stay put when the weather's bad, and then hustle down the Autobahn at flank speed when the clouds part and you feel like making time. The bottom line is that *you* are in charge. And, if you forego fancy hotels in favor of campgrounds, you can get by on $30 per day. That's a lot less than you'll pay for commercial tours, which usually run $100 to $200 per day.

Crating and pickup will run another $100 to $150 on the average. If the gas tank, battery and carburetors are removed, shipping rules are more lenient, and you may be able to save 20 to 30 percent by consolidating the bike with other cargo. Contact Burlington Air Express, 8900 Bellanca Avenue, Los Angeles, CA 90045, (213) 649-0012; or Circle Air Freight, 300 N. Oak Street, Inglewood, CA 90301, (213) 673-7720.

PLANNING AN ITINERARY

If you plan to tour on your own in the United States, pick up a copy of the Harley Davidson touring guide, *America's Best Roads*. It lists 50 of North America's best motorcycle routes. When selecting an itinerary, don't try to cover too much ground in one day. In a car, 300 miles a day is an easy task, but it is a lot of distance on a bike, particularly if you take time to enjoy the sights along the way.

LICENSING & INSURANCE

If you plan to tour in a foreign country, either on your own machine or on a rental bike, make sure you get an international driver's license endorsed for motorcycles. You will also need special insurance to tour in most European countries. This can be arranged by Budget Rent-a-Car, which rents motorcycles at seven locations in Germany. Send FAX inquiries to (011 49) 69 296 238 in Frankfurt. When traveling, remember to keep your passport with you at all times. Don't leave it in a hotel room. And never leave your helmet or riding jacket on the bike unsecured, even for a few minutes.

OVERSEAS SHIPPING

Beach's Motorcycle Adventures, (716) 773-4960, can coordinate crating of your bike and shipment to Europe from most large US cities. Cost for delivery in Europe (Switzerland or Spain) averages about $1.10 per pound, plus insurance. Von Thielmann Tours, (619) 463-7788, can also arrange to have your bike shipped to Europe in connection with one of its tours.

Because of fuel residues, used motorcycles are considered hazardous cargo (officially labeled "restricted articles"). For this reason, few, if any, air carriers will accept bikes directly, so you will need a freight forwarder such as Burlington Air Express or Circle Air Freight to supervise air shipping. As do most freight forwarders, Burlington and Circle require the motorcycle to be crated before shipping. One-way costs are about $1.80 per pound from Los Angeles to Auckland, New Zealand, $.95 per pound from Los Angeles to London, and $1.05 per pound from Los Angeles to Switzerland.

BUY-BACKS & RENTALS

If you own a typical big-bore touring motorcycle, you'll probably be shipping 650 pounds or more, including crating. Your air freight costs to Europe will therefore run $1,200 to $1,500 on a European tour, and more than double that if you plan a tour Down Under.

Unless you plan to ride at least three weeks, you're better off renting a motorcycle at your destination. The Harley Owners Group, Von Thielmann Tours, and mhs Motorradtouren all rent large-displacement bikes on the Continent. Prices start at about $55 per day, plus insurance. Another good option is buying a BMW at the Bavarian factory, and then bringing it home. BMW will arrange for shipping to America. If you plan an extended tour closer to home, Western States Motorcycle Tours, 1823 West Seldon Lane, Phoenix, AZ 85021, phone/FAX: (602) 943-9030, offers a purchase/sell-back program for all makes of bikes that can be more cost-effective than renting. (For shorter tours, Western States also rents BMWs, Goldwings and Harley FLHTCs for $65-$95 per day, or $400-$600 per week.)

MOTORCYCLE TOURING

TRAINING PROGRAMS

MSF Training

The Motorcycle Safety Foundation (MSF) offers an innovative and effective training course for new motorcyclists. The beginners' course costs $120-$145 for a 16-hour program conducted over 2 or 3 days. The price includes use of an insured 175cc to 250cc machine for your roadwork. As an added incentive, many insurers offer a 5 to 15 percent discount for successful completion of an MSF course.

For those with previous street-riding experience, MSF offers a 1-day Advanced Riders' Course, which costs about $60. Every seasoned rider we know who tried the Advanced Course recommended it highly. And, like the entry-level course, it will qualify you for an insurance discount. Call the MSF at (800) 833-3995 to locate the MSF training course nearest you.

High Performance Programs

■ **CALIFORNIA SUPERBIKE SCHOOL**
P.O. Box 3107, Hollywood, CA 90078, (213) 484-9323; FAX: (213) 484-9323.

Rated by Sports Illustrated as the "best buy in America" for high-performance training, Superbike is also the only school which provides bikes and leathers to its students. Chief instructor Keith Code supervises classroom sessions followed by timed track practice aboard 600cc Kawasaki ZX-6 Ninjas.

Superbike School now operates at 10 tracks nationwide April through August: Road America (WI), Mid-Ohio, Memphis Motopark (TN), West Palm Beach (FL), Road Atlanta (GA), Watkins Glen (NY), Loudon (NH), and Willow Springs, Sears Point and Laguna Seca in California. (For dates at each track, call the Superbike School in California).

The Superbike School provides instruction for all levels of riders. The basic 1-day program (40 miles on track) with onboard audio costs $250. The regular expanded (full-day, 100 track-miles) program costs $450, while the expanded line-tech school and race training program, available at Wil-

RICH COX

low Springs only, costs $475. Finally, the 2-day video camp for advanced riders and novice racers, which features onboard videos of the students on the track, costs $1,050. All students must be at least 18 and possess a valid motorcycle license. (Note: Prices may increase in 1992.) Rating: ★★★★

■ **CLASS, INC. SAFETY SCHOOLS**
1495 Palma Drive, Suite B, Ventura, CA 93003, (805) 642-7228; FAX: (805) 642-5856.

The is not a racing school, although it is conducted on a track and is designed to improve high-speed riding skills. Instructor Reg Pridmore, three-time AMA Superbike champion, emphasizes body control, execution of the proper line through turns, and braking skills. The object is to produce skilled, confident riders.

Pridmore's students are mostly BMW owners, but Class is open to all riders. Students must provide their own motorcycles, although Class students are permitted to test-ride new BMW motorcycles on the track. The basic Class programs last for 1 day, cost about $275 and are held at a dozen tracks nationwide. For previous Class graduates, Pridmore offers an advanced 1-day school at California's Laguna Seca and Willow Springs tracks at the same cost. Rating: ★★★

RIDER ORGANIZATIONS

Goldwing Road Riders Assoc. (GWRRA) P.O. Box 14350, Phoenix, AZ 85063, (800) 843-9460, or (602) 269-1403 in Arizona.

BMW Motorcycle Owners Association P.O. Box 489, Chesterfield, MO 63006-0489, (20,000 members nationwide).

Harley Owners' Group P.O. Box 453, Milwaukee, WI 53201, (800) 258-2464, (414) 935-4522; call collect from Alaska and Hawaii.

The American Women Road Riders' Alliance (AWRRA) P.O. Box 536, Santa Monica, CA 90406, (213) 395-1171.

RESOURCES

Motorcycle Touring, an International Directory 1991/92, is a one-of-a-kind resource for commercial motorcycle tours worldwide. You won't find maps or suggested routes however, and some of the listings are a bit dated. Cost is $19.95 from Whitehorse Press, 154 West Brookline Street, Boston, MA 02118, (800) 842-7077, or (617) 482-3350.

America's Best Roads, by Harley-Davidson, is a short (98 pages) but useful guide to 50 of America's best touring routes. This book contains color photos and detailed maps of all 50 routes. Available from your local Harley dealer, or from Whitehorse Press for $18.95.

Nature & Wildlife

ART WOLFE

*Let us permit nature to have her way; she understands
her business better than we do.*
-Michel de Montaigne

▼

Nature tours give us a chance to appreciate the wonder and diversity of the natural world, while escaping the noise and hassles of urban life.

Today dozens of companies and guide services conduct nature tours and photo safaris virtually everywhere wild creatures are to be found. There are polar bear odysseys in the Canadian Arctic, whale-watching cruises in Mexico, and tiger-tracking safaris in India. We introduce you to all these adventures and more, reviewing the best nature tours on all seven continents, ranging from bird-watching weekends to serious jungle expeditions. These trips cover the complete vacation spectrum, from barebones to ultra-luxurious. However, you'll find that the typical nature or wildlife tour is aimed at a demanding clientele, and accordingly offers a fair amount of creature comfort.

To avoid duplication, this chapter only covers nature tours outside Africa. If you want to see lions, elephants, zebras, gorillas, and other African game, consult Chapter 17, Safaris.

CHAPTER
13

Giant tortoises, Alcedo Volcano, Galapagos Islands/FRANS LANTING, MINDEN PICTURES

A WILDLIFE TRIP NEED NOT BE AN EXPENSIVE OR LABORIOUS UNDERTAKING. However, if you want to see the greatest variety and numbers of wild species, you'll want to head to the hinterlands, where mankind has not yet driven the wild creatures from their natural habitats. We review seven of the prime wildlife-viewing venues in the world, where you can observe nature at its finest.

GALAPAGOS ISLANDS

Ecuador's Garden of Eden

It's easy to lapse into superlatives when describing Ecuador's Galapagos Islands. Many believe that the Galapagos comprise the single richest sanctuary for land and aquatic wildlife on the planet. This place has it all--fantastic bird populations, sea lions, unusual flora, giant tortoises, and marine iguanas, creatures found nowhere else in the world. For ardent naturalists, the Galapagos may well be the ultimate destination.

A trip to the Galapagos is a true adventure. The entire chain of islands is maintained as a wilderness preserve, with only a few small settlements. After arriving in Quito, Ecuador, you will fly 600 miles west to the landing strip at Baltra. From there most tourists transfer to a waiting yacht, their home for the next 3 days to 3 weeks. On some trips, tourists will spend a few days in hotels or camping, but most of the tour will be spent onboard, sailing from one island to another to observe the full spectrum of wildlife.

You will want to visit a number of different islands in the chain--each has its own distinctive attractions. Outlying Hood and Tower Islands are home to the exotic marine iguanas, and large populations of blue and red-footed boobies. South Plaza Island hosts a large number of land iguanas, and colonies of sea lions. The sea lions are remarkably unafraid of humans, allowing face-to-face encounters. Santa Cruz Island, site of the Charles Darwin Research Station, is one of the largest islands in the chain, and one of the few with acceptable hotel accommodations.

Floreana Island is a divers' favorite, with extensive corals, sand beaches and vast numbers of tropical fish. James Island is noted for its bird species, including the Galapagos hawk, and its colonies of playful fur seals. Dominated by the still active Alcedo Volcano, Isabela Island is perhaps the most fascinating isle in the chain. Many tours offer a backpack trip on Isabela. After ascending the volcano's 3,000' flanks, the hikers camp in the four-mile wide caldera, an otherworldly landscape of lava flows and steamy fumaroles where hundreds of giant tortoises live and breed.

A number of outfitters conduct nature

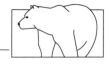

Seven Ultimate Wildlife Adventures

study tours in the Galapagos Islands, ranging from 1 to 3 weeks in length. Our favorite tour is Wilderness Travel's 18-day Ultimate Galapagos trip which visits a dozen islands and includes a 3-day Alcedo Volcano backpack adventure. Trips depart January through July, at a cost of $3,090 to $3,550 depending on group size. For those with less time, Wildland Adventures offers a fine 11-day tour that covers 10 islands; unfortunately, Isabela is not among them.

The price is a reasonable $1,860. Both trips feature comfortable sailing yachts and expert naturalist guides from the Darwin Research Station. Contact Wilderness Travel, 801 Allston Way, Berkeley, CA 94710, (800) 368-2794, or (510) 548-0420; or Wildland Adventures, 3516 NE 155th, Seattle, WA 98155, (800) 345-4453, or (206) 365-0686.

The widest variety of Galapagos trips is offered by Inca Floats, which schedules more than 80 departures to the Galapagos each year. On a typical trip, you'll travel with eight to 10 passengers on a large sailing or motor yacht, guided by a licensed naturalist. Prices range from $1,995 to $3,595 for 11 to 20-day itineraries. Trips depart virtually year-round with many different variations. Inca Floats' 18-day April trip is very similar to Wilderness Travel's Ultimate Galapagos trip.

Quite popular are the chartered, specialty dive trips (11 or 18 days). Contact Inca Floats, 1311 63rd Street, Emeryville, CA 94608, (510) 420-1550; FAX: (510) 420-0947.

Marine iguana/FRANS LANTING

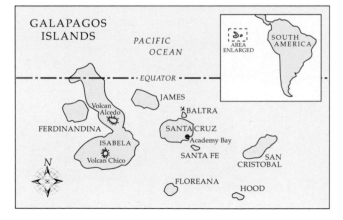

GALAPAGOS ISLANDS
PACIFIC OCEAN
AREA ENLARGED
SOUTH AMERICA
EQUATOR
JAMES
Volcan Alcedo
BALTRA
FERDINANDINA
SANTA CRUZ
Academy Bay
ISABELA
SANTA FE
Volcan Chico
SAN CRISTOBAL
FLOREANA
HOOD
N

YELLOWSTONE

America's Wildlife Headquarters

Yellowstone Park is the richest wildlife preserve in the Lower 48. In its 2.2 million acres of geysers, meadowlands and mountains are found all of North America's great wildlife species: deer, moose, elk, bears and buffalo. The sheer numbers of animals in Yellowstone are impressive--30,000 elk, 2,100 bison, an estimated 200 grizzlies and countless other smaller species. Though the summer crowds almost overwhelm the park's major tourist attractions, if you're prepared to venture into Yellowstone's 3,500 square miles of backcountry, it's surprisingly easy to escape the crowds.

Hiking the backcountry is the best way to view Yellowstone's animals. With 1,210 miles of trails, the park offers endless options for travelers on foot. At the top of any day-hiker's list is a walk through the Hayden Valley, Yellowstone's garden, and home to its largest bison herds. The day-hiking on the Mary Mountain Trail is equally scenic. A good overnight excursion is the Pebble Creek trail which starts off a mile or so from the northeast entrance. Here you will find large groups of elk, moose and buffalo, while black and grizzly bears may be observed as well. For a longer trip, take five days to walk the length of the Thorofare trail. From a trailhead on East Entrance Road, it winds along the shore of Yellowstone Lake, providing good views of eagles and ospreys, and possibly bears.

Yellowstone is a high-altitude wilderness, and conditions can be fairly inclement as late as June. The best time to hike the backcountry is August and September. The rivers and streams will be much lower, the bug count is down, and the weather will be more hospitable. Because of the altitude, snow flurries are possible any time of year, so always bring warm clothes and a good tent, no matter what the weather forecast. More details on wilderness hiking in Yellowstone can be obtained from Backcountry Information, Yellowstone National Park, WY 82190, (307) 344-7381, ext. 2296.

In the summertime it's hard to justify the cost of a commercial tour when you can easily see most of the park's wildlife on your own. However, come winter, many of the main roads within the park are closed, so it makes sense to go with a guide. Our favorite winter wildlife tour is offered by Van Os Photo Safaris. Noted lensmen David Middleton and Perry Conway lead small groups of amateur photographers to observe elk, deer, bison, bighorn sheep and other wild species. This photo safari has been rated one of the best in North America. Seven-day tours operate in February, and cost roughly $1,350, departing from Bozeman, Montana. Van Os also offers an 8-day autumn tour in Yellowstone and the Grand Tetons. Trips depart in September and cost about $1,600. Contact Joseph Van Os Photo Safaris, P.O. Box 655, Vashon Island, WA 98070, (206) 463-5383.

BAHAMAS

Swimming with Dolphins

While there are a number of swim-with-dolphin programs which use captive creatures in enclosed pens, at present the

Bull Elk in Yellowstone Park, after the summer fire/ART WOLFE

Bahamas is the only place where tourists can interact with dolphins in the open ocean.

Since 1979, UNEXSO (Underwater Explorers' Society), a Freeport-based dive center, has conducted a unique program that allows humans to swim with dolphins both in salt-water pens and the open ocean. For $59, participants can swim with the creatures in a protected bay for 15 to 30 minutes. The big attraction, however, is the ocean dive program. Several times a week, UNEXSO's dolphins are released to sea. The participants, who must be certified divers, board a launch to rendezvous with the dolphins at a coral reef a mile offshore. The divers swim with the dolphins for an hour or so, taking turns feeding the mammals and hitching rides. The dolphins are friendly and quite responsive, having been taught hand commands used by the divers. The ocean dolphin encounters cost $70 on top of the $30 charge for a regular dive. Contact UNEXSO, P.O. Box F-2433, Freeport, Grand Bahama, (809) 373-1244, or (800) 922-DIVE.

If UNEXSO's program is intriguing, even more exciting is the prospect of swimming with truly wild dolphins. Oceanic Society Expeditions conducts 8-day cruises between May and August to study wild spotted and bottlenose dolphins off Grand Bahama Island. Non-disruptive communication with the dolphins is a goal on each expedition, conducted as part of an ongoing research effort. One past participant described her experience: "After frantic scrambling for our gear, we plopped one by one into the water into a scene unlike anything I have experienced before. The world was dolphins, everywhere I looked. The water was the temperature of my skin, and I lost all sense of boundaries. A five-foot dolphin calf came to me and started corkscrew turns down to the ocean floor. I circled with him, down, then catapulted to the surface, exhausted and delighted."

Participants will sail to the dolphin grounds on a comfortable 70' schooner. The 1992 trips will cost roughly $1,450. Contact Oceanic Society Expeditions, Ft.

Bengal tiger/ART WOLFE, ALLSTOCK

Mason Center, Building E, San Francisco, CA 94123, (415) 441-1106. A very similar program is offered by the Wild Dolphin Project. Participants will join marine researchers on a 60' catamaran for a week of swimming with dolphins off Grand Bahama Island. Trips depart June through September at a cost of about $1,450. Contact Wild Dolphin Project, 21 Hepburn Avenue, Suite 20, Jupiter, FL 33458, (407) 575-5660.

INDIA

Tracking the Bengal Tiger

India is the "Land of the Tiger." The Bengal tiger, a proud but threatened species, is now sheltered in India's Ranthambhor, Kanha, and Sariska Game Reserves, where despite the ever-present danger of poachers, the animals' numbers are actually on the rise. The Indian game parks are large and well managed, with a great diversity of animal life. In addition to tigers, you'll be able to observe leopards, elephant, rhinos and countless smaller species. For those interested in big game, India is second only to East Africa.

Of the many Indian wildlife safaris available, SafariCentre's 18-day package probably offers the best opportunities for tiger-viewing, with a total of 9 days in Ranthambhor, Kanha, Nagarhole National Park, and other game parks. In Ranthambhor and Corbett game parks,

along with tigers you'll probably see a few leopards, caracals and other big cats. The Nagarhole National Park features all the major Indian big game, including elephants, leopards and tigers, along with 250 species of birds. This park is a good choice for off-season, and is less heavily touristed than most other game reserves in India. The tour, which visits the Taj Mahal and other major Indian cultural sites, runs November through April each year, with a land cost of $2,200 to $2,500 depending on accommodations. Longer or shorter itineraries are available. Contact SafariCentre Int'l, 3201 N. Sepulveda Blvd., Manhattan Beach, CA 90266, (800) 223-6046, or (800) 624-5342 in CA.

On GEO Expedition's tiger trip, you visit the Ranthambhor Tiger Reserve, the Indian one-horned rhino reserve at Kaziranga, and a number of spectacular palaces, including the Taj Mahal. Cost for 17 days in January 1992 is estimated at $2,490. International Expeditions will take you to three or four of the leading tiger reserves along with a number of cultural sites. Trips last 16, 18 or 22 days with an optional Nepal extension. These trips are not inexpensive--they start at $3,598--but you have a wide choice of departures between October and April. Contact GEO Expeditions, P.O. Box 3656, Sonora, CA 95370, (800) 351-5041, or Int'l Expeditions, One Environs Park, Helena, AL 35080, (800) 633-4734, or (205) 428-1700.

If you're looking for a truly exotic Indian wildlife-watching trip, consider Victor Emanuel Nature Tours' unique 21-day elephant safari. Participants will travel on elephant-back through rural wilderness areas, overnighting in tented camps, or at rest houses where the last non-Indian signature in the guest book dates back to the days of the Raj. The wildlife-viewing opportunities, including tiger-tracking, rival the best in Africa. The elephant safari departs in late January; the 1992 land cost was $3,695. Contact Victor Emanuel Nature Tours, P.O. Box 33008, Austin, TX 78764, (800) 328-VENT.

MADAGASCAR

Zoological Wonderland

Situated 250 miles off the East African coast, Madagascar has been called "one of the most remarkable zoological districts in the world," by famed naturalist Alfred Russell Wallace. It is a wildlife treasure-trove, home of countless exotic plant and animal species, 80 percent of which are indigenous. The world's fourth largest island, Madagascar remains virtually untouched by Western tourism. The best time to travel is from April to October, when the weather is relatively cool and dry. However, the climate varies around the island--cool in the central highlands, humid on the east coast, dry in the southern desert areas.

Among wildlife enthusiasts, Madagascar is best known for its remarkable lemurs--endemic species of long-tailed primates that look like a cross between a raccoon and a teddy bear. These creatures, which range in size from the giant indris, as large as a chimp, to the tiny mouse lemur, inhabit the dense jungles and high mountains of Madagascar. This island nation has dedicated much of its interior as parklands or wildlife reserves, affording excellent opportunities to view lemurs, chameleons and Madagascar's other unique species.

Any Madagascar itinerary should include Montagne D'Ambre National Park, and the Perinet, Ranomafana, and Berenty Wildlife Reserves. Montagne D'Ambre is situated on the northernmost tip of the island. A beautiful rainforest, it boasts fantastic orchid gardens, a major waterfall, dozens of bird and reptile species, and many different types of lemurs. The Perinet Reserve is one of the most accessible tropical rainforests in Madagascar. It is home to nine species of lemurs (including the giant indris lemur), numerous bird species, and large chameleons. The Berenty Reserve (Fort Dauphin), situated on the banks of the Mandrare River, is an internationally acclaimed wildlife refuge boasting very rare flora and fauna. Here you will find ring-tailed lemurs, the rare sifakas, flying foxes and exotic bird species.

There are many naturalist travel options for Madagascar, located three hours by air from Nairobi, Kenya. Lemur Tours is the Madagascar specialist, offering a variety of trips, from 7 to 13 days, with year-round departures. Prices vary widely based on the particular itinerary, so call or write for specifics. For those looking to add a Madagascar adventure to an East African safari, we recommend the 7-day Perinet-Berenty tour, a good value at about $1,260. Lemur Tours also offers custom itineraries, such as bird-watching, diving and anthropology. Contact Lemur Tours, 2562 Noriega Street, #203, San Francisco, CA 94122, (800) 73-LEMUR, FAX: (415) 681-6274. A preview video is available for $23.00.

Journeys offers some of the best in-depth nature study programs in Madagascar, and would be our first pick for a longer tour. Journeys' most rewarding trip is its 3-week Exploratory Expedition, which is conducted in both April and September. Led by an experienced English-, French-, and Malagasy-speaking guide, participants will travel by air, rail, boat, foot and jeep to visit some of the most remote and scenic areas of the island--including many places visited by no other Westerners. This is probably the most complete nature tour presently offered in Madagascar. It is limited to 10 participants, and will cost roughly $3,000. Shorter, less demanding trips are scheduled year-round, and custom itineraries can be arranged.

Contact Journeys, 4011 Jackson Road, Ann Arbor, MI 48103, (800) 255-8735.

ALASKA & CANADA

The Land of the Caribou

The 19.5-million-acre Arctic National Wildlife Refuge, America's largest, is probably the finest wildlife-viewing area in North America. Dozens of the major mammal species, including bear, dall sheep, wolves and caribou, thrive in this vast wilderness, where there are no permanent human settlements. The Refuge is the site of one of nature's great spectacles, the annual migration of the 180,000-strong Porcupine caribou herd. Each June, the herd moves northward through the Refuge to calving grounds on the Arctic coast. A number of small Alaskan outfitters can guide you to the herd on a custom basis, or you can sign up with Mountain Travel's 11-

Ring-tailed lemur and cub/FRANS LANTING

Caribou, Arctic National Wildlife Refuge/TOM WALKER, ALLSTOCK

INDONESIA

The Dragons' Lair

Indonesia, a vast archipelago of islands, is home to some of the most exotic creatures on earth. Many species are endemic, including the rare and threatened Javanese rhino. (The last 40 to 50 creatures survive in the confines of Ujung Kulon National Park on the west end of Java.) Indonesia is also the last sanctuary of the orangutan and the Komodo dragon, a much-fabled link to the age of the dinosaurs.

If you've wondered about the Komodo dragons--here's the straight dope. These giant monitor lizards are found only on Komodo, a small volcanic island 200 miles south of Bali in Indonesia. They grow to 12 feet in length, and have been known to attack humans, although birds and small mammals are their favorite fare. We've looked for the best dragon trip, and have come up with the Adventure Center's 20-day Indonesian sea-trek. On a 165' schooner you will visit the islands of Java, Bali, Lombok, Subawa, Komodo and Flores. On each island you stop for a day or two to explore villages, snorkle in the warm, clear water, or trek inland. Highlights are dragon-viewing on Komodo, and visiting the Kelimutu crater lakes on Flores Island. The price will be roughly $2,370; food and on-board accommodations are good, but hardly luxurious. Contact the Adventure Center, 1311 63rd Street, Suite 200, Emeryville, CA 94608, (510) 654-1879.

For those who want to see the widest spectrum of Indonesian animals, we recommend a trip that includes Borneo or Sumatra, in addition to Indonesia's smaller islands of Bali, Lombok and Komodo. The best we've found is GEO Expeditions' 19-day Indonesian wildlife expedition. This trip manages to pack a vast amount of adventure into a relatively short period of time. You can explore the remnants of the famous Krakatoa volcano, then take a river trip through the jungle to the Tunjung Puting orangutan reserve operated by Dr. Birute Galdikas and Rod Brindamour. In addition to the red apes, you'll find gibbons and a host of other primates. After Borneo, you visit Bali, Lombok and Komodo Islands. On Komodo, participants will trek inland to view the dragons in the wild. Land cost will be $2,090, with June and August departures. Contact GEO Expeditions, P.O. Box 3656, Sonora, CA 95370, (800) 351-5041, or (209) 532-0152.

day Arctic Refuge wildlife trip. After flying from Fairbanks to a wilderness basecamp, participants spend 6 days in the wild, watching tens of thousands of animals move across the tundra within walking distance of the group's tents.

With sunlight almost 24 hours a day, you can pack more wildlife observation into a week that you might think possible. Bring plenty of film. And be prepared for rough weather. Situated above the Arctic Circle, the Refuge can be cold and inhospitable even in the middle of summer (trips run in both June and August, but June is the best time to see the caribou). Cost for the 11-day trip is $2,390, plus $650 for Alaskan charter flights. The price isn't cheap, but this trip is well sorted out (caribou sightings are virtually guaranteed in June), and a privately guided trip would cost as much or more. Contact Mountain Travel/Sobek, 6420 Fairmount Avenue, El Cerrito, CA 94530, (800) 227-2384.

If you don't have 11 days to spend in the high arctic, Canada is a good alternative for caribou-watching. Every August, Canada's Adventure Northwest leads an 8-day wilderness tundra trip to view the Bathurst caribou herd during its southward migration. From Yellowknife in the Northwest Territories, participants are carried by bushplane to a tent basecamp situated along a known migration route. Seven days will be spent observing and photographing the herds at close range. You'll probably see more animals (including newborn calves) than on an Alaskan trip, as the Bathurst herd numbers 500,000, and the migration is continuous throughout the month. Cost for the program will be about $3,500 CDN, including round-trip charter flights from Edmonton, Alberta. Contact Adventure Northwest, P.O. Box 2435, Yellowknife, NWT, Canada X1A 2P8, (403) 920-2196. If you want to arrange an independent caribou-watching trip, see Chapter 28 for listings of wilderness flying services in the Northwest Territories.

TOP NATURE & WILDLIFE TOURS

Breaching humpback whales/JAMES D. WATT, EARTHVIEWS

I T SEEMS THAT EVERYBODY IS RUNNING A NATURE TRIP THESE DAYS. HOWEVER, WE'VE found too many wildlife tours are poorly planned or overpriced--you either don't see very many animals, or you have to fight a pack of tourists to get close to the action. The trips described here are something quite different. These are time-tested programs run by experienced outfitters or wildlife organizations. In most cases the trips are guided by trained naturalists who know their stuff.

MARINE MAMMALS

GRAY AND HUMPBACK WHALES

By most criteria, Baja Mexico is the best whale-watching destination in the world. Every winter, hundreds of whales migrate down the Pacific coast to winter in Southern Baja's warm lagoons. On the west coast, Magdalena Bay is the focus of activity, while on the Sea of Cortez side, Isla Espiritu Santo north of La Paz is a favorite whale hangout. The whales congregate in great numbers and stay in the same lagoons for days on end, making for easy viewing.

For a top-flight Baja experience, a good choice is Biological Journey's Magdalena Bay to La Paz·tour. As many as 10 whale species have been spotted in recent years, including scores of grays in Magdalena Bay. The 8-day voyage costs $2,295. Contact Biological Journeys, 1696J Ocean Drive, McKinleyville, CA 95521, (800) 548-7555, or (707) 839-0178.

For whale-watchers on a tighter budget, we recommend Baja Expeditions' Mexican cruises. Using inflatables launched from a large motor yacht, participants observe gray, blue and humpback whales in their winter harbors. The cruises run January through April, starting at $1,250 for 4 days. Contact Baja Expeditions, (800) 843-6967.

Outside Baja, we again recommend Biological Journeys. Having led marine mammal tours for over 20 years, no outfitter has more expertise. In addition to its Mexican trips, this outfitter runs whale-watching cruises to Australia, Alaska, British Columbia, Ecuador, and the Galapagos. The Alaska trips feature spectacular Glacier Bay and Admiralty Island.

Outer Edge Expeditions runs a remarkable trip featuring diving with humpbacks off Australia's Great Barrier Reef. After a helicopter ride to an offshore live-aboard, participants cruise to Platypus Bay, where the entire stock of South Pacific humpback whales congregate during breeding season. There, certified divers can swim with the whales, while enjoying visibility up to 150'. Price ranges from $3,400 to $4,400 for 15 days. Contact Outer Edge Expeditions,

45500 Pontiac Trail, Walled Lake, MI 48390, (800) 322-5235.

Every year migrating families of humpbacks visit the Hawaiian Islands, their winter breeding grounds. The best value in Hawaiian whale-watching is a $70-$110 half or full-day trip with Captain Zodiac. Captain Zodiac uses small, motorized inflatables to get within 100 yards of the creatures--close enough to feel the spray kicked up when they breech. Trips run January through April from Kauai, Maui and the Big Island. Contact Captain Zodiac, P.O. Box 456, Hanalei, Kaui, HI 96714. Call (800) 422-7824, (808) 667-5862 (Maui), (808) 329-3199 (Big Island).

For those looking for more than a day-trip, Eye of the Whale offers an Earth, Fire and Sea Hawaiian holiday which combines sailing, wilderness hiking and volcano exploration. A lovely 54' sailing yacht is used to observe migrating gray and humpback whales off the Big Island. The 5-day trips cost about $1,000 with departures January through mid-April. Contact Eye of the Whale, P.O. Box 1269, Kapa 'Au, HI 96755, (800) 657-7730, or (808) 889-0227.

KILLER WHALES (ORCAS)

The best locales to view orcas are the bays and inlets of the Canadian Northwest. While orcas can be observed from large vessels, nothing beats a sea kayak for close encounters. Some of the best orca trips are led by Larry Roy of Discovery Kayaks. Discovery's 6 and 8-day kayak tours explore the Inland Passage along Vancouver Island to Robson Bight, spending four days in close proximity to the whales. Discovery has this trip wired--for the past three years running, Roy has been able to lead his customers to the same family of Orcas. Contact Discovery Kayaks, 2755 Departure Road, Nanaimo, BC, Canada V9S 3W9, (604) 758-2488. If Discovery's trips are booked, Northern Lights Expeditions, 5220 NE 180th, Seattle, WA 98155, (206) 362-4506, also offers kayak trips to the Northwest's prime orca grounds.

If you want to view orcas from a larger craft, we recommend Adventure Canada's 8-day Whale and Wildlife trip on the comfortable 65' sailing yacht Ocean Light. The vessel will navigate the protected inland waters of Johnstone Straight, Desolation Sound and Robson Bight, following three or more orca pods. Hydrophones are fitted to the vessel, allowing participants to hear the whales communicate. Trips cost $950 CDN and depart from Port Hardy in BC in September. Contact Adventure Canada, 1159 W. Broadway, Vancouver, BC, Canada V6H 1G1, (604) 736-7447; FAX: (604) 736-6513. In June, Biological Journeys offers a 3-day orca-watching cruise in Puget Sound aboard a 50' yacht for $1,295. Call (800) 548-7555.

SEALS & SEA LIONS

We couldn't publish this book without a baby seal trip. Our favorite is Seal Watch '93, operated by Natural Habitats Wildlife Adventures. This 4 to 5-day tour takes you to Canada's Gulf of St. Lawrence to watch newborn harp seals. You'll be transported by helicopter to the ice floes of the Magdelen Islands. There, participants can walk within touching range of the newborn "whitecoats." Your money goes to a good cause--part of the proceeds of the Seal Watch tours will be used to offset revenues lost to Eskimo communities by the banning of baby seal hunting. Six departures are planned between February and March, and the 1992 price was $1,495 4 nights, $2,395 5 nights. Contact Natural Habitats, 1 Sussex Station, Suite 110, Sussex, NJ 07461, (800) 543-8917, or (201) 702-1525. Adventure Canada (604) 736-7447 (address above) offers a similar Magdelen Island harp seal trip every March. The 5-day tours cost $1,150 US in 1992.

Alaska's St. Paul Island is home to 800,000 northern fur seals, as well as over 200 species of birds. Still relatively unknown, the St. Paul/Pribilofs area is a prime, undisturbed natural habitat which receives few visitors each season. When it comes to sheer numbers of seals, nothing tops the Pribilofs. You will be amazed. World Express Tours, 7879 Greenback Lane, #240, Citrus Heights, CA 95610; 200 W. 34th Avenue, Suite 393, Anchorage, AK 99503-3969 (800) 544-2235, or (907) 562-4600 offers 3, 4 and 6-day expeditions to St. Paul Island each summer, with land costs from approximately $699 to $1,149.

California's Channel Islands National Park is perhaps the best place in the Lower 48 to view seals, sea lions and elephants seals. The most popular Channel Islands tour is a day-trip to Anacapa Island. Here you can observe sea lions hauling out on rocks, and playing in the island's many coves. Serious seal-watchers will want to head farther offshore to Santa Barbara Island, a major sea lion hangout. Overnight camping is possible on both islands.

To the north lies San Miguel Island, the ultimate seal haven. Five different species of seals, sea lions and elephant seals inhabit the rugged shoreline by the thousands. Though you can explore San Miguel on foot, the largest rookeries, including the elephant seal breeding grounds at Pt. Bennett, are off limits to hikers, so you'll actually see more if you stay on board. Island Packers, a national park concessionaire, provides transport to all the Channel Islands. Day-trips start at $37, overnights on the boat per night run $215. Contact Island Packers, 1867 Spinnaker Drive, Ventura, CA 93001, (805) 642-1393.

Sea lion pups, Galapagos Islands/ART WOLFE

Alaskan brown bear (grizzly), with catch, McNeil River/ART WOLFE

BEARS

POLAR BEARS

∎

Churchill, Manitoba is the undisputed polar bear capital of the world. Each summer, as the pack ice of Hudson Bay retreats, the bears congregate by the hundreds along the Bay's southern shore to hunt seals and fish. Just south of Churchill the bears make their maternity dens, giving visitors a chance to view mothers and their cubs. The best time for bear-watching is in October, just before the winter freeze, when seals concentrate in the few remaining open waterways, attracting large numbers of bears. The most serious polar bear trip is run by Joseph Van Os Photo Safaris. After flying into Churchill, participants board giant 4WD tundra buggies that allow bear-watchers to view the animals at close range in warmth and safety. For avid photographers who want to view the bears in the most favorable early morning and late afternoon light, Van Os also offers a tundra bunkhouse option. Cost for 1 week is $2,145, while the 9-day bunkhouse trip runs $3,095, all-inclusive from Winnipeg, Manitoba. Departures are scheduled for October and November. Contact Van Os Photo Safaris, P.O. Box 655, Vashon Island, WA 98070, (206) 463-5383.

If the Van Os tour is a bit beyond your means, Adventure Canada (604) 736-7447 (address above), also offers 6-day October polar bear expeditions to the western shores of Hudson Bay near Churchill. Tundra buggies will be used for transport, and the guide and photo instructor is noted Arctic explorer Mike Beedel. Cost is $1,395 US.

ALASKAN BROWN BEARS

∎

The best spot in the world to watch Alaskan brown bears is along the banks of the McNeil River in Kamishak Bay, part of Katmai National Park. During the annual salmon runs, scores of Alaskan browns (part of the grizzly family) come down to the riverbanks to fish and feed. It is not uncommon to see as many as 30 bears in a stretch of just 100 yards.

Visitors at McNeil can observe the bears safely from a few yards away. This is due to three factors: the animals are accustomed to being watched, they have not learned to associate humans with food (feeding the bears is strictly prohibited), and the salmon streams are so productive that the bears would rather fish than beg for handouts.

Access to the McNeil River is closely controlled by the National Park Service. Only 10 visitors are allowed each day, by permit only. To apply for the lottery-drawn, 4-day permits, send $50 to Alaska Department of Fish and Game, 333 Raspberry Road, Anchorage, AK 99518-1599, (907) 344-0541. Apply before May 1. Last year, 1,800 applications were received for 140 permits. Standby applicants pay $25 and can camp for one week at the McNeil River ranger station while waiting. (Your chances are pretty good, as a third of the permit days go unclaimed.) Air shuttles, and camping permits for the nearby Chenik Bear Camp, can be handled by the Kachemmak Bay Lodge, China Poot Bay, P.O. Box 956, Homer, AK 99603, (907) 235-8910.

If you don't want to organize your own bear-watching trip, or are concerned about availability of McNeil permits, you can join one of Joseph Van Os' summer Brown Bear Photo Safaris. These popular 6-day tours visit the Brooks River in Katmai Park, June through July. Like their McNeil River brethren, the Brooks River bears are intent on their fishing, allowing visitors to observe from close range. Long Alaskan summer days allow participants to photograph the bears under a variety of lighting conditions. The tour is based at the Brooks Lodge, situated just a few hundred yards from some of the bears' favorite salmon runs. The 6-day trips cost $1,945 from Anchorage. Contact Van Os Photo Safaris, (206) 463-5383.

GRIZZLIES & KODIAKS

∎

British Columbia's Khutzeymateen region, just below the southern tip of Alaska, is a prime breeding ground for the North American grizzly bear. Each spring, mothers and cubs descend from mountain birthing dens to the valley floor, drawn to the water's edge by large salmon runs. North/South Expeditions leads 4, 8 and 14-day tours aboard the 65' sailing yacht Ocean Light to observe the Khutz grizzlies fishing and foraging along the shore. On the 8-day trip, participants will also visit the Prince William Islands to view the rare white Kermodie bear and other wildlife. Cost for the 4, 8 and 14-day grizzly trips are $925,

$1,400 and $2,200 CDN, respectively. The guide is Charlie Russell, whose father Andy wrote the classic book *Grizzly Country*. Four and 14-day trips depart in May and June, while the 8-day tour runs in September. Contact David Freese, director of North/South Expedition Services, 1159 West Broadway, Vancouver, BC, Canada V6H 1G1, (604) 736-7447

PREDATORS

MOUNTAIN LIONS

■

If you're enthralled by the power and beauty of America's big cats you can join a unique mountain lion research program in Idaho's Albion mountains. As part of an effort to stem the decline of the species, scientists from Idaho State University will lead teams to capture wild cougars, fit them with radio collars, and then track their movements. The lions' habitat is an alpine wilderness of deep canyons, 7,500' peaks, and forests of aspen, pine and Douglas fir. This is a working program; during the day helpers will record the animals' movements using radar-equipped vans. The cougar-tracking program offers 11-day sessions June through August ($1,295 fee), and January through February ($1,195 fee). Contact Earthwatch, 680 Mt. Auburn St., Box 403, Watertown, MA 02272, (617) 926-8200.

Aside from the Earthwatch cougar program, it's quite unlikely that you'll be able to spot mountain lions in the wild unless you're prepared to spend days or even weeks tracking the elusive animals. However, for those who really want to see the big cats in open country, Van Os Photo Safaris has organized a unique program employing captive cougars in special game preserves. Participants will observe the big cats from portable, camouflaged enclosures in natural settings near Glacier National Park. Along with mountain lions, black bear, wolves, fox, wolverine and lynx prowl the park grounds. Van Os offers big cat photo trips in February, June and October. Wintertime offers serene, snowy backgrounds, while June is the best time to observe mothers and cubs. The

cost will be $1,695 for 6 days (3 days with the animals). Call (206) 463-5383.

JAGUARS

■

Widely known as the world's richest habitat for birds, Peru's Manu National Park is also probably the best place in the world to see jaguars and ocelots in the wild. While a number of outfitters run trips to Manu National Park, we recommend Wilderness Travel, (800) 247-6700, and Oceanic Society Expeditions, (415) 441-1106 (1993 programs only). The 16-day Wilderness Travel trips depart in July and August for about $3,090. Neither of these trips concentrates on predator-tracking, but you will have a good chance to see big cats during your tour, and you won't be disappointed with Manu even if you don't--both these tours have won kudos from past clients.

Belize, along the western Caribbean, hosts the world's only jaguar preserve, which also serve as sanctuary for four other big cats--margay, ocelot, jaguarundi and mountain lion. Unfortunately, it's tough to see the jaguars on the prowl as they hunt mostly at night. However, Belize, the heartland of the Mayan civilization, has much to recommend it in other respects. One zoologist was recently following a radio-collared jaguar into the wild and discovered a previously unknown Mayan archaeological site. We can't guarantee that kind of adven-

ture, but this should give you a sense of how wild Belize remains. International Expeditions, the leading tour operator for Belize, offers an 11-day natural history tour for $2,000 with air from Miami; the Jaguar Preserve may be added as a 3-day option. Int'l Expeditions, One Environs Park, Helena, AL 35080, (800) 633-4734, or (205) 428-1700.

WOLVES

■

Elk-hunting is an important sport and food source in the Bieszczady Mountains in southeastern Poland. However, in recent times, hunters have claimed that wolves, a protected species for the past 10 years, have been taking too many of the hunters' trophy stags. To help settle the controversy, Earthwatch will lead a team of scientists and volunteers to the 12,000-acre Bieszczady National Park to examine the wolves' behavior and their impact on the elk population. For $1,470 in shared expenses, participants will help track wolves in the wild, and count deer herds in mountain forests. During the 2-week programs, team members will also observe bear, wild boar, and many other species in the field. Research sessions are conducted in March, May, July, September, October and December in 1992. Contact Earthwatch, 680 Mt. Auburn Street, Box 403, Watertown, MA 02272, (617) 926-8200.

Cougar cubs, Sawtooth Mountains, Idaho/DAVID STOECKLEIN FOR DUTCHER PROD.

Bird-watching is an industry unto itself, one dominated by three major tour companies: Field Guides, Inc.; Victor Emanuel Nature Tours; and Wings. All feature excellent (in many cases renowned) guides, and a vast selection of itineraries worldwide.

In choosing a bird tour, don't be overly swayed by the promise of a big name tour guide. Although there is a temptation to go with the person who "wrote the book," many customers may have a better experience with a more people-oriented trip leader, even if his academic credentials are not as impressive. We've found that the most famous ornithologists are not necessarily the most personable of trip leaders--in the field they may well prefer birds to humans.

■ FIELD GUIDES, INC.

P.O. Box 160723, Austin, TX 78716-0723, (512) 327-4953; FAX: (512) 327-9231.

Field Guides, started a number of years ago by Allan Griffith and other former Victor Emanuel guides, now offers trips to more than 70 destinations worldwide. For birders looking to view hundreds of different species during a single tour, Griffith recommends the tours to Ecuador, Manu Park in Peru, Costa Rica, and Kenya. On each 2-week trip, you can expect to see 300 to 600 species. Field Guides' tours tend to be a bit more hardcore than Victor Emanuel's--you spend more time in the field, with less free time at the lodge. Field Guides' also follows a different philosophy than Victor Emanuel in selecting trip leaders. Rather than hiring the big names, Field Guides tends to employ younger naturalists who have lived and worked in the region visited, who love guiding, and enjoy working with people. Field Guides enjoys strong customer loyalty and repeat business. It would be our first choice for many destinations. Rating: ★★★★

■ VICTOR EMANUEL NATURE TOURS

P.O. Box 33008, Austin, TX 78764, (800) 328-VENT, or (512) 328-2919; FAX: (512) 328-5221.

Started in 1975, Victor Emanuel Nature Tours (VENT) is the oldest and largest of the bird-watching tour companies. VENT offers over 100 tours on virtually every continent. Its associates include many of the most respected ornithologists in the world, including Roger Tory Peterson, author of the classic *Field Guide to Western Birds*. Compared to Field Guides, VENT's tours are more creature comfort-oriented, and VENT offers many general wildlife tours, in addition to its birding expeditions. VENT's prices tend to be somewhat higher than Field Guides' or Wings', but you must compare itineraries carefully and remember that VENT's food and lodging are often superior. Among VENT's 1992 offerings, we recommend the following trips: Southeastern Brazil (September, 23 days, $3,695 from Rio de Janeiro) with Steven Hilty, author of the *Field Guide to the Birds of Columbia*; Peru's Manu Park (July, 18 days, $3,595 from Lima), also with Steven Hilty; Kenya (July and October, 24 days, $4,950 from Nairobi); Australia (October, 33 days, Grand Australia Tour, $5,650 from Cairns) with Len Robinson. Rating: ★★★★

■ WINGS TOURS

P.O. Box 31930, Tucson AZ 85751, (602) 749-1967; FAX: (602) 749-3175.

Now in its 20th year, Wings offers nearly 100 bird-watching tours to over 35 countries on six continents. Four of the most popular destinations are Alaska, Thailand, Kenya and Costa Rica, but Wings will also take birdwatchers to some truly exotic venues including Papua New Guinea and Borneo. Wings' North American Tours, some of which are led by founder Davis Finch (yes, the name is for real), are of a consistently high quality. Wings is not as strong in South America as Field Guides or Victor Emanuel, although its programs in Costa Rica are among the very best. Wings' prices are very similar to Field Guides', typically $1,900 to $2,600 for an 18-day foreign trip. Before you book any trip, write for Wings' 169-page catalog. Along with lovely artwork, it has very detailed itineraries for every trip. Rating: ★★★★

In addition to birding's Big Three listed above, two other specialty outfitters are worth mentioning: Motmot Nature Tours, and Australia's Monarch Tours.

■ MOTMOT NATURE TOURS

101 W. Upland Road, Ithaca, NY 14850-1415, (607) 257-1616.

Motmot (formerly McHugh Ornithology Tours) runs fewer trips than the Big Three, but it goes to many exotic destinations--such as Russia, Hungary, Czechoslovakia, and Austria--not served by Wings, Field Guides, or Victor Emanuel. The emphasis tends to be a bit more scientific than most of the competition--many of Motmot's tours are co-sponsored by the

Cornell Ornithology Lab. We particularly recommend the Trinidad and Tobago trip led by Richard ffrench (sic), author of the definitive field guide for the region. Other top destinations are Equador, the Galapagos Islands and Costa Rica overseas, and south Texas in the States. Domestic trips start at about $500, while foreign trips begin at about $750 per week. Rating: ★★ to ★★★

■ MONARCH BIRDING & WILDLIFE TOURS

P.O. Box 890, Belconnen A.C.T. 2616, Australia, or call ATS Tours at (800) 423-2880, SPRINT Dept.

Monarch Tours is the leading birding outfitter Down Under. Monarch offers a far greater selection of Australian tours (at somewhat lower prices) than its American competitors. All budgets and schedules can be accommodated, with tours from 1 to 30 days, and lodging ranging from tents to deluxe hotels. Aviculture tours can also be combined with wildlife and marsupial study programs. Prices for a 3-day tour start at about $369. Rating: ★★

EAGLES

For viewing eagles in the wild, there's no place better than Alaska's Chilkat Valley. Here, more than 3,000 bald eagles gather each year during the November salmon run. A prime aviary habitat, the Chilkat is also home to thousands of swans, terns, cranes, geese and songbirds. Two recommended outfitters leading eagle tours in the Chilkat Valley are Chilkat River Guides, P.O. Box 170, Haines, AK 99827, (907) 766-2491, (1-day float trip, $100) and Van Os Photo Safaris, (address above), (206) 463-5383, (6-day lodge program, November, $1,595.)

Another major eagle nesting ground is Alaska's Prince William Sound. Along with eagles you'll find peregrine falcons, wild swans, puffins, and more than 270 other bird and mammal species. The best way to see the Sound is by boat. We recommend Choice Marine Charters, (907) 243-0069 (50' cruiser). To get really close to the action, rent a Zodiak boat from Sound Inflatables, (907) 333-9043 (Anchorage). Contact the Alaska Div. of Tourism, (907) 465-2010, for land-based programs.

American bald eagle, Alaska/JIM SIMMEN, ALLSTOCK

CHOOSING THE RIGHT NATURE TOUR

Virtually anywhere you can imagine, from Alaska to the Antarctic, there's a tour operator ready, willing and able to lead paying customers into the animal kingdom. However, with so many options available, choosing the right trip and outfitter can be a daunting experience. Here are tips on getting back to nature without getting ripped off.

■ *Consider all the options*

The most popular wildlife destinations, such as Alaska, Baja and the Galapagos, are each served by a dozen or more major tour operators. Before you settle on an expensive tour, compare all your options. Prices vary widely depending on the level of luxury. Consider a Baja whale-watching trip, for example. By kayak it will cost $100 per day, by cruise ship, up to $300 per day.

■ *Find out who is running the trip*

In many cases, the company which advertises a trip is not the actual operator in the field. Before you put down a deposit, find out who really runs the trip, and how many times it has done so. Don't be a guinea pig.

■ *Look for special expertise*

If getting good pictures of animals is a prime concern, a specialized photo safari may suit you better than an ordinary tour. Recommended photo tour operators include: Joseph Van Os, (206) 463-5383, Joe McDonald's Wildlife Photography, (215) 433-7025, Big 5 Expeditions, (800) 541-2790, and Voyagers, (607) 257-3091.

■ *Choose the right season*

If you're hoping to see one of the great annual wildlife events, such as a caribou migration, or the hatching of sea turtles, you have to travel at just the right time of year. There is often a very small time-window, and if you miss it, you will be sorely disappointed.

■ *Find out the full price*

To make their trips attractive, many outfitters advertise a rock-bottom price that omits many unavoidable expenses. Some of the additional charges you need to consider are: small group supplement (typically $300-$400 extra), inland air charter ($200-$300), ground transport, and meals.

Ocean Kayaking

West Coast Vancouver Island, British Columbia/JOEL W. ROGERS

▼

*S*ea kayaking is a great way to explore remote coastal waters from the Arctic to the tropics. More stable and considerably more comfortable than whitewater kayaks, modern sea kayaks will hold two people and plenty of gear. The forgiving craft can be paddled easily by novices, and on most guided trips the pace is slow and easy.

Sea kayaking is the aquatic equivalent of backpacking. You travel light, under your own power, and journey close to nature. An ideal platform for observing whales and other wildlife, a kayak allows you to navigate waterways inaccessible to any other craft. Some of our favorite kayak cruising grounds are the islands of the South Pacific, the inlets of the Pacific Northwest and the golden coast of Mexico's Baja Peninsula. In this chapter, we feature trips to these and other great sea kayak destinations. In addition, we provide a complete listing of sea kayak outfitters around the world, and offer tips on choosing the right craft for your ocean adventures.

CHAPTER

14

Paddling a folding kayak in the Sea of Cortez/JOHN PLUMMER, F-STOCK PHOTOGRAPHY

SEA KAYAKS AREN'T JUST FOR ESKIMOS. TOURING BY KAYAK, WHETHER ON YOUR own or with a commercial outfitter, doesn't require months of training or superior strength. Like backpacking, sea kayaking takes you to realms beyond the reach of mechanized transport, to the wild places not yet spoiled by civilization. And for the adventurer on a budget, the price is right. Most organized sea kayak trips cost under $120 per day--a bargain in today's economy.

BAJA

Kayaking the Gulf of Cortez

If there is an ideal sea kayaking destination, Baja Mexico may be it. The water is warm, the wildlife is varied and abundant, and there are countless inlets and beaches to explore. A host of quality outfitters lead kayak trips to Baja year-round, though most tours are conducted during Mexico's warm winters. Some tours focus on wildlife and whale-watching, while others emphasize exploration of remote coves and out-of-the-way beaches.

Baja is the winter breeding ground for a number of large whale species, with the largest concentrations of gray whales found in Magdalena Bay on the Pacific coast. Baja Expeditions conducts very popular 9-day kayak trips to Magdalena Bay January through March each year. Support boats carry the gear and are used for close encounters with the big whales (in some places you can even reach out and touch the resting creatures). Past customers have given these trips rave reviews, and many participants have returned a second time. Baja Expeditions also takes sea kayakers to Isla Espiritu

Santo, a beautiful, isolated island on the Gulf Coast near La Paz. With a major sea lion rookery, crystal-blue waters and numerous sea caves, this little island is a snorkelers' paradise. The Magdalena trip costs $1,200, including airfare from Los Angeles, Tucson or San Diego, while the Espiritu Santo expedition runs $1,200 with airfare from the same cities.

Trudi Angel's Paddling South runs great 6 and 9-day trips along the Sea of Cortez November through May. Trudi is a legend in Baja, a soft-spoken lady who knows every inch of the coast from Conception Bay to La Paz. Tours start in Loreto, and work south along 40 miles of very remote, unspoiled coastline. Some trips visit Don Zante and Carmen islands, both rich with marine life. The meals are a highlight of Paddling South's tours, especially the local seafood. Paddling five miles per day, there is plenty of time for snorkeling on the reefs and day-hiking. Cost for 9 days is about $800. Compared to Baja Expeditions, the program is more adventurous--no motor support boat is used, and Paddling South avoids the

Eight Great Sea Kayaking Adventures

highly touristed destinations.

Canada's Tofino Expeditions runs more than a dozen guided kayak trips to the Sea of Cortez every winter. Starting from Mulege, Tofino's tours visit remote hideaways where you'll never have to compete with other voyaging gringos. The tours are self-contained (no noisy outboard launches), and emphasize low-impact camping, though the food is surprisingly deluxe. The pace is easy, seven to eight miles per day, making Tofino's program a good choice for novice kayakers. Trips last 8 days, and cost about $800 US.

The National Outdoor Leadership School (NOLS) has operated sea kayak training courses in Baja for more than a decade, and NOLS' trip leaders know the best secret spots on both sides of the Sea of Cortez. The NOLS program, offered November through March, is not just a holiday. Running for 21 days, the NOLS Baja kayak program is designed to teach outdoor survival and leadership skills, and offers five hours of college credit to participants. Expect more time paddling or day-

hiking with NOLS than you might spend with another outfitter, and a bit less luxury. At $1,900, NOLS' 3-week trip is a good value. A 2-week, over-25 course featuring

Magdalena Bay whale-watching is also offered in March and April for roughly $1,700.

For tour information on Baja kayaking, contact: Baja Expeditions, (800) 843-6967; NOLS, (307) 332-6973; Paddling South, 4510 Silverado Trail, Calistoga, CA 94515, (707) 942-4550 (winter), or (707) 942-4796 (summer); Tofino Expeditions, (604) 737-2030; FAX: (604) 737-6468. Full addresses, and listings of other Baja kayak tour operators, are provided on page 211.

COSTA RICA

River and Ocean Combo Trip

Costa Rica is Central America's natural wonderland, a unique showcase of scenery and wildlife. Anything you can imagine--volcanoes, cloud forests, raging whitewater, beautiful beaches, you name it--Costa Rica has it. This ecological diversity makes Costa Rica a great paddling destination.

Baja Expeditions, in conjunction with Rios Tropicales, Costa Rica's top paddling outfitter, offers a 9-day combo trip featuring inland river and lake travel with a sea

Gulfo Dulce, Costa Rica/JOEL W. ROGERS

NEW ZEALAND

Bay of Islands & Marlborough Sounds

Outside magazine called the New Zealand Adventures' (NZA) Bay of Islands kayak cruise one of the best trips of 1989; and in the '90s, it remains a top choice for a sea kayak tour. We would add, however, that NZA's other New Zealand kayak tours are equally rewarding. Our favorite trip runs from Matauri Bay to Whangaroa Harbor, along a remote and almost completely undeveloped stretch of the northeast coast. The Bay of Islands itself, located about 12 miles farther south, is beautiful, but you will see a lot of tourist activity there in the Kiwi summer from December through March. The upper northeast coast, by contrast, is wild and unspoiled; the only evidence of man is an isolated farmhouse or two. On the Matouri Bay trip you'll spend 2 days on the Motukawuni Islands, about two miles offshore, then explore the volcanic rock gardens of the Mahinepua Peninsula. Expect excellent snorkeling and beachcombing, and NZA takes great pride in the sumptuous beach picnics it lays out for its paddlers.

In addition to its standard kayak tours, NZA offers a masters tour for those over 50, as well as a kayak-equipped yacht cruise for those who prefer a little luxury along with their kayaking. Basic tours cost $1,200 for 10 days, the masters tour costs $800 for 5 days, while the 5-day yacht/kayak adventure is $1,100. Prices include all food and equipment. Contact New Zealand Adventures, 11701 Meridian Ave. N., Seattle, WA 98133, (206) 364-0160.

If you've already visited the Bay of Islands, or would like to explore an even more remote corner of New Zealand, we recommend a kayak cruise through the Marlborough Sounds. This region, a sheltered archipelago on the northern tip of New Zealand's South Island, boasts over 1,400 square kilometers of hidden inlets, secret coves and pristine beaches. Paddling in the Sounds is easy; since there is always another small island or sheltered harbor only minutes away, you never have to make long passages across open ocean. With its calm waters, and many good campsites, this little-known part of New Zealand is a great destination for a self-guided tour--easily one of the best sea kayaking areas in the Southern Hemisphere. And when you feel like trading your sleeping

kayak exploration of the Costa Rican shoreline. Depending on water levels and tidal conditions, the trip will begin either with a run down the Rio Bebedero through Palo Verde National Park, or, alternatively, with a voyage across Lake Arenal in the Western Mountains. Both freshwater options take you through wild jungles inhabited by howler monkeys, iguanas, coatimundis and other exotic species. Once the paddlers reach the sea, they'll transfer to sea kayaks for a week exploring the tropical coast. The group will camp on black sand beaches, and venture to offshore islands for snorkeling, fishing and beachcombing. Trips run from December through June. The cost will be roughly $1,275 without air. Call Baja Expeditions at (800) 843-6967, or (619) 581-3311 in California. Participants on the December 1991 trips gave high marks to outfitter Rios Tropicales and praised the trip as a great winter getaway.

bag for a bed, you can cruise to a nearby island farm where homestay lodging is available at reasonable rates.

Both kayak rentals and guided tours can be arranged through local outfitter Marlborough Sounds Adventure Company, R.D. 1, Picton, New Zealand, (011 64) 57 42301. Cost for a guided trip is $100 per day for the group's guide, and about $40 per person per day for kayak and all provisions. Independent paddlers can rent kayaks for about $25 per day. Custom itineraries and power boat shuttles to distant islands can be arranged on request.

THAILAND

Mystery Adventures

Exotic, beautiful and little known to Westerners, the Phang Nga (pronounced "pong naw") region of southwest Thailand is perhaps the most unique tropical kayaking destination in the world. Here, you'll find mangrove forests, hundreds of uninhabited islands, and huge limestone monoliths that rise like giant fingers from the quiet waters. Narrow breaks in the island walls open into mysterious sea caves and rock gardens. There is nothing else like it anywhere on earth.

Amazingly, many of Phang Nga's largest sea caves were only recently discovered during exploratory tours of the region by John Gray, director of the Phuket Sea Canoe Center (PSCC). Because some cave entrances were so narrow that only a kayak could pass through, even local Thai fishermen had no idea what lay behind the sheer limestone walls of Phang Nga's islands.

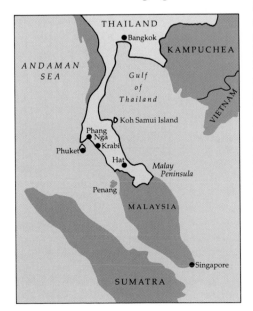

Bulia, Fiji/COURTESY SOUTHWIND SPORTS RESOURCES

While you can visit Phang Nga for a day or two by booking a motorized longboat trip with local tour brokers in Phuket (a popular beach resort in South Thailand), to see Phang Nga's most exotic features, and the sea caves in particular, you must have a kayak. At present, PSCC's package tours are the only way to go, unless you ship your own kayak to Thailand and hire your own guide. That's out of the question for most of us, and the PSCC tour will probably offer a better kayaking experience than you could arrange yourself, without a great deal of advance planning.

Before exploring Phang Nga Bay, paddlers can visit Koh Samui, a palm-covered island in the Gulf of Siam that boasts some of the finest beaches in the world. Unfortunately, Koh Samui has become all too popular with vacationing Europeans (an airport is going in this year) and the tourism is starting to take its toll, though Koh Samui is still a wilderness compared to, say, Waikiki. You *will* have a chance to experience the unspoiled Thailand, however, during a visit to the Angthong National Marine Park. This region, with its crystalline waters and beautiful rock formations, has been justly hailed as one of the world's finest underwater preserves.

After Koh Samui, you will be ferried to the mainland, and then taken by minivan to PSCC's base in Phuket. Depending on the itinerary, the next 3 or 7 days will be spent exploring Phang Nga's myriad islands, sea caves and grottos in PSCC's forgiving inflatable kayaks. You will spend your evenings in tourist hotels or rustic bungalows, some of them on the water.

Thailand, despite the rapid expansion of tourism in the past 15 years, remains a very special destination, a place to be treasured for its unique culture and natural beauty. And there is no better time to visit Phang Nga than now. In another few years, many of the secret spots visited by PSCC will have been added to a hundred package tours, and kayakers will no longer be able to ply the waters of Phang Nga in quiet solitude. PSCC's Thailand sea kayak tours depart November through May, and cost roughly $300 for 2 days, $500 for 3 days, or $1,000 for a full week. Contact PSCC directly at Box 276, Phuket 83000, Thailand, (011 66) 76 212 172; FAX: (011 66) 76 212 252, or call its US agents: Adventures in Paradise, (800) 736-8187, or Ecosense Adventures of Seattle, (206) 325-3720.

FIJI

South Sea Adventure

If you're looking for a true Polynesian paradise, forget Hawaii or Tahiti, and head for Fiji. Long recognized as a world-class dive venue, Fiji is also an excellent kayaking destination, with its scores of idyllic islands, warm, crystal-clear waters, and spectacular coral reefs. Apart from the main island of Viti Levu, most of Fiji has escaped commercial tourist development. On the outer islands, life is quiet and simple, free from the burdens and pressures of the civilized world. You can still walk down a perfect white sand beach and not see another soul--or wade out on the reef at sunset and pick up a lobster for your dinner.

If ever there were an antidote to civilization, Fiji is it. Most Westerners visiting Fiji go there to dive, or just sit on the beach. However, with so many islands situated so close together, Fiji was made for sea kayak cruising. Unless you bring your own craft, however, you must go with a commercial outfitter, as there is no rental inventory on any of the islands. Two companies presently offer sea kayak programs in Fiji: Worldwide Expeditions of Australia, and Taveuni Sea Canoe Center, a Fiji-based outfitter.

For novice paddlers who want a relatively slow-paced adventure, Worldwide Expeditions' tour is the best choice. You spend 13 days in the Yasawas, a chain of 16 small islands covering a 50-mile stretch of the Pacific. For 9 days you will paddle and sail double kayaks among the islands, camping on pristine beaches and visiting small island villages. Azure waters within the reefs defy description--with visibility of 150' to 200', it's like paddling in a giant swimming pool. Highlights of the trip include Turtle Island (site of the movie *Blue Lagoon*), and the wild limestone caves of Sawa-i-Lau island. Trips cost about $1,500 US, with June and July departures. Call Worldwide Adventures, which represents World Expeditions in North America, at (800) 387-1483.

More seasoned kayakers should opt for the Taveuni/Rainbow Reef tour offered by Taveuni Sea Canoe Center. After spending a few days on Viti Levu, you will depart for the idyllic island of Vanua Levu. Here you paddle and snorkel along some of the most spectacular coral reefs in the world. Next you will fly to the island of Taveuni, a remote hideaway famed for world-class diving. From Taveuni you will make a 4-day, 3-night island circumnavigation, exploring waterfalls and jungle rivers.

Participants can choose between a smooth-water passage inside the surround-

Surf kayaking, La Push, Washington/JOEL W. ROGERS

ing reef, or a challenging open-ocean route. The second option requires some skill and stamina as you must navigate narrow passages with complex currents. During the round-island tour, the group will camp out on isolated, wilderness beaches. For most paddlers, the wilderness camping is the highlight of the trip--a chance to get away from it all in a true tropical paradise. Price without airfare is $2,100 for 15 days, with departures March through November. Contact the Taveuni Center's US agent, Adventures in Paradise, (800) 736-8187. Two excellent California-based outfitters that may also offer Fiji kayak trips in 1992 are Paddling South, (707) 942-4796, or (707) 942-4550, and Southwind Sports Resources, (714) 730-4820.

BRITISH COLUMBIA

Inside Passage Orca Odyssey

The sheltered waters of the Inside Passage between Vancouver Island and mainland British Columbia provide a near-perfect venue for kayak touring. The summer weather is warm, calm and dry, and there are hundreds of great campsites along the remote stretches of the BC coast. Navigating the hundreds of inlets and small islands between Vancouver and the northern coast, the kayaker enjoys unrivalled natural beauty and close contact with wildlife. Eagles soar overhead, and schools of porpoises are common. The big thrill, how-

sites, which may include old Kwakiutal Indian villages, you're treated to fresh-caught salmon, crab and other regional delicacies.) Trips run virtually every week from July through mid-September, and will cost about $725 US, all-inclusive.

If you're looking for a slightly longer tour, Discovery Kayaks leads 6 and 8-day orca-watching trips each July and August. You'll navigate the Johnstone Strait near Robson Bight, where the largest groups of orcas congregate. It's not uncommon for the paddlers to see whales every day, and guide Larry Roy has been able to rendez-vous with the same orca family for three years running. Discovery's trips feature day-hikes in nearby forests, eagle-watching and salmon-fishing. The trips are afford-able--$650 CDN for 6 days, $850 CDN for 8 days--and no special skills are required.

Another outstanding sea kayak outfit-ter is Canada's Tofino Expeditions. In addi-tion to whale-watching trips, Tofino's guides lead kayak cruises through British Columbia's Inside Passage (Queen Char-lotte Straight), and along the west coast of Vancouver Island (Barclay Sound, Clayoquot Sound). These 6-day, $675 trips are true wilderness expeditions; you are unlikely to see other paddling groups on your journey.

If you're yearning to do more exploring after a week with the whales, consider Northern Light's annual Mystery Tour. Each year Northern Lights leads experi-enced kayakers to some of the more remote and wild stretches of the BC coast. Most of the campsites are abandoned Indian vil-lages, and the paddling will be more strenuous than on the Inside Passage trips. Of the exact destination, Northern Lights will only say: "It's an area that has rarely seen kayakers in the past, and we want to keep it that way for as long as possible. So its exact location will remain a mystery until you arrive." Six days of mystery cost about $725 US.

For information on these programs, contact: Northern Lights Expedi-tions, 5220 Northeast 180th, Seattle, WA 98155, (206) 483-6396; Discovery Kayaks, 2755 Departure Bay Road, Nanaimo, BC, Canada V9S 3W9, (604) 758-2488; Tofino Expeditions, 320 Main Street, P.O. Box 620, Tofino, BC, Canada V6J 1M4, (604) 737-2030.

ever, is the orcas. Attracted by the mass summer salmon runs, over 200 orcas visit the Inside Passage each summer, traveling in family groups called pods. Sea kayakers can accompany an orca pod for days, often venturing within a paddle's distance of the big creatures. Experienced tour leaders can often identify particular whales, which re-turn to the same waters each year.

Seattle's Northern Lights Expeditions has offered outstanding orca-watching kayak trips since 1983. Northern Lights knows the best places to find orcas, and even fits its kayaks with microphones so you can hear the whales communicate. Northern Lights' 6-day trips require no special kayaking skills, only a love of na-ture and a hearty appetite. (At your camp-

MAINE

Acadia National Park

The President goes to Maine to recharge his batteries, and once you've had a chance to explore the rugged but beautiful Maine coast, you'll understand why. Stands of pines run right to the water's edge, and hundreds of tiny islands dot the coastline. Snug harbors are found everywhere, per-fect for coastal exploring. The seaside vil-lages and fishing ports remain small and quiet, a reminder of New England's past. Even the most popular resort areas are relatively unspoiled, and Maine remains a peaceful haven for the touring paddler.

Most sea kayaking in Maine is done in Acadia National Park and along the Maine Island Trail. Here, any reasonably fit pad-dler can range easily from island to island, camping in the park and visiting small harbor towns to replenish supplies, or per-haps bed down for a night in a seaside inn. While Maine's waters are calm and pad-dling is easy, good equipment and careful preparation are essential. With so many islands clustered around a jagged coastline, navigation also requires some skill. If this is your first coastal cruise, we recommend that you stay within the main Mt. Desert Is-land section of Acadia Park, not venturing too far offshore. Notify the Parks Depart-ment of your itinerary, and keep your daily paddling distances fairly short. Detailed land maps are available from park offices, but you should also obtain navigational charts and tide tables before you go.

Maine has two good kayak outfitters: Explorers at Sea, and Coastal Kayaking. Explorers at Sea runs 1 to 9-day tours for kayakers of all skill levels, using both single and double kayaks. Trips depart June through September from the south end of Deer Isle and explore nearby Jericho and Penobscot Bays. This region offers an

Totems, Queen Charlotte Islands, BC/JOEL W. ROGERS

abundance of cruising options, with over 100 small islands within easy reach of the paddlers. Day-trips cost about $75, and longer cruises cost approximately $115 per day, including food. Call (207) 367-2356 for detailed itineraries.

Coastal Kayaking's base at Bar Harbor within Acadia Park gives it access to a number of small islands in Frenchman Bay to the north, as well as the park's main cruising grounds to the southwest (Otter Cove, Cranberry Island, Bass Harbor). While shorter 1 and 2-day trips comprise the bulk of Coastal's business, it also offers 3-day multi-island camping expeditions for $300 to $400, depending on destination. Contact Coastal Kayaking at (800) 526-8615, or (207) 288-9605.

PATAGONIA

Fjordland Wilderness Voyage

Patagonia, at the southern tip of South America, is the ultimate destination for the skilled ocean kayaker. Here, in Chile's famed Torres Del Paine National Park, paddlers can journey from mountain to ocean on an adventure of unique beauty and challenge. Starting from high glacial lakes beneath razor-edged towers of granite, you descend through forested valleys, then navigate icy fjords to the sea. The coastal edge is rugged, windswept and as wild as any place on earth. Paddling the Patagonia coastline requires intelligence, strength and great skill. This is one of the most rewarding journeys in the world of paddling.

At present, no American kayak outfitter runs trips to Patagonia. However, in March, World Expeditions of Australia conducts a unique 16-day Patagonia kayak expedition. (This trip ran for the first time in 1990 to rave reviews.) The land/sea journey begins with a walking trek from the Torres Park entrance to Laguna Amarga. There, the group will assemble the folding kayaks, and paddle to the junction of the Rio Paine and Lago Njordenskold. For the next 7 days the group will work their way along a system of lakes and rivers, moving down from the highlands all the way to the ocean. Hikes to side valleys will be made and, weather permitting, the group will climb Donoso Peak and traverse the rugged Tyndell Glacier.

During the last 4 days, the kayakers will paddle along ocean fjords to the Lago Azul area, exploring the edge of the Patagonian icecap. Sea lions, seals, dolphins, whales and dozens of sea bird species can be observed in this area.

Because of the strong winds, tough currents, and unpredictable weather encountered in this far-flung locale, tour participants must have a high level of fitness and strong basic paddling skills. To complete the passage to the sea, a number of short portages will be made, requiring the paddlers to haul all their gear, including the kayaks, from one valley to the next. Though the trip will run in March, the best season, biting Katabatic winds can rise off the glaciers at any time. The weather is erratic, and it is not unusual to see sun, sleet, snow and rain all within half an hour.

For all the rigors one must endure, Patagonia remains an incredible destination. A kayak veteran who ran the trip last year reported that the Torres Del Paine odyssey was "the most stunning kayaking I have done anywhere in the world, including Alaska. The scenery is overwhelming." Call World Expeditions at (011 61) 2 264 3366, or its North American agent, Worldwide Adventures, at (800) 387-1483. The 1992 price is about $2,200 US if booked in Australia, $2,500 if booked with Worldwide.

CHRIS NOBLE

JOEL W. ROGERS

The Top Ocean Kayak Outfitters

HERE'S OUR LIST OF THE TOP SEA KAYAK COMPANIES AND SOME OF THEIR featured offerings. Operating both close to home and in the far corners of the globe, these outfitters can take you to sunny, tropical paradises, or to wild and unspoiled northern bays and inlets. Many popular sea kayak trips are sold out by summertime, so you should book well in advance. See page 212 for tips on selecting the right outfitter.

ALASKA

■ ALASKA DISCOVERY
369 South Franklin, Juneau, AK 99801, (907) 586-1911; FAX: (907) 586-2332.

Alaska Discovery holds the exclusive concession for sea kayak trips in Glacier Bay National Park. (Other companies may advertise Glacier Bay trips but Alaska Discovery will likely be running the show.) The 5, 7 and 10-day Glacier Bay kayak trips range from $800 to $1,100 plus $300 for floatplane charter. Other great kayak itineraries include Icy Bay (10 days, $1,400 plus $300 air), Hubbard Glacier (7 days, $1,200 plus $150 air) and Endicott Arm (7 days, $1,050 plus $300 air). Kayak trips can be combined with rafting and inland canoe excursions. Rating: ★★★★

■ ADVENTURES & DELIGHTS
414 K Street, Anchorage, AK 99501, (800) 288-3134, or (907) 276-8282 in AK.

Adventures & Delights offers kayak voyages to Kenai Fjords National Park. Camping on islands, kayakers will enjoy scenery and wildlife as spectacular as anything in North America. Kayaking can be combined with backpacking, rafting and summer skiing. Five-day trips start at $675 including water taxi. Rating: ★★

■ SPIRIT WALKER EXPEDITIONS
P.O. Box 240, Gustavus, AK 99826, (907) 697-2266.

Spirit Walker leads fully outfitted kayak voyages through the remote inlets and bays of southeast Alaska. Three and 5-day whale-watching trips through Icy Strait off the Alexander Archipelago cost $550 to $750. If you're looking for phenomenal wildlife, we recommend the 8-day Myriad Islands expedition. Price is about $1,400, including wilderness floatplane drop-off and pick-up. Leaders are trained naturalists. Rating: ★★★

■ ALASKA EXPEDITION COMPANY
P.O. Box 675, Cordova, AK 99709, (512) 467-2603, or (907) 424-4317 in summer.

Alaska Expedition Co. (AEC) conducts 3 and 7-day sea kayak tours along the Bering Glacier in southeast Alaska. Proper meals, bunkhouse lodging and hot showers are provided at AEC's own wilderness lodge between forays to the glacier. Trips cost $975 for 3 days, $1,700 for 6 days. Rating: ★★

CALIFORNIA COASTAL

■ SANTA BARBARA WATERSPORTS
119 State Street, Santa Barbara, CA 93101, (805) 564-8815.

This outfitter offers 1 and 2-day sea kayak trips to Channel Islands National Park off the southern California coast. The park's waters are a rich marine habitat, and paddlers can view sea lions, otters and other marine mammals up close. On Santa Cruz Island you'll also have a chance to explore the largest natural sea cave in the world-- 130' high at the entrance and almost a quarter-mile in length. Cost for 1 day is $125, all-inclusive, while 2-day overnight trips range from $180-$260. Rating: ★★

■ SEA TREK OCEAN KAYAKING CENTER
85 Liberty Ship Way, Suite 110, Sausalito, CA 94945, (415) 332-4457.

Sea Trek runs a variety of sea kayak programs in Richardson Bay, Drakes Bay, Tomales Bay, and other sheltered regions of the northern California coast. Sea Trek offers summer programs for teens, and specialty programs for the whole family--ages 8 and older. Introductory classes and weekend trips run $55 to $80 per day. Sea Trek also books kayak tours with many other outfitters worldwide. Rating: ★★★

■ SOUTHWIND SPORTS RESOURCES
1088 Irvine Boulevard, Suite 212, Tustin, CA 92680, (714) 730-4820.

Southwind runs a very professional operation, with a strong emphasis on training. It features challenging trips to Catalina Island and Anacapa Island (Channel Islands Nat'l Park) designed for intermediate to advanced paddlers. The Anacapa trip is a real adventure. You paddle all 12 miles to the island and camp for 3 days. Southwind also offers programs suitable for novice paddlers including a Morro Bay trip and a terrific kayak tour of Lake Mead. For those with whitewater skills, Southwind offers an ad-

Punta Pulpito, Sea of Cortez, Baja/JOEL W. ROGERS

vanced San Simeon trip featuring wave-riding and surf landings. Rating: ★★★

CARIBBEAN & SOUTHEAST

■ BLUE PLANET ADVENTURES
P.O. Box 8325, Cruz Bay, St. John, USVI 00831, (604) 669-7741.

New (since 1991) outfitter Blue Planet offers guided tours in the US and British Virgins. Either camp out on isolated beaches or paddle from resort to resort. Rating: ★★

■ ECOSUMMER EXPEDITIONS LTD.
1516 Duranleau St., Vancouver, BC, Canada V6H 3S4, (604) 669-7741; FAX: (604) 669-3244.

Ecosummer offers 8 and 14-day kayak tours of the Exumas Land and Sea Park in the Bahamas. This area of unihabited cays boasts some of the clearest water and loveliest beaches in the world--plus fantastic sea caves. Sails will be fitted to the kayaks, making light work of the 7 to 10-mile daily passages. Trips cost $1,200 or $2,000, with departures in March and April. Rating: ★★★

■ HURON KAYAK ADVENTURES
P.O. Box 78, Paisley, ONT, Canada N0G 2N0, (519) 353-5572.

In March, Huron Kayak offers 6 days of beach-camping and exploring in the Florida Everglades or Georgia's Barrier Isles for just $530. Huron Kayak's premier offering is an 8-day Bahamas cruise in June. A deluxe 64' sailboat serves as a floating hotel, providing amenities such as private berths, refrigeration and showers. Rating: ★★

CENTRAL AMERICA

■ BAJA EXPEDITIONS
2625 Garnet Avenue, San Diego, CA 92109, (800) 843-6967, or (619) 581-3311.

Baja Expeditions offers 9-day sea kayaking trips in Costa Rica for $1,295 without air, December through June. (See trip featured on p. 203.) Rating: ★★★

■ ECOSUMMER EXPEDITIONS LTD.
(Address at left), (604) 669-7741; FAX: (604) 669-3244.

Ecosummer Expeditions offers an outstanding 14-day sea kayak program in Belize. The tour visits pristine tropical islands, situated along the world's second largest coral reef. Fishing, snorkeling and beachcombing are world class. You will also visit Mayan temples on the Belize mainland. Cost is roughly $1,575, with departures in February. Ecosummer also offers a 26-day Belize Explorer trip that gives you more of everything--island-hopping, temples and jungle exploring. Cost will be about $2,700 with departures between March and April. Highlights include a river descent to the ocean and a horseback trek to remote waterfalls. Rating: ★★★

■ SLICKROCK ADVENTURES
Box 1400, Moab, UT 84532, (801) 259-6996; FAX: (801) 259-8698.

Slickrock organizes sea kayak trips to Belize which feature reef exploration and camping on tropical islands. The Belize trip runs from February through May at a cost of about $950. This is a well-run trip, and Slickrock is one of the most experienced outfitters in Belize. Rating: ★★★

HAWAII

■ KAYAK KAUAI
1340 Kuhio Highway, Ka Paa, Kauai, HI 96746, (808) 822-9179, or (808) 826-9844.

At least once in their lifetime, everyone should experience the Na Pali coast, an area of awesome scale and unique beauty. With sheer 1,000' cliffs, pristine beaches accessible only by sea, and spectacular waterfalls, the Na Pali coast is as impressive a destination as you will find anywhere on the planet.

From May through September, Kayak Kauai runs daily guided trips for $120 per person. In the winter, when ocean conditions are too rough for paddling, you can explore Kauai's inland river system. Basic rentals cost $35–$75 per day (the rate decreases with time). Kayak Kauai also offers "muleskinner" service--for $150 per day per group, Kayak Kauai provides a guide who will arrange permits and assist with navigation. The kayakers make their own camp and cook their own food. Rating: ★★

■ KONA KAI-YAKS
74-5563 Kaiwi Street, Kailua-Kona, HI 96740, (808) 326-2922.

Kona Kai-Yaks on the Big Island enjoys great paddling conditions year-round. Day-trips to Kealakekua Bay run $95 per person, while the adventurous will enjoy overnight expeditions to remote, unspoiled beaches along the Kona Coast or Waipio and Waimano Valleys. For seasoned paddlers, custom off-island trips to Molokai are available, weather permitting. The guides are skilled and enthusiastic, and do a good job matching itineraries to clients' skills, interests and time constraints. Rating: ★★

IRELAND

■ INTERNATIONAL ADVENTURE
9 Teasdale Close, Royston, Hertfordshire, England SG8 5TD, (011 44) 763 42867.

This British outfitter offers weeklong sea kayak tours from Little Killary Harbor on the Connemara Coast in Ireland's County Galway. The Connemara Coast is notable for its long, sheltered inlets and myriad small islands and bays--perfect sea kayak country. Few places in North America can match the west Irish coast for sheer, rugged beauty. We're certain you'll be impressed with Ireland, a new sea kayaking frontier for Americans. The weeklong program includes day-trips, a 3-day overnight expedi-

tion, and instruction in kayak handling and rescue technique. Cost is about $75 per day. (No rating.)

MAINE

■ **COASTAL KAYAKING TOURS INC.**
P.O. Box 405, Bar Harbor, ME 04609, (800) 526-8615, or (207) 288-9605.

Coastal Kayaking, with 10 years of experience in Maine waters, offers half-day, full-day, or multi-day island camping trips along the Maine Island Trail (Deer Island, Jericho Bay). Day-trips cost $50-$70, while 3-day tours run from $300-$400. Coastal has a great location in Bar Harbor, close to the best cruising grounds. Travelers' Note: in the winter season, Coastal Kayaking has plans to premiere commercial kayak tours through the US and British Virgin Islands. Call for details. Rating: ★★★

■ **EXPLORERS AT SEA**
P.O. Box 51-0, Stonington, ME 04681, (207) 367-2356.

Explorers at Sea leads 1 to 9-day sea kayaking trips in Maine's Penobscot Bay between May and September. Trips feature paddling instruction, island camping and gourmet meals. With smaller groups and more personalized attention, Explorers at Sea gets the nod over competitor Coastal Kayaking for longer trips. Prices, including food and gear, begin at $50 for a half-day, and run about $120 per day for the multi-day tours. Rating: ★★★

MEXICO

For a description of Baja kayaking, see the featured trip on pages 202-203. The leading outfitters for Baja include:
BAJA EXPEDITIONS, *2625 Garnet Avenue, San Diego, CA 92109, (800) 843-6967, or (619) 581-3311 in CA.* Rating: ★★★★
ECOSUMMER EXPEDITIONS, *1516 Duranleau Street, Vancouver, BC, Canada V6H 3S4, (604) 669-7741; FAX: (604) 669-3244.* Rating: ★★★
NATIONAL OUTDOOR LEADERSHIP SCHOOL (NOLS), *P.O. Box AA, Lander, WY 82520, (307) 332-6973.* Rating: ★★★$
PADDLING SOUTH, *4510 Silverado Trail, Calistoga, CA 94515, (707) 942-4550, (Loreto base; also horseback tours).* Rating: ★★★★$
SEA TREK OCEAN KAYAKING CENTER, *85 Liberty Ship Way, Sausalito, CA 94965, (415) 332-4457).* Rating: ★★★
TOFINO EXPEDITIONS, *#114-1857 West 4th Avenue, Vancouver, BC, Canada V6J 1M4, (604) 737-2030; FAX: (604) 737-7348.* Rating (for Baja): ★★★

■ **OUTBACK EXPEDITIONS**
P.O. Box 16343X, Seattle, WA 98116, (206) 932-7012.

Outback leads sea kayak trips to La Manzanilla on the Mexican mainland, south of Puerto Vallarta. These excellent tours feature snorkeling in Tenacatita Bay (known as "the aquarium" for its sea life), plus wildlife-watching in Manzanilla Lagoon. Outback also serves Baja. Rating: ★★★

PACIFIC NORTHWEST

■ **GEOFF EVANS' KAYAK CENTRE**
Box 97, Cultus Lake, BC, Canada V0X 1H0, (604) 858-6775.

Goeff Evans leads outstanding summer

Broken Islands, Barclay Sound, British Columbia/JOEL W. ROGERS

kayak trips in the protected waters of Johnstone Strait and Robson Bight in the Canadian northwest. Seven-day trips will cost around $700 US. Evans also offers a $365 weekender program in May and June which combines 2 days of whitewater instruction on Cultus Lake with a 3-day tour of the Gulf Islands. This is a good option for those seeking an introduction to surf kayaking. Rating: ★★★

■ NORTHERN LIGHTS EXPEDITIONS
5220 NE 180th, Seattle, WA 98155, (206) 483-6396; FAX: (206) 483-1554.

Northern Lights has been leading sea kayak trips along the coast of Washington and British Columbia since 1983. Trips are conducted throughout the summer with small groups using stable two-person kayaks. In addition to its popular Northwest Passage and Mystery trips, (see pp. 206-7), Northern Lights offers a unique 7-day fly-in kayak vacation at a deluxe lodge in Northern BC's Farewell Harbor. Roughly $1,450 covers food, lodging, kayaks and the floatplane trip in and out. Rating: ★★★★

■ TOFINO EXPEDITIONS
#114-1837 West 4th Avenue, Vancouver, BC, Canada V6J 1M4, (604) 737-2030; FAX: (604) 737-7348.

Tofino, one of BC's most respected sea kayak companies, leads 6-day tours each year to the west side of Vancouver Island (Barkley Sound, Clayoquot Sound) as well as the Queen Charlotte Straight at the northern end of the Inside Passage. Cost will be about $675 US. Each winter, Tofino also conducts 7-day kayak trips to Baja and Tenacatita Bay (near Puerto Vallarta) for $750 US. Rating (for Northwest): ★★★★

■ MARLBOROUGH SOUNDS ADVENTURE COMPANY
R.D.I., Picton, New Zealand, (011 64) 57 42301.

The Adventure Company offers kayak rentals and guided kayak tours starting at $25 per day. (See p. 204.)

■ NEW ZEALAND ADVENTURES
11701 Meridian Ave. N., Seattle, WA 98133, (206) 364-0160.

New Zealand Adventures operates 5 and 10-day sea kayak tours in New Zealand's Bay of Islands December through May (summer and fall Down Under). (See the featured trip on p. 204.) Cost for 10 days is $1,200 from Auckland, NZ. Rating: ★★★

■ OCEAN RIVER ADVENTURE CO.
P.O. Box 216, Motueka, New Zealand, (011 64) 524 88 823.

Ocean River offers 4-day guided sea kayak tours in Abel Tasman National Park, at the north end of New Zealand's South Island. Untouched by development, Abel Tasman enjoys some of the best (and most consistent) weather in New Zealand. As a kayaking destination, Abel Tasman may even be better than the Bay of Islands. There is less wind to contend with, the water is crystal clear, and there are fewer signs of civilization. You will be able to explore remote bays and harbors, and camp on sandy beaches, with no other soul for miles. Price for a 4-day guided tour is about $250 US, and longer tours can be arranged. Independent paddlers can rent touring kayaks for about $30 US per day. Rating: ★★

■ PHUKET/TAVEUNI SEA CANOE CTR.
c/o Adventures in Paradise, (800) 736-8187.

John Grey's Sea Canoe Centers, formerly Pacific Outdoor Adventures, offer sea kayaking tours in Fiji and Thailand, complete with discount air travel. Custom kayak expeditions can be arranged for other South Pacific islands on request. Grey has run kayak trips in the South Pacific for six years, and while his tours are not always the most well organized, the destinations are world class. Rating: ★★

■ WORLDWIDE ADVENTURES
920 Yonge Street, Suite 747, Toronto, ONT, Canada M4W 3C7, (800) 387-1483, in Australia: (011 61) 2 264 3366; FAX: (011 61) 66 562 109.

World Expeditions (known as Worldwide Adventures) offers sea kayak trips in Northern Queensland (Coral Sea / Barrier Reef area), Tasmania, the Solomon Islands and Fiji. The weeklong Queensland trips run twice monthly from May through October and cost about $850 US, including equipment, food, and shuttle from Cairns to Hinchinbrook Island. Waters are warm and clear, allowing world-class snorkeling over coral reefs. The Fiji trip runs 13 days at a cost of about $1,500 US. (See pp. 205-6.) A true wilderness voyage, the $1,400 Solomons trip is new for 1992. In Tasmania the kayakers will fly into Bathhurst Harbor, a remote and beautiful wilderness preserve on the southwest coast. Rating: ★★★

CHOOSING A KAYAK OUTFITTER

The Trade Association for Sea Kayaking (T.A.S.K) advises that you consider the following factors when selecting a kayak outfitter:

➤*How long has the company been in business?* (There is no substitute for experience. Many of the best outfitters have run trips for seven years or more.)

➤*Does the company maintain adequate liability insurance?* (While sea kayaking is relatively safe, it is important to have proper coverage.)

➤*Are the guides safety-conscious?* (Some guides forgo their life vests--this sets a bad example for customers.)

➤*What will the wind and weather conditions be on the trip?* (You don't want to struggle against strong winds and currents, particularly if this is your first trip.)

➤*Will the outfitter provide references from past customers?* (Talking to a veteran of a previous trip is the most important bit of trip planning you can do.)

➤*What kind of personal equipment should you bring?* (E.g. paddles, spray skirts, wetsuits.)

➤*Does the outfitter lead its own trips?* (Many American firms use less skilled local outfitters in remote locales.)

➤*Be sure to get a complete itinerary.* (Good outfitters will be able to tell you exactly where you are going and when.)

Referrals for member outfitters in North America can be obtained by contacting T.A.S.K. at P.O. Box 84144, Seattle, WA 98124, (206) 621-1018. You may also request a free brochure, "Before You Go," which covers paddling technique, equipment selection, safety and trip planning.

OCEAN KAYAKING

KAYAK BASICS

Modern sea kayaks are constructed from polyethylene (Frisbee material), Kevlar or fiberglass. Fiberglass and Kevlar boats are strong, long-lasting and very rigid, but you must use care to avoid impact damage during transport and when landing on rocky shores. Polyethylene construction sacrifices stiffness and performance for impact resistance and economy.

Most touring kayaks have an enclosed cockpit, with a spray skirt to keep the water out. Open cockpit designs are more comfortable, but are suitable for warm water touring only. Solo kayaks range from 14' to 18' in length, while doubles run from 18' to 23'. Narrow kayaks are faster, but wider boats are more stable and hold more gear. And generally, the shorter the kayak, the easier it is to turn. Novices should look for a relatively flat-bottomed design which offers greater stability than a round-bottomed hull form. Some "Vee" in the design will improve tracking, making the kayak run straighter with less steering input.

IMPORTANT FEATURES

A rudder will help you paddle straight in crosswinds and when you need your hands free. Hatches should be absolutely watertight, yet big enough to hold all your gear. Good kayaks will also feature watertight bulkheads; these add strength and will prevent the craft from swamping if it is capsized.

Perhaps the most important cruising item is a well-formed, comfortable seat with decent back support. Don't buy any kayak with an uncomfortable seating position-- it will only feel worse with every mile you paddle.

SINGLE VS. DOUBLE

Cruising singles are light and agile in the surf. Double kayaks offer greater speed, comfort and stability. However, they are harder to turn than singles, and doubles can be more difficult to right when capsized. Doubles are a good choice for a couple if the man is stronger and his partner would have trouble keeping up in her own kayak. Rudders are fitted to most doubles, and sailing rigs are popular as well.

JOEL W. ROGERS

COLLAPSIBLE KAYAKS

For far-flung touring, try a collapsible kayak. Folding kayaks such as the Feathercraft and the Klepper can be broken down and stored in a case not much larger than an expedition backpack. Collapsible boats cost more than rigid kayaks, however, and their design sacrifices both speed and ease of handling. A good compromise is a rigid kayak that breaks down into 3 to 4 sections for transport.

HANDBOOKS

The Hidden Coast--Kayak Explorations from Alaska to Mexico, *by Joel W. Rogers,* Alaska Northwest Books, is one of the nicest sea kayaking books in print. Covering virtually all the major sea kayaking destinations along the West Coast of North America, Rogers offers informative first-person destination reports, maps and superlative photography.

Paddling Hawaii, *by Audrey Sutherland,* is the best guide to Hawaii's coastal coves and jungle streams. This 240-page volume covers a multitude of itineraries, with recommended campsites and scenic highlights. $12.95 from the Boat People, (408) 258-7977.

Sea Kayaker magazine, 6327 Seaview Avenue, N.W., Seattle, WA 98107. This fine quarterly publication offers useful articles on kayaking destinations, equipment, navigation and paddling skills.

Sea Kayaking--A Manual for Long Distance Touring, *by John Dowd,* (3rd Ed. 1988), U. Wash. Press, Seattle, WA. Sometimes Dowd gets a bit too pedantic, but his book is still an excellent guide for planning a long kayak journey.

A Coastal Kayaker's Manual, *by Randall Washburn,* (1989), Globe Pequot Press, P.O. Box Q, Chester, CT 06412. Washburn's up-to-date guide contains many useful tips, particularly for wilderness camping.

KAYAK COMPARISON CHART

Here are some recommended sea kayaks of various types, both double and single. All but the Prism have an enclosed cockpit. Rudders, compasses and other deluxe features can be added to most rigid models.

BRAND	TYPE	FEATURES	MANUFACTURER	LENGTH/WIDTH
Libra Major	Rigid double	Twin hatches bulkheads	Current Designs (604) 655-1596	21'8"/30"
Feathercraft K-2	Folding double	Twin hatches Aluminum frame	Feathercraft Products (604) 681-8437	20'/30"
Tofino	Rigid double	Twin hatches bulkhead	Necky Kayaks (206) 743-9252	20'/31.5"
Feathercraft K-1	Folding single (single bag)	Aluminum frame hypalon hull	Feathercraft Products (604) 681-8437	16'4"/23.5"
Mariner XL	Rigid single	Twin hatches bulkheads	Mariner Kayaks (206) 822-7299	17'1"/23.5"
Prism	Rigid single open cockpit	Twin hatches	Prism/Aquaterra (803) 859-7518	14'2"/27"

Oregon ridge-running/DAVID STOECKLEIN

ditions

▼

*F*our-wheel drive vehicles have enjoyed an enormous surge in popularity in recent years. Rugged and reliable, the latest generation of off-road vehicles will take you just about anywhere you want to go in high style and surprising comfort. To help you get the maximum enjoyment out of your new 4WD vehicle, we've compiled a detailed guide to North America's top off-road destinations. In these all-star 4WD touring areas and off-road parks you can get back to nature with your 4WD vehicle, without incurring the wrath of farmers or bureaucrats. To help you find fellow 4WD enthusiasts, we've included a complete list of 4WD clubs nationwide.

We've also selected a number of exciting 4WD adventures worldwide, allowing you to explore the backroads of every continent but Antarctica. You'll find a wide variety of jeep safaris and fully outfitted overland odysseys to some of the most exciting and exotic venues around the globe, from Tasmania to Timbuktu.

CHAPTER
15

Off-Roading Near Lake Mead/MARC MUENCH

IF THE BMW WAS THE QUINTESSENTIAL YUPPIE VEHICLE FOR THE 1980S, THEN THE new breed of deluxe 4WD vehicles (Jeep Cherokee, Ford Explorer, Isuzu Trooper, etc.) is the livery of choice for upscale urban road warriors of the '90s. However, all that traction wasn't intended just for runs to the market and the childcare center. Isn't it about time you put your shiny new 4WD to good use? Here's a selection of some of the best off-road destinations in North America.

GRAND CANYON

Arizona and Utah

The northwest corner of Arizona, along the Northern Rim of the Grand Canyon, is an off-roader's dream, with 7,600 square miles of high desert wilderness, scores of accessible jeep trails, and the splendor of the Grand Canyon. From St. George, Utah, a rough road takes you south toward the Canyon overlook at Tuweep Point. There you can see the Colorado River snaking along 3,000' beneath you. Heading back

north, you will connect with paved Highway 67 at Jacob's Lake. This can take you to the North Rim in summer, but the road is usually closed in winter. If you've got the time, continue east to the Marble Canyon area. You'll find pretty scenery and a number of fun routes over reservation roads and through sand washes near the banks of the Colorado.

You can also book a river float trip from Marble Canyon or continue up to Lake Powell, worth a visit by itself. Camping information and maps can be obtained from the BLM, Arizona Strip District Office, 390 North 3050 East, Saint George, UT 84770, (801) 673-3545. Good guidebooks include Roger Mitchell's *Grand Canyon Jeep Trails I: North Rim,* (La Siesta Press), and Thelma Heatwole's *Arizona Off the Beaten Path,* (Golden West Publishers). All Grand Canyon National Park visitor centers offer resource materials as well.

RUBICON TRAIL

California Sierra Nevada

The Rubicon Trail runs for 65 miles over the crest of the Sierras from Georgetown in the west to Lake Tahoe in the east. Along this challenging and historic route, an old wagon road, you'll test your patience and your machine's low-speed agility through lengthy sections of steep boulders. The rocks can be so tough in places that we've actually seen dirt-bikers get fed up and turn around. Once you've passed the rocky sections, the rest of the run is relatively easy, but it still offers great views and excellent campsites in the Eldorado National

America's Best 4WD Destinations

Forest. If you'd like some company on the Rubicon Trail, you may want to try out the Jeepers Jamboree, held each summer since 1953. This is traditionally one of the premier 4WD tours in California. For further details, contact Jeepers Jamboree, Box 308, Georgetown, CA 95634.

BAJA CALIFORNIA

Mexico

Baja is a four-wheeler's dream, with any kind of terrain you could want, from snowy ridges in the Sierra Madres to high dunes on the west coast. You can explore the coast along the Sea of Cortez, camping on the beach, or venture overland via some of the most rugged, rock-strewn routes you'll find anywhere. Along the coast road to San Felipe you can cruise for miles on lake beds, a dustier version of the Bonneville flats. There's endless variety for any 4WD taste, from mild to wild. You can even sample desert racing during the San Felipe 500, one of off-roading's premier competitions. Run in late May and early June, this race draws hundreds of competitors every year.

If you like nightlife with your adventuring, head all the way south to Cabo San Lucas. You can enjoy great surfing and fishing beaches with your 4WD, and still be back at your hotel by nightfall for the evening's party. Another nice spot is halfway up the coast at Bahia De Los Angeles. There are major overland routes to explore from here, plus you'll find superior fishing and diving offshore. Cut across to Santa Rosalita on the west coast and explore miles of deserted beaches, or camp out at nearby Scammon's Lagoon for winter whale-watching.

AAA offices throughout California have a good general guide for motor tourists in Baja, available free to all AAA members. *The Baja Book III*, by Tom Miller and Carol Hoffman (Baja Trail Publications, Inc.) describes campsites and contains maps illustrating jeep trails, as well as the best spots for fishing and diving.

ANZA BORREGO

California State Park

Encompassing over half a million acres with dozens of tempting dirt and gravel routes, Anza Borrego State Park is one of Southern California's prime off-road playgrounds. Much of the park can be negotiated in an ordinary car, but many road sections are so narrow that you have to thread your way, especially if you've got one of the bigger 4WDs. Anza Borrego is also open to ATVs and dirt bikes, or was when this was written--meaning that you will have to contend with some noisy competition in sections of the park near the main roads. But with 500,000 acres, there's room for everyone, and you can camp at roadside, as well as at designated campsites. Just remember this is a desert, so bring plenty of water with you. For maps, and official information, write to Anza Borrego State Park, Borrego Springs, CA 92004. A good book describing the region, with descriptions of popular jeep trails, is Lowell and Diana Lindsay's *Anza Borrego Desert Region,* available from Wilderness Press.

MONUMENT VALLEY

Arizona and Utah

Everyone should visit Monument Valley at least once in a lifetime. You'll be awestruck the first time you enter the valley and drive beneath giant sandstone pinnacles formed by millions of years of wind and erosion. The valley's scenery is otherworldly--straight out of the age of the dinosaurs. A network of jeep trails runs through the valley, accessing the best scenic vistas and a variety of old Indian sites. For a nominal fee you can take your own 4WD, or for about $20 per day you can book a guided 4WD tour at the Tribal Park headquarters, which overlooks the entrance to the valley.

Try to visit at sunrise or sunset to experience the rich colors and rugged beauty that have attracted countless Hollywood film crews to this area. Accommodations and camping sites are limited, so it is wise to book in advance if you're planning to stay more than a day or two. Monument Valley is only a few hours' drive from the Grand Canyon and other major southwestern parklands. For further details and maps, contact: Superintendent, Monument Valley Tribal Park, Box 93, Monument Valley, UT 84536.

MAUI & THE BIG ISLAND

Hawaii

If you're thinking about a vacation to Hawaii, be sure to include time for a little tropical four-wheeling. The two best islands for off-roading are Maui and the Big Island of Hawaii. Both have high peaks, lush valleys, and rugged coastal sections that can only be reached by 4WD vehicle. Get yourself a good map of the island, showing fire and ranch roads, and you're ready to go. Most of the major car rental agencies now rent Suzuki Samurais or equivalent small 4WDs.

On Maui, you'll want to take the spectacular road to Hana. This is paved, but mudslides are common, so you'll be glad you're in a jeep. From Hana, proceed southwest toward the edge of Haleakala

Monument Valley/DAVID MUENCH

National Park. As you proceed down the coast, you'll soon find yourself in real 4WD country with thick jungle, and rugged stretches of lava. Continue along the shore, passing the Highway 31 junction, while keeping to the coastal dirt road. You'll have fun exploring the windswept, wild southern end of the island, which is not passable by normal cars. You can call the Haleakala National Park Service office at (808) 572-7749 for information about other island areas open to off-road vehicles.

The Big Island is also a fine 4WD destination. Two of the island's best backcountry routes are the Saddle Road between Hilo and Waimea, and the Waipio Valley Trail. You'll definitely want to check these

out, plus the southern approaches leading up to Mauna Kea and the Kilauea volcano. The latter is great for lava-watching, although the Park Service may have the road blocked off close to the coast. Call the National Park Service Visitor Center at the Kilauea Crater for current road conditions, (808) 967-7311.

GREAT SMOKY MOUNTAINS

Tennessee

Great Smoky Mountain National Park extends into four separate states: Kentucky, Tennessee, and both North and South

218

Carolina. While the park itself is closed to most off-road travel, it is bordered on all sides by National Forest lands with numerous good 4WD routes. Some of the most popular trails are found in Tennessee's Cherokee National Forest. The wide assortment of jeep roads here attracts 4WD fans from around the country. In the Nolichucky district, take the Horse Creek Rock road to Cold Spring Mountain. At the summit you'll enjoy great views and access to the Appalachian Trail.

In the Carolinas, routes along the headwaters of Tellico River are very popular, and there are many good trout streams nearby. Call the local ranger in North Carolina at (704) 837-5152 for more details. The

Great Smoky Mountains are still relatively unspoiled, but you're never too far from civilization, making it easy to locate a good campground or country inn. For maps and wilderness permits, write to: Cherokee National Forest, Supervisor's Office, 2800 North Ocoee Street, Cleveland, TN 37312, (615) 476-9700. To get practical assistance on the best roads to run, contact the local rangers, whose phone numbers are available from the Forest Service office in Cleveland, Tennessee.

SAN JUAN MOUNTAINS
Colorado

The San Juan Mountains in southwestern Colorado have been called the "Switzerland of America." Here you'll find plenty of old mining trails and abandoned railroad beds perfect for backcountry forays. One scenic and challenging trail is the high route from Telluride to Silverton via the 12,350' Ophir Pass. From Silverton, another great run crosses the 12,500' Stony Pass, a route that carried thousands of miners and covered wagons in its heyday. To get to Stony Pass, head north from Silverton to Howardsville, then turn south through Cunningham Gulch. Follow the signs to Cunningham Pass, another name for the Stony Pass route. You'll start climbing right away, as you begin a 28-mile journey through forests and alpine meadows. Along the way you'll encounter some of the best overlooks in the Rockies.

From the summit, you'll want to continue down toward Creede, but don't miss the network of 4WD trails near Forest Service Road 520. From this point you can head to Lost Lakes, Regan Lake or other wilderness destinations. There are very few folks up here, and you're likely to have the roads to yourself most times of year. Take Highway 149 to return to Creede.

When you start your trip, pick up a Rio Grande National Forest map from area rangers. It will clearly indicate the Stony Pass Route, as well as lesser used fire roads and jeep trails to lakes and camping areas. To obtain the best local trail guide, *Jeep Roads and Ghost Towns of the San Juans*, contact the Silverton Chamber of Commerce, Box 565, Silverton, CO 81433, (303) 387-5654. The Chamber also has information on local 4WD outfitters and off-road events.

UPPER PENINSULA
Michigan

Michigan's Upper Peninsula is a prime outdoor recreation area, with excellent hunting, fishing and camping in the Ottawa and Hiawatha National Forests. With over a million acres of forest lands, it's easy to head off for a weekend and really get away from the crowd. There's good vehicle access via Forest Service routes and dirt roads constructed by the lumber and mining companies that once ruled the roost here. Abandoned railroad right of ways will also take you deep into the heart of the peninsula, though be prepared for some heavy slogging on some of the most remote routes.

Before you go, pick up one of the local recreational guide books. There's so much good fishing in this region that you should allow at least a day or two to sample the angling. Stick to the smaller streams for trout; head to the lakes for bass. For information about the Ottawa and Hiawatha National Forests, (and suggestions about the best fishing destinations), write to the Regional Forester, US Forest Service, 2727 North Lincoln Road, Escanaba, MI 49829, (906) 786-4062 (Hiawatha); or 2100 East Clover Land Drive, Ironwood, MI 49938, (906) 932-1330 (Ottawa). You may also contact the Upper Peninsula Travel and Recreation Association, P.O. Box 400, Iron Mountain, MI 49801.

WENATCHEE FOREST
Washington

If you're looking for a real test of your 4x4's abilities, consider a trek through the backwoods of the Wenatchee Forest in Washington. Some really hair-raising trails

The classic American Jeep/DAVID STOECKLEIN

are found here, with tricky sidehills, tough slopes, sheer ridgelines, and lots of rocks and streams. You'll want to check out the trails in the southwest part of the Forest, northeast of Highway 410. Ask about the Shoestring Trail near Cliffdell, route of the annual Northwest 4WD Jamboree. We're told it's rougher and more challenging than California's Rubicon, which is really saying something. The Devil's Gulch area is also a hotspot for off-roading. The trails are not as forbidding, but the scenery is great. Throughout the Wenatchee Forest, you should be prepared for rain any time of year. Be especially careful in the spring, when the snowmelt run-off can present some real problems. You'll need all the ground clearance you can get. To obtain maps, permits and general information, write to Wenatchee National Forest, 301 Yakima Street, P.O. Box 811, Wenatchee, WA 98801, (509) 662-4335. For tips on routes, call the Forest Service office at (509) 662-4201 and ask for Mike Dolfay, ORV Specialist.

OWYHEE COUNTY

Idaho

Owyhee County is one of the most appealing 4WD destinations in the Rockies. With ghost towns galore, impressive canyons, rocky peaks and even dunes, this is 4WD paradise. There are more good trails than you can count, plus you're right next to the Snake River, one of the world's best rafting runs. A great drive begins at the town of Murphy on Highway 38. Take a rough but exciting old gold mining road through the mountains west to the Oregon border where you'll end up at US 95. You'll have 45 miles of real wilderness off-roading over tough, wet and rocky tracks, a real challenge for man and machine. Don't try this if you want to keep your 4x4 showroom-clean. A map showing dirt roads and jeep trails in Idaho is available from the Idaho Travel Council, Statehouse, Boise, ID 83720, (800) 635-7820.

CANYONLANDS

Utah

For colorful rock formations and sheer rugged beauty, we can't think of a better destination than the Canyonlands. What's more, you won't find a more scenic daytrip than a tour through nearby Arches National Park. With hundreds of richly colored sandstone spires and arches

Colorado River, Canyonlands/DAVID MUENCH

carved by eons of wind and erosion, Arches National Park is a high desert wonderland. No nature-loving off-roaders should miss this spot.

The main route through Arches is suitable for all vehicles. However, there are sandy tracks through adjoining wilderness areas especially designated for 4x4s. Salt Valley and Klondike Bluffs are the most popular 4WD routes. Bring plenty of water, because you'll be quite isolated on many of your excursions throughout this region. One lure of the Canyonlands area is that you are within a few hours' drive of other great southwestern destinations, including

Bryce Canyon and Capitol Reef National Park. For information on off-road trails and campsites, contact Superintendent, Arches National Park, P.O. Box 907, Hwy 191, Moab, UT 84532, (801) 259-8161. Good maps and regional guidebooks are available at various national park offices in Utah. Useful information on jeep touring is also available from the Moab Chamber of Commerce, Moab, UT 84532.

CAPITOL REEF

Utah

In Capitol Reef National Park you'll find stunning red rock canyons, huge sandstone rock formations, one of the world's largest natural arches and many other remarkable geological features. There is an excellent campground in the middle of the Park, one of Utah's best. The Park boasts a good network of hiking trails, as well as a number of dirt and gravel roads laid out expressly for 4x4 touring. You can easily spend a week exploring the network of wilderness roads, and if you're adventurous, there's plenty of open country to run. Check with the Park Service before you venture off designated routes, however. If you're planning to camp, make reservations early. The nearest motels are 13 miles away, and they are often booked. For maps, reservations and permits, write to Capitol Reef National Park, Torrey, UT 84775. A good resource is Wade Roylance's *Seeing Capitol Reef National Park*, (Wasatch Publishers).

PANHANDLE

Florida

No, you don't need a prop-driven skimmer or swampbuggy to have fun in Florida's Panhandle Wilderness. Between the Gulf Coast and the southern edges of Alabama and Georgia, you'll find lots of good 4WD destinations in the Apalachicola and Osceola National Forests.

These regions are found near Tallahassee and Lake City on your map, and can be reached via Interstate 10. Both forests contain a good network of off-road trails, along with many camping and fishing spots. Florida game management areas on the Panhandle also allow 4WD use over a network of fairly rugged and often muddy roads. You'll need a permit to venture into the game preserves, which are operated by the Game and Fresh Water Fish Commission, Department of Natural Resources, 620 S. Meridian, Tallahassee, FL 32399-1600, (904) 488-4676. Permits are available from local tackle shops. For further information about the Apalachicola and Osceola forest trails, contact the Regional Forester, US Forest Service, 227 North Bronough Street, Suite 4061, Tallahassee, FL 32301, (904) 681-7265.

FLAMING GORGE

Utah and Wyoming

Just the name should give you an idea of the spectacular scenery in this destination, situated along the Wyoming-Utah border. You'll find every kind of terrain in the Flaming Gorge National Recreation Area--arid and desert-like in the north, verdant and forested in the south. There are lakes, streams and good campsites throughout the region, which is controlled by the US Forest Service and the Bureau of Land Management. A relatively small portion of the Recreation Area is restricted, leaving acres to explore by 4WD. For an off-road trip combining fishing, hiking and wilderness camping, this is one of the top destinations. Unlike most parts of Utah or Arizona, there's plenty of water here, so you won't feel like you're on a desert patrol. It's hard to find good maps of the area for 4x4 travel, so obtain topographical maps from the Forest Service or local mountain shops. You'll also want to talk to local outfitters for tips on the best fishing holes and campsites within the Flaming Gorge region. An added bonus is that you're close to Yellowstone, a great place to view wildlife and fish high mountain lakes. For further information and maps, contact Flaming Gorge National Recreation Area, P.O. Box 157, Dutch John, UT, 84023, (801) 885-3315.

CONTINENTAL DIVIDE

Colorado

You'll find a host of great 4WD runs across the Continental Divide in northern and central Colorado. Fire roads, logging trails and old railroad beds comprise an ideal off-road trail system. One fine run begins at Rolinsville, on State Highway 119; look for the abandoned railbed in the west. Known as the Moffat Road, this will take you over Rollins Pass to the 11,400' Corona summit, and then to US 40 on the other side of the Great Divide. Another great trail is Mosquito Pass, which runs for 20 miles between Fairplay and Leadville. You'll hit 13,186' at the summit, making

Boulder, Colorado/DAVID STOECKLEIN

this the highest off-road trail in the continental United States. Along the way, there are plenty of good opportunities for camping and fishing. Just be prepared for snow flurries, even in summer.

A good, though dated guide to ridge-running in the Rockies is *Jeep Trails to Colorado Ghost Towns*, by Robert Brown (Caxton Printers). Check US Forest Service offices in the area for topographical maps and wilderness permits.

BLACK HILLS

South Dakota

Famed site of Custer's Last Stand, and home to hundreds of abandoned mines and ghost towns, South Dakota's Black Hills offer a playground for off-road adventures. Old mine trails crisscross the

area, and most of the 1.25 million acres of public land in the Black Hills is open to off-roading, including much of the Black Hills National Forest. You can also visit the famed Homestake Mine, the single largest producer of gold in the world over the past century. But don't think the Black Hills contain nothing but ghost towns and mining centers. The Black Hills offer excellent camping, fishing and canoeing in many unspoiled and uncrowded parks and wilderness areas. The most popular spots are Sheridan Lake, Deerfield Lake and Pactola Reservoir. In winter, the Black Hills become a haven for snowmobiling as well. For ideas on specific off-road destinations, pick up a copy of the *Guide to Black Hills Ghost Mines*, available from North Plains Press. Trail maps and general information can be obtained from the Black Hills National Forest Headquarters, RR2, Box 200, Custer, SD 57730, (605) 673-2251.

WIND RIVER RANGE

Wyoming

Most of the extremely wild and rugged Wind River Range is wilderness sanctuary, off limits to all motorized vehicles. However, you can experience the splendor of this region in sections of the Shoshone National Forest, very close to the protected reserves. Take US 287 to Lander, Wyoming, and pick up forest maps from the rangers there. They can show you which areas are open to 4WDs, and suggest the most popular routes. If you plan to camp, fish or build fires, be sure to obtain the necessary permits. (The fly-fishing is superb in this area.) From Lander, you'll probably want to take Highway 131 into the mountains. Follow this gravel road into the high country where you can explore a wide selection of smaller jeep trails. (You must stay on designated roads while in the National Forest lands.) For more information, contact: Shoshone National Forest Headquarters, P.O. Box 2140, Cody, WY 82414, (307) 527-6241; Lander Ranger District, 600 N. Hwy. 287, Lander, WY 82520, (307) 332-5460; and BLM, Lander Resource Area, P.O. Box 589, Lander, WY 82520, (307) 332-7822.

Off-roading in Africa/THE ADVENTURE CENTER

THE OVERLAND EXPERIENCE

FOR MOST AMERICANS, FOUR-WHEELING IS A FORM OF WEEKEND RECREATION. Elsewhere in the world, where paved roads are the exception rather than the rule, 4x4 transport is a necessity. If you want to get to the most remote reaches of Africa, South America and Asia, a 4WD vehicle is often your only alternative to saddling up a yak or making your way on foot. Able to cover 250 miles a day over poor roads, 4WDs have made long-distance travel possible even in the most far-flung destinations. These days, 4WD tours go just about anyplace you can imagine, on an adventure from a few days to a matter of months. (How does a four-month road trip from London to Kathmandu grab you?)

An overland 4WD tour is one of the last great getaways. You travel deep into the heart of foreign continents, far from the resorts and tourist traps frequented by westerners. On a trans-African overland trip, for example, you'll probably see fewer westerners in two months than you would on a weeklong trek through the Annapurna region of Nepal. These trips may be the best way to explore the hinterlands on a shoestring budget. Many overland tours cost less than $40 per day, all-inclusive.

Exploring the Wild Outback

Trans-Continental Safaris offers 1 to 37-day off-road expeditions into Australia's central outback. Notable destinations include Ayers Rock, the opal mining fields, the Simpson Desert, Litchfield Nat'l Park and the Flinders Range. The expedition vehicles are air-conditioned and fitted out with all necessary camping equipment. Driving duties are handled by expert local guides who double as chefs during the tours. Crocodile Dundee may be an invention of Hollywood, but these outback drivers come close. Snakes, wild boars, flash floods and dust storms won't phase them, and their enthusiasm for their work is unbounded. Trans-Continental Safaris, James Road, Clare, S. Aus. 5453, Australia, (011 61) 88 423 469; FAX: (011 61) 88 422 586.

If you're heading Down Under, but plan to stay on Australia's east coast, you still have many excellent off-road opportunities. Numerous 4WD outfitters run jeep treks out of Cairns into Queensland's tropi-

cal rainforests, and out of Darwin into the desolate northern outback. Australia's leading adventure outfitter, World Expeditions, runs a trip from Cairns to Cape York, Australia's northernmost frontier. This 15-day expedition takes you from the Marlin Coast, across the Jardine River, and past old gold mines and aboriginal villages on the route to Cape York. On the return, journey through the Daintree Rainforest, a World Heritage area, and visit Cape Tribulation before returning to Cairns. Contact Worldwide Adventures, Suite 747, 920 Yonge Street, Toronto, ONT, Canada M4W 3C7, (800) 387-1483. Other Northern Australian 4WD tours are offered by: Ausventure Holidays, P.O. Box 54, Mosman, NSW 2088, Australia, (011 61) 2 960-1188; FAX: 2 969-1463 (destinations--Kakadu, Cape York, Flinders Range, north-central deserts); Australia-Pacific AAT King's Tours, Burbank, CA, (800) 821-9513 (destinations--all Australia); or Adventure Center, 1311 63rd Street, Suite 200, Emeryville, CA 94608, (800) 227-8747, (800) 228-8747 in CA (destinations--Kakadu, Ayers Rock, Queensland).

AFRICA

Trans-African Expedition

If you're looking for the most ambitious 4WD experience on earth, this is it: a 15-week overland expedition across the heart of Africa from Morocco to Kenya, passing through Algeria, Niger, Cameroon, the Central African Republic, Zaire, Rwanda, Burundi and Tanzania along the way. The trip is run by Tracks Africa, a leader in African trips for the past 20 years. Much of the route will be through open country with no charted roads--only "pistes," tracks on the ground left by previous vehicles. This is not a trip for luxury-seekers. Everyone joins in on the work to be done, whether changing a tire, or sharing cooking duties.

The trans-African trip will be run in military-spec 4WD expedition vehicles, driven by experienced guides. For the most part, you will sleep in tents during the journey until you reach Kenya. We can safely say that this is a trip of a lifetime--tough, long, intense, but in all likelihood one of the most rewarding things you could ever do. The expeditions depart from

London in January, with a return trip via a similar route in May. Total land cost is a reasonable $4,000 or so. Contact Tracks Africa's US agent, Himalayan Travel, Inc., P.O. Box 481, Greenwich, CT 06836, (800) 225-2380, or (203) 622-6777.

We promised you Timbuktu, and Dragoman's 19-week Trans-Africa expedition will take you there, along with West Africa and most of the destinations on the Tracks tour. Price is about $4,290 plus another $840 for the food kitty. Dragoman (a Turkish word for "guide") is an experienced British company that uses excellent Mercedes expedition vehicles. You can book a Dragoman trip through the Adventure Center, (address at left), (800) 227-8747, or (800) 228-8747 in CA.

SOUTH AMERICA

The Andes Express

Imagine traversing the entire length of South America in specially equipped military-class Mercedes 4WD vehicles. You'll ford jungle streams, penetrate dense, remote rainforests, and scale 17,000' passes. Offered by Forum Travel International for the first time in 1990, the Andes Express runs all the way from the headlands of the Amazon to the tip of Patagonia, covering over 5,000 miles of wilderness in 5 months. If you don't have time to complete the full expedition, you can join the tour for any period, from 11 days on up, meeting the Express as

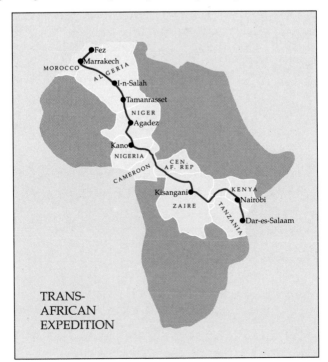

TRANS-AFRICAN EXPEDITION

it passes through small villages. When the tour visits populated areas, you'll stay in inns or villagers' homes. In the wild, participants camp in tents.

The Andes Express commences in November, and is divided into 11 stages, each averaging 12 days. The 1991-1992 cost, including local transport to rendezvous with the tour, was roughly $1,740 per stage, or about $145 per day. Contact Forum Travel International, 91 Gregory Lane, Suite 21, Pleasant Hill, CA 94523, (510) 671-2900; FAX: (510) 946-1500.

Dragoman, the IBM of overland trips, offers a similar, if less exotic, 7-week journey down the length of the Andes. The trip begins in Quito, Ecuador, and finishes in Santiago, Chile. Along the way, you'll hit all the major highlights, including Machu Picchu, Cuzco and Chile's Atacama Desert. This trip traverses more main roads than does the Andes Explorer, but the price ($1,900 plus $130 food kitty) is a bargain by comparison--roughly $40 per day. Book through the Adventure Center, (800) 227-8747, or (800) 228-8747 in CA.

BOLIVIA & CHILE

Deserts and Mountains

Explore the remote wildlands and deserts of Bolivia on a 14-day jeep safari offered by adventure outfitter SafariCentre. The first organized 4WD tour of its kind offered in Bolivia, this tour takes participants to the most remote and geologically unique regions of Bolivia. You start in La Paz, then depart for famed Lake Titicaca. Next the tour ventures to Uyuni, site of the highest salt flats in the world. Proceeding south, you head into the mountains, climbing to Potosi, a fabled mining town situated at 13,350'. The next two days are spent visiting country markets before looping back to La Paz. During the tour you will stay in small villages, with modest hotel accommodations. Trips depart monthly May through October and cost roughly $2,500. An optional extension to Chile's starkly beautiful Atacama high desert is available. (Wilderness Travel, (800) 247-6700, hopes to offer a similar 19-day 4WD trip in 1993 that includes the Atacama, the Altiplano Wildlife Preserve, and Chile's rugged Pacific coast, all well worth visiting.)

If you're curious about other South American 4WD options, Safaricentre offers a number of good overland trips ranging from the Amazon to Patagonia. Many different itineraries and prices are available. Contact Safaricentre International, Inc., 3201 N. Sepulveda Boulevard, Manhattan Beach, CA 90266, (800) 624-5342 in CA, (800) 233-6046 in Canada, (800) 223-6046 nationwide.

Jeep Trekking in Paradise

If you don't know already, New Zealand boasts some of the most beautiful and unspoiled scenery on earth. There are lush tropical forests in the North Island and rugged snow-capped mountains in the South Island. Because New Zealand is relatively small, access to most areas is good, with jeep trails and outback farm roads crisscrossing most regions.

New Zealand can be an off-roader's dream. The average country Kiwi relies on his Land Rover or Toyota for his livelihood, so the government doesn't view off-roaders as some kind of fringe group. It seems perfectly reasonable to the Kiwis that tourists would enjoy jeep trekking, so a host of opportunities exist. In the North Island, you can explore volcanic craters and dense coastal bush country. In the South Island, drive alpine ridges in glacier country, or enjoy 2 to 12-day overland wilderness safaris. One popular trip will take you over shingle river beds and mountain passes all the way from Queenstown to Dunedin, staying at remote ranch stations along the route. Leading North Island operators include: Cross Country Tours (NZ's largest company), P.O. Box 10224, Hamilton, NZ, (011 64) 7 849-3949; FAX: 7 849-3320; Aotearoa Adventures, RD1, Whitianga, NZ, (011 64) 843 63-808. In the South Island, contact Edgewater Resort Adventures, P.O. Box 61, Wanaka, NZ, (011 64) 3 443-8311; FAX: 3 443-8323. Typical 2 to 6-day trips cost $150-$250 per day. Many smaller operators, e.g. Collingwood Safaris in Nelson (South Island), run day-trips. Call the NZ Tourist Office for more details: (800) 388-5494.

The Undiscovered Australia

The green island of Tasmania, Australia's southernmost territory, is a land of wild rivers, quiet rainforest and unspoiled wilderness. Off-road travel is an everyday thing in sparsely populated Tasmania, so visitors have a wide range of 4WD options. If you're feeling intrepid, rent a sturdy 4WD vehicle, grab an armload of topo maps, and set out to circumnavigate the island in 10-15 days. Make sure to hit the major parks: Cradle Mountain/Lake St. Clair, Ben Lomond and Freycinet, a peninsula on the east coast.

If you prefer a guided trip, Bushventures 4WD Tours offers a 4-day run through the Heritage Wilderness Area and Lake St. Clair Nat'l. Park at a cost of about $710. Call (011 61) 02 236 910. Tas-Trek leads a 10-day tour that covers most of the island's parks and takes you deep into the Tasmanian interior to explore dense rainforest and isolated waterfalls. Land cost is

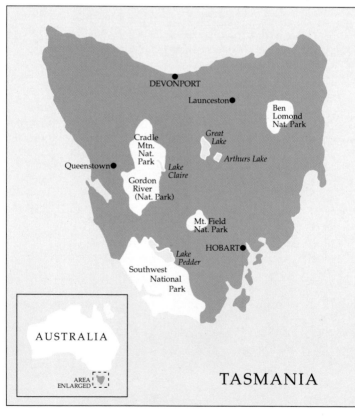

AUSTRALIA

AREA ENLARGED

TASMANIA

about $1,400. Call (011 61) 03 341-787. 4WD Tours takes customers to the Cradle Mountain/Lake St. Clair area and then visits remote, west coast beaches. These 6-day camping tours run a reasonable $600 or so per person. (All prices are subject to ex-

change rate changes.) For further information, contact the Tasmanian Travel Centre, 80 Elizabeth Street, Hobart, Tasmania, 7000, Australia, (011 61) 08 309 011, or the Australian Tourist Office, 2121 Avenue of the Stars, Suite 1270, Los Angeles, CA 90067, (310) 553-6352.

Jungle and Mountain Exploring

Himalayan Travel, a major adventure outfitter, offers trips to the remote jungles and mountains of Peru using specially equipped 4WD expedition vehicles. The tours feature bilingual guides, familiar with the local culture and environment. The 16-day tour begins in Lima, Peru, a resort located near a major wildlife refuge. You then visit Nazca, site of the huge, mysterious forms left by ancient civilizations. Chariots of the gods? You decide. Next, you'll visit Colca Canyon, three times the depth of Arizona's Grand Canyon. You'll proceed on through the Andes to Lake Titicaca and Cuzco, capital of the Inca empire. From there you can tour ancient ruins at Machu Picchu, or join optional river-rafting trips and Amazon jungle cruises. Land cost is approximately $1,395. Contact Himalayan Travel, Inc., P.O. Box 481, Greenwich, CT 06836, (800) 225-2380.

A similar 3-week Peru trip is offered by Great Britain's Exodus Expeditions, a world leader in overland touring. Highlights include Colca Canyon, Cuzco, Machu Picchu, and an optional 3-day Inca Trail sojourn. Price is approximately $1,950. Exodus offers a wide variety of other South American overland trips, including a 22-week full circuit of the continent--one of the last great adventures. On this remarkable 5-month odyssey, you'll visit all the major Latin countries: Columbia, Venezuela, Brazil, Argentina, Chile, Bolivia and Peru. Total price, including all food, is approximately $5,400, roughly $35 per day. Contact Exodus' US Agent: Force 10 Expeditions, P.O. Box 34354, Pensacola, FL 32507, (800) 922-1491; FAX: (904) 492-6661.

OVERLAND & 4WD

TRIP PLANNING

If you're considering a lengthy 4WD expedition, by all means do your homework. A long overland trek can be hell on wheels if the guide is inexperienced or if the vehicle isn't up to the task. Remember that your transport, typically a large 4WD truck outfitted with special camping and cooking equipment, will be your home for weeks or even months. Choose an established international outfitter like Tracks, Dragoman or Exodus that uses sturdy military-grade 4x4s, fitted with long-range fuel and water tanks. The big Mercedes trucks will get you through just about anything. For long trips, insist on a vehicle that provides real seats, not just benches. We recommend rigs that offer an outside seating option so you can enjoy the view when the weather is good. Enclosed coaches are less romantic, but if you plan to cover many miles in extreme temperatures or dusty conditions, this is the best.

Most long overland trips are cooperative exercises. You will be expected to assist in the cooking and other daily duties. If you want to be pampered, pick another vacation. There are no first-class compartments on the road to Xanadu. You also have to put up with a certain lack of privacy. On an overland trip, you may be banging elbows with a dozen other travelers, mostly foreigners, for 1,000 miles or more. Hot showers will be few and far between. Whether this kind of adventure is a burden or a blessing is really up to you. If you are used to creature comforts, you will be disappointed. On the other hand, there is something very special about a shared challenge of this kind, and you just might make some of the best friends of your life.

INFORMATION SOURCES

For literature on minimal impact off-road driving procedures, write to *"Tread Lightly,"* **USDA Forest Service**, 324 25th Street, Ogden, UT 84401.

JIM ELDER

OFF-ROAD CENTERS

A list of federal lands where off-road driving and ATV riding is permitted is available from the **Bureau of Land Management (BLM)** regional office in your area. Check with your local state legislator for lists of state lands open to 4x4s and ATVs. You'll find that many coastal states operate parks near large dune areas where 4WD use is not only tolerated, but is encouraged. Check your State Parks Department.

MAPS

Sidekick Maps, *12475 Central Avenue, No. 352, Chino, CA 91710, (714) 628-7227.* Don't venture off-road in California without one of Sidekick's slick topo maps. Areas covered include Big Bear, Rubicon Trail, Orocopia Mtns., Santiago Canyon and Dunes, and Dumont Dunes. All maps include trail difficulty ratings and campground listings.

The Map Catalog: Every Kind of Map and Chart on Earth, from Vintage Books, is a valuable resource for those traveling to remote and exotic places. The Map Catalog features listings of all map varieties, from marine charts to CIA aerial photo maps. The greatest feature is a comprehensive appendix telling you how to get the right map for any spot on the globe. This can be especially handy if you are headed to communist nations or third world countries where foreigners can have trouble obtaining accurate or current maps. Send $14.95 to *Vintage Books, 400 Hahn Road, Westminster, MD 21157, (301) 848-1900,* or try your local bookstore.

VIDEOS

The Searchers, *P.O. Box 1445, Cortez, CO 81321, (800) 274-1455.* The Searchers offer excellent 90-minute videos on some of the West's top 4WD destinations including the Rubicon Trail, Black Bear Road, Moab Rim, Arch Canyon, and Canyonlands National Park. These tapes will lead you along the best backroads, with expert commentary. Cost is $35 plus $3 shipping for each destination.

4WD CLUBS AND ASSOCIATIONS

For the name and address of a 4WD club in your area, contact the **United Four Wheel Drive Association** at *(800) 44U-FWDA,* or write to *105 Highland Avenue, Battle Creek, MI 49015.* (For $25, you can join the UFWDA and receive discounts on 4WD supplies, plus a year's subscription to a 4WD magazine.) Some of the active 4WD clubs around the country include:

Arizona State Assoc. of 4WD Clubs, *P.O. Box 23904, Tempe, AZ 85282, (602) 258-4BY4.*

Cal. Assoc. of 4WD Clubs, *910 Florin Road, #209, Sacramento, CA 95831, (916) 974-3984.*

Colorado Assoc. of 4WD Clubs, *P.O. Box 1413, Wheat Ridge, CO 80034, (303) 321-1266.*

East Coast 4WD Assoc., Inc., *101 S. Miami Avenue, Cleves, OH 45002, (513) 941-1450.*

4WD Assoc. of British Columbia, *Box 284, Surrey, BC, Canada V3T 4W8, (604) 534-0215.*

Great Lakes 4WD Assoc., *11495 W. Burt Road, Chesaning, MI 48616, (517) 585-3356.*

Midwest 4WD Assoc., *RR2, Box 70, Lake Crystal, MN 56055, (507) 726-2598.*

Montana 4x4 Assoc., Inc., *23 Border Lane, Bozeman, MT 59715, (406) 587-8307.*

Pacific Northwest 4WD Assoc., *946 18th, Longview, WA 98632, (800) 537-7845.*

Southern 4WD Assoc., *P.O. Box 3473, Oak Ridge, TN 37831, (615) 482-6912.*

Utah 4WD Assoc., Inc., *P.O. Box 20310, Salt Lake City, UT 84120.*

Wisconsin 4WD Assoc., *203 Gruenwald Ave., Neenah, WI 54956, (414) 722-3777.*

Rafting

Colorado River, Crand Canyon, Arizona/CHRIS NOBLE

I do not know much about gods; but I think that the river is a strong brown god--sullen, untamed and intractable.
-T.S. Eliot, "The Dry Savages"

▼

Whitewater rafting is synonymous with high adventure. It combines physical challenge, raw excitement, and the chance to explore pristine wilderness areas. Rafting also offers a special measure of camaraderie; you make friends quickly when you have to rely on your fellow paddlers to make it through serious whitewater.

Hundreds of rafting companies now operate around the world. By and large these outfitters have skilled crews and enviable safety records. Choosing where to go and who to go with can still be a difficult task. This chapter should make the selection process a bit easier. We have compared the operations of more than 100 outfitters running scores of rivers worldwide. For each destination we've listed the river guides with the top skills, experience, and highest levels of customer satisfaction. With this book you'll be able to plan exactly the kind of trip you want, and be assured that the rafting company you select will be a good one.

CHAPTER
16

Zambezi River, Africa/STEVE GILROY

RAFTING OFFERS ANY KIND OF VACATION EXPERIENCE YOU COULD WANT, FROM half-day trips near home to 200-mile wilderness expeditions in the remote jungles of South America. If you are looking for an ultimate river trip, one with the biggest rapids or the most incredible scenery, here are ten very special adventures, each the trip of a lifetime.

ZAMBIA / ZIMBABWE

Zambesi River Adventure

A trip down the Zambezi from Victoria Falls to Lake Kariba, 80 miles downstream, is one of the greatest adventures on earth. For those looking for thrilling whitewater, unique scenery, great wildlife and exotic foreign culture, the Zambezi is in a class by itself. Photographer Steve Gilroy, who has run most of the world's classic rivers and who shot the photos on these pages, reports: "Absolutely nothing tops the Zambezi for the sheer power, number and size of rapids--even the Colorado at peak flood."

The trip begins at the base of massive Victoria Falls (known to natives as Mosi-O-Tunya, the Smoke that Thunders), 350' high and over a mile wide. On the first day, the Zambezi cuts through a deep gorge where rafters encounter the world's wildest runnable whitewater--ten of the world's biggest rapids, including the notorious boat-launcher, Number 5. The upper sections of the Zambezi also boast two spectacular waterfalls cascading from 20-foot basalt cliffs. Short portages will be made over these sections. The balance of the 10-day trip alternates between rollicking Class IV and Class V whitewater and quiet stretches teeming with wildlife, including crocodiles, hippos, eagles and antelope.

Along the way, rafters will camp on the sandy river banks and visit Zambian fishing villages.

On the Zambezi, the choice of outfitters is simple--Sobek Expeditions Zambia. Since it pioneered the Zambezi in 1981, Sobek has been the premier outfitter on the river, and it is the only one we can recommend wholeheartedly. (Sobek Zambia is a sister company of US-based Mountain Travel/Sobek, but it is independently owned and operated.) Sobek enjoys a commendable safety record, and its equipment and river guides are first rate. The boatmen have an average of six years of experience, and all are trained in CPR and swift-water rescue.

At present, Sobek offers three options on the Zambezi. One-day trips featuring the hottest rapids just below Victoria Falls are offered for $85 January through March and mid-June through December. Two-day trips are offered once each month, August through November, at a cost of $200. The full 10-day river trip, with 6 days spent rafting, costs $1,575, with departures June through November. Maximum thrills are to

Ten Ultimate Rafting Trips

be had during the high water seasons--January through March, and July to mid-August. Contact Mountain Travel/Sobek, 6420 Fairmont Ave., El Cerrito, CA 95222, (800) 227-2384, or Sobek Exped. Zambia, Ltd., P.O. Box 60957, Livingstone, Zambia, (011 260) 3 321432; FAX: (011 260) 3 323542.

If you want to run the Zambezi, don't hesitate too long. Plans are afoot to dam the river in two places, which would wipe out the most exciting stretches of whitewater. The Zambezi's flow to the ocean is already interrupted by the Kariba Dam, which impounds a 120-mile stretch of the river. A new dam is proposed below Kariba, and another dam at the Batoka Gorges which would drown the river between Kariba and Victoria Falls.

ARIZONA

Grand Canyon of the Colorado

By almost anyone's reckoning, a rafting trip down the Grand Canyon is America's greatest river odyssey, one that ranks among the three finest river trips in the world (other consensus picks are the Zambezi, and either the Bio-Bio or the Indus). The 279-mile journey takes you through 161 named rapids and some of the most spectacular scenery on earth--the geological legacy of billions of years of history. Sheer walls rise a mile above the river, creating stunning contrasts of light and shadow below. There are mysterious side canyons and inviting waterfalls. The canyon's scale defies description, and its rugged beauty is truly awe-inspiring.

Running the Grand Canyon has become big business. More than 20 concessionaires take thousands of visitors down the Colorado every year. In planning a trip, your primary concerns should be the length of the trip, the type of craft (motor,

Zambezi River, Africa/STEVE GILROY

Late afternoon on the Colorado/CHRIS NOBLE

oar, paddle or dory), and price. If you want to see the entire canyon, which we strongly recommend, it will take 7 to 9 days in a motor-raft, and up to 2 weeks in an oar-boat. If you are on a tight budget, you may want to choose a 4 to 6-day motorized trip covering half the river. Most folks doing a partial trip prefer the Upper Canyon, from Lee's Ferry southward, as this contains most of the major rapids, and you don't have to hike down into the canyon. However, the second half has less river traffic and contains some of the most spectacular side canyons. Though it still includes some sizable rapids, the second half of the river is gentler, and may be more suitable for the old or very young.

Some Upper Canyon trips venture 185 miles or so, well over half the river's length, so as to include Lava Falls, which is by far the wildest rapid on the Colorado. While most Grand Canyon rafting brochures emphasize the thundering waters of Lava Falls and other major rapids, such as Crystal or Horn Creek, this is a bit deceptive. Most of your time on the river will be spent floating long stretches of relatively still water. For this reason your decision as to what type of craft to take can be all-important.

Big motor-rafts travel fast, enabling you to see more canyon in less time. Carrying upwards of 20 passengers, these huge 30 to 40-footers can seem like cattle-boats, however, and there is the noise of the motor to consider. (Actually, most folks get used to the motor within a few hours, and it ceases to bother them.) Oar-rafts provide a more personal experience and, in our view, they are more exciting in the rapids. Paddle-rafts are the most adventurous option, but unless you're a fitness freak, you'll quickly get tired of paddling through the long flatwater sections of the canyon. Last but not least, dories offer the most traditional Grand Canyon experience. Dories are pretty to look at and can be very exciting in big rapids, but they aren't the most comfortable of craft, and they are slow. It takes 14 to 21 days to run the Grand Canyon from top to bottom in a dory.

For a motorized trip, we recommend Adventures West, (800) 828-WEST; Western River Expeditions, (800) 453-7450; and Mike Denoyer's Grand Canyon Expeditions Co. (GCE), (800) 544-2691. For an oar-raft trip, the top outfitters are GCE, O.A.R.S., (209) 736-4677; and Colorado River & Trail Expeditions (CRTE), (801) 261-1789. If you're really hardcore, you can paddle your own raft with O.A.R.S., CRTE,

or Arizona Raft Adventures, (800) 786-7238. Grand Canyon Dories (a sister company of O.A.R.S.), (209) 736-0805, is the clear choice for dory trips on the Colorado.

Since it is dam-controlled, the Colorado is runnable year-round. However, the best time to go is probably the late spring (April/May), and early fall (September/October). During these times the river is less crowded, and temperatures will be in the high 80s as opposed to 100+ in mid-summer. Prices for Colorado River trips vary considerably. A short 3 or 4-day motorized trip will average between $650 and $800. A 6 to 8-day, full-canyon motor journey costs between $1,500 and $1,800. A half-river oar-boat trip of 7 to 8 days runs about $1,100-$1,200, while a full-river oar-boat or paddle-boat trip ranges in price from $1,500 to $2,100.

WEST VIRGINIA

Class V Fury

For those seeking continuous action, with back-to-back Class IV to V rapids (Class VI is considered unrunnable), West Virginia offers America's best whitewater experience. Rivers such as the New, the Gauley, the Tygart, the Cheat and the Upper Youghiogheny rank among the most challenging and thrilling river runs in the world. The upper section of the Gauley is a solid Class V, with huge waves and very high water volumes during the October dam release. The Tygart boasts Glens Falls, the most powerful, runnable rapid in the Appalachians. The Upper Yough--a challenging, technical run from top to bottom--is the steepest waterway east of the Rockies.

What makes West Virginia rivers unique are the steep drops, the nonstop rapids and the narrow passages, which require the utmost in boat-handling skill by the guide and careful coordination by the team of paddlers. During the spring run-off and late-season dam releases, rafters will encounter some of the most powerful water flows in the country. All this puts a premium on river skills and safety. It is essential to have first-class equipment (preferably a self-bailing

raft), and expert boatmen to run these rivers at high water levels.

Having fairly short runs--no more than 15 miles or so--most West Virginia rivers are rafted on a day-trip basis only. Some

Cooling off/CHRIS NOBLE

outfitters do offer overnight river tours, but these generally consist of a double run of the same river, or a two-river combination with overnight accommodation in a lodge. Since the West Virginia rafting industry is so competitive, prices have remained quite

Making camp/CHRIS NOBLE

reasonable, considering the quality of the whitewater. A typical day's run on the New or Gauley will cost $75 to $85 per person, including lunch. The Upper Yough may cost a bit more because it is more remote and difficult.

There are numerous good outfitters operating in West Virginia. On the Upper Yough, top choices include Appalachian Wildwaters and North American River Runners. On the New, the Gauley and the Cheat Rivers, Class VI River Runners, and Mountain River Tours are among the best. Contact Class VI River Runners, Ames Heights Road, P.O. Box 78, Lansing, WV 25862-0078, (304) 574-0704; Mountain River Tours, P.O. Box 88, Sunday Road, Hico, WV 25854, (800) 822-1386, (304) 658-5266; North American Riverrunners, Inc., P.O. Box 81, Hico, WV 25854, (800) 950-2585, or (304) 658-5276; USA Whitewater, (Appalachian Wildwaters), P.O. Box 277, Rowlesburg, WV 26425, (800) 872-7238 or (304) 454-2475. For a complete listing of accredited rafting companies, call West Virginia's rafting hotline, (800) 225-5982.

IDAHO

Best of the Rockies

Idaho is North America's premier destination for multi-day river vacations. Boasting many fine rivers--including two of America's best, the Selway and the Salmon Middle Fork--Idaho is an unbeatable river venue for those seeking both exciting whitewater and wilderness solitude.

The Selway

The Selway is Idaho's gem, a waterway of exceptional beauty and diversity. A designated Wild and Scenic River that flows through the Bitterroot Wilderness Area, it is the least crowded and most serene of Idaho's waterways. Thanks to Park Service policies severely limiting use by commercial outfitters, even in peak season you can travel the entire waterway and not see another rafting group. The typical trip on the Selway lasts 4 to 6 days, running a distance of 50 miles or so. After the remote put-in, you descend through steep canyons topped by tree-lined ridges, passing through excellent fishing areas and camping along sandy river banks. The wildlife is as good as you'll find outside of Alaska--elk, moose, bears and large birds of prey. The scenery is pristine and very beautiful; even outfitters who run other rivers concede that rivers don't get any better than the Selway.

The Selway provides excitement via a tight, narrow riverbed that passes 18,000 cubic feet per second of water, with drops as steep as 120 feet per mile. The solitude is guaranteed by US Forest Service regulations that allow only one launch per day. The best times to experience the Selway are June and July when the water is up, but the waterway is so exceptional that you should not hesitate to run the river in late summer or early fall as well.

There are four licensed river guide services on the Selway. All are good, but ARTA and Northwest River Company (NRC) are our top picks. Both are very professional and employ highly skilled guides. Neither offer the super-deluxe amenities and cuisine of Idaho's finest outfitters, such as Holiday River Expeditions and Rocky Mountain River Expeditions, but those who have rafted the Selway with ARTA and NRC have come away impressed--commonly observing that their trip on the Selway was the best vacation they have ever had. Another recommended outfitter with decades of experience is Elwood Masoner of Twin Falls. Masoner pioneered river-rafting in Idaho, and his trips, though hardly lavish, are solid, well-run adventures. Masoner offers oar-boat trips only, unlike ARTA and NRC which can service paddle-rafters as well. Contact ARTA River Trips, Star Route 73, Groveland, CA 95321, (800) 323-ARTA; Northwest River Company, P.O. Box 403, Boise, ID 83701, (208) 344-7119; Elwood Masoner's Whitewater Adventures, 1953 San LaRue, Twin Falls, ID 83301, (208) 733-4548.

The Salmon Middle Fork

After the Selway, the Middle Fork of the Salmon is probably Idaho's finest rafting

Middle Fork of the Salmon, Idaho/CHRIS NOBLE

destination. It has everything that makes a great river--wilderness solitude (it runs through the largest wilderness area in the lower 48 states--over 20,000 square miles), exciting Class III to IV rapids and outstanding wildlife, with big game (bear, lynx, elk) and birds of prey. The water is crystal clear and there are numerous hot springs along the way. Because the Middle Fork flows in a circle, access is convenient; you can take a 6-day journey that starts and finishes near the same point. The voyage begins with a descent down a steep alpine section. For the next 5 days, you will pass spectacular rocky gorges, sandy beaches and hot springs. In the calm stretches there is excellent fishing for rainbow, cutthroat and Dolly Varden trout--among the best in Idaho.

The Middle Fork is an ideal choice for those looking for a luxury rafting holiday. Some of America's finest river outfitters operate on the Middle Fork. Perhaps the best of the bunch is Dave Mills' Rocky Mountain Tours. Along with his wife Sheila, Dave fields a superb operation, with outstanding attention to detail and phenomenal food. Dave runs virtually all his trips himself, ensuring a very high level of quality throughout the season. His boats are first class, and Mills' crew is the most experienced in Idaho (the average age of the boatmen is 40 years). Another outstanding husband and wife operation is Middle Fork Wilderness Outfitters run by Kurt and Gail Selisch. The Selisch's trips cost a bit less than Rocky Mountain's, but the quality level is still very high. One particularly nice feature of the Selisch's trips is that a large "sweep" boat runs the river before the customer boats, arriving at the campsite in time to set everything up before hand. When the rafters pull in at day's end they are greeted with hors d'oeuvres and cocktails. Two other superior, well-established outfitters are Hughes River Expeditions and Sevy Guide Service. Jerry Hughes and Bob Sevy are two of the most knowledgeable guides in Idaho, their trips are always well run, and they treat their customers like family.

A typical trip on the Middle Fork of the Salmon lasts 6 days, except in the early high-water season of June, when most outfitters run 4-day trips. Prices for a full trip on the Middle Fork run between $800 and $1,100 depending on the outfitter. For further information, contact Hughes River Expeditions, P.O. Box 217, Cambridge, ID 83610, (208) 257-3477; Middle Fork Wilderness Outfitters, P.O. Box 2222, Haley, ID 83333, (208) 788-9168; Rocky Mountain River Tours, P.O. Box 2552, Boise, ID 83701, (208)

345-2400; Sevy Guide Service, P.O. Box 24, Stanley, ID 83278, (208) 774-2200.

If fishing is your first love, you should also consider Dave Helfrich Outfitters for a Middle Fork trip. The Helfrich family has decades of experience running the rivers of Oregon and Idaho in classic McKenzie driftboats. Though fairly expensive, Helfrich's Middle Fork trips are acknowledged, even by his competitors, as the very best for serious anglers. Contact Dave Helfrich River Outfitters, 47555 McKenzie Highway, Vida, OR 97488, (503) 896-3786.

THE USSR

Glasnost River Running

Commercial rafting has come of age in the USSR. Westerners can now choose from a variety of Soviet river trips run by experienced North American outfitters. In the past few years, the Soviet Union has become, if not a mainstay of the international rafting scene, an active and vital rafting frontier where vacationers can experience world-class river-running on a host of superb waterways. Here are three of Russia's best.

The Chatkal

The most popular Soviet river, and our pick as the best overall, is the Chatkal. A 2-week journey down the Chatkal combines stunning scenery, remote cultures and the exotic nature of central Asia. A major, fast-flowing Class IV to V river, the Chatkal runs through isolated gorges beneath the Tien Shan mountains, where the borders of the Soviet republics of Uzbekistan, Kirghizia, Kazakhstan and Tadjikistan meet. This is the homeland of Russia's ethnic subgroups, and you'll have plenty of opportunities to meet with local villagers along the route. The journey begins on the turquoise Sandalsh River, a Chatkal tributary which flows through deep canyons of red sandstone. Along the riverbanks nomadic Kirghiz tribesmen live in yurts, tending large herds of horses. After two days of highly technical Class IV rapids, the trip becomes increasingly difficult as it passes through five major gorges with rapids up to Class V. This is a very rewarding trip in all respects. Just don't expect deluxe cuisine, or five-star hotels in the cities. Chatkal trips

Project Raft Siberian Expedition/STEVE GILROY

are offered by Steve Currey Expeditions, P.O. Box 1574, Provo, UT 84603, (800) 937-7238, or (801) 224-6797, (17 days, September, $3,200 land cost), and Mountain Travel/Sobek, (address on p. 229), (800) 227-2384, (15 days, August or September, $4,370 with airfare from New York, or $3,250 land only).

The Obihingou

For those looking for serious whitewater, Russia's Obihingou, one of the most

COURTESY RICHARD BANGS, SOBEK

difficult commercially run rivers in the world, offers all the challenge one could possibly want. This remote and demanding river flows beneath the glacier-clad peaks of the Pamir Range, which tower as high as 24,000'. The trip begins with a helicopter lift to the put-in on the westernmost flanks of the Himalayas. The Obihingou boasts miles of continuous Class IV and V rapids, cutting beneath snow-capped peaks. The countryside is quite beautiful, with alpine meadows and turquoise lakes within easy hiking range of the river.

Currey Expeditions is presently the only western guide service running the Obihingou. As with all Steve Currey's Soviet trips, the Obihingou descent is made jointly by an American team and a group of Soviet rafters. We can't say enough about this feature of Currey's USSR program. Even if the river was not so spectacular, we would recommend this adventure just for the opportunity to share the experience with Russian paddlers. Participants will have a chance to test-drive the Russian catarafts on the river and swap stories around the campfire each evening. The 17-day journeys depart in May with a land cost of $3,200. Travelers' Note: The Obihingou descent is a very rugged and demanding journey. The guides caution that participants should have previous whitewater experience and be prepared to endure extreme weather.

The Katun

For those looking for a kinder, gentler Russian rafting experience, the Katun is a smart choice. Flowing through the remote Siberian hill country, the Katun offers a good blend of exotic cultures, alpine scenery and moderate whitewater, mostly Class III with a few notable Class IV sections. As with the Obihingou, the trip begins with a helicopter flight to the glacial source of the Katun, below 14,000' Mt. Belucha, the tallest peak in the region. According to Sobek, one of the two American outfitters running the Katun, the verdant countryside "comes as a pleasant shock to those who imagine only a Siberia of gulag and tundra."

The rafters will journey over 150 miles through deep, tree-lined canyons, staying in Soviet villages along the way. The Sobek trip commences with a tour of Moscow and other Soviet attractions. Currey meets his clients in Helsinki, and the group visits Leningrad before being transported to the remote put-in by chartered helicopter. Both trips run in July, the best time for clear skies and warm weather. Currey Expedition's Katun trip is priced at $2,900 land cost for 16 days, while the Sobek trip is offered for $3,150 land cost for 15 days, or $4,450 including air from New York.

COSTA RICA

Tropical Rafters' Paradise

Costa Rica is Central America's outdoor playground. Over one-tenth of its interior has been set aside as national parks or wilderness preserves, and the enormous variety of plant and animal species has earned Costa Rica the title "Eden of the Americas." With its tropical climate and reliable winter water levels, Costa Rica makes a great off-season getaway, offering world-class rafting on four major waterways: the Reventazon, the Chirripo, the Rio General and the Pacuare. All these rivers boast lush scenery, abundant wildlife and exciting whitewater.

The Reventazon offers the most challenging rafting in Costa Rica, with numerous major rapids, including the Class V Land of 100 Holes, Burning Rocks and El Horrendo. The river's remarkably steep gradient (it drops over 100 feet per mile in the first three miles) generates back-to-back rapids that test the most expert boatmen. Because the river is dam-controlled, water flow on the Reventazon is consis-

TIM BROWN

tent season to season, allowing good paddling year-round. By contrast, the Chirripo is best in the second half of the year. The Chirripo is considered the most diverse of Costa Rica's rivers, with 50 miles of rapids, waterfalls, lush foliage and a full panoply of exotic fauna, including otters and iguanas.

The Rio General is a good choice for a family vacation, as few of the rapids exceed Class III, and there are many opportunities to explore nearby villages and scenic waterfalls. However, there is still plenty of action. With a gradient of over 50 feet per mile, the Rio General offers close to 100 runnable rapids in a 40-mile stretch.

One of our favorite rivers is the Pacuare. A drop of 60 feet per mile produces continuous challenging rapids over a 2-day run. Very remote, the shores of the Pacuare are prime habitats for jungle wildlife such as tapirs, jaguars, ocelot and South American deer. The Pacuare is considered a Class IV+ river at high water, but it also has many smooth stretches where you can relax and enjoy the beauty of the tropical jungle. Many feel that, overall, the Pacuare

TIM BROWN

offers the best combination of raucous whitewater and jungle scenery in Central America. Sadly, there are plans to dam the Pacuare in the near future.

Generally, the best time to raft the rivers of Costa Rica is the July through December wet season. However, rafting is possible year-round, particularly on the Pacuare and Reventazon. You can run Costa Rica's rivers with a number of reputable outfitters. The leading local company, Rios Tropicales, P.O. Box 472-1200, San Jose, Costa Rica, (011 506) 33 645, has the lowest prices and runs all the top rivers 12 months a year. The major US outfitter, Sobek Expeditions, offers a two-river adventure, running the Pacuare and Reventazon December through June, and the Chirripo and Pacuare from June through December. The 8-day Sobek trips will cost roughly $1,300--land only. Call (800) 227-2384. Another top American company, Nantahala Outdoor Center, offers a multi-river Costa Rica trip every October for both rafters and kayakers.

Contact Nantahala, 41 US 19W, Bryson City, NC 28713, (800) 232-7238.

CHILE

Last Hurrah on the Bio-Bio

Mile for mile, the Bio-Bio is considered by many to offer the finest river experience available anywhere, at any price. This adventure combines outrageous Class V rapids, dramatic scenery, comfortable camping and fine weather. The trip begins deceptively, with easy passages through rolling, open countryside. Then the landscape changes abruptly, as massive granite gorges narrow the river's flow, creating furious Class IV and V rapids, many of which have become legendary: Lava South, Yahoo, Suicide King and One-eyed Jack. During the 8-day descent, rafters will encounter over 100 rapids, but most are fairly short so there is still plenty of time to enjoy the Chilean countryside. The scenery is dramatic and diverse--rugged volcanic peaks, large waterfalls, soft beaches, and lovely alpine lakes that can be reached on a day-hike. Trips run December through early March, the Chilean summer, so conditions are typically sunny and warm.

Along with boat-flipping hydraulics and scenic beauty, a descent of the Bio-Bio offers a rewarding cultural experience. Most Bio-Bio trips feature a day or two exploring the cities of Santiago and Victoria before the group heads up-country to begin the river odyssey. And during the balance of the trip, participants will have a chance to meet a cross-section of Chile's citizens--farmers, cowboys and Indian villagers. The Chileans are warm, curious and friendly, and most participants will remember the cross-cultural friendships they make long after the adrenalin wears off.

If you have dreamed of running the Bio-Bio, don't hesitate. The 1992 expeditions may well be the last ever as the river is threatened with a major dam project. The road is in, and construction has begun. If the project continues on schedule, winter '92-'93 may be the final opportunity to run one of the world's greatest rivers.

A number of outfitters run the Bio-Bio. Our top picks are Steve Currey Expeditions, Sobek Expeditions, and White Magic Unlimited. Steve Currey's operation is first class, with great attention to detail. Sobek is the biggest operation on the Bio-Bio, its guides are excellent, and it provides personalized videos shot by a professional cameraman who accompanies each trip. White Magic's trips are led by ace river guide Jack Morrison, who was on the first descent of the Bio-Bio, and probably knows the river as well as any man alive. Bio-Bio river expeditions run December through March, last 9-13 days and cost roughly $2,300-$2,600 without airfare. A choice of paddle or oar-raft is normally available with advance notice. Contact Steve Currey Expeditions, Inc., P.O. Box 1574, Provo, UT 84603, (800) 937-7238, or (801) 224-6797; Mountain Travel/Sobek, 6420 Fairmont Ave., El Cerrito, CA 95222, (800) 227-2384; or White Magic Unlimited, P.O. Box 5506, Mill Valley, CA 94942, (415) 381-8889; FAX: (415) 383-5232.

The Bio-Bio, Chile/STEVE GILROY

GREAT NORTH AMERICAN RAFTING RIVERS

F OR EACH RIVER LISTED, RAPIDS ARE GRADED I-VI, WITH VI BEING THE MOST DIFFICULT. RAPIDS
gradient represents the average vertical drop of the river per mile. A high gradient is
a good indicator of continuous rapids, although there may also be a series of steep drops
and flat pools. Percentage Whitewater (% WW) indicates the portion of a river trip which
involves some rapids. A Wild and Scenic River (WSR), as classified by the Department of
the Interior, is a pristine wilderness waterway with limited recreational traffic. Note that
river conditions can vary considerably from year to year, and season to season. A river
may be Class III most of the summer, but Class VI and unrunnable during a dam-release
or spring flood. CODES: Wild and Scenic River (WSR); Whitewater (WW); Raft (R);
Motorized Raft (MR); Twin-hulled cataraft (CR); Passenger (P); Guide (G); Kayak option
(KO). River locations are shown on the map on page 239.

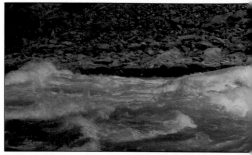

Hermit rapid, Mile 95, Grand Canyon/LIZ HYMANS *This photo was shot with a Fuji Pa...*

RIVER	RAPIDS CLASS/ GRADIENT/ % WW	SCENERY & FEATURES	TRIP MILES/TRIP DAYS/SEASON	RAFT TYPE/# PASSENGERS
ALASKA Tatshenshini/Alsek	I-III/mild/low	Primitive wilderness; wildlife & waterfalls, Elias Mtns., spectacular Glacier Bay on Alsek.	160 miles/11 days/Summer	16' raft, rowing frame/ 5 P+ 2G
Kongacut	I-III/mild/low	High mtns., Arctic Nat'l Wildlife Refuge, caribou migration. 24-hour daylight.	100 miles/10 days/June-July	14' paddle R 4 P + 2G
ARIZONA Colorado (Grand Canyon)	I-VI/9/10%	Awesome scenery; 161 rapids, many huge with steep drops. Canyon is one mile deep, 4-18 miles wide.	Up to 280 miles/6-7 days typical/Mar-Nov	37' pontoon MR /20 P + 2 G 20' oar R, 4P + 2G
CALIFORNIA Kern (Upper & Forks)	IV-V/55-60/65%	Kern Forks has 4,000' cliffs, snow-capped mtn. background. Upper is dry and lightly forested. WSR.	17-20/1-3 days/Apr-Aug	16'-18' paddle R 5-8 P + G
Stanislaus (North Fork)	IV/65/65%	4,000' Sierra forest. Superb scenery in Calaveras Big Trees State Park. Goodwin Canyon option.	10 miles/1-2 days/Apr-June	14'-16' paddle R 5-8 P + G
Toulumne (Upper & Lower)	Up:V/120-200/95% Low:IV/40-60/60%	Upper: steep canyons, rock walls. Lower: rolling hills, wild flowers in spring, ghost towns. WSR.	9 Upper; 18 Lower/ 1-3 days/Mar-Oct	14'-16' oar or paddle R 2-6 P + G
American (North Fork)	III-IV+/50-35/55%	Cliffs, gorge, pine forests. Major waterfall. Middle Fork has tunnel. WSR.	9 or 18 (repeat)/1-2 days/ Apr-May	14'-16' oar or paddle R 5-8 P + G
COLORADO Animas (Upper)	IV-V (VI at very high water)/85/90%	High forested mountains then San Juan desert. Return via Durango/Silverton Railroad.	28/2/Summer	16' CR 4-5 P + G .
Arkansas (Leadville to Canon City)	III-V/100 upper, 55 aver./45%	14,000' peaks. Open and closed canyons. Wild granite formations. Crowded on weekends.	100 (Many run options)/ 1-3 days/May-Sept	14'-16' paddle R KO
Gunnison (Black Canyon Nat'l Mon.)	II-III/25/55%	Put-in at 5,000'; black rock walls. Bighorn sheep, eagles. Xlnt. trout fishing. Horse/hike access only.	14-20/1-3 days/May-Nov	14' paddle or oar R 5-6 P + G; KO
Colorado (Westwater Canyon)	III-IV/NA/25%	Black basalt canyon, historic, remote wilderness, desert canyon trip. Campsites can be crowded.	20-30/2-3 days/May-Aug	16' oar R; paddle R option
Cache La Poudre	II-V/varies/85%	CO's only WSR. Narrow, fast alpine stream, put-in at 7,000', rocky shores. Upper run Class IV-V.	18/1/2-1 day/May-Aug	14'-16' paddle R 4-6 P + G
IDAHO Salmon (Middle Fork)	III-IV/NA/35%	Mountains, rocky gorges, sparse forest, beaches and hot springs. Consider inflatable kayak. WSR.	100/5-6 (or flyout)/June-Sept	14'-18' paddle or oar R 2-6 P + G/Inflatable KO
Salmon (Main)	III-IV/NA/20%	Similar to Middle; slower with fewer hot springs. Blend of smooth stretches and WW. Scenic. WSR.	96/6 days/June-Sept	16' oar R, paddle opt., 4 P + G Inflatable KO; WW Dory
Selway	III-IV/30-50/35%	True wilderness. Remote river put-in. Steep can- yons, narrows with big boulders. Uncrowded. WSR.	48/4-5 days/May-Aug	14'-18' paddle or oar R, 2-4 P Decked Canoe and KO
Snake (Hell's Canyon)	IV-V/10-15/10%	Deeper than Grand Canyon. 10,000' mountains. Slow pools and wild drops. Great fishing. WSR.	32-85/3-6 days/May-Oct	12'-16' paddle or oar R, McKenzie drift boat; WW do...
MAINE Penobscot (West Fork)	IV/60/75%	90' gorge, 12 waterfalls on river, very scenic, views of Mt. Katadin, continuous rapids.	14/1 day/May-Oct	16' paddle R 4-8 P + G
MONTANA Flathead Middle & North	II-IV/22/20%	Stunning alpine wilderness in Glacier Nat'l Park. Moose, elk, bighorn sheep. Fine fishing. WSR.	10-50/1-4 days/May-Sept	14'-18' paddle or oar R 4 P + G
NEW MEXICO Rio Grande	II-IV/NA/50%	Taos and La Junta Box Canyons. Lava Gorge and sandy haul-outs. Indian ruins & petroglyphs. WSR.	18-35/1-3 days/Mar-Sept	14'-16' oar R, 3-4 P + G, paddle R on request
Rio Chama	II-III/8/25%	7,000' forested mountains. Georgia O'Keefe Country--wild southwest.	24-32/2-3 days/May-Aug	12'-16' paddle or oar R 3-6 P + G/Canoe & KO
NEW YORK Moose	IV-V/85 max/50%	Pool and drop; very challenging, technical rapids. Flat, open terrain. Little wildlife.	12/1 day/Apr-May	16' paddle R 4-8 P + G
OREGON North Santiam	III-V/30/50%	Steep canyon, spectacular rock formations beneath fir forest. Narrow chutes and steep drops.	13 /1 day/May-Nov	14' paddle R 6 P + G
Upper Owyhee	III-V/25/25%	Deep, narrow desert canyon. Richly colored rock formations, sandy beaches and warm nights. WSR.	35/3-4 days/Apr-June	14' paddle or oar R 3-4 P + G
Rogue	III-IV/15/20%	A bit of everything. Great scenery, riverside inns, dense forests, fine fishing. Good for families. WSR.	40-45/3-5 days/May-Sept	12'-14' paddle R 16'-18' oar R/inflatable KO
SOUTH CAROLINA Chattooga	III-IV+/30/35-50%	The *Deliverance* river. Remote, mysterious, diverse. Sections 3 and 4 are most scenic. WSR.	10-21 (Sec. 3&4)/1-2 days	16' paddle or oar R 5-8 P + G, KO
TENNESSEE Nolichucky	III-IV/30-60/60%	Dramatic steep-walled gorge, topped by rich forested hills.	8.5/1 day/Mar-July	13' paddle R, 4-6 P + G; low water infl. KO
Ocoee	III-IV/60/85%	Controlled dam-release through Cherokee Nat'l Forest. Summer all week; spring & fall weekends.	5/1-2 days/Apr-Oct	13' paddle R 4-6 P + G

Cost Range	Accommodations	Best Outfitters	Comments	Rating
$1200 (Tat),$1400 (Alsek); + $300-$400 air	wilderness camp	Alaska Discovery, Sobek, Can. River Expeditions	Extraordinary scenery and wildlife: "most beautiful river trip in the world" acc. to Sobek	★★★★★
$1400 + $900 air	wilderness camp	Alaska Discovery	Very dramatic, stark scenery. Abundant wildlife. Fine day-hikes and fishing.	★★★★
$225/day MR $150/day Oar R	luxury camping meals	Adven. West, Colo. River & Trail Exp., Gr. Cnyn. Exp., OARS, Western Riv. Exp.	For big water, awesome scenery, and off-river exploring, the Grand Canyon is the very best.	★★★★★
$100-250 Upper $200-500 Forks	riverside camp deluxe meals	Whitewater Voyages--(800) 448-4238 Kern River Tours	Forks is particularly scenic & challenging. Upper offers many good single day options.	★★★
$100-250	riverside camp quality meals	All-Outdoors, Beyond Limits Adven., Whitewater Voyages	One of the best Sierra short runs. Continuous big rapids. Lower run recently reopened.	★★★
$200 Upper $125-400 Lower	riverside camp deluxe meals	Upper: ARTA, Sierra Mac Lower: ARTA, ECHO	Upper Tuolumne is the "best whitewater in the Sierras" acc. to ARTA. Very exciting.	★★★★
$95-120	riverside camp quality meals	All-Outdoors, ARTA, ECHO, OARS	Very strong river for lots of big rapids. Middle Fork is enjoyable, but not so wild.	★★★
$350	camping railroad ride home	Mountain Waters Peregrine Outfitters--(303) 385-7600	New destination. Big drop and non-stop major rapids. Only 2-day Class V in West.	★★★★
$30 (half-day) $75-190 (1-2 days)	camp or motels and lodges	Dvorak, Adrift Adven., Mad River Rafting	Most popular river run in CO. Royal Gorge section is a "hot" Class V.	★★★
$120 1-day/$250 2-day $415 3-day	wilderness camp deluxe meals	Dvorak, Far Flung Adven., Gunnison River Expeditions	True wilderness adventure. Considered by many to be among top 10 in US.	★★★★
$265-390	riverside camp deluxe meals	Dvorak, Sheri Griffith River Exp.	Steep first stage with thundering continuous WW, followed by float trip out through red rock canyon.	★★★★
$30-70	snack or deluxe lunch	Adrift Adventures	Half-day is good for family. Full day has fast dropping, technical, nonstop rapids--experience required.	★★★
$800-1625 (less with early fly-out)	wilderness camp deluxe meals	ARTA, ECHO, Hughes Riv. Exp., Rocky Mtn. River Tours	Good getaway trip offering fishing, sunbathing and hiking along with WW thrills.	★★★
$650-1000	wilderness camp deluxe meals	ARTA, ECHO, Northwest Dories, River Odysseys, Orange Torpedo	Suitable for family vacation. Wide choice of watercraft. Luxury amenities on most trips.	★★★
$900-1000	wilderness camp deluxe meals	ARTA, Northwest River Co., Elwood Masoner Outfitter	Primitive, remote and unspoiled. Abundant wildlife and good fishing. Back to nature.	★★★★
$490-800	wilderness camp deluxe meals	Northwest Voyagers, Hughes River Exp., River Odysseys West	One of America's great adventures. Hell's Canyon combines stunning scenery with super WW.	★★★★
$80-90	day-trip deluxe lunch	Eastern River Exp., Unicorn Rafting, New Engl. WW Cntr.--(800) 766-7238	Great challenge and enjoyment--rated among top 10 in US. Most technical rapids in East.	★★★★
$50-300	riverside tent camps, dlx. food	Glacier Wilderess Guides, Wild River Adventures	Superlative scenery and wildlife. Mostly smoothwater with early-season Class III & IV.	★★★★ (scen.) ★★ (WW)
$80-265 $760 week	Taos Box day-trip/ overnight forest camp	Dvorak, Far Flung Adv., Sierra Outfitters & Guides	Taos Box trip is an American classic. Continuous rapids up to Class V in spring.	★★★
$200-300	wilderness camp	Dvorak Expeditions, Far Flung Adv., Arkansas River Tours	Good intro river for family vacation, and canoe/kayak training. Warm, sunny.	★★/★★★
$85-95	day-trip restaurant meal	Eastern River Exp., Unicorn Rafting, Adirondack Outfitters--(315) 369-3536	Very exciting, technical rapids in a pleasant, but unspectacular setting. A fine day-trip.	★★★
$75	day-trip with lunch	Take Me Rafting	A great run, which rewards skill and daring. Still relatively unknown, a top Western WW river.	★★★
$400	riverside camp & cabins, hot springs.	Take Me Rafting	Southwest-style rugged wilderness. High excitement & tough WW. Good physical cond. required.	★★★★
$395-600	riverside camp and lodges	ARTA, ECHO, Rogue River Outf., Orange Torpedo	A fine, long weekend choice. Good WW plus creature comforts and multi-sport options.	★★★
$50-70 (1 day) $200 (2 days)	day-trip or overnight river camp	Nantahala Outdoor Center, Wildwater Ltd.--(800) 451-9972	Sec. 3 is moderate, Sec. 4 is one of the most thrilling and difficult of all river runs.	★★★★
$50-60	day-trip with lunch	Nantahala Outdoor Ctr., Appalachian Wildwaters, Wildwater Ltd.	One of the best southern rivers, especially during spring highwater.	★★★/★★★★
$30-40	day-trip no lunch	Nantahala Outdoor Ctr., Appalachian Wildwaters, Wildwater Ltd.	Big waves, constant action. A good, short starter river with lots of rapids.	★★★

RIVER	RAPIDS CLASS/ GRADIENT/% WW	SCENERY & FEATURES	TRIP MILES/TRIP DAYS/SEASON	RAFT TYPE/# PASSENGERS
TEXAS RIO GRANDE (BIG BEND)	II-III/low/low	Massive limestone canyons, 1500' stony cliffs, Chihuahua desert. Easy float trip. Good fishing. WSR.	10-85/1-7/Varies with trip	14'-16' paddle or oar R 3-4 P + G/Canoe option
VIRGINIA RUSSELL FORK	V+/200/90	Steep wooded hills. Back-to-back intense rapids. River runs along Kentucky border.	7/1 day/Sep-Oct	12' paddle R 4 P + G, KO
UTAH GREEN	II-IV/20/20%	Red rock canyons, Indian country, sparse forests, sandy beaches, Dinosaur Nat'l Monument.	42/2-4 days/May-Sept	14'-16' paddle or oar R 5-6 P + G
WASHINGTON KLICKITAT	II-IV/47/90%	Cascade forests to semi-desert. Deep canyons. Rugged, isolated scenery. True wilderness. WSR.	16/1-2 days/May-July	16' paddle R 4-6 P + G
SAUK	III-IV/38/75%	7,000' Cascade Mountains, lush fir forest, much wildlife. WSR.	8.3/1 day/June-Aug	16' paddle R 6-8 P + G
WHITE SALMON	IV/45/80%	Mt. Adams snowmelt. Deep, narrow canyon, lush vegetation. Husum Falls portage. Double run option.	7.2/1 day/June-Aug	16' paddle R 6-8 P + G
WEST VIRGINIA CHEAT	IV-V/26/65%	Mine run-off, orange rocks, scenic spring run-off 7500 cfs, pool and drop. Most rapids in 2nd half.	11/1 day/Mar-July	12-16' paddle R inflatable KO
NEW	III-V/18/50%	Wooded hills, bridges, ghost town. First half mellow, second half rough. Typical Allegheny terrain.	15 or 30/1 or 3 days/Apr-Nov	16' paddle R 6-9 P + G
UPPER GAULEY	III-V+/38/90+%	Canyon, wooded hills. Wild flowers and waterfalls. Almost continuous rapids. Very challenging.	15/1 day/Sep-Oct	16' paddle R 6-9 P + G
UPPER YOUGHIOGHENY	IV-V/115/70%	Rocky gorge beneath wooded hills. Narrow, fast and beautiful. Short pools; very technical and intense.	11/1 day/Apr-Nov	12' paddle R 2-3 + 1 or 2 G
WYOMING NORTH PLATTE	III-IV/25-30/65%	Wilderness forest. 4WD access. Rock canyons, wildlife, fishing.	40+/2-3 days/May-July	12'-16' paddle or oar R, 4-6 P + G
CANADA JACQUES-CARTIER (QUEBEC)	IV/100/60%	Boreal forest, beautiful valley with 3,000' hills. Fine fishing and wildlife.	8/1 day/June-Oct	14'-16' paddle R, 6-8 P + G
KICKING HORSE LOWER CANYON (B.C.)	IV/steep/70%	Narrow, rocky canyon in heart of BC Rockies near Lake Louise. Wild flowers and wild animals.	7/1/Aug-Sep	16' paddle or oar R 6 P + G, (Oar 2 P + G)
ROUGE (QUEBEC)	III-V/35-47/55%	Laurentian hills, upper run has rock gardens, lower boasts big rapids and waterfalls.	8-16/1 or 2 days/June-Oct	14'-18' paddle R, 6-8 P + G, infl. KO
CHILCO/CHILCOTIN (FRASER OPTION) (B.C.)	IV/20/35%	Tremendous variety: canyons, pools, long stretches of WW. Fly-in expedition with 3-river option.	120+/6-11 days/Jun-Sep	22' oar CR with motor on big rapids, 8-12 P + G

TRIP PLANNING

In planning a rafting holiday, you should think carefully about the kind of experience you are looking for. Do you want to paddle, or have a guide row the raft? Do you want mostly gentle sections, or will only the biggest rapids do? Is it important to have continuous whitewater, or will two or three big drops daily suffice? Do you want to cover a lot of distance, or just a few miles a day? How important is sunbathing and general relaxation?

When you contact outfitters, give them your answers to these questions, and they will help select the best river for your interests. In general, rivers in the Northern Rockies offer the longest continuous runs, while California and Oregon rivers are more suited for weekend tours. The best whitewater rivers in the East (Maine, West Virginia) have relatively short but intense runs, with nearly continuous, Class IV-V rapids. One cannot generalize about foreign rivers except to say that they can be the most wild and since they are not run on a regular basis, unexpected conditions can present special challenges.

To help with your planning, you may wish to contact the following organizations:

America Outdoors, *P.O. Box 1348, Knoxville, TN 37901, (615) 524-4814.* (This merges the former Eastern Professional River Guides Association and Western River Guides Association.)

Colorado River Outfitters Association, *P.O. Box 1032, Buena Vista, CO 81211, (719) 395-8949.*

Eastern Canadian River Outfitters Association, *c/o Sean Mannion, Exec. Dir., Quebec City, QUE, Canada, FAX: (418) 848-4562.*

Idaho Outfitters and Guides Association, *P.O. Box 95, Boise, ID 83701, (208) 342-1919.*

BOOKING AGENCIES

In addition to guides' associations there are specialty agencies that book rafting adventures for a variety of outfitters. These services can be quite helpful in finding a raft trip that suits your particular needs. When you contact them, let them know where you want to raft, how many days you want to spend on the river, how much challenge you're looking for (Class I rapids are the easiest, Class V the most dangerous), and how much you want to spend.

High Desert Adventures, *5400 Am. Earhart Drive, Salt Lake City, UT 84116, (800) 345-RAFT.*

All-Outdoors Adventure Trips, *2151 San Miguel Drive, Walnut Creek, CA 94596, (510) 932-8993, or (800) 942-7238 in CA.*

USA Whitewater, *P.O. Box 277, Rowlesburg, WV 26425, (304) 454-2475, or (800) 872-7238.*

West Virginia/KEVIN O'BRIEN

COST RANGE	ACCOMMODATIONS	BEST OUTFITTERS	COMMENTS	RATING
$85-700	riverside campsites	Far Flung Adventures, Dvorak Expeditions	Great southwestern scenery. Relaxing--mostly smooth water. Good wildlife and fishing.	★★★
$170-200	day-trip average meal	Appalachian Wildwaters	One of the wildest short river runs in US. Very tough. Newly offered.	★★★★
$290-700	riverside camp average meals	Adrift Adventures, Sheri Griffith	North section has large waves, many rapids. Lower, Desolation Canyon is mostly smooth; colorful scenery.	★★★
$60-80	day-trip with lunch	Take Me Rafting	New, outstanding river run with great WW, unique wilderness beauty and isolation.	★★★★
$65-90	day-trip with lunch	Orion Expeditions, Downstream Riv. Runners	Scenic wilderness. Challenging WW requires previous river experience. Uncrowded.	★★★
$65-90	day-trip with 2nd run option	Orion Expeditions, Downstream Riv. Runners, Take Me Rafting	Steep gorge requires cable raft launch. Very scenic and challenging. Superb but icy WW.	★★★
$40-70	day-trip with br. & lunch	USA Whitewaters	Varies acc. to water level. With possible boat-flipping hydraulics, previous exp. vital.	★★★
Day: $50-80 3-Day: $250-300	3-day camp or country inn; deluxe meals	Appalachian Wildwaters, Class VI River Runners	Enjoyable, both relaxing and challenging (lower half). Very busy on summer weekends.	★★★
$75-90	day-trip deluxe meal	Appalachian Wildwaters, Eastern River Exp., Class VI River Runners	Crowded on weekends, but worth it. Over 100 rapids. Very exciting. Top 10 day-trip.	★★★★
$110-180	day-trip deluxe meal	Appalachian Wildwaters, Youghiogheny Outfitters	World class, peak experience. Steepest drop east of Rockies. Wild, continuous rapids.	★★★★★
$180 2-day $280 3-day	wilderness camp quality meals	Dvorak Expeditions, Adrift Adventures	River flows north from CO into WY. Northgate (CO) has best WW.	★★★
$45-70	day-trip; dinner BBQ at lodge	New World River Exp., Excur. Jacques-Cartier	Great weekend trip with abundant WW and pretty scenery. Nearby resort facility.	★★★
$85-90	day-trip with steak BBQ	Alpine Rafting Co., Glacier Rafting Co.	Very scenic and challenging. Combo trip options (biking, horseback rides).	★★★★
$65-85	day-trip or over-night river camp	New World River Exp., Eau Vivre Rafting	Upper and lower Rouge are separate day-trips. Lower has best WW. Nearby resort facility.	★★★
$1175 (6 days) $2175 (11 days)	riverside camps deluxe meals	Clearwater Expeditions, Canadian Expeditions	Must be physically fit. Intense rapids for miles. One of Canada's finest outdoor experiences. Superb scenery.	★★★★★

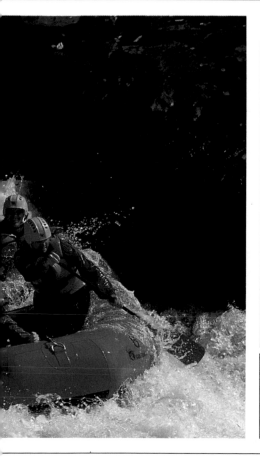

RAFTING RIVERS OF NORTH AMERICA

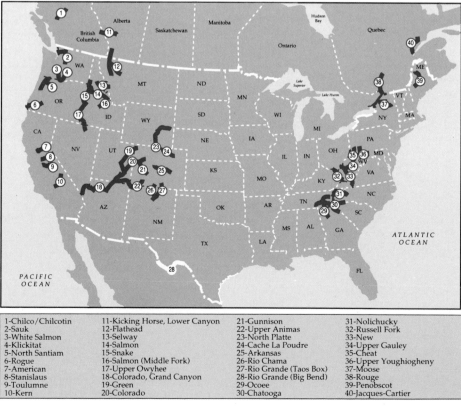

1-Chilco/Chilcotin	11-Kicking Horse, Lower Canyon	21-Gunnison	31-Nolichucky
2-Sauk	12-Flathead	22-Upper Animas	32-Russell Fork
3-White Salmon	13-Selway	23-North Platte	33-New
4-Klickitat	14-Salmon	24-Cache La Poudre	34-Upper Gauley
5-North Santiam	15-Snake	25-Arkansas	35-Cheat
6-Rogue	16-Salmon (Middle Fork)	26-Rio Chama	36-Upper Youghiogheny
7-American	17-Upper Owyhee	27-Rio Grande (Taos Box)	37-Moose
8-Stanislaus	18-Colorado, Grand Canyon	28-Rio Grande (Big Bend)	38-Rouge
9-Toulumne	19-Green	29-Ocoee	39-Penobscot
10-Kern	20-Colorado	30-Chatooga	40-Jacques-Cartier

Recommended Outfitters Worldwide

GOOD ORGANIZATION, SKILLED, PERSONABLE GUIDES AND QUALITY EQUIPMENT are the hallmarks of a top outfitter. On the roughest Class IV to V rivers, state-of-the-art boats are essential. Choose a company that uses modern self-bailing rafts, so you won't struggle through the rapids half-submerged. On longer river tours, particularly those with lengthy flatwater stretches, the interaction between guide and customers is what makes or breaks the trip. Look for a company that employs guides who understand the local history, archaeology and ecology of the river you're running.

We use the following codes: M (Large, motorized raft); O (Oar-raft); P (Paddle-raft); K (Raft-supported kayak trip). Trip durations are listed in days (3,4,5 etc.).

Alaska

■ ALASKA DISCOVERY
369 S. Franklin St., Juneau, AK 99801, (907) 586-1911.
Rivers: Tatshenshini, Alsek, Noatak, Kongacut.
Alaska Discovery is generally regarded as the best wilderness river outfitter in Alaska. It operates multi-day excursions along the major Alaskan rivers plus Discovery Bay. Most trips are flatwater runs, with few rapids. Raft trips average about $100 per day, plus floatplane charges of another $300 or so on longer trips. Rating: ★★★

■ NOVA RIVERRUNNERS OF ALASKA
P.O. Box 1129, Chickaloon, AK 99674, (907) 745-5753.
Rivers: Chickaloon, Talkeetna, Lionshead, Matanushka, Copper.
With 16 years experience, Nova Riverrunners offers 2 to 14-day wilderness excursions ranging from mild (Matanushka), to Class V whitewater on Six-mile Creek. Nova's guides are very skilled and knowledgeable. Rating: ★★

■ SOURDOUGH OUTFITTERS
P.O. Box 90, Bettles, Alaska 99726, (907) 692-5252.
Rivers: Noatak, Kobuk, Alatna, John, Wild River, North Koyukuk, Nigu into Colville, Killik.
Sourdough has run rivers in the Brooks Range area for the past 18 years. Rafting and canoeing can be combined on the same trip. The Noatak is the most popular trip. Rating: ★★

■ SOBEK EXPEDITIONS
P.O. Box 1089, Angels Camp, CA 95222, (800) 777-7939.
Rivers: Alsek, Talkeetna, Tatshenshini.
Unlike many of the large adventure companies, Sobek runs its own Alaskan raft trips, which, though basically float trips, are outstanding. Rating: ★★★

EAST

Maine

■ EASTERN RIVER EXPEDITIONS
P.O. Box 1173, Greenville, ME 04441, (800) 634-7238, or (207) 695-2411.
Rivers: Penobscot, Kennebec, Dead (ME); Moose, Hudson (NY).
Operated by John and Sandy Connelly, Eastern River Expeditions (ERE) has been a mainstay of New England rafting for many seasons. The Penobscot and Kennebec runs are the most popular, with the Penobscot arguably being Maine's most exciting rafting river. ERE also offers kayak trips on most of the rivers it runs. Rating: ★★

■ UNICORN EXPEDITIONS
P.O. Box T, Brunswick, ME 04011, (207) 725-2255.
Rivers: Penobscot, Kennebec, Dead (ME); Moose, Hudson (NY).
Unicorn, with over 10 years of experience, is the other big player in the Maine whitewater industry, offering popular river trips April through October. Unicorn operates two deluxe basecamps where you can unwind after riding the rapids. Rating: ★★★

North Carolina

■ NANTAHALA OUTDOOR CENTER
US19W, Box 41, Bryson City, NC 28713, (704) 488-6900, or (704) 488-2175; FAX: (704) 488-2498.
Rivers: Nantahala, French Broad, Nolichucky, Chatooga, Ocoee, Grand Canyon Colorado, Rio Grande, also Costa Rica and Mexico.
Nantahala is a world leader in river-running, most notably for canoeing and kayaking, although its rafting operations are equally good. Choose from weekend or day-trips on southeastern rivers (the Ocoee or Section 4 of the Chatooga offer the best whitewater), or destination tours throughout North America. Nantahala employs outstanding guides and operates one of the best paddling schools in the country. Nantahala is an obvious first choice for the rivers of Southern Appalachia. Rating: ★★★★

West Virginia

■ CLASS VI RIVER RUNNERS
Ames Heights Road, P.O. Box 78, Lansing, WV 25862-0078, (304) 574-0704.
Rivers: New, Gauley (WV), Rio Grande (TX).
Class VI concentrates on two of the finest West Virginia rivers, the New and the Gauley. For its scenery and big water thrills the New has been called the "Grand Canyon of the East," while the Gauley has been rated one of the 10 best whitewater runs in the world. For maximum thrills, hit the Gauley during the fall dam-release. Class VI maintains its own lodge. Rating: ★★★

■ NORTH AMERICAN RIVER RUNNERS, INC.
Box 81, Hico, WV 25854, (800) 950-2585, or (304) 658-5276.
Rivers: New, Cheat, Gauley (WV), Upper Youghiogheny (MD).
North American River Runners (NARR) offers quality trips at competitive prices, with a wider selection of rivers than Class VI. Thrill-seekers will enjoy the Upper Youghiogheny, a boat-flipping Class V run as challenging as anything in America. NARR uses self-bailing boats,

and offers inflatable kayak trips on the New and Gauley. Rating: ★★★

■ MOUNTAIN RIVER TOURS
P.O. Box 88, Sunday Road, Hico, WV 25854, (800) 822-1386, or (304) 658-5266.

Rivers: New and Gauley.

With 17 years of experience, Mountain River Tours has long been regarded as one of the very best outfitters in West Virginia. The guides are very skilled and most of the larger rafts are self-bailing. Very popular are the $145-$170 Saddle and Paddle trips combining horse-riding with 1 or 2 days on the river. Day-trips start at $65. Rating: ★★★

■ USA RAFT (APPALACHIAN WILDWATERS, ROUGH RUN EXPEDITIONS)
P.O. Box 277, Rowlesburg, WV 26425, (304) 454-2475, or (800) 872-7238.

Rivers: Cheat, Gauley, New, Tygart (WV), Upper Youghiogheny, Potomac (MD), Nolichucky, Ocoee (TN), French Broad, Nantahala (NC), Russell Fork (KY).

USA Whitewater represents a variety of quality outfitters, such as Appalachian Wildwaters and Rough Run Expeditions, which collectively run a dozen rivers in the Southeast. One call can arrange any kind of river experience from family float trips to advanced, steep creeks. The most popular rivers are the New, Gauley, Nolichucky, Upper Yough and Cheat, all classic whitewater runs, some rated as high as Class V. Most rafts are self-bailing, and the guides are excellent. Rating: ★★★ to ★★★★

NORTHWEST

Idaho

■ Hughes River Expeditions
P.O. Box 217, Cambridge, ID 83610, (208) 257-3477.

Rivers: Salmon (Middle and Lower Fork), Snake (Hell's Canyon), Owyhee, Bruneau Canyonlands.

Hughes River Expeditions is a small family-run operation, and owner Jerry Hughes still guides most of the trips himself. Those in the know say Hughes' trips on the Middle Fork of the Salmon and Snake River/Hell's Canyon are among the very best in all respects---guides, food, equipment and service. A 3-day trip costs about $580, and longer trips run roughly $180 per day per person. Rating: ★★★★

■ MIDDLE FORK WILDERNESS OUTFITTERS
P.O. Box 2222, Haley, ID 83333, (208) 788-9168.

River: Salmon Middle Fork.

Middle Fork Wilderness Outfitters runs excellent 4 to 6-day trips on the Salmon Middle Fork. The tours cover 105 miles, with 80 major rapids, a quarter of which are Class IV. Husband and wife team Kurt and Gayle Selisch run all the trips themselves, providing first-class service, new self-bailing rafts and top-quality food. On every trip a large gear boat precedes the paddlers downriver. When the rafters arrive at day's end, they are greeted with hors d'oeuvres and cocktails. Kurt really knows the history and ecology of the region. Trips cost $850-$1,050. Rating: ★★★

■ NORTHWEST RIVER COMPANY
P.O. Box 404, Boise, ID 83701, (208) 344-7119.

River: Selway.

Run by Doug Tims, President of the Idaho River Guides Association, and Mike McLeod, the North-west River Company is a solid choice for Idaho's Selway, a Wild and Scenic River that combines exciting rapids, unspoiled wilderness and superb scenery. Access to the Selway is more tightly controlled than other Idaho rivers, making this the perfect destination if want to spend your vacation in solitude, not dodging other rafters. Rating: ★★

■ RIVER ODYSSEYS WEST
P.O. Box 579, Coeur D'Alene, ID 83814, (800) 451-6034.

Rivers: Salmon (Middle & Main), Snake, Lochsa, Owyhee.

River Odysseys West runs virtually all the major Idaho rivers. The Salmon River trips are ideal for first-timers, while the Lochsa River expedition offers almost continuous Class IV and V rapids. Both oar and paddle-rafts are available, and you can switch from one to the other during the trip. Programs range from $60 day-trips to $1,000 6-day tours. Food and service are average. Rating: ★★

■ ROCKY MOUNTAIN RIVER TOURS., INC.
P.O. Box 2552, Boise, ID 83701, (208) 345-2400.

Rivers: Salmon (Middle Fork).

CHRIS NOBLE

A family operation with a 16-year track record, Rocky Mountain River Tours is renowned for its fabulous cuisine and great guides. This is a superb small company that has earned rave reviews from past customers. The crew is the most experienced in Idaho, the boatmen averaging 40 years of age. Sheila Mills' cooking is legendary. Trips run from June through September each year, and cost $745 for 4 days, $1,145 for 6 days. June's high water means maximum whitewater excitement, but kids and older folks should go later in the season. Definitely book well in advance. Rating: ★★★★★

■ SEVY GUIDE SERVICE, INC.
P.O. Box 24, Stanley, ID 83278, (208) 774-2200.

Rivers: Salmon (Middle, Lower).

Even his competitors will tell you that Bob Sevy runs one of the best river operations in Idaho. The trips are well organized, and run by responsible, friendly guides who make every trip memorable. Almost all of Sevy's business comes from repeat customers and referrals, testimony to his operation's quality. Rating: ★★★★

■ ORANGE TORPEDO TRIPS
P.O. Box 1111, Grants Pass, OR 97526, (800) 635-2925, or (503) 479- 5061.

Rivers: North Umpqua, Rogue (OR), Salmon, (Main & Lower, ID), Lower Klamath (OR), Grand Canyon (CO).

Orange Torpedo pioneered commercial duckie (inflatable kayak) trips and now is a major force in the river industry, chalking up over 100,000 paddle miles each year on Class II and III waterways. Orange Torpedo maintains a fine lodge on the Klamath for those who want real comfort after a day on the river. Most river trips don't offer ultimate whitewater thrills, but they make fine intros to solo paddling, and good family vacations. Rating: ★★★

■ TAKE ME RAFTING
P.O. Box 1330, Springfield, OR 97477, (800) 524-9977, or (503) 741-2780.

Rivers: Owyhee, Grande Ronde (ID/OR), Deschutes, McKenzie, Rogue, Minam, John Day, North Umpqua, Upper Klamath (OR), White Salmon, Klickitat (WA), Cal. Salmon, Klamath (CA).

With 18 years of experience, Take Me Rafting (formerly Sierra Whitewater) provides some of the most exciting rafting on the west coast, including the Class V Upper Klamath, Upper North Santiam, and California Salmon. It has first-rate boatmen and offers more tours on more rivers than any other Oregon outfitter. All things considered, you won't find a better rafting company in the Pacific Northwest. Prices are moderate. Rating: ★★★★

Washington State

■ DOWNSTREAM RIVER RUNNERS
12112 NE 195th, Bothell, WA 98011, (800) 732-7238 (in WA), or (206) 483-0335.

Rivers: Klickitat, Methow, Sauk, Skykomish, Suiattle, Tieton, Wenatchee, White Salmon, Noosack, Green (WA), Grande Ronde, Owyhee (OR).

The rivers of Washington may be the best kept secret in the rafting world. Rivers such as the Klickitat and White Salmon offer exciting rapids in pristine wilderness settings. Most of the runs are fairly short, however, eight to 12 miles on average. Downstream is a very professional operation with an 18-year spotless safety record. All guides are certified in swiftwater rescue. Most rafts are self-bailing. Prices average $60-$80 per day. Rating: ★★★

■ ORION EXPEDITIONS, INC.
1516 11th Avenue, Seattle, WA 98122, (800) 553-7466, or (206) 322-9130.

Rivers: Methow, Sauk, Skagit, Skykomish, Tieton, Wenatchee, White Salmon (WA), Middle Salmon (ID), Deschutes (OR).

Orion offers the full spectrum of river-running, from gentle floats to serious whitewater. The Sauk has the liveliest stretch of runnable whitewater in Washington, while the Skykomish offers natural beauty and a great run beneath Mt. Index. The roller coaster Wenatchee is the most popular run, with continuous Class III conditions. Orion has 14 years of experience and uses quality equipment. Orion's guides tend to be older and more experienced than Downstream's boatmen. Rating: ★★★

Class IV action, West Virginia/KEVIN O'BRIEN

Montana

■ GLACIER WILDERNESS GUIDES
P.O. Box 535Y, West Glacier, MT 59936, (800) 521-7238, or (406) 888-5333.

Rivers: Flathead (North and Middle Fork).

The Flathead, which runs through some of the most impressive scenery in North America, is the specialty of Glacier Wilderness Guides, a family operation based near Glacier National Park. The 1 to 4-day trips offer excellent fishing and wildlife-viewing opportunities. What makes these trips really special, however, is owner/guide Randy Gayner, whose knowledge of the Glacier Park region's ecology and fauna is without peer. Late spring is best for whitewater. Rating: ★★

■ WILD RIVER ADVENTURES
P.O. Box 272, West Glacier, MT 59936, (406) 442-7809.

Rivers: Flathead (North and Middle Fork).

You'll find exceptional scenery and serenity (albeit few rapids) on Wild River Adventures' 1 to 3-day trips in the Glacier National Park region, along the US-Canadian border. Three-day trips featuring great food, prime fishing and wildlife galore cost $250 per person. Rating: ★★

SOUTHWEST

Arizona

■ ADVENTURES WEST, INC.
P.O. Box 9429, Phoenix, AZ 85068, (800) 828-WEST, or (602) 493-1558.

Rivers: Grand Canyon Colorado (M; 3,6).

With over 30 years of experience, Adventures West is one of the premier motorized raft operators on the Colorado. The quality of the food and service is well above average, and its rafts are more comfortable and less crowded than most on the river. The prices--$1,100 for 6 days, $535 for 3 days--are a good 15 percent less than you might pay with other companies. Overall, Adventures West simply tries harder than some other operations, and this attitude has paid off. Book well in advance. Rating: ★★★★

■ ARIZONA RAFT ADVENTURES, INC.
4050 E. Huntington, Flagstaff, AZ 86004, (800) 786-RAFT.

Rivers: Grand Canyon Colorado (M,O,P,K; 6,8,9,13,14). Also Costa Rica and Idaho.

Arizona Raft Adventures (AzRA) is a major Grand Canyon concessionaire that is used by a number of other companies which market Colorado river trips. While AzRA runs mostly motor trips, it is also offers more paddle-raft and kayak support trips on the Grand than just about anybody. Rating: ★★★

■ CANYONEERS, INC.
P.O. Box 2997, Flagstaff AZ 86003, (602) 526-0924, or (800) 525-0924 .

Rivers: Grand Canyon Colorado (M,O,K; 1,3,4,7,14).

One of the pioneers of Grand Canyon rafting, Canyoneers has been operating on the Colorado since 1936. Grand Canyon trips are offered on both oar-boats (17' and 22') and large (37') motorized rafts. Canyoneers' river trips are quite good, but the cuisine is less than the best, and much of the equipment has seen better days. Canyoneers runs a lot of trips, however, so you have a good chance of getting a place, even late in the season. Rating: ★★

■ GRAND CANYON DORIES
George Wendt or John Vail, P.O. Box 216, Altaville, CA 95221, (209) 736-0805.

Rivers: Grand Canyon Colorado (O,Dory,K; 5-13,15-18,20).

Purists argue that the best way to run the Grand Canyon is in classic wooden dories. The overall pace is leisurely, but the action in the major rapids (see the photo on page 6) is wet and wild to say the least. Grand Canyon Dories (GCD) has been running the best trips of this kind for years. Itineraries range from 5 days to 3 weeks at a cost of roughly $150 per day including food. (GCD is listed as an Arizona outfitter because it runs only the Grand Canyon.) Rating: ★★★

Colorado

■ ADRIFT ADVENTURES OF COLORADO, INC.
1816 Orchard Place, Ft. Collins, CO 80521, (800) 824-
0150, or (303) 493-4005.

Rivers: Yampa (Dinosaur), Green (UT), Dolores, Gunnison, North Platte, Arkansas, Cache La Poudre.

Unlike the mass amphibious assaults of some companies, Adrift Adventures runs small trips that manage to preserve the serenity of the backcountry. The Yampa trip is a true wilderness journey on Colorado's last free-flowing river. The Gunnison is a good fishing river, with little tourist traffic. For serious whitewater, try the upper Cache La Poudre, a Wild and Scenic River that is Class V at high water. Raft-supported kayak trips are also offered. Sample prices: Yampa 5-day $490; Green 4-day $420; Gunnison 2-day $195. Rating: ★★★★

■ DVORAK'S KAYAK AND RAFTING EXPEDITIONS
17921-S Highway 285, Nathrop, CO 81236, (719) 539-6851, or (800) 824-3795.

Rivers: Arkansas, Dolores, Gunnison, North Platte, Green (UT), Rio Grande and Rio Chama (NM), Salmon (ID), Grand Canyon Colorado (AZ).

Dvorak's Expeditions, a husband and wife team, is one of the premier river outfitters in the business, and its trips down the Arkansas, Gunnison and Dolores are the standard of the industry. A 3-day raft trip begins at $290. One unique offering is a 5-day rafting, mountain biking and horse-packing package program for $555 (Arkansas River). Weeklong trips are offered on the Salmon and Colorado. Prices subject to change. Rating: ★★★★

■ MAD RIVER RAFTING
P.O. Box 650, Winter Park, CO 80482, (800) 451-4844, or (303) 726-5290.

Rivers: Upper Colorado float, Arkansas (Browns Canyon, Texas Creek, and Royal Gorge).

There are more than 20 outfitters on the Arkansas, but you won't go wrong with Mad River. It employs full-time professional guides, and uses high-tech, self-bailing rafts. The best time to run the Arkansas is late May through June. During high water, the Royal Gorge run offers the best rapids on the Ark--Class IV to V. Families will enjoy floating the upper Colorado, a dam-controlled river with good water all season. Rating: ★★

■ MOUNTAIN WATERS
P.O. Box 2681, Durango, CO 81302, (800) 748-2507, or (303) 259-4191.

Rivers: Upper and Lower Animas, Piedra.

Mountain Waters is a small, family operation, but it runs two great rivers, the Upper Animas, the only 2-day Class V run in the Rockies, and the Class IV Piedra, one of the undiscovered jewels of American rafting. These are very serious rivers; customers must have prior river-running experience and a swimming test is mandatory for the Upper Animas. Owner Casey Lynch uses high-tech catarafts and modern 14' self-bailers. Cost is $350 for 2 days on the Upper Animas, including transport on the Durango-Silverton Railroad to and from the river. Peak water flow is mid-June for the Animas, mid-May for the Piedra. Rating: ★★★

■ ROCKY MOUNTAIN OUTDOOR CENTER
10281 Highway 50, Howard, CO 81233, (800) 255-5784, or (719) 942-3214.

Rivers: Arkansas (Brown's Canyon, Parkdale, Royal Gorge, Upper Canyons), Dolores.

Rocky Mountain Outdoor Center (RMOC) is our favorite outfitter on the Arkansas. Its guides are personable and very skilled, and it uses new, high-quality boats. For non-stop major rapids, we recommend the Royal Gorge section or the Upper Canyons, which are run only at high water in the spring. Inflatable kayaks are offered on the easier sections of the Ark. Rating: ★★★

Texas

■ FAR FLUNG ADVENTURES
P.O. Box 377, Terlingua, TX 79852, (800) 359-4138, or (915) 371-2489.

Rivers: Salt (AZ), Arkansas, Gunnison (CO), Rio Chama and Rio Grande Gorge (NM), Big Bend and Lower Canyons (TX).

Far Flung Adventures offers a diverse range of river experiences, from Class IV whitewater on the Rio Grande Gorge to gentle floats in Big Bend National Park. The guides are all experienced boatmen and talented cooks. Modern self-bailing rafts are used on the whitewater runs. We recommend Far Flung's specialty programs--photo workshops, naturalist workshops and music trips. Rating: ★★★

■ BIG BEND RIVER TOURS
P.O. Box 317, Terlingua, TX 79852, (800) 545-4240.

Rivers: Rio Grande (TX), Usumacinta (Mexico).

With 12 years of experience, Big Bend is Far Flung Adventure's main competition on the Rio Grande. Specialty gourmet, naturalist, and photo trips are popular, and a combo raft/horseback trip is available. Big Bend provides raft support and outfitting for canoeists. Rating: ★★

Utah

■ COLORADO RIVER & TRAIL EXPEDITIONS
P.O. Box 57575, Salt Lake City, UT 84157, (800) 253-7328, or (801) 261-1789.

Rivers: Colorado (Grand Canyon M,O,P,K; 3,5,6,8,13; Cataract & Westwater Canyons); Green (Desolation Canyon); Also Alaska.

David Mackay's Colorado River & Trail Expeditions (CRTE), now in its 21st season, is one of the top five outfitters for the Grand Canyon. A small, family-run business, CRTE offers better service and prices than most of its high-volume competitors, plus less-crowded motor rafts. CRTE also offers some of the best oar and paddle-raft journeys on the Colorado. CRTE stresses personal service and quality as the bottom line, as opposed to hauling the maximum number of customers. CRTE's boatmen are among the best. Rating: ★★★★

■ GRAND CANYON EXPEDITIONS COMPANY
P.O. Box 0, Kanab, UT 84741, (800) 544-2691.
Rivers: Grand Canyon Colorado (M,O; 8,14).

Mike Denoyer's Grand Canyon Expeditions (GCE) is not one of the biggest operations on the Grand, but it is one of the best. This is an owner-operated business and the attention to detail really shows. Denoyer employs great guides, and customers can request a boatman with special expertise in photography, geology, archaeology or other outdoor science. Though options are limited--there is basically one full-river itinerary, either 8 days for motor or 2 weeks for oar-boat--GCE's program is clearly a top choice for the Grand. Rating: ★★★★

■ SHERI GRIFFITH RIVER EXPEDITIONS
P.O. Box 1324, Moab, UT 84532, (800) 332-2439, or (801) 259-8229.

Rivers: Colorado (Cataract, Westwater Canyons), Green (UT).

Sheri Griffith, three-time President of the Western River Guides Association, offers excellent raft and canoe trips on Utah's most scenic rivers. Particularly recommended are Griffith's Cataract Canyon and Westwater Canyon trips on the Colorado River, and the Desolation Canyon trip on the Green River. Both trips feature moderate rapids, great scenery, and truly superb food. In business 21 years, Griffith runs a solid program overall, although the equipment could be more modern. Rating: ★★★

■ HOLIDAY RIVER EXPEDITIONS
544 East 3900 South, Salt Lake City, UT 84107, (800) 624-6323, or (801) 266-2087 in UT.

Rivers: Colorado, Green, Yampa, San Juan (UT), Salmon (Main & Lower), Lochsa, Snake (ID).

River guides Dee and Sue Holladay offer very high-quality wilderness raft trips on the Green and Colorado Rivers in Utah, and also in Idaho. This is an outstanding operation in all respects. Holiday's highly-rated 1 to 6-day trips average about $130 per day. This is above average, but the trips are superb, with skilled boatmen, excellent food and great attention to detail. This company sets the standard for professionalism in the river industry. Something for everyone is offered--from rugged big-water runs to gentle family floats. Rating: ★★★★★

■ WESTERN RIVER EXPEDITIONS
7258 Racquet Club Drive, Salt Lake City, UT 84121, (800) 453-7450, or (801) 942-6669 in UT.

Rivers: Colorado (Grand, Cataract Canyon, Westwater Canyon) (M,O; 3,4,6,12), Green.

Western River Expeditions (WRE) is the nation's largest rafting company, and has over 35 years of experience on the Grand Canyon. It uses big J-Rig motor-rafts, the best craft for negotiating the Colorado's major rapids. WRE offers a range of itineraries, but we recommend the full-river trip if you can afford it. WRE's boatmen, trip organization, and cuisine are superior. Most trips begin with a helicopter flight, and WRE maintains its own lodge atop the Canyon Rim. For a Grand Canyon motor trip, WRE is an excellent choice. However, WRE packs a lot of people into its boats, and the pace on the 6-day trip is a bit hurried. Rating: ★★★

California

■ ARTA RIVER TRIPS
Star Route 73, Groveland, CA 95321, (800) 323-ARTA.

Rivers: American, Tuolumne, Merced, Salmon (CA); Klamath, Illinois, Rogue, Umpqua (OR); Yampa (CO); Green (UT); Salmon and Selway (ID).

Since 1963, ARTA has been one of the country's finest rafting companies. ARTA selects guides not only for their whitewater skills, but also their knowledge of wilderness ecology and geology. This is a class operation with great boatmen, and good prices to boot. ARTA is probably the best outfitter on the Selway, (see pages 231-232). Custom trips can be arranged for experienced paddlers. Rating: ★★★★

■ BEYOND LIMITS ADVENTURES
P.O. Box 215, Riverbank, CA 95367, (800) 234-RAFT in CA, or (209) 529-7655 elsewhere.

Rivers: American, New, Salmon, Scott, Stanislaus (3 Forks), Trinity, Yuba (3 Forks) (CA).

Beyond Limits, a great small outfitter, runs some of the most exciting rivers in the country. The Wild Plum section of the Yuba offers non-stop Class IV to V rapids for nine solid miles. The scenic New River is a supreme test of paddling skills--technical, with serious Class V drops. Beyond Limits also offers many moderate 1 and 2-day trips, such as the Stanislaus, suitable for families. Water levels are best in late spring, so book early. Rating: ★★★

■ ECHO: THE WILDERNESS Co.
6529 Telegraph Ave., Oakland, CA 94609, (800) 652-ECHO in CA, or (510) 652-1600.

Rivers: Salmon (ID), Rogue (OR), Tuolumne, American (CA). (All both raft and kayak support.)

ECHO boasts top-quality equipment, very good food, and some of the best guides in the business. Prices range from $405 for a 3-day trip on Oregon's Rogue river to $1,625 for a 12-day Salmon River expedition. Specialty programs (naturalist trips, photo tours) are first class. Many regard ECHO as the best operation in California. Rating: ★★★★

Catarafting the Class IV-V Payette, Idaho/SCOTT SPIKER

O.A.R.S., INC.

P.O. Box 67, Angels Camp, CA 95222, (209) 736-2924, or (209) 736-4677.

Rivers: Colorado (O,P,K; 5,6,9,13); Cal. Salmon, American, Kern, Merced, Tuolumne, Upper Klamath (CA); Main and Middle Fork Salmon, Snake, Selway (ID); Rogue (OR); Snake to Grand Teton (WY); Dolores, Green, Yampa, San Juan (UT).

Now in its 20th year, O.A.R.S. is a major player in the rafting industry. O.A.R.S.' guides, service and cuisine have earned high praise from its customers, although some trips can be crowded. The O.A.R.S. staff does a good job of helping you plan the ideal river vacation, from a family float on Oregon's Rogue to a high-adrenaline outing on the Class V Tuolumne. O.A.R.S. works with Holiday Expeditions in Utah, and offers dory trips on many western rivers with Grand Canyon Dories. Rating: ★★★★

WHITEWATER VOYAGES

P.O. Box 20400, El Sobrante, CA 94820, (800) 488-7238.

Rivers: American (All Forks), Cal. Salmon, Kern (All Forks), Upper and Lower Klamath, Merced, N. Fork Stanislaus, Tuolumne, Trinity (Burnt Ranch Gorge), Yuba (All Forks).

Now in its 16th year, Whitewater Voyages (WWV) runs more trips on more rivers than any other California outfitter. WWV offers everything from Class V white-knuckle runs (Cherry Creek or Giant Gap) to specialty family trips on the lower Klamath(kids under 16 go for half price). Equipment is state-of-the-art, with new boats every season. While not all of the guides are seasoned veterans, most are quite good and a third are EMTs and/or Swiftwater Rescue certified. The food is first rate, and prices are moderate, starting at $85 per day. The most popular river is the Kern, just 3 hours from Los Angeles. Rating: ★★★

FOREIGN RAFTING

Africa and Asia

STEVE CURREY EXPEDITIONS, INC.

P.O. Box 1574, Provo, UT 84603, (800) 937-7238, or (801) 224-6797.

Destinations: China/Tibet (Upper Yangtse).

Veteran river guide Steve Currey pioneered rafting on the mighty Yangtse, and we wouldn't consider using anyone else on this potentially dangerous river. (Sobek and other companies contract with Currey in China.) The June trips last 3 weeks and cost $6,000. About 10 days is spent rafting, with balance spent visiting Chinese cities and cultural sites. Rating: ★★★★

MOUNTAIN TRAVEL/SOBEK

(Address on page 360), (800) 227-2384.

Destinations: *(Africa)*--Ethiopia (Omo), Tanzania (Rufiji), Zambia (Zambezi); *(Asia)*--China (Min, Dadu), Tibet (Tsangpo), Nepal (Sun Khosi), Indonesia (Alas), Papua New Guinea (Watut).

Sobek's African river trips are some of the most unique and rewarding adventures in the world. You can read about the Zambezi on pages 228-29; see our Safari Chapter for a review of the Omo River trip. Sobek offers a wide selection of Asian rivers, some run by its own guides, some by other outfitters. There are challenging Class IV rapids on the Dadu, while the Min offers Grand Canyon-scale standing waves. The Tsang Po trip takes paddlers deep into central Tibet. Sobek's China trips run 18 to 21 days, and average about $4,500. Descents of the exotic

Alas and Watut are world-class Sobek exclusives. Rating: ★★★ to ★★★★, depending on guide used.

WHITE MAGIC UNLIMITED

P.O. Box 5506, Mill Valley, CA 94942, (415) 381-8889.

Destinations: China (Dadu, Min, Tsan Tao Pai, Er Dao Chiang), India (Tons), Nepal (Sun Khosi, Tamur, Trisuli, Seti, Karnali), Tibet (Tsang Po), Costa Rica (Pacuare, Reventazon, Generale, Chirripo), Guatamala (Cahabon, Usumacinta), Chile (Bio-Bio).

White Magic runs many of the world's most exotic rivers. White Magic is used by Sobek and Overseas Adventure Travel in Nepal and China, and no American outfitter has more experience in the Asian sphere. White Magic's trips are hard to top for serious whitewater, combined with exotic cultures. We recommend the Tamur in Nepal, the Tons in India, and the Bio-Bio in Chile. (White Magic has an extensive program in Latin America.) Rating: ★★★

Canada

ALPINE RAFTING COMPANY/ MOUNTAIN TOURS

P.O. Box 1409, Golden, BC, Canada V0A 1H0, (800) 663-7080, (604) 344-5016 in Canada.

Destinations: Kicking Horse, Illecillewaet Rivers, Blaeberry.

Golden BC is the center of Canadian whitewater rafting, and Alpine is the top operator in this scenic part of the Rockies. The Kicking Horse is a Class III-IV run that made it onto our top 40 list. Rating: ★★★

CANADIAN RIVER EXPEDITIONS

3524 W. 16th Avenue, Vancouver, BC, Canada V6R 3C1, (604) 738-4449.

Destinations: Chilcotin, Fraser (BC), Tatshenshini/Alsek (BC/Yukon/Alaska), Firth (Yukon).

Canadian River Expeditions (CRE) offers some of the most spectacular river runs in the world. Sections of the Chilco/Chilcotin rival the Grand Canyon for big water excitement, and the Tatshenshini/Alsek is the ultimate, far northern float trip. On the Firth trip you can observe the caribou migration. CRE has very skilled guides and decades of experience. Rating: ★★★★

CLEARWATER EXPEDITIONS

613 Bissette, Kamloops, BC, Canada V2B 6L3, (604) 674-3354, or (604) 579-8360 in Kamloops.

Destinations: Clearwater, Thompson, Chilco/Chilcotin (BC).

The Clearwater and Thompson are excellent day-trip rivers with lovely scenery and powerful rapids. If you live in the Northwest, it is worth crossing the border to sample these runs. Clearwater Expeditions is very experienced, and its prices are quite reasonable. Rating: ★★★

NEW WORLD RIVER EXPEDITIONS

2360 Rouge River Road, Calumet, QUE, Canada J0V 1B0, (800) 361-5033, or (819) 242-7238.

Destinations: Jacques-Cartier, Rouge, Batiscan Rivers (Quebec).

There is plenty of great whitewater in eastern Canada, though you are limited to short day-trips or overnighters. Good water flow allows long seasons, and many runs finish at cozy lodges where you can enjoy fishing, hiking or canoeing. New World runs two of the best short rivers in Quebec. Rating: ★★

Europe

ATALANTE

36/37 Qual Arloing, 69009 Lyon, France, (011 33) 78 64 16 16; FAX: (011 33) 78 64 60 62, or 72 00 96 33.

Destinations: France (8 rivers), Austria, Turkey (also Canada, Morocco, Nepal, Zimbabwe).

Atalante is the number one French rafting company, a very experienced outfitter with world-class

Hermit Rapid, Grand Canyon/LIZ HYMANS

guides and operations around the globe. Write for a full catalog, or contact Mountain Travel/Sobek (800) 227-2384, which can book trips with Atalante on request. Rating: ★★★

FASZINATOUR MAGERBACH

1, A-6425 Haiming, Tirol, Austria, (011 43) 52 66 81 88; FAX: (011 43) 52 66 83 11.

Destination: Austria.

Faszinatour is one of Austria's leading adventure companies, offering half-day to weeklong river adventures on the glacier-fed rivers of the Tirol. Day-trips run about $80 US, while overnight excursions cost about $120 per day, including indoor lodging. Rafting can be combined with rock-climbing and mountain biking. Rating: ★★

■ **Norwegian Wildlife & Rafting (NWR)**
2655 Heidal, Norway, Phone/FAX: (011 47) 66 38727 (summer), (011 47) 62 38727 (winter).

Destinations: 8 major rivers in Norway.

NWR, the leading rafting service in Northern Europe, offers 1 to 4-day runs on eight wilderness rivers, rated Class II to V. NWR has great boats (new self-bailers and catarafts), and was the first in Norway to run Class V rivers commercially. The scenery can be stunning. Be ready for steep, steady gradients and icy water, even in summer. Rating: ★★★

■ Both **Steve Currey Expeditions**, (800) 937-7238, and **Sobek Expeditions**, (800) 227-2384, have extensive Soviet Union rafting programs, described on pages 367-68. Earth River runs the Katun, Bashkaus/

Chulishman, Chatkal, Murgab and Obihingou, while Sobek runs the Katun, Rioni and Chatkal. Sobek offers rafting on Turkey's superb Class IV Çoruh.

Mexico

■ **Dvorak's Kayak and Rafting Expeditions**
(address on p. 242), (800) 824-3795.

Destinations: Mexico (Rio Jatate, Rio Usumacinta).

The Jatate and Usumacinta, both great rivers, are profiled in our canoe and kayak chapter. Either makes for an exotic and memorable tropical vacation. The Jatate is the better whitewater river, while the Usu offers Mayan temples and the world's second largest rainforest. Rating: ★★★★

■ **Far Flung Adventures**
(address on p. 242), (915) 371-2489.

Destinations: Mexico (Yucatan), (Rio Antigua, Rio Usumacinta).

Far Flung Adventures enjoys a strong reputation in the industry, and its Mexican river trips have been among its most popular. Customer satisfaction has been very high. Rating: ★★★

■ **Slickrock Adventures**
P.O. Box 1400, Moab, UT 84532, (801) 259-6996.

Destinations: Mexico (Rios Jatate, Usumacinta, Chancala--kayak only).

See our canoe and kayak chapter for a description of Slickrock's trips on the Jatate and Usumacinta. Slickrock's owner is a talented river guide with a vast knowledge of the culture and ecology of the Mexican jungle interior. These trips are highly recommended. Rating: ★★★

Pacific

■ **Raging Thunder**
P.O. Box 1109, Cairns, 4870 Queensland, Australia, (011 61) 70 311 466, or 70 514 911 (reservations).

Destinations: Tully, Barron, and North Johnstone rivers, Queensland.

If you're in Cairns, take a day or two to run a river with Raging Thunder. The Class II-III Tully is the most popular trip, and this $95 (Australian) day-trip offers nice drops with great rainforest scenery. Raging Thunder produces custom videos of its daily Tully trips. For jungle sun-worshiping, check out the 5 to 7-day journey down the North Johnstone, ($660-$810 Australian). Rating: ★★

■ **Danes Shotover Rafts**
P.O. Box 230, Queenstown, New Zealand, (011 64) 3 4427-318; FAX: 3 4426-749.

Destinations: New Zealand (Landsborough, Kawarau and Shotover Rivers).

One of the top three Kiwi rafting operations, Danes specializes in half-day to 3-day trips on the South Island, roughly $50-$350. Advance reservations are not needed, just sign up when you get to Queenstown. Danes' guides are fearless, and less safety-conscious than most American crews. (This is true of all NZ outfitters.) Rating: ★★★

■ **Kawarau Raft Expeditions**
P.O. Box 266, Queenstown, New Zealand, (011 64) 3 4429-792; FAX: 011 64 3 4427-876.

Kawarau's operation is virtually the same as Danes', from the prices to the destinations. You won't go wrong with either. The Landsborough is New Zealand's best multi-day trip. Rating: ★★★

■ **Worldwide Adventures/World Expeditions**
Suite 747, 920 Yonge Street, Toronto, ONT, Canada M4W 3C7, (800) 387-1483, or (416) 963-9163.

Destinations: New South Wales (Nymboida, Murray, Mitta Mitta), Tasmania (Franklin), Victoria (Snowy River), Queensland (Herbert, Johnstone).

World Expeditions is Australia's leading adventure company. It should be your first choice for New South Wales and Tasmania (in Queensland, Raging Thunder is tops). The Franklin River run in Tasmania may be the finest multi-day wilderness river trip in Australasia. Rating: ★★★

South America

■ **Steve Currey Expeditions, Inc.**
(Address Above), (800) 937-7238.

Destinations: Chile (Bio-Bio), Patagonia (Futaleafu).

This will be Currey Expedition's 14th season on the Bio-Bio, and it has recently added the Futaleafu River in Patagonia, a new world-class run featuring azure waters, stunning scenery, and five times as many major rapids as the Bio-Bio. Rating: ★★★★

■ **Rios Tropicales**
Contact Rafael Gallo, or Fernando Esquivel, P.O. Box 472-1200, San Jose 3183, Costa Rica, (011 506) 33 645.

Destinations: Costa Rica (Pacuare, Reventazon, General).

Rios Tropicales is Costa Rica's largest river outfitter, and one of its owners, Rafael Gallo, co-wrote *The Rivers of Costa Rica* (Menasha Ridge Press), the definitive whitewater guidebook for this region. Rios Tropicales is used by many US-based adventure companies, particularly for combo trekking/rafting, or rafting/sea kayaking adventures. You may cut costs by booking directly. Rating: ★★★

■ **Mountain Travel/Sobek**
(Address above), (800) 227-2384.

Destinations: Chile (Bio-Bio), Costa Rica (Chirripo, Pacuare, Reventazon).

Sobek has as much experience in South America as anybody. Call White Magic Unlimited, (415) 381-8889, or Currey Expeditions, (see above), for destinations Sobek does not serve. Rating: ★★★ to ★★★★

Safaris

Botswana/FRANS LANTING, MINDEN PICTURES

*There is something about safari life
that makes you forget your troubles
and feel the whole time as if you had drunk
half a bottle of champagne--bubbling over
with heartfelt gratitude for being alive.*
-Karen von Blixen as Isak Dinesen, *Out of Africa*

▼

The number and variety of commercial safaris is enormous, ranging from whirlwind wildlife tours, to monthlong odysseys visiting a half-dozen or more African nations. Most modern safaris are well planned and expertly guided, allowing the first-time African traveler to concentrate on the wildlife and scenery.

The biggest challenge in East African travel today is finding the untamed places where great herds still roam, and tourists are few and far between. While Kenya and Tanzania remain the most popular venues, the high volume of tourism in these areas has driven much of the game away. The resourceful safari traveler should consider visiting other destinations such as Botswana, Zambia and Namibia, which have superior concentrations of many species, including elephants and rhinos. In this chapter, we review the most popular safari venues, as well as the less-touristed areas where the "real" Africa survives.

CHAPTER
17

Hippo in Zaire/ FRANS LANTING, MINDEN PICTURES

IN THIS SECTION WE FEATURE BOTH CLASSIC SAFARIS--BIG-GAME VIEWING IN traditional lodges--as well as more exotic adventures that will take you to the most remote reaches of the African continent. Be aware that the trips reviewed represent but a small fraction of the safaris available in East and Southern Africa. There are safaris for all budgets--from bargain camping expeditions to luxury safaris costing as much as a small car. Whatever your resources permit, however, you won't be disappointed.

KENYA AND TANZANIA

The Classic Wildlife Safari

A tour of the great game parks of Kenya and Tanzania remains the quintessential safari experience. And though poaching and elimination of grazing lands have taken their toll on East Africa's game herds, during the annual migrations you can still see animals by the tens of thousands in the parklands of Kenya and Tanzania.

Modern safaris are carefully orchestrated. After arriving in Nairobi or Mombasa, Kenya, you will be transported by air or van to staging points in Amboseli in Kenya or Arusha in Tanzania. Typically you will be housed in large, permanent lodges situated near watering holes, natural drawing points for all types of wildlife. Increasingly popular, however, are tent camps, semi-permanent facilities that may be situated closer to the largest groups of animals. You sacrifice some luxury in a tent camp, but the experience is far from rugged.

Each day, you will board Land Rovers or minivans to search out the wildlife. As the game parks are often situated great distances apart, you can expect long passages over dusty, bumpy roads. When you reach your destination, other tour vehicles will likely be there, or will soon arrive. Be aware that the game reserves are busy places, particularly in the peak seasons. If you go to East Africa expecting solitude, you may be disappointed.

Kenya

The game parks of Kenya are the best known safari destinations. Kenyan lodges and tent camps are comfortable and sophisticated, generally the finest in Africa. Any Kenyan itinerary should include the Maasai Mara National Reserve, an extension of the Serengeti Plain. The Mara offers the greatest quantity and diversity of big game in Kenya. In August, vast herds of zebra and wildebeest, pursued by lions, migrate northward, stretching across the dusty landscape as far as the eye can see.

Amboseli Game Reserve and Tsavo West are two other recommended Kenyan safari venues. Amboseli, at the base of Mt. Kilimanjaro, was one of the old crossroads of East Africa. Watering holes in this area

Six Great African Adventures

are few and far between, so those places with exposed ground water are good bets for spotting lions, elephants, rhinos, giraffes and other game. Tsavo West Park is famous for its large herds of elephants.

Good lodges are found throughout Kenya, but two complexes near Mt. Kenya deserve special mention. In the Nyeri area are several hotels built above the ground near popular watering holes and salt licks. The game-viewing here is superlative. About 40 miles away is the Mt. Kenya Safari Club, a classic luxury lodge with few rivals in East Africa.

Tanzania

While Kenya is the overwhelming choice of most tourists, those in the know seem to prefer Tanzania, even if its tourist facilities aren't quite as refined. Tanzania's primary attraction is the Serengeti Plain. Covering 5,610 square miles, it is home to more than three million animals--35 major species in all.

Any visit to Tanzania should also include the Ngorongoro Crater, probably the best single spot for game-viewing in all of East Africa. The 2,000' walls of the crater's rim, the remnants of the world's largest volcano, shelter the largest non-migratory concentration of wildlife in Africa: over 20,000 animals. From atop the mountainous rim, the land below looks like a Garden of Eden, with green forests and open savannah surrounding a soda lake. The luxury lodges are situated on the rim. However, if you're willing to rough it a little, tent camping at one of the four campsites within the crater will save you money and put you closer to the wildlife--black rhinos, lions, zebras, wildebeests, cape buffalo, elephants, hippos, gazelles, impalas, cheetahs, hyenas, bushbuck, ostriches and flamingos.

A typical 14-day safari in Kenya or Tanzania will visit four or five different game parks, each featuring particular types of game. A wide variety of safaris is available, ranging from about $125 to more than $300 per day. When choosing a sa-

fari, it pays to shop around. Prices for similar itineraries (the same game parks, lodges and tent camps) can vary by thousands of dollars. You can often save by using a lesser-known safari agency, such as SafariCentre, as opposed to one of the name brands, such as Abercrombie & Kent. Substantial savings

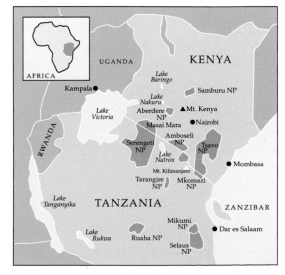

249

can also be had by traveling in East Africa's spring, September through October. (Tourism peaks during the cooler winter, May through August.)

RWANDA & ZAIRE

Gorilla-Tracking Safaris

"You get a funny feeling when you first see these 'wild hairy men.' They're animals all right, but the way they look at you makes you think twice."
-Dr. David Livingston

In Rwanda and neighboring Zaire, the endangered mountain gorilla makes its last stand against extinction. The gorillas' numbers have dropped drastically in this century, from over 1,000 to about 350. Despite their fearsome reputation, the gorillas are quite gentle creatures. Traveling in family groups of five to 30, they are generally curious and unafraid. Humans can come within a few yards of them and will not be attacked (unless the gorillas are severely

provoked). The adolescent animals are particularly playful.

Since the release of the movie *Gorillas in the Mist*, which chronicled the courageous efforts of Diane Fossey to save the mountain gorilla from extinction, interest in visiting these creatures has run high. In fact, the film has done wonders for tourism in Rwanda and Zaire, and the hottest thing in African tourism today may well be the specialized gorilla-tracking safari.

Rwanda's gorillas are found in the misty forests of Volcanoes National Park. Here, at 7,000', the air is cool and the trails wind precipitously beneath twisted trees six stories high. When you finally encounter the elusive gorillas, you approach slowly, mimicking their eating behavior so as to reassure them. These Rwandan gorillas are the largest primates. The males average 5'6", 430 pounds; the females, 4'7", 220 pounds. The number of visitors allowed to see the gorillas is strictly limited by the National Parks Department of Rwanda to only six persons per day per gorilla group.

In Zaire, several tours visit the rainforests of Virunga and Kahuzi Biega National Parks, home of the lowland gorillas, smaller cousins of the mountain gorillas. Here, the gorillas are less mobile, and therefore easier to track. The going can still be strenuous, with lengthy hikes through steep, dense rainforest. However, as the lowland gorillas live in a fairly small preserve, and are disinclined to wander far, they are generally easier to locate than the mountain gorillas in Rwanda or Uganda.

What should you expect on a gorilla trek? First, you will be hiking through bush, on hilly terrain. It is vital to have a good guide as there are few trails. It usually takes two to four hours before you find a gorilla family. You will spend an hour or two observing the gorillas then return to your vehicle. Which is best for gorilla viewing, Rwanda or Zaire? In Rwanda, your trek is at high altitude, 9,000', and the hike will probably be longer and more difficult than in Zaire. The Rwandan gorillas

Okavango Delta, Botswana/ FRANS LANTING, MINDEN PICTURES

tend to be a bit bigger that their Zairean cousins--but only by 50 pounds or so. In either case, you'll be impressed.

Most gorilla treks run 4 to 6 days at $1,800 to $2,500, with 3 or 4 days of actual gorilla-tracking. Himalayan Travel, Overseas Adventure Travel (OAT), and SafariWorld all offer fine gorilla-tracking safaris. Many travelers add a 3 to 5-day gorilla trek to a standard safari itinerary. Three-week tours with an add-on gorilla trek average $4,000.

For hardy travelers, OAT offers a superb new 23-day Mountains of the Moon primate safari. Starting in Zaire, trekkers will observe chimpanzees in the new Tonga Reserve, and mountain gorillas in the Djomba Reserve. Next the group will hunt with pygmies before commencing a 5-day trek to the top of 15,000' Mt. Stanley. From the summit the group crosses into Virunga Park (see p. 260) and Uganda's Ruwenzori Park. The Lake Edward camp in Virunga offers hippos by the thousands and spectacular views. The cost is $3,000, with June and January departures. Call (800) 221-0814.

Mountain gorilla, Rwanda/MICHAEL NICHOLS

ETHIOPIA

Rafting the Queen of Rivers

A raft voyage down Ethiopia's Omo River, the "Queen of Rivers," ranks as one of the most rewarding adventures offered anywhere, at any price. This trip, Sobek Expeditions' hallmark river journey, runs a full 28 days, and has been called a "cornerstone of adventure travel." Unlike so many packaged African tours which shuttle tourists from one modern lodge to another, the Omo River journey carries you through some of the most remote regions on earth, where civilization has not yet taken hold. If you want to experience the undiscovered Africa, this trip is as good as it gets.

The voyage begins at high altitudes, in cool, green surroundings. From the start, whitewater action is the watchword. Within an hour of the put-in, you will encounter rugged Class III and IV rapids, winding through a 5,000' deep canyon. The rafts pass through turbulent cataracts, 300' sheer-walled gorges, and natural rock amphitheaters. You will stop to explore large waterfalls, swim in the Omo's tributaries, and hike to villages in the nearby forests. Camps are made at riverside, where you will be surrounded by waterfowl and lush vegetation. Hippos, antelope, baboons and even lions can be observed nearby.

The second part of the trip takes you through lower elevations, with warmer temperatures, more open scenery and slower water. Though some major rapids remain, the pace slackens considerably, and the focus turns to wildlife. This is hippo country. The creatures bask in great numbers in the quiet waters, and occasionally cruise over to have a closer look at the rafts.

During the final stretches of the trip you'll visit at least five different tribes including the Bodi, Mursi, Nyangatom, Karo and Bacha. Living as they have for centuries, these river peoples greet you in distinctive tribal dress--beaded skirts, elaborate head decorations and giant lip-plates. Sobek's guides speak the native languages, so you are able to communicate with the locals, trading stories, and bartering for native crafts and artwork.

We recommend doing the whole trip, but if time is limited you can do either half separately. Sobek runs the Omo in October on a custom basis. The latest prices were $4,000 for the full trip, $2,600 for the upper half, and $3,200 for the lower half. Contact Mountain Travel/Sobek, 6420 Fairmont Ave., El Cerrito, CA 94530, (800) 227-2384.

BOTSWANA

Delta Wildlands & the Kalahari

In many ways, Botswana offers an unspoiled safari experience available nowhere else in Africa. This landlocked nation in southern Africa straddles the Tropic of Capricorn and is about the size of France, with just over one million people. Independent since 1966, it is one of the fastest developing countries in the third world. Brochures tout Botswana as the real Africa, "more incredible than any movie on the silver screen," and Botswana does indeed offer a diversity and richness of wildlife and flora that is hard to match in any other safari venue. Almost one-quarter of the country has been set aside as national park lands and game preserves. Though facilities are generally less deluxe than those found in Kenya or Tanzania, if you can forgo a little comfort, Botswana should not be missed.

Most of Botswana is covered by the Kalahari Desert, the world's largest mantle of sand. Herds of zebra, springbok, gemsbok and desert antelope can be seen in the desert's salt pans. At the edge of the Kalahari is the vast Okavango Delta. The flood plain is actually the inland terminus of a river that begins in the Angolan high-

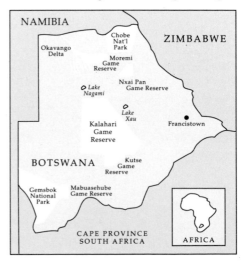

lands 600 miles away. In the delta, the waters run crystal clear through floating gardens of palms, reeds, papyrus, bulrushes, giant leadwoods and acacia. Safaris travel by truck, plane and boat. Some venture through the delta in mokoros, traditional canoes punted by Okavango boatmen. All manner of life thrives in the delta, an incredibly rich ecosystem. Hippos swim through the tree-lined lagoons, and the birdlife is staggering.

Situated north of the Okavango, scenic Chobe National Park is a must for any Botswana itinerary. Here you will find very large herds of elephant (more than you're likely to see in Kenya), as well as buffalo and other game, including rare puku and red lechwe. Some safaris stop to see Bushmen rock paintings. Another highlight of a Botswana safari is Victoria Falls, just across the border with Zimbabwe. The falls, on the Zambezi, are twice the height of Niagara Falls and half again as wide.

There are many options for the tourist wishing to visit Botswana. Capricorn Safaris, a leading Botswana-based company, offers fine tented safaris led by experienced bush guides. Capricorn's most complete safari covers the Kalahari, Okavango, Chobe, the Zambezi and Victoria Falls in 12 (land) days for about $2,650. Capricorn trips can be booked through the SafariCentre, (800) 223-6046. Another recommended

budget-priced Botswana adventure is offered by the Adventure Center, (800) 227-8747. Over a 3-week span, you explore the delta by dugout, and visit remote villages and the Kalahari desert by 4WD vehicle. Lodging is basic, camping-style, but the price is a low $1,850 for 22 days.

If you prefer a deluxe Botswana experience, the clear choice is Ker Downey Selby (KDS), (800) 231-6322, which has been operating its own safari camps in Botswana for decades. KDS has fine lodges and equipment, and some of the best guides in the business. The trips aren't cheap (a 2-week, first-class tent safari runs about $3,500), but there is no better operator in the region.

WINGS OVER AFRICA

The Flying Boat

If you're looking for the ultimate African adventure and price is no object, the Catalina Safari Company offers one of the most remarkable tours available anywhere--a 23-day, 4,700-mile trans-African odyssey by flying boat. You fly from Cairo to Victoria Falls, hopscotching across seven countries--Egypt, the Sudan, Kenya, Tanzania, Zanzibar, Botswana and Zimbabwe--along the route. Your transport is a vintage Catalina Flying Boat extensively

modified and lavishly outfitted for 16 passengers. The rear of the aircraft contains a sitting room with a map and reference library, a bar, and huge bubble-shaped observation windows. The galley serves gourmet meals and French wines.

The trip is conducted in a dozen stages, along a route pioneered by Imperial Airways in the first half of the century. Accommodations range from fine hotels to deluxe lodges and game camps. You'll have ample time for land exploring, spending roughly two days at each destination. Flights are made at low altitudes, allowing game-watching from the air, and most landings are made on lakes and rivers.

The itinerary reads like an atlas. After visiting the Pyramids, you take off from Cairo, bound for Luxor, and the Valley of the Kings. Two days are spent touring the tombs of the Pharaohs and the Karnak Temple, and then you fly down the Nile to visit the temple at Abu Simbel, landing on the river just below the great statues of Ramses II. Leaving Egypt, the Catalina follows the Nile to Khartoum in the Sudan. After visiting Khartoum's museum and temples, you land on Lake Turkana in Northern Kenya's Rift Valley. The group transfers here to Land Rovers for an overland land passage across the Chalbi desert to aptly named Lake Paradise. At the lake you rejoin the aircraft for the flight to Nairobi.

Departing from Nairobi, the Catalina circles Mt. Kilimanjaro, and then lands at Manyara, where you depart for two days of game-viewing in the Ngorongoro Crater. Following a flight offshore to the island of Zanzibar, you return to tour the Okavango Delta and Chobe National Park in Botswana. The last stop is Zimbabwe's spectacular Victoria Falls. This one-of-a-kind expedition costs $17,000, and may be booked through Mountain Travel, (800) 227-2384, or Abercrombie and Kent, (800) 323-7308. It's also possible to do half the trip for $8,500--either Cairo to Nairobi, or Nairobi to Victoria Falls. Trips depart in March, September and November.

Black rhino and young/ FRANS LANTING, MINDEN PICTURES

TANZANIA

Mt. Kilimanjaro Climb

Mt. Kilimanjaro, Africa's highest peak, dominates the horizon for vast distances. Rising from the Tanzanian plains to 19,340', this solitary, snow-capped mountain has become a symbol of the African continent. When Kilimanjaro's lower flanks are hidden by morning clouds, the summit seems to float high above the real world, as if in a dreamscape. Despite its great height, Kilimanjaro is the easiest of the world's great peaks to climb, and the summit can be reached in a few days by any reasonably fit person, even one without previous mountaineering experience. Nonetheless, climbing Kilimanjaro remains one of the world's classic adventures.

Climbing Kilimanjaro is a study in contrasts. Starting out from dry savannah, you ascend through a series of different ecosystems--rainforest and moorlands--to emerge at a mile-wide volcanic caldera, covered in snow. When you reach the nearly four-mile high summit, you'll think you've been transported to another continent. It's unlike anything you'd expect in Africa, and the view from the top is extraordinary.

You can organize a Kilimanjaro climb yourself, starting from either the Kenyan (northwest) or Tanzanian (south) flanks. You'll be at very high elevations at the summit, so spend a couple of days between 9,000' and 12,000' to acclimatize. There are no steep pitches requiring special technical skills or equipment, but it helps to have made a few alpine trips before. Good solid boots are a must, and an ice ax is useful--on the actual ascent you'll spend at least two days hiking through snow with some sections of ice. Foreign climbing groups must hire a local guide. The staff at the Marangu Hotel will help you obtain one, as well as porters should you want them. The best times to climb Kilimanjaro are January through March, and July through October.

For those preferring to climb with an organized group, Journeys offers a 7-day trip departing from Arusha in Tanzania. You spend 5 days on the mountain, and two in the Marangu Hotel. You should be reasonably fit, but porters will carry your gear. Land cost, including guide, porters and provisions is about $1,000, a major bargain. (Wilderness Travel charges over $4,000 for a 19-day combo Kili climb and wildlife safari.) Contact Journeys, 4011 Jackson, Ann Arbor, MI 48103, (800) 255-8735. A good second choice is Mountain Madness' 8-day climb--$1,350 with native guides, or $2,100 with European guides. Contact Mountain Madness, 4218 S.W. Alaska, Suite 206, Seattle, WA 98116, (206) 937-8389. Treks depart year-round.

If you want to climb Mt. Kenya as well, Himalayan Travel offers an 18-day twin peak expedition for $2,600. Call (800) 225-2380. For wildlife fans, Mountain Travel offers a 16-day Kilimanjaro trip that starts with a 3-day safari to Lake Manyara, the Rift Valley, and the Ngorongoro Crater in Tanzania. Price is steep--$3,200 to $3,600--plus $240 in park fees, but this includes porters. Call Mountain Travel at (800) 227-2384.

Fifteen Leading Safari Companies

Elephants' watering hole, Chobe Park, Botswana/STEVE GILROY

L ISTED BELOW ARE FIFTEEN RECOMMENDED SAFARI AGENCIES IN NORTH AMERICA. Most of them contract with African guide services who actually run the tours in Africa. When studying what these agencies have to offer, ask lots of questions. Learn what kind of vehicles you'll be using and how many people they will carry. Find out how close to the animals you'll really get, and what species you can actually expect to see. Read the brochures carefully; many "16-day safaris" may include as little as 11 days in the wild--you spend the rest of the time in a city hotel, or on an airplane.

■ ABERCROMBIE & KENT
1520 Kensington Road, Oak Brook, IL 60521-2141, (800) 323-7308, or (708) 954-2944.

This is an upper-end operation, with years of experience in Africa. Trips are deluxe and the prices reflect it. Customer service is excellent. Rating: ★★★★

■ ADVENTURE CENTER
(Guerba Expeditions), 1311 63rd Street, Suite 200, Emeryville, CA 94608, (800) 227-8747, or (510) 654-1879.

Adventure Center books reasonably priced trips for many excellent foreign outfitters. They offer many multi-nation 4WD overland safaris. Rating: ★★$$

■ BIG FIVE TOURS, LTD.
110 Route 110, South Huntington, NY 11746, (800) 445-7002, or (516) 424-2036.

Big Five is a good, general agency with its own safari guides and vehicles in Africa. Photo safaris are a specialty. Rating: ★★★

■ BORTON OVERSEAS
5516 Lyndale Ave. South, Minneapolis, MN 55419, (800) 843-0602, or (612) 824-4415.

A top outfitter for Tanzania, Borton runs its own show in East Africa. Rating: ★★★

■ GAMETRACKERS INTERNATIONAL
1000 E. Broadway, Glendale, CA 91205, (800) 444-BUSH, or (818) 507-8401.

With 19 years' experience, Gametrackers is highly recommended for Botswana, Namibia and South Africa. A wide range of prices is offered. Rating: ★★★

■ HIMALAYAN TRAVEL
(Tracks), P.O. Box 481, Greenwich, CT 06836, (800) 225-2380, or (203) 622-6777.

Like the Adventure Center, Himalayan Travel principally books value-oriented trips for very solid, foreign safari operators. Rating: ★★$

■ INTERNATIONAL EXPEDITIONS, INC.
One Environs Park, Helena, AL 35080, (800) 633-4734, or (205) 428-1700.

This company offers serious wildlife tours featuring plenty of time in the bush and trained naturalist guides. Rating: ★★★

■ KER DOWNEY SELBY
(Botswana), 13201 Northwest Fwy., Suite 800, Houston, TX 77040, (800) 423-4236, (800) 231-6352, or (713) 744-5222; in Kenya, contact: Ker & Downey, Box 41822, Nairobi, Kenya, Phone: (011 254) 2 556466.

One of the stalwarts that runs its own programs, Ker Downey offers a wide variety of safaris at medium to high prices. Nobody does Botswana better. Rating: ★★★★

■ **MOUNTAIN TRAVEL/SOBEK**
6420 Fairmont Avenue, El Cerrito, CA 94530, (800) 227-2384; FAX: (415) 525-7710.

One of the largest, all-in-one tour companies, Mountain Travel/Sobek offers some of the more unique African itineraries, including walking safaris, river trips and mountain climbs. Rating: ★★★

■ **OVERSEAS ADVENTURE TRAVEL (OAT)**
349 Broadway, Cambridge, MA 02139, (800) 221-0814, or (617) 876-0533. East Africa office: OAT, Arusha Conf. Centre, P.O. Box 6074, Arusha, Tanzania. Phone and FAX: (011) 255 57 6694.

OAT is a major player in the safari market, with its own offices and guides in Africa. Highly recommended. Rating: ★★★★

■ **SAFARICENTRE INTERNATIONAL, INC.**
3201 N. Sepulveda Blvd., Manhattan Beach, CA 90266, (800) 223-6046 USA & Canada, (800) 624-5342 in CA, or (213) 546-4411.

SafariCentre has a very wide range of itineraries, from very low priced to super-deluxe. Rating: ★★★$

■ **SAFARIWORLD**
425 Madison Avenue, New York, NY 10017, (800) 336-0505, or (212) 486-0505; FAX: (212) 486-0783.

Safariworld uses its own operators, and its Kenya and Tanzania trips visit the top lodges. A good, solid choice with many safaris at moderate prices. Rating: ★★★

■ **TRAVCOA**
P.O. Box 2630, Newport Beach, CA 94530, (800) 992-2003, or (800) 992-2004 in CA.

TRAVCOA specializes in luxurious lodge-based safaris using the top operators in East and South Africa. Rating: ★★★$

■ **WILDERNESS TRAVEL**
801 Allston Way, Berkeley, CA 94710, (800) 247-6700 nationwide, (415) 548-0420 in CA.

This popular company has very good safari guides and challenging itineraries. Prices are fairly high. Rating: ★★★

■ **WILDLIFE SAFARI**
346 Rheem Boulevard, Moraga, CA 94556, (800) 221-8118; FAX: (510) 376-5059.

This well-established broker offers mainly medium to high-end trips to all popular safari destinations. Rating: ★★★

CHOOSING AN AFRICAN SAFARI

If you're preparing to shell out $3,500 to $6,000 (with airfare) for a couple of weeks on safari, you owe it to yourself to comparison shop. Competing outfitters often run virtually the same safaris, with a wide range of prices. We've found that many of the domestic safari companies actually use the same guides and overland services in Kenya and Tanzania, so you may be mistaken if you automatically assume that the most expensive trip is the best.

We don't recommend venturing all the way to Africa unless you can stay a minimum of two weeks. Get to more than one country if you can. You'll be happiest with a safari that combines multiple destinations--Kenya and Tanzania, or Tanzania and Botswana, for example. We'd also look for a trip that offers something more than riding around in a van for five to 10 days. Some safari companies offer balloon rides, canoe trips or flight-seeing as options.

Be realistic about what you are looking for and what you can afford. If you want to stay in luxury lodges, go with an elite safari, such as those led by Ker Downey Selby (Botswana), or Abercrombie & Kent (Kenya, Tanzania). If you want more challenge, try a trip that includes a walk into the bush, or an ascent of Mt. Kilimanjaro or Mt. Kenya. Mountain Travel and the Adventure Center organize such programs.

While most who have gone to Africa have loved the experience, we think many of the organized tours are too soft, that most insulate you from the real Africa, and that virtually all are overpriced. What is best about Africa remains wild and free. In our view, you should go there to experience an untamed world, not to luxuriate. We think if you are prepared to rough it a little, your trip will ultimately be much more rewarding.

> *Travel stripped of all unpredictability is inevitably monotonous; without it the traveler moves through strange lands untouched and touching nothing.*
>
> -Caskie Stinnett

Maasai dancers/FRANS LANTING, MINDEN PICTURES

PHOTO SAFARI

COURTESY VAN OS PHOTO SAFARIS

*A*LL AFRICAN SAFARIS CATER TO PHOTOGRAPHY TO SOME EXTENT BECAUSE ALMOST EVERYONE WANTS TO take pictures. However, if you're really serious about getting those once-in-a-lifetime shots, consider a specialized photo safari led by a recognized wildlife photographer. With such a trip you spend more time in the field when the conditions are best for picture-taking. As Maine-based East African Photographic Safaris explains, "One thing that we feel separates us from the [ordinary safaris] is our search for the light that gives Africa her magic. No matter who you go with, you will see lots of animals. But in each African day, there are a few hours when the light is just right."

Before you chose a photo tour, check the itinerary to make sure you'll be viewing the particular species you want to shoot. Next, find out the ratio between participants and guides--you'll want this to be less than 10 to 1. Ask about equipment--can the tour operator provide specialty lenses, tripods and basic camera repair? Find out what the price covers. Most photo tours are expensive and should include food, lodging, and all ground transportation.

Probably the leading photo safari operator is Joseph Van Os Photo Safaris. Its photographers/guides are world class. Van Os Africa programs include: Kenya (16 days, July); Namibia (19 days, July); Zimbabwe (19 days, Aug./Sept.), and Botswana (16 days, fall). All trips cost about $4,000. East African Photo Safaris

offers 18-day Kenyan and Tanzanian tours in February, March and September. Trips range in price from $4,300 to $5,200 with air from New York, and an optional Rwanda extension. PhotoTravel (Big Five Tours) offers 18-day photo safaris to Zimbabwe and Botswana for $4,750, including airfare from New York. International Expeditions (see p. 254) also offers 3-week photo safaris in Kenya, Rwanda and Tanzania.

Joseph Van Os Photo Safaris, *P.O. Box 655, Vashon Island, WA 98070, (206) 463-5383; FAX: (206) 463-5484.* Rating: ★★★★

East African Photographic Safaris, *45 Rawson Avenue, Camden, ME 04843, (207) 236-4244.* Rating: ★★

Photo Travel, *110 Route 110, South Huntington, NY 11746, (800) 445-7002, or (516) 424-2036.* Rating: ★★

COURTESY VAN OS PHOTO SAFARIS

GETTING THE MOST OUT OF YOUR PHOTO SAFARI

by John Shaw, Van Os Photo Safaris

Speak of wildlife photography and many people automatically think of an East African safari. The image of vast herds of animals streaming across the savannah is ingrained in our minds from countless articles, books and movies. However, for the first-time traveler to Kenya or Tanzania, the reality can be overwhelming. This is especially true when you compound problems by venturing out early and late to photograph in the good light, burdened with cameras and long lenses.

What general preparations should you make? When it comes to clothing, make it comfortable. Since almost all your photography will be from a vehicle--it's illegal to get out of vehicles within any of the game parks and reserves--you'll spend long hours in Nissan vans or Land Rovers. Don't bring fancy togs. The roads are dusty beyond belief, and "formal" at most game lodges means a clean shirt at best. Jeans or khakis, a long-sleeved shirt, sweatshirt and windbreaker (it can get cool at night since most East African parks are at fairly high elevations), and a good hat--that's about all you need. Add toiletries, sun block, and a pair of small binoculars. Pack light. Luggage space in the vehicles is at a premium and you can do laundry in the lodges.

CAMERAS

What camera gear should you bring? First of all, don't take anything, camera or lens, that you have not tested out at home first. Make sure it's all working, and make sure you know how to work it. The Serengeti is no place to learn what all those buttons really do. Run several rolls through the camera, practice loading and rewinding film, and test that new lens.

Don't even think of going to Africa with only one camera. Bring at least two bodies, preferably with motor drives, and a third body for backup wouldn't hurt. You'll probably be happiest with one standard body, and one autofocus. If your one and only camera quits, you have no options. For practical purposes, there will be no possibility of camera repair on your safari. Take lots of batteries for the camera and motor drives. Such things will just

not be available. (This is true for virtually everything in your camera bag.)

LENSES

As to lenses, you won't need many short focal lengths. A medium wide-angle or normal, in the 35-50mm range, will do, particularly if you have a popular camera and can borrow a true wide-angle for one or two shots. Otherwise, slip a small 28mm in your bag. Absolutely bring a zoom in the 80-200mm or 70-210mm range. Zooms are great for safaris as you'll be doing almost all your shooting from the vehicles, and the ability to crop in the camera is paramount.

Bring any big lenses you have. If you double up on any focal lengths, make it the long ones. The most useful lens is a rea-

Maasai Mara, Kenya/RONNA NELSON

sonably fast 400mm, f3.5 or f4. A 300mm is worth bringing as well. A 200-400mm zoom, such as the f4 Nikon can be ideal, particularly if it has constant aperture throughout the zoom range. A 500mm lens is as big as you'll ever want, but avoid a mirror lens such as a 500mm f8--it's just too slow. By all means bring a 1.4X teleconverter. This will take your 300mm to 420mm, offering great versatility. A 2X converter sacrifices too much light and image quality.

ACCESSORIES

Pack your camera gear in a good case which you hand-carry onto the airplane. I'm partial to the soft, padded bags since you can fit more into them than the foam-filled

hard-sided cases. I would suggest a bag where the top not only closes with a zipper, but also with a large flap. With this you can leave the top unzipped, and the flap will keep the dust out when you're in the field.

Pack your tripod in your suitcase. You'll want it at the lodges, but in the vehicles it's useless. For working out of the vans, you'll want a bean bag about the size of a loaf of bread. You can easily make one out of an old pair of jeans with velcro sewn on one end. Buy the beans in Nairobi, and offer them to your driver at the end of the trip. Fancy window mounts do work fine, but bean bags are more handy and versatile.

One very important item is a dust bag. Dust will be your major enemy in East Africa. When you're on a game drive, you'll want your camera ready with long lens attached. Unfortunately your gear will quickly become coated with a thick layer of dust. An easy solution is to keep it all ready, but inside a bag. A finely woven pillowcase works fine if you keep it clean. Plastic bags hold static electricity, attracting the dust you want to avoid. A nightly camera cleaning routine is advisable. Take a squeeze-bulb blower, lens tissue, lens cleaner, some Q-tips, and an old toothbrush for cleaning.

FILM

As to film, take whatever you normally like to shoot. You don't really need several kinds of film, although you may want to shoot both some print film and slides. A belt pouch to carry extra film is very handy. How much film to bring? Take double what you think you would shoot. An absolute minimum would be three rolls per day in the field. You can always bring the film back home with you, but don't count on buying any in Africa. Take all your film as carry-on luggage, and ask for a hand inspection. Don't mail it home from Nairobi.

As a final tip on getting the shots you'll prize for a lifetime, my advice is to shoot freely when you have a good subject and the conditions are right. The price of film is a tiny fraction of the cost of your trip. The attitude you should have is that your next shot will be the definitive photo of your subject.

TOP TWENTY SAFARI DESTINATIONS

Lion cubs, Maasai Mara, Kenya/ART WOLFE

IF YOU'RE DESIGNING YOUR OWN AFRICAN SAFARI, USE THIS SHORTHAND LIST TO plan an ideal itinerary. We've selected 20 of the best destinations, with the most weight given to the quantity and variety of wildlife in each area. Since crowds can spoil any safari, we also emphasize lesser-known areas where tourism is low but the game-viewing is still outstanding.

BOTSWANA

Chobe National Park

Chobe remains an untouched wilderness where game runs free and the park is not yet overrun with safari tourism. A particularly scenic area, Chobe features very large herds of elephant and sable antelope, plus strong populations of giraffe. Some lion and cheetah follow the antelope herds, and you can expect to see white rhinos, although their numbers are small.

Okavango Delta

The Okavango Delta, a 7,000-square-mile inland floodplain, hosts one of the richest concentrations of wildlife in Africa. On the plains, there are large herds of buffalo, kudu, oryx and sable antelope. In the waters of the delta, which can be visited only by mekoros (dugout canoes), you'll find crocodiles and countless hippos. Elephants, lions and leopards are common, but in lesser numbers than in the large game parks of Tanzania.

KENYA

Amboseli Game Reserve

Kenya's Amboseli Game Reserve sits beneath snow-capped Mt. Kilimanjaro. Although the reserve is quite dry, there are many water holes which attract elephants, rhinos, lions, giraffe and countless bird species. Being close to Nairobi, and having many permanent lodges, Amboseli suffers from heavy tourism and lacks some of the wilderness ambience you can find better elsewhere. It's worth the visit to see Kilimanjaro, however--something best done at dawn or dusk.

Lake Nakuru

Centrally located in the Great Rift Valley, Lake Nakuru is famed for its huge flocks of lesser and greater pink flamingos. (Over half of the world's five million flamingos nest in the Rift Valley, with the largest populations at Lake Nakuru.) The soda lake is ringed by acacia groves and dense forest. There are herds of waterbuck, gazelle and impala at water's edge, along with many shorebirds including pelicans, storks and the fish eagle. Giraffe herds range close by. Lake Nakuru has also been recently designated as a sanctuary for the endangered black rhino.

Maasai Mara Game Reserve

The Maasai Mara is the best big-game park in Kenya. Located on the northern edge of the Serengeti Plain, at an elevation of

5,200', the Mara justly enjoys its fame as one of the few areas left in Africa where game can still be observed in vast numbers. The diverse terrain (savannah, rolling hills, forests and water courses) supports a wide variety of animals, including the big cats--lions, leopards and cheetahs--which prey on migrating herds. If you visit during the August wildebeest migration, you can see as many as 150,000 animals in one area. The Maasai Mara is also home to virtually all of the other popular species--elephants, rhinos, giraffe, zebras and gazelles.

Mt. Kenya National Park

At 17,058', Mt. Kenya is East Africa's second highest summit. The surrounding foothills and lowlands are among the most scenic regions in Kenya, with lakes, rainforests and dense woodlands. The Mt. Kenya area is one of the best spots in East Africa for a walking tour. Game-viewing is not as good as at Samburu or Maasai Mara to the south, but you can still expect to see elephant, buffalo, bushback, and a rhino or two if you're lucky. If you can afford it, spend a night or two at the Mount Kenya Safari Club, a classic colonial-era lodge.

Samburu National Park

Samburu (and nearby Buffalo Springs and Shaba) are considered by many to compose the best game-viewing area north of Nairobi. All the major big-game species are here, plus hippos and crocodiles. There are large herds of zebra and antelope, many giraffe, and ostrich are quite common. Try to visit a Samburu village. The women wear elaborate colorful necklaces, and the tribal dances are inspiring.

Tsavo National Park

A huge (8,034-square-mile) and very arid park, Tsavo has some of Africa's largest elephant herds, but they can be hard to locate. Tsavo West, dominated by the Yatta Plateau, an ancient lava flow, contains the more interesting terrain, but more wildlife is found in Tsavo East which is mostly open savannah. Along with elephants, look for rhinos, lions and lesser kudus. Don't miss the Mzima Springs oasis, where hippos and crocodiles can be viewed from a submerged tank and observation platform.

NAMIBIA

Etosha National Park

One of the largest game parks in the world, Etosha is the wildlife spectacular that Kenya and Tanzania were 25 years ago. Centered around the Etosha Pan, a 72-mile lake bed, the park features a number of spring-fed water holes that attract game year-round. You'll find kudus, wildebeest, oryx and zebras in very large numbers, along with elephant, lions, springbok, giraffes, ostrich, cheetahs and leopards. As yet, Etosha is relatively undiscovered; tourism is a drop in the bucket here compared to the annual activity in the major Kenyan or Tanzanian game parks. And, since humans do not overwhelm their environment, the animals are relaxed, affording excellent photo opportunities. This is a definite must-see destination--the way Africa is supposed to be.

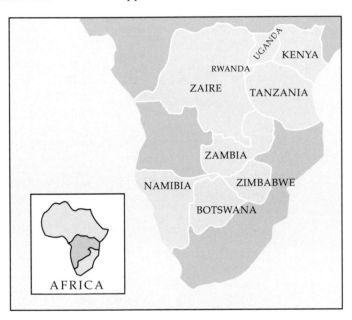

Namib Desert/Damaraland

The otherworldly landscape of the Namib desert--massive dunes, high mesas and giant rock formations--is quite unlike anything else in Africa. The world's tallest sand dunes, hundreds of feet high, are found at Sossusvlei. At Sandwich Harbor, huge red sand hills tower over a lagoon filled with thousands of flamingos, pelicans and other species. To the north of the Kuiseb River, the sand gives way to the windswept isolation of the skeleton coast. Farther inland is Damaraland, a land of stark contrasts--desert, grasslands and high mountains. There you'll find elephant, the rare Hartmann's mountain zebra, springbok and rhino.

RWANDA

Akagera National Park

Akagera, one of Africa's oldest game parks, encompasses 980 square miles of savannah, hills, lakes and marshes along Rwanda's northeast border. Over 500,000 animals coexist in this scenic and water-rich habitat. Hoofed and water-dwelling mammals are especially abundant, although you'll also find lions and leopards. This is a great spot for a walking tour, or getting good shots of hippos and crocodiles. Over 525 species of birds live in the park.

Volcanoes National Park

Volcanoes Park is the principal habitat of the rare mountain gorilla. Unfortunately, the area is increasingly overrun with tourists, and you may have some trouble locating more than a few gorillas. When you do however, it's quite an experience. Richard Attenborough has written, "There is more meaning and understanding in exchanging a glance with a gorilla than with any other animal I know." Reaching the gorillas can be tough, requiring strenuous hiking at high altitudes. Most safaris spend only a day or two in the park (you'll likely visit other preserves in Zaire or Uganda as well), and visits to the gorilla sanctuary are strictly limited to a few hours per day. Other park highlights include hippos on the Rutshuiro River, and lions on the Rwindi plains.

TANZANIA

Gombe Stream National Park

If you want to see chimpanzees in the wild, Gombe Stream, one of Tanzania's lesser-known parks, is probably your best bet. However, Tanzanian chimps remain quite wild and elusive, and are a good deal harder to locate than the gorillas of Rwanda or Zaire. Another chimpanzee habitat you may wish to explore is the Tanzania's Mahale Mountains National Park.

Lake Manyara National Park

Situated in Tanzania's Rift Valley, Lake Manyara Park is known for its big cats and abundant birdlife. The many lions in the park can often be found resting in the acacia trees, high above the ground. A rise in tourism has made it more difficult to find a tree-climbing lion in recent years, however. The relatively small park also boasts the highest concentration of elephants in East Africa, though they do not roam particularly close to the permanent lodges. The lake's alkaline waters attract numerous bird species--over 340 varieties have been observed in the park. Monkeys and baboons also abound in this region. For some great photos, head to a hippo pool, where you'll see these creatures cavorting in the mud, while buffalo, zebra and giraffe congregate nearby.

Ngorongoro Crater

Ngorongoro was once the site of the world's largest volcano--a giant peak over three times the height of Mt. Everest. In a catastrophic explosion, the volcano erupted, leaving a huge, 100-square-mile crater with a rim reaching to 7,000'. The crater now harbors the greatest concentration of wildlife species on the planet. On the plains of the crater you will find huge herds of wildebeest, antelope and zebras, which also attract the large predators (lions, leopards and cheetahs) in considerable numbers.

The lakes and rivers within the crater abound with hippos and waterfowl. Protected by the crater's high, mountainous rim, elephants and rhinos have managed to elude the poachers here, surviving in great numbers. No trip to Tanzania should omit Ngorongoro, a one-of-a-kind wildlife preserve. To get closest to the action, we would opt for a tent camping safari in the heart of the crater, but you can also stay at luxury lodges on the crater rim.

Serengeti National Park

Perhaps the most famed of all the African game parks, the Serengeti adjoins the Maasai Mara Reserve to the north. Embracing over 6,000 square miles of plains and savannahs, the Serengeti is unrivaled for sheer number of migratory animals and big game. With over 35 species of large game and 350 species of birds, the Serengeti is without peer in the African wildlife world. Here you'll find antelope of all varieties, and huge herds of gazelle, zebra and wildebeest. The Serengeti plains are home to more lions than any other park in Africa, and leopard, cheetah and other predators are also found in abundance. The Serengeti is a must for any Tanzanian safari.

Tarangire National Park

Tarangire Park is Tanzania's newest and wildest game reserve. It's refreshingly free of development and offers fine game-viewing, especially along the Tarangire

Sunset at Ngorongoro Crater, Tanzania/ FRANS LANTING, MINDEN PICTURES

River where elephants, lions, buffalo and kudus all congregate to cool off in large, muddy pools. Tarangire is a good choice for ornithologists, as over 260 species of birds populate the park, including the bateleur eagle, secretary bird and the Maasai ostrich.

ZAMBIA

South Luangwa National Park

The Luangwa Valley, part of the 6,000-mile long Great Rift Valley, is known as the Valley of the Elephants. The 3,500-square-mile South Luangwa National Park, in addition to its elephant herds, probably holds the highest concentration of hippos and crocodiles in all of Africa. The Luangwa River, which runs through the center of the park, has numerous lagoons and mudholes which attract large wildlife populations year-round. Luangwa Park remains wild, and the game herds have not yet been driven out by excessive tourism. This destination ranks high on our list of little known but outstanding African destinations.

ZAIRE

Virunga National Park

Virunga, Zaire's first national park, is known for its beautiful scenery (mountains, lakes and rivers) and extremely large, diverse wildlife populations. One of Africa's oldest and best-planned parks, Virunga boasts the world's largest hippo populations--30,000 or more. Along the many waterways there are thousands of water buffalos and five species of antelope. Monkeys and baboons congregate in the forestlines. In the Virunga Volcanoes area gorilla safaris are offered, although Rwanda is probably your best bet for mountain gorillas. Hundreds of bird species nest in the park, while elephants, lions and leopards are present in limited numbers.

ZIMBABWE

Victoria Falls

Twice as high as Niagara Falls, and over a mile wide, Victoria Falls is considered one of the Seven Wonders of the World. Originally known as "Musi-O-Tunya" (the smoke that thunders), the falls were discovered in 1955 by explorer David Livingston and christened after Queen Victoria. The falls are located just across the border from Botswana in Zimbabwe, and many Botswana safaris include a trip to the falls as an option. A flight-seeing excursion over Victoria Falls is highly recommended.

SAFARIS

GETTING TO AFRICA

When selecting a package trip, choose one that gets you to Africa without delay. Many safari packages actually include as much as 4 days total travel time as part of their itinerary--on a "10-day safari" you may spend less than a week in Africa. With careful planning, you can spend more time in the bush and less in transit. You may want to arrange your own flights, and not leave this up to your safari broker, who will probably charge you $2,200 or more for a round-trip ticket to East Africa. You can save hundreds by combining a discount ticket to London with a London-Nairobi charter flight. See Chapter 28 for details.

WHAT TO BRING

Bring lightweight, durable cotton clothes, comfortable walking shoes, two pairs of quality sunglasses, and a hat for the sun. Pack a sweater or windbreaker for the evenings, which can be quite cool in the highlands. In the rainy season (April and May in Kenya), a small folding umbrella is your best friend. Those staying at luxury lodges should bring one "better" outfit (sport coat and tie for men, lightweight dress for women). Bring all the personal items you will need, as cosmetics, medicines, etc. are difficult to obtain outside Nairobi or Mombasa. If possible, limit your luggage to one medium-size bag under 25 pounds, plus a daypack or shoulder bag.

GROUND TRANSPORT

Virtually all safari operators transport their guests in small minivans or Land Rovers. If the vehicle is seriously over-crowded, it can spoil your whole vacation. Ask your outfitter the maximum number of persons per vehicle--if it's more than five or six, go with somebody else. Some outfitters guarantee a window seat, a good practice. We prefer open safari trucks for photo-taking, but they are less comfortable than minivans in the heat and dust.

FRANS LANTING, MINDEN PICTURES

WHEN TO GO

KENYA/TANZANIA

Most tourists visit Kenya and Tanzania in the winter, June through August, when highs are in the 70s and lows in the 50s. We prefer the spring, September through November, when you can see blossoms and newborn animals, and temperatures reach the upper 80s. December through March is hot (90-100) on the plains, but pleasant in the higher altitudes where many of the game reserves are located. Summer is the time of the great migrations on the Serengeti--a good reason to brave the heat. April and May are considered the rainy months, but the weather rarely turns very severe, and this is the time for off-season rates and reduced tourism in the field.

NAMIBIA

The best time to visit Namibia is probably September or October. Game herds have congregated, and you'll see newborn animals and wild flowers. The least crowded period is the summer rainy season from November through March.

You'll see fewer tourists then, but the wildlife tends to be more dispersed. The concentrations of game around Etosha's water holes are the highest in the dry season from April until the rains come. Along the rugged Skeleton Coast it can be cold and windy year-round, due to cooling currents from Antarctica.

RWANDA AND ZAIRE

Rainy season in the highlands is from March to May, and again in October and November--the fall and spring in these Southern Hemisphere countries. Gorilla-tracking can be more difficult in the October through December period, when the gorillas are moving about in the wild, foraging for bamboo.

ZAMBIA

You'll want to visit Zambia in its winter and spring, June to September. Rain will be rare then, daily highs will be in the 70s to 80s, and evenings in the 50s and 60s. October and November is also a good time to travel, but the heat can be oppressive.

ZIMBABWE

Zimbabwe is best traveled in the Southern Hemisphere's fall and winter (March to September). Days are dry and sunny then, with highs in the 60s and 70s.

BOOKS

The African Safari, The Ultimate Wildlife and Photographic Adventure, by P. Jay Fetner is the biggest and most complete resource for safaris throughout Africa. $60 from most major booksellers.

East Africa, a Travel Survival Kit, is the detailed Lonely Planet guidebook to Kenya, Tanzania, Zaire and Botswana. If you plan to spend any time on your own in East Africa, this book is essential.

A Field Guide to the National Parks of East Africa, by J.G. Williams, is the best standard text on big-game viewing in Kenya and Tanzania. $24.95 from Collins Press.

Fielding's African Safari Guide, provides comprehensive descriptions of 65 different African safaris for all budgets. It also contains wildlife, health and safety information. $17.95 at travel bookstores.

Charter Sailing

▼

Cruising on a sailboat is one of life's greatest pleasures. With water covering three-quarters of the earth's surface, the variety of possible adventures is endless.

Bareboating, i.e. skippering your own boat, is generally the least expensive, and most liberating kind of sailing holiday. You're free to plan your own itinerary, sailing when the wind is good, relaxing along a deserted beach when you want a break. While operating a large yacht is not child's play, most people with some keelboat experience will be able to charter in a destination like the Virgin Islands, although you may have to put a skipper on board for the first day or two.

In the following pages, noted sailing author Brian Fagan will introduce you to seven of the world's great bareboat cruising grounds. You'll also find a comprehensive chart covering more than 20 great sailing destinations worldwide, a directory of recommended charter companies around the globe, and a guide to windjammer cruises worldwide.

CHAPTER

18

Sunrise in the tropics/RONNA NELSON

I F YOU TRULY WANT TO GET AWAY FROM IT ALL, INCLUDING THE CONFINES OF a land-based resort, a bareboat charter cruise is an ideal vacation. If your cruising skills are a bit rusty, you can hire a skipper for a few days, or you might prefer flotilla sailing. In a flotilla, you sail with a group of boats, following a leader who handles the navigation chores. While you can have fun in any boat 25' or larger, we recommend a yacht in the 34' to 44' range. At this size, you can get private cabins for two or three couples--a big plus on an extended cruise.

VIRGIN ISLANDS

Cruising Mecca

Many cruising sailors rate the American and British Virgin Islands (BVI) as the best bareboating area in the world. The Virgins have everything to offer--superlative sailing in relatively sheltered water, predictable winds, exceptional diving and snorkeling, and all the social life ashore you could possibly want.

A Virgin Island charter usually starts in St. Thomas in the American Virgins, or at Road Town on Tortola Island in the BVI. Both are excellent charter bases with all needed facilities close by, and there are excellent anchorages within a half-day's sail. St. Thomas and St. John lie at the south-western end of the Sir Francis Drake Channel, the waterway that bisects the Virgins. Mountainous Tortola dominates the north side of the Channel, while a string of lesser islands, the largest of them Virgin Gorda, protect the southern edge. The islands run

east to west, protecting you from the Atlantic swells that sweep down on the Lesser Antilles from thousands of miles of open water. This allows novice crews to enjoy tradewind sailing in relatively flat water, with plenty of safe anchorages close by.

There are so many possible highlights of a Virgins vacation, that it's hard to know where to begin. For pure sailing fun, we recommend the beat to windward in the sheltered waters of the Sir Francis Drake Channel, or reaching across from Tortola to nearby Jost Van Dyke Island. Wherever you sail, the choice of anchorages is endless. For evening entertainment, check out Foxy's Beach Bar on Jost Van Dyke, or Stanley's at Cane Garden Bay on Tortola. There are internationally famous resorts, too, like the Bitter End on Virgin Gorda. A visit to the Bitter End is the climax of many bareboat cruises. Anchor or moor offshore, and treat yourself to lobster at the resort.

Smart sailors will work their way to windward against the prevailing trades from St. Thomas and Tortola over the first few days, then take their time sailing home

Seven Great Charter Sailing Vacations

by Brian Fagan

downwind. This gives you time to snorkel the wreck of the Royal Mail Ship Rhone, or to enjoy dinner at Marina Cay, where the evening social life is always fast and furious. Those craving peace and quiet will find it at the Bight on Norman Island, alleged to be the prototype for Robert Louis Stevenson's *Treasure Island*, or in the quiet nooks of Gorda Sound, where your only companions will be sea creatures, and the gentle sough of the trades.

The Virgin Islands are the bareboating capital of the world, which means that anchorages and resorts are crowded during high season from December through early April. There is a bewildering array of charter companies from which to choose. The Moorings is famous for its fine service, and well-maintained fleet. Sunsail, formerly Stevens Yachts, is based on West End, an easy ferry ride from St. Thomas. Other recommended companies include La Vida and CSY, both based at St. Thomas.

It's best to work with a larger company in these waters, especially on a first-time charter. If ever there was a vacation experience where you get what you pay for, a Virgins cruise would be it. The larger companies have the facilities to back up their yachts, and if there is a real problem, they can bring you another boat. The most popular charter yachts are in the 38' to 50' range, and many charter parties of six people divide up the cost to make for an affordable vacation. Consult our chart for details on prices and yacht features.

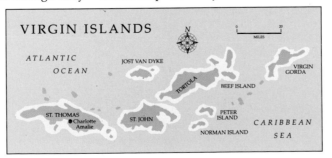

NEW ZEALAND

Southern Sojourn

New Zealand is the only charter destination in the world where you can sail in the morning and ski in the afternoon. It is also perhaps the most distant cruising ground accessible to the bareboater--14 hours flying time from the US West Coast. But the country that awaits you at the other end more than compensates for the long hours aloft.

You will want to spend a minimum of two weeks in New Zealand, at least one of them ashore (you shouldn't miss the sights of the South Island), the remainder afloat. Most charterers land at Auckland, spend a day there, rent a car, then drive three and a half hours north to the Bay of Islands. You can sail from Auckland or take a weeklong coastal charter, but we strongly recommend starting in the Bay of Islands your first time around. The charter base, located at the village of Opua, has a good selection of yachts in the 27' to 40' range. The first stop on most

cruises is the old whaling town of Russell, a short sail away. Take time to visit the museum and the church, which is the oldest in New Zealand. Across the water lies Waitangi, New Zealand's most important historical site. The Treaty House and Maori meeting house are national monuments well worth a visit.

The anchorage off Russell can be uncomfortable, so you are best off sailing into the sheltered waters in the Bay of Islands itself. You beat out into the prevailing winds and anchor in any one of six coves in nearby Manawaora Bay. The Bay of Islands offers everything from uninhabited islands to small coves hemmed in by steep hills. You can sail around Cape Brett to Whangamumu Harbor, which was a whaling station until the 1930s. But the highlight of your charter is a visit to Kerikeri, where missionary Samuel Marsden founded a mission station in 1819. The stone mission store still stands beside a quiet pool reached by a long, tidal channel. High overhead broods the great "pa" (fortified village) of the Maori chief Hongi Hika. Spend a day here, touring the mission and the pa.

The Bay of Islands is a compact cruising ground, so much so that Kerikeri Inlet is only seven miles from Russell. Few charter areas offer such variety in so small a compass, with so many unique sights and fine beaches close at hand.

GREECE

Classical Adventuring

Greece is a magical place for chartering, especially if you have an interest in colorful ports and archaeology. This is the land of a gregarious, friendly people who welcome tourists and sailors alike with open arms. You can anchor in the shadow of a classical temple, explore remote islands, dance till dawn in local tavernas, or simply relax on sandy beaches to your heart's content.

This all sounds heavenly, and indeed it is. But Greece is not a cruising ground for the novice. The weather, even in summer, can be stormy, frustrating, and at times downright uncomfortable. For a first-time visit, try a week's flotilla charter. You sail from port to port in the company of a half-dozen or more yachts, under the supervision of an experienced flotilla leader. You can flotilla charter in the Ionian Islands, in the Saronic Gulf, and in the Sporades in the northern Aegean, and along the Turkish Coast. Flotilla charters are especially popular with British and German sailors, and you will find plenty of attractive package deals in European sailing magazines. If you prefer to bareboat by yourself, you cannot go wrong with Kavos, an Athens-based company recently merged with the Moorings of Caribbean fame. Other recommended charterers in Greece are Sunsail and GPSC.

Experts prefer to charter in May or early June, or in September, at either end of the high season. The sheltered waters of the Saronic Gulf are an ideal introduction to Greek waters. Your first stop is the island of Aegina, a short sail from Athens. In late afternoon, take a cab to the ancient Temple of Aphaia high on a hill to the northeast. The fluted columns of the temple shine pink in the sunset as you gaze out over the mountains and bays of the Peloponnesus.

Aegina is a half-day's sail from Epidauros, a small port close to the world-famous classical amphitheater and shrine of Aeskepios, the God of Healing. The acoustics in the theater are so perfect that you can hear a whisper even when seated on the upper tier. After a half-day of archaeology, sail east to Poros, a charming old town perched above a narrow channel that takes you east toward one of the highlights of a Saronic charter--Hydra.

Hydra is invisible until you are just outside the harbor entrance, a tiny semicircular cove hemmed in by house-covered slopes that has been a trading center for many centuries. A stone quay shelters the tiny port where you moor among a crowd of yachts large and small. There are no automobiles on the island, only heavily laden mules, which wend their way through the narrow streets. This picturesque harbor is busy with ferries and tourists by day, but wonderfully quiet at night.

Your Saronic cruise takes you as far as Naplion, an old Venetian town overlooked by an imposing fortress--the Palamidi. Your passage homeward will bring you to the island of Spetsae, where you can wander through small boatyards where they still build traditional wooden fishing craft. There are quiet anchorages, too, places where you will be alone except for the wind. On the last day, sail along the eastern shore of Aegina to Agia Marina and perhaps savor another visit to the Temple of Aegina.

Greece is addicting, a place where the magic of history comes to life. The great thing is that you can return again and again, exploring different charter grounds each time. Sailing Greece is truly a lifetime's work.

Princess Louisa Inlet, British Columbia/NEIL RABINOWITZ

NORTHWEST

Gunkholer's Paradise

To many people, the Pacific Northwest is a land of gray skies, fir trees and driving rain. True, it does rain more often here than in other parts of North America, but the summers can bring weeks of predictable winds, calm seas and brilliant blue skies. For sailing, the best winds are in spring and fall, before and after the high season between Memorial and Labor Days. Summer winds are lighter and tend to blow from the southwest through northwest, with calms and light land breezes in evening, night and early morning hours, and a pleasant sea breeze that comes up about noon. This is a cruising ground for people who like rugged unspoiled scenery, superb fishing and sailing among a myriad of small islands.

Most US charterers take a boat out of Anacortes, Washington, while Canadian fleets operate from Vancouver and Vancouver Island. Distances can be large here, so many people prefer to rent a diesel trawler rather than a sailing yacht in these waters, particularly if they are bound for British Columbia.

Anacortes is a superb base for exploring the San Juan Islands, only 10 miles away across the Rosario Strait. The tides run strongly through the Strait, which should only be crossed in clear weather. Once among the islands you will find a good anchorage every few miles. Friday Harbor is the only town,

a small and crowded tourist community where you can buy supplies, and clear customs if inbound from the Canadian-owned Gulf Islands to the north. Roche Harbor, on the northwest coast of San Juan Island, is a popular destination with local sailors, famous for its resort hotel and many sheltered coves. There are no less than 11 state parks in the San Juans, all of them accessible from your yacht. One of the best is Spencer Spit, just over 10 miles from Anacortes.

You can explore the San Juans in a week, but a longer charter will tempt you to sail north across the border into the Gulf Islands. Clear customs on South Pender Island, then head north into a paradise of islands. The Gulfs are more sparsely populated than the San Juans, and you should be prepared to motor during the calm summer months. However, the lovely anchorages are worth it, places like Glenthorne Passage or Conover Cove on Saltspring Island. Some people spend but a day or two in the Gulf Islands, then head west for Victoria, at the southern end of Vancouver Island.

Many charterers plan more ambitious cruises north from Anacortes and Vancouver along the mainland Sunshine Coast. If you have the time, you can also cross the Strait of Georgia--but watch the tides and the weather. One favorite cruise takes you up the narrow Agamemnon Channel to Egmont, then 40 miles inland up spectacular Jervis Inlet, through the narrow Malibu Rapids at slack water, and into Princess Louisa Inlet, with its gorgeous 120-foot waterfall. If you have the time, make your way back down Jervis Inlet and head north again, this time into Desolation Sound, where there are so many scenic anchorages that you need months to explore them all.

WINDWARDS

The Other Caribbean

Sooner or later, you'll tire of the Virgins and think of exploring other Caribbean cruising grounds. We believe the more rugged Windward Islands, from St. Lucia in the north to Grenada in the south, offer some of the finest sailing in the West Indies.

Most bareboat charters in the Wind-

NEIL RABINOWITZ

wards start in St. Lucia or St. Vincent. St. Lucia is our favorite, for you can anchor in Anse des Pitons on the first evening of your charter. Anse des Pitons is one of the most spectacular anchorages in the world, with sugarloaf-shaped peaks towering 2,000' above the ocean. Anchoring is quite a challenge, for there is 600' of water only 400 yards from the beach. You should anchor 50 yards offshore and secure a stern line to a nearby tree.

From Anse des Pitons, most people sail south to Blue Lagoon or Young Island at the southern tip of St. Vincent, before taking off for the Grenadines. The prevailing trades allow you to reach comfortably down-island, even if the inter-island passages can be a trifle bumpy. Coming home, you'll be hard on the wind, so allow plenty of time to work your way up north.

The best time to sail here is between November and April, when the northeast trades blow steadily at a constant 15 to 25 knots. You sail down the westerly side of the islands, spending your first night at Bequia, only about nine miles from Blue Lagoon. Admiralty Bay, off the town, is a fine anchorage, and there are simple restaurants ashore. No visit to Bequia is complete without an excursion to Friendship Bay and the island of Petit Nevis off the south coast.

Most charterers head south from Bequia to Tobago Cays and Union Island. Tobago Cays consists of four islands inside Horse Shoe Reef. Avid snorkelers spend days here, either anchored off Baradal Island, or in the narrow cut between Petit Rameau and Petit Bateau Islands. You can walk ashore and

COURTESY THE MOORINGS

admire the aloes, collect shells on island beaches, or simply snorkel for hours on end. Nearby Palm Island, Union Island and Petit Saint Vincent offer a pleasant mix of island resorts, with the best anchorage in Clifton Harbor sheltered behind the reefs, just off the resort hotel.

From Union Island, it's a comfortable day's run south to Grenada, a superlative cruising ground by any standards. The best anchorages are along the southwestern coast, so plan to visit St. George's first. This is a good shopping town, and the public market on Wednesdays and Saturdays is always a treat. The Dutch-like architecture of the town is well worth a leisurely tour. The southwestern coast is a gunkholer's paradise with many sheltered anchorages. The anchorage west of Hog Island is among the best. At Hog Island, you eyeball your way between reefs, conning the ship from the bow through brilliantly clear water. Once inside, anchor in about 25 feet of water, and use your dinghy to explore the channel into Clarke's Court Bay and to snorkel local reefs. Most sailors work their way as far east as Bacaye Harbor, having explored many secluded anchorages like Port Egmont. The reefs are tricky here, so enter the harbor when the sun is high so you can detect changing water colors.

TONGA
South Pacific Paradise

Tonga's Vava'u islands in the South Pacific offer a unique opportunity to experience tropical sailing at its best. The people are friendly, there is plenty to do ashore, the tradewind sailing is magnificent, and the snorkeling and diving are beyond peer. This is a small cruising ground that inspires confidence. If you can sail the Virgins, you can charter here. All that's needed is some expertise with eyeball navigation through reefs and in shallow water. Anchoring presents few problems, and you can always check your set with a pair of goggles and a snorkel. You can charter anytime, but January through March is the hurricane season, and best avoided.

The islands are a scenic mixture of the Bahamas and the Virgins, but with a profusion of shallow coral reefs and fine white beaches. You'll find yourself sailing in the last independent monarchy in the Pacific, still largely untouched by modern civilization. The missionary influence here is very strong, and the islanders observe the Sabbath with Victorian rigor.

The highest islands are in the north and west, offering plenty of deep water anchorages and an ever-changing vista of cliffs, beaches and sheltered coves. The people live in small clusters of huts among extensive copra plantations. Sail to the east to view the great coral reefs that protect Vava'u. Inside the reef, you sail among tiny islets capped with a few palm trees and surrounded with gleaming white beaches. Many visitors spend their nights in the sheltered anchorages to the north and west, then sail down to the reef during the day for snorkeling and beachcombing.

The Moorings, the charter company of choice here, will supply you with a modern Beneteau yacht, and with a professional crew if you prefer. There is much to be said for hiring a Tongan skipper, especially if you want to fish or dive. They know all the best spots, and have excellent contacts in local villages. The charter base at Neiafu lies up the five-mile-long, fjord-like waterway that virtually bisects Vava'u. There are plenty of places to anchor along the fjord, and be sure to allow time for a visit to Swallow Cave on Kapa Island. The late afternoon sun shines into the water inside, illuminating coral formations deep under water.

Take a couple of days to get used to local conditions before sailing eastward into shallower water. The Fanua Tapu Passage takes you to the heart of the reefs, an easy trip provided you have a rising tide under you and high sun to see the shallows

COURTESY THE MOORINGS

Spend a night at nearby Makave village, and visit the Ofu village, a marvelous example of Tongan life, with the thatched huts laid out around a gently curving beach where fishermen mend their nets.

You can spend a fascinating day sailing the 10-mile passage inside the chain of reefs and islands to Maninita. You will need a local guide to anchor at Maninita. He will eyeball you into a small, sandy cove surrounded by coral heads and a beach. Alternatively, head over to Euakafa five miles away, a higher island where you can tramp over a 300' summit plateau and get some exercise. The more ambitious charterer can sail to Hunga Lagoon on the western island of Ava Pulepulekai. The entrance is narrow, and should only be attempted on a high tide.

Vava'u is one of the few charter areas where you can still experience tropical sailing as it was in the Caribbean before the days of package tours and large charter fleets. Visit soon before the word gets out.

WHITSUNDAYS

Down Under Cruising Haven

The Whitsundays lie near Townsville in northern Queensland, a tropical region with year-round sunshine and warm, clear waters. The charter fleet is based at Shute Harbor, which can be reached by air from Sydney or Brisbane. On the other side of the Whitsunday Channel is the Great Barrier Reef, one of the world's natural wonders. Crewed charters are quite popular here, and there are many fine yachts to choose from, including the Apollo, a former maxi ocean racer. More adventurous sailors venture out on their own, on a bareboat in the 30' to 45' range. Reserve a yacht well ahead of time, as the local demand is strong year-round.

The Whitsundays themselves are not part of the Barrier Reef. They are craggy islands with indented bays, rugged hills and snow-white sandy beaches, rimmed by protective coral reefs. The trade winds blow steadily here, lighter in summer and with greater, more predictable force during the Australian winter (May through August). You can sail year-round, but we prefer the southern winter months, even if the winds are stronger. Temperatures will be comfortable, and the sailing is simply better.

This is not a cruising ground for beginners, as the currents run strongly between islands and sudden downslope winds can put you on the coral at the entrance to an anchorage in seconds. A newcomer is best advised to engage a local skipper, at least for a couple of days, until you are used to Whitsunday sailing. Having said that, anyone with solid anchoring experience, and some familiarity with eyeball navigation and reefing should adjust rapidly to these waters. Anchoring in the Whitsundays requires care, and you will find yourself using plenty of anchor chain, and running your engine rather more than you might in home waters.

Note, incidently, that the Barrier Reef is 15 to 40 miles offshore, and that bareboats are forbidden to visit it. However, Air Whitsunday will actually pick you up in a seaplane from your yacht and take you for a half-day excursion to the low, sandy cays and reefs far offshore.

The Whitsundays are like the Virgins in one sense: you can combine days of quiet solitude with occasional congenial evenings ashore at the various resorts, such as Hamilton Island, that dot the area. Many maintain moorings for floating visitors, and dinner and a few drinks is a wonderful way to meet the locals on their own turf. They are some of the friendliest people in the world. If your tastes run to the unspoiled, have no fear. There are 74 Whitsunday Islands, and you can lose yourself for days among them. This is a "lunch hook" charter area where you can anchor off any number of pristine white beaches and walk ashore, your feet scuffing sand that may not have seen another soul for months. The choice of overnight anchorages is unending, including such famous spots as Butterfly Bay and Macona Inlet, where you can lie in solitude and snorkel among colorful coral heads, or simply climb ashore to admire the view.

RONNA NELSON

269

The Top Bareboat Charter Companies

NEIL RABINOWITZ

*H*ERE IS OUR LIST OF THE MAJOR PLAYERS IN THE WORLD OF BAREBOAT CHARTERING. While all these companies are good, their prices vary considerably, as do the features of the yachts they offer for charter. Remember that your boat will be your home for a week or more. It must be comfortable and reliable. In general, the newer the boat the better. You'll also find that the latest French designs (Beneteau, Centurian, Jeanneau, Oceanis) offer superior comfort and privacy.

We use the following codes to describe features: BB (Bareboat), CB (Chaseboat), CC (Crewed charter), DIO (Dinghy with outboard included in price), MH (Multihull available), PROV (Provisioning plan), REFR (Onboard refrigeration), TRAV (Air/land package can be arranged). The price for comparison purposes is a 42' to 45' monohull in the Caribbean during the week of January 20-26, 1992.

■ ATM YACHTS
2280 University Drive, Ste. 120, Newport Beach, CA 92660, (800) 634-8822.

4 years in business, 200 yachts, 32' to 50' (aver. 3 years), BB & CC, CB, DIO, MH, PROV basic, REFR all boats, TRAV. Bases: Tahiti, Martinique, Guadeloupe, St. Martin, Grenadines. Best Boats: Lagoon 42' Cat, Jeanneau 442, Oceanis 515. Pricing: Below Average (44' $3,000). Boat Rating: ★★★★ Overall Rating: ★★★★ (Pacific); ★★★ (Carib.)

ATM runs an outstanding program in French Polynesia, and it is building a strong reputation in the Caribbean. ATM's French-designed yachts are spacious and comfortable, though they are not quite as well equipped as similarly sized craft from The Moorings or CSY. ATM's big catamarans are superb vessels for cruising, offering great stability, roomy interiors and acres of deck space. Our first choice for a Polynesian charter would be an ATM multihull.

■ CARIBBEAN SAILING YACHTS (CSY)
P.O. Box 152379, Tampa, FL 33684, (800) 631-1593, or (813) 886-6783.

25 years in business, 48 yachts, 42' to 51' (aver. 2 years), BB, CB, CC, REFR + inverter, TRAV. Bases: St. Vincent (17), Tortola (31). Best Boats: CSY 51, CSY 50, CSY 445. Pricing: Average (44' $2,370 until 1/31; $3,150 High Season). Boat Rating: ★★★★ Overall Rating: ★★★★

Many sailors would rank CSY among the top three in the Caribbean. One of the most experienced companies around, it runs a very professional operation in the Grenadines and Tortola. Its yachts are fitted out with complete charter equipment, and it offers attractive rates during some periods, such as mid-January, which are considered high season by other operators. You should definitely check out CSY before booking any Caribbean charter.

■ CARIBBEAN YACHT CHARTERS (CYC)
P.O. Box 583, Marblehead, MA 01945, (800) 225-2520, or (617) 599-7990 in MA.

24 years in business, 42 yachts, 38' to 52' (aver. 2 years), BB, CB, CC, REFR, FLO on custom basis, PROV deluxe, TRAV. Bases: St. Thomas (42). Best Boats: Frers 51, Frers 44, S&S 47. Pricing: Low (44' $2,795). Boat Rating: ★★★ Overall Rating: ★★★★

The oldest and largest operation in St. Thomas. CYC is one of the stalwarts in the USVI cruising trade. Its charters can be considerably cheaper than The Moorings during certain periods, yet the standard of boat maintenance and customer service is high. As with any charter in the Virgins, expect crowded anchorages during peak season.

■ GPSC CHARTERS, LTD.
600 St. Andrews Road, Philadelphia, PA 19118, (800) 732-6786, or (215) 247-3903; FAX: (215) 247-1505.

14 years in business, 150+ yachts, 30' to 250' (aver. 1.5 years), BB, CB some locations, CC, MH, PROV split, full, or custom, REFR larger yachts, TRAV. Bases: Guadeloupe, Greece (70-Athens, Rhodes), Italy (10-Sardinia), Spain (12-Palma, Mallorca), Turkey (20-Kalkan, Marmaris), Thailand (25), Yugoslavia (20-Split, Dubrovnik). Best Boats: Express 510 (51'), Sun Magic 44', Baltic 40'. Pricing: Below Average (44' $3,000). Boat Rating: ★★ to ★★★★ Overall Rating: ★★★

GPSC, a Greek-based company, offers one of the biggest charter operations in the world. GPSC has recently added many new vessels to its Caribbean inventory, including some of the very popular French boats. GPSC is a very good choice for a flotilla charter in the eastern Mediterranean, although Kavos (affiliated with The Moorings) offers stiff competition in Greece.

■ (LA VIDA MARINA) FIRST CLASS CHARTERS
Suite 237, Red Hook Plaza, St. Thomas, USVI 00802, (800) 835-7719.

12 years in business, 24 yachts (sail & power), 44' to 51' (aver. 2 years), BB, CB, CC, DIO, PROV basic & deluxe, REFR all, some AC. Bases: St. Thomas (24). Best Boats: Centurian 47, Sun Magic 44, Sun Odyssey 51. Pricing: Above Average (44' $3650). Boat Rating: ★★★★ Overall Rating: ★★★★

First Class Charters at La Vida Marina is the former La Vida operation, and is still one of the best in the USVI. This is a small, but high-quality charter service. Client satisfaction has been well above average, and the yachts are roomy and comfortable. Although prices are generally on a par with

The Moorings, you should compare rates carefully. For certain weeks, First Class Charters may be less expensive, or vice versa.

■ THE MOORINGS

19345 US 19 North, Ste. 402, Clearwater, FL 34624, (800) 535-7289, or (813) 535-1446 in FL.

24 years in business, 600+ yachts, 27' to 51' (aver. 2 years), BB, CB, CC, DIO, PROV split or full, REFR, TRAV. Bases: Tortola (137), St. Martin (23), Grenada, Guadeloupe, St. Lucia (41), Baja (11), France, Greece, Italy, Spain, Turkey, Tonga (14), Tahiti (14), Thailand. Best Boats: Moorings 510, Moorings 32 S5, Moorings 433. Pricing: Above Average (43' $3,700). Boat Rating: ★★★★ Overall Rating: ★★★★★

A world leader in bareboating, The Moorings is *the* company to beat in the BVI, and is the only large operator in Tonga and the Sea of Cortez, two great cruising destinations. The Moorings' prices are fairly high, but its yachts are fitted with many features, such as power winches and extra ventilation, that really make a difference. The Moorings is very responsive to the needs of novice charterers--among other things, it has added a number of smaller yachts to its fleet, and it offers a free skipper for the first two days of your cruise. It also runs the innovative Club Mariner program for those who want to combine a land-based resort holiday with a cruise aboard a skippered yacht. We've heard some complaints about minor equipment problems in the Caribbean late season, but otherwise, The Moorings is at the top of the class.

■ PRIVILEGE CHARTERS INC.

1650 S.E. 17th Street, Suite 204, Ft. Lauderdale, FL, 33316, (800) 262-0308, or (305) 462-2706; FAX: (201) 342-7498.

3 years in business, 42 yachts, 39' to 48' (aver. 2 years in Carib.), BB, CB some locations, CC, PROV split or full, REFR, AIR and cook on larger boats. Bases: Bahamas (Marsh Harbor), St. Lucia, Galapagos, the Grenadines (Union), Guadaloupe, St. Martin, Tahiti. Best Boats: Privilege 39 Cat, Privilege 43 Cat, Privilege 48 Cat. Pricing: High (39' $4,950). Boat Rating: ★★★★★ Overall Rating: ★★★★

For well-to-do charterers looking for the most comfortable and luxurious charter craft around, Privilege is hard to beat. Its fleet is composed entirely of fast, stable and beautifully appointed catamarans. Very shallow draft makes anchoring a snap. Families with small children will appreciate the vast deck space and absence of heel while underway. All boats carry windsurfers and electric refrigeration. The larger boats come with skippers and superb cooks.

■ SUN YACHT CHARTERS

P.O. Box 737, Camden, ME 04843, (800) 772-3500, or (207) 236-9611.

14 years in business, 78 yachts, 36' to 51' (aver. 1.5 years), BB, CB, CC, DIO, MH, PROV std. & gourmet, REFR, TRAV. Bases: Camden (ME), Antigua, St. Martin (90 percent of fleet in Caribbean) Best Boats: Jeanneau 51, Centurian 42, Pajot 45 Cat. Pricing: Above Average (44' $3,970). Boat Rating: ★★★★ Overall Rating: ★★★

Sun operates very roomy, comfortable French boats, mostly new or nearly new. The yachts come very well equipped, as they should; Sun's prices aren't cheap. Sun offers some nice extras such as untippable dinghies, and a complimentary skipper to the first anchorage. Great new 39' and 45' multihulls may join the fleet this winter. These are some of the fastest yet most comfortable craft in the Caribbean, and are ideal for large groups and families.

■ SUNSAIL

3347 N.W. 55th Street, Ft. Lauderdale, FL 33309, (800) 327-2276, or (305) 484-5246.

16 years in business, 500 yachts, 24' to 55' (aver. 1.5 years), BB, CC, CB, DIO, FLO, MH, REFR on most, PROV basic split or full, TRAV. Bases: Tortola, St. Lucia, Grenada, Greece, Corsica, Sardinia, Turkey, Thailand, Yugoslavia (120 boats in Caribbean, 100+ in Med.). Best Boats: Beneteau 38-S5, Beneteau 45-F5, Oceanis 500. Pricing: Average (45' $3,295). Boat Rating: ★★★ Overall Rating: ★★★★

Sunsail (formerly Sunsail Stevens) recently combined with Bahamas Yachting Services (BYS), and now maintains one of the largest fleets of bareboat yachts in the world. It is a top choice for the Mediterranean; it maintains a large fleet in the Caribbean; and it has the best bareboat operation going in Thailand, a hot new destination. Sunsail runs a very professional program and its peak season rates are lower than its leading competitors such as The Moorings.

CHOOSING A CHARTER COMPANY

Here are the most important factors to consider before you book any bareboat trip. Attention to these details will help you avoid the most common problems bareboaters encounter.

■ *Choose a charterer with a proven track record.*

Look for a bonded company that has been in business for at least 10 years. Although longevity is no guarantee of quality, you will avoid the typical problems associated with start-ups.

■ *Ask about the age and condition of the yachts.*

Pick a company that can give you a boat under five years old, if at all possible. Bareboats take a lot of abuse, and a craft can become a real headache after just a few seasons of use.

■ *Learn the hidden costs in advance.*

Know what you'll be spending *before* you set sail. Your bareboat fee typically omits provisioning, charter taxes, land accommodations, and extras such as windsurfers or dive gear. You may even have to pay extra for insurance--an absolute necessity.

■ *Find out what qualifications are required.*

Almost all charter companies will ask you to provide a sailing resume establishing that you have previous experience on a yacht of the size you plan to charter. Having an ASA certificate helps, but this is no guarantee that you'll be allowed to bareboat. When you arrive in your destination, you'll be checked out on the water, and a skipper will be put on board if necessary.

■ *Find out the best season to sail.*

Just because you pay high season prices doesn't mean conditions will be ideal. Ask about wind, weather and water temperatures before you go. In many parts of the Caribbean, the best sailing is in the late spring when prices are much lower and the anchorages are far less crowded.

■ *Ask for references from past customers.*

Before you put down a deposit, talk to customers who recently chartered the same type of yacht in the same area. You will learn vital facts no brochure would reveal.

■ *Don't be too cheap.*

Seasonal discounts notwithstanding, you generally get what you pay for when bareboating. Don't be overly swayed by low prices--saving a few dollars can result in a miserable vacation if your boat is a lemon.

BEST BAREBOAT OPERATIONS WORLDWIDE

T HIS CHART FEATURES THE LEADING BAREBOAT OPERATIONS IN THE MOST POPULAR CRUISING GROUNDS worldwide. Due to space constraints, many good charter companies are not covered, particularly in the Caribbean (see our World Directory). However, if you stick to the listings in this chart, you can count on a top-flight charter holiday. You are also likely to get a better, newer boat, and a wider range of options. Where a charterer offers a variety of vessels, we have selected the best and/or most modern in the fleet. In general, the French boats (Jeanneau, First, Beneteau) offer the most usable space and privacy in their class.

Codes: Fuel included (FI); Dinghy included (DI); Dinghy with outboard (DIO); Flotilla (FLO); Sailing instruction (SI); Dive gear option (DV); Windsurfer option (WS); Cook (CK); Multihull (MH); Spinnaker (SP); High season/Low season (HS/LS); Per person (pp). SKILL: This rates the skill required to sail and navigate safely; 1 is the easiest, 4 is the most difficult. NOTE: High season rates are for winter 1992. Prices or discount programs are subject to change and currency fluctuations.

R. RILEY, COURTESY THE MOORINGS

LOCATION	CHARTER OPERATOR	PHONE	YACHTS (BERTHS/PRIVATE CABINS/HEADS)	SKILL
ALASKA	58'22" NORTH	(907) 789-7301	Catalina 30 (6/2/1), Catalina 36 (6/2/1)	3
ANTIGUA	SUN CHARTERS	(800) 772-3500	Centurian 40 (6/2/2), Jeanneau 44 (6/3/2), Jeanneau 51 (10/5/4)	2
AUSTRALIA	WHITSUNDAY RENT A YACHT	(800) 551-2012	Columbia 27 (5/2/1), Chieftan 38 (8/3/1), Beneteau 430 (8/4/4)	1
BAHAMAS	SUNSAIL	(800) 327-2276	Endeavor 33 (5/2/1), Endeavor 40 (7/2/2), BYS 52 (10/4/4)	1
	ABACO BAHAMAS	(800) 626-5690	Newport 33 (6/1/1), CSY 33 (5/1/1), CSY 44 (7/2/2)	1
BAJA (Sea of Cortez)	THE MOORINGS	(800) 535-7289	Moorings 38 (5/2/2), Moorings 433 (7/3/3), Moorings 51 (8/4/4)	2
CALIFORNIA (Channel Is.)	SANTA BARBARA SAIL. CNTR.	(800) 350-9090	Catalina 30 (6/2/1), Catalina 36 (7/2/1), Moorings 50 (9/4/2)	3
CHESAPEAKE BAY	AYS	(800) 452-6287	Pearson 33 (6/2/1), Beneteau 390 (6/2/1), Pearson 422 (7/3/2)	2
	NORTH-EAST WIND CHRTRS.	(800) 638-5139	Ericson 38 (6/2/1), Morgan 41 (7/3/2), Tayana 42 (6/2/1)	2
FLORIDA KEYS	FLORIDA YACHT CHARTERS	(800) 537-0050	Hunter 30 (5/2/1), Hunter 35 (5/2/1), Passage 42 (6/2/2)	1
	SW FLORIDA YACHTS	(800) 262-7939	Catalina 34 (6/2/1), Crealock 37 (6/2/1), Irwin 41 (6/2/2)	1
GREECE	GPSC	(800) 732-6786	GPSC 40 (6/3/2), 51 (9/4/3), 54 (9/5/5)	2-4
	SUNSAIL	(800) 678-7044	First 305 (5/2/1) FLO, First 345 (6/3/1), First 375 (8/3/1)	2-4
GRENADA	THE MOORINGS	(800) 535-7289	Moorings 38 (6/2/2), 433 (7/3/3), 500 (10/5/5)	3
	CSY	(800) 631-1593	CSY 42 (6/3/2), CSY 445 (7/3/2), CSY 50 (9/4/2)	3
GUADELOUPE	ATM YACHTS	(800) 227-5317	ATM 403 (6/3/2), ATM 442 (5/4/2), 42' MH (7/3/2), 48' MH (10/5/4)	3
	THE MOORINGS	(800) 535-7289	Moorings 38 (6/2/2), Moorings 445 (8/4/2), Moorings 500 (10/5/5)	3
ITALY (Corsica, Sardinia)	SUNSAIL	(800) 678-7044	Oceanis 32 (4/2/1), Oceanis 35 (6/3/1), Oceanis 43 (6/3/2)	3
MAINE	HINCKLEY CHARTERS	(207) 244-5008	Sabre 34 (5/2/1), Hinckley 42 (7/2/1), Mason 44 (6/2/1)	3
	SUN CHARTERS	(800) 772-3500	Pierson 30 (5/1/1), Baltic 38 (6/2/1), O'Day 40 (6/2/2)	3
MARTINIQUE	ATM YACHTS	(800) 227-5317	ATM 403 (6/3/2), ATM 442 (5/2/2), 42' MH (7/3/2), 48' MH (10/5/4)	3
NEW ZEALAND	CHARTER LINK	(011 64) 9-535-8710	Carpenter 29 (5/1/1), Raven 31 (7/2/1), Beneteau 35 (8/3/1)	2
	RAINBOW CHARTERS	(800) 227-5317	Davidson 28 (4/1), Farr 34' (6/2/1), Farr 40 (6/3/2)	2
PACIFIC NW (Canada)	PACIFIC QUEST CHARTERS	(604) 682-2205	C&C 30 (5/1/1), C&C 33 (6/2/1), C&C 38 (7/2/1)	2
	ANACORTES YACHT CHTRS.	(800) 233-3004	Catalina 30 (6/2/1), Beneteau 35 (6/3/1), Beneteau 38 (8/3/2)	2
ST. LUCIA	THE MOORINGS	(800) 535-7289	Moorings 38 (6/2/2), Moorings 433 (6/3/3), Moorings 500 (10/5/6)	2
	SUNSAIL	(800) 678-7044	Beneteau 39 (6/2/2), Oceanis 500 (8/4/4)	2
ST. MARTIN (St. Maarten)	CARIBBEAN SAILING CLUB	(800) 444-3996	Cent. 36 (5/2/1), Jeanneau 44 (6/3/2), Jeanneau 51 (9/4/5)	3
	PRIVILEGE CHARTERS	(800) 262-0308	Privilege 39 MH (8/4/4), Privilege 43 MH, Privilege 48 MH (9/5/5)	3
	THE MOORINGS	(800) 535-7289	Moorings 38 (6/2/2), Moorings 430 (8/4/4), Moorings 500 (10/5/5)	2
	SUN CHARTERS	(800) 772-3500	Centurian 40 (6/2/2), Centurian 42 (7/3/2), Centurian 47 (8/4/2)	2
ST. VINCENT	CSY	(800) 631-1593	CSY 42 (6/3/2), CSY 445 (7/3/2), CSY 50 (9/4/2)	3-4
	BAREFOOT YACHT CHARTERS	(800) 677-3195	Barefoot 44 (8/3/3), Jeanneau 12.5m (6/3/2), Jeanneau 41 (6/3/2)	3-4
TAHITI	THE MOORINGS	(800) 535-7289	Moorings 38 (6/2/2), 432 (6/3/3), 510 (10/5/5)	2
	ATM YACHTS	(800) 227-5317	ATM 403 (6/3/2), ATM 515 (10/4/4), 48' MH (10/5/4) with skipper	2
THAILAND	SUNSAIL	(800) 768-7044	Sundance 36 (6/3/2), Suncharm 39 (6/3/2) (10-day charter)	3
TONGA	THE MOORINGS	(800) 535-7289	Moorings 38 (6/2/2), 433 (7/3/3), Moorings 510 (10/5/5)	2
TORTOLA (Brit. Virgins)	CSY	(800) 631-1593	CSY 42 (6/3/2), CSY 445 (7/3/2), CSY 50 (9/4/2)	2-3
	THE MOORINGS	(800) 535-7289	Moorings 38 (6/2/2), Moorings 433 (6/3/3), Moorings 500 (10/5/5)	2-3
TURKEY	GPSC	(800) 732-6786	Sundance 36 (6/3/1), Sun Magic 44 (9/4/2), Sun Odyssey 50 (9/4/5)	2-3
	SUNSAIL	(800) 678-7044	Oceanis 320 (6/2/1), 38' (8/3/1), 390 (7/3/1) (Prices for 14-day charters)	2-3
U.S. VIRGINS	CYC	(800) 225-2520	Frers 44 (6/2/2), S&S 47 (8/3/2), Frers 51 (8/3/2)	2
	FIRST CLASS CHARTERS	(800) 835-7719	Jenneau Sun Magic 44 (7/3/2), Sun Odyssey 51 (8/4/5)	2
YUGOSLAVIA	GPSC	(800) 732-6786	Sundance 36 (6/3/1), Sun Magic 44 (9/4/2), Sun Odyssey 50 (9/4/5)	2-4
	SUNSAIL	(800) 678-7044	First 29 (4/2/1) FLO, Oceanis 35 (6/3/2), Oceanis 39 (7/3/2)	2-4

ONNE VAN DER VAL, STOCK NEWPORT

RONNA NELSON

R. RILEY, COURTESY THE MOORINGS

Cost/Week HS	Cost/Week LS	Skipper Cost/Day	Hotel Avail.	Deposit or Insurance	Provision Cost/Day	Features	Rating
30' $1200, 36' $1750	Same	$175	Yes	$1000	NA	FI, DI, SI	★★★
44' $3970, 51' $5300	44' $1870, 51' $2700	$100	Yes	$1500, $18/day	$19 pp	FI, DIO, SI, WS	★★★
38' $2800, 43' $4760	Same	$130 AUS	Yes	$500	$19 pp	FI, DI, DV, WS, CK	★★★
33' $1890, 40' $2600	33' $1050, 40' $1595	$85	No	$500	$18 pp	FI, DI, WS	★★
33' $1450, 44' $2000	2 weeks for price of 1	NA	Yes	$500	$18 pp	FI, DI	★★
38' $2185, 433 $2700	38' $1491, 433 $1757	$70	Yes	$14/day	$20 pp	FI, DIO, WS, CK $70/day	★★★★
30' $865, 36' $1245	Same	$150	Yes	$500 30', $1000 36'	NA	FI, DI, SI	★★
33' $940, 390 $1380	33' $850, 39' $1245	$150	No	$500	NA	FI, DI $12/day, SI	★★
38' $1395, 41' $1610	38' $1250, 41' $1450	$140	No	$500	Avail.	DI ($75/week)	★★
35' $1550, 42' $2500	35' $1400, 42' $2200	$100	Yes	$1500 35', $2000 42'	$25 pp	DI (oars)	★★
34' $1379, 41' $2334	34' $1103, 41' $1867	$100	No	$650 34', $1300 41'	NA	DI	★★
40' $2275, 51' $4515	40' $1820, 51' $3640	$100	Yes	$1000	NA	FI, DI, WS	★★★★
305 $3865, 375 $5337 (2 wks)	305 $1945, 375 $2153 (2 wks)	$100	Yes	25%	NA	DI, WS, SI	★★★
38' $3052, 433 $3906	38' $1603, 433 $2051	$80	Yes	$14/day	$21 pp	FI, DIO, DV, WS, CK $60/day	★★★★
44' $3150, 50' $3570	44' $2020, 50' $2280	$80	Yes	Inquire	$20 pp	FI, DI, DV, WS	★★★
403 $3180, 42' $5138	403 $2300, 42' $3693	$130	Yes	$1100 to $2900	$30 pp	FI, DI, DV, WS, SP, CK $84/day	★★★
38' $3206, 445 $4165	38' $1680, 445 $2275	$115	Yes	$14/day	$21 pp	FI, DIO, WS, SP, CK $80/day	★★★★
32' $3988, 35' $4910	32' $2147, 35' $2761	$100	Yes	25%	NA	DI, WS, SI	★★★
34' $1750, 42' $3000 (1991)	34' $1375, 42' $2375 (1991)	NA	Yes	$65 to $130 ins./wk	Inquire	FI, DI	★★★
30' $1500, 38' $2300 (1991)	30' $1400, 38' $2100 (1991)	$125	No	$1000	NA	DI, SI	★★
403 $3180, 42' $5138	403 $2300, 42' $3690	$126	Yes	$2200 to $3200	$28 pp	FI, DI, DV, WS, SP, CK $84/day	★★★
31' $1910, 33' $2205	29' $1115, 33' $1365	$60	No	$350 $NZ	$17 pp	FI, DI, WS, SI	★★
28' $1550, 40' $2900	28' $900, 40' $1800	$110	Yes	33%	$20 pp	FI, DI, DV, WS, SP, CK ($70)	★★★
30' $1500, 38' $2100	30' $900, 38' $1290	Call	No	$1100 to $2000	NA	DI (Price includes 13% GST)	★★
30' $950, 38' $1575 (1991)	30' $715, 38' $1200 (1991)	$150	No	$500 to $1000	$23 pp	DI, CB	★★
433 $3406, 500 $5509	433 $2051, 500 $2842	$80	Yes	$14/day	$21 pp	FI, DIO, DV, WS, CK $60/day	★★★
39' $3200, 500 $5200	39' $1700, 500 $2700	$85	Yes	$500, $12/day	$17 pp	FI, DI, DV, WS, CK $65/day	★
44' $800 pp, 51' $800 pp	44' $500 pp, 51' $500 pp	$110	Yes	$250, $15/day	Incl.	FI, DIO, WS, CK $55/day, DV	★★★
39' $4950, 48' $9950	39' $2950, 48' $8600	$100 or incl.	Yes	Included	Incl.	FI, DIO, WS, DV, SP, CK on 48'	★★★★
38' $3206, 500 $5509	38' $1680, 500 $2842	$105	Yes	$14/day	$19 pp	FI, DIO, WS, CK $80/day	★★★
40' $3370, 47' $4390	40' $1700, 47' $2500	$100	Yes	$1500, $18/day	$24 pp	FI, DIO, SI, WS	★★★
42' $2765, 50' $3570	42' $1386, 50' $2282	$50	Yes	$500	$20 pp	FI, DI, DV, WS	★★★
41' $2855, 44' $3595	41' $1555, 44' $2595	$100	Yes	$500 dep., $15/day	$20 pp	DIO, WS, CK $65/day, DV	★★
38' $2380, 432 $2807	38' $2177, 432 $2709	$95	Yes	$14/day	$25 pp	FI, DIO, WS, CK $85/day	★★★★
48' $7950, 515 $5400	48' $6620, 515 $4500	Incl.; $130	Yes	$1100 to $2900	$30 pp	FI, DI, DV, WS, SP, CK $90	★★★
36' $4000, 39' $4550 (10 day)	36' $2370, 39' $2730 (10-day)	$100	Yes	25%, $75/week	$20 pp	FI, DI, WS, SI, CK $80/day	★★★
38' $2534, 432 $3052	38' $2303, 432 $2744	$60	Yes	$14/day	$29 pp	FI, DI, WS, CK $50/day	★★★★
44' $3150, 50' $3570	44' $1575, 50' $1785	$80	Yes	Inquire	$20 pp	FI, DI, DV, WS	★★★
38' $3052, 433 $3906	38' $1603, 433 $2051	$80	Yes	$14/day	$18 pp	FI, DIO, DV, WS, SI, CK $70/day	★★★★
36' $2415, 44' $3920	36' $1610, 44' $2415	$85	Yes	$1100 to $2500	Optional	DI, WS	★★★
320 $3926, 390 $5706 (2 wks)	320 $2147, 390 $2761	$100	Yes	$500 dep., $20/day	$23 pp	FI, DIO, DV, CK $85/day	★★★
44' $3095, 47' $3695	44' $1995, 47' $2195	$75	Yes	$10/day	$19 pp	FI, DI, WS	★★
44' $3650, 51' $5250	44' $2185, 51' $3330	$100	Yes	Inquire	$23 pp	FI, DI, WS, SI, CB	★★★
36' $2500, 50' $5845	36' $1680, 50' $4200	$85	Yes	$1100 to $2500	Optional	DI, WS	★★★
29' $3037, 39' $5828	29' $1656, 39' $3374	$100	Yes	25%, $47-75/day	NA	FI, DI, WS, FLO, CK $80/day	★★★

COURTESY THE MOORINGS

BELOW WE PROVIDE COMPLETE LISTINGS FOR CHARTER COMPANIES AROUND THE WORLD THAT DID NOT QUALIFY FOR OUR DEtailed profiles on the preceding pages. In general, you will find the best companies in the more competitive markets, such as the Caribbean and the Mediterranean. A check mark denotes a specially recommended company. The codes BB, CC, and SK stand for bareboat, crewed charter, and skippered charter respectively.

ALASKA

◆

58'22" North, P.O. Box 32391, Juneau, AK 99803, (907) 789-7301. Summer sailing, BB or SK. Cruising grounds: Southeast Alaska, Glacier Bay.

AUSTRALIA

◆

Queensland Yacht Charter; Whitsunday Rent a Yacht. BB, SK & CC. For both, contact US agent SO/PAC Travel Marketing, 7080 Hollywood Blvd., Suite 201, Hollywood, CA 90028, (800)551-2012; FAX: (213) 871-0811. Cruising grounds: Whitsunday Islands, various bases.

ASIA

◆

Asia Isles Yacht Charters, 70 Shenton Way, Unit 19-03, Marina House, Singapore 0207, 2222

879. BB, FLO, SK & CC. Cruising grounds: Singapore, Malaysia, Thailand, or call Jubilee Yacht Charter, (800) 922-4871.

Thai Yachting Co., Ltd., Rajdamri Arcade, 7th Floor, Rajdamri Road, Bangkok, Thailand, (011 66) 251 6755; FAX: 251 6920. Or call GPSC in the US, (800) 732-6786. FLO, SK, & CC. Cruising grounds: Thailand, Malaysia, Penang.

BAHAMAS/FLORIDA KEYS

◆

Abaco Bahamas Charters, 10905 Cowgill Place, Louisville, KY 40243, (800) 626-5690, or (502) 245-9428. 30+ yachts, 33'-44', BB. Cruising grounds: Abaco Bahamas ONLY; bases in Hope Town and Abaco.

Eleuthera Bahamas Charters, 190 Widgeon, Drive, Eastham, MA 02642, (800) 548-9684; FAX: (508) 255-8971. 25 yachts, 35'-44', BB, SK & CC. 2 weeks for 1 off-season rates. Cruising grounds: All Bahamas; based in Hatchet Bay, Eleuthera.

Florida Yacht Charters & Sales Inc., 1290 5th Street, Miami Beach Marina, Miami Beach, FL 33139, (800) 537-0050, (305) 532-8600. 20 yachts, BB & SK, 27'-60'. Cruising grounds: East Florida.

Southwest Florida Yachts, 3444 Marinatown Lane, NW, N. Fort Myers, FL 33903, (800) 262-7939, or (813) 656-1339. 28 yachts, 24'-44', BB & SK. Cruising grounds: all Florida; bases in Ft. Meyers and Punta Gorda.

BRITISH ISLES/IRELAND

◆

Clyde Offshore Sailing Centre, Kip Marina, Inverkip, Renfrewshire, Scotland PA16 0AS, (011 44) 475-521210. 12 yachts, BB & SK. Cruising grounds: Scotland, Azores.

Hebridean Cruising Co. Ltd., Dunsteaffnage, Yacht Haven, Near Oban, Argyll, Scotland PA37 1PX, (011 44) 631-65616; FAX: 0631 66725. 14 yachts, 25'-42', BB & SK. Spring through fall. Cruising grounds: Scottish coast, lochs.

Jersey Yacht Charters, P.O. Box 531, Caledonia House, Caledonia Place, St. Helier, Jersey, Channel Islands, (011 44) 534 78522; FAX: 534 71032. March through October, 6 very well-equipped yachts, 35'-50', BB & SK. Cruising grounds: Normandy and Brittany coast, Channel Islands.

Yachting Int'l Ireland, Trident Hotel, Kinsale, Co. Cork, Ireland, (011 353) 61-333206; FAX: 353 21-774173. 11 yachts, 32'-42', BB, SK & CC. Cruising grounds: South Ireland, also Canaries.

CARIBBEAN

◆

Barefoot Yacht Charters, 2550 Stag Run Blvd., No. 111, Clearwater, FL 34625, (800) 677-3195; FAX: (813) 797-3195. 1 year. 8 yachts; new fleet April 1992, BB & SK, 40'-44'. Cruising grounds: St. Vincent, The Grenadines. Base in St. Vincent.

Caribbean Sailing Charters, 3883 Andrews Crossing, Roswell, GA 30075, (800) 824-1331, or (404) 641-9640. 27 years. 18 BB yachts, 33'-50'. CC to 200'. Cruising grounds: USVI, St. Thomas base.

Caribbean Yacht Owners Assn., Box 9997, St. Thomas, USVI 00801, (800) 524-2073; FAX: (809) 774-6910. 12 years, 25 yachts, 34'-51', BB, SK & CC. Excellent sailing school. Cruising grounds: US and British Virgins, St. Thomas base.

Nautor Swan Charter, c/o Lynn Jachney Charters, P.O. Box 302, Marblehead, MA 01945, Phone: (800) 223-2050. Beautiful Swan yachts, 36'-65', BB, SK & CC. Cruising grounds: Leeward Islands; base in St. Martin.

Soleil et Voile, c/o Le Boat Inc., P.O. Box E, Maywood, NJ 07607, (800) 922-0291, or (201) 342-1838; FAX: (201) 342-7498. 65+ yachts, BB & CC, 30-50' (aver. 2 years) New, roomy French boats, including fast 34'-50' multihulls. Cruising grounds: Guadeloupe, Martinique, St. Martin.

CENTRAL/GREAT LAKES

◆

Bay Breeze Yacht Charters, 12935 W. Bayshore Drive, Traverse City, MI 49684, (616) 941-0535. 27 yachts, 27'-65', BB & SK. Cruising grounds: Lake Huron and Lake Michigan.

Canadian Yacht Charters Ltd., R.R. 2, Minesing, ONT, Canada L0L 1Y0, (705) 721-4297. 21 yachts, 27'-40', BB & SK. Cruising grounds: North Channel (Lake Huron), Georgian Bay and Gore Bay.

Discovery Yacht Charters, 1 Port Street East, Mississauga, Ontario L5G 4N1, (416) 891-1999. 12 yachts, 26'-38', BB & SK. Cruising grounds: Manitoulin Island, Little Current.

Harbor North, 400 Huron Street, Huron, OH 44839, (419) 433-6010. 14 years, 30 yachts, 27'-40', BB & SK. Cruising grounds: Lake Huron.

EAST COAST

◆

AYS Charter and Sailing School, 7416 Edgewood Road, Annapolis, MD 21403, (800) 452-6287, (301) 267-8181. 7 years, 25 yachts, 30'-46', BB & SK. Cruising grounds: Chesapeake Bay. ✓

Carolina Wind Yacht Sales & Charters, P.O. Box 967, Washington, NC 27889, (800) 334-7671.

10+ yachts, 30'-50', BB & SK. Cruising grounds: Pamlico and Albemarle Sounds, Cape Hatteras.

Hinckley Yacht Charters, Bass Harbor Marine, Bass Harbor, ME 04653, (207) 244-5008. 26 years, 38 yachts, 30'-44', BB & SK. Hinckley Caribbean--contact Proper Yachts, P.O. Box 70, Cruz Bay, St. John, USVI 00830, (809) 776-6256. 12 yachts, 38'-51', BB, SK & CC. Cruising grounds: Maine, US and British Virgins.

McKibben Sailing Vacations, 176 Battery, Burlington, VT 05401, (800) 522-0028. 8 years, 12 yachts to 38', BB & SK. Cruising grounds: Lake Champlain.

North-East Wind Yacht Charters, P.O. Box 4220, 306 Second Street, #27, Annapolis, MD 21403, (800) 638-5139. 11 years, 24 yachts 30'-52', BB & SK. Cruising grounds: Chesapeake Bay.

EUROPE (NORTH)

◆

First Class Charters, c/o Le Boat, Inc., (800) 922-0291; FAX: (201) 342-7498. Cruising grounds: Sweden and Norway.

Poseidon Yacht Charters, c/o Le Boat Inc., P.O. Box E, Maywood NJ, 07607, (800) 922-0291;

COURTESY THE MOORINGS

FAX: (201) 342-7498. 13 years, 100+ yachts BB, SK & CC. Cruising grounds: Denmark, Holland, Sweden, Turkey, Yugoslavia.

MEDITERRANEAN

◆

Jubilee Yacht Charters (agency), 51 White Oak Shade Road, New Canaan, CT 06840, (800) 922-4871, (203) 655-7227. BB, SK, CC & FLO all sizes. Cruising grounds: France, Greece, Italy, Turkey, Yugoslavia.

Russell Yacht Charters (agency), 2750 Black Rock Turnpike, Fairfield, CT 06430, (800) 635-8895. Hundreds of yachts, 32'-53', BB, SK, CC & FLO. Cruising grounds: France, Greece (Corfu, Rhodes, Lesbos, Mykonos, Crete), Italy, Turkey.

SOUTH AMERICA

◆

Angra Yacht Charter, Rio De Janeiro, Brazil. (011 55) 11-256-5691, or 11-258-8887.

Quasar Nautica SA, P.O. Box 1036, Punta Gorda, FL 33951, (800) 247-2925, or (813) 637-4660 in Florida. CC 30'-50'. Cruising grounds: Galapagos Islands.

SOUTH PACIFIC

◆

Charter Link NZ, P.O. Box 82-111, Highland Park, Auckland, New Zealand, (011 64) 9 535-8710; FAX: 9 537-0196. 15 years, 18 yachts 29'-40', BB & SK. Cruising grounds: Auckland, Bay of Islands, Marlborough Sounds. ✓

Rainbow Yacht Charters, P.O. Box 8327, Symonds Street, Auckland, NY, (011 64) 9 780-719. 21 yachts, 25'-40', BB, CC & SK. Cruising grounds: Auckland, Bay of Islands, Marlborough Sounds. Note: Freedom Yacht Charters of Russell has been combined with Rainbow's charter base in Opua, just across from Russell. The US agent for Rainbow is: Pacific Destination Center, 3471 Via Lido, Ste. 206, Newport Beach, CA 92663, (800) 227-5317. ✓

WEST COAST

◆

ABC Yacht Charters, 1905 Skyline Way, Anacortes, WA 98221, (800) 426-2313, or (206) 293-9533, or 293-0313. 75+ yachts, 25'-70', BB & SK. 43 years--Pacific Northwest's most established charter operation. Cruising grounds: San Juan Islands, Gulf Islands. ✓

Anacortes Yacht Charters, P.O. Box 69, Anacortes, WA 98221, (800) 842-4002, or (800) 233-3004 in WA. 100+ yachts, 28'-55' (sail & power), BB & SK. Cruising grounds: San Juan Islands, Gulf Islands. ✓

Blue Orca Sailing, 1818 Maritime Mews, Granville Island, Vancouver, BC, Canada V6H 3X2, (604) 683-6300. 43 yachts, 20'-48', BB & SK. Cruising grounds: Gulf Islands, Inside Passage, San Juan Islands.

Club Nautique, 1150 Ballena Boulevard, Alameda, CA 94501, (415) 865-4700, or (415) 332-8001. 50 yachts, 23'-47', BB & SK. Cruising grounds: SF Bay and nearby offshore; also bluewater cruising in Virgins, Fiji, Whitsundays.

Pacific Quest Charters, 1521 Foreshore Walk, Granville Island, Vancouver, BC, Canada V6H 3X3, (604) 682-2161; FAX: (604) 682-2722. 20+ yachts, 27'-45', BB & SK. Cruising grounds: Gulf Islands, Inside Passage, San Juan Islands.

Santa Barbara Sailing Center. The Breakwater, Santa Barbara, CA 93109, (800) 776-0700, (805) 962-2826. 30 yachts, 25'-50', BB & SK. Cruising grounds: Channel Islands.

Harbor Sailboats, 2040 Harbor Island Drive, San Diego, CA 92101, (800) 854-6625 out of CA, (619) 291-9568; FAX: 291-1473. 21 years, 45 boats, 14'-39', 34' $275/day. BB & SK. Cruising grounds: West Coast from Ensenada to Pt. Conception. ✓

WINDJAMMERS

St. Barts, French West Indies/DARRELL JONES

IF YOU WANT TO RECAPTURE THE ROMANCE OF THE AGE of sail, while letting a skilled crew do all the work, we recommend a windjammer vacation. Tall ship cruises are available worldwide, from the snug harbors of Maine to the tropical islands of the South Pacific.

CALIFORNIA

■ **NAUTICAL HERITAGE SOCIETY**
24532 Del Prado, Dana Point, CA 92629, (800) 432-2201 in CA, or (714) 661-1001.

The Nautical Heritage Society offers winter and spring day-cruises aboard the 145' tall ship California, an authentic replica of an 1849 revenue cutter. This is the only regularly scheduled windjammer program on the West Coast. Programs range from a 4-hour, $75 day-sail, to a 4-day offshore cruise around the Channel or Farallon Islands ($595). During winter the cutter is based in Southern California, while in summer she sails from San Francisco. Eleven-day training cruises are also offered for students aged 15-20.

CARIBBEAN

■ **WINDJAMMER BAREFOOT CRUISES**
P.O. Box 120, Miami Beach, FL 33119, (800) 327-2600.

If you're looking for a floating Club Med, this is it. Windjammer Barefoot Cruises (WBC) operates five luxury 200'-282' windjammers, all set up for serious partying. The ships sail only at night, allowing you time to frolic on the beach or party down at more than a dozen Caribbean ports of call (St. Martin, Antigua, Grenada, Tortola, St. Lucia, St. Vincent, Martinique, Dominica, St. Barts, Anguila, Saba, Statia, St. Kitts and Nevis). The island ports you actually visit vary from trip to trip, but all cruises take you to a new destination each day. WBC's 6 or 13-day cruises start at a reasonable $675, including food. Each ship carries windsurfing and snorkeling gear, and scuba diving is available at extra charge.

MAINE

Maine is the center of windjammer sailing in the United States. A fleet of classic 70'-140' sailing vessels ply the waters of Maine every summer, under the guidance of skilled skippers and professional crews. The typical schooner cruise lasts 3 or 6 days, averaging $300 for the shorter trip and $550 for a 6-day voyage. Between 20 and 35 customers will be accommodated on each vessel, usually in private cabins. The food is consistently excellent, and many vessels offer traditional lobster-bakes to cap off every cruise.

You'll have more fun if you book your cruise to coincide with one of the summer windjammer events. On the last Wednesday in June, Boothbay hosts the Windjammer Days, featuring a sail parade and onshore festivities. During the Fourth of July week, the Maine Windjammer Association

conducts the Great Schooner race, an all-day run from the island of North Haven to the Rockland Breakwater. Last but not least, the second week of September sees the fleet converge on the headquarters of WoodenBoat magazine on Eggemoggin Reach for a waterfront celebration.

For literature or information on Maine cruises, contact the *Maine Windjammer Association, P.O. Box 3178, Rockport, ME 04856, (800) 624-6380, or (207) 374-5400; FAX: (207) 374-2417*. The Association represents 11 superb sailing ships: the American Eagle (92'), the Angelique (95'), the Heritage (95'), the Isaac H. Evans (65'), the J.& E. Riggin (89'), the Lewis R. French (64'), the Mary Day (90'), the Nathaniel Bowditch (82'), the Mercantile (78'), the Roseway (137'), and the Grace Bailey (80').

Among the 15 or so Maine windjammers in service, these are our favorites.

The American Eagle is a classic schooner recently returned to service after an extensive two-year refitting. It now looks and feels like a new boat, and offers very comfortable accommodations. Home Port: Rockland.

The Heritage is the newest windjammer on the Eastern Seaboard, having been built in 1983 for the summer cruising business. It is one of the more comfortable vessels in Maine waters. Home Port: Rockland.

The Mary Day, launched in 1962, was the first windjammer to be built specifically to carry passengers on coastal cruises. Equipped with a centerboard, it can explore some harbors which are too shallow for other craft. *To book directly, contact Capt. Steve Cobb, P.O. Box 798, Camden, ME 04843, (207) 236-2750*. Home Port: Camden.

The Nathaniel Bowditch, a classic racing schooner from the 1920s, was extensively refitted in the 1970s for the windjamming trade. Equipped with 11 cabins for 24 guests, it is a handsome, fast-sailing vessel with a noteworthy heritage and fine captain, Gib Philbrick. Home Port: Rockland.

The Roseway, at 137' overall, is one of the largest vessels operating on the Maine coast. Custom options are available for those who want to combine bicycle touring or other land-based adventures with their sailing. The Roseway is the only schooner to offer 2-week cruises. It also sails in the Virgin Islands during the winter. Contact Yankee Schooner Cruises, *P.O. Box 696, Camden, ME 04843, (800) 225-4449, or (207) 236-4449*. Home Port: Camden.

MASSACHUSETTS

■ COASTWISE PACKET COMPANY, INC.
P.O. Box 429, Vineyard Haven, MA 02568, (508) 693-1699.

Coastwise Packet operates the 152' clipper schooner Shenandoah on 6-day cruises through New England waters, visiting destinations such as Block Island, Mystic, Nantucket and New Bedford. One of the largest windjammers on the Eastern Seaboard, the Shenandoah makes a grand sight under full sail--over 7,000 square feet of canvas. She is also a comfortable vessel, having been purpose-built in 1964 for carrying passengers. Cost for 6 days is about $600. Home Port: Martha's Vineyard.

VERMONT

■ VERMONT SCHOONER CRUISES
P.O. Box 800, Bristol, VT 05443, (802) 453-4818.

From May through October, the 77' schooner Homer W. Dixon navigates the blue waters of Lake Champlain. On cruises of 2, 3 and 4 days, you will explore the 110-mile-long lake, anchoring each evening in a quiet cove or beside a small island. (A gunkholer's dream, Lake Champlain has more than 100 islands to visit.) Past customers have raved about this Lake Champlain cruise, one of the most relaxing sailing vacations available anywhere. You can combine a sailing trip with a bike tour around the lake.

LIZ HYMANS

WORLDWIDE

■ CLYDE OFFSHORE SAILING CENTRE
Kip Marina, Inverkip, Renfrewshire, Scotland PA16 OAS, (011 44) 475 521210.

This is one of the few programs offering true long-distance ocean passages to the general public. In addition to its regular coastal sailing courses, the Clyde Centre sponsors a 15-month, round-the-world sail voyage, as well as a trans-Atlantic cruise. Unlike most of the tall ship cruises featured above, these are hands-on voyages, with participants expected to stand watch and sail the vessel as regular crew members.

■ OCEAN VOYAGES
1709 Bridgeway, Sausalito, CA 94965, (415) 332-4681.

Ocean Voyages books both individuals and groups aboard large sailing vessels operating in the Caribbean, Mediterranean, Galapagos Islands, Mexico, Australia, New Zealand and South Pacific. These bluewater cruises, which last from a week to a month, are ideal for persons who may lack the skills to charter a boat on their own, or who prefer to sail in faraway destinations not served by charter bases. Prices typically run between $100 and $150 per day.

■ WINDSTAR SAIL CRUISES
300 Elliot Avenue West, Seattle, WA 98119, (800) 258-7245; FAX: (206) 281-0627.

Windstar offers luxury cruises in Tahiti, the Caribbean (Lesser Antilles and Grenadines), and the Mediterranean (Athens to Istanbul, and Rome to Venice). Don't expect any hands-on sailing--computers control all sail-handling on Windstar's fleet of three 440' ultramodern tall ships. Each vessel carries 148 passengers in high style--everyone gets a private window cabin. A 7-day cruise runs $2,200-$2,800 per person. This price includes all food, along with waterskiing and windsurfing.

■ WORLDWIDE ADVENTURES
1920 Yonge Street, Suite 747, Toronto, ONT, Canada M4W 3C7, (800) 387-1483.

Worldwide Adventures offers tall ship voyages in Australia, Greece, New Zealand, Fiji and the Maldives. For $800-$1,000 per week per person, you can book either individual holidays or a group charter. Most cruises last a week, but monthlong voyages are also available in New Zealand and Fiji. The most popular trips are the Coral Trekker cruise in Australia, and island-hopping tours in Greece.

TOP SAILING SCHOOLS

■ **ANNAPOLIS SAILING SCHOOL**

P.O. Box 3334, Annapolis, MD 21403, (301) 267-7205, or (800) 638-9192.

Now in its 33rd year, the Annapolis Sailing School conducts programs in Annapolis, St. Petersburg (FL), the Florida Keys and St. Croix (USVI). Annapolis offers a full range of instructional seminars including some of America's best bareboat charter certification programs. Courses range from 2 to 9 days, at a cost of $355-$1,800, depending on location and length. Highly recommended are Annapolis' learn to sail cruising vacations, offered at all locations. This is a great way for novices to explore the Virgins for the first time--with an experienced instructor on board. Rating: ★★★

■ **CHICHESTER SAILING CENTRE**

Chichester Marina, Sussex, England PO20 7EL, (011 44) 243 512557.

Since 1954, the Chichester Sailing Centre has offered sailing instruction year-round in Chichester Harbor, the Solent, the English Channel, and off Brittany. Along with day classes, offshore training cruises are offered starting at $225 for 5 days, all-inclusive. The Chichester Centre is a traditional, full-service sailing academy located in the heart of England's yachting world. It is a member of the Royal Yachting Association (RYA), and the Royal Ocean Racing Club. Rating: ★★★

■ **CLUB NAUTIQUE**

1150 Ballena Boulevard, Alameda, CA 94501, (510) 865-4700.

With 50 yachts from 23'-47', Club Nautique (CN) operates one of the larger training fleets on the West Coast. CN runs basic classes on windy San Francisco Bay, as well as intensive offshore cruising courses in the Bay and nearby waters. CN's Bareboat Certification course, one of the few such programs that carries much weight with big charter companies, is highly recommended. Rating: ★★★

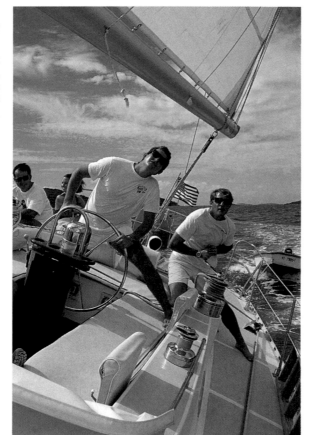

NEIL RABINOWITZ

■ **J WORLD, PERFORMANCE SAILING SCHOOL**

P.O. Box 1500, Newport, RI 02840, (800) 343-2255, or (401) 849-5492.

J World offers the most thorough race training available in a weekly program. J World instructors are world-class sailors, with strong teaching skills. Seminars are offered year-round at San Diego (CA), January through April in Key West (FL), and May through August, Newport (RI). While the mainstay of J World's programs are racing clinics conducted in J-24s (5 days, $650), J World also offers a limited number of Big Boat Cruising classes in J-35s and J-40s. Cost will be roughly $650 for 5 days. Rating: ★★★★

■ **OFFSHORE SAILING SCHOOL**

16731-110 McGregor Boulevard, Ft. Meyers, FL 33908, (800) 221-4326, or (813) 454-1700; FAX: (813) 454-1191.

No finer school is available for East Coast and Caribbean sailors than Colgate's Offshore Sailing School (OSS), now in its 27th year. Training programs include Learn to Sail, Bareboat Cruising Preparation, Live-aboard Cruising, Advanced Sailing, and Introductory and Advanced Racing. We recommend the Caribbean learn to sail program--a great way for novices to enjoy the bareboat experience without the worries. OSS operates from five bases: Captiva Island (FL), Cape Cod (MA), City Island (NY), and St. Lucia and Tortola in the Caribbean. Prices start at $995 for a week, including lodging. OSS is an extremely professional operation, with well-maintained 27'-43' yachts, and talented teachers. Rating: ★★★★

■ **SANTA BARBARA SAILING CENTER**

The Breakwater, Santa Barbara, CA 93109, (800) 248-1244, ex. 7245, or (805) 962-2826.

Among the many West Coast sailing schools, the Santa Barbara Sailing Center (SBSC) deserves mention because of its proximity to the Santa Barbara Channel Islands. Though a popular cruising destination, the Channel Islands demand true bluewater sailing skills--ocean navigation, heavy-weather sailing, and advanced anchoring technique. Learn to sail here successfully, and you should be able to cruise just about anywhere. SBSC, the largest A.S.A. school in Southern California, offers a variety of courses, including Learn to Sail, Bareboat Certification, Navigation, and Offshore Cruising. We recommend the full offshore course, which will put you head and shoulders above the average novice bareboat skipper in the Caribbean. Rating: ★★

■ **WOMANSHIP**

410 Severn Avenue, Boathouse B, Annapolis, MD 21403, (800) 342-9295, or (301) 267-6661.

Now in its seventh year, Womanship is a unique sailing program run by women for women. Expert female instructors teach lady sailors cruising, navigation, sail trim, docking and maintenance. A.S.A. Bareboat Certification programs are also available. Class sessions range from 2 to 7 days, at an average cost of $200 per day. The teaching is personalized and noncompetitive--Womanship's directors promise that "nobody yells." Womanship operates in the Virgin Islands, Chesapeake Bay, Florida, Long Island Sound and the Pacific Northwest. Rating: ★★

TRAVELERS' GUIDE

CHARTER SAILING

CREWED CHARTERS

Selecting a great crewed charter is a challenge. With bareboat operators, company size generally assures a certain level of quality and service. However, some of the best crewed charter operations are small, perhaps just a husband and wife team. And finding a top-flight small operator isn't easy, since the good ones don't need to advertise--they get all the business they can handle from word of mouth. Here it is essential to get the advice of a reputable charter broker. We list five of the best crewed charter agencies below.

While a 34'-40' yacht is ideal for a two-couple bareboat vacation, we prefer crewed charters in the 50'-70' range. With a yacht of this size, three couples can each have a private cabin, there will be a full-time cook aboard, and the vessel can carry fishing tackle, dive gear and windsurfers.

RONNA NELSON

CREWED CHARTER AGENCIES

Nicholson Yacht Charters, *P.O. Box 302, Marblehead, MA 01945, (800) 223-2050, or (203) 655-7227.* The oldest, and probably the best source for deluxe crewed charters. All boats have full-time crew and cook. Hundreds of yachts in Caribbean, Mediterranean, South Pacific. Rating: ★★★★

Lynn Jachney Charters, *P.O. Box 302, Marblehead, MA 01945, (800) 223-2050, or (617) 639-0787.* Outstanding reputation in the industry. Excellent choice of yachts in the Caribbean and Mediterranean. Rating: ★★★

Jubilee Yacht Charters, *51 White Oak Shade, New Canaan, CT 06840, (800) 922-4871, or (203) 655-7227.* A top choice for the Med with superb yachts in France, Greece, Turkey. Rating: ★★★

Ann-Walis White, *326 First Street, Annapolis, MD 21403, (301) 263-6366.* Very knowledgeable, with strong fleet in Antigua and the Leewards. Rating: ★★

Blue Water Yacht Charters, *2130 West Lake North, Seattle, WA 98109, (800) 732-7245, or (206) 286-3618 in WA.* Good choice for Pacific NW, Alaska, Mexico, South Pacific. Rating: ★★

BAREBOAT CERTIFICATION

If you've never bareboated before, it's a good idea to take an American Sailing Association (A.S.A.) bareboat certification course. While earning your A.S.A. bareboat certificate will not guarantee that you will be allowed to charter on your own (you must still satisfy the charter company of your skills), a bareboat course is a logical start. At present, there is no standardized curriculum for bareboat certification, and the courses available range from superb to

superficial. A good program will span a couple of weekends and include an off-shore cruise. You will be trained in sail handling, anchoring, coastal navigation, radio etiquette, emergency procedures, and boat maintenance and repair. A basic bareboat course will train you to operate a boat up to 30'. After chartering a 30-footer two or three times, you may want to pursue your advanced bareboat certificate, which covers yachts up to 50' overall.

BOOKS

Chartering Fundamentals, by Brian Fagan, is the American Sailing Association's textbook for coastal cruising and bareboat chartering courses. $14.95 from Tab Books Inc., Blue Ridge Summit, PA 17294, (800) 822-8138.

The Cruising Guide to the Maine Coast, by Hank and Jane Taft, is the definitive (382 pages, hardcover) guide to Maine cruising grounds. $39.50 from Tab Books.

Cruising Guide to the Virgin Islands, by Simon and Nancy Scott, is one of the best guides to the most popular chartering destination in the Caribbean. Good navigational diagrams and anchorage guides. $14.95 from Cruising Guide Publications, P.O. Box 13131, Station 9, Clearwater, FL 34621, (813) 796-2469.

Cruising Guide to the Leeward Islands, by Chris Doyle, is a new, detailed resource, with good listings of uncrowded anchorages. $12.95 from Cruising Guide Publications.

Exploring the Windward Islands, by Chris Doyle. Not just a cruising guide, this 224-page book covers windsurfing, diving and land accommodations, as well as anchorages. $11.95 from Cruising Guide Publications.

Yachtsman's Guide to the Bahamas (40th ed. 1990). This 454-page classic has everything you need to know about sailing the Bahamas, including anchorages, dive sites, tide tables, etc. $18.95 from Tropic Isle Publishers, Inc., P.O. Box 610935, North Miami, FL 33161, (305) 893-4277.

North Puget Sound, South Puget Sound, and **The San Juan Islands Afoot and Afloat** (three books), by Marge and Ted Mueller. These three 240-page guides cover marina facilities and regional highlights. $9.95 each from The Mountaineers, 306 2nd Ave West, Seattle, WA 98119.

Greek Waters Pilot, by Rod Heikell. Hard to find, and expensive at $34.50, this is still the most thorough guide to cruising in the Aegean. From Imray, Laurie et al, Ltd., Cambridgeshire, England, (011 44) 480 62 114.

VIDEOS

Cruising Under Sail (Annapolis Book of Seamanship Video Series--Vol. I). The single best video introduction to bluewater sailing. 72 minutes, $49.95. Other recommended Annapolis videos include **Heavy Weather Sailing (Vol. II)** and **Safety at Sea (Vol. III.)** Order from C.P.I., 30 E. 60th St., N.Y., NY 10022, (800) 426-4962.

279

Performance Sailing

Hull-flying on Hobie 18s, Tahiti/NEIL RABINOWITZ

Once I'd sailed at 75 miles an hour,
I didn't see much point in going slow anymore.
Speed is addictive.
-Colin Palmer,
world land yacht champion

▼

Conventional keel-boat sailing is a gentleman's sport, challenging but slow. Even a multimillion-dollar America's Cup Yacht is lucky to approach 12 knots in the best of conditions. Thankfully, for those who relish speed, there are faster ways to harness the wind. Modern racing catamarans can hit 30 miles per hour under spinnaker. Land yachts, streamlined three-wheelers with high-tech wingsails, have been clocked at over 90 miles per hour. And iceboats, the fastest wind-powered machines on earth, regularly eclipse the century mark, screaming over frozen lakes.

High-speed sailing, whether on water, land or ice, is one of the most exhilarating forms of recreation around. This chapter tells you how to select the right equipment, and get started on your quest for speed. We also review a number of destinations worldwide where you can enjoy a performance sailing holiday.

CHAPTER
19

Catamarans
ECONOMICAL EXCITEMENT

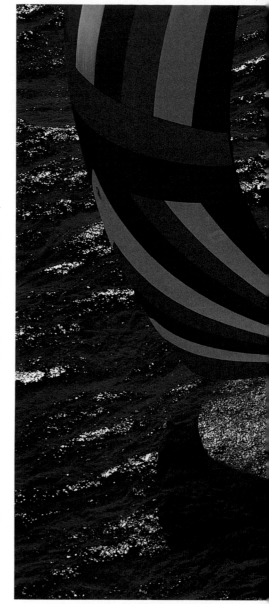

*I*F YOU'RE LOOKING FOR THE MOST SAILING EXCITEMENT FOR YOUR DOLLAR, TWO hulls are better than one. Ever since Hobie Alter introduced the little Hobie 14, the first really successful off-the-beach playboat, the sailing world has never been the same. Big multihulls now dominate the world of professional sailing, holding virtually all open ocean sailing records. And beach catamarans from 16'-20' overall, the smaller cousins of these ocean racers, are now the most popular recreational sailboats in most parts of the world.

In many harbors around the country you'll be able to rent small catamarans. Unfortunately, most aren't in particularly good condition, and lack the performance features, such as trapezes, that make these boats really go. At present, no company offers any point-to-point sailing vacations on small multihulls, presumably because of the liability problem, even though many areas, such as the Florida Keys and the Bahamas, would be ideal. Thus, if you're looking to really experience the thrill of catamaran sailing, plan to purchase your own boat, perhaps with a partner. We've selected the best of the bunch below.

BEST OPEN CLASS

NACRA 6.0 (20') is the class of the field, the ultimate production catamaran. Rigged with 260 square feet of Mylar sails plus optional spinnaker, a 6.0 can easily sail at 10 knots upwind, and 20 knots off-the-wind in moderate breezes. With fine, buoyant bows, the NACRA 6.0 can be driven very hard into chop and waves with very limited risk of pitchpoling (a somersault capsize). You don't need to be an expert to enjoy this boat because it steers easily and has lots of reserve flotation to keep you out of trouble. However, to realize the full potential of the NACRA, including spinnaker technique, you should probably have a season or two of experience.

Cost of a new NACRA 6.0, fully rigged with trailer, is approximately $8,500. A good used boat can be found for $5,000 without spinnaker. The NACRA 5.8, an earlier design, offers similar performance without all the high-tech goodies. This is a tough, sturdy boat that has circumnavigated Australia. A good used 5.8 can be had for $3,000-$4,000 with trailer and stock sails.

Honorable Mentions: The new Hobie Miracle 20 keeps pace with the NACRA 6.0. However, the Hobie's hulls are less forgiving in heavy seas, and it has a metal boom to hit your head, unlike the NACRAs. The DART 20 is very fast and comes standard with a spinnaker for fast reaches.

BEST RACING CLASS

If you want to race every weekend, get a Hobie 18 or 16. Hobie has the biggest fleets, and the most races and weekend gatherings. Each year Hobie also sponsors exciting international regattas, often providing free boats to qualified sailors. The Hobie 18, particularly the SX-18 version with racks, is a good boat, but quite heavy. The Hobie 16 is a lightweight classic, but most beginners find it very hard to tack. It also pitchpoles often and early. We'd take the 16 in a warm water area, where capsizing is no big deal. The Hobie 18 is a better boat for big crews (two grown men), or for sailing in areas with cold water or high winds.

boomless design without centerboards. Stay with an established class such as Hobie, Prindle or NACRA.

BEST OCEAN BOAT

If you live in a windy area like Hawaii or San Francisco, you'll want a tough, bulletproof boat with pitchpole-resistant hulls and a smallish sailplan. You'll need all the buoyancy you can get from the hulls. The NACRA 5.8 is a good choice because you have to be a real maniac to pitchpole it, but the tall rig can be a handful in high winds. The Hobie 21 has racks which keep the crew dry, but it is costly (over $12,000 with spinnaker), and it weighs a ton. If you can find one, a Supercat 20 with its 12' beam and huge, buoyant hulls is probably the ultimate. Look for a clean used boat for around $4,000 with trailer. This is a boat to leave on the beach because it must be broken down for trailering, and is quite heavy. Early models had some hull-cracking problems, but the Supercat 20 is basically a big, tough cruiser that thrives in the heavy stuff. You can sail it with a crew of three, and if you manage to pitchpole it, you've probably got a major death wish.

If you want further information on any of the catamarans reviewed above, contact the following class associations or manufacturers' representatives:

Dart--Sail Sports Ltd., 198 W. Main Street, Rockville, CT 06066, (203) 872-1961.

Hobie Class Association--c/o Hobie Cat, P.O. Box 1008, Oceanside, CA 92054, (619) 758-9100.

NACRA/Prindle Class Association, 1810 E. Borchard Avenue, Santa Ana, CA 92705, (714) 835-6416.

Supercat Association--Diane Haberman, 118 Hickory, Mahtomedi, MN 55115, (612) 426-3922.

Spinnaker reaching on a NACRA 5.8/NEIL RABINOWITZ

Honorable Mention: Tornado. This 20' Olympic-class cat is for serious racers. It's light and fast, but requires a lot of technique. You'll spend a minimum of $10,000 for a competitive new boat and trailer.

BEST COUPLES BOAT

The new Prindle 18-2 is the boat if you and your honey want to combine recreational sailing with a weekend race now and then. The Prindle 18-2 has fine, easily driven hulls, retractable centerboards, and pretty Mylar sails. It's a lot lighter than the big NACRAs or Hobies, so it's easy to put on the trailer or haul up the beach. This design hasn't been out for long, so you'll have to pay close to the $6,000+ factory purchase price for boat and trailer.

BEST NOVICE BOAT

This is a tough choice. You want a boat that is light, simple and forgiving. The Dart 15 meets the requirements, but you won't find much of a fleet in most parts of the United States. The Hobie 16 is light and easy to rig, but it doesn't tack well and pitchpoles easily. The NACRA 5.0 is a good choice, especially with its boomless rig, but it's heavy for its size. The best thing to do is to find out what 16-footer is popular in your area, and try to pick up a good, used boat for around $2,500. We recommend a

Prindle 19/COURTESY PERFORMANCE CATAMARANS

BUYING YOUR OWN CAT

Most modern production catamarans are solid, well built, and will provide many seasons of sailing with a minimum of maintenance. Some particular design features really do make a big difference, however, and you should look for these when selecting a boat, particularly if you are buying new.

Sails--Get a boat that has high-quality, durable sails. Some of the early Hobies used stretchy sailcloth that would bag out in a hurry. A Mylar reinforced mainsail could last the life of the boat, by contrast.

Hulls--Older style boats with a lip connecting the deck to the underside of the hull tend to trip and stall when the hull is submerged at high speed. This can result in a vicious and often instantaneous capsize.

Look for a boat with rounded decks and lots of buoyancy (volume) in the bows.

Boom--A boomless rig is light, simple and doesn't hit you in the head. There is really no reason for any beach boat to be rigged differently.

Hobie 17s/PATRICK McDOWELL

Centerboards--Boats with centerboards tack (change direction) and sail to windward much better than boardless designs. Get a centerboard boat if you like to race. For a beach boat, a boardless design is lighter and much easier to get in and out of the surf. Choose a symmetrical boardless design, such as the Dart, which doesn't sacrifice too much windward ability.

Trapezes--Look for a boat with double trapezes. Once you get the hang of it, it's a lot more fun, and you'll stay drier.

Racks--Hobie pioneered the use of racks. They make daysailing much more comfortable, and allow lightweight crews to sail in heavier winds. They work best on the bigger boats (18'-21').

HOW TO FIND A GOOD USED CAT

Do a little homework before you go shopping. Find a Hobie or Prindle/NACRA dealer and get phone numbers for the local cat fleets. Hitch rides on different boats, comparing their features. When you're looking at used boats, check out the sails. They must be in very good shape if you want to race. The condition of the hulls is important, but a little sanding and simple fiberglass work can fix most common problems. The rudders and centerboards should be smooth and undamaged. Inspect all the wire rigging and trapeze gear. If any wires are broken or rusty you'll have to replace them at $25-$40 each.

Once you've found a good boat, see if the owner will throw in a few free lessons. Remember that most people selling their boats are quite motivated to sell. Don't hesitate to start with a pretty low offer. Make sure you get a trailer with a storage box, even if you plan to keep the boat on the beach. If the lights or wheel bearings are shot, you could

be looking at a $200-$400 repair job. Keep this in mind when you are bargaining.

Resist the urge to put a lot of racing gear on

NACRA 5.8/PAUL McMENAMIN

the boat right away. You'll have the most fun if you concentrate on your sailing skills at first. Invite one of the local hotshots along--he'll probably be happy to show you how to get the most out of your new boat.

RESOURCES

Multihull Magazine, 421 Hancock Street, Quincy, MA 02171, (617) 471-0118, covers multihull racing worldwide and reviews the latest catamaran and trimaran racing and cruising designs.

Catamaran Sailing from Start to Finish, by Phil Berman, is the best guide for beginning catamaran sailors. Berman covers everything from boat maintenance to racing strategies. $13.00 from Murray's Marine, P.O. Box 490, Carpinteria, CA 93013, (805) 684-8393.

The Catamaran Book, by Brian Phipps, uses good photo sequences to illustrate the fine points of cat sailing including tacking, trapezing and downwind sailing. $17.50 from Murray's Marine.

Hobie Hotline is a colorful, informative magazine not just for Hobie sailors. Call (619) 758-9100.

PERFORMANCE DINGHIES

Laser on a full plane/NEIL RABINOWITZ

AUSTRALIAN 18

For traditionalists who just can't see themselves on a catamaran, planing dinghies offer a full measure of speed and thrills. The ultimate racing dinghy is the Australian 18. These outrageous 250-pound machines top 30 mph on a screaming spinnaker reach. Sailed by professional crews of two or three, who perform their duties suspended from trapezes on 10' aluminum racks, Aussie 18s are the most demanding sailing craft ever invented. In Australia, commercially sponsored teams race for money prizes, and public wagering is popular for many race series.

LASER

The leading one-person dinghy is the Laser. This sturdy, simple craft is sailed throughout the world by both novices and Olympic-caliber skippers. It's light enough to cartop, and class rules keep the hardware so simple that you won't ever have to spend a lot of money to keep the boat competitive. You can find a very clean late-model Laser, with trailer, for about $2,000.

Aussie 18 under full sail/NEIL RABINOWITZ

OLYMPIC 470

There are dozens of good two-person high-performance dinghies, but the boat of choice for both recreational sailing and racing applications is the 470. With a trapeze for the crew and a small spinnaker, this Olympic-class boat offers plenty of challenge. However, with its light weight, and strong, self-bailing hull, it is also a safe, fast daysailer that is easily trailered by small cars. While an Olympic-quality 470 can cost well over $10,000, you can find a very clean used model for under $4,000.

LAKE SCOW

If you live near midwestern lakes, another high-performance alternative is scow sailing. The big "Class A" scows approach 20 knots in the hands of experts. Scows come in a variety of classes and sizes, but all share the same basic hull form--wide and flat. They can be tricky to master, as they must be heeled over at all times to keep drag to a minimum. Virtually all production scows are built by the Melges Boat Works, P.O. Box 1, Zenda, WI 53195, (414) 248-6621.

PERFORMANCE SAILING VACATIONS

You can sail Hobie cats at most Club Meds, and you can rent a variety of small cats at popular beach resorts in Florida, Australia and Puerto Rico. The Moorings' Club Mariner program offers small boat sailing at resorts in St. Lucia, Tortola and Grenada in the Caribbean. Dinghy sailing and windsurfing can be combined with a 4-day holiday on a fully crewed 51' yacht. Call **Club Mariner** at *(800) 334-2435.* Many other popular resorts offer vacation packages featuring sailing in both catamarans and dinghies. Here are a few programs to consider.

Caribbean Watersports, *(011) 590 875866, ext. 5151, or FAX: (011) 590 542571,* based at St. Martin in the West Indies, rents new Hobie 16s and 18s for $40 per hour or $160 per day. This is a great place to sail, with reliable tradewinds and warm, crystal-clear waters. Windsurfers and dive gear are available as well. Rental offices are located at La Belle Creole Hotel and the Radisson Hotel, two of St. Martin's nicest resorts.

Caribbean Watersports, *Sheraton Key Largo, P.O. Box 781, Key Largo, FL 33037, (305) 852-4707; FAX: (305) 451-4095.* Catamaran-sailing holidays are offered by this American company, (which has no connection with the St. Martin operation above). Package prices start at $190 per day per person for hotel and Hobie Cat--choose from Hobie's full line: 14', 16', 17', and 18'. All boats are fully equipped, including trapezes, and are available for daily rental at $85-$130 per day. With water temperatures in the 70s and 80s, you won't need wetsuits. Qualified sailors can overnight in the nearby Keys. This is a fine program, however, room prices more than double December through March.

Falcon Sailing, *13 Hillgate Street, London, England W8 7SP, (011 44) 71 727 0232,* offers performance sailing vacations in Greece, Turkey and Sardinia. Dinghy and windsurfing package holidays are available starting at $500, including airfare from London and Royal Yachting Association (RYA) instruction. The Greek destinations, with light winds, are best suited for novices, while seasoned sailors will revel in the strong breezes of Turkey or Sardinia. Programs are offered for all skill levels.

Hobie Cat Aventure, *Espl. Jean D'Arc, 17000 La Rochelle, France, (011 33) 46 50 55 84; FAX: (011 33) 46 50 60 59.* This French company offers catamaran sailing vacations at many great destinations worldwide, including Florida, France, Greece, Martinique, the Philippines, Sierra Leone, and Tahiti. A single price covers airfare, hotel, and rental of a late-model Hobie Cat. Programs like this are the latest trend in recreational sailing. Prices start at about $140 per day. Make the first contact by FAX as the staff does not speak particularly good English.

The Greek Islands Sailing Club offers high-performance dinghy and catamaran sailing holidays on the islands of Paxos, Zakynthos and Ithaca. Choose Ithaca for high winds, the other two islands for smooth water. Package vacations including boat rentals, RYA instruction and lodging are available starting at about $500 per week from London. Contact The Sailing Club at *66 High Street, Walton-on-Thames, Surrey, England KT12 1BU, (011 44) 932 220477.*

PRO SAILING

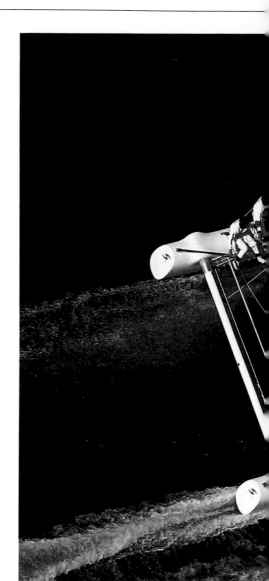

ULTIMATE CAT RACING
The World 1000

What ranks as the ultimate small boat racing challenge? For adventurers with paid-up life insurance? Over the past 15 years, campaigning a 20-footer in the World 1000 has been sailing's greatest test for small boat sailors. Since the mid 1970s, the World 1000 (formerly the Worrell 1000) has been run on the East Coast between Florida and Virginia. Racers sail between check points along the coast or offshore islands, beaching their boats on shore every night. During an offshore leg, a team may spend as long as 18 hours on the water, often battling big seas and high winds. When it's blowing, racers will spend hours in the trapeze, blasting over ocean swells at 20 knots. This experience is not for the faint of heart or weak of body. The race lasts a full

The Pro 40 Superlube on San Francisco Bay/NEIL RABINOWITZ

off the California Coast. "The wind was a solid 30, the swells an easy 10', maybe more. We were making over 20 knots, flying airborne from the crest of one swell into the back of the one ahead. We were on the absolute edge of control, expecting to crash and burn any moment. I kept thinking, this is insane. It was, without a doubt, the most outrageous thing I have ever done."

FORMULA 40 & HOBIE 21

Formula 40 is the rage in Europe, where high-tech composite 40' cats and trimarans blaze around harbor courses with big money at stake, and prime-time live television coverage. The rules are simple: your boat must not exceed 40' in length, weigh less than 1,800 kg (3,960 lbs), and must use the same mast and mainsail in all races. Purses can exceed $10,000 per race, but the big money is in sponsorship--top French skippers earn as much as $250,000 per year in salary and endorsements. The American trimaran *Adrenalin* finished second in 1988, while American Randy Smyth skippered his cat to the championship in Formula 40's debut season. Formula 40 boats, known as ProSail 40s in the US, are becoming popular over here as well, but the rules are tighter, allowing only catamarans, and limiting overall cost. If you're interested in campaigning, be prepared to spend a cool half-million dollars per season. Unfortunately, the current domestic series is in doubt until a major sponsor can be found.

For a much lower investment, roughly $13,000 for boat, racing license and registration fees, you can compete for major prize money in Hobie 21 competition. In 1990, sailors garnered over $130,000 in winnings in the multi-race series, which attracted crowds as large as 45,000. Contact Hobie Catamarans, (619) 758-9100.

two weeks. The punishment the body takes over that period of time is enormous.

The weapon of choice has been a 20' catamaran, raced basically stock (Production 20 Class) or modified with added beam, and perhaps hiking racks and spinnaker poles (Open Class--Formula 20). Extra safety equipment required includes compasses, emergency transponders, and back-up shrouds.

Most teams raced NACRA 6.0s or Prindle 19s, equipped with full spinnaker and ocean-racing hardware. Out of the box, this cost $10,000-$12,000 all up, more for custom features used on some of the Formula 20 boats. Teams also required a support van, and a pit crew of at least two good boat mechanics who can double as crew. Unless they just won the lottery, most racers relied on a commercial backer to finance the campaign. The heavy hitters were sponsored by the likes of 7-Eleven, Domino's Pizza and British Airways. The World 1000 is on hold this season, but it is hoped it will be revived by summer 1993, perhaps with $20,000 or more in prize money.

What's an offshore catamaran race really like? We asked past NACRA world champion Larry Harteck, the second place finisher in the 1986 Pacific Coast version of the World 1000. Larry recalls running flat-out under spinnaker on the backside of Santa Cruz Island, 27 miles

Hobie Cats, Lake Powell/PATRICK McDOWELL

Land Yachts

OF WHEELS AND WIND

*I*MAGINE SAILING ACROSS THE DESERT AT SPEEDS UP TO 80 MPH, IN A SAILING machine that accelerates as fast as a Porsche 928. No, we're not dreaming. Such performance is possible in production land yachts that can be purchased for less than $2,500 new. Though some design features vary, all modern land yachts are three-wheelers, with a narrow central fuselage, and a single sail, often connected to a wide, airfoil mast. Some of the latest designs use solid foils, with no sailcloth at all.

The smallest land yachts, such as the one-design Manta class, are constructed of simple steel tubing, with small, aircraft-like wheels at the three corners. Mantas are light enough to car-top, cost only $900, and can reach 50 mph. Other lightweight one-design racers include the Freedom ($1,850, 49 sq.ft.), and the Spirit ($2,500, 59 sq.ft.), both capable of speeds up to 80 mph. Large custom yachts may be made from aerospace composites, or honeycomb aluminum, and hit peak velocities exceeding 100 mph.

On all land yachts, the skipper or pilot steers via rods or pulleys connected to the front wheel. He controls his speed by trimming the sail or wing as on a boat, but adjustments must be very rapid and precise. Slight overtrimming can interrupt the airflow, cutting speed from 70 mph to 35 mph in a matter of seconds. Land yachts race over desert triangle courses, rounding marks at high speeds with all three tires in a controlled skid if the pilot knows what he's doing. It's not easy to keep the craft at peak power, but

when you get the hang of it, the sport is addictive. Many of the best land sailors got their start on the water, but once having tasted real speed, they have trouble going back to conventional sailing.

In addition to the smaller production yachts, there are four active development classes, restricted only by total sail area: Class V--49 sq.ft., Class IV--59 sq.ft., Class III--79 sq.ft., and Class II--121 sq.ft. Nord Embrodden of Pinon Hills, California holds the land yacht speed record at 88.4 mph, set with a small Class IV rig. Embrodden has actually gone much faster, but not over a measured course during a clocked run. The latest Class II monsters regularly hit speeds over 100 mph during windy races. Embrodden still uses a soft-sail rig set on a wingmast, but he has been challenged by Phil Rothrock of Oregon, who has created beautiful all-metal racers with solid wingsails. Rothrock's designs, which look like they came from NASA, probably represent the future of land yachting.

BEHIND THE WHEEL—WARP SPEED, MR. SULU

You snake your legs into the streamlined fuselage, feeling as though you're about to take a ride in a missile. The analogy isn't misplaced. As you tighten the racing harness and slip on your helmet, it dawns on you that you

are about to pilot a machine that can exceed 100 mph, but has no brakes.

If the wind is pumping, you can simply climb in and go, but most land sailors push their yachts for a few yards to get the wind

flowing over the sails—it's like cranking the engine on a car. Once you're moving, things happen fast. Hauling on a 10:1 sheeting system, it takes a few seconds to strap the sail in, but when you do, it's as though a silent but powerful motor has come to life. Within 10 seconds you are cruising quickly.

At around 50 knots, the sweat starts forming. Lying almost horizontal in the cockpit, you can hardly see ahead. To make matters worse, your helmet is bouncing as the yacht speeds over ripples in the lake bed. Looking over your shoulder, you can't even see the horizon. Your peripheral vision is filled only with a plume of dust. The roostertail now streams 100 feet or more behind your wheels. You are a bullet, a wind propelled bullet. You catch a glimpse of the windward wheel getting airborne. Adrenalin responds before you can think. Two feet of mainsheet leap out of your hand, and with a thump the machine settles down. You overreacted, but that's far better than dumping a $20,000 carbon fiber racer that doesn't even belong to you.

With practice, the delicate process of reaching maximum speed becomes easier. You're able to anticipate wind changes, and you start to sense when the machine wants to move out—the chassis squats down under load and the mainsheet tension increases. But mastery of the straights won't prepare you for the turns. At high speeds, you must carve a broad arc, letting the tires scrub off some velocity in a controlled drift. As you turn, dust from the wheels billows away in thick clouds. The jibe is quick, two, three seconds at the most, but you must push hard with your foot pedals to keep the machine in the turn. The sail swings through the wind and with an audible pop, the battens change camber. Then it's time to hit the gas again. To chase the wind. In search of speed.

How to Get Involved

If this sounds like your kind of adventure, you'll want to contact a local land yachting club for further information and, if you're lucky, a test-ride. Land sailing is not a big sport in the United States yet, but there are active clubs in the Western States and Texas. The North American Land Sailing Association, (NALSA), c/o James Braslow, Chase Indus., 2100 Gaylord Street, Long Beach, CA 90813, (310) 437-8585, can put you in touch with the land yachting club nearest you. You can also get regatta schedules for the most active groups including the Pacific Land Yacht Club, and the Desert, Bay Area, Texas, and Oregon landsailors' clubs.

For further information on both one-design and development-class land yacht racing, call Jim Goss, past President of the Manta Association, 6739 Devonshire Drive, San Jose, CA 95129, (408) 867-2200, ext. 7071; or contact Nord Design, 9079 Green Road, Pinon Hills, CA 92372, (619) 868-4484, builder of Nord Embrodden's 1989 championship yacht.

Silver Bullet, Nord Embrodden's championship land yacht, on Ivanpah Dry Lake/PAUL McMENAMIN

Just when it starts to seem easy, a puff suddenly hits. Don't swing into the wind, you remember--the twisting of the sharp turn will flip the craft. Instead you drive away from the wind, sheeting in as your speed increases. It's all very counter-intuitive. You are running away from the wind, all the time increasing your speed, and thereby raising the airflow velocity over the sail. You go faster, then faster still. The acceleration snaps your helmet back, and the desert floor becomes a blur. You are now exceeding the legal speed limit, and your head is a mere 18 inches off the ground.

60 mph across Ivanpah Dry Lake/PAUL McMENAMIN

NORTH AMERICAN LAND YACHTING

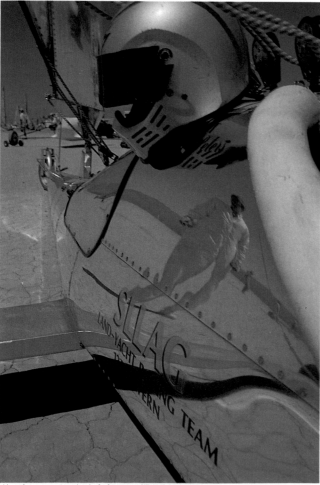

Aircraft-type construction is the latest trend/PAUL McMENAMIN

MOST LAND SAILING IS DONE ON DRY LAKE BEDS, ALTHOUGH flat, windy beaches are coming into their own. Winter provides the strongest, most consistent winds in the high desert, while summertime is best for beach sailing. Listed below are the top spots in North America.

California
Mile Square Park, Fountain Valley; El Mirage Dry Lake; Rabbit Dry Lake; Superior Dry Lake; Harper Dry Lake; Cuddeback Dry Lake; Silurian Dry Lake; Ivanpah Dry Lake; Soggy Dry Lake; Pismo Beach; Crows Landing

Nevada
Roach Dry Lake; El Dorado; Blackrock Desert; Delamar; Mud Lake

Arizona
Red Dry Lake

Utah
Great Salt Lake

Florida
Daytona Beach

Virginia
Hilton Head Island

Oregon
Coos Bay Beach; Alvord Dry Lake

Washington
Long Beach

Texas
Padre Islands

Mexico
Ensenada, San Felipe

To have a firsthand look at top land yachts in action, head for the America's Gold Cup Regatta, held annually at Ivanpah Dry Lake on the California/Nevada border in April. The Regatta usually runs as a world championship race, attracting top land yacht pilots from around the world. Over 150 racers from France, Germany, Great Britain, Argentina, Belgium, New Zealand, Australia, the United States and Canada can be expected to attend the event.

FOREIGN LAND YACHTING

AMERICA'S WINDSWEPT DRY LAKES ARE IDEAL FOR LAND YACHTING. HOWEVER, few other countries have such terrain, so most foreign land sailing takes place on beaches. In Europe and New Zealand, two hotbeds of land yachting, races are held on long stretches of hard-packed sand exposed during low tides. Belgium and France produce the fastest land sailors in the world, and the sport is very popular in these countries. The European land yacht championship is televised in France every year. If you want to learn more about foreign land yachting, contact the following organizations.

■ **AUCKLAND LAND YACHT CLUB (NEW ZEALAND)**
c/o Bruce Wood , 32 Mountbatton Ave., Auckland 10, NZ, (64) 09 418 4983; FAX: (64) 09 277 7635.
■ **AUSTRALIAN LANDSAILING FEDERATION**
c/o Barry Dixon, 2 Rawe Court, Redwood Park, South Australia, (61) 08 396 0264.
■ **BELGIUM FEDERATION OF LAND YACHT CLUBS**
c/o Pierre Nyssens, 4 Boskee, B-3061 Leefdaal, Belgium, (32) 2 767 8096.
■ **BRITISH FEDERATION OF SAND AND LAND YACHT CLUBS**
c/o John Andrews, 10 Chatsworth Road, St. Annes-On-Sea, Lancashire, England, FY8 2JN, (44) 253 725 981.
■ **FRENCH FEDERATION DE CHARS A VOILE**
B. Lambert, 143 Blvd. De Boulogne, F-62600 Berck , France, (33) 218 44904; FAX: (33) 218 47355.

Five Square Meter Class/PAUL McMENAMIN

New Zealand Class III yacht between races/PAUL McMENAMIN

Downhill Skiing

On the edges in Taos, New Mexico/DAVID STOECKLEIN

There's a fine line between great skiing and insanity.
-Greg Stump, ski moviemaker

▼

There are over 600 ski resorts in North America alone. Some of the best remain relatively unheralded, and are surprisingly uncrowded. How do you choose a destination? It's not always easy. Ask even an experienced skier where to go, and you're likely to come up with a list of a half-dozen or so resorts, usually near his or her hometown. Also, ask your skiing friends to compare one ski site to another and you're likely to get a lot of subjective opinions and not too many facts. We can help you plan your trip more logically, with greater confidence that you're making the right choice.

In this chapter we rate the top 25 North American ski centers and provide essential information on each, including number of runs, snow conditions and toll-free numbers. We review 10 outstanding destinations for novices, and 10 leading European ski areas. You'll also find a comprehensive report on summer skiing and heli-skiing throughout the world.

CHAPTER
20

The Ten Best Training Resorts

Margie Noble in spring powder/CHRIS NOBLE

LET'S FACE IT: IF YOU'VE ONLY SKIED a season or two, you don't need the longest runs, the deepest powder or the biggest moguls. Novices need gentle gradients, consistent, well-groomed trails, and plenty of room to practice their turns without being run down by maniacal racers. Here's a list of the best locations in North America to improve your skills. (See p. 310 for ski resort numbers.)

BRECKENRIDGE, COLORADO

■

Breckenridge almost made it into our top 25, but it's not just for the experts. The Peak Nine area, with its host of wide, well-groomed runs, is one of the best training areas in Colorado for novices and lower intermediates. Smooth, dry snow makes it easy to work on those parallel turns, and a high-speed quad chair means more time on the snow and less waiting.

BUTTERMILK, COLORADO

■

Buttermilk took top honors in *SKI* magazine's ski school rankings, and finished a close second to Snowmass as the country's best family destination. With over 200 instructors, classes are small, even the best guides will teach beginning skiers. All the runs are easy to ski, though it can be a challenge to avoid the other beginners who make up half of Buttermilk's customers.

COPPER MOUNTAIN, COLORADO

■

A perennial favorite weekend resort, Copper Mountain boasts some of the most economical packages in the Rockies. Copper Mountain knows that occasional skiers are its bread and butter, and it delivers with a fine network of long, wide novice trails. You don't have to choose between short bunny hills and steep sections that will send you sprawling. Located close to Vail, Copper Mountain shares that resort's superb high-altitude snow conditions.

CRESTED BUTTE, COLORADO

■

Crested Butte offers a superb network of long, smooth, "easy blue" runs, perfect for advanced novices looking to practice their parallel turns. Long known as a great choice for intermediates, Crested Butte has really pulled out the stops to attract first-timers. For three weeks after Thanksgiving, the resort offers free lifts, lessons and rentals to all those who've never skied before. Their companions receive half-priced lessons and rentals, plus a bargain-basement $15 lift ticket. Discount accomodations are also available.

DEER VALLEY, UTAH

■

Deer Valley is known for smooth, well-groomed, wide-open slopes that offer plenty of fun without pushing novices or intermediates past their limits. You can improve your skills without thrashing yourself or losing face. Deer Valley also boasts the best food and customer service of any Rockies resort.

MT. SNOW, VERMONT

■

Mt. Snow's broad and smooth lower slopes make up one of the best areas in the East to move out of the novice ranks. And while some resorts lavish all their hardware budget on lifts for advanced runs, Mt. Snow features a wide variety of fast lifts on its gentler trails. Mt. Snow's fine cruising runs will keep the better skiers in your party happy as well.

NORTHSTAR-AT-TAHOE, CALIFORNIA

■

All of the major resorts in California have plenty of runs suitable for novices and intermediates. However, Northstar is Northern California's clear destination of choice for the not-ready-for-prime-time skier. The terrain is predominantly intermediate, and the lower blue runs are as good as you'll find in the West, with reliable, superbly groomed snow. Northstar has recently expanded its snowmaking and added new quad lifts.

PARK CITY, UTAH

■

With 3,100' of vertical drop, Park City may seem like an experts' resort, but the sheer size and diversity of the facility means there's ideal skiing for everyone, even those just working out of their wedge turns. The wide-open quality of the intermediate runs allows easy traversing if things get a bit steep. A number of new lifts have been added, which will leave more of the central runs free for entry-level skiers.

STRATTON, VERMONT

■

Although snow conditions can get a bit icy, the gentle slopes and wide-as-can-be trails at Stratton beckon novice skiers. With the hot dogs headed to Killington, there's plenty of room here to practice your skills. The gondola and pleasant ski village are special bonuses that commend Stratton for all levels of skiers. You'll find excellent nordic skiing nearby as well.

SUNDAY RIVER, MAINE

■

Sunday River, though one of the best training hills in the East, rarely gets overcrowded. Its smooth, well-groomed slopes and great snowmaking (covering 80 percent of the runs) put Sunday River at the top of the class in the East. Though most of the slopes are intermediate, *Skiing* magazine included Sunday River among its East Coast ten best--for all skiers, not just beginners.

Groomed slopes in Utah/SCOTT MARKEWITZ

NORTH AMERICA'S TOP TWENTY-FIVE SKI RESORTS

Here are North America's best of the best. Our rankings are based on reports from the major ski industry magazines, input from ski writers and our own experiences on the slopes. When choosing a resort, be aware that certain data, such as the number of lifts, may have changed.

Codes: Snowmaking (SM), High-Speed (HS), High-Speed Detachable Quad Chair (HSQ), Regular, Fixed-Grip Quad Chair (RQ), Gondola (GON), Night Skiing (NS), Main Phone (M), Reservation Phone (R).

CHRIS NOBLE

	RESORT	PHONE	VERTICAL DROP	RUNS–%/BEG./INT./ADVANCED
ROCKIES	ASPEN MOUNTAIN P.O. Box 1248, Aspen, CO 81612	M-(800) 525-6200 R-(800) 262-7736	3,300'	625 acres of wide, well-groomed trails up to 3 miles, for intermediate to advanced. Adjacent Buttermilk Resort for novices. 0/35/65.
	BEAVER CREEK P.O. Box 915, Avon, CO 81620	M-(303) 949-5750 R-(800) 525-2257	3,340'	59 runs on 940 acres, up to 4.6 miles. Mostly intermediate, wide & groomed, but also challenging expert runs. 18/39/43.
	COPPER MOUNTAIN P.O. Box 3001, Copper Mtn., CO 80443	M-(303) 968-2882 R-(800) 458-8386	2,760'	76 runs, 4 bowls, on 1,200 acres (plus 350 extreme). All types of terrain. Share lift ticket with Breckenridge, A-Basin and Keystone. 25/40/35.
	KEYSTONE/A-BASIN P.O. Box 38, Keystone, CO 80435	M-(303) 468-2316 R-(800) 222-0188	2,360'	50 runs on 680 acres, open bowl, glade and superbly groomed trails. North Peak moguls. 25/60/15.
	STEAMBOAT SPRINGS 2305 Mt. Werner Circle, Steamboat Sprgs., CO 80487	M-(303) 879-6111 R-(800) 525-BOAT	3,600'	106 runs up to 3 miles on 2500 acres (1,500 groomed), with great advanced powder, glades & race trails. Open slopes. 15/54/31.
	SNOWMASS P.O. Box 1248, Aspen, CO 81612	M-(800) 525-6200 R-(800) 525-6200	3,615'	72 runs on 2,100 acres. Fantastic array of wide-open intermediate runs up to 4.16 miles. Great expert runs. 9/51/40.
	VAIL P.O. Box 7, Vail, CO 81658	M-(303) 476-5601 R-(800) 525-2257	3,250'	120 trails. 3,800 acres. 32/36/32, but many green runs up top. Long, wide runs. Best bowls in CO. Backside is challenging. 0/36/64.
	ALTA P.O. Box 8007, Alta, Utah 84092	M-(801) 742-3333 R-(801) 942-0404	2,000'	Powder and groomed trails; mostly open & bowl skiing, best for strong skiers. Great expert areas. 25/40/35.
	DEER VALLEY P.O. Box 1525, Park City, UT 84060	M-(801) 649-1000 R-(800) 424-3337	2,200'	54 trails on 900 acres, no long catwalks, just good open downhills. Superb groomed powder. 15/50/35.
	PARK CITY P.O. Box 39, Park City, UT 84060	M-(801) 649-8111 R-(800) 222-7275	3,100'	83 trails on 2,200 acres, 5 bowls, groomed runs, mogul and tree runs, long lighted NS run. 20/50/30.
	SNOWBIRD Snowbird, UT 84092	M-(801) 742-2222 R-(800) 453-3000	3,100'	48 trails, up to 2.5 miles, huge 2,000-acre bowls. Groomed lower novice/intermed. runs from chairlifts. 20/30/50.
	SUN VALLEY Sun Valley, ID 83353	M-(208) 622-4111 R-(208) 635-8261	3,400'	73 trails on 1,275 acres. Great groomed intermed. runs. Black diamond bowls. Nearby Elkhorn novice resort. 38/45/17.
	TAOS SKI VALLEY Taos Ski Valley, NM 87525	M-(505) 776-2291 R-(800) 635-8261	2,610'	73 lift-served runs on 1,051 acres. Great snow. Challenging expert runs. Lower trails can be crowded during xlnt. learn-to-ski weeks. 24/25/51.
	JACKSON HOLE P.O. Box 290, Teton Village, WY 83025	M-(307) 733-2292 R-(800) 982-7669	4,139'	66 trails on 2,500 acres. Major steep and deep expert runs. Casper Bowl great for intermed. Best snow on top. 10/40/50.
WEST	HEAVENLY VALLEY P. O. Box AT, S. Lake Tahoe, CA 95705	M-(916) 541-1330 R-(702) 588-4584	3,600'	20 square miles of trails, groomed, open bowls with expert tree runs on Nevada side. Most beg. runs at top. 25/50/25.
	MAMMOTH MOUNTAIN P.O. Box 24, Mammoth Lakes, CA 93546	M-(619) 934-2571 R-(800) 367-6572	3,100'	150 trails, mostly intermediate, up to 2.5 miles, 200 acres SM. Major ski school with 300 instructors. 30/40/30.
	NORTHSTAR/TAHOE P.O. Box 129, Truckee, CA 96160	M-(916) 562-1010 R-(800) 533-6787	2,200'	50 trails, up to 3 miles, north-facing bowls with good powder, newly opened backside with steep tree runs. 25/50/25.
	SQUAW VALLEY P.O. Box 2007, Olympic Valley, CA 95730	M-(916) 583-6985 R-(800) 545-4350	2,850'	4,000 acres of open bowls, most runs groomed, xlnt. advanced runs. Great lift network. NS. 25/45/30.
	MT. BACHELOR P.O. Box 1031, Bend, OR 97709	M-(503) 382-2442 R-(503) 382-7888	3,100'	54 runs on 3,200 skiable acres. Mostly groomed & intermed. 360-degree trails from summit. Spring is best. 15/60/25.
EAST	SUGARLOAF R.R. 1, Box 5000, Kingfield, ME 04947	M-(207) 237-2000 R-(800) 843-5623	2,837'	70 trails on 400 acres. Varied terrain from double diamond to 3-mile cruising run. Mostly groomed, but many expert glades. 38/29/33.
	KILLINGTON Killington, VT 05751	M-(802) 422-3333 R-(800) 621-6867	3,175'	6 mtns., 107 trails, 77 miles. Most intermed., but ultra-steep runs for experts and novice trails from summit. Great SM, xlnt. diversity. 45/20/35.
	STOWE (MT. MANSFIELD) 5781 Mtn. Road, Stowe, VT 05672	M-(802) 253-7311 R-(802) 253-6617	2,360'	45 trails on 378 acres. Great pro runs plus long trails for novice/intermed. Excellent grooming and SM. 16/59/25.
CANADA	MONT STE. ANNE, QUEBEC P.O. Box 400, Beaupre, QUE, G0A 1E0	M-(418) 827-4561 R-(800) 463-1568	2,050'	50 trails, 396 acres, trails newly widened, mostly well-groomed good intermed. cruising runs. Can be cold and icy. NS. 23/42/35.
	LAKE LOUISE, ALBERTA P.O. Box 5, Lake Louise, AL, T0L 1E0	M-(403) 522-3555 R-(403) 256-8473	3,250'	50 named runs on 4,000 acres. Heaps of powder, long cruising runs. Novice runs off almost all lifts. 25/45/30.
	WHISTLER/BLACKCOMB, B.C. P.O. Box 67, Whistler, BC, V0N 1B0	M-(604) 932-3434 R-(604) 932-4222	5,020'	130 marked trails, plus 5 alpine bowls on 4,000+ acres. Superb grooming, heaps of snow. Plenty of off-piste and steep chutes for experts. 20/55/25.

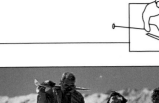

COURTESY HEAVENLY SKI RESORT

BOB PERRY, COURTESY KILLINGTON RESORT

BOB WINSETT, COURTESY KEYSTONE RESORT

Lifts	Heli-skiing	Season–%Snowmaking	Comment	Rating
Summit GON, 1 HSQ, 2 RQ, 4 doubles	None, but snowcat	Nov-Apr 35%	Flashy crowd. Bell Mtn. is expert hotspot with moguls, trees and deep powder.	★★★
Very new and modern. 2 HSQ, 5 triples, 4 doubles, short lift lines	None	Nov-Apr 26%	Underrated; great intermediate skiing. well-organized & cheaper than parent Vail.	★★★
2 HSQ, 6 triples, 8 dbls, 4 surface-- faster run to bowls than before	Colorado Heli-Ski (800) HELI-SKI	Nov-Apr 23%	No weaknesses. Mountain divided naturally for various skill levels. Good value.	★★★
GON, 4 triples, 12 dbls, 4 surface lifts (incl. Arapahoe Basin)	Rocky Mtn. Heliski (303) 468-8253	Oct-June 75%	Great intermed. trail system. With SM, opens Halloween. Share lift tickets with other resorts.	★★★
GON, 1 RQ, 7 triples, 10 doubles, 2 surface. 29,300 skiers/hr. capacity	Steamboat Powdercats (303) 879-5188	Nov-Apr 15%	Short waits, great verticals. Now major jet service. Better than average clientele.	★★★★
3 HSQs, 2 triples, 9 doubles, 2 surface. Short lift lines	None	Nov-Apr 55 acres	Hugh complex, very popular intermediate runs & moguls. Crowd-pleaser. A real cruisers' mountain.	★★★★
GON, 7 HSQ, 2 RQ, 2 triples, 9 doubles, most high speed lifts in West	Colorado Heli-Ski (303) 668-5600	Nov-Apr 332 acres	Maybe the best. Easy top three in US. New China Bowl offers great backcountry powder.	★★★★
1 triple, 7 doubles, 3 tows Trail to Snowbird	Wasatch Powderbird Guides (801) 742-2800	Nov-Apr 10%	Skiing the way God intended it. Wild, open expert areas, great powder, plus fine novice runs. A bargain.	★★★★ $
1 HSQ, 9 triples, 1 double	Utah Powderbird Guides (801) 649-9739	Dec-Apr 25%	Better cruising runs, shorter lift lines than Park City. Pricey, but with all amenities--great food and service.	★★★
GON, 1 HSQ, 1 RQ, 5 triples, 5 doubles	Utah Powderbird Guides (801) 649-9739	Nov-Apr 35%	Most variety in Utah. Nice long mogul runs. Fine bowl skiing. Home of US Ski Team.	★★★
125 person tram (inter/adv. terrain), 7 dbls., chute to Alta	Wasatch Powder Guides (801) 742-2800	Nov-June Inquire	Huge skiable area, full range of terrain and conditions good for all skill levels. Easy top 10 in U.S.	★★★★
3 new HSQ, 6 triples, 5 dbls., 10 min. to top	SV Heli-Ski Guides (208) 622-3108	Nov-May 25%	New lifts reduce wait time for superb, long runs. Good value compared to top Colorado resorts.	★★★★
2 RQ, 5 dbls, 1 triple, 2 surface	None	Nov-Apr 85% easy runs	SKI magazine's writers rank Taos #2 in US. Excellent terrain, but much of mtn. is quite difficult.	★★★
60-seat tram, 1 RQ, 1 triple, 5 doubles	High Mtn. Heli-Ski (307) 733-3274	Dec-Apr 5%	Major verticals, wild chutes, plus good cruising routes. Try Yellowstone snowmobiling.	★★★★
62-person tram, 6 triples, 10 doubles, 9 surface lifts	Heavenly Ski School (916) 541-1330 ext. 255	Nov-May 30%	Fantastic expert runs, but even novices can ski the top of the mountain.	★★★★
2 GON, 1 HSQ, 4 RQ, 7 triples, 14 doubles, plus t-bars	None	Nov-June 20%	Great runs, snow conditions and weather. Four stars even with the crowds. Very long season.	★★★★
GON, 2 HSQ, 3 triples 3 doubles, 2 surface	None	Nov 21-Apr 35% of runs	Good diversity. Excellent grooming and snow quality. User-friendly for intermediates and great for families.	★★★
2 GON, 3 HSQ, 7 triples, 16 dbls, 4 surface. 47,400 skiers/hr. capacity	None	Nov-May Minimal	One of the best resorts for skilled skiers in US. Great diversity, fast lifts, vistas galore and plenty of room.	★★★★
3 HSQ, 1 HS triple, 4 reg. triples, 2 doubles	None	Nov-July No SM	Best resort in Pacific NW. Summit can be cold, but 360-degree views and runs are great.	★★★
1 GON, 1 triple, 8 doubles, 2 quads, 2 t-bars	None	Nov-Apr 80%	Big mountain with wide choice of black runs. Most complete SM in East. Ho-hum scenery.	★★★
GON, 2 HSQ, 2 RQ, 4 triples, 7 doubles, 2 surface	None	Oct-June 72%	10-mile Juggernaut is longest run in US. Most trails, lifts and longest season in East. Superb for all levels.	★★★★
HS GON, 1 HSQ, 1 triple, 6 doubles, 1 surface	None	Nov-May 72%	50+% of lifts exceed 1 mile. Big mountain skiing and New England charm; top 10 candidate.	★★★★
3 HSQ, GON, 1 triple, 2 doubles, 5 surface. 10 min. to top on HSQ	None	Nov-May 85%	Eastern Canada's most complete resort, with modern lift network. Great night skiing.	★★
2 HSQ, 1 RQ, 2 triples, 4 doubles, 3 surface	See Heli-ski directory	Nov-May 40%	Spectacular setting. Great for all levels. Adjacent Sunshine Vill. & Mt. Norquay also good.	★★★
Ultra-modern lifts; GON, 5 HSQ, 8 trpls, 8 dbles, 6 surface (Total--both resorts)	Whist. Heli-skiing (604) 932-1405	Nov-June 45% at Blackcomb	SKI magazine writers' poll No. 1--the best. Great skiing variety. Major new snowmaking at Blackcomb.	★★★★

Ten Great European Ski Resorts

With so many fine ski areas in Europe, it's hard to select a destination, particularly if you've never skied the Alps before. Here are 10 resorts that all offer world-class skiing, fine accommodations and a memorable ambience. All are solid four or five-star resorts, but some are best for experts, while others are suitable for all levels of skiers.

In general, France offers the biggest resorts, with the steepest verticals and most challenging off-piste skiing. The Swiss ski areas have more charm, but the mountains are still big and impressive. Austria offers good value, countless skiing options and the charm of small villages. Italy has the lowest prices, the friendliest locals and the most consistent snow in the Alps.

Where possible we have provided local contact numbers. You should check with your long distance carrier to obtain regional area codes as necessary if they are not listed below. All prices are subject to change.

AUSTRIA
St. Anton

St. Anton, in the Arlberg region of the Tirol, is one of the oldest and busiest of Austria's resorts. You can ski dozens of runs from St. Anton proper, plus hundreds of other runs in the nearby resorts of St. Cristoph, Stuben, Zurs and Lech. St. Anton offers Austria's largest ski school and perhaps the best skiing for intermediates in the Tirol. From St. Anton, take the cable car to the Valluga summit and you'll enjoy a 9,000', half-hour cruise to the valley below. The intermediate run from the Gampberg summit is outstanding, while experts will be challenged by the large mogul field accessed from the Tanzboden lift.

St. Christoph offers fine intermediate runs off the Kampall summit. Zurs is the expert's choice in the St. Anton area, with the steepest verticals and some of the best off-piste powder skiing on the Continent.

St. Anton is a charming but bustling community, with a wide variety of accommodations. Co-op apartments and small guesthouses are preferred by bargain-hunters, with the lowest prices in the small village of Stuben. If you want to go first class, try the Hotel Schwarzer Adler in St. Anton, or the Hotel Post in Lech. A 6-day lift ticket good for the entire Arlberg area costs about $150. To get to Arlberg, fly to Zurich, then take the express train to St. Anton or the Swissair skibus to Lech. The tourist office is located at A-6580 St. Anton, Arlberg, Austria, (011 43) 5446 22690. Package tours to St. Anton (and all Austrian resorts) are offered by Alphorn Tours, (800) ALP-HORN.

Kitzbühel

Kitzbühel boasts the best night life among Austrian resorts, a wide selection of mostly intermediate runs, and easy access from Munich. The town of Kitzbühel, founded in the Middle Ages, has a unique charm that draws skiers back time and again, though the snow can be thin on the relatively low-altitude slopes (2,500'-6,500'). The focus of Kitzbühel skiing is the

The late extreme skier, Patrick Vallencant, South Face of the Grandes Jorasses, Courmayeur, Italy/CHRIS NOBLE

Hahnenkamm, the site of World Cup races each January. If you want to avoid the crowds, however, ski the Ehrenbachhohe in nearby Kirchberg, or try the 6,500' Kitzbüheler Horn which features long but relatively easy intermediate trails.

Despite the attention paid to the World Cup, Kitzbühel is mostly an intermediate destination, at least when it comes to prepared trails. Off-piste fans can go with guides to more challenging sections (about $120 per day), and the Red Devil ski school gives group classes in off-track skiing for about $35 per day. If you haven't booked a package tour, you can save quite a bit with the joint Kitzbühel/Kirchberg lift pass--3 days for about $75, 6 days for about $135.

All kinds of accommodations can be found in Kitzbühel, but we would recommend finding a room ("zimmer") in a private home, farm or apartment. These are universally spotless, warm and cozy, and you can often get by for under $35 per person per day, including breakfast. If you opt for a hotel, one of the best is the Tiefenbrunner ($100+ per night), while the Hotel Seehof

in Kirchberg is wonderfully situated by a lake and the rooms are a bargain. Budget hotel packages begin at $320 for a week, with lifts an additional $140 or so.

To get to Kitzbühel/Kirchberg fly to Munich and take the train straight through. Contact the local tourist office at Fremdenverkehrsverband, Hinterstadt, 18, A-6370 Kitzbühel, Austria, (011 43) 5356 2155, when you reach Munich.

Zell Am See

With its multitude of options--groomed trails, World Cup downhills, off-piste runs and glaciers--Zell Am See offers the complete Alps ski experience. Most of the best runs are accessed via the Schmittenhohe lifts. There is an outstanding network of intermediate trails, but experts can challenge themselves on the World Cup runs, and a superb run down from the Kapellenlift summit. Nearby Kaprun, located 10 kilometers from Zell Am See, is famous for its high-altitude glacier skiing. Reach the Alpin Center via a cablecar, or the Stanseil-

bahn tunnel route. Ski from here, or those with strong legs can go all the way to the 10,000' top station via aerial tram.

All this great skiing comes cheap. A joint Zell/Kaprun 7-day pass good for all 52 lifts at both resorts runs about $125. There are plenty of places to stay in the Zell Am See/Kaprun area. Most of the hotels and pensions are situated close to the lifts, and you can even stay at a mountain hotel right on the Kaprun glacier. The nearby village of Thumersbach, scenically located beside a lovely alpine lake, is another good choice if you have a rental car.

In low and mid-season, Zell Am See offers a good all-in-one ski package, the "Schnee-Okay." Starting at around $550 you get a regional 6-day lift pass, 7 nights' first-class lodging and use of the regional ski shuttles. There are also cheaper plans, starting at $350, which book you in "pensions" (family hotels), or B&Bs (lifts are extra). Local accommodations can be booked directly through the Zell Am See Kurverwaltung, Brucker Bundestrasse, A-5700 Zell Am See, Austria, (011 43) 6542 2600; Prodinger Travel, (011 43) 6542 2170; or Apartment service, (011 43) 6542 7539.

FRANCE
Chamonix

In the European Alps, France offers the biggest lift networks, the steepest verticals, and the most challenging off-piste and powder runs. And among the French resorts, if there is a king of steep and deep, it is Chamonix. This was the first home of the winter Olympics, and once you visit the place, you'll understand why. Near the town's edge, the terrain rises abruptly into a wonderland of white verticals, topped by 15,800' Mt. Blanc.

Though Chamonix boasts six separate ski resorts, this area is primarily geared for strong intermediate to advanced skiers. The showcase run is the 11-mile glacier descent from the Aiguille du Midi, skiable after February each year. You must have strong skills, and a guide is required ($130 for a group of four), but those who've done it say the passage down the Vallee Blanche and Mer De Glace is simply one of the best skiing experiences on the planet. Another great expert run is the descent from the 10,600' station at Les Grandes Monets.

Non-experts can still have fun at Chamonix, notably on the intermediate runs at Planpraz, and good blue trails at Les

Chamonix, France/SCOTT MARKEWITZ

Houches, but if you really want to know what all the fuss is about, you should have black trail skills.

Lift tickets at Chamonix are priced about the same as the major Austrian resorts--$140 or so for 6 days. Lodging will cost a bit more than in Austria, with two-star hotels starting at about $450 per week. The best hotels, such as the Mont-Blanc, Auberge du Bois Prin and the Alpina, run $130 and up per night, though prices are discounted in the low season. Ski apartments start at about $300 per week. A weekend-to-weekend stay is usually required.

Information on Chamonix and all major French resorts can be obtained from the French National Tourist Office (see page 311), or contact Chamonix directly at Office du Tourisme, place de L'Eglise, F-74400 Chamonix, France, (011 33) 50 53 00 24.

Les Trois Vallées

Les Trois Vallées, the largest ski area in the world, encompasses four distinct deluxe resorts: Courchevel, Meribel, Les Menuires and Val Thorens. Courchevel is the biggest and most cosmopolitan, with facilities and a run selection on a par with Vail. It offers mostly intermediate skiing on superbly groomed slopes, though the Col de Chanrossa routes will challenge even the best of skiers. Meribel is also largely composed of intermediate trails, but it offers easy access to the other ski areas in the region. Val Thorens and the newer resort of Les Menuires are the experts' destinations of choice. Val Thorens also offers some of the best summer skiing in France.

The key feature to Les Trois Vallées is diversity. With over 175 interconnected lifts, and 280 miles of marked runs, skiers can find exactly what they want, no matter what their skill level. For the average skier, Les Trois Vallées is an excellent choice because there are plenty of wide-open, relatively easy trails, all groomed to perfection, especially at Courchevel. Lifts in Les Trois Vallées are modern and efficient, keeping lines to a minimum.

Joint lift tickets valid for all area resorts run about $170 for a week. If you stick to one resort, prices are lower. Most skiers choose to stay in ski apartments, which outnumber hotel rooms by at least four to one. Expect to pay about $530 per week for a small two-person chalet. Hotel rooms begin at about $650 per week. Both apartments and hotel rooms are discounted heavily during special "White Week" periods. Contact the local tourist offices for complete details:

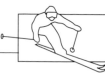

Val Thorens--73440 Val Thorens, France, (011 33) 79 00 08 08; Courchevel--La Croisette, 73120 Courchevel, France, (011 33) 79 08 00 29; 73550 Meribel, France, (011 33) 79 08 60 01; Les Menuires--73440 Les Menuires, France, (011 33) 79 08 20 12.

ITALY
— Cervinia —

With the Matterhorn looming above, you'll think you're in Switzerland, but Cervinia is definitely Italy, offering both something more and something less than you'll get elsewhere in the Alps. On the plus side, you'll see more sun and generally better weather than at the nearby French or Swiss resorts. And, in recent years, the snow has been much more reliable on the Italian side. Lift tickets and food are cheaper, as are accommodations. The downside is that Cervinia's lifts lack the speed and capacity found in France or Switzerland, (although a fine new gondola now runs to Plan Maison, the main ski center), and many of the best expert runs are not open until late in the season. Still, this relatively new resort is earning new converts each season (even the French are crossing the border to ski Cervinia), and Cervinia is now considered by many to offer the best overall skiing in the Alps, at least for the average skier.

Most of Cervinia's slopes are broad, wide-open and not too steep--ideal conditions for lower intermediates. Grooming is excellent. The lift system is interconnected with Val Tournache, giving skiers a choice of 65 miles of marked trails serviced by six cable cars, a gondola and 30 smaller lifts. The big thrill on the hill is the descent from Plateau Rosa to Val Tournache. Where else can you cruise for 20 kilometers, enjoying a 5,000' vertical drop on a single run? Those looking for greater challenges can ski the Zermatt side of the mountain, which offers steeper verticals and narrower runs.

Italian skiing's big attraction is its affordability. One nice feature is that a week's lift at Cervinia gives you a day's skiing at Courmayeur (reviewed below). Smart shoppers can find fantastic package bargains. Central Holiday Tours offers a week's skiing in the Italian Alps starting at under $200 per person, including lodging and lift tickets. That's under $30 per day, complete, less than a lift ticket alone in Vail. Call Central Holiday Tours at (800) 526-6045 for details. If you book your own hotel, try to stay at the Hermitage, easily the best in the area. Daily rates range from $70-$150, with two meals.

To get to Cervinia, fly to Geneva or Milan and then drive. The local bus connections to Cervinia are unreliable, so it's wise to get your own rental car. If you come from Geneva, be ready for the $25 toll at the Mont Blanc tunnel.

—— Courmayeur ——

Courmayeur, located on the Italian side of Mont Blanc, is Italy's premier resort. With lifts running as high as 11,000', one can always find skiable snow, and there is a wide choice of runs, although most are best suited for strong intermediates. Courmayeur is split into two major sections, the biggest across the Val Veny from Mont Blanc. There, skiers take cable cars up to high bowls served by chairlifts. Beginners won't find much to their liking here, but the terrain inspires confidence in intermediates who can rest on a number of plateaus separating the steeper sections. Snowmaking has been added recently to keep the lower sections runnable even in dry years. The 8,500' Cresta Youla is the highest an intermediate will want to go, allowing a solid 3,600' vertical drop to Zerotta. Experts with guides can take the cable car all the way up to 9,000' Crest Arp.

High-altitude fans will want to venture across the valley to ski the slopes of Mont Blanc. From the highest cable stop at 11,000', advanced skiers have a number of options--ski back to Courmayeur (some of the best runs are among the trees), traverse the glacier face or head off to Chamonix.

Lift tickets run about $140 for six days--not bad, but you're still better off with a package which includes lifts and accommodations. Central Holiday Tours, (800) 526-6045, offers bargain packages, starting at about $260 per person for lodging and transfers, or $475 with meals. (Discount airfare can be arranged as well.) The cheapest accommodations in Courmayeur are in large apartment complexes, the Residence Les Jumeaux and the Residence Universo. The best rooms in town are at the Hotel Pavilion, ideally situated near the lifts.

Courmayeur is served by a single, private tourist agency: VV Tours, Strada Regionale, Courmayeur, Italy, (011 39) 165 842061.

— Madonna Di Campiglio —

While Cervinia and Courmayeur are big, and getting bigger every season, Ma-

donna Di Campiglio has managed to retain the charm of a small, alpine ski village. Four local ski resorts encircle the town, and it's quite possible to circumnavigate the entire area via the 34 lifts and 65 miles of trails. The biggest ski area is Groste, famous for the world's longest gondola ride (three miles) and correspondingly long cruising runs from a high point of 7,500'. You'll find tougher trails in nearby Spinale, among them rugged World Cup runs. If you've exhausted the central ski basin, ride the linked lifts to the Folgarida and Marilleva resorts for another 20 lifts and more than 30 miles of prepared trails.

While the Madonna area isn't noted for its off-piste pleasures or powder, you can get into some pretty wild backcountry via a helicopter service run out of Campo Carlo Magna, one of the few in the Italian Alps.

No report on Madonna would be complete without some mention of the ambiance. Yes, there is great skiing, world-class at least for intermediates, but there is so much more. The village, situated on the shores of a scenic lake, is genuinely beautiful. The people of Madonna are warm, helpful and friendly. Its traditional architecture is a refreshing change from the concrete high-rises of the purpose-built resorts.

A package vacation is probably the best way to ski Madonna Di Campiglio (as well as the other Italian resorts). Central Holidays Tours offers 7-day package tours to Madonna for about $400 per person including lodging and transfers. Add about $160 per week for lifts. Call Central Holidays at (800) 526-6045, or contact the Italian Tourist Board at (212) 245-4822, or (415) 392-6206.

SWITZERLAND
Verbier

Many advanced skiers who've sampled resorts throughout Europe consider Verbier the best of the best. Verbier has earned this reputation for its slopes (steep and challenging), its size (there are 88 lifts connecting four separate valleys), and its setting (Verbier is nestled among the highest and most scenic peaks in southwest Switzerland). Though Verbier can hardly be called a single-focus resort, it is a destination best suited to skilled skiers. Beginners and novices will find little to ski but short bunny slopes. But for the experts looking for a real challenge, plus unexcelled off-piste thrills, Verbier delivers.

The Verbier resort is the hub of the ski area, with the smaller resorts of Thyon, Veysonna, Haute Nendaz and Mayens clustered nearby. Verbier proper offers the most modern lifts and longest trails. On Verbier's major expert runs, such as the Tortin descent from Col des Gentines, you find 30+ degree gradients, through narrow corridors requiring quick, perfect turns.

Those looking to push the off-piste envelope can sample deep powder and steep chutes on the upper reaches of the ski area. Easier skiing is to be found in Nendaz and Thyon. Lifts are a bit slower, but the slopes are much less crowded, particularly on weekends. Nendaz also offers cheaper accommodations than Verbier.

The best time to ski Verbier is during the latter halves of January and March when "White Week" promotions are in effect. During White Weeks you'll get 7 nights lodging with two meals a day, a 6-day lift pass, and 6 half-days of instruction, for about $900 (four-star hotels), or about $600 (two-star hotel). A four-star hotel would normally run at least $120 per night for a double. During other periods, your most affordable lodging option is to rent a ski apartment through Verbier's efficient, computerized booking system. Many package tours utilize these facilities, which are modern and ultra-clean in typical Swiss fashion. Expect to pay about $550 per week (dbl. occupancy), with lifts an additional $150 per week.

Verbier is conveniently served by direct train from the Geneva airport, and is an easy hour's drive from other major Swiss ski resorts and the charming cities of Montreaux and Lausanne--both worth a visit when you've finished skiing. For further information, contact the local Tourist Office at 1936 Verbier 1, Verbier, Switzerland, (011 41) 26 76222, or 77181.

Zermatt

Zermatt wins top honors in almost every category. Situated beneath the Matterhorn, Zermatt is a classic, picturesque alpine village. As no cars are allowed, you arrive in town by narrow gauge railway or horse-drawn sleigh. Zermatt has few equals as a ski destination that will please any level of skier. Beginners can practice on the gentle slopes of the Klein Matterhorn glacier and Gornergrat-- real alpine country, not bunny hills. There are dozens of great alternatives for intermediates. Sunnegga offers sunny slopes with snowmaking. The Kumme area has long, wide-open trails, with short lift lines. Take the long cable car ride all the way to 12,500' to ski down from the Klein Matterhorn. The views are spectacular from this summit, the highest cable car-served point in Europe. From the top you can descend the glacier (skiable year-round), or cross the ridge and ski down to Cervinia on the Italian side. (To get back via the Italian lifts, you must first purchase a special ticket in Zermatt.)

Zermatt offers all the excitement an advanced skier could want. There are dozens

COURTESY AUSTRIAN NATIONAL TOURIST OFFICE

of serious chutes and couloirs in the Sunnegga and Gornergrat areas, and the Unterrothorn's Kumme side. Mogul lovers have plenty to cheer about, especially in the Stockhorn and Rote Nasse sections of the Gornergrat. Anything you want off-piste is available--deep powder, cornice jumping, even an overland run to Saas-Fee. Hardcore adventure skiers may want to try out the Haute Route, a classic backcountry circuit between Saas-Fee, Zermatt, Courmayeur and Chamonix. Guided Haute Route tours cost about $650 in Switzerland, including guides, hut accommodations, and lift/transportation costs. Skiers must be strong in deep powder and steep terrain, and be able to climb 3,300' per day on skins. A rec-

ommended Haute Route guide is John Hogg, Alpine Adventures, CH-6490, Andermatt, Switzerland, (011 41) 44 68353.

Lodging in Zermatt does not come cheap, but $120 per night will buy you a great deal more charm and luxury than you can find in the United States for the same price. The very best hotels in Zermatt are the Mont Cervin and Zermatterhoff ($170+ per night, mid-season); cheaper but still excellent choices are the Hotel Alpenhof and Hotel Monte Rosa (both under $130). There are over 10,000 apartment beds in Zermatt, and you should be able to find something you can afford. Apartment prices begin at about $380 per person per week, double occupancy. Add $155 for a 6-day lift ticket.

The most desirable location is in the Obere-Steinmatte district, close to the Sunnegga lifts. Night life in Zermatt is active, but not as wild as in Kitzbühel or some of the French resorts. Top aprés-ski pubs are the Old Zermatt and the Popular Pub. In the evening, try the jazz bar in the Hotel de Poste. Package tours to Zermatt are offered by a number of operators, such as Joli Tours, (800) 333-5654, and Value Holidays, (800) 558-6850. Check with your travel agent, or call (800) 662-0021 to request Swissair's ski package tour directory, the "Alpine Experience," available free. For further information, consult the Swiss Tourist Board or the Zermatt Tourist Office at CH-3920, Zermatt, Switzerland, (011 41) 028 661181.

Summer Skiing

Glacier skiing in the Selkirks, Canada/MARK GALLOP

WHERE DO YOU GO WHEN THE season's over at your favorite American resort? Here are the best places in the world to make tracks between June and September.

ARGENTINA

The leading ski resort in South America is Las Lenas, located at Mendoza, Argentina in the Andes. A true world-class resort, Las Lenas has 11 lifts, 40 miles of trails, and 4,000' of vertical drop, beginning at 10,000'. Receiving 250 inches of snow annually, Las Lenas offers excellent powder conditions and reliable snow from June through October. The quality of the skiing has made Las Lenas the summer choice of the US, French and Swiss Olympic teams. The bowls will remind you of Colorado's best, while the verticals are as good as anything in the States.

Las Lenas is located 90 minutes from Buenos Aires. Package tours and advance reservations are handled through Las Lenas North America, Inc., 9592 Harding Avenue, Second Floor, Surfside, FL 33154, (305) 864-7545, or (800) 862-7545; FAX: (305) 861-2895. A 10-day tour with 7 days skiing cost about $1,900 in 1991, including lifts, four-star hotel and round-trip airfare from Miami.

CHILE

Chile has four principal ski resorts, all offering great snow and uncrowded slopes. The most popular resort is La Parva, choice of Santiago's upper class and the Canadian Ski Team. It offers dozens of well-marked runs, all above 9,000', and miles of open terrain for experts. Lifts are basic, but prices are a bargain; $500-$700 buys lodging, lifts and meals for a week.

Next door to La Parva, Valle Nevado is being developed by the French operators of Les Trois Vallées. When complete, it will be one of the largest ski areas in the world, able to serve 30,000 skiers. At present, you can enjoy the vast ski area and superb dry, snow almost all to yourself. Visitors say the resort is like four Vails combined, offering the solitude of cross-country skiing with the convenience of lifts. Package tours run $2,500-$3,100 per week with round-trip air from Los Angeles. Heli-skiing is available.

Portillo is Chile's oldest resort, and its world-class downhill runs are favored by European experts. Portillo offers a low-key setting with some of the most challenging skiing in the Southern Hemisphere, including great heli-skiing. A week's skiing starts at $700, or $2,300 with round-trip air. Chillan is another quaint resort, but it boasts South America's longest chairlift, a mile and a half in length. From the top you can ski 15,000 virgin acres with nobody else in sight. Package prices range from $550-$900 per week.

Contact the Chilean National Tourist Board, 510 W. 6th Street, Suite 1210, Los Angeles, CA 90014, (213) 627-4293, or call Path Tours, (818) 980-4442.

AUSTRIA

■

If you missed Austria in the winter, don't worry; there's plenty of skiing in the summertime too. Choose from any of five 9,000' destinations: Hintertux at the end of the Ziller Valley, above Innsbruck in the Stubai Valley, above Solden in the Oetz Valley, at the end of the Pitz Valley, and under Weissee Peak in the Kauner Valley. Contact the Austrian National Tourist Board for details, (212) 944-6880 or (310) 477-3332. If you're curious about summer snow conditions or current lift ticket prices, you can dial the Tirolian Tourist Board directly at Bozner Platz 6, A-6010 Innsbruck, (011 43) 5222 20777 0, or 5222 20777 111 for the 24-hour snow report. Visit Kaprun if you're looking for the easiest way to ski Austria in the summertime. Lifts run year-round on the wide-open slopes of the glacier beneath the 10,506' Kitzsteinhorn. For information, contact Verkehrsverein Kaprun, A-5710, Kaprun, Austria, or call the Austrian Tourist Board.

CANADA

■

Canada's Whistler and Blackcomb resorts, located side-by-side north of Vancouver, offer the most popular and extensive summertime skiing opportunities in North America. The longest running program is the Dave Murray Summer Ski Camp, which recently relocated from Whistler to Blackcomb Mountain. Both adult and junior sessions are offered for any particular interest area--freestyle, racing, recreational skiing and snowboarding. The

adult program, which also features tennis, mountain biking and windsurfing, costs about $1,200 per week. Contact the Dave Murray Summer Ski Camp, Box 98, Whistler, BC, Canada V0N 1B0, (604) 932-3141 or (604) 687-1032 (Vancouver).

Other summer programs at Blackcomb cover virtually every type of skiing. Racing clinics are offered by Rossignol, (604) 932-8325, and Technica, (802) 888-3272. Snowboard skills are taught by the Canadian Snowboarding Association, (604) 983-3839, while freestyle instruction is offered by World Mogul Camp, (303) 879-2202. Contact Blackcomb Skiing Enterprises, Box 98, Whistler, B.C., Canada V0N 1B0, (604) 932-3141; FAX: (604) 932-5988.

FRANCE/SWITZERLAND

■

With a number of large glaciers in the French and Swiss Alps, you can ski there year-round if you don't mind snow conditions that can be a bit unpredictable. (The recent series of hot, dry summers have caused many of the glaciers to recede, although there is still plenty of snow up high.) For scenic splendor, head to Zermatt, Switzerland, and ski the Klein Matterhorn Glacier, served by a 12,000' cable car, the world's highest. In France, the Tignes resort operates an 11,000' lift year-round to the top of La

DAVID STOECKLEIN

Grande Motte. Package tours to these and other destinations can be arranged by Adventures on Skis, 815 North Road, Route 202, Westfield, MA 01085, (800) 628-9655 nationwide; FAX: (413) 562-3621.

If you're looking for the ultimate summer ski experience in the Alps, a helicopter is the only way to go. Air Zermatt offers alpine heli-trips to some truly inspirational ski runs. Just the view from the drop points

is worth the (hefty) price of admission-- $350-$600 per day. Contact Air Zermatt, 3290 Zermatt, Switzerland, (011 41) 2867 3487; FAX: (011 41) 2867 4004.

NEW ZEALAND

■

Seasons are reversed south of the equator, so there is always good summer skiing Down Under. The Mt. Hutt resort is the expert's choice for New Zealand's most challenging skiing. However, high winds can close the resort a few days a month, explaining its Kiwi nickname, Mt. Shut. The best intermediate skiing is found at the Cardrona resort, a great place to improve your skills with 3,200 vertical feet and wide-open bowls. Nearby Treble Cone, with 2,800 vertical feet of drop and lots of moguls, is for rough-and-ready types.

A couple of hours away is Queenstown, the winter sports hub of the South Island. Regular bus service takes skiers to the Remarkables and Coronet Peak resorts. Snow conditions are likely to be better at the Remarkables, which offers some excellent and challenging black runs, although the slopes can get icy in August and September. Lift tickets at most New Zealand ski resorts cost about $24-$28 US per day ($30-$35 NZ).

New Zealand heli-skiing is some of the best in the world, with deep powder, top-notch guides and extraordinary views. Harris Mountain Heli-skiing offers 1 to 3-day heli-skiing packages starting at about $270, while $2,800 buys a mind-boggling 50,000 Odyssey Week--7 days of guided heli-skiing, 50,000 vertical feet of runs, and all meals and accommodations. Contact Harris Mountain Heli-skiing, P.O. Box 177, Wanaka, New Zealand (011 64) 3 443 7930.

For those wishing to sample a number of ski areas, Ski New Zealand, Inc., 150 Powell Street, Suite 407, San Francisco, CA 94102, (800) 822-KIWI, or (415) 421-3171 offers an excellent 14-day tour covering most of the Kiwi ski centers. Round-trip airfare, accommodations and local transport are included in the $1,695 price, with meals and lift tickets extra. For the same price, you can try 2 full weeks of heli-skiing; $1,695 buys everything except the actual helicopter flights (about $275 per day), guides and meals. A similar 7-day heli-ski package is available for $1,395-$1,595.

Exotic Skiing

GREECE, MOROCCO, HAWAII, USSR, YUGOSLAVIA

S O YOU'RE TIRED OF THE SAME OLD RUNS AND WANT to combine a little world exploration with your skiing? Then consider venturing beyond North America and Western Europe. Excellent, uncrowded ski sites are also to be found in many less developed or Socialist countries, usually at bargain rates. And many warm weather regions such as Hawaii have at least one high, skiable mountain. The facilities may not be as deluxe as you are accustomed to, but dealing with a bit of challenge is all part of the adventure. Here are some far-flung possibilities.

GREECE
▲

Mts. Olympus and Parnassus

Equipped with modern lifts and facilities, Mt. Parnassus, Greece's most popular ski center, is relatively close to Athens. More challenging is 9,750' Mt. Olympus, the tallest summit in Greece. Basic lift services are available, and lodging is available in the nearby village of Litohoro. Further information can be obtained from the Greek National Tourist Organization, 645 Fifth Avenue, New York, NY 10022, (212) 421-5777 or (212) 826-6940. Bookings can be arranged by Arvanitis Travel, 36 Voulis Street, Athens 10557, Greece, (011 30) 1 32 32 375, or 32 31 130; FAX: (011 30) 1 32 32 340.

HAWAII
▲

Mauna Kea

At almost 14,000', Hawaii's Mauna Kea volcano holds decent snow from May through December and boasts a 5,000' vertical drop. You won't have to wait for lifts because there aren't any. Ski Guides Hawaii hauls skiers up the slopes in 4WD vehicles for $150 per day, guides included. You will be picked up at your hotel on the Big Island, and full gear rental is available for $30. For details, contact Ski Guides Hawaii, P.O. Box 1954 Kamuela, HI 96743, (808) 885-4188, or the Hawaii Visitors Bureau, 180 Kinoole Street, Hilo, HI 96720, (808) 961-5797.

MOROCCO
▲

Atlas Mountains

Morocco may seem an unlikely ski venue, but its High Atlas Mountains, Africa's highest range, get skiable snow every winter, despite the southerly latitude. At 13,000', the ski resort at Oukaimeden offers decent, dry ski conditions from December through March, and attracts many Europeans to its slopes every year. Accommodations and lifts are similar to those in smaller resorts in the States. Because Oukaimeden and one smaller neighboring resort cater to European tourists, you'll find your ski experience surprisingly civilized. The biggest problem is transportation.

Heli-skiing, Himachal Pradesh, India/CHRIS NOBLE

pressive, a steep summit flanked by other large peaks. Close to Cheget is Mt. Elbrus, Europe's highest peak at 18,481'. Mt. Elbrus' snowfields are accessible by a cable car located a few minutes drive from the ski area. Most of the ski area here remains a wilderness, unspoiled and untamed.

Expect the trip to be an adventure. There is no hotel for foreign tourists in Cheget, so you'll be housed at Dombai, a newer resort servicing the Elbrus area. You must bring all your own equipment. There is no ski equipment to rent, and what you might be able to buy, you wouldn't want to use. There are no regular alpine ski packages organized for Cheget. However, Intourist, the USSR's foreign tourist agency, can arrange lodging (you'll have to get to the mountain on your own), while the Citizen Exchange Council coordinates nordic ski holidays in the Cheget area. Contact Intourist, 630 Fifth Avenue, New York, NY 10111, (212) 757-3884; and The Citizen Exchange Council, 18 East 41st Street, New York, NY 10017, (212) 889-7960.

YUGOSLAVIA

▲

Europe's Best Bargain

Even before the recent political turmoil, Yugoslavia offered the best skiing values in Europe. Hopefully, by winter 1992-1993, the situation will have stabilized to the extent that skiers can return. Site of the 1984 Winter Olympics, Yugoslavia boasts a number of fine resorts, good intermediate skiing and bargain prices. Yugoslavia's mountains trap moisture-laden Mediterranean air, making for abundant, reliable snow every winter. In the north, where Yugoslavia shares the Alps with Italy and Austria, you'll find the Kranjska Gora resort, which boasts well-groomed trails and no lift lines.

In the central region, Sarajevo offers the most skiing options. Novices will enjoy Johorina, with a dozen short runs served by 11 lifts. A wide variety of accommodations is available, and you can enjoy night skiing under lights. Strong intermediate skiers will find more challenge at nearby Bjelasnica. The runs are much longer, and the hills much steeper--up to 3,700' of vertical.

Yugoslavian skiing is a great bargain. A 6-day lift ticket at most Yugoslavian ski areas costs under $80, and under $150 with ski school. In 1990, Yugotours offered 9-day package tours for under $850, including round-trip airfare from New York, lodging and most meals. Call Yugotours at (800) 872-5298, or (800) 872-8598 on the west coast.

There is very limited bus service to Oukaimeden, so do what the French tourists do--rent a car in Marrakech and drive. Both Avis and Hertz have modern offices in Marrakech with English-speaking staffs. Package tours for Morocco can be arranged through most French-based travel agencies. The *Let's Go Guide to Spain, Portugal and Morocco* is an invaluable resource.

USSR

▲

Cheget & Gudari

Gudari, the Soviet Union's most modern and complete ski resort, offers an impressive number of runs from mild to wild, along with up-to-date lifts and very good (by Eastern bloc standards) accommodations and support facilities. Challenging off-piste skiing is available via reasonably priced heli-ski services. For a full run-down on the glasnöst Gudari skiing experience, check out the November 1989 issue of *Powder* magazine.

Though Gudari is the USSR's showcase resort, chances are if you meet anyone who has skied the Soviet Union, it will have been at Cheget, situated in the Caucasus mountains, close to Turkey. Though it's been around since 1964, Cheget has few lifts, and mostly unimproved terrain. However, it does boast an impressive 3,100' vertical drop, along with wide-open bowls where you can ski in virtual solitude.

The main mountain at Cheget is im-

HELI-SKIING WORLDWIDE

GARY BRETTNACHER

HERE ARE SOME OF THE BEST HELI-SKIING OPERATIONS WORLDWIDE. MANY OF these companies had not set their prices at the time of printing, so you may expect costs to move upward about 5 to 10 percent. Add 7 percent GST surcharge to most Canadian prices. Consult our Top 25 ski resort comparison list (p. 296) for other heli-skiing operators in North America.

CANADA

Canada is the heli-skiing center of North America. Here you'll find most of the top heli-skiing operations in the business. If 15,000 vertical feet ("VF") a day sounds good, contact one of the operators below. March offers the best overall conditions. Note: most programs are priced in Canadian funds ("CDN"); multiply by .85 to get the approximate price in US dollars.

Alberta

■ **CANADIAN MOUNTAIN HOLIDAYS**
P.O. Box 1660, Banff, ALB, Canada T0L 0C0, (800) 661-0252, or (403) 762-4531.

Twenty-five years' experience in Canadian Rockies: Bugaboos, Gothics, Bobbie Burns, Cariboos, Monashees, Revelstoke, Selkirks, Galena. Most routes for experts only. Grades of 40-60 percent are not uncommon. One of the most radical runs, Steep and Deep, is 3,300 VF at a 78 percent average grade! Seven days, with meals and lodging: 100,000 VF, $2,430-$4,930 CDN. An Intro-Week is also offered for strong intermediates, with 7 days' skiing on more moderate terrain. Rating: ★★★★

■ **KOOTENAY HELICOPTER SKIING, LTD**
P.O. Box 717, Nakusp, BC, Canada V0G 1R0, (800) 663-0100, or (604) 265-3121; FAX: (604) 265-4447.

Fifteen years operating in Kootenay and Monashee ranges. With 140 runs, two-thirds deep powder, tree skiing for experts and very strong intermediates. Seven days with meals and lodging: 80,000 VF guaranteed, roughly $3,500, including ground transfers from Spokane. Extra runs $13 CDN per thousand VF. Package tours from Washington state are available. Rating: ★★★★

■ **MIKE WIEGLE HELICOPTER SKIING**
P.O. Box 249, Banff, ALB, Canada T0L 0C0, (800) 661-9170, or (403) 762-5548.

Monashees and Cariboos. Deep, dry powder. Chutes, tree runs and glacier routes for experts only. Among the most challenging heli-skiing in the world. Packages with meals and lodging: 3 days: 42,000 VF (30k guaranteed), $1,210-$2,176 CDN; 5 days: 70,000 VF (50k guaranteed), $1,981-$3,563 CDN; 7 days: 100,000 VF (80k guaranteed), $2,700-$4,495 CDN. For his clientele, Wiegle offers 16 chalets and a large, comfortable lodge with European chefs. The experience is quite deluxe. Rating: ★★★★★

British Columbia

■ **PURCELL HELICOPTER SKIING, LTD.**
P.O. Box 1530, Golden, BC, Canada V0A 1H0,

(604) 344-5410; FAX: (604) 344-6076.

With 150 routes in Purcell Range for experts and strong intermediates. Full-day, 3 runs: $345 CDN. Packages with meals and lodging: 3 days: 27,000 VF, $1,300-$1,500 CDN; 5 days: 45,000 VF, $2,165-$2,500 CDN; 7 days: 65,000 VF, $3,030-$3,500 CDN. Additional runs $50 CDN for 3,000 VF. December through May. Rating: ★★★

■ **SELKIRK TANGIERS HELI-SKIING, LTD.**
P.O. Box 1409, Golden, BC, Canada V0A 1H0, (800) 663-7080, or (604) 344-5016.

Selkirk and Monashee Ranges. 1,550 square miles of bowls, trees and glaciers, all with deep, dry powder. Seven days with meals and lodging, 30+ runs: 100,000+ VF, $3,160-$3,360 CDN; 6 days: $2,780-$2,930 CDN; extra runs: $45 CDN for 3,000 VF (GST included). Rating: ★★★

Quebec

■ **CHIC-CHOC WILDERNESS RESORT**
Case Postale 458, Cap-Chat, QUE, Canada G0J 1E0, (418) 786-2134.

Gaspe Peninsula, chutes and bowls, corn snow. Intermediate to expert, 2,700 VF/run. One-day, 11,000 VF, approx. $450 US. Three-days with meals and lodging, 24,000 VF, should be under $1,000 US. 5-7 skiers per guide. Helicopters and snow-cats. Rating: ★★

UNITED STATES

Many large domestic ski resorts in the Rockies and Sierra Nevada offer heli-skiing for around $350 per day per person.

Colorado

■ **COLORADO HELI-SKI**
P.O. Box 64, Frisco, CO 80443, (800) HELI-SKI.

High alpine bowls, chutes and glades in Eagle and Summit Counties region. Advanced, 5 guided runs: $375; Intro Day, 2 guided runs: $300; single half-run, 2,000-3,000 VF: $150. Also programs for handicapped skiers. (1990 prices) Rating: ★★

■ **TELLURIDE HELITRAX**
P.O. Box 1560, New Sheridan Hotel Lobby, Telluride, CO 81435, (303) 728-4904.

San Juan and Uncompahgre National Forest high-altitude (13,000') powder. Five runs, full day: $380, 12,500 VF; add'l. runs: $70. Rating: ★★

Idaho

■ **SUN VALLEY HELI-SKI**
P.O. Box 978, Sun Valley, ID 83353, (208) 622-3108.

Sawtooth and Pioneer Ranges. Virgin

corn powder. Only three skiers per guide. Five runs, 12-20,000 VF: about $375 per day. Three-run half-day program: about $275. Also heli-lift ski touring and ski mountaineering. Rating: ★★

Nevada

■ **RUBY MOUNTAIN HELI-SKI**
P.O. Box 1192, Lamoille, NV 89828, (702) 753-6867; FAX: (702) 753-7628.

Open, high-altitude bowls--great dry, light powder, good for novice to expert heli-skiers. Three days, with food and lodging, 39,000 VF guaranteed: $1,400 ($1,100 late season). One day, 1 night, 13,000 VF: $490. Snowcat backup for bad weather. Rating: ★★★

Utah

■ **WASATCH POWDERBIRD GUIDES**
P.O. Box 57, Snowbird, UT 84092, (801) 742-2800.

Wasatch Range. Small groups with guide. Dry, light powder. Full-day, 6 runs, 15,000 VF: $325-$385; extra runs $35-$45. Sis-

John Falkiner, Zermatt, Switzerland/ACE KVALE, CLAMBIN PROD.

ter Company: Utah Powderbird Guides, Park City, (801) 649-9739. Rating: ★★

Washington

■ **NORTH CASCADE HELI-SKIING**
P.O. Box 367, Winthrop, WA 98862, (509) 996-2148, or (800) 422-3048 in WA.

Eighty routes through Okanagan National Forest. Full-day, five runs with guide, 10,000 VF: $350. Three-day package (with

lodging & meals), 30,000 VF: $1,400. One-day heli-lift nordic telemark program, 4,000 VF: $90. Rating: ★★

Wyoming

■ **HIGH MOUNTAINS HELICOPTER SKIING**
P.O. Box 2217, Jackson, WY 83001, (307) 733-3274.

Snake River and Palisades ranges; powder bowls good for both experts and intermediates. Full-day, 6 runs, 14,000 VF: $375. Guided nordic telemark heli-tour: $125. (1991 prices.) Rating: ★★

WORLDWIDE

Austria

■ **HELICOPTER VUCHER**
A-6713 Ludesh, Austria, (011 43) 55 502261.

■ **HELISKI TIROL**
A 6563 Galtur, Tirol, Austria, (011 43) 54 43440.

Chile

■ **ANDES POWDER GUIDES**
Casilla 48, Correo San Enrique, Santiago, Chile, Phone/FAX: (011 56) 2772 758.

Himalayas

■ **HIMACHAL HELICOPTER SKIING**
P.O. Box 920108, Snowbird, UT 84092-0108, (801) 742-2735.

■ **ADVENTURES ON SKIS**
Leo Demelbauer, 815 North Road, Route 202, Westfield, MA 01085, (800) 628-9655.

Italy

■ **LACADUR HELI-SKI**
Jean Marie Duriaux, 1010 Val Grisenche, Italy, (011 39) 165 97138; in summer: (011 33) 50540 840 (France).

■ **AUGUSTINO PERROD HELITUR**
P.O. Box 78, Courmayeur, Italy, (011 39) 165 843 737 or 165 884 828.

New Zealand

■ **Harris Mountain Heli-skiing**, *P.O. Box 177, Wanaka, New Zealand, (011 64) 3 433-7930.*

■ **Alpine Guides**, *Box 20, Mt. Cook, New Zealand, (011 64) 3 435-1834. Prices average $350 US per day for 4-5 runs with guide.*

Switzerland

■ **AIR GLACIER SA**
3822 Lauterbrunnen, Switzerland, (011 41) 30 51 321; FAX: (011 41) 36 55 2224.

■ **AIR ZERMATT**
3290 Zermatt, Switzerland, (011 41) 28 67 3487; FAX: (011 41) 28 67 4004.

DOWNHILL SKIING

SKI RESORT CONTACT NUMBERS

Use these numbers to contact over 70 ski resorts around the country. Where two numbers are provided, call the first for information on runs, prices, ski schools and weather; call the second to reserve accommodations and/or a rental car.

The Weather Channel now provides snow reports as part of its 24-hour 900 weather hotline.To obtain current ski conditions at more than 400 US resorts, dial (900) WEATHER. Separate reports, updated daily November through June, can be accessed for the West Coast, New Mexico and Arizona, Idaho and the Rocky Mountains, the Midwest, the Southeast and New England.

UNITED STATES

Alaska
Alyeska:	(907) 783-2222

California
Alpine Meadows:	(916) 581-8225
	(800) 824-6348
Bear Mountain:	(714) 585-2519
	(714) 866-7000
Dodge Ridge:	(209) 965-3474
	(800) 446-1333
Heavenly:	(800) 243-2836
Homewood:	(800) 824-6348
Kirkwood:	(800) 288-2463
Mammoth Mountain:	(619) 934-2571
	(800) 367-6572
Northstar:	(916) 562-1330
	(800) 533-6787
Squaw Valley:	(916) 583-6985
	(800) 545-4350

Colorado
Aspen:	(800) 525-6200
Breckenridge:	(303) 453-5000
	(800) 221-1091
Copper Mountain:	(303) 968-2882
	(800) 458-8386
Crested Butte:	(303) 349-2259
	(800) 544-8448
Keystone:	(800) 222-0188
Steamboat Springs:	(303) 879-6111
	(800) 922-2722
Telluride:	(303) 728-4424
	(800) 525-3455
Winter Park:	(303) 726-5514
	(800) 453-2525
Vail/Beaver Creek:	(303) 476-3239
	(800) 525-2257

Idaho
Sun Valley:	(800) SUN-VALY
	(800) 634-3347

Maine
Saddleback:	(207) 864-5671
Sugarloaf:	(207) 237-2000
	(800) 843-5623
Sunday River:	(207) 824-3000
	(800) 543-2SKI

Massachusetts
Butternut:	(413) 528-2000
	(413) 443-9186

Montana
Big Mountain:	(800) 858-5439
Big Sky Resort:	(406) 995-4211

Big Sky Resort: *(cont.)*	(800) 548-4486
	(800) 824-7767 in MT
Bridger Bowl:	(800) 223-9609
Red Lodge Mountain:	(406) 446-2610
	(800) 444-8977

Nevada
Diamond Peak:	(702) 832-1120
	(800) 468-2463
Ski Incline:	(702) 832-1120
Mt. Rose:	(702) 849-0704

New Hampshire
Attitash:	(603) 374-2368
	(800) 223-7669
Cannon:	(603) 823-5563
Loon Mountain:	(603) 745-8111
	(800) 433-3413
Waterville Valley:	(603) 236-8311
	(800) 468-2553
Wildcat:	(603) 466-3326
	(800) 334-7378

New Mexico
Angel Fire Resort:	(505) 377-6401
	(800) 633-7463
Pajarito (Los Alamos):	(505) 662-7669
Red River Ski Area:	(505) 754-2223
	(800) 331-7669
Santa Fe Ski Area:	(505) 982-4429
	(800) 982-7669
Taos Ski Valley:	(505) 776-2291
	(800) 992-7669

New York
Hunter:	(518) 263-4223
	(518) 263-3827
Whiteface:	(518) 523-1655
	(800) 833-2521
	(800) 942-7547 in NY

Oregon
Mt. Bachelor:	(503) 382-2442
	(800) 547-6858
Ski Ashland:	(503) 482-2897
Mt. Hood Meadows:	(503) 337-2222
Timberline:	(503) 231-7979
	(800) 547-1406 (Northwest)

Pennsylvania
Blue Knob:	(814) 239-5111
	(800) 222-1834 in PA
Hidden Valley:	(814) 443-6454
	(800) 458-0175
Shawnee Mountain:	(717) 421-7231
	(800) 742-9633 (PA, VA, D.C.)
Seven Springs:	(814) 352-7777
	(800) 458-2313 (East Coast)
	(800) 452-2223

Utah
Alta:	(801) 742-3333
Brian Head:	(801) 677-2035
Brighton Ski Bowl:	(801) 943-8309
Deer Valley:	(801) 649-1000
	(800) 424-3337
Park City:	(801) 649-1111
	(800) 222-PARK
Snowbird:	(801) 742-2222
	(800) 453-3000
Sundance:	(801) 225-4100
	(800) 634-5911

Vermont
Jay Peak:	(802) 988-2611
	(800) 451-4449
Killington:	(802) 422-3333
	(802) 773-1330
Okemo Mountain:	(802) 228-4041
	(802) 228-5571
	(802) 228-5222 (snowphone)
Mount Snow:	(802) 464-8501
	(800) 245-7669 (outside New England)
Smuggler's Notch:	(802) 644-8851
	(800) 451-8752 USA
Stowe:	(802) 253-7311
	(800) 253-7321
Stratton Mountain:	(802) 297-2200
	(800) 843-6867 (outside VT)
Sugarbush:	(802) 583-2381
	(800) 537-8427

Washington
Crystal Mountain:	(206) 663-2265
Mission Ridge:	(800) 422-3048 WA
	(509) 996-2148 USA
Alpental/Ski Acres/Snoqualmie:	(206) 232-8182
	(800) 528-1234

Wyoming
Grand Targhee:	(307) 733-2292
	(800) 443-8146
Jackson Hole:	(800) 443-6931

CANADA

Alberta
Lake Louise:	(403) 522-3555
	(800) 661-1676
	(403) 256-8473
Mt. Norquay (Banff):	(403) 762-4421
	(800) 661-1676
Sunshine Village (Banff):	(403) 762-6500
	(800) 661-1676

British Columbia
Blackcomb:	(604) 932-3141
	(604) 932-4222
Whistler:	(604) 932-3434
	(800) 944-7853

Ontario
Blue Mountain:	(705) 445-0231
	(705) 445-0748

Quebec
Gray Rocks:	(819) 425-2771
	(800) 567-6767
Mont Ste. Anne:	(800) 463-1568
Mont Sutton:	(514) 538-2338
	(514) 538-2646
Mont Tremblant:	(800) 461-8700

TRAVELERS' GUIDE

EUROPEAN TOURIST OFFICES

AUSTRIA
500 Fifth Avenue, New York, NY 10110, (212) 944-6880; 11601 Wilshire Blvd., Ste. 2480, Los Angeles, CA 90025, (310) 477-3332. Austrian snow reports (24 hours): (212) 944-6917.

FRANCE
610 Fifth Avenue, New York, NY 10020, (212) 757-1125; billed information line: (900) 420-2003; 9401 Wilshire Blvd., #840, Beverly Hills, CA 90212, (213) 271-6665.

GERMANY
747 Third Avenue, New York, NY 10017, (212) 308-3300; 444 S. Flower Street, #2230, Los Angeles, CA 90071, (213) 688-7332, or (213) 688-7574.

ITALY
630 Fifth Avenue, New York, NY 10011, (212) 245-4822; 360 Post St. #801, San Francisco, CA 94108, (415) 392-6206; 3 Place Ville Marie, Montreal, Quebec, Canada, (514) 866-7667.

SWITZERLAND
608 Fifth Avenue, New York, NY 10020, (212) 757-5944; 222 North Sepulveda Boulevard, Ste. 1570, El Segundo, CA 90245, (213) 335-5980; 260 Stockton Street, San Francisco, CA 94108, (415) 362-2260. 150 N. Michigan Avenue; Chicago, IL 60601, (312) 630-5840.

YUGOSLAVIA
Yugotours Int'l: (800) 223-5298 (West Coast), (800) 872-8598 (West Coast). Yugotours serves Russia and Hungary as well as Yugoslavia.

BOOKS

The Audi Ski Guide, by London's *Daily Mail*. Though it's not geared for hardcore bargain-hunters, this is still the best Euro ski book. Order from the Traveler's Bookstore, (212) 664-0995.

Ski Europe: A Budget Guide, by Charles Leocha and William Walker. The best handbook for discount schussing on the Continent. Order from the Traveler's Bookstore, (212) 664-0995.

Skiing Europe, Frommer's Dollarwise Guide. Features complete listings for the top ski centers in Austria, France, Switzerland and Italy, including runs, hotels, discount options.

Insider's Guides to the Best Skiing (California, Colorado, Utah). These up-to-date guidebooks cover all the top resorts, with maps and plenty of hot insider tips. If skiing's your passion, buy these books. $9.95 each at most bookstores.

Ski Resorts of North America (Fodor Guides). This resource offers 391 pages of solid, practical information. We'd like to see trail maps and more data on ski conditions, but you'll find a good summary of runs, lifts, lodging and off-the-slope facilities. $14.95 at most bookstores.

CHRIS NOBLE

SKI TRAVEL AGENCIES

The agencies listed below specialize in package ski vacations (hotel, air and lift tickets). Most of these agencies book trips to destinations in North America and abroad, and many can arrange off-piste, heli-skiing and wilderness skiing tours. It is wise to call two or three agencies to compare prices. We use the following codes to describe specialty tour offerings and foreign packages: off-piste (OP), heli-skiing (HS), ski mountaineering (SM); Austria (AUS), France (FR), Hungary (HU), Italy (IT), Japan (JP), Germany (GDR), Morocco (MO), Nepal (NP), New Zealand (NZ), North America (NA), Norway (NO), South America (SA), Spain (SP), Switzerland (SW), Yugoslavia (YU).

Adventures on Skis, Westfield, MA, (800) 628-9655 nationwide; FAX: (413) 562-3621. OP, HS; AUS, FR, IT, SW.

Alphorn Ski Tours, Inc., Lahaska, PA, (800) ALP-HORN; FAX: (215) 794-7199. HS, SM; AUS, FR, HU, IT, SW. *Austrian specialist.*

Alpine Skills International, Norden, CA, (916) 426-9108. SM and OP in FR, NA, NZ, SW.

American Express Vacations, Norcross, GA, (800) 241-1700. AUS, FR, GDR, IT, SW.

Central Holidays Tours, Los Angeles, CA, (800) 248-9378. AUS, FR, IT, SW.

Eduards International, Bakersfield, CA. (800) 828-9801 in CA, (800) 332-6823 nationwide or (805) 325-7899. HS, OP, SM; AUS, FR, IT, JP, MO, NP, NZ, SP, SA, SW, USSR.

Holidaze Ski Tours, Belmar, NJ, (800) 526-2827. AUS, FR, GDR, NP, SP, SW.

Joli Tours, Inc., Hudson, NY, (800) 333-5654, or (518) 828-2929. OP, HS; AUS, FR, HU, IT, SW.

Sportours, Huntington Beach, La Canada, Mission Viejo, San Diego, CA, (714) 848-4696, (213) 684-1978, (818) 790-4882, (619) 224-3185. OP, HS; AUS, FR, IT, JP, NA, NP, NZ, SA, SW.

Value Holidays, Mequon, WI, (800) 558-6850; FAX: (414) 241-6379. HS, SM; AUS, FR, GDR, SW, NZ.

VIDEOS

Skiing Extreme I-IV, takes you to the ragged edge and back again with North Face's Extreme Team, challenging the wildest slopes in North America. To order, call (800) 726-7003.

Steep and Deep, Warren Miller's worldwide powder odyssey offers truly inspiring footage of powder blasting on remote slopes in Asia, Europe and New Zealand. 92 minutes, $24.95 from Warren Miller, (800) 523-7117.

Apocalypse Snow, a French video, has a ridiculous plot, but features the most remarkable snowboarding and tandem skiing shots you'll ever see. Check your local ski shop.

Nordic and Wildernes

Deut du Midi, Glacier du Trient, Switzerland/MARK SHAPIRO, CLAMBIN PRODUCTIONS

Skiing

In wilderness is the preservation of the world.
-Henry David Thoreau

▼

*P*opular interest in nordic and backcountry skiing has been growing rapidly, as more people seek out a less expensive, simpler alternative to downhill skiing. Nordic skiing is easy to learn, costs relatively little, and offers excellent fitness benefits. (Sports physicians say that cross-country skiing is a nearly ideal aerobic sport.)

When skiing the backcountry, you travel closer to nature, experiencing a greater serenity and solitude than is possible with any other winter sport. Skilled downhillers can don a pair of mountaineering skis to escape the lift lines and enjoy untracked slopes with virgin powder. And, both novices and experts can have fun on the many thousands of miles of groomed, tracked trails found at nordic centers throughout North America and Europe.

In this chapter we feature 10 great cross-country ski trips around the world, review 20 top nordic ski areas in North America, and describe a variety of backcountry skiing programs--from weekend seminars to advanced ski mountaineering expeditions.

CHAPTER
21

Over the Sierra Crest on skinny skis/GORDON WILTSIE

MANY OF US TEND TO FORGET THAT THERE WAS SKIING LONG BEFORE THERE were ski resorts, and that skis were originally used for travel, not sport. Nordic skiing unlocks the vast, undeveloped reaches of the backcountry to the winter explorer. One can venture freely into the wildlands, away from the crowds and hassles of downhill resorts. For those who enjoy touring the backcountry in winter, here are 10 great tours to consider.

GRAND CANYON

North Rim Ramble

There are few sights more dramatic than the North Rim of the Grand Canyon in winter, a spectacle of richly colored rock improbably covered with snow. Off limits to winter travelers for many years, the North Rim opened to ski touring in 1989 with the debut of the North Rim Nordic Center.

The Nordic Center offers more than 25 miles of groomed trails along the top of the 9,000' Kaibab Plateau. Skiers are shuttled in by snowvan from Jacob Lake (some 30 miles away), and housed in the Kaibab Lodge, or in heated yurts. Once you arrive, getting to the canyon's edge will be your prime objective, something accomplished by taking the snowvan to the boundary of the North Rim Park and then skiing 13 miles to the lookout at Bright Angel Point.

The Nordic Center operates from December through April. Home-cooked meals are offered in the lodge, which is open to all guests, including those staying in the yurts. A 2-night package with yurt lodging, snowvan transport and all meals, starts at $175. Equipment rentals are available, but you should bring your own touring shoes. Advance reservations are required. Contact the Canyoneers/North Rim Nordic Center at P.O. Box 2997, Flagstaff, AZ 86003, (800) 525-0924.

AUSTRIA

Tirolian Inn to Inn

Austria's Tirol region offers one of the largest networks of cross-country ski trails in the world. Miles of groomed tracks connect the picturesque villages of the Tirolian Alps. Many major downhill resorts offer nordic programs, both in the valleys, and on higher elevations served by lifts and cable cars. Even in the high country, you're never far from a country inn or heated climbers' hut. And with many reasonably priced rooms in small hotels and private homes, you can enjoy a ski holiday in Austria for less than $50 per day, if you use your own equipment.

A variety of itineraries are available for skinny-ski fans. One recommended tour takes you over well-maintained trails through the foothills of the Karwendel Alps.

Ten Great Backcountry Ski Tours

After a day's warm-up just outside of Innsbruck, follow the Leutasch River Valley to the village of Scharnitz, then cross by car into Germany, skiing back across the border to the village of Hinterriss. From there drive to Lake Achensee, your starting point for a 30-mile circuit through beautiful valleys. Take your time on this route, spending evenings in Steinberg am Rofan or Thiersee--both noted for their baroque architecture.

For a comprehensive list of nordic ski areas and recommended hotels in Austria, contact the Austrian National Tourist Board at 500 Fifth Avenue, Suite 20009-2002, New York, NY 10110, (212) 944-6880, or 11601 Wilshire Boulevard, Suite 2480, Los Angeles, CA 90025, (310) 477-3332.

NORTH CASCADES

Methow Valley Backcountry

Rendezvous Outfitters operates a set of five huts in the Methow Valley on the eastern slope of the Cascades. Here you'll find great scenery, nice dry snow and 90 miles of groomed trails. You can ski from hut to hut, or explore old logging roads and high meadows. The Methow Valley offers something for everyone--flat trails for beginners, and deep powder and steeper slopes in the Rendezvous Peak and Fawn Peak areas--a perfect setting for telemarking.

You can book the huts for a self-guided tour, or sign up with Rendezvous Outfitters for a 2 to 5-day guided backcountry trip. Either way, Rendezvous can transport your gear by snowmobile, freeing you to ski with only a daypack. Hut rental runs about $130 per day, for up to eight people. Gear shuttle costs $70 per trip. New this year is the Panther Basin alpine hut, accessible only by snowcat or helicopter. Cost is roughly $275 per person for 2 nights, $375 for 3 nights, including food, guiding and heli-lift. Nature nuts will enjoy the solitude, while ski mountaineers will enjoy being close to the steepest, most scenic parts of the mountain. To reserve a hut, or book a guided trip, contact Rendezvous Outfitters, P.O. Box 728, Winthrop, WA 98862, (509) 996-3299.

COLORADO ROCKIES

The Tenth Mountain Trail

The Colorado Rockies offer boundless options for wilderness ski enthusiasts. Experts will enjoy the Tenth Mountain Trail, a 270-mile network of ski routes atop the Rockies. The most popular stretch is the 50-mile run from Vail to Aspen. All of the routes offer superb views, great powder, and the opportunity to ski the best of the Rockies in almost complete solitude.

Along the way you can bed down at 10 well-equipped huts maintained by the Tenth Mountain Trails Association (TMTA), and three private cabins. Two more huts are slated to open in 1992, which will make this the most extensive hut network in the country. A few huts, such as Janet Cabin near Copper Mountain resort, can be reached directly from ski lifts, saving you hours of hard climbing. At most huts, a night's lodging runs from $20 to $30 per person. To reserve a hut, contact TMTA,

Gulmarg, Kashmir, India/ACE KVALE, CLAMBIN PRODUCTIONS

1280 Ute Avenue, Aspen, CO 81611, (303) 925-5775.

Experienced ski mountaineers can make the trek unguided, but most skiers are best off hiring an experienced guide. Paragon Guides, P.O. Box 130, Vail, CO 81658, (303) 949-4272; Elk Mountain Guides, P.O. Box 10327, Aspen, CO 81612, (303) 927-9377; and Aspen Alpine Guides, P.O. Box 7937, Aspen, CO 81612, (303) 925-6618 all offer fine Tenth Mountain tours and other adventures in the Rockies. Tours average $145 per day, all-inclusive.

If your telemarking and climbing skills are a bit weak, you may prefer to sample the Rockies Grand Tour--90 miles of trails between the major ski resorts. You will use lifts to get up to the major passes, and from there you can traverse from resort to resort with relative ease. We like the idea of letting the lifts do the work, but you'll be overnighting in downhill resorts, so some of the wilderness appeal is lost. Grand Tour trips are offered by the US Backcountry Association, P.O. Box 30-B, Montezuma/St. John, CO 80435, (303) 468-5378.

USSR

Glasnost Getaway

If you want the most exotic ski holiday available anywhere, consider Wintergreen Adventures' Siberian Arctic tour--a traverse of the Chukotka Peninsula using skis and reindeer sleighs. After arriving in Northern Siberia, tour members will be helicoptered to a remote village basecamp where they will stay in the homes of native Chutkotkans, nomadic reindeer herders. These people still maintain their traditional culture, herding caribou, and driving sleighs made of antler and driftwood. Next, the group will take "vizdahotes," heated half-tracks, to the jumping-off point for the ski crossing. The guide will be Paul Schurke, leader of the 1989 Bering Bridge dogsled expedition, and co-leader of the 1986 North Pole dogsled expedition.

With clothing loaded in backpacks and gear stowed on reindeer sleighs, the group will make a 100-mile passage on skis from the Chukotkan interior plateau to the Arctic Ocean. The snow conditions are excellent, and Chukchi sled-drivers can provide lifts for tired skiers. Along the way the group may camp with Chukchi families in their yurangis, fur-lined yurts. At journey's end, the skiers will be treated to a traditional Eskimo celebration. The 12-day trip runs in late April, a time of long days and moderate weather. Cost will be about $3,500 with airfare from Alaska. Contact Wintergreen Adventures, 1101 Ring Rock Road, Ely, MI 55731, Phone/FAX: (218) 365-6602.

NEW ZEALAND

Touring the Southern Alps

For a world-class hut to hut vacation, ski New Zealand's Southern Alps. You'll traverse high mountain passes, learn the basics of ski mountaineering, and get a taste of glacier skiing. Ski tours are conducted by Alpine Guides in May through September--winter Down Under. Six-day trips cost

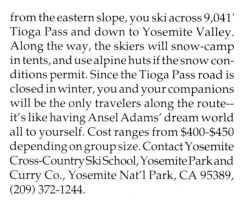

about $80 per day. Accommodation is in provisioned, heated huts, so you carry a minimum of gear. Routes can be customized for all skill levels, and private guides can lead you to virgin wilderness areas. For those with the financial wherewithal, a variety of heli-skiing options are available.

Having traveled so far in search of alpine adventure, while you're in New Zealand you might want to set aside a few extra days for one of Alpine Guides' excellent courses in winter camping and ice-climbing. Contact Alpine Guides, Mt. Cook Ltd., P.O. Box 20, Mt. Cook Nat'l Park, New Zealand, (011 64) 3 435-1834; FAX: 3 435-1898.

NEW YORK

Adirondack Hut to Hut

Hut to hut skiing in the Adirondacks is a great winter getaway. You'll start in the Gore Mountain Ski Area and ski to comfy cabins or lodges located about 10 miles apart in New York's Adirondack State Park. The backcountry trails take you through virgin forest and across frozen lakes in the Siamese Ponds Wilderness Area. Adirondack Hut to Hut Tours has run ski trips in this area for the past 10 years and maintains its own network of heated log cabins.

While you'll typically travel just six to nine miles per day, most of the time you'll be breaking ground in untracked snow, so intermediate skills are required. Your gear and food are separately transported to wilderness cabins, so you can travel light. Two guides tour with each group of 10 to 12 skiers, and at day's end, your guides even cook dinner--a real touch of luxury. Cost for 2 days is roughly $135 per person, while a 5-day tour runs about $390 per person, all-inclusive. Contact Walter Blank at Adirondack Hut to Hut Tours, R.D. 1, Box 85, Ghent, NY 12075, (518) 828-7007.

CALIFORNIA

Sierra Hut to Hut Adventures

Rock Creek Winter Lodge, situated at 9,373' near Bishop, California, offers one of the Sierra's best backcountry ski programs. Rock Creek maintains two huts, three miles apart, above 10,000'. You can ski the

relatively flat trails between huts, or venture off into powder bowls with nobody else in sight. Self-guided hut trips cost a reasonable $30 per day, with a two-person minimum per hut. Four-day guided hut tours run roughly $225, which includes snowcat transport for your supplies. Contact Rock Creek Lodge, Route 1, Box 12, Mammoth Lakes, CA 93546, (619) 935-4452.

If you prefer groomed track, the nearby Tamarack Lodge in Mammoth Lakes offers 25 miles of tracked trails starting at 8,600'. Programs start at $55 per night for winterized cabins, plus $13 trail fee. There is regular shuttle bus service to the cozy lodge. Contact Tamarack Lodge, P.O. Box 69, Mammoth Lakes, CA 93546, (800) 237-6879.

In the Lake Tahoe area, Alpine Skills Int'l (ASI), P.O. Box 8, Norden, CA 95724, (916) 426-9108, offers a wide variety of nordic programs from its own deluxe lodge. ASI's backcountry itineraries range from mild to wild, and custom trips can be arranged for about $85-$110 per day.

Telemarking in Austria/AUSTRIAN NATIONAL TOURIST OFFICE

YOSEMITE

Touring Ansel Adams Country

If the summer crowds get you down, try Yosemite in the winter. There are 90 miles of marked trails in the valley, with daily nordic classes available for all ages and skill levels. Telemark training is also offered at nearby Badger Pass ski area. If you want to get into the high country, overnight hut trips to Glacier Point and Ostrander Lake can be booked at a cost of $90 for one night, $130 for two.

The ultimate Yosemite skiing adventure is a 6-day trans-Sierra crossing. Starting

from the eastern slope, you ski across 9,041' Tioga Pass and down to Yosemite Valley. Along the way, the skiers will snow-camp in tents, and use alpine huts if the snow conditions permit. Since the Tioga Pass road is closed in winter, you and your companions will be the only travelers along the route--it's like having Ansel Adams' dream world all to yourself. Cost ranges from $400-$450 depending on group size. Contact Yosemite Cross-Country Ski School, Yosemite Park and Curry Co., Yosemite Nat'l Park, CA 95389, (209) 372-1244.

OREGON

Crater Lake Ski Odyssey

Crater Lake in winter is one of the most beautiful sights in North America. The jagged white peaks of the crater's 6-mile wide rim are mirrored in the lake's icy waters--a fantastic sight that puts any Sierra Club calendar shot to shame.

A mecca for summer tourism, Crater Lake is deserted in the winter. The Crater is best approached from the east, ascending fairly gentle grades to the top, after you park your 4WD vehicle a few miles from the crest. The best touring is on the 33-mile Rim Drive. Connecting snowmobile trails allow easy skiing, even with packs.

Organized Crater Lake ski tours are offered each winter by Mountain Madness of Seattle. Departing from Portland, small groups will drive to the edge of the national park, and then ski to the top. Snow-camping in tents on the upper sections of the mountain, the group will spend a week circling the entire rim. Along the way, the group can climb to the Watchman, Hillman Peak and Cloudcap summits high above the Lake. Stronger skiers will be able to telemark down the crater's slopes, away from the rim basecamps. While intermediate backcountry skiers will get the most out of this trip, Mountain Madness customizes each outing according to participants' abilities, so novices can have a good time as well. Price for the 6-day February trip will be about $920, including food, group gear and transport from Portland. Contact Mountain Madness, 4218 S.W. Alaska, Ste. 206, Seattle, WA 98110, (206) 937-8389.

317

Galena, Idaho/DAVID STOECKLEIN

TWENTY TOP NORTH AMERICAN NORDIC SKI CENTERS

EAST

MAINE

Carrabassett Valley

If it's too icy at Sugarloaf for down-hilling, try out your skinny skis at nearby Carrabassett Valley Ski Touring Center. You'll find comfortable warming huts, and 55 miles of some of the best machine-made tracks in the East. There's even a 7.5 km racing loop for the speed freaks, plus a fine ice-skating rink for diversion. Carrabassett Valley is still uncrowded and unspoiled--a favorite refuge from the urban rat race. Contact Carrabassett Valley Ski Touring Center, (207) 237-2205. Rating: ★★

NEW HAMPSHIRE

Jackson Nordic Resorts

Jackson is the hub of New England ski touring. Under the aegis of the nonprofit Jackson Ski Touring Foundation, Jackson offers 90 miles of premium trails suitable for all skill levels. The trails cover a wide variety of terrain and connect a number of small and medium-sized touring centers ranging from country inns (e.g. Inn at Thornhill, Nestlenook Farm, Whitney's Inn) to large destination resorts (Nordic Village). Contact Jackson Ski Touring Foundation, P.O. Box 216, Jackson, NH 03846, (603) 383-9355 (ski report), or (603) 383-9356 (lodging). Rating: ★★★

NEW YORK

Mt. Van Hoevenberg XC Center

This ski center near Lake Placid boasts 35 miles of Olympic-quality groomed trails with 7 kms of snow-making, expert instruction, and 13 racing loops for all levels. Trail fees and ski rental runs $7-$15 per day. The Mt. Van Hoevenberg Center is linked with two regional trail systems, and the renowned 25-mile Jackrabbit Trail is also nearby. Contact Olympic Authority, Olympic Center, Lake Placid, NY 12946, (518) 523-2811; or the Lake Placid Visitors Bureau, Main Street, Lake Placid, NY 12946, (800) 44-PLACID (447-5224), or (518) 523-2445. Rating: ★★★

VERMONT

Bolton Valley

At an average altitude of 2,100', Bolton Valley's 65 miles of groomed trails are the highest in New England. This, combined with 250 inches of annual snowfall, guarantees a long season. The trails run through pristine, mostly wooded terrain. Visitors can choose between trailside condos and a deluxe lodge (starting at $150 for two nights). Contact Bolton Valley Resort, P.O. Box 500, Bolton, VT 05477, (800) 451-3220, or (802) 434-2131. Rating: ★★★

Mountain Top Inn

Situated in the Green Mountains, the Mountain Top boasts 110 miles of trails, mostly groomed and tracked, with 5 kms served by snow-making. The Mountain Top Inn offers top-flight training seminars and many recreational options, including sleigh rides and ice-skating. Prices are expensive. Contact Mountain Top Inn, P.O. Box 402, Chittenden, VT 05737, (800) 445-2100, or (802) 483-2311. Rating: ★★★

WEST VIRGINIA

White Grass Ski Touring Center

West Virginia's White Grass Ski Touring Center offers excellent nordic skiing in the scenic Dolly Sods Wilderness Area, situated on a 4,000' plateau. The Touring Center is based at a former downhill resort, which means you'll find plenty of challenging hills if you want to practice your turns, though most visitors come to enjoy the miles of groomed flats on the open plateau. Contact the White Grass Ski Touring Center, Rt. 1, Box 299, Davis, WV 26260, (304) 866-4114. Rating: ★★

CENTRAL

MICHIGAN

Garland Resort

Garland is a new, upscale nordic resort boasting high-quality facilities and first-class luxury accommodations. Excellent skiing is found on 40 miles of groomed tracks through 3,000 acres of pristine backcountry. With its own private airstrip and charter jet, this is the first nordic center they'll feature on "Lifestyles of the Rich and Famous." Price for room, skiing and two meals will be roughly $150-$190 per person per night. Garland Resort, County Road 489, Lewiston, MI 49756, (800) 968-0042, or (517) 786-2211. Rating: ★★★

Traverse City

Traverse City is a nordic supermarket, with hundreds of miles of groomed public and private trails, and six nearby nordic resorts which offer instruction, and accommodations from basic to deluxe. The trails cover a wide variety of terrain--hills, valleys, even frozen waterways at the Sleeping Bear Dunes National Lakeshore. Recommended resorts include the Shanty Creek-Shuss Mountain Resort, (800) 748-0249; the Sugar Loaf Resort (downhill also), (800) 748-0117;

Group touring in Idaho/DAVID STOECKLEIN

and the Grand Traverse Resort, (800) 748-0303. Contact the Grand Traverse Convention & Visitors Bureau, 415 Munson Ave., Suite 200, Traverse City, MI 49684, (800) TRAVERS. Rating: ★★★

MINNESOTA

Bearskin Lodge

The Bearskin Lodge is located along the northern end of the Boundary Waters Canoe Area. From the lodge, you can ski 30 miles of groomed trails, or go off-track to explore hundreds of nearby lakes. The relatively flat terrain and numerous frozen waterways make it easy to cover lots of ground, even when you venture off the prepared trails. This is a true wilderness area, so you won't encounter a 7-Eleven at every trailhead, or have to put up with the buzzing of snowmobiles. The lodge itself is spacious and run by a gracious staff. A lighted trail and ice-skating are offered as well. Contact the Bearskin Lodge, 275 Gunflint Trail, Grand Marais, MN 55604, (800) 338-4170, or (218) 388-2292; FAX: (218) 388-4410. Rating: ★★★

ROCKIES

COLORADO

The Aspen Lodge

Even if the facilities and accommodations weren't so nice, we'd go to the Aspen Lodge just for the superb scenery. In the heart of Rocky Mountain National Park, ski groomed private trails, or venture into truly wild backcountry. This resort also offers all the amenities--sleigh rides, ice-skating and great downhilling a few minutes away. The Aspen Lodge, 6120 Highway 7, Longs Peak Route, Estes Park, CO 80517, (800) 332-MTNS, or (303) 586-8133. Rating: ★★★★

The Great Divide Nordic Complex

Run by the folks at Breckenridge, this complex offers any kind of nordic and backcountry skiing you could want. Ski 50 miles of groomed track, or head off the track to traverse mountain ranges between old mining towns. Great Divide makes it easy with courtesy shuttles to trailheads, and ski instruction for all levels. Contact Breckenridge Nordic Ski Center, 1200 Ski Hill Road, Box 1776, Breckenridge, CO 80424, (303) 453-6855. Rating: ★★★

IDAHO

Busterback Ranch

No, it's not a big, fancy resort, but the Busterback Ranch offers great snow, 30 miles of splendid trails, both flat and hilly, and old-fashioned hospitality. Experts will enjoy the telemark hill and the easy access to wide-open skiing in the nearby Sawtooth National Recreation Area. This is the West the way it should be--no crowds or concrete condos. Roughly $160 per person per day covers everything, including all meals. The Busterback Ranch, Star Route, Ketchum, ID 83340, (208) 774-2217. Rating: ★★★

MONTANA

∎

Isaac Walton Inn

Frankly, when we ski, even nordic style, we like to see real mountains--not those East Coast hills. If you feel the same way, head to the Isaac Walton Inn, located next to Glacier National Park in Montana's Rockies. You can cruise 31 miles of groomed trails, or venture into the park and nearby wilderness areas. The Inn is an outstanding base for winter camping and wildlife-watching, and a lighted 1km trail has recently been completed. Rustic accommodations are also available within the park, but you must contact the Park Service for room availability. Isaac Walton Inn, P.O. Box 653, Essex, MT 59916, (406) 888-5700. Rating: ★★

Lakeview Ski Ranch

Diversity is the hallmark of the Lakeview Ski Ranch. You can traverse flats on narrow skis, on a 2 to 4-night, hut to hut tour. Or try telemarking in remote bowls accessed by helicopter. (Dry and deep, the powder lasts well into May.) Many visitors to the ranch combine nordic skiing with downhilling, often on the same day. While most customers are veteran skiers, ski programs and PSI-certified instruction are available for all skill levels. Proprietor and guide Pat McKenna can also arrange custom ski trips. The Ski Ranch is situated about 50 miles from Yellowstone Park. Contact Lakeview Ski Ranch, Monida Star Route, Lima, MT 59739, (406) 276-3278. Rating: ★★★

W E S T

CALIFORNIA

∎

Kirkwood XC Ski Area

Part of a major ski complex, Kirkwood offers 45 miles of machine-groomed track at an average altitude of 7,800'. Along with flat valley trails, you'll find extensive alpine and mountaineering routes for the experts. This is a perfect place to combine nordic and alpine skiing in a single vacation. Operating December through the end of April, Kirkwood's Nordic Center provides three warming huts, and high-quality instruction for all levels. Contact Kirkwood Cross Country, P.O. Box 1, Kirkwood, CA 95646, (209) 258-6000. Rating: ★★★

Montecito-Sequoia XC Ski Center

Montecito-Sequoia Ski Center offers 50 miles of beautiful trails running between Sequoia and Kings Canyon National Parks. This is a good choice for a strong backcountry skier, or a novice looking for superb scenery. After you've hung up your skis for the day, try the lighted night ice-skating on nearby Lake Homavalo. Lodging prices are reasonable--dinner, bed and breakfast is about $75 per night. Contact Montecito-Sequoia Cross Country Ski Center, 1485-B Redwood Drive, Los Altos, CA, (800) 451-1505, or (800) 227-9900 in CA. Rating: ★★★

Telemarking in powder/JOHN KELLY

Royal Gorge Nordic Ski Resort

You could stay a month at Royal Gorge, and never ski the same trail twice. Located at 7,000', Royal Gorge enjoys one of the longest ski seasons around, and with 317 km of groomed tracks, it is the biggest cross-country resort in the country. Facilities are top rate, with two lodges, a full-time ski school, and seven warming huts. We recommend the 3-day program at the Wilderness Lodge. For $225 you get three nights' lodging, meals, instruction and a sleigh ride to the lodge and back again. Located about three hours from San Francisco, Royal Gorge is a good selection for West Coasters planning a 3-day nordic weekend. Royal Gorge Nordic, P.O. Box 1100, Soda Springs, CA 95728, (800) 634-3086, or (916) 426-3871. Rating: ★★★★

OREGON

∎

Mount Bachelor Nordic Center

The spring training center for the US Nordic Ski Team, Mount Bachelor offers 40 miles of machine-laid tracks ideal for the nordic racer-in-training. Located in central Oregon away from the constant coastal drizzle, you'll find good dry snow and plenty of sunshine. Along with the excellent training loops, groomed trails run through the scenic Deschutes National Forest in the Cascades, offering great backcountry skiing through verdant pine forests and alpine meadows. Instruction and competition programs are among the best in the West. For more information, contact Mt. Bachelor, P.O. Box 1031, Bend, OR 97709, (800) 829-2442, or (503) 382-2442. Rating: ★★★

C A N A D A

BRITISH COLUMBIA

∎

Wells Gray Provincial Park

Wells Gray Provincial Park is an outstanding choice for those seeking a wilderness cross-country experience with abundant snow and spectacular scenery. Operating from two deluxe ski chalets and two cabins, Wells Gray offers both track-set trails and backcountry routes; choose from either guided or unguided options. Snowcats or helicopters can drop you off for spectacular alpine traverses. This is Rockies ski touring at its best. For more information, contact Wells Gray Park Backcountry Chalets, P.O. Box 188, Clearwater, B.C., Canada V0E 1N0, (604) 674-3317. Rating: ★★★★

QUEBEC

∎

Villa Bellevue

Situated in the scenic Laurentian Range, just three miles from Mont Tremblant, Villa Bellevue offers 70 miles of groomed trails connecting quaint villages, and inviting country inns. In addition to the premium double-set tracks, there are 40 miles of wilderness routes, plus recreational loops for all levels of skiers. Weather can be bone-chilling, but there's almost always plenty of snow. A 5-day package at the resort costs about $370. Contact Villa Bellevue Resort, Mont Tremblant, Quebec, Canada J0T 1Z0, (800) 567-6763, or (819) 425-2734. Rating: ★★

SKI MOUNTAINEERING

Scott Schmidt jumps the backside, Mt. Fort, Verbier, Switzerland/MARK SHAPIRO, CLAMBIN PRODUCTIONS

I F YOU'RE LOOKING TO SKI THE MOST VIRGIN SNOW, IN THE WILDEST TERRAIN, ski mountaineering represents the final frontier. The equipment is a blend of nordic and downhill--steel edges, but with a randonée boot/binding system that can be freed at the heel. Ascents are made with skins, or on foot. The hallmark of ski mountaineering is the ability to go anywhere--to ascend, traverse and come down virtually any terrain, no matter how steep or difficult.

HIGH SIERRAS

▲

Summit Skiing Adventures

Alpine Skills International, based in the California Sierra, offers a full range of ski mountaineering programs, from short introductory seminars to 10-day haute route odysseys through the Alps. Ideal for novice ski mountaineers with some downhill experience are ASI's 2-day climb/ski trips to major western peaks, such as Mt. Lassen and Mt. Shasta. On the first day you ascend to a high elevation basecamp. The next day you bag the summit, then ski downhill until you run out of snow. Cost runs roughly $200. If this seems tame, sign up for the 3-day Mt. Shasta descent, offering 8,000 vertical feet of skiing for about $250. Contact Alpine Skills International, P.O. Box 8, Norden, CA 95724, (916) 426-9108; FAX: (916) 426-3063. (Prices are subject to change.) Rating: ★★★

ALASKAN ADVENTURE
▲
The Ruth Amphitheater

Spilling down the East Buttress of Denali (Mt. McKinley), the Ruth Glacier winds its way for miles between sheer walls of granite and ice. The great peaks of the Alaska Range rise above it on every side, and the deep powdery snow on their flanks creates matchless conditions for ski mountaineering.

Seattle's Mountain Madness leads week-long ski trips to the Ruth Amphitheater each April. After a flight into the heart of the Ruth Glacier wilderness, the group will settle into a snug backcountry hut complete with wood stove. Glacier travel skills and telemarking technique will be taught by experienced guides. While this trip is suited for all levels of skiers, those with previous backcountry skiing experience and good telemark technique will get the most out of the program. Though glacier travel is featured, downhilling is the major focus. Using ice axes and crampons, participants will ascend nearby slopes, then ski back to the valley floor using telemark equipment. Cost will be about $1,000. Contact Mountain Madness, 4218 S.W. Alaska, Suite 206, Seattle, WA 98116, (206) 937-8389. Rating: ★★★

THE HAUTE ROUTE
▲
Europe's Great Challenge

Europe's classic Haute Route connects the ski resorts of Saas-Fee and Zermatt in Switzerland, with Courmayeur and Chamonix in France. The Haute Route through the Alps may be the ultimate alpine adventure, a test of stamina, skiing skill and determination. Haute Route skiers will have to climb 30+ degree slopes with heavy packs, ascending as much as 3,300' per day. Strong powder skills are vital. Haute Route tours normally run in the late spring, May to June, when the high-altitude snow conditions are most suitable. Avoid the busiest holiday periods however, when the huts are packed. Qualified alpine guides operate from the major resorts along the route. We recommend Canadian John Hogg of Alpine Adventures, P.O. Box 106, CH-6490

Ruth Glacier, Alaska/CHRIS NOBLE

Andermatt, Switzerland, (011 41) 44 68353; FAX: (011 41) 44 68243. Rating: ★★★★

For those wanting a package tour, Alpine Skills International (ASI) offers a 10-day trek across the Route from Chamonix to Zermatt. It begins with a 2-day off-piste skiing seminar at Chamonix featuring glacier travel and ski mountaineering. Then you set off for a full week climbing the cols,

and making steep descents from the Aiguille du Midi, Mt. Blanc and the Grandes Jorasses. You eventually arrive at Zermatt via the Matterhorn. Last year's price was about $1,300, with early spring departures. Contact ASI, (916) 426-9108. Rating: ★★★

Summits, operated by famed mountain guide Peter Whittaker, also offers a 10-day Haute Route Ski Mountaineering Tour in May, traversing 11 glaciers in the Alps, from west to east. Contact Summits, P.O. Box 214, Ashford, WA 98304, (206) 569-2992. Rating: ★★★

NORTHWEST PASSAGES
▲
Cascade Ski Mountaineering

Mountain Ski Ventures, P.O. Box 2974, Bellingham, WA 98227, (206) 647-0656, offers 2 to 5-day nordic and randonée skiing, ski mountaineering, and snow, ice and rock-climbing courses in the North Cascades. Three and 5-day telemark camps, skiing expeditions, and trips worldwide are also available. The ski mountaineering courses, offered both winter and summer, cover a combination of skiing and technical mountaineering skills, and are conducted along various North Cascades high routes and traverses. Notable programs this year include a Mt. Baker circumnavigation on skis, and ski descents of several major northwest peaks. Skiing experience is required, but novices are welcome in the basic courses. Rating: ★★★

Rainier Mountaineering, Inc., 535 Dock Street, Tacoma, WA 98402, (206) 627-6242, or (206) 569-2227 in summer, runs 5-day ski mountaineering seminars each April on the lower slopes of Mt. Rainier. In addition to backcountry ski techniques, you'll practice roped glacier skiing and crevasse rescue. Cost for the seminar or the circumnavigation is $460; you bring your own skis and boots. Rating: ★★★

NORDIC & BACKCOUNTRY SKIING

GEAR

Clothing

In the backcountry, keeping warm and dry is vital. Wool and synthetics such as thermax, Capilene, Polarfleece and Synchilla are best. These fabrics retain very little moisture and dry from the inside out when wet. By contrast, when cotton gets wet, it acts like a towel, keeping saturated fibers next to your skin and drawing out body heat and energy.

You should wear layers of clothing rather than one bulky sweater or jacket. By wearing a number of loose, lighter layers (fleece over a thermax undershirt, for example) you can most efficiently trap air, which will be warmed by your body. For layering to be effective, you must peel off a layer before you begin sweating heavily.

Skis

For groomed trails, or relatively flat areas, conventional narrow nordic skis are all you'll need. Waxless skis perform well, but a good coat of wax will improve your glide. For true backcountry exploration involving steep grades, icy sections and deep powder, you'll want mountaineering skis--commonly called telemark skis. Telemark skis are heavy-duty, metal-edged skis that are designed for maximum control on variable, difficult terrain. They tend to be wider than most touring skis, enabling them to float better in powder and to provide a more stable platform for skiing on uneven ground while wearing a heavy pack. The metal edges do add weight, but they are invaluable when downhill control is important, or when the conditions are icy.

Bindings

Heavy-duty, three-pin or cable bindings are the best choice regardless of the type of ski you use. Three-pin bindings, designed for telemarking and backcountry skiing, are made of strong metal alloys and are considerably stronger than standard touring bindings. Getting stranded with a mangled lightweight aluminum binding when you are miles from nowhere should

DAVID STOECKLEIN

convince you that heavy-duty bindings are worth the investment. Cable bindings are less aesthetic, but they are strong and simple, and can be easily adapted to a variety of boots.

Poles

Most people just use their regular cross-country poles for backcountry skiing. However, on steep trails these will be too long and can throw you off balance. A good solution are the adjustable probe poles sold by many manufacturers. These collapse or extend, depending on the demands of the terrain--long for uphills, short for descents. Interchangeable baskets and grips are available. The poles can also be joined to form an 8' avalanche probe, an important safety feature.

Climbing Skins

When skiing steeper sections, or traveling with a heavy pack, climbing skins can be a godsend. Climbing skins are ski-length strips of fabric with one-directional 'hairs' which grip the snow when the ski starts to slide backward. Today's skins are made of nylon, mohair or plastic. The plastic is the least expensive and most durable, but mo-

hair and nylon offer better glide. You can think of skins as a safety item. On a difficult tour, skins may make the difference between reaching the shelter of a hut and spending the night outside.

Packs

Internal frame, or frameless packs that sit close to your back are best for ski touring because they move as you move. Sternum (chest) straps are useful in keeping the pack molded to your body. On uphills, keep your hip belt snug and shoulder straps loose. On downhills, tighten the shoulder and sternum straps to keep the pack from swaying. Your skiing will be greatly affected by the center of gravity of the pack. Keep the weight low, and pack the heaviest items near the bottom. Pack only the essentials. Most of us can manage a 35-pound pack when hiking on foot, but on skis, even 25 pounds can be a real struggle.

BOOKS

The Best Ski Touring in America, by Steve Barnett. $10.95 from Sierra Club Books, 1987. This is the best resource for North American ski touring. An enormous variety of nordic ski venues, both popular and lesser known, are listed, and Barnett's commentary is full of practical insights.

Classic Backcountry Skiing: A Guide to the Best Ski Tours in New England, by David Goodman. $11.95 from Appalachian Mountain Club Books, 5 Joy Street, Boston, MA 02108, (617) 523-0636; 1988. Less comprehensive than the Barnett book, this guide is equally well written and provides excellent trail maps.

VIDEOS

American Haute: Skiing the High-Country Trails, is a well-made, 20-minute introduction to alpine ski touring in the Colorado Rockies. Order from Paragon Guides, P.O. Box 130, Vail, CO 81658, (303) 949-4272.

The Telemark Movie, by Dick Hall and John Fuller. Telemark Movies, Inc., P.O. Box 44, Waitsfield, VT 05673, $34.95. With great cinematography by John Fuller (Warren Miller's cameraman), and solid, but lighthearted instruction by Dick Hall, this is a fine introduction to the mysteries of telemark techniques and control of touring skis in deep powder.

Skydiving & Paragliding

Stepping into space over the Swiss Alps/DIDIER GIVOIS

▼

*I*n this chapter, we feature the parachute sports: skydiving and paragliding. For many of us, skydiving represents the ultimate thrill--the quintessential risk sport. Hardened adventurers, who have tried every action sport under the sun, say that nothing offers a greater adrenalin rush than hurtling into the air, two miles above the ground, and freefalling downward at more than 100 miles per hour.

For those looking for a kinder, gentler parachuting experience, we also cover the new sport of paragliding-- using foot-launched parachutes to fly from a hillside or mountaintop. Paragliding is the rage in Europe, as well you can understand once you give it a try. It's relatively easy (you can fly the first day), and the equipment is simple, lightweight and modestly priced. In this chapter, we introduce you to basic paragliding skills, list the top flight schools, and review the best paragliding tours worldwide.

CHAPTER
22

Skydiving

THE ULTIMATE ADVENTURE

This is it. The real thing. Jumping out of an airplane with only a few ounces of nylon between you and the great beyond. For many of us, skydiving represents the danger line we just won't cross. But surprisingly, modern training methods and closely supervised instruction have made the sport of parachuting far safer than you might imagine. In 1988, 115,000 persons made over 2.25 million jumps in the United States with less than 25 fatalities. Over the last five years, only one jump in 80,000 has resulted in death. Statistically, you're safer skydiving than driving to work in many parts of the country.

TOM SANDERS

Jump schools are better than ever before, equipment is safer and easier to use, and new techniques such as tandem jumping and Accelerated Freefall (AFF) have made it possible for novice jumpers to enjoy the most exciting aspects of the sport. Today, on a tandem jump, even a first-timer can enjoy the thrill of freefall in the secure grasp of two expert jumpmasters.

SELECTING A JUMP SCHOOL

❖

Sport parachuting is carefully regulated by the United States Parachuting Association (USPA). Most USPA jump schools are reputable and maintain high professional standards. However, there are differences between schools, so you want to choose a training program carefully. The most important factors to consider when selecting a jump school are: safety record, quality of instruction, aircraft, equipment and scheduling convenience.

Safety--Ask about the number and seriousness of any mishaps associated with the training program. High-quality jump centers will have logged thousands of training jumps without serious injury. Programs using static lines tend to have more minor injuries such as twisted ankles.

Instruction Quality--It's best to go with a well-established jump school with full-time professional jumpmasters/instructors.

Mass exit from DC-3s/TOM SANDERS, AERIAL FOCUS

The most qualified instructors will have logged a thousand jumps or more. Tandem and AFF instruction should be done only by jumpmasters specifically certified in these disciplines.

Aircraft--Two engines are better than one. Turbocharged or multi-engined planes can take you higher, in less time, than can small, normally-aspirated Cessnas or similar aircraft. With larger aircraft, you typically jump from higher altitudes (12,500' versus 9,000'), allowing more freefall time. And, as big planes climb faster, it takes less time to get to your jumping elevation.

Equipment--Don't enroll in a school that uses old-style round canopies. In fact, the USPA now requires the softer-landing "squares" and easy-to-manage piggyback chute packs for all its group member schools. Square parachutes fly better, and land more easily. Select a jump school that keeps its equipment (chutes, harnesses, jumpsuits) in top condition--your life depends on it.

Scheduling--Many smaller schools are part-time operations that may run only a few days a month. This can be inconvenient, and will slow down your progress as a jumper. Major jump centers such as AFF, Inc. in the east, or Perris Valley Skydiving in the west, operate 6 or 7 days a week, and always have jumpmasters and aircraft ready to go.

YOUR FIRST JUMP

❖

All training programs, whether traditional static line or AFF, begin with ground school. You will spend approximately five hours learning the principles of skydiving, basic safety techniques, rigging and landing skills. In most modern training centers, gone are the days of jumping off 10' concrete walls to practice a hard-impact landing and ground roll that you used to see in films of WWII paratroopers. With square parachutes, you descend slowly enough to land easily on your feet.

After completing ground school, you have three choices for your first actual jump: tandem, AFF or static line. Static line jumping is the simplest--you are physically attached to your aircraft by a tether which opens your chute as soon as you are clear of the plane. Because this allows for no freefall time, however, most jump centers are phasing out static line jumping and concentrating instead on tandem and AFF training.

Freefall over Hawaii/TOM SANDERS, AERIAL FOCUS

STATIC LINE JUMPING

❖

During conventional static line training, your parachute is opened by a tether attached to the aircraft. You will make a minimum of five solo jumps with the automatic static line, leaving the aircraft at about 3,000'. After a half-dozen or so static line jumps, you will make your first free jump from about 4,000', experiencing about 10 seconds of freefall. You then jump from progressively higher altitudes, working up to 9,000'+ and 45 seconds of freefall. It typically takes about 15 jumps before you complete your training and are certified to jump without supervision. The entire 15-jump static line training program costs about $1,500 at most jump schools.

TANDEM JUMPING

❖

Tandem jumping is a reassuring way to make your very first jump. With this recently devised method of skydiving, a person with absolutely no prior jumping experience can enjoy the thrill of freefall without worrying about making a mistake in the air. His or her instructor makes all the critical decisions, and deploys the canopy after the freefall.

After an introductory ground session, the tandem instructor and the student board the plane together. While airborne over the drop zone, the two will physically link their jumping harnesses, front to back. High-strength metal carabiners secure the student's harness webbing to the instructor's rig. The jumpmaster/instructor carries an extra-large, two-person parachute designed expressly for tandem jumps. At the instructor's command, teacher and student jump from the aircraft, like Siamese twins, with the student in front. The two will freefall for 30 to 60 seconds before the instructor pulls the ripcord. Before touching down, the tandem team will fly for about four minutes under the deployed canopy as the instructor demonstrates how to steer the parachute.

Tandem jumping is ideal for those who feel they'd never have the nerve to leap out of a plane on their own. Using the tandem method, people of all ages and walks of life have been able to experience skydiving's excitement.

While not all jump centers offer tandem jumping yet, it is becoming increasingly popular. Some schools now even require a tandem jump as a prerequisite to a student's first freefall jump. Over 15,000 tandem jumps were made last year, with a remarkable safety record. If you're looking for the best way to sample skydiving for a minimal investment, tandem jumping is for you. An introductory class session and one tandem jump will cost between $90-$150, including all equipment and basic insurance.

ACCELERATED FREEFALL

❖

After you've tried a tandem jump, the next step for most students is an Accelerated Freefall jump. This technique has eclipsed the conventional static line training method in North America's top jump schools. By utilizing AFF, a novice has a chance to enjoy freefall right away--the most exciting aspect of the skydiving experience.

During initial AFF training, you will jump with two specially certified jumpmasters from about 9,000'. All three of you exit the plane at once, with your instructors holding on to your arms and/or harness during the freefall. When you have reached minimum altitude, the jumpmasters will tell you to pull your ripcord. If you have problems, your instructors will pull the ripcord for you. As a final safety measure, all students (whether AFF or otherwise) must use an automatic back-up ripcord device that activates the ripcord at minimum altitude, in the event the student becomes distracted.

After three to four jumps with two instructors, you will shift to one-on-one AFF. Typically, after about 10 one-instructor AFF jumps (about 12 total AFF jumps), you will be approved to jump solo. At this point you are off student status and can jump without any air-to-air supervision. You will still carry your back-up ripcord safety device however.

The next stage in your training is obtaining your Class A parachute license. Most beginners require about 20 total jumps, including the initial AFF jumps, to reach this level. The Class A license is your ticket to fly. It will permit you to pack your own chute and make unsupervised jumps at USPA jump centers throughout the country. You will also be eligible for USPA liability insurance as a Class A licensee.

Initial AFF jumps, including ground school, cost about $250. Additional jumps average $130 with two jumpmasters, $90 with one jumpmaster. Typically, it will cost between $1,300 and $1,800 to complete the dozen or so AFF jumps you must make before you are allowed to solo jump. By contrast, traditional static line training costs $100-$150 for the first jump, and about $25-30 for additional jumps, plus $90 or so per hour for the jumpmaster.

EQUIPMENT

❖

After 10 to 20 jumps, if you continue with the sport, you'll want to purchase your own equipment. As with any risk sport, choose top-quality gear. Here's what you'll have to pay for quality new equipment: primary parachute, $800-$1,000; reserve parachute, $400-$600; harness, $500-$600; altimeter, $140-$175; jumpsuit, $150; helmet, $25;

goggles, $25. Used equipment is available, but you should have it thoroughly inspected and certified before you purchase.

PRICE OF ADMISSION

❖

Skydiving is not an inexpensive sport. However, once you've completed your initial training and can jump without instructor assistance, the cost is comparable with other action sports such as rafting or scuba diving—about $50-$100 per day, depending on the number of jumps. Once you're certified to make solo freefall jumps, expect to pay about $1.25 per thousand feet of altitude, which translates to $15-$20 per jump.

At organized jumpfests, this can drop to as little as $10 per jump. Add to this the cost of rental equipment which can range from $15 to $30 per day.

INSURANCE

❖

Virtually all formal first-jump programs include a 90-day USPA membership, which offers jumpers' insurance for liability, property damage and major medical coverage. You should check your own medical insurance to see if it applies to minor injuries (such as sprained ankles) that are not covered by the USPA group policy. Look to see whether skydiving is an excluded activity.

All-women's jump team practices for a world-record canopy stack/TOM SANDERS

Jan Davis making the first women's jump of Angel Falls/TOM SANDERS

JUNGLE JUMPING ADVENTURE

Looking for the ultimate parachuting thrill? How about base-jumping the world's tallest cascade, Venezuela's Angel Falls? Jumping from the top, 3,200' above the jungle floor, should be attempted by only the most skilled and fearless skydivers. In recent years, Tom Sanders and Jan Davis of Santa Barbara, California have led jumping expeditions to Angel Falls in October, at the end of the wet season. Along the way, the chartered Venezuelan 727 makes a spectacular pass through the canyon below the falls.

After arriving at a jungle camp, near Conaima, Venezuela, one day is spent reconnoitering the falls, and another climbing to the top--with parachutes in hand. When they reach the summit, the parachutists must carefully check the weather conditions--gusting winds could push the jumpers against ragged rock walls. Then, one by one, they jump, sailing their bodies outward from the sheer rock face for a few tense seconds before deploying their chutes. With canopies open, the team floats down through mist and rainbows to the jungle floor. This is one of the world's great adventures. If you've got the nerve, and plenty of jumping experience, contact Tom Sanders or Jan Davis at (805) 966-1230.

JUMP SCHOOLS

There are hundreds of jump centers wh you can receive skydiving training from tified instructors. Not all jump schools o AFF and tandem jumping yet, so be sur ask about these options before you mak long drive to a jump site. The yellow pa contain jump school listings under "Pa chute Schools," or sometimes "Skydivin centers.

Below, we list 30 of the most active ju centers registered with the USPA as Gro Members. (USPA Group Members ha pledged to follow USPA Basic Safety Requi ments and recommendations for student a advanced skydivers, and to offer first-ju courses taught by USPA-rated instructo You can obtain a complete directory USPA Group Member jump centers across country by contacting the USPA at 1440 D St., Alexandria, VA 22314, (703) 836-34 FAX: (703) 836-2843.

CENTRAL

Accelerated Freefall Iowa, *Boone Munici Airport, Boone, IA 50036, one mile north of Hwy. (515) 232-8212, or 432-1018.*

Des Moines Skydivers, Inc., *RR4, Box 234 Winterset, IA 50273, (515) 244-1834.*

Horizon Skydiving School, *8608 E. 32nd Str Kansas City, MO 64129, (816) 923-7006.*

Skydive Greene County, Inc., *177 S. Mor Siding Road, Xenia, OH 45385, (513) 372-0700.*

Sky Nights, *East Troy Municipal Airport, E Tory, WI, (414) 542-9143, or 642-9933.*

Wisconsin Skydivers, Inc., *W 204 N 5(Lannon Rd., Menomonee Falls, WI 53051, (414) 2 3434.*

NORTHEAST

AFF East/Skydive Chambersburg, Inc., *3! Airport Road, Chambersburg, PA 17201, (800) 5. 3497, or (717) 264-1029; FAX: (717) 264-0726.*

Connecticut Parachutists, Inc., *Elling Airport, Rt. 83, Ellington, CT 06029, (203) 871-00*

Long Island Skydivers, Inc., *Spadaro's Airp Montauk Highway, East Moriches, NY 11940, (5 589-2910, or (516) 653-9184.*

Pepperell Skydiving Center, Inc., *Peppe Airport, Rt. 111, Nashua Rd., Pepperell, MA 014 (508) 433-9222, or (603) 673-5867.*

The Ranch, *P.O. Box 121, Gardiner, NY 125. (914) 255-4033, 255-9538.*

United Parachute Club, Inc., *New Hano Airport, Rt. 663/Swamp Pike, Gilbertsville, PA 195 (215) 323-9667, or (215) 323-8565.*

Rockies

Front Range Skydivers, P.O. Box 26290, Colo-Springs, CO 80918, (800) 624-3773; FAX: (719) 1890. (Drop zone 30 miles northeast of Colorado ngs, in Calhan, CO.)

Skydive Colorado, Ft. Collins-Loveland Airport, land, CO 80538, (303) 669-9966, or 667-2113.

Utah Sky Ranch, Airport #2, 7200 South 4450 t, West Jordan, UT 84084, (801) 255-JUMP, or) 322-JUMP.

South

Aggies Over Texas, Inc., Coulter Field, 6120 A, j. 21 East, Bryan, TX 77803, (409) 778-0245, or) 693-0415.

Air Adventures Florida, Air Glades Airport, j. 27, Clewiston, FL 33440, (813) 983-6151.

FreeFall Ranch, Inc., Roosevelt Memorial Air-, Hwy. 27-A, P.O. Box 39, Warm Springs, GA 30, (404) 655-3373.

Hartwood ParaCenter, Inc., 194 Cropp Road, twood, VA 22405, (703) 752-4784.

Oklahoma Parachute Center, Inc., Cushing nicipal Airport, Cushing, OK 74110, (918) 225-2, or (918) 836-8888.

Raeford Parachute Center, P.O. Drawer R.A., ford, NC 28376, (919) 875-3261.

Skydive DeLand, Inc., P.O. Box 3071, DeLand, 32723, (904) 736-1742.

Skydive Spaceland, Houston Gulf Airport, 2750 1266, League City, TX 77573, (713) 337-1713.

West

California City Skydive Center, 5999 Curtiss :e, California City, CA 93505, (619) 373-2733.

Kapowsin Air Sports Ltd., 27611 146th Avenue t, Kapowsin, WA 98344, (206) 847-5766.

Perris Valley Skydiving Center, 2091 Goetz d, Perris, CA 92370, (714) 657-9576, or 657-3904. l (800) 832-8818 for P.V. Skydiving School.

Skydive Oregon, Inc., Skydive Oregon Airport, 50 S. Hwy. 211, Molalla, OR 97038, (503) 829-/E, or 829-5867.

Snohomish Parachute Center, Harvey Airfield, homish, WA 98290, (800) 338-JUMP in WA, or 5) 568-5960.

Skydive Arizona, 4900 N. Taylor Rd., Eloy, AZ 31, (602) 466-3753.

Skydive Hawaii, Dillingham Airfield, 68-760 rington Hwy., Honolulu, HI 96791, (808) 521-4404.

PARACHUTING CLUBS & CENTERS WORLDWIDE

Below you'll find contact information for parachuting clubs and/or jump centers for 20 countries worldwide. If no particular jump center is listed, contact each foreign country's official Parachuting Association. (Note: addresses are supplied by the USPA.)

Worldwide

Argentina: **Fed. Argentina de Paracaidismo**, Anchorena 275, Buenos Aires.

Australia: **Australian Parachute Fed.**, P.O. Box 144, Curtin, ACT 2605, Australia.

Austria: **Aeroklub**, Prinz Eugen Strasse 12-P, A-1040 Wien, Austria. Jump Center: **Jonathan Air Sport** (Multiple DZs in Austria and France.) (011 43) 8327-1370, or 8327-1379.

Belgium: **Aero Club**, 1 rue Montoyer, B-1040, Brussels, Belgium. Jump Center: **Paraclub Moorsele**,

An AFF jump/TOM SANDERS

Ledegem-straat 142, 8640 Moorsele, Belgium, (011 32) (56) 50 00 92.

Denmark: **Dansk Faldskaerms Union**, Romergade 19, III, DK-1362, Kobnhavn, Denmark.

Finland: **Aero Club**, Malmin Lentoasema, SF-700 Helsinksi, Finland.

Germany: **Deutscher Aero Club c.v.**, P.O. Box 710123, D-6000, Frankfurt, 71, Germany. Jump Center: **Aero Fallschirm Sport, Inc.**, Flughafen, 3527 Calden, Germany, (011 49) 5674 4119; **Fallschirm-sprungausbildung**, Flugplatz Saarlouis, Duren, Germany, (011 49) 6837-7375; FAX: (011 49) 6837-74373.

Great Britain: **British Para. Assn.**, 47-P Vaughan, Leicester, LE1 4SG, England. Jump Center: **Border Parachute Centre**, Dunstanburgh House, Embleton, Northumberland NE66 3XFA-1, (011 44) 665 76 588; **Swansea Parachute Club**, Swansea Airport, Fairwood Common, Swansea, West Glamorgan, SA2 7JU, (011 44) 792 296464 (AFF and static line. One of Britain's largest jump centers.)

Indonesia: **AVES SPC**, Djuanda 262-P, Bandung, Indonesia.

Ireland: **Irish Aviation Club**, Dublin Airport, Republic of Ireland. Jump Center: **Wild Geese School of Adventure**, 27 Drumeil Road, Aghadowey, Coleraine, Co. Londonderry, Northern Ireland. (011 358) 265 868 669.

Italy; Jump Center: **Pro Skydiving**, c/o The Sky Shop, Via Canturino 22, 22070 Vertemate, Como, Italy, (011 39) 182 582-924, or (011 39) 31 900-935.

Japan: **Japan RW Assn.**, 302 Sansahira Yotsuya 2-9-15, Yotsuya Shinjyuku-ku, Tokyo, Japan. (011 81) 3 3350-5655, or 3 3350-5825.

Mexico: **Club Para. De Mexico**, Lerdo No. 210, Mexico 3, D.F.

New Zealand: **NZ Para Fed.**, P.O. Box 10109, Balmoral, Auckland, NZ. Jump Center: **Parakai Parachute Centre, Ltd.**, (Same Address), (011 64) 9 836 6963.

Norway: **Norges Lufsportforbund**, P.O. Box 9514, N-0159, Oslo 1, Norway.

Spain; Jump Centers: **Centro de Paracaidismo Costa Brava**, Apartado de Correos 194, Ampuriabrava, Gerona, Spain, (011 34) 72 45 01 11; **Centro Int'l de Paracaidismo-Castellon**, Apartado Postal 37, 12100 Grao-Castellon, Spain, (011 34) 33 64 22 29 68.

Sweden: **SPA, KSAK**, Malgomajvagen 17, S-12172 Johanns, Sweden.

Switzerland: **Aero Club of Switzerland**. Jump Centers: **Para Centre Sa Locarno**, Aeroporto Cantonale, 6596 Gordola, Switzerland, (011 41) 93 67 26 51; **Para-Club Beromunster**, Postfach, 6215 Baromunster, Switzerland, (011 41) 42 21 65 72.

USSR: **Aero Club**, P.O. Box 395, Moscow, CCCP 123362.

Venezuela: **Para Club Caracas**, Apartado 80016-P, Caracas, Venezuela.

NATIONAL JUMPING ORGANIZATIONS

The United States Parachuting Association SPA) is the central clearing-house for para-ating information nationwide. It has the most -to-date information on USPA-approved np schools, as well as scheduled jumpfests l skydiving competitions.

Contact the **USPA** at 1440 Duke Street, Alex-andria, VA 22314, (703) 836-3495; FAX: (703) 836-2843.

The Canadian Sport Parachuting Association, RR#3, 4195 Dunning Road, Navan, ONT, Canada K4B 1J1, (613) 835-3731, regulates all aspects of skydiving in Canada, much as the USPA does in the United States.

Paragliding

THE NEW WAVE OF FLIGHT

"Paragliding is like living a dream of flying.
Anyone who has flown in their dreams will understand."
-Vicki Peck,
parapente pilot in training

A trio of flyers in the French Alps/MARK SHAPIRO, CLAMBIN PRODUC

You stand on the crown of a 1,000' dormant volcano, looking at the desert floor far below. With a quiet prayer, you propel yourself down the slope, straining against a 250 square foot nylon wing rising up behind you. Then suddenly, the wing comes to life, hauling you airborne. You are free of the bounds of gravity, soaring outward into the void, rising aloft on the warm desert winds.

TILL GOTTBRATH

This is paragliding, American-style, the new wave of flying. Pioneered in the Swiss and French Alps, paragliding--flying with a foot-launched parachute from ridge or mountaintop--has emerged as one of Europe's hottest adventure sports, and if America follows suit, paragliding (called "parapenting" in Europe) will likely become the most popular aerial sport ever devised.

Paragliding is less expensive than hanggliding, and much easier to learn. In Europe, paragliding enthusiasts already outnumber hangglider pilots 10 to one. Every summer weekend in the Alps, hundreds of paragliders take to the air for 30-minute to two-hour flights over snow-covered glaciers and green valleys.

THE QUICK AND EASY WAY

▼

Paragliding offers immediate gratification. The learning process is much faster than with other forms of flying, and most people will be up in the air in virtually no time. According to Mark Chirico, veteran hangglider pilot and President of Parapente USA, no aerial sport is easier to learn than paragliding. New flyers don't have to spend months and thousands of dollars learning the basics: "It is much better for the average person who doesn't have a lot of time or money to put into a sport before they can have fun. We can start with complete novices, and by the end of a weekend they will be flying off moderately sized hills in the Cascades."

The compact size and light weight of paragliding gear makes it easier than ever before to fly. There is no large rig to as-

After a 10 to 20-yard run, if you manage to keep the canopy centered overhead, the wing lifts you from the ground, one last kick launching you into flight.

Wind, "the invisible hazard," is the paraglider pilot's best friend *and* his worst enemy. With no wind, it's extremely difficult to inflate the canopy. But if the wind is too strong, the canopy assumes a mind of its own, and can veer violently to one side, or even drag the pilot embarrassingly (and painfully) up the slope. However, with the right breeze--a steady, 5 to 10 mph head wind--a good pilot can inflate his canopy with a few strong tugs and no more than a brief sprint, lifting his legs into the air within a few yards of his starting point.

Once airborne, the pilot controls his flight by steering the wing above him. The parapente is equipped with two control lines, called brakes, running to either side of the pilot's harness. To turn left, the pilot pulls down on the left brake toggle line. To turn right, he does the opposite. To descend, and ultimately to land, the pilot pulls on both brake toggles, stalling the canopy just as he contacts the ground.

For novices the first flights will be exciting, but undeniably brief. You remain airborne for only a minute or so as you glide over the training slope towards the landing zone at the bottom of the hill. On your initial flights, you're rarely more than 60 feet above the ground, and are always within the watchful eye of an instructor.

Once you make the progression from the bunny slopes to higher altitude launch sites, flights of 20 minutes or longer can be accomplished. And, when you learn how to locate and work rising columns of air (thermals), it is possible to paraglide over long distances, staying in the air for hours in the right condition. Because they can make such tight spirals in the air, paragliders can ascend small thermals even better than hanggliders or sailplanes.

EQUIPMENT EVOLUTION

▼

Paragliding started in Europe when some crazy mountain climbers conceived of a faster and easier way down from the summits they labored so hard to scale. For Swiss, French, and Austrian mountaineers, it was not enough to merely reach the summit. If you were a true sportsman, you climbed up, then soared back down under a brilliantly colored parapente, catching thermals in the company of hawks.

semble, and you don't need a car to get to your launch site. The equipment weighs only 15 pounds or so, and can be easily carried on your back to your take-off point. In Europe, many fliers simply hop on an alpine cable car with their gear and ride to the top of the mountain. The pilot picks a smooth, grassy slope, and deploys his canopy on the ground. As soon as the wind is right, he can inflate his canopy, running down the slope until he is airborne. If he finds rising currents of air, a good pilot can stay aloft for an hour or more.

PARAGLIDING PRIMER

▼

Paragliding, also known as slope-soaring, is not child's play, but it is certainly the easiest and least expensive way to fly. Most novices manage at least a brief flight on the first day, and for about $700, you can get your basic paragliding pilot's rating, typically after just 4 to 5 weekends of flying. By contrast, most hangglider pilots spend many months, and considerably more money, before they complete their training.

.A paragliding flight begins with reassuring terra firma beneath your feet. The first task is to deploy your specially designed canopy or "parapente" (pronounced para-pawnt) behind you, facing the prevailing wind. After checking the forward and rear risers (the canopy lines), and hoisting them above your head, you run down a slope. In fact you run like hell, and keep running until you finally feel your weight lift off your toes. To the observer, it looks awkward, and it is at first. The canopy can inflate and then rotate backwards, making a launch appear like a running tug of war. If all goes well, the parapente should inflate within a few seconds, taking shape as the scoops in its forward edge fill with air.

The European pioneers started with old-fashioned round canopies, but soon adopted the square canopies that most parachutists now use. The wing shape offers superior lift, and is more maneuverable. Modifying skydiving canopies by trial and error, the Europeans settled on a design with large open cells or slots on the leading edge, which taper to a close on the rear of the canopy. This the French dubbed the "parapente." When air enters the leading edge of the canopy it fills the separate compartments, and inflates the parapente into its recognizable wing shape.

Parapentes are most commonly foot-launched from grassy slopes, but skis can be used to descend snow-covered hillsides. Ski paragliding is especially popular in Europe where flying is possible year-round on the lift-served glaciers of Switzerland, France and Austria. From these launch sites, spectacular 5,000' vertical descents are commonplace.

Typical sport parapentes measure 25' to 30' from wingtip to wingtip, with a narrow cross-section from front to rear, creating a

Taking off/TOM SANDERS, AERIAL FOCUS

high aspect-ratio wing similar to a sailplane's. Training parapentes (called PA or Class I canopies) are smaller and more boxlike, making them easier to inflate. Class

I canopies are more stable and forgiving in the air, making them much safer for novices. Class II canopies fly faster and soar better, but their high-performance wings can be prone to collapse, requiring expert piloting skills. These high-lift parapentes boast lower sink rates, and higher flight speeds. These qualities permit longer, higher flights and allow pilots to fly in stronger wind conditions, when lift is best. In expert hands, mountain flights of well over 50 miles are possible with a modern Class II canopy.

Parapente canopies and harnesses are colorful, well made and surprisingly durable. The sun's UV radiation will degrade the fabric over time, but with proper care, a quality sail can last many years. Most parapentes are manufactured in Europe, where design and manufacturing standards are strictly regulated. A quality European canopy with harness and backpack from ITV (France), Condor (Switzerland), or Pro Design (Austria) runs about $1,700 to $2,400. This is about $700 more than a skydiver's parachute. You can purchase wings from most of the schools reviewed below.

A pilot's perspective in the Alps/TILL GOTTBRATH

End of the day at the Sheba Crater, Arizona/TOM SANDERS, AERIAL FOCUS

Paragliding Training Centers Worldwide

*A*S WITH ANY AERIAL SPORT, LEARNING TO PARAGLIDE IS SERIOUS BUSINESS. ANY beginner should enroll in a formal course of instruction taught by certified professionals. Like any form of aviation, paragliding can be hazardous, even fatal. In the past few months a number of serious accidents have occurred both in the US and abroad. Make no mistake: this is a life-threatening sport. Do not underestimate the hazards involved.

An introductory flight session costs about $100 per day at most schools. To obtain your paragliding pilot's rating, allowing you to fly without supervision, you'll need to pass a written test, log a number of high-altitude flights (500'+ above the ground), and master specified flight skills in the air. This typically takes 4 to 5 weekends, at a cost of approximately $600 to $800. For more information, contact the American Paragliding Association (APA), 25 Goller Place, Staten Island, NY 10314, (718) 698-5738. The APA regulates paragliding nationwide and maintains listings of more than fifty certified instructors.

NORTH AMERICA

■ AIRTEK PARAGLIDING SCHOOL
425 Bonair Street, Suite 4, La Jolla, CA 92037, (619) 454-0598; FAX: (619) 551-9355.

Airtek runs one of the most professional paragliding schools in America. Instructor Marcus Salvemini is patient and thorough, his equipment is first rate, and he uses one of the best private flying sites in Southern California. Marcus is also the principal instructor for the Torrey Pines Flight Park, a full-service flight center just north of San Diego, (619) 452-3202. Rating: ★★★

■ ASPEN PARAGLIDING
P.O. Box 2432, Aspen, CO 81612, (303) 925-7625, or (303) 927-3258.

Aspen Paragliding conducts one of the few true mountain-flying operations in the country. Both flight training ($375 for 3 days) and tandem rides are available. Ski paragliding is offered in winter. Instructors Jan Stenstadvold and Dick Jackson are both among the nation's best. Rating: ★★★

■ CHANDELLE HANGGLIDING CENTER
488 Manor Plaza, Pacifica, CA 94044, (415) 359-6800.

You can enjoy spectacular ocean views and soft-sand landings in Pacifica, California, site of the Chandelle Hanggliding Center's weekend parapente classes for novices. Chandelle, probably one of the top 10 hanggliding schools in the country, has offered classes in slope-soaring for the past two years. A 1-day class costs $100, while a 5-day program runs $500. Chandelle pro-

vides personalized instruction with a strong emphasis on safety. Rating: ★★★

■ GLIDING FLIGHT (ABOVE & BEYOND)
3314 West 11400 South, South Jordan, UT 84065, (801) 254-7455.

Operated by Fred and Claudia Stockwell, Gliding Flight offers 1-day introductory courses for $85, and 6-day full certification programs for $450. All classes are conducted at the Point of the Mountain, a superb grassy knoll suitable for both beginners and intermediates. Fred Stockwell is the former president of the APA, and also publishes Paragliding magazine. The instruction could be better organized, but the training hill is one of the best. Rating: ★★★

■ MORNINGSIDE FLIGHT PARK
RR 2, Box 109, Claremont, NH 03743, (603) 542-4416.

Morningside, New England's oldest hanggliding center, offers half-day introductory paragliding lessons for about $75. We strongly recommend you request instructor John Bouchard, one of America's best pilots. He makes the program worthwhile, even though the flying conditions could be better. Rating: ★★

■ MULLER HANGGLIDING LTD.
R.R. 2, Cochrane, ALB, Canada T0L 0W0, (403) 932-6760.

Willy Muller operates the most experienced paragliding program in Canada. Training flights are made on the prairies west of Calgary, while advanced training includes mountain flights in the Rockies. A weekend intro course costs $95 CDN, while a 5-day intermediate program, including mountain flights, costs $295 CDN.

This is an excellent program that has introduced over 500 new pilots to the sport in the past five years. Rating: ★★★

■ **PARAPENTE USA**

2442 N.W. Market Street, No. 31, Seattle, WA 98107, (206) 467-5944.

Mark Chirico's Parapente USA, a very active paragliding school, operates both in Washington and Arizona. From May through October, classes are held outside Seattle in the Cascades. Most winter classes are conducted outside Flagstaff, at the Sheba Crater, a 1,000' volcanic cinder cone. Sheba is an ideal flying site that allows first-time pilots to launch from any direction. Classes feature two-way radios, and a jeep to take you up the hill. From November through April, contact Mark Chirico at P.O. Box 30773, Tucson, AZ 85731, or call (602) 292-1136. Parapente USA uses a European pilot rating system, although Chirico is an APA-certified instructor. Rating: ★★

■ **RAVEN ADVENTURES**

P.O. Box 1887, Palmer, AK 99645, (907) 745-3097.

Located one hour north of Anchorage, Raven Adventures conducts paragliding programs in spectacular mountain ranges. APA-certified instructors Clark and Norma Saunders offer both basic flight training for novices and mountain flight adventures for experienced pilots. Rating: ★★

■ **SKYDANCE PARAGLIDING COMPANY**

332 Richardson Drive, Mill Valley, CA 94941, (415) 332-1928.

Skydance's Curtis Woodman offers a complete training program from beginner to advanced, including coastal ridge soaring and inland thermal flying. Basic classes, conducted in the Sonoma foothills, cost $100 per day. A 6-day Class I certifi-

cation package costs $695, including 2 days of mountain flying at various sites near Mt. Shasta. For qualified pilots, Skydance will offer custom paragliding tours to Baja Mexico, Mt. Shasta, Big Sur and Europe. Skydance runs a quality, safety-conscious program, and Woodman is an excellent instructor. Rating: ★★★

■ **TEXAS PARAGLIDING**

1437 Waseca, Houston, TX 77055-4411, (713) 973-9536.

Texas Paragliding is probably the premier tow-launch and cross-country flying center in the country. Using a truck-mounted winch with a mile of tow line, flyers are lifted over flatlands to altitudes of 1,500'. This permits both novices and experts to practice many maneuvers that are simply impossible at most foot-launched sites. Outstanding thermal lift allows advanced flyers to make cross-country flights of up to 2 hours in duration. (The school supplies a radio-equipped chase vehicle.) A complete 3 to 4-weekend Class I flight certification program costs $750. Rating: ★★

■ **OREGON PARAGLIDING**

1012 N.W. Wall Street, Bend, OR 97701, (503) 389-5411; Phonemail/FAX: (503) 389-8010.

Oregon Paragliding is a serious, full-time school run by able instructor Kevin Arends. Both individual and group training is available complete with video reviews. This is a solid program--a very good place to learn. You'll find a full selection of high-quality wings and accessories, which can be purchased without sales tax. The shop also offers flying tours throughout Oregon. Rating: ★★★

EUROPE

If you want to try your hand at paragliding in Europe, you may wish to contact one of the following flight schools or paragliding clubs:

AUSTRIA

■ **CLUB ALPIN EXTRA**

c/o TraWell Reisen, Frankenberggasse 14, A-1040 Vienna, Austria, (011 43) 1 505 0457; FAX: (011 43) 1 505 1224.

One-day basic course is about $55; 5-day course with high flight, about $460.

■ **FLUGSCHULE ZILLERTAL**

Andreas Gerber, Atlas Sportalm, A-6283 Hippach, Austria, (011 43) 5282 3720, or 3721.

Paragliding above Chamonix Valley, France/CHRIS NOBLE

■ **STV UND PARAGLEITSCHULE**

Ernst Steger, Gschwandt 293, A-6100 Seefeld, Austria, (011 43) 5213 5287.

For a complete list of Austrian paragliding schools, contact the Austrian National Tourist Office, 500 Fifth Avenue, New York, NY 10110, (212) 944-6880; or 11601 Wilshire Boulevard, Suite 2480, Los Angeles, CA 90025-1760, (310) 477-3332. Request the 12-page air sports brochure. See page 338 for information on Austrian paragliding holidays.

FRANCE

■ **CHAMONIX PARAPENTE**

278 Rue Pacard, 74400 Chamonix, France, (011 33) 50 55 98 50.

This is one of Europe's leading schools, with skilled, English-speaking instructors, and instruction year-round. The emphasis

cluding equipment, instruction and farmhouse accommodation.

■ NORTHERN HANG GLIDING & PARAGLIDING CENTRE
Dunvegan Lodge, Front Street, Barmby Moor, York, England YO4 5EB, (011 44) 759 304 404.

SWITZERLAND

There are 32 registered paragliding schools in Switzerland. For addresses, contact the Aero Club of Switzerland, Dept. Paragliding, Lidostrasse 5, 6006 Lucerne, Switzerland, (011 41) 41 31 21 21. One recommended school is:

■ CENTRE DELTA-PARAPENTE
PH Bernard Immeuble Turbulences, CH 1936, Verbier, Switzerland, (011 41) 26 31 68 18, or Box 20 1256, Troinex, Geneva, Switzerland, (011 41) 022 784 33 33.

This is a well-established operation with top-quality equipment and skilled instructors. Flight training begins at roughly $90 per day, more expensive than French or Austrian schools.

SOUTH PACIFIC

AUSTRALIA
■ PARAGLIDING CENTRE
P.O. Box 413, Charlestown, NSW 2290, Australia, (011 61) 049 498 946. Ask for Director Ian Ladyman.

NEW ZEALAND
■ ALPINE GUIDES (MT. COOK)
P.O. Box 20, Mount Cook, New Zealand, (011 64) 3 435-1834; FAX: 3 435-1898.

Alpine Guides offers both introductory and advanced paragliding courses in New Zealand's scenic Southern Alps. See page 339 for a more complete description.

is on advanced flying, so you may want to do your initial training elsewhere.

■ ECOLE FRANÇAISE VOL LIBRE
Le Grand Chalet, 06420 Valdeblore, France (011 33) 9302 8350.

Open year-round. About $55 per day, or $250 for 6 days. Insurance and lodging is available.

■ LES ADVENTURIERS DES L'AZURE
St. Jalle 26610, Nyons, France, (011 33) 7527 3238.

This is one of the leading schools in the central region of France and offers flight training for all skill levels.

■ OFFICE DU TOURISME
Immeuble La Ruade, 06660 Auron, France, (011 33) 9323 0266; FAX: 9323 0509.

The tourism office can recommend local schools. An intro flight runs about $55, with a weeklong seminar roughly $250.

GREAT BRITAIN
■ CAIRNWELL HANG GLIDING & PARAGLIDING SCHOOL
Cairnwell Mountain, Braimar, Aberdeenshire, Scotland AB3 5XS, (011 44) 3397 41331.

■ HIGH ADVENTURE
Tapnell Farm, Isle of Wight, England PO41 0YJ, (011 44) 983 754 042.

High Adventure, Britain's largest paragliding/hanggliding school, offers day classes and weeklong paragliding holidays, in-

Inflating the canopy, Verbier, Switzerland/MARK SHAPIRO, CLAMBIN PRODUCTIONS

PARAGLIDING HOLIDAYS WORLDWIDE

HAVE PARAPENTE, WILL TRAVEL. PARAGLIDING IS THE PERFECT AERIAL SPORT for nomads. No larger than a medium-sized backpack, a complete parapente outfit can easily be transported just about anywhere.

At present, Europe remains the premier paragliding vacation destination. In the Alps, you'll find ideal high-altitude launch sites served by an extensive network of cable cars and ski lifts operating year-round. In Europe, small villages are also linked by good train and bus systems, so you can fly from one area to another, and get back to your original starting point without great difficulty. There's no need for a chase vehicle to meet you at your landing zone.

If you're seeking a winter flying holiday, there are many attractive options. The American Southwest--Utah, New Mexico and Arizona--offers beautiful flying sites, and fairly consistent flying conditions year-round. Baja Mexico is also emerging as a great off-season paragliding venue, with warm weather and many recreational options. If you're really adventurous, you can fly New Zealand's spectacular Southern Alps between November and March, summer in the Southern Hemisphere.

EUROPEAN ALPS

If you dream of flying the European Alps, consider **Parapente USA's** 14-day Alpine paragliding tours. Expect to pay about $2,500 for airfare, lodging and 2 weeks of flying at a dozen sites in the French and Swiss Alps. Call (206) 467-5944 in Seattle, or (602) 292-1136 in Arizona. **Compact Wings** of California offers a summer paragliding tour visiting Verbier, Chamonix and other famous sites in France and Switzerland. The 11-day trip will cost about $2,400, including airfare, lodging, guides, lifts, and over-water maneuver clinic. You should have previous flying experience. Contact Compact Wings, 1271 Avenida Floribunda, San Jacinto, CA 92383, (714) 654-8559.

Going with an American-run tour is not the only way to paraglide in the Alps. France, Switzerland and Austria all have well-established paragliding centers. Austria in particular has dozens of excellent, licensed parapente schools that offer parapente rentals and training at quite reasonable rates, ranging from $50 to $90 per day. Contact the Austrian National Tourist Office at 500 Fifth Avenue, New York, NY 10110, (212) 944-6880; or 11601 Wilshire Boulevard, Suite 2480, Los Angeles, CA 90025-1760, (310) 477-3332 and request the list of paragliding centers.

A 5-day, learn-to-fly package in the Austrian Alps is offered by **TraWell Reisen**, a sports travel agency based in Vienna. If conditions are good, you can earn your European pilot's rating in the course of the week. The price, including instruction, equipment and lodging in a modest alpine hotel, is about $625 for the week. Contact TraWell Reisen, Frankenberggasse 14, 1040 Wien, Austria, phone: (011 43) 1 505 0457; FAX: (011 43) 1 505 1224. It's best to send a FAX, but the director speaks English.

Alphorn Ski Tours offers a summer adventure package to Innsbruck in Austria, with optional paragliding. The $1,150 price includes round-trip airfare on Lufthansa from the East Coast, 7 nights in four-star hotels, mountain hiking guides, and ground transfers. Paragliding and/or rafting is available for $50-$90 per day extra. Experienced flyers can fly from high-altitude sites. Contact Alphorn at 5788 Route 202, P.O. Box 356, Lahaska, PA 18931, (800) ALP-HORN; FAX: (215) 794-7199.

AMERICAN WEST

Each summer, **Gliding Flight** operates highly regarded "Above and Beyond" paragliding tours to a number of scenic flying sites in Utah and nearby areas. These tours, designed for proficient pilots, range from 3 to 7 days, with customized itineraries selected by the participants. The Above and Beyond tour program has been ranked as one of America's best adventures. Call (801) 254-7455 for details.

For those looking for a terrific Wild West flying vacation, **Parapente USA** offers 5-day tours to Idaho's scenic Lemhi mountain range in the last two weeks of May. From the Twin Peaks dude ranch, the flyers ride to mountain launch sites on horseback. Then they will paraglide 2,500' down to the Salmon River, where rafts await to carry them on a whitewater journey back to the ranch. The tour costs about $950, including food, lodging and all equipment. Call (206) 467-5944, or (602) 292-1136.

To fly the peaks of the Sierra Nevada overlooking scenic Lake Tahoe, contact **Adventure Sports**, 3680 Research Way, #8, Carson City, NV, (702) 883-7070. Spring and summer flying tours for both novice and experienced flyers, start at $75 per day, including wing. The 1 to 3-day tours are offered on a custom basis with overnights in Reno. Adventure Sports also offers guided flying expeditions to the Alps, the Andes and the Himalayas.

MEXICO

Parapente USA offers weeklong winter paragliding tours to southern Baja. Pilots (novices are welcome) will stay aboard the 60' sailing yacht *Nagual*, which will cruise along the Sea of Cortez to a variety of flying sites. When customers aren't in the air, they can sample the fishing, swimming and snorkeling for which Baja is famous. Trips depart in December and April, and will cost $1,200, or $1,000 if you bring your own wing.

California-based **Skydance Paragliding,** (800) 845-4337, leads a number of flying expeditions to Baja and mainland Mexico each year. The tours are designed for seasoned flyers, but training can be arranged. Flying sites may include Cabo San

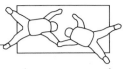

Lucas, Puerto Vallarta, and one or more of the Mexican volcanoes. Each winter Skydance also offers flying tours to the Caribbean, and paraskiing programs in the Rockies. Prices start at $100 per day.

Ken Baier's **Air Junkies**, 151 Tamarack Avenue, Carlsbad, CA 92008, (619) 7230-9775, offers guided flying safaris to northern Baja for both novice and advanced flyers. The 1 and 2-day trips visit a variety of warm-weather sites just across the border, including La Salina, a beautiful 600' coastal cliff site, and the Cantamare Dunes, a superb training hill. Price for novices is $100 per day including instruction, equipment and transport. A rated pilot with his own wing pays just $25. Trips are offered on a custom basis year-round.

NEW ZEALAND

If you're looking for a great winter paragliding adventure, head to New Zealand. **Alpine Guides**, the Southern Hemisphere's best mountain guide service, offers 3-day basic and advanced paragliding courses in New Zealand's Southern Alps. This is a terrific area to fly, with phenomenal alpine scenery. The novice programs follow a safe, logical progression--starting with low-level flights, and progressing to a high-altitude flight on the third day. Helicopters will be used extensively during the advanced course, allowing spectacular high-altitude glacier launches. Programs run November through March, at a cost of roughly $450 for beginners, $650 for advanced pilots. Contact Alpine Guides, P.O. Box 20, Mt. Cook, New Zealand, (011 64) 3 435-1834; FAX: (011 64) 3 435-1898.

RESOURCES

Paragliding magazine is North America's leading paragliding periodical. Available to APA members, or contact 3314 W. 11400 South, South Jordan, UT 84065.

Paragliding USA (magazine). This new, fairly technical publication is produced by manufacturer Performance Designs, 12650 Softwind Drive, Moreno Valley, CA 92388.

Paragliding Flight, *by Dennis Pagen*. This 208-page manual by the author of the hang-gliding "bible" is must reading for all new paraglider pilots. $19.95 from Paragliding magazine.

Paragliding In America, *by Marcus Salvemini*, covers 40 major US flying sites, providing site descriptions, photos and contact information. 120 pages, $12.00 from Airtek Paragliding, (619) 454-0598.

Jean-Marc Boisvin flying the south face of the Grand Jorasses into Courmayeur Valley, Italy/CHRIS NOBLE

Snowmobiling

Powder blasting in Jackson Hole, Wyoming/MITCH KEZAR, COURTESY ARCTCO INC.

*Consciousness is always open
to many possibilities
because it involves play.
It is always an adventure.*
-Julian Jaynes

▼

Snowmobiling of-
fers speed and
excitement, but it is also one of the
most pleasurable ways to experience
America's backcountry in winter. The
mobility and freedom provided by a
snowmobile allows a traveler to reach
farther into the forests and outlands
than is possible on skis, or with any
other mode of transport.

With the extensive network of trails
available in the United States and
Canada, the snowmobiler can explore
hundreds of thousands of square miles
of scenic, remote territory virtually inaccessible by other means. To help you
enjoy these opportunities, this chapter
describes six ultimate snowmobile
trips worldwide, and reviews 16 of the
top snowmobile destinations in North
America. We also review and rate
North America's top snowmobile tour
operators.

CHAPTER
23

Ridge-running in the Rockies/COURTESY YAMAHA MOTOR CORP.

FOR THOSE WHO LIVE OUTSIDE OF THE SNOWBELT, TOURING BY SNOWMOBILE may seem a strange concept. Yet for anyone who wants to cover more than a few miles a day in a winter wilderness, snowmobiling is the only way to go. You can cruise slowly, concentrating on the scenery, or enjoy a turn of speed on hard-packed trails. You don't need to be experienced to enjoy a snowmobile trip; driving a sled comes second nature to most folks. All you need is a sense of adventure, a love for the outdoors, and, of course, some good warm clothes.

JACKSON HOLE

Teton Powder Holiday

One of America's skiing hotspots, Jackson Hole is also a superior snowmobiling venue. Tucked up against imposing peaks of the Teton Range, Jackson Hole boasts a good network of groomed trails, but the most fun is to be had roaming off-trail through wide open bowls, alpine meadows, or up steep mountain passes. You can explore the Gros Ventre Valley, cut across to Green River Lakes basin, or if you're feeling adventurous, climb to the Continental Divide over 10,000' Union Pass.

For confirmed trail-runners, the best routes take you through Grand Teton National Park and the high country in the Gros Ventre region. Our favorite cross-country run begins in Togwotee, and runs overland to West Yellowstone and Yellowstone Park. You can't do this in a day, so you'll need to book at least one night in Yellowstone, although the sledding's so good there, you'll probably want to spend at least a couple of days before you make the run back to Jackson Hole.

Your best bet for a package snowmobile tour in the Jackson Hole area is the Togwotee Mountain Lodge, located 50 miles northeast of Jackson Hole. Situated high in the pines at 8,500', Togwotee Lodge offers everything a sledder could need, including sled rental, hot tubs and saunas. You can literally park your sled in front of your door. The rental equipment is excellent, brand-new Arctic Cat 440 Jags. The most popular program is an 8-day, 7-night program that features 5 days of sledding, which costs about $1,100 per person. For approximately $80 more, the lodge staff will transport your sled down to Yellowstone Park for 2 days of exploring. Or, for an additional $120, you can spend a full 3 days in the park on a guided tour visiting Old Faithful and other scenic highlights. Along the way you'll see moose, bison, elk and other wildlife. (Both options are still part of the 8-day program; you pay more to spend part of your holiday in Yellowstone.) To make reservations, contact

Six Ultimate Snowmobile Adventures

the Togwotee Mountain Lodge, P.O. Box 91, Moran, WY 83013, (307) 543-2847.

Sno-World Snow Tours also offers a package tour based out of the Togwotee Lodge. Cost for the 8-day tour through the nearby Tetons and Yellowstone country, is about $1,000-$1,200 including lodging, sled rental, most meals, and ground transfers. Past customers have raved about this tour: "A snowmobiler's dream with breathtaking scenery and miles and miles of trails that you must experience to believe." For details, contact Sno-World Snow Tours, 3701 Buttrick Road S.E., Ada, MI 49301, (616) 676-3313. Decker's Sno-Venture Tours offers a 6-night package to Jackson Hole that features 5 days of snowmobiling, including 2 days in Yellowstone Park. Price is approximately $750, with sled rental an additional $350.

For competitive types, each April Jackson Hole hosts the leading snowmobile hillclimb event in the West. For hillclimb information, contact the Jackson Hole Area Chamber of Commerce, P.O. Box E., Jackson, WY 83001, (307) 733-3316.

Decker's Sno-Venture Tours offers a special 7-day Hillclimb Championship holiday tour. Price is about $700 per person, plus $350 for a rental sled. Contact Decker's Sno-Venture Tours, P.O. Box 1447, Eagle River, WI 54521, (715) 479-2764.

ICELAND

Mysterious Land of the Far North

For a unique, exotic sledding destination, Iceland is hard to beat. This 100-mile-long volcanic island, located just below the Arctic Circle, boasts an environment ideal for snowmobiling. Iceland is formed from the lava flows of over 200 volcanoes, many still active. You'll find all imaginable terrain--flat rangeland, rolling hills, glaciers, even steep peaks, and of course volcanic craters both large and small. The snow conditions are superb. Smooth and firm, the snow permits you to venture just about anywhere you want to go without any worries of getting bogged down (most of the landscape is covered with snow year-round). If your idea of great snowmobiling is riding off-trail, yet on well-packed snow, Iceland is the place. Riders

who've ridden the top areas in Canada, Wyoming and Minnesota claim that Iceland may be the best of all.

Iceland's far northern latitude makes for long days in the late spring--ideal for touring around at your own pace, and stopping to enjoy the scenery. Amateur photographers will have their hands full, as there are fine views on just about any route. Iceland is a land of contrasts. Next to glaciers you'll find

Wyoming winter/MITCH KEZAR, ARCTCO, INC.

geysers. It's not unusual to travel cross-country for a few hours, then take a dip in a natural hot spring, right out in the wilderness. When you're out on the trail you can also warm yourself at the many climbers' huts located near lakes and other scenic points in the Icelandic interior.

To arrange a regular holiday in Iceland, contact Icelandair at (800) 223-5500, or (312) 956-3100. Icelandair can book accommodations, and give you sources for snowmobile rentals in Reykjavik, Iceland's largest city. Icelandair can arrange a customized itinerary including snowmobiling, or Decker's Sno-Venture Tours can set up a custom tour for an organized group. In past years, an Iceland tour cost about $1,700 per person, including lodging, most meals, snowmobile rental, guides, and airfare from New York. Contact Decker's Sno-Venture Tours, (715) 479-2764.

COLORADO ROCKIES

High Alpine Adventure

Sun, warm temperatures, and buckets of perfect powder snow--this is what brings skiers to the Colorado Rockies, and it also produces some of the best snowmobiling anywhere. In Colorado, you can find any kind of riding, from wide groomed valley trails to high ridges in Rocky Mountain National Park. The hub of Colorado snowmobiling is Grand Lake, a resort town that receives 140 inches of snow each

COURTESY BOMBARDIER, INC.

year. Grand Lake is a snowmobiling paradise, offering 300 miles of trails (100 groomed), and even a snowmobile racetrack. Most of the better lodges can arrange snowmobile rentals for you, and trail access couldn't be better--you can ride right down the town's main street to some of the area's best trails.

It's just a few miles along groomed trails to Rocky Mountain National Park. There you're treated to spectacular views from trails that rise to the top of the Continental Divide, at over 12,000'. Another great route is Stillwater Pass. From the top, you can see 50 miles or more on a clear day. The off-trail riding is hard to resist. The snowbase is deep, but the consistency of the powder allows even novices to sled the wildlands with confidence. Some of the prettiest runs are in nearby Arapahoe National Forest, but you'll also find great conditions just a few minutes away in the Meeker, Colorado, and White River National Forests.

If you can break free from the Superbowl, don't miss the annual Grand Lake Winter Carnival, held during the third weekend in January. Along with dogsled and snowmobile races, festivities include balloon races, skating and organized trail rides with outdoor cookouts. For lodging and sled rental, contact the Grand Lake Chamber of Commerce, P.O. Box 57, Grand Lake, CO 80447, (303) 627-3402; the Driftwood Lodge, P.O. Box 609, Grand Lake, CO 80447, (303) 627-3654; and The Overland Station, 801 Grand Avenue, Box 1527, Grand Lake, CO 80447, (303) 627-3077. Figure on at least $90 per day for a room and rental of a late model snowmobile.

Many sledders who have visited this part of Colorado believe it offers the best combination of quality snow, great scenery, and moderately priced accommodations in the country.

ALASKA

Cross-Country Tours

Alaska remains a wild frontier. A state grand in scope, it is the home of the highest mountains, biggest snowfields, and the most abundant wildlife in America. For those looking for a tour destination of unmatched natural beauty, Alaska delivers.

Daily snowmobile rentals are available in Anchorage. However, if you've spent the money to travel this far, you should head farther inland, away from the cities, where tourists are few and far between. A good choice is the rustic Eureka Lodge, situated 125 miles northeast of Anchorage, in the heart of Alaska's Gold Rush country. Both Sno-World Snow Tours and Decker's Sno-Venture Tours offer 9-day snowmobile outings from the Lodge in March. We'd probably

JIM ELDER

go with Sno-World, as it has timed its tour to coincide with the famed Iditarod dogsled race. The first three days are spent following the mushers in the day, and partying with them in the evenings. Both tours take sledders through remote backcountry, home to moose, caribou and arctic wolves. A highlight of both programs is a ride across the Scott Ice Field, a 6,000' glacier, to visit the tanker port at Valdez. After your 5 days of riding, you return to Anchorage for a flightseeing trip of the nearby Chugach Mountains and the Kink Glacier.

Cost for either tour is about $1,900, all-inclusive, except air travel. Contact Sno-World Snow Tours, 3701 Buttrick Road, SE, Ada, MI 49301, (800) 383-9863, or Decker's Tours, (address above), (715) 479-2764.

YELLOWSTONE

Snowmobilers' Paradise

What Wimbleton is to tennis, Yellowstone is to snowmobiling. Whatever kind of experience you seek--whether speed runs on marked trails, or slow rambles

Valcourt Snowmobile Festival

Every February, Valcourt, Quebec becomes a mecca for snowmobiling. The Valcourt International Snowmobiling Festival has grown in 10 years to be the largest and most successful event of its kind in the world. Every year hundreds of sledders gather for trail rides, races and a host of other winter sports. Valcourt is also the site of the world's only snowmobile museum, where you can see the very first motorized sled, built fifty years ago by Canada's Armand Bombardier.

Quebec Snow Cruises offers a 5-day tour scheduled to coincide with the Valcourt Festival. Before joining the weekend festivities at Valcourt, you'll cover over 500 miles of pristine trails in four major regions of Quebec: the Beauce, Quebec City, Central Quebec and the eastern townships. Cost, including everything except sled rental, is about $810, double occupancy. Snowmobile rental will run another $75-$100 per day, including insurance. The tour price is a bit steep, but remember, you'll be riding some of the best trails in the world. The Trans-Quebec Snowmobile Trail system links all the major scenic areas in Quebec with over 15,000 miles of trails--all marked, groomed and double-laned. You can cover a lot of ground in a day, and there's always a country inn or lodge nearby when you feel like taking a break.

Snow cover in February is usually good, but conditions have been a little thin in recent years. However, the trail system in Quebec is so extensive that you will never lack for riding options. Contact Quebec Snow Cruises, P.O. Box 338, Masson, Quebec, Canada J0X 2H0, (819) 986-2223; FAX: (819) 986-9743. For general information on the Festival, contact Tourisme Quebec, P.O. Box 20,000, Quebec City, Quebec, Canada G1K 7X2, (800) 363-3777, or (819) 778-2222.

through alpine wilderness--it's possible here. From your hotel you can explore over 400 miles of groomed trails, and the off-trail opportunities are virtually limitless. Powder hounds can venture through 10,000 square miles of wilderness in two national parks and seven nearby national forests.

In the wintertime, the little town of West Yellowstone becomes a haven for sledders. You can take your snowmobile just about anywhere, even on city streets. At the edge of town is the gateway to Yellowstone National Park, probably the most unique snowmobiling destination in the world. Riding in the park is restricted to marked trails, but these provide excellent access to the park's thermal sites and abundant wildlife. Elk and moose graze and drink in Yellowstone's free-flowing rivers, and herds of bison can be seen close to the trails. And of course there is Old Faithful, one of 10,000 thermal sites within park boundaries.

For those seeking open country, the seven national forests adjoining the park are ideal. You can easily cruise 100 miles without running into vehicular traffic. Popular trips include the Continental Divide Route, and the run to Two Top Mountain. Hire a guide if you plan to overnight in the backcountry.

A number of snowmobile operators offer guided tours and sled rentals in the Yellowstone Park region. Two of the best are Yellowstone Adventures, Inc., P.O. Box 669, West Yellowstone, MT 59758, (800) 231-5991, or (406) 646-7614; and Yellowstone Tour and Travel (YT&T), P.O. Box 369, West Yellowstone, MT 59758, (800) 221-1151, or (406) 646-9310. Yellowstone Adventures offers daily sled rentals as well as package tours. Its 4-day package, including lodging (double occupancy), snowmobile rental and clothing rental, costs $380 per person. The same program for a full week costs $720 per person. YT&T offers complete packages from 4 to 7 days ranging in price from $460 to $890 including sled rental, and full board and lodging.

COURTESY YAMAHA MOTOR CORP.

The Top North American Snowmobile Tour Operators

■ DECKER'S SNO-VENTURE TOURS

111 W. Pine St., P.O. Box 1447, Eagle River, WI 54521, (715) 479-2764; FAX: (715) 479-9711.

Sno-Venture Tours is a family operation, run by Richard and Audrey Decker. With over 25 years of experience, the Deckers have a wealth of knowledge about the best snowmobiling destinations. Machines and tour routes are selected for riders of all skill levels--both those who like speed, and those who prefer a more tranquil ride. Sno-Venture Tours offers a complete range of trips. Destinations include the Wisconsin Northwoods, Yellowstone Park/Jackson Hole, the Black Hills of South Dakota, Crater Lake in Oregon, Western Utah and Ontario. Trips range in price from $550 to $700 per week, with sled rental an additional $350 on the average.

The Deckers also offer outstanding trips to the far north--the Alaskan interior, and Canada's NW Territories. Rating: ★★★★

■ NORTH AMERICAN SNOW TOURS

P.O. Box 1016, Meredith, NH 03253, (603) 279-3985.

North American Snow Tours (NAST) specializes in package snowmobile vacations in Maine and Quebec. Now in its sixth year, NAST leads wide-ranging tours on an excellent network of well-groomed trails. You'll travel far and wide on these trips--the 7-day Lac St. Jean loop tour covers over 950 miles of scenic Canadian backcountry. Other trips include the Maine "God's Country" tour (5 or 6 days, 800 miles), and a special Formula Club Ride co-sponsored by Bombardier. Prices for the Canadian tours range from $750 to $950 for 5 to 7 days (double occupancy). The Formula Club Tour costs $885 for 6 days. These prices cover gas, accommodations and guides, but not snowmobile rental.

Of NAST's tours, the Lac St. Jean loop is probably the most scenic. The route follows high cliffs above a lovely river basin. NAST's tours all feature experienced guides and a 4x4 support truck. We recommend NAST programs for sledders seeking to pack the most riding into their holiday--these are fast-paced trips designed primarily for

---

CHOOSING A TOUR

When choosing a tour, look for a company that takes small groups (5-10 people), and has experienced guides able to deal with mechanical breakdowns on the trail. It is also desirable to have a support vehicle. Ask the following questions before you go.

How long has the tour company been operating?
How much riding will be done each day, and what is the average speed?
Who pays for repairs if the sled breaks, and will a spare be provided?
How much can you expect to pay for gas and oil during the trip?
What are the trail conditions like, and what happens if there's no snow--can you get your money back?

Will there be a support vehicle to carry food, supplies, and backup sleds during the trip?
What kind of machines will you be riding, and how new will they be?
Does the tour price include all lodging and food costs?
Can you get a discount for organizing a group of riders?
Will the tour operator trailer your sled to the destination for a fee?

Warming up on the trail/MITCH KEZAR, COURTESY ARCTCO, INC.

those with some previous snowmobiling experience. Many of NAST's Quebec tours were sold out last year by early fall, so you should book well in advance. New destinations will be added next year. Rating: ★★★

■ ROCKY MOUNTAIN SNOWMOBILE TOURS
9918 71st Ave., Edmonton, ALB, Canada T6E 0W7, Canada, (403) 439-4987; FAX: (403) 439-0017.

With premium riding sites, a state-of-the art, 52-sled transporter and reasonable prices, Rocky Mountain Snowmobile Tours (RMST) is hard to beat. Tours run November through March in the Canadian Rockies and West Yellowstone, Montana. The Canadian tour locations, Valemount, Revelstoke, and Hunters Range in BC, and Blairmore in Alberta, are all superb. Valemount boasts three separate mountain ranges with well-marked trails. Revelstoke, with an annual snowfall over 52 feet, offers riders all the powder snow they can handle. Hunters Range in the BC interior offers high alpine wilderness routes as well as easy trail running. The Blairmore site promises sunny skies, and scenic ridge-running atop Crowsnest Pass. Canadian tours run 3 to 5 days, and cost about $130 per day including ground transport but not sled rental.

RMST also runs 6-day Yellowstone programs perfect for Canadians wanting to bring their own sleds. $750 CDN covers all transport and lodging. For 1993, RMST plans programs in the French Alps and Norway--both spectacular new destinations. Rating: ★★★★

■ SNO-WORLD SNOW TOURS
3701 Buttrick Road, S.E., Ada, MI 49301-9328, (800) 383-9863, or (616) 676-0397.

Sno-World Snow Tours (SWST) offers complete snowmobile vacation packages in Wisconsin, Ontario, Colorado and Wyoming. Sno-World's premier tour is based at the Togwotee Mountain Lodge near Jackson Hole, Wyoming. From this spot, 8,500' high in the Tetons, you'll experience challenging alpine runs above treeline, blast through virgin powder, or just enjoy miles of touring on established trails. The tour will also visit Yellowstone Park. Cost for 8 days is $1,000-$1,100, including lodging, all meals and five days of sled rental.

Also recommended is Sno-World's Ontario Snow Train adventure. After a train passage to Northern Ontario, you explore Ontario's fine trail system from your base hotel. Past customers have loved this trip: "Snowmobiling was fantastic--some of the best groomed trails that I have seen in a long time." Approximately $600 covers your transport, trail permits and accommodations for 6 days. An exciting new destination is Grand Mesa, Colorado, the remnants of an ancient volcano. For 5 days and 6 nights sledders will enjoy great panoramas and super snow conditions. Price will be about $1,100. Rating: ★★★

■ YELLOWSTONE ADVENTURES, INC.
131 Dunraven Street, P.O. Box 669, West Yellowstone, MT 59758, (800) 231-5991, or (406) 646-7735.

Yellowstone Adventures (YA) is a leading Yellowstone/Grand Teton snowmobile rental operation. While single-day snowmobile rentals comprise the lion's share of its business, YA also offers complete package vacations from 4 days to 2 weeks. YA features new Ski-doo machines, from basic to high performance. Prices range from $70 per day for a Safari 377 to $100 per day for the Formula MXLT. All sleds have heated handlebars and the first tank of fuel is free. A 4-day package tour, including lodging (double occupancy), snowmobile rental and clothing rental, costs $380 per person. The same package for a full week costs $711 per person. You won't find a better place to ride than Yellowstone, and YA is one of Yellowstone's best package tour operators. Rating: ★★★

■ YELLOWSTONE TOUR & TRAVEL
P.O. Box 369, West Yellowstone, MT 59758, (800) 221-1151, or (406) 646-9310.

Yellowstone Tour & Travel (YT&T) runs 4 to 7-day complete snowmobiling vacations from West Yellowstone, Montana. The 4-day Explorer trip, a good choice for the novice snowmobiler, offers 3 days of guided riding through Yellowstone National Park. The $450 price (per person, dbl. occ.) includes lodging, snowmobile rental with a free tank of gas each day, and all sledding gear (suit, boots, gloves, goggles and hat). The 6 and 7-day Adventurer and Rough Rider programs, at $720 and about $890 respectively, provide the same items, while allowing more riding time to explore the Grand Canyon of Yellowstone, and powder snow in the Gallatin and Targhee National Forests. Groups of 10 or more get 10 percent off. Rating: ★★

Note: All trip prices are for the spring 1992 season, and are subject to change.

Idaho Rockies picnic/DAVID STOECKLEIN

Running in the high country, Wyoming/JIM ELDER

GREAT NORTH AMERICAN SLEDDING SITES

CALIFORNIA

Lake Tahoe

Location: Lake Tahoe, CA and Reno, NV.

Trails and Conditions: Groomed and ungroomed logging roads and trails. Deep powder, often steep terrain. A number of groomed trails run from Zephyr Cove which are suitable for all riders.

Top Destinations: Tahoe Vista, Toiyabe National Forest, and for experienced sledders, ski resort to ski resort.

Attractions: World-class downhill skiing, Nevada gambling, watersports on lake.

Snowmobile Rentals/Guides: Snowmobiling Unlimited, P.O. Box 1591, Tahoe City, CA 96145, (916) 583-5858; Zephyr Cove Snowmobiling Center, 760 Hwy. 50, Zephyr Cove, NV 89448, (702) 588-3833.

Contact: Tahoe North Visitors Bureau, P.O. Box 5578, Tahoe City, CA 95730, (800) 822-5959 in CA, (800) 824-8557 nationwide.

CANADA

Haliburton, Ontario

Location: Haliburton County is just across the border, four hours from Niagara Falls.

Trails and Conditions: Great system of 450 miles of groomed trails, with night grooming on weekends. Extensive trail marking and sign-posting. Primarily flat, open country, plus frozen lakes. Over 100 inches of snow annually.

Attractions: Large, active snowmobiling club. Good nordic skiing. Winter carnival each February.

Snowmobile Rentals/Guides: Loralea Inn, RR#2, Minden, ONT, (705) 489-2048; Wedgewood Marina, (705) 489-2320.

Contact: Haliburton County Snowmobile Association, c/o Ontario Federation of Snowmobile Clubs, 98 Marshall St., Barrie, ONT, Canada L4N 4L5, (705) 739-7669.

Lanaudiere, Quebec

Location: Access trails from St. Donat, 75 miles north of Montreal.

Trails and Conditions: 100 miles of groomed trails with superb sign-posting. Linked to 5,000-mile, trans-Quebec trail system. Varied terrain--mountains, lakes, forests.

Top destinations: Lake Ouereau, Mont Tremblant Park.

Attractions: Possibly best snowmobiling in Canada. Fine network of small inns and warming huts, numerous wilderness preserves and parks to tour. Mont Tremblant Park trails are superb.

Snowmobile Rentals/Guides: Gephaneuf Inc., 148 Beauchesne, Repentigny, Quebec, J5Y 1X5, (514) 582-0473, sled and clothing rentals, 45 machines; Sport & Marine MV, Inc., 1108 Principale, St.-Donat, Quebec, J0T 2C0, (819) 424-3433.

Contact: Club Moto-Neige St.-Donat, Inc., Box 401, St.-Donat, Quebec, J0T 2C0, (819) 424-2263, 424-3433.

IDAHO

Mountain River Country

Location: Northeast Idaho near Island Park area.

Trails and Conditions: 200 miles of groomed trails, over varied terrain--flatlands, forests, mountains. Deep powder in high country.

Top Destinations: Two Top and Lionhead Mountains, Island Park trail system; you can cross to Yellowstone Teton region.

Attractions: Spectacular scenery, deep powder, long season. Excellent downhill ski resorts nearby.

Snowmobile Rentals/Guides: Contact Sawtell Sales & Rentals, 1941 Balboa Drive, Idaho Falls, ID 83403.

Contact: Yellowstone Teton Travel Council, Box 50498, Idaho Falls, ID 83405-0498, (800) 634-3246, request maps and brochures on Mountain River Country.

MAINE

Millinocket

Location: Millinocket is north of Bangor on I-95, at the foot of Mt. Katahdin.

Trails and Conditions: 300 miles of groomed trails take you to nearby Baxter and Lilly Bay State Parks, or north into Canada. High mountain trails tend to be uncrowded, with good snow all winter.

Top Destinations: Mt. Kineo, Baxter State Park, and Double Top Mountain. (Note--Baxter Park may be restricted.)

Attractions: Robinson's Twin Pine Camp caters to sledders and sponsors annual snowmobile Fun Fest.

Snowmobile Rentals/Guides: Robinson's Twin Pines Camp, P.O. Box 152, Millinocket, ME 04462, (207) 723-5523.

Contact: Millinocket Chamber of Commerce, P.O. Box 5, Millinocket, ME 04462, (207) 723-4443; Baxter Park Authority, (207) 723-5140.

MICHIGAN

Houghton Lake

Location: Houghton Lake, North Central Michigan, on US 27.

Trails and Conditions: 175 miles of groomed runs through mountains and around 22,000-acre Houghton Lake. Heaps of snow all winter.

Top Destinations: Leota Trail and Prudenville Trail, Houghton Lake State Forest.

Attractions: January winter festival, March snowmobile safari.

Snowmobile Rentals/Guides: Hacker's Yamaha and Honda, 3901 Houghton Lake Drive, Houghton Lake, MI 48629, (517) 366-7015.

Contact: Houghton Lake Chamber of Commerce, 1625 W. Houghton Lake Drive, Houghton Lake, MI 48629, (800) 248-LAKE, or (517) 366-5644 (MI).

Keweenaw Peninsula

Location: Northwest corner of Michigan's Upper Peninsula.

Trails and Conditions: 21' of annual snowfall. Over 200 miles of groomed, marked trails. Mostly rolling hills and backwoods.

The day's last run/JIM ELDER

Top Destinations: Copper Harbor, Agate Beaches, Calumet, Firesteel River Gorge.

Attractions: Numerous quality resorts and active nightlife in Houghton. Organized snowmobile rallies.

Snowmobile Rentals/Guides: Dan's Polaris, M-26 S., Houghton, MI 49931, (906) 482-6227, 15 machines.

Contact: Keweenaw Tourism Council, P.O. Box 336V, Houghton, MI 49931, (800) 338-7982, or (906) 482-2388 in MI.

MINNESOTA

Hiawathaland

Location: Lake City, MN, 100 miles from Minneapolis.

Trails and Conditions: 350 miles of groomed, well-marked trails connect to 950 miles of trails statewide. Most trails are in scenic river valleys with large wildlife populations. You can ride Wisconsin trails by crossing the lake.

Top Destinations: Whitewater State Park, Lake Zumbro, Hiawatha River Valley, Zumbro Valley, Dells of the Mississippi.

Attractions: Memorial Harwood Forest, eagles and wildlife, January winterfest--sled drag racing, ice-skating, winter parade.

Snowmobile Rentals/Guides: No rentals. Sunset Motel, 1515 North Lakeshore Drive, Lake City, MN 55041, (612) 345-5331 (trail map and trail orientation only).

Contact: Minn. Office of Tourism, 375 Jackson St., 250 Skyway Level, St. Paul, MN 55101, (800) 657-3700, or (612) 296-5029.

Superior Snow Country

Location: Northeast MN bordering Lake Superior and Voyageur National Park.

Trails and Conditions: Hundreds of miles of groomed trails in interconnected wilderness parks--Boundary Waters Canoe Wilderness Area, Voyageur National Park. Trails through forests and along lakeshores.

Top Destinations: Gunflint Trail, Burntside, Vermillions, Namakan, Crane Lake. Attractions: nordic ski-touring, winter camping, downhill skiing.

Snowmobile Rentals/Guides: Scenic Trails Snow Guide Service, 4311 Isle of Pines Drive, Tower, MN 55790, (218) 753-4722, or (218) 753-3218. Guiding only; no rental.

Contact: Grand Rapids Visitor & Convention Bureau, P.O. Box 157, Grand Rapids, MN 55744.

MONTANA

West Glacier

Location: West Glacier, MT, accessible by commercial airline.

Trails and Conditions: 150 miles of groomed trails through alpine meadows, and over high ridges. Deep powder off trails, rarely crowded. Can be very cold.

Top Destinations: Hungry Horse Reservoir, Desert Mountain, Flathead Lake, Emery Bay.

Attractions: Glacier National Park is spectacular. High-altitude passes offer extraordinary views. Big Mountain downhill ski area is 15 miles from West Glacier.

Snowmobile Rentals/Guides: Martin City Polaris (Steve Brown), (406) 387-5266; Fun Unlimited Yamaha, 1805 Hwy. 2 West, Columbia Falls, MT 59912, (406) 892-7676, 10 machines, group discounts; Flathead Adventures, 9215 Hwy. 2 East, Hungry Horse, MT 59926, (406) 387-9090.

Contact: National Park Service, Glacier National Park, West Glacier, MT 59936.

NEW HAMPSHIRE

■

North Country

Location: Located just south of the Canadian border, New Hampshire's North Country is reached from Pittsburg, NH.

Trails and Conditions: 500 miles of groomed trails, mostly logging roads, are available and connect to other trail systems in Canada, Maine and Vermont. Many frozen lakes and rivers are passable. Terrain is mountainous.

Top destinations: Stub Hill, Magalloway Mountain, and Mt. Pigsah.

Attractions: Good fishing, ice-skating, skiing nearby, many small towns for rest stops. Easter Seals snowmobile ride-in each February.

Snowmobile Rentals/Guides: Sportsman's Lodge Snow Tours--RR 1, Box 167, Diamond Pond, NH 03576, (603) 237-5211, 22 machines.

Contact: New Hampshire Snowmobile Assoc., P.O. Box 38, Concord, N.H. 03302, (603) 224-8906; FAX: (603) 226-3880.

NEW YORK

■

Hamilton County

Location: Lake Pleasant, NY, in the Adirondacks.

Trails and Conditions: 750 miles of groomed, well-marked trails. Nearby Inlet, NY boasts another 300 miles of groomed trails. Nice mountains, many scenic lakes.

Top destinations: Long Lake, Blue Mountain Lake, Moose River Plains (superb wide trails--some of the best in the East), and Indian Lake near Inlet. Diverse scenery with many small towns to visit.

Attractions: Countless touring possibilities, good ice-skating and cross-country skiing. Inexpensive accommodations.

Snowmobile Rentals/Guides: Ask for guides at the Willis Lodges, Rt. 28, Seventh Lake, Inlet, NY 13360, (315) 357-3904. No rentals are available in Hamilton County.

Contact: Speculator Lake, Lake Pleasant Chamber of Commerce, P.O. Box 184, Speculator, NY 12164, (518) 548-4521.

Old Forge

Location: 50 miles north of Utica, NY, turnpike exit 31.

Trails and Conditions: 500 miles of groomed, marked trails, rolling hills and woodlands. Powder off trails most of the season. An excellent novice destination.

Top Destinations: Stillwater Reservoir, Enchanted Forest, Moose River Bottoms, and Ice Cave Mountain.

Attractions: Numerous small restaurants and resorts near well-patrolled trails. Skiing, skating and ice fishing nearby.

Snowmobile Rentals/Guides: Old Forge Sport Tours, Old Forge, NY 13420, (315) 357-5594 (Polaris, $275-355 for 2 days). Contact: Tourist Information Center, P.O. Box 68, Old Forge, NY 13420, (315) 369-6983.

UTAH

■

Wasatch Mountain

Location: Midway, UT, near Park City.

Trails and Conditions: Over 100 miles of groomed trails in 22,000-acre Wasatch State Park. Three to six-foot powder off trails. Open meadows, woods, high ridges, elevation 6,000' to 10,000'.

Top Destinations: Bonner Hollow, Cascade Springs, Little Deer Creek.

Attractions: Great alpine running on open ridges, super off-trail powder. Good skiing in nearby Park City. Best place to stay is Homestead Resort--spa, sleigh rides, guided tours, etc.

Snowmobile Rentals/Guides: Homestead Resort, 700 N. Homestead Drive, Midway, UT 84049, (801) 654-1102, (800) 327-7220.

Contact: Park City Chamber of Commerce, Park City, UT 84060, (800) 453-1360.

WISCONSIN

■

Oneida County

Location: Runs are accessed from Minocqua, WI.

Trails and Conditions: Huge network of groomed trails--hundreds of miles to countless destinations. There are over 1,000 lakes accessible by sled, with trails running through open country. Oneida is special--still undiscovered and uncrowded. Season is from middle December through March.

Top Destinations: Corridor 10, Bearskin Trail, Upper Peninsula overland trek.

Attractions: Annual World Series of Snowmobile Drag Racing. XC skiing at Minocqua Winter Park and Nordic Center.

Snowmobile Rentals/Guides: Minocqua Sport Rental, Highway 70 W., Minocqua, WI 54548, (715) 356-4661.

Contact: Minocqua Chamber of Commerce, P.O. Box 1006, Minocqua, WI, 54548, (800) 33-NORTH in WI, (800) 44-NORTH nationwide.

Wisconsin Dells

Location: Wisconsin Dells is at the center of a five-county recreation area in south-central Wisconsin.

Trails and Conditions: 570 miles of marked, mapped and professionally groomed trails. Frozen lakes, meadows and hills. Trails are mostly wooded. (Good snow through the first of March.)

Top Destinations: Castle Rock Lake, Corridor 21 Trail, Devil's Lake.

Attractions: Nearby state parks with 25 miles of XC ski trails. Christmas winter carnival and sled dog racing. Downhill skiing at Christmas and Cascade Mountains.

Snowmobile Rentals/Guides: Chula Vista Resort, P.O. Box 30, North River Rd., Wisconsin Dells, WI 53965, (800) 38-VISTA, (608) 254-8366, (Polaris 340 sports; 2-hour tours cost $55 for single, $85 for double).

Contact: Wisconsin Dells Visitor & Convention Bureau, 115 Wisconsin Dells, WI 53965, (800) 22-DELLS, or (608) 254-8088 in WI.

COURTESY BOMBARDIER, INC.

SNOWMOBILING

RIDING SKILLS

Driving a snowmobile is a bit like riding a motorcycle, a bit like driving a car, and a bit like piloting a Flexible Flyer sled. It's easy to get started, since you steer with handlebars just as on a bicycle. You need to remember that snowmobiles are heavy (500-700 pounds), so you won't be able to pick up your machine easily if you take a spill. Stick with the smaller, lighter machines while you're learning basic skills. Keep your speeds down at first. However, when going through deep snow, it is important to keep up a moderate pace so you don't get bogged down. The biggest challenges are steep hillsides and descents. When you are traversing a steep slope ("sidehilling"), you need to keep your weight in towards the slope. When descending a steep grade, keep your weight back on the sled to avoid submarining the front skis.

Most regional snowmobiling organizations offer introductory programs to teach beginners the basics of snowmobile operation and trail safety. Contact your local dealer for dates and locations.

EQUIPMENT

Sleds come in two-person and solo models. The solos are smaller, lighter and generally more maneuverable. Larger sleds offer luxuries such as electric starters and heated grips. Look for these features when you rent a sled. You'll want independent front suspension if possible. The most common type uses A-arms and springs. Yamaha and some other manufacturers fit their sleds with telescopic front tubes, as used on motorcycles. This system is the most responsive in rough terrain. Virtually all machines use light, powerful two-stroke engines. Try to pick a machine that has automatic oil injection. This way you won't have to struggle with fuel/oil mixing when you're out in the wild and it's 10 below. Electric starting is a big plus, but a backup manual starter is great to have if your battery is weak.

CLOTHING

Obviously, dress warmly. Layering is the best way to go. Start with a bottom layer of polypropylene or thermax close to the skin. On top, you need a good snowmobiling suit. Make sure your boots are completely waterproof and well insulated. If your toes still get chilly, purchase thermal inserts such as Hot Feet, and wear polypropylene socks. Electric socks, vests and mittens are another option, but your sled must have the necessary wiring. Wear good insulated gloves of Goretex, or other breathable, waterproof fabric. Silk inner gloves add comfort and warmth.

By all means, wear a helmet, preferably a full-face model. If you ride bare-headed, even a low-speed fall can cause serious injury. Helmets keep your head warm, make it easier to see, and reduce wind noise. An electric intercom, voice-activated, will allow you to speak with your passenger or another rider. The best, but most expensive, is the Collett Model 40, originally designed for snowmobiles. It is fully guaranteed for three years and costs $169. Basic intercoms, such as the Maxon 49-H5, cost about $75.

VIDEOS

Sno-World Snow Tours will loan you a 30-minute video of one of its 1989 tours based at Togwotee Mountain Lodge, featuring journeys through Yellowstone and Jackson Hole. *Sno-World Snow Tours, 3701 Buttrick Road, S.E., Ada, MI 49301, (616) 676-0397, or 676-3313.*

Each year, **Snowmobile** magazine produces its **Rode Reports Video Annual,** featuring touring/sled-testing footage from premier snowmobiling destinations, such as Grand Lake, CO (1990) and Yellowstone Park (1989). Highly recommended. Videos are available for $29.95 from *Rode Reports, P.O. Box 611, Wayzata, MN 55391,* VHS or Beta, add $10 US for Canadian delivery.

FURTHER INFORMATION

The National Snowmobile Foundation, *P.O. Box 1453, Merrifield, VA 22118,* provides information on snowmobile training and safety, and maintains files on snowmobiling trail networks.

Get your hands on a copy of **Snowmobile** magazine's **Annual Vacation Guide,** available at newsstands for $3.50, or $4.00 from *Ehlert Publishing, 319 Barry Avenue S., Wayzata, MN 55391, (612) 476-2200.* This 150-page resource describes snowmobile destinations throughout North America, reviews new sleds, and calendars important snowmobile events.

Bivouac high above Palisade Glacier on Temple Crag in the Sierras/GORDON WILTSIE

erness Training

▼

*I*n recent years much media attention has been given to so-called survival schools, training centers that teach city folks how to subsist in the wilderness with a minimum of equipment. The press has focused on the "ordeal" aspect of these programs, i.e. extended sessions spent in the wilds, often alone, with little or no food and water. As a result of such reporting, when many people think of Outward Bound and similar programs, what may come to mind are these celebrated solo ordeals. In fact, this is only part of the picture.

Wilderness living instruction falls into two categories: true survival training, and general outdoor skills programs. In a survival school, students learn to live off the land, with virtually no assistance or equipment. The object is to find food and water, make a fire, and construct a shelter. The skills come from a variety of sources, from American Indian lore to military manuals.

By contrast, in a general outdoor skills program, although you will still learn how to fend for yourself in the wilderness, you will also learn other skills more suitable to general outdoor recreation. This may include organizing an extended

The art of fire-making/DAVID WESCOTT, BOSS

backpacking trip, telemarking in the Tetons, paddling a canoe, sailing, or scaling a mountain peak. In this chapter, we review the leading wilderness living programs of both categories-- true survival schools, as well as the general outdoor skill centers.

CHAPTER
24

SPECIALIZED SURVIVAL SCHOOLS

Learning to snag dinner/BRANSON REYNOLDS, BOULDER OUTDOOR SURVIVAL SCHOOL

TO BECOME TRULY SELF-SUFFICIENT IN THE WILD, ONE MUST LEARN "ABORIGINAL" skills such as building a fire, food-gathering and shelter-making. These things were second nature to American Indians and to pioneers, but they are lost arts to contemporary city dwellers. Today, you can learn what it takes to survive in the wild from a number of specialty survival schools around the world.

■ **BOULDER OUTDOOR SURVIVAL SCHOOL**
P.O. Box 3226, Flagstaff, AZ 86003-3226, (801) 335-7404 (summer), or (208) 356-7446 (winter).

For more than a decade, Boulder Outdoor Survival School (BOSS) has been the place to go to gain primitive survival skills--living off the land as Indians did. BOSS conducts 1-week primitive arts and skills courses in the Snake Valley, Idaho; 1-week marine and desert skills courses in Mexico; and 1 to 3-week intensive field courses in Canyon Country, Utah. BOSS's curricula features native cultures' clothing-making methods, tool and hunting-weapon construction, food-gathering, shelter building and ecological awareness.

Both basic earth skills and aboriginal skills courses are offered at $525, and this year a winter living skills and nature awareness course has been added to the curriculum. Students will learn how to construct winter shelters, make snowshoes, lead a dogsled team, navigate overland and administer winter first aid. Cost is $565. The weeklong Mexico desert and marine training course covers surf and spear fishing, boat operation, snorkeling and surf diving, wilderness food selection/preparation, water gathering, and desert survival techniques. The $600 course is conducted in small groups, using 14' inflatables to navigate through the

Kino Bay area in Sonora, Mexico.

The most challenging and notable of BOSS's operations is its $1,225, 27-day field course in the Utah high desert and mountains. The goal of the program is to travel light, with little use of modern technology, and minimal environmental impact. The course consists of four phases after initial orientation. The first few days is spent on a rigorous "immersion" hike, carrying no food, water or modern equipment. The second 10 to 12 days are spent traveling overland, with the class learning and practicing all basic survival skills along the way. During phase three, each student spends 3 to 4 days on a solo survival quest, carrying only minimal tools, and little modern equipment. During the final phase of the course, student teams without instructors make a 5-day wilderness trek, their "graduation expedition."

Sports Afield has labeled the BOSS Field Course the "most challenging and toughest school in the nation," and America magazine has called it "the supreme challenge."

Yet despite the rigor, despite the pain, most participants have found these programs enormously rewarding. One student declared, "It was hard...the most intense experience I have ever had. But it made me appreciate a lot of things. I don't believe I have ever felt more alive." Rating: ★★★★

■ BREAKAWAY SURVIVAL SCHOOL
17 Hugh Thomas Avenue, Holmer, Hereford, England HR4 9RB, (011 44) 432 267 097.

The Breakaway School offers a true, military-style survival training experience in the Welsh countryside. This is the real thing--staying alive in the bush, Rambo-style. Taught by former SAS commando Mike Tyler, this is the ticket if you really want to learn how to live off the land with a minimum of equipment, and aren't squeamish about eating the local fauna. Breakaway's weekend and 5-day courses encompass all the hardcore survival techniques, including building a weatherproof shelter, making a fire, and hunting by bow and arrow. Price is about $100 for a weekend, $220 for a full 5-day course. All instruction is carried out in the wilds of Brecon Beacons National Park, Wales' scenic waterfall country. Participants must supply their own rucksack and sleeping bag. Rating: ★★$

■ GREEN MOUNTAIN WILDERNESS SURVIVAL SCHOOL
P.O. Box 125, Waitsfield, VT 05673, (802) 496-5300.

Mike Casper leads wilderness training courses each summer in the Green Mountains. Skills taught include fire-making, tracking, trapping, fishing, hunting, tool-making and wilderness food preparation (no pots, no stoves). You'll also be shown how to recognize edible plants, how to find and purify water, and how to construct summer and winter wilderness shelters. During the program, students will camp out in Vermont state parks and wilderness areas. Green Mountain's 10-day courses are offered three or four times each summer, and are suitable for persons with

BOULDER OUTDOOR SURVIVAL SCHOOL

or without previous backcountry experience. Cost for the 10-day program will be roughly $950. Rating: ★★

■ THE HARDT SCHOOL OF WILDERNESS LIVING AND SURVIVAL
P.O. Box 231-A, Salisbury, VT 05769, (802) 352-1033.

The Hardt School, located in the Green Mountain National Forest, specializes in 6-day outdoor skills courses for people of all ages, with or without prior wilderness experience. You will be taught all the essential survival skills: building a fire, finding water, constructing a shelter, finding natural food sources, tracking and hunting animals, and wilderness cooking. Complete self-reliance is the goal--using just your hands, your imagination, and the tools you can find in nature.

You won't be expected to endure long periods in the outdoors however. There are no prolonged solos requiring you to forage for food or water. When the classes are in camp, students stay in comfy cabins, with three home-cooked meals a day. Programs are offered twice a month, June through August, for $525. A new, 2-day weekend intro program will also be offered for about $200. Participants have praised the school, including one recent graduate who observed that "one week with Ron [Hardt] is like reading one hundred books on how to survive in a wilderness area." Rating: ★★★

■ INTERNATIONAL ADVENTURE
7 Melbourne Street, Royston, Hertfordshire, England SG8 7BP, (011 44) 763 242 867.

International Adventures offers 10-day survival training courses in the Varmland region of southern Sweden in both summer and winter. With pristine lakes, rolling hills and verdant forests, Sweden is an ideal location to practice wilderness survival skills. In Sweden, unlike much of America, your survival course won't be a dry and dusty marathon in the hot sun. Instead you can enjoy pleasant alpine conditions while practicing your fire-building and rabbit-catching skills.

The instructor is Preben Mortensen, advisor to the Swedish and US Armed Forces. Prices start at around $1,000 for 10 days, exclusive of airfare. No rating.

Celebratory mudbath/RAY GRASS, BOULDER OUTDOOR SURVIVAL SCHOOL

O U T D O O R   S K I L L S

Mt. Rainier/SCOTT SPIKER

BEFORE TACKLING A MAJOR SUMMIT, OR SETTING OFF ON AN EXTENDED WILDERness expedition, you should learn the essential skills from experts. Whatever your particular interests, whether climbing, backcountry skiing or sea kayaking, training centers such as Outward Bound and NOLS can provide you with the techniques and conditioning you need.

■ NATIONAL OUTDOOR LEADERSHIP SCHOOL (NOLS)

P.O. Box AA, Lander, WY 82520, (307) 332-6973; FAX: (307) 332-3031.

Want to learn how to be a mountain guide, how to teach winter camping skills, or how to lead a sea kayak expedition? If so, NOLS may be just the place for you. This is the only wilderness institute specifically set up to train future guides. Programs are conducted year-round in mountaineering, backpacking, sea kayaking, telemark skiing and winter camping. Certain courses even offer college credit. School directors lead 2-week to 3-month expeditions in Wyoming, Alaska, Argentina, Canada, Kenya, Mexico and Washington. If Outward Bound is boot camp, NOLS is officer's candidate school. You learn by doing, and you're shown how to teach what you've learned.

NOLS is not a survival school where you learn to live off the land, or undergo rugged conditioning treks and solos. Rather NOLS strives to "teach the skills and judgment that should prevent you from ever getting yourself into a survival situation." You'll get this kind of training through hands-on experiences in the wilderness. Mountaineering is taught through monthlong courses conducted in the North Cascades, the Wind River Range (Wyoming), Alaska, British Columbia and Kenya. Shorter courses are available for those over 25. NOLS also offers climbing expeditions to Aconcagua in the Andes, and Denali (Mt. McKinley) in Alaska. The Denali Expedition is a serious high-altitude climb for those who have already completed one of the NOLS courses. Cost is $2,850 and seven hours of college credit are available.

Kayak training programs range from 14-day tours of Baja, the Rio Grande or Alaska, to a full semester (83 days) in Baja, during which you'll learn sailing and climbing skills as well. Other multi-activity semester programs (16 to 20 hours of credit) are run in Alaska, Wyoming, the Cascades, Africa and Patagonia. These cost around $5,500 and feature kayaking or rafting, rock- or ice-climbing, and alpine hiking and camping. Shorter monthlong wilderness courses combine hiking with kayaking or rock-climbing and cost about $2,100. Once you've completed one of these basic wilderness classes, you can apply for the NOLS instructor's course (34 days, $2,100).

For those without a lot of time, we recommend NOLS's 2-week specialty courses.

KURT MITCHELL, VOYAGEUR OUTWARD BOUND

These include a $1,700 rock-climbing session in the Wind River Range in Wyoming, a Wilderness Horsepacking Course ($1,850), and our favorite, the Wyoming Winter Ski course, available in both standard (2 weeks $1,250) and age 25+ (8 days, $950) versions. In these programs, you'll learn how to telemark in powder, build snowcaves and igloos, and how to navigate through open wilderness areas.

NOLS is a unique program, with highly qualified instructors and a vast range of activities--44 different courses, in five countries and three continents. If you're serious about learning outdoors skills in sufficient depth to teach others, contact NOLS. Getting college credit was never so exciting or so rewarding. Rating: ★★★★

■ OUTWARD BOUND

384 Field Point Road, Greenwich, CT 06830, (800) 243-8520, or (203) 661-0797 (national office).

Founded in 1941, Outward Bound now encompasses 31 schools and training centers worldwide. It is by far the most well-established outdoor skills school, the holder of the patent if you will. While the core of the Outward Bound curriculum remains a 2 to 3-week wilderness adventure, during which students learn to be self-sufficient in the outdoors, and then make 1 to 3-day solos, there are now many variations on the theme. Various courses focus on ocean skills, rock-climbing, river-rafting, winter camping or canoeing. There are also specialty programs for families, young adults, even corporate or business groups.

All Outward Bound programs feature four distinct training stages. First, students are led through an initial instruction and conditioning program during which they'll learn specific skills needed for their principal activities, whether paddling, rock-climbing or hiking. Next, the students (in groups of 8 to 12) set off with their instructors on an extended wilderness journey--down a river, up a mountain, or into a forest. As they make their way along the route, the students practice and refine their wilderness skills.

Phase three is the solo, the aspect of Outward Bound that has received the most attention. It may seem risky, but the students are monitored daily by instructors, in the interest of safety. The solo is designed to be a challenge, not an ordeal. It is a chance to get away from everything, with a minimum of equipment, and just reflect on one's own feelings and capabilities. Many Outward Bound alumni credit the solo as the best part of the course. At the conclusion of the solos, the last phase begins. The students are divided into smaller groups to complete short expeditions without instructors. When all the student groups have completed their group trek, there is one final group activity--a hike, climb, or paddle--and then participants depart to home, family and civilization.

Outward Bound has an excellent reputation for safety and professionalism. All instructors are Red Cross and CPR trained. Forty percent are Emergency Medical Technicians. Typical staff to student ratio is one to four. Technical programs, such as rock-climbing, are staffed by experts, many with world-class credentials.

With five schools nationwide, Outward Bound offers an enormous variety of courses. Some of our favorites are: ski mountaineering in the Rockies (Colorado School, 18 days, Dec/Jan, $1,300); combined mountaineering, canyon trekking and whitewater rafting in Utah (Colorado School, 21 days, April-Sep, $1,800); canoe expedition and trekking (Voyageur School, 7-29 days, summer, $800-$2,100); combined mountaineering and whitewater rafting in Cascades and Deschutes River, Oregon (Pacific Crest School, summer, 21 days, $2,095); backpacking and rock-climbing (North Carolina School, summer, 9 days, $1,000). Prices are approximate.

Outward Bound also conducts leadership courses offering college credit. Ranging from 4 days to a full semester, these programs are designed for professional educators and would-be outdoor guides. Contact the Kurt Hahan Leadership Center in North Carolina at (704) 437-6112.

■ **COLORADO OUTWARD BOUND SCHOOL**
945 Pennsylvania Street, Denver, CO 80203, (303) 837-0880, or (800) 547-3312.

■ **HURRICANE ISLAND OUTWARD BOUND SCHOOL**
P.O. Box 429, Rockland, ME 04841, (800) 341-1744, or (207) 594-5548.

COURTESY PACIFIC CREST OUTWARD BOUND

■ **NEW YORK CITY OUTWARD BOUND CENTER**
450 Park Avenue South, New York, NY 10016, (212) 340-3500.

■ **NORTH CAROLINA OUTWARD BOUND SCHOOL**
121 N. Sterling Street, Morganton, NC 28655, (704) 437-6112.

■ **PACIFIC CREST OUTWARD BOUND SCHOOL**
0110 S.W. Bancroft Street, Portland, OR 97201, (800) 547-3312, or (503) 243-1993.

■ **VOYAGEUR OUTWARD BOUND SCHOOL**
10900 Cedar Lake Road, Minnetonka, MN 55346, (800) 328-2943, or (612) 542-9255.

Outward Bound Overall Rating: ★★★ to ★★★★ (depending on program)

■ **STONEHEARTH OPEN LEARNING OPPORTUNITY (SOLO)**
RFD 1, Box 163, Conway, NH 03818, (603) 447-6711; FAX: (603) 447-2310.

Where do NOLS and Outward Bound staffers get advanced outdoor rescue training? They go to SOLO, short for Stonehearth Open Learning Opportunity, a wilderness training institute that offers 2-day seminars for about $100 at sites in California, Colorado, New Hampshire, New Mexico, North Carolina and Wyoming. For $1,200, SOLO also offers a 4-week complete wilderness Emergency Medical Technician Certification (EMT) course. Basically, SOLO is geared to teach seasoned outdoor guides how to cope with wilderness emergencies, i.e. how to get themselves and their students out of tough situations that require specialized skills and medical knowledge.

The three cornerstones of the SOLO curriculum are climbing rescue, backcountry medicine (treating altitude sickness and exposure cases), and emergency medicine (advanced first aid, including setting fractures and treating major wounds). Though SOLO is not geared primarily for the general public, its training programs will benefit any individual involved in high-risk, outdoor sports. Rating: ★★★

Indian Creek, Utah/CHRIS NOBLE

SURVIVAL SCHOOLS & WILDERNESS TRAINING

WHAT YOU CARRY HOME

You don't need survival school to learn how to enjoy the outdoors, certainly not like you need basic training to stay alive as a combat soldier. Modern outdoor equipment has made it possible for the average person to complete a weeklong backpack with no major calamities besides sore feet. One need not be a modern-day Daniel Boone to have a good time in the wilderness. Why then subject yourself to the rigors of a wilderness training school? Because you'll probably end up a better, stronger person-- one who sets higher goals in life, and has the self-confidence to achieve them.

One student called Outward Bound her "most meaningful personal experience...more cerebral and spiritual than anything else. In every way, I learned I was much greater and more capable than I thought." Another student noted: "I think my Outward Bound experience was just as much a course 'inward-bound' as it was 'outward' into the wilderness. I was able to sort out some questions of the heart, as well as my physical and mental capacities. My solo was largely responsible for this. It was one of the greatest, most peaceful times of my life." This echoes the words of famed climber Reinhold Messner: "I don't climb mountains simply to vanquish their summits. What would be the point of that? I place myself voluntarily into dangerous situations to learn to face my fears and doubts, my innermost feelings."

Will all this really help in the years to come? Most who have completed a wilderness training course say yes, emphatically. A NOLS student observed of her experience: "The work you are doing goes far beyond the extent of the trip. It shapes attitudes, affects lives, and inspires careers." Outward Bound and programs like it tap human potential, and open people's eyes. And that, perhaps, is the great reward of all adventure--it forces us to summon our courage, and thereby find new limits.

Sunset watch in Canyonlands/SCOTT MARKEWITZ

GETTING READY

Survival schools involve tough, strenuous activity--mountaineering and backpacking over long distances with limited supplies of food and water. The object, to a great degree, is to live off the land as primitive peoples did. This can be quite a shock to those used to sending out for pizza, or even to experienced backpackers, who still carry their food with them. The average weight loss on a BOSS 3-week survival course is 10 to 15 pounds.

You don't have to be a decathlete to endure these courses, but you should do your best to arrive fit, and mentally prepared for what lies ahead. Remember it is your courage and your will, more so than your physical abilities, that will pull you through these programs and make them a success. As much as these survival schools challenge your body, they test your spirit. And that is why you can achieve an inner strength through these programs that no gym could ever provide. But you must be ready to push your limits, otherwise you'll resent what you're being asked to do. This is supposed to be a vacation, after all.

PUBLICATIONS

Outdoor Survival Skills, by Larry Dean Olson. Official text of the Boulder Outdoor Survival School (BOSS). $9.95 plus $2.75 handling from BOSS, P.O. Box 3226, Flagstaff, AZ 86003-3226.

Primitive Outdoor Skills, by Richard Jamison. Available from BOSS, $12.50 plus $2.75 for handling.

Backwoodsman magazine. Useful articles on wilderness skills, emergency shelters, hunting and fishing.

VIDEO

Land of One Season--The Basics of Mountain Safety is an award-winning video that covers the most important wilderness survival techniques. Survival and rescue skills are explained and demonstrated by mountain guides and backcountry medicine experts. Topics covered include hypothermia, avalanche survival, overland navigation, weather, shelter-building, and selection of proper food, fuel and clothing. $19.95 plus $3.50 shipping from Trade Northwest, Inc., 8259 SW Sirrus Drive, Beaverton, OR 97005, (800) 828-9816.

Trekking

Machapuchare at sunset, Dhampus Ridge, Annapurna Region/BARBARA ROWELL

360

*Walking is the way the serious traveler moves.
It sets him down in the midst of the action,
homelander to visitor, eye to eye.*
-Virginia Barton Brownback

▼

*L*oosely defined, a trek is a walking tour through wild or primitive areas. Unlike a backpack trip, you typically stay in shelters along the way, eliminating the need to carry full camping gear. Without tents, stoves and food to transport, your load is only a few pounds. The classic Himalayan trek takes you from village to village, over high alpine trails. You lodge with the locals, eating with them in the evenings, and getting to know their way of life. A trek through the Alps is similar, although you're more likely to spend the evenings in huts or chalets than in villages.

It's very easy to organize your own locally guided trek in many locations around the world, or you can book one of the hundreds of package treks offered by the large, commercial outfitters. Whatever your preference, this chapter will help make your trekking holiday the trip of a lifetime.

CHAPTER
25

Trekker on Khumbu Glacier, Khumbu Himal, Nepal/CHRIS NOBLE

YOU CAN EXPECT A RICH CULTURAL EXPERIENCE ON MOST TREKS IN LESS developed countries. Walking brings you into much closer contact with the reality of foreign cultures than is possible with other modes of travel. Remember, most people in the world don't have cars. They use their feet, or if they're lucky, a donkey or horse. When you walk, you enter their world, and see it through their eyes.

PERU

The Inca Trail to Machu Picchu

The Incas once ruled over an empire that rivaled that of Rome. Today, the Camino Inca (the Inca Trail), still carries travelers to the famed Lost City of the Incas, Machu Picchu. For 400 years Machu Picchu eluded western searchers until it was discovered by a Yale archaeologist in 1911.

On most Machu Picchu treks Quechua Indian porters and mules carry the bulk of your gear and look after your needs in camp. The route follows ancient Inca roads and tunnels through cloud forests, condor habi-tats and orchid zones, rising up through the jungle and crossing the spectacular 13,700' Warmihuanusca Pass. After about 5 days of hiking, you pass at last through the stone archway called Intipunku--the Gate of the Sun. There, below you, is the sacred city of Machu Picchu, looking even more exotic than any Hollywood set designer could have imagined.

A Machu Picchu trek is typically part of a longer 12 to 14-day itinerary that includes Cuzco and Lake Titicaca. Even if you're anxious to get to Machu Picchu, it's important to stay in the cities for a few days to acclimatize to the high altitudes. Though pack animals will carry your gear on the trek, this is still a demanding hike.

Many American outfitters operate Inca Trail treks. A good, moderately priced trip is offered by Wildland Adventures from April through September. On the $1,495 14-day itinerary you trek to Machu Picchu in 5 days, visit Cuzco and Lima, and may elect an optional excursion to Peru's Manu National Park, considered by many naturalists to be the finest nature preserve in the Western Hemisphere. (If you have *any* interest in exotic wildlife, Manu shouldn't be missed.) Wildland has very good contacts in Peru, and offers a richer cultural experience than many of its competitors. Wildland also operates an 11-day Inca Trail Preservation Trek each year. Cost is a reasonable $1,295; call (800) 345-4453, or (206) 365-0686 for details.

While Machu Picchu is a magnificent destination in every respect, its very popularity means that you will probably encounter many other trekkers along the way. To avoid the crowds at peak season, consider Overseas Adventure Travel's (OAT) Highland Trek. This itinerary follows little-used

Eight Great Trekking Adventures

pathways, and offers two days of rafting on the Vilcanota River in the Sacred Valley of the Incas. After the whitewater segment, the serious walking begins outside of Mollepata overlooking the Apurimac Valley. The trek continues to a 15,100' high camp beneath the massive south face of 20,600' Mt. Salcantay. From there you explore high glaciers and remote Incan trading routes before boarding a train to Machu Picchu. Cost is about $1,900 for 17 days, with 8 days spent hiking. Call OAT at (800) 221-0814. (Full outfitter listings are found on pages 370-71.)

Travelers' Watch: Travelers may be at risk in remote mountain regions of Peru due to political activity. However, the itineraries described above are considered safe, if you travel with an organized group.

NEPAL

The Annapurna Circuit

Many veteran trekkers consider the 200-mile Annapurna Circuit the ultimate long-distance trek in Nepal. The route encircles the Annapurna Range--a collection of mas-sive, snow-covered summits, many over 26,000'. While walking the circuit, you will encounter 17,000' passes, glaciers, the world's deepest valley, pine forests, rice paddies, tundra, remote villages and an-cient monasteries. Most trips start up the Marsyandi River, then continue north in the wooded Manang Valley through Chamje, Pisang and Braga (or other villages in the valley). You must take your time initially, getting used to the elevation. Midway through the trip, you will encoun-ter 17,771' Thorong La Pass, one of the most formidable passes in trekking. You must start up the pass in the middle of the night, but when you clear the pass at daybreak, your reward is a breathtaking view of the world's tallest mountains glowing in the pastel light of dawn.

On the other side of the pass, it is a steep descent to the Hindu and Buddhist shrines at Muktinath (12,500'). From there, you pass through the Kali Gandaki Gorge, a rugged valley three times as deep as the Grand Canyon. As you descend the Kali Gandaki towards Pokhara, there are continuous views of 26,796' Dhaulagiri, and other 20,000'+ peaks in the Annapurnas. Take time to en-joy the view, as Pokhara is the last stop on the circuit before returning to Kathmandu.

A host of seasoned outfitters can take you around the Annapurna Circuit. Hima-layan Travel is the budget leader; it offers

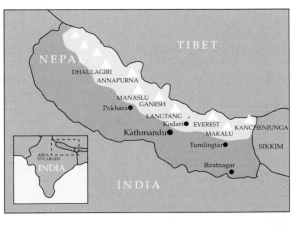

Dhaulagiri, Nepal/GALEN ROWELL

a 27-day full circuit trip (19 days on the trail) for just $1,550. Journeys' 28-day trek (21 walking days) avoids the busy camps and trail bottlenecks; it is offered in March, April, October and November for $1,895.

Worldwide Adventures, one of the most experienced outfitters in Nepal, does the circuit in 31 days, allowing trekkers some layover days while up in the high country. The cost is about $2,300. Last but not least, Mountain Travel has been running the circuit for years, and its program has been praised by customers as "a terrific experience, well planned and organized." Trips run spring and fall and cost $2,190 to $2,490 depending on seasons.

THAILAND

Hilltribe Odyssey

In the northwest corner of Thailand, near the junction of the Burmese, Thai and Laotian borders, live Thailand's celebrated hilltribes.

A visit to the Thai hilltribes is a unique cultural odyssey. In their remote mountain retreats, the people live in a world without laws, taxes or governments. While in recent years the hilltribes have been increasingly drawn into the modern world (some vil-

lages now have electricity, and a motor-bike or truck is occasionally seen in larger settlements), there are still many village tribes that retain their ancient culture relatively intact.

The center for hilltribe trekking is the

CHRIS NOBLE

city of Chiang Mai in northern Thailand, a day's bus ride from Bangkok. A busy commercial center, Chiang Mai is a haven for budget travelers. At one of the many guest houses, you can book a clean room with a private bath for under $10 per night. To find a trekking agency, head for the Old City, a walled enclosure on the eastern side of town. There, along Chaiyapoom Road, you'll find a dozen agencies offering guided hilltribe treks. The competition keeps prices incredibly low. Expect a 5-day, 4-night trek to run roughly $40 to $70.

Following a ride by long-tail boat or bamboo raft to the trailhead, you will hike about 15 miles each day. Lunch will be served up in one village and dinner cooked at your evening's destination. As you will stay inside village huts, you only need to take a daypack with your own personal gear. In the winter, however, it is advisable to bring a sleeping bag. The thatched walls of the huts provide no insulation against the cold night air, and you will be provided with the thinnest of blankets.

There are many decent trekking companies, but Folkways Trekking or Summit Tribal Treks are among the most popular, and both have skilled guides who will take you to places not overrun by tourists. You

can also book a hilltribe trek with an American company, but such a trip could easily cost you ten times what you might pay in Thailand, and not be as good. (Most western companies use local Thai outfitters anyway, and the best are busy with their own trips.) Our Folkways guide in Thailand spoke Thai, English, German, Chinese and two tribal dialects. Over the course of our weeklong trek, we had three helpers who spoke another four tribal languages between them. The ability to communicate with native peoples, via the guides, was the highlight of the trip.

An absolutely essential piece of equipment for any trip to Thailand is the guidebook, *Thailand--A Travel Survival Kit*, from Lonely Planet Publications. This single resource is more useful than all the other Thailand travel guides combined.

AUSTRIA

Tirolian Hut to Hut

Trekking through the Alps offers spectacular scenery, and none of the logistical hassles or health risks associated with Asian trekking venues. Trekking in the Alps without a guide is also very easy; this can't be said about the Himalayas. While commercial programs in the Alps have concentrated on Switzerland (Bernese Oberland), and France (Chamonix Haute Route), Austria would be our first choice for an Alpine trek. Compared to Switzerland or France, the people are friendlier, the prices are lower, and the huts will be less crowded in the summer--a vital consideration.

The Austrian hut system is remarkable. There are over 120 huts in the Tirol region alone, ranging from deluxe to bare bones. All provide blankets and mattresses, and food is served at most of the facilities. The cost is a reasonable $10 to $15 per night. Compared to huts in Switzerland and France, the Austrian "huttes" are definitely the most comfortable. Some are even lavish, and Austrian hospitality is legendary. Even the largest huts can get very busy,

however, particularly during summer weekends in August.

The range of hiking options is enormous. Many huts can be reached on short day-hikes from ridges served by cable cars or ski lifts. Although many huts are just a few hours in from the nearest road, hiking in the Alps does require good conditioning. Most of the trails are located above 6,000', and you may have to climb 2,500' or more to reach your destination. Adventurous trekkers will want to sample the Weitwanderweg--a 750-mile pathway traversing all of Austria from one end to the other. Not all of the Weitwanderweg is appropriate for trekking, but the section from Innsbruck south passes through the Stubai, Zillertal and Gross Venediger

Balti, Karakoram Himalaya/GALEN ROWELL

Alps, all premier trekking locales.

Planning your own Austria Alps trek is easy. A comprehensive directory of huts and alpine clubs can be obtained from the

Austrian National Tourist Office, 500 Fifth Avenue, Suite 2009-2022, New York, NY 10110 (212) 944-6880, or 11601 Wilshire Boulevard, Suite 2480, Los Angeles, CA 90025, (213) 477-3332. (Request the Tirol Summer Vacation Guide for hikers, and an application for the Austrian Alpine Club--membership in the club will entitle you to a 50 percent discount off hut fees.)

If you prefer a commercially guided trek, Mountain Travel offers 8-day hut to hut alpine tours in the Tirolian Alps (5 days hiking) for $890. Call (800) 227-2384 for details. The Austrian Alpine Club, Wilhelm-Greil-Strasse 15, A-6020 Innsbruck, Austria, (011 43) 5222 24107 can direct you to Austrian commercial outfitters which offer guided treks from 2 days to 2 weeks.

JALJALE HIMALAYA

The Other Nepal

Trekking activity in Nepal has increased dramatically in the past two decades. In 1972, 2,000 Nepali trekking permits were issued. In 1988, the figure was 54,000. Now, in the peak season of October-November, the busiest trails in the Annapurna area resemble Yellowstone Park in summertime. Some villages in the lower Annapurna region will see as many as 250 trekkers camped out each day.

Thankfully, however, many regions of Nepal remain relatively undiscovered. (Eighty percent of the commercial trekking is confined to 10 percent of the trails.) A fine alternative to the trekking superhighways is the Jaljale Himalaya, a region of eastern Nepal that sees very little trekking activity. Above the Clouds Trekking (ACT) pioneered walking tours to the Jaljale region in 1988, and it is the clear choice for a guided trek in the Jaljale today. ACT has refined its Jaljale itinerary very well over the past three years, and employs some of the finest guides in Nepal.

The Jaljale trek follows a high ridge trail, allowing easy walking and nearly continuous views of four of the world's five highest peaks: Everest, Kanchenjunga, Lhotse and Makalu. The trek begins with a flight into Biratnagar, Nepal's second largest city. From here the traverse of the ridge begins, first through isolated hill villages, then through a dense rhododendron forest. Upon reaching the Jaljale itself, a spiny mountain that runs north-south for over 25 miles, the trekkers will stay above 14,000' for nearly a week.

Coming off the ridge, the group will descend along the Mewa River to the rarely visited town of Topke Gola. An ancient Tibetan trading center, few outsiders have been to this remote outpost, where the rhythms of life have changed little over the centuries. The walking part of the tour concludes at Shidua. From there, the group drives to Dharan and then Biratnagar for the return flight to Kathmandu.

The total adventure lasts 30 days, of which 19 are actually spent hiking. Trips depart in March and October each year; those who travel in the spring will be treated to beautiful wild flower displays, while fall is the greenest period. Anticipated land cost is $2,275. We highly recommend this program, as well as ACT's other Nepal treks. ACT has a strong commitment to low-impact trekking,

NEW ZEALAND
The Milford Track

New Zealand's Milford Track is frequently called "the finest walk in the world." This 5-day walk covers 33 miles of superb scenery through the Alps and fjords of New Zealand's South Island. Along the way, you'll stay at guest lodges, hut-style, so you need only a daypack with your personal gear--clothes, camera, umbrella (don't laugh), and toiletries. The trip is not particularly strenuous. It can, however, be very wet; this part of the South Island is infamous for its long rainy seasons.

The trek starts with a boat ride across Lake Te Anu, the gateway to Fjordland National Park. The trail follows the course of the Clinton River along deep canyons and glaciated valleys, and through rainforests of tree ferns and beeches. From atop McKinnon Pass, there are great views of the park's fjords and the massive snow-capped peaks of the Southern Alps.

The Milford Track is so popular that it can be booked up months in advance, and most of the spaces are controlled by New

Fitzroy Climb, Patagonia/GALEN ROWELL

ed 5-day tour. You carry only a daypack and stay in deluxe chalets; everything from meals to sleeping quarters is prearranged. If this sounds a bit too expensive, sign up for the $95 Freedom Walk, a self-guided 4-day walk. You stay in modest huts and carry all your own gear, including food and camping equipment. The Freedom Walk is essentially a backpack trip, although you do sleep indoors. Packs and other equipment can be rented from a number of shops in Queenstown, your departure point for the bus to Lake Te Anu.

Both kinds of Milford Track outings can be booked in America through the NZ Tourism Office, 501 Santa Monica Boulevard, Suite 300, Santa Monica, CA 90401, (800) 388-5494. Request the Milford Track information packet and specify whether you want a guided or an independent tour.

USSR
From Kamchatka to the Caucasus

For those of us who remember the Berlin Airlift and the Cuban Missile Crisis, the changes in the Soviet Union and Eastern Europe have been almost overwhelming. The positive result of all these changes however, is that the Soviet Union has finally opened its doors in a major way to western tourist activity, including trekking.

The leading trekking operator for the Soviet Union is REI Adventures of Seattle.

Khumbu Himal, Nepal/CHRIS NOBLE

and preservation of the traditional Nepali way of life. Contact Above the Clouds Trekking, P.O. Box 398, Worcester, MA 01602, (800) 233-4499, or (508) 799-4499 in MA.

Zealand tour companies. To hike the Milford Track, you have two options, both requiring at least six months' advance notice. For roughly $700 you can book a guid-

Among this summer's Soviet adventures, REI will offer wilderness treks in Central Asia and an exploratory photo-trek in the remote Kamchatka Peninsula.

The Kamchatka trek is the most unique and exciting of REI's offerings. Off limits to westerners until recently, the Kamchatka peninsula is a land of stunning natural beauty--a realm of glaciers, geysers, volcanoes and spectacular wildlife. The land and river expedition begins with a helicopter lift to the Zhupanova River, the starting point for a 4-day trek to the Kronotsky Nature Preserve, home to Siberian bighorn sheep, sable, marmots and arctic brown bears. The trip concludes with 3 days of rafting on the Zhupanova, a prime salmon fishery. Participants on this adventure will be among the very first westerners to visit the Kamchatka wilderness. The cost of the 12-day trip will be about $3,000 with departures July through September.

If Kamchatka is too pricey, consider a $1,300 2-week trek through the heart of the rugged Turkestan range in Central Asia. From the Aksu Valley in Kirghizia, the group crosses two high passes, overnighting in wild flower carpeted valleys with Kirghiz herders. The scenery is impressive, with massive granite faces and glaciers rivaling the Alps. The trip concludes in colorful Samarkand--a step back in time. Contact REI Adventures, P.O. Box 88126, Seattle, WA 98138, (800) 662-2236.

PATAGONIA

Latin Wilderness

It is hard to describe Patagonia without resorting to adjectives like "breathtaking" or even "mind-boggling." Imagine the Alps, Yosemite and Alaska rolled into one, and you get the idea. In the Towers of Paine National Park, you will find razor-sharp pinnacles of granite rising more than a mile straight up into the clouds. Alaskan-scale glaciers cut through forested valleys to the sea, spilling huge blocks of ice violently into the cold waters. The Moreno Glacier, a sheer wall of white the size of a city, dominates the horizon for miles as it pushes its way into the Pacific.

Although Patagonia couldn't be considered a mainstream trekking destination, you still have a wide range of commercially led options. The ultimate Patagonian adventure may be Overseas Adventure Travel's (OAT) 17-day Patagonia Explorer trip, which offers trekking in Paine National Park, a 3-day raft trip down the Grey and Serrano Rivers to the Pacific, and a 4-day cruise on a motorsailer through the fjords of the Chilean Archipelago. Condor sightings are virtually guaranteed and you will observe many other indigenous species including pumas, guanacos (Chilean llamas) and Andean foxes. Trips depart November through March at a cost of $2,790. Call OAT at (800) 221-0814.

Mountain Travel runs a moderately priced 16-day camping trek that covers both Paine and Glacier National Parks. You spend 3 days hiking and camping among the granite needles of the Towers of Paine. Horses will transport all the gear, freeing the trekkers to carry only daypacks. Then in Glacier National Park, you will camp in the shadow of the 11,073' Fitzroy Massif, which towers a full 6,000' over the glaciers at its base. Price for the program will range from $2,100 to $2,400 with departures in February, March, October and November.

Call (800) 227-2384 for details.

Wilderness Travel offers a similar 24-day trekking-camping expedition that has won very high praise from past customers. Along with 4 days in Paine National Park, and 4 days camping near the Fitzroy Massif, Wilderness Travel offers a visit to Lapatia National Park along the Beagle Channel, and a boat trip up Last Hope Sound to the face of Balmaceda, the southern tip of Patagonia's continental icecap. This program runs in January and February for roughly $2,590. Call (800) 247-6700.

Any first-time visitor to Patagonia should come prepared for a harsh climate. Patagonia is noted for its bone-chilling winds, and extremely changeable weather conditions. You can experience rain, snow, sleet and sunshine all within the course of an hour. As long as you keep this in mind, and don't expect to come home with a suntan, you won't be disappointed.

The 'Horns of Paine,' Chilean Patagonia/STEVE GILROY

30 Great Treks Around The World

This is only a small sampling of the commercial treks available. Most trekking companies offer dozens of fine treks worldwide, so use this chart only as a starter for your trip planning. Treks are rated 1-5 for difficulty, 1 being the easiest; ★ to ★★★★★ for quality; $ or $$ for special value. Codes used are: AIR (Price includes airfare); BP (Backpack--trekker carries all gear, up to 40 lbs.); DP (Trekker carries gear in daypack); RFT (Raft trip); BT (Boat trip); NP (National Park); TR (Trekking segment). All prices are per person, double occupancy, and are subject to change. For African treks (Mt. Kilimanjaro, Rwanda gorilla-tracking etc.), consult the Safari Chapter. For jungle destinations (Amazon, Costa Rica, Papua New Guinea, Irian Jaya), consult the Jungle Chapter.

BILL ABBOTT, WILDERNESS TRAVEL

Location	Description	Max. Alt.
ALPS (EUROPE)		
Mont Blanc Circuit	Inn to inn alpine hikes, climbing options, light packs, "better" lodging & food.	8,500'
Swiss Traverse	Chamonix to Zermatt, hut to hut. Alpine passes, lakes, meadows.	9,750'
Alpine Pass Route	200 stunning miles from Lichtenstein to Lake Geneva, 14 high passes, climbers' huts & inns.	9,180'
BHUTAN/SIKKIM		
Dragon Kingdom	True medieval kingdom. Few trekkers. High meadows, ancient monasteries, very pristine with traditional native culture. Trips coincide with spectacular spring & fall religious festivals.	15,800'
Sikkim Kanchenjunga	Darjeeling-Gangtok, Tista River, high meadows, view Kanchenjunga (28,200') and many 20,000'+ peaks. Unspoiled, new area for trekking.	16,000'
Sikkim Trek	High remote passes, lakes and glaciers, monasteries, view Kanchenjunga from 17,500'.	17,500'
CHINA		
Ghengis Khan Trek	Moscow, Ulan Bator (Mongolia) Nat'l Festival, Khanghai Mtns. TR, Gobi Desert, Great Wall, Beijing.	8,000'
ECUADOR		
Andean Highlands Cultural Trek	Alpine trek among remote villages and snow-capped volcanoes (Mt. Chimborazo). Amazon option.	16,000'
FRANCE		
Burgundy Chateaux	Easy walking tour from chateaux to chateaux. Wine-tasting. Michelin eateries. Short hikes.	4,000'
GREECE		
Pindos Peaks	Ioanina to Lake Pamvotis, Vikos Gorge, high passes, 9,000' peaks. Ionian Coast.	7,900'
INDIA		
Garwahl (Land of Gods)	Delhi, Mussoorie (Hindu shrines), 9-day pilgrimage route to source of Ganges, 19,500' Mt. Meru.	14,500'
Dhaula Dhar Traverse	India's best scenery--lush valleys, wild flowers, and monster peaks of the Himachal. Few trekkers.	15,000'
LADAKH		
Across Zanskar	New trekking areas, Zanskar range, nomadic tribes, palaces, Buddhist shrines.	18,000'
Zanskar Trek	High (15,000') passes, monasteries & palaces. Very unspoiled. Superb guides.	18,000'
MOROCCO		
M'Goun Massif	Marrakech-Iskattafern, high pass to Imazayn, Tissili gorge, ascend M'Goun Massif.	13,347'
EASTERN NEPAL		
Everest East Face	Remote trail--Arun River valley, Salpa Pass, view Makula, Everest. Depart Lukla.	16,500'
Everest Walk-in	Bhandar Pass, forests, monasteries, Khumbu Glacier, Kala Pattar, Everest base.	18,200'
Himal. Discovery Safari	Gorkha Valley east of Annapurna--new area to trekking, Chitwan NP safari, RFT.	11,000'
WESTERN NEPAL		
Annapurna Short Circuit	Features all circuit highlights (see p. 363), while avoiding congested trails. Spectacular vistas.	17,700'
Annapurna Sanctuary	Kathmandu, Kali Gandaki, sanctuary, view 12 20,000' peaks, Modi Khola valley.	13,500'
Best of Nepal	Annapurna Circuit 9-day TR, 2-day RFT Trisuli, Chitwan safari, 8-day Lukla TR.	15,000'+
NEW ZEALAND		
South Island	Abel Tasman NP, Matukituki Valley (Mt. Aspiring, Rob Roy Glacier), Mt. Cook, farm stays. Car travel between alpine hikes. Either backpacking or day-hiking programs.	7,000'
NORWAY		
Fjords and Isles	Olso-Nordfjord Fjord, Arctic Circle flight, Lofoten Isles, North Cape tundra trek.	NA
Alps & Fjords	Boat up Sognefjord, Jotunheimen Mtns. (highest in No. Europe), Mt. Huts, glaciers.	8,000'
PAKISTAN		
K2/Concordia Trek	Shigar Valley, Braldu gorge, Baltoro glacier traverse, Concordia & K2 basecamps.	17,000'
PATAGONIA		
Patagonian Wildlands Safari	Short treks from camps and inns, Valdez Peninsula (penguins), Moreno Glacier and Patagonia Icecap, Magellan Straits BT, Tierra Del Fuego NP. Outstanding wildlife.	NA
Trek on the Wild Side	Backpack trip through Glacier NP, Fitzroy Massif, Cordon Moyano traverse, Lago Argentino condor area, Upsala Glacier, Estancia Christina. Very scenic, new area for trekking.	NA
PERU		
Incas and Amazon	Cuzco, Sacred Valley, Inca Trail, Machu Picchu, rafting, Tambopata Rain Forest Wildlife Preserve.	15,000'
Ultimate Andes	Lima-Cuzco, Sacred Valley, Mt. Salcantay, Machu Picchu, view Auzangate (20,644').	15,300'
TURKEY		
Mt. Ararat Ascent	Kackar Mtns., 4-day Ararat ascent, Noah's Ark site, Lake Van camp, Istanbul.	16,946'

CHRIS NOBLE *GALEN ROWELL* *GORDON WILTSIE*

TRIP DAYS (Trek Days)	PORTERS/VAN/PACK ANIMALS	COST	OUTFITTER	DIFFICULTY	SEASON	RATING
15	No (DP)	$2000 Est.	Mountain Travel	3	Summer	★★★
16 (10)	No (DP)	$1100	Himalayan Travel	3.5	Summer	★★★
15 (12)	Van	$1150	REI	3.5	Summer	★★★
16 (10)	Yes	$3500–3900	Overseas Ad. Travel	3.5	Mar, Apr, Sept	★★★★
21 (11)	Yes	$3400	Himal. Travel	3	Mar, Sept	★★★★
22 (12)	Yes	$2590	Mountain Travel	3.5	Apr, Sept, Oct	★★★
22 (6)	Yes	$4200 with air from UK	Himalayan Kingdoms	2.5	July	★★★★
15 (7)	Yes	$1495	Wildland Adventures	3	July, Aug	★★★★
8 (6)	Van	$2100	Progressive Trav., (800) 245-2229	1.5	June-Oct	★★★
17	Part van	$975	Himalayan Travel	3	June, Sept	★★
18 (9)	Yes	$1750	Adventure Center	3	June	★★
21 (15)	Yes	$1550	Himalaya Trekking	4	Oct	★★★
31 (21)	Yes	$3190	Wilderness Travel	4.5	July	★★★
31 (20)	Yes	$2395	Journeys	4	July, Aug	★★★★
16	Yes	$925	Himalayan Travel	3.5	Aug, Sept	★★
30	Yes	$2250	Above the Clouds	4	Sept	★★★★
27	Yes	$1725	Himal. Travel	3.5	Spr, Fall	★★
20 (9)	Yes	$1695	Journeys	3	Oct, then May	★★★
23 (16)	Yes	$1900	Himalaya Trekking	3.5	Apr–May, Oct–Nov	★★★
20 (13)	Yes	$2190	Wilderness Travel	3	Apr, Oct–Nov	★★★★
29	Yes	$2417	World Expeditions	3	Sept–May	★★★
20 (18)	No	$2000–2400	NZ Travelers (802) 985-8865	3.5	Nov–Apr	★★★
17 (13)	Yes	$3690	Wilderness Travel	2	Summer	★★★
17 (12)	No	$1790	Mountain Travel	4	July, Aug	★★★
29	Yes	$3400	Himalayan Travel	4	Spr, Summer	★★★
19 (4)	Yes	$2200	Wildland Adventures	2	Jan, Feb	★★★
17 (13)	No	$2900 Est.	Ecosummer Exp. (604) 669-7741	4	Dec–Jan	★★★
15 (7)	Yes	$2000 Est.	Overseas Ad. Travel	3	Apr–Aug, Nov–Dec	★★★
19 (12)	Yes	$2290	Wilderness Travel	3.5	May–Aug	★★★
12–16	Yes	$1550–2200	Mtn.Trav., Wildland Adv.	4	May–Oct	★★

Trekking in the Biafo Valley, Baltistan, Pakistan/GALEN ROWELL

The Top Ten Trekking Companies

*E*ACH OF THESE COMPANIES RUNS OUTSTANDING, WELL-ORGANIZED TREKS TO A host of exotic destinations worldwide. Some specialize in particular destinations--Above the Clouds Trekking, for example, built its reputation on trips to Asia and the Himalayas. Other companies, such as the Adventure Center, can take you virtually anyplace in the world. Before leaving on a trek, even if you plan to go alone, or to obtain a guide abroad, we recommend that you contact the trekking companies below, and study their catalogs carefully. The literature will give you not only some good basic itineraries, but also a sense of what routes are done to excess these days. If you find 10 companies going to the same place at the same time of year, you know you'll see more tourists than you'd probably care to. Consider all the options; remember, there is plenty to see in Nepal or the Andes without hiking the same route as everyone else.

■ ABOVE THE CLOUDS TREKKING
P.O. Box 398, Worcester, MA 01602-0398, (800) 233-4499, or (508) 799-4499 in MA; FAX: (508) 797-4779.

Destinations: Costa Rica, Botswana, Patagonia, Kenya (Mt. Kenya), Madagascar, Ireland, Alps (Mt. Blanc), Nepal (Everest, Kanchenjunga, Sanctuary, Annapurna), India (Kashmir/Ladakh), Bhutan, Pakistan (Hunza Valley, Shimshal Valley), Thailand. Highly Recommended.
20 Days Nepal: $1,650. Rating: ★★★★

■ ADVENTURE CENTER
1311 63rd Street, Suite 200, Emeryville, CA 94608, (800) 227-8747, (800) 228-8747 in CA, or (510) 654-1879.

Destinations: Virtually everywhere-- Egypt, Israel, Spain, Portugal, Yugoslavia, the Alps, Iceland, Greece, Turkey (Lycia), Morocco (Atlas Mtns.), Rwanda/Zaire, India, Nepal (Everest approach, Annapurna, Langtang-Jugal, Chitwan Nat'l Park), Pakistan (K2, Concordia), Thailand, Malaysia, Borneo, Peru (Inca Trail), Patagonia, Australia, New Zealand.
26 Days Nepal: $1,760. Rating: ★★ to ★★★

■ HIMALAYAN TRAVEL, INC.
(Sherpa Expeditions), P.O. Box 481, Greenwich, CT 06836, (800) 225-2380, (203) 622-6777 (CT).

Destinations (highlights): Africa (Morocco, Kilimanjaro), Bhutan/Sikkim, China (Heavenly Mountains), European Alps, Greece, India, Ladakh, Pakistan (K2, Karakoram), Peru (Huayhuash, Machu Picchu), Nepal (Everest, Kanchenjunga, Annapurna), Spain (Pyrenees, Sierra Nevada), sTurkey (Mt. Ararat).
28 Days Nepal: $1,550. Rating: ★★ to ★★★

■ JOURNEYS/WILDLAND ADVENTURES
4011 Jackson Road, Ann Arbor, MI 48106, (800) 255-8735; (800) 345-4453 for Wildlands Adv.

Destinations: Nepal (Annapurna), Tibet, Ladakh, Kenya, Peru, Ecuador (Andes), Costa Rica, Madagascar, Patagonia. Journeys offers Africa and Himalayas; Wildland specializes in South America. Strong emphasis on ecology and native culture.
30 days Nepal: $2,195. Rating: ★★★★

■ MOUNTAIN TRAVEL/SOBEK, INC.
6420 Fairmont Avenue, El Cerrito, CA 94530, (800) 227-2384.

Destinations (highlights): Africa (Botswana, Kenya, Tanzania), Alaska, Austria, Bhutan/Sikkim, European Alps (Mt. Blanc circuit, Haute Route), Greece (Pindos Range), Himalaya Traverse, India (Peimonte), Kashmir, Ladakh, China (Karakoram), Nepal (Everest trail, Arun Valley, Annapurna), Norway (Fjordland), Pakistan (Baltoro, K2), Papua New Guinea, Peru (Inca Trail, Cordillera Blanca), Patagonia, Poland (Tatras), Scotland, Spain, Thailand, Tibet (Everest East), Turkey (Ararat), Venezuela (Lost World), USSR.
30 days Nepal: $2,300-$2,800. Rating: ★★ to ★★★★, depending on local guide.

■ REI ADVENTURES
P.O. Box 88126, Seattle, WA 98138-0126, (800) 622-2236, or (206) 395-7760.

Destinations (highlights): Nepal (Everest, Dolpo, Annapurna), USSR (Caucasus, Pamir Ranges), Alps (Mt. Blanc, Alpine Pass Route), Ecuador (Machu Picchu), India, Mexico (Mayan regions), Thailand.
30 days Nepal: $2,025. Rating: ★★★, ★★★★ for USSR

■ SIERRA CLUB OUTING DEPARTMENT

730 Polk Street, San Francisco, CA 94109, (415) 923-5630 (voice mail).

Destinations (highlights): China (Bhutan), Nepal (Annapurna, Makalu, Sanctuary, Kanchenjunga), European Alps (Tirol, Dolomites), Iceland, Norway (fjord region), Scotland (walking tour), Mexico, Romania, Thailand. Also hundreds of backpack and walking tours in North America.

20 Days Nepal: $1,560 (However, treks vary considerably in price; check competitive trips before you book.)

Rating: Varies widely depending on trip and leader. Normally ★★

■ OVERSEAS ADVENTURE TRAVEL

349 Broadway, Cambridge, MA, 02139, (800) 221-0814.

Destinations (highlights): East Africa (Kenya, Botswana, Tanzania), China, Morocco, European Alps, Fiji, Papua New Guinea, Norwegian Arctic, Irian Jaya, Pakistan (Karakoram), Nepal (Everest Valley, Annapurna), Kashmir/Ladakh, Sikkim, Thailand, Turkey, China, Andes (Inca Trail), Peru (Inca Trail, Cordillerra Vilcabamba), Venezuela (Angel Falls).

20 days Nepal: $2,400

Rating: Varies from ★★ to ★★★★ (depending on the destination)

■ WILDERNESS TRAVEL

801 Allston Way, Berkeley, CA 94710, (800) 368-2794, or (510) 548-0420 in CA.

Destinations (highlights): Africa (Kilimanjaro, Kenya, Zambia), Australia, Portugal, Basque Country, Turkey (Mt. Kackar), Alps (Mt. Blanc, Chamonix Haute Route, Bernese Traverse), Peru (Machu Picchu, Urubamba Valley, Auzangate), Patagonia, Nepal (Annapurna, Everest Valley, Kanchenjunga), Tibet (Everest, Lhasa), India (Kashmir, Ladakh).

20 days Nepal: $1,600-$2,000.

Rating: ★★★ to ★★★★

■ WORLDWIDE ADVENTURES

(World Expeditions), Suite 747, 920 Yonge Street, Toronto, ONT, Canada M4W 3C7, (800) 387-1483, or (416) 963-9163.

Destinations (highlights): Kashmir/Ladakh, Nepal (Everest trek, Annapurna Circuit and Sanctuary, Langtang Valley, Makalu Base Camp), Pakistan (K2 Base Camp), Thailand, East Africa (Kenya, Tanzania, Zanzibar/Selous), Andes (Machu Picchu, Cordillera Vilcabamba), Argentina (Patagonia), Canadian Yukon, Australia (Tasmania). (Very high volume in Nepal.)

30 Days Nepal: $2,230. Rating: ★★★

Honorable Mentions: HIMALAYAN KINGDOMS, *(011 44) 272 237163,* (Quality UK firm with unique treks and major summit climbs); HIMALAYA TREKKING & WILDERNESS EXPEDITIONS, *(800) 777-TREK* (very knowledgeable staff); FORCE 10 EXPEDITIONS, *(800) 922-1491,* (agent for UK's Exodus Expeditions--very good prices).

WHAT TO EXPECT ON AN OUTFITTED TREK

On virtually all commercial treks, you will be accompanied by a guide familiar with the region you'll be hiking. A good guide will have personally hiked the route at least once, and will have made advance arrangements for lodging in the villages or outposts along your itinerary. It is very important that your guide speak the local language(s), or have a native assistant who does. This is the downfall of some otherwise good treks.

You can actually get a good night's sleep on an organized trek, even if you've never been able to do so when backpacking. Typically you'll stay in a hotel on the first and last nights of the trip. While in the field, you'll be accommodated in tea houses, mountain huts or, in some cases, in movable shelters such as yurts or tents. You'll sleep on mats, or thin mattresses, with bedding provided by the outfitter. If you are going to a cold area, you should bring a quality sleeping bag to ensure that you are warm enough. Also consider bringing a traveler's pillow.

When you're walking 10-20 miles a day, you get hungry. On a trek, meals become the major focus of each day's travels. Your guide and/or village host will prepare meals

Yaks in Nepal/CHRIS NOBLE

for the whole group, with hearty, hot food for breakfast and dinner. Before you leave on your trip, you should stuff your pack with edible goodies that you can't find along the trail. A week without sweets is enough to drive many chocoholics crazy. For cold nights, it's nice to bring a small flask with some firewater.

The latest trend in commercial treks is the multi-activity tour. Today, many combo treks seem more like a trip to Disneyland than a walk in the wild. In Thailand, treks now feature elephant rides, and bamboo raft or long-boat cruises. In South America, river-rafting and flightseeing are featured on some deluxe treks. Tours in New Zealand combine trekking with mountain biking and rafting. These options are fun, but they often boost the price of an ordinary trek by 20 percent or more.

Before you set off on a commercial tour, try to talk with a past customer. You'll get vital information you won't find in your outfitter's catalog. Ask about what to wear, how much pocket money you'll need, what the weather's like, how steep and how crowded were the trails, and how was the food and lodging. Satisfy yourself that this is really the experience you want.

In this regard, however, we think the biggest mistake you can make is deciding against a tour because you think it may be too rough. The best treks, in our view, are those that go to the most remote areas, where you meet people who don't see a lot of westerners. Naturally, treks to such regions can be more arduous. You may have to walk more miles, up steeper hills, carrying more weight. The days may be hotter, the nights colder, and your bed harder. But when enduring a few hardships gives you the chance to experience cultures not yet changed by the modern world, we think it's all worth it.

Trekking on Your Own

[A good walk demands]... endurance, plain clothes, old shoes, an eye for nature, good humor, vast curiosity, good speech, good silence, and nothing too much.
-Ralph Waldo Emerson

GREAT DO-IT-YOURSELF TREK DESTINATIONS

If you don't like traveling in large groups, a commercial trek can be a big disappointment. Some of the big operators run virtual pack trains of 20 people or more on the most popular routes. This isn't our idea of getting away from it all. Remember that there are options besides booking a packaged trek with an American company. In many areas, you can easily contract with a local outfitter, or hire your own guide and/or porters at your destination. This usually costs much less than booking

STEVE CONLON, ABOVE THE CLOUDS TREKKING

a trek with an American outfitter. Plus, when you hire your own guide, you can decide the size of the group, how far you want to go, and at what pace.

Below we've listed some of the best spots in the world for do-it-yourself treks. For each destination we've noted some suggested itineraries and recommended guidebooks that will help you start planning your trip. The outfitters' literature will also describe the most popular routes and the cultural highlights of each region.

CANADA

▼

No Guide Needed

Recommended Treks: Near the BC/Alberta border there are literally hundreds of superb trails through Glacier, Yoho, Kootenay, Banff and Waterton National Parks. Pick up a good guidebook for selections. The towns of Golden and Radium Hot Springs in BC are important staging points.

When to Go: Hike the high country any time from mid-May through mid-September. August offers the best weather.

Best Guidebooks: *Climbing and Hiking in S.W. British Columbia*, Bruce Fairley, Gordon Soules Book Publishers Ltd.; *103 Hikes in Southwestern British Columbia*, Mary and David Macaree, the Mountaineers, Seattle; *Canadian Rockies Trail Guide*, Brian Patton and Bart Robertson, Summerthought Publishers.

Contact: Tourism British Columbia, (800) 663-6000; Tourism Alberta, (800) 661-6888; Mt. Equipment Co-op (Vancouver), (604) 872-7858.

Heli-Hiking: This is the newest way to explore the high country of BC and Alberta. Contact **Golden Alpine Holidays,** *(604) 344-7273* in Golden, BC; or **Panorama Heli-Hiking,** *(604) 342-6494*, in Panorama, BC. Golden's cost is roughly $415-$690 US for 4-8 days with alpine chalet lodging and meals. Hikers carry only a daypack.

FRENCH AND SWISS ALPS

▼

Guide Needed for Glacier Routes Only
Recommended Treks: Mt. Blanc Circuit, Chamonix Haute Route, Bernese

On the Annapurna Circuit/BRUCE KLEPINGER

Greece, the Walkers' Guide, Tim Salmon, Cicerone Press, GB; *Let's Go Greece*, Harvard Student Agencies.

Contact: Greek National Tourist Organization, 645 Fifth Avenue, New York, NY 10022, (212) 421-5777.

JAPAN
▼
No Guide Needed

Recommended Treks: Kita Alps, Mt. Fuji.

When to Go: Late spring when the flowers are in bloom is a lovely time to travel, but the entire summer through mid-fall is good.

Best Guidebooks: No trekking books readily available in English; for general information use *Japan: A Travel Survival Kit*, by Ian McQueen, Lonely Planet Publications.

Contact: Japan National Tourist Organization, 624 S. Grand Avenue, Suite 2640, Los Angeles, CA 90017, (213) 623-1952. (Trail maps available.)

NEPAL
▼
Local Guide Recommended

Recommended Treks: Annapurna Circuit, Annapurna Sanctuary, Everest valley approach, Gorkha area loop.

When to Go: Travel in Nepal is possible year-round, but the high passes are best crossed in the early fall and late spring. December and January are best for trekking in the lower elevations, below 10,000'. Summertime is the rainy season.

Guidebooks: *Trekking in the Himalayas*, by Tomaya Iozawa, translated by Michiko and David Kornhauser, Heian Int'l Inc., P.O. Box 1013, Union City, CA 94587; *Trekking in Nepal Himalaya*, by Stan Armington, Lonely Planet Publications.

Contact: Numerous guide services are available in Kathmandu, or contact Tibet Travels and Tours, Box 1397, Thamel, Kathmandu, Nepal.

NEW ZEALAND
▼
No Guide Required
Advance Reservations Recommended

Recommended Treks: Nelson Lakes Nat'l Park, Mt. Aspiring Nat'l Park, Mt. Cook Alps Traverse, Routeburn Track.

When to Go: Seasons are reversed Down Under, so summer runs from late November through February. Late February to early March is probably the best time for

Oberland (Alpine Pass Route).

When to Go: May through September; August is very crowded.

Best Guidebooks: *Walking Switzerland the Swiss Way*, Marsha and Philip Lieberman, the Mountaineers, Seattle; *Tour of Mt. Blanc*, Andrew Harper, Cicerone Press; *Walks and Climbs in the Pyrenees*, Kev Reynolds, Cicerone Press.

Contact: Swiss National Tourist Office, 222 N. Sepulveda Boulevard, Suite 1570, El Segundo, CA 90245, (213) 335-5980; Federation Francaise de la Rondonee Pedestre,

8 Avenue Marceau, 75008 Paris, France. (Will provide maps of Grand Randonnee ("G.R.") trails throughout France.)

GREECE
▼
No Guide Needed
Recommended Treks: Crete, Pindos Peaks, Mt. Olympus.

When to Go: April through October.

Best Guidebooks: *Greece on Foot: Mountain Treks and Island Trails*, Marc S. Duein, the Mountaineers, Seattle; *The Mountains of*

hiking. The sunshine is more consistent, and most of the tourists have gone home by then.

Best Guidebooks: *New Zealand Travel Survival Kit,* Lonely Planet Publications; *Tramping in New Zealand,* by Jim DuFrense (avail. from AYH Travel Center, 335 W. 7th Street, San Pedro, CA 90731 (213) 831-8846).

Contact: NZ Tourism Office, 501 Santa Monica Boulevard, Suite 300, Santa Monica, CA 90401, (800) 388-5494; Department of Conservation, P.O. Box 10-420, Wellington, NZ (parks information); NZ Mountain and Safety Council, c/o Department of Internal Affairs, Private Bag Wellington, NZ, (011 64) 4 726 556.

TASMANIA
▼
No Guide Required
Recommended Treks: Overland Track (Lake St. Clair Nat'l Park), Cynthia Bay-Mt. Ossa, South Coast Track.

When to Go: November through March.

Best Guidebooks: *100 Walks in Tasmania,* Tyrone Thomas, Hill of Content Press, Melbourne, Aus.; *Aus-*

Prayer flags/CHRIS NOBLE

tralia, a Travel Survival Kit, Lonely Planet Publications; Adventure Travel `89, Vol. 12, No. 1 (magazine--Rodale Press, (215) 967-5171).

Contact: Tasbureau, 2121 Avenue of the Stars, Los Angeles, CA 90067, (213) 552-3010; The Department of Lands, Parks and Wildlife, 134 Macquarie St. GPO Box 44A, Hobart, 70000, Tasmania, Australia; Tasmanian Highland Tours, P.O. Box 168, Latrobe 7307, Tasmania, Australia, (011 61) 04 26 9312.

TURKEY
▼
Local Guide Useful
Recommended Treks: Lycia Nine Lakes District, Tauras Mountains/Alagdaglar, Mt. Ararat.

When to Go: Travel is possible year-round, but late spring/early summer offers temperate conditions, and the chance to see wild flowers.

Best Guidebooks: *Trekking in Turkey,* by Mark Dubin & Enver Lucas (avail. from AYH Travel Center); *Turkey Travel Survival Kit,* by Tom Brosnahan, Lonely Planet Publications.

Contact: Turkish Government Tourism Office, 821 United Nations Plaza, New York, NY, 10017, (212) 687-2194.

TREK FREE—WHEN AND WHY TO DO IT YOURSELF

Most commercially run treks cost $70-$125 per day. This covers your guide, land transport, food and lodging. If you're willing to carry your own sleeping bag and some minimal cooking gear, you can follow the same routes as many of the commercial treks for a fraction of the price. In Nepal, for example, you can very easily hire your own guide in Kathmandu, who will arrange lodging in villages along your route, and cook your meals. Total cost, including your lodging, will be less than $20 per day per person for a group of three or more. In New Zealand, where some companies charge $100 or more per day to walk the Routebourne or Milford Track, you can do the same routes self-guided, and stay at alpine huts for less than $20 per night. You'll have to carry your own food (there's cooking gear in the huts) and sleeping bag, but aside from that, you're really not giving up very much in comparison to a costly, fully outfitted trip. In Austria or Switzerland, if you do a little homework and advance planning, you can also put together a great self-guided hut to hut trek, for under $30 per day including food.

Economy is obviously the big reason to organize your own trek, but you should also consider the extra freedom you will have. If the weather's turned bad in the high country, you can stay in town for another day or two, or try your hand at something else--rafting or sailing perhaps. Conversely, if you find that you're really enjoying an area, you can stay a few extra days if you like, or add a sidetrip to a new destination. This isn't possible with most organized treks which have to follow a rigid schedule.

You can also customize a trek to suit your own special interests. If you like rock-climbing or glacier exploring, you can hire a guide in the Alps who will take you up to the mountain. If you're an avid angler, you add a few days fishing to your trek. (New Zealand, Canada and Patagonia are particularly good alpine trout fishing destinations.) All it really takes is some research and preparation on your part.

TREKKING

EQUIPMENT

On most commercial treks, porters or pack animals will carry all communal gear and most of your equipment (sleeping bags, etc.), so you can make do with a small backpack. A fanny pack is handy for cameras and water bottles. If your trip is not porter-supported, and you will be carrying all your own gear, you need a sturdy, comfortable backpack. Internal-frame packs are best for very steep trails, but they tend to make you sweat because they fit so close to your back. Choose an external-frame pack if you will be carrying very heavy loads. If you plan to be making a number of airplane flights, choose a "travelers' pack" with a zippered cover to enclose the waistbelt and shoulder straps. The more your pack looks and acts like a suitcase, the easier it will be to manage in an airport.

FOOTWEAR

Modern lightweight hiking boots are ideal for trekking, although you should break them in thoroughly before you hit the trail. While the Goretex/leather models are lighter and more comfortable than all-leather models, fabric boots (despite the advertising claims) will let the water in, and should not be used in areas such as New Zealand where you cross many streams. For low to medium-altitude treks, leather high-top tennis shoes work as well as boots on soft ground, and if you plan to take only one pair of shoes on your journey, tennis shoes will be more versatile.

BILL ABBOTT, WILDERNESS TRAVEL

MAPS

A good map is the key to a great trek. Most mountaineering shops have maps of the most traveled areas in the Alps and the Himalayas. Make sure your map shows elevations, and important features such as river crossings. For a comprehensive list of maps worldwide, consult **The Map Catalog: Every Kind of Map and Chart on Earth.** This resource has a comprehensive appendix telling you how to get the right map for any spot on the globe. From **Vintage Books,** *400 Hahn Road, Westminster, MD 21157, (301) 848-1900.*

BOOKS

Before you go to any third world trekking destination, pick up the appropriate **Travel Survival Kit** handbooks by Lonely Planet. These invaluable little books are the best resources for dealing with transportation, food and lodging in faraway places. If you can't find them in your local book store, you can order them from the American Youth Hostels Travel Catalog, 335 W. 7th Street, San Pedro, CA 90731, (213) 831-8846.

Adventuring in the Andes, by Charles Frazier and Donald Secrest, Sierra Club Books.

A Guide to Trekking in Nepal, by Stephen Bezruchka, The Mountaineers.

Hut Hopping in the Austrian Alps, by William Reifsnyder, Sierra Club Books,

Trekking in Indian Himalaya, by Garry Weare, Lonely Planet Publications.

Trekking in Nepal Himalaya, by Stan Armington, Lonely Planet Publications.

Trekking in the Himalayas, by Tomaya Iozawa, translated by Michiko and David Kornhauser. This is the most thorough Himalayan trekking book, with outstanding maps and lists of local guides and outfitters. Heian Int'l Inc., P.O. Box 1013, Union City, CA 94587.

Walking Europe from Top to Bottom, by Susanna Margolis and Ginger Harmon. An inspiring account of hiking Europe from the Netherlands to the south of France, Sierra Club Books, 1986.

HEALTH & MEDICINE

Consult your physician about the immunizations you will need. For the most primitive areas, such as Tibet, you should get a full battery of inoculations before you depart--typhoid, tetanus, meningitis and gamma globulin. Both aspirin and the diuretic Diamox can help reduce the effects of altitude sickness. Make sure your medical insurance covers you when overseas.

Gastrointestinal disorders caused by impure water are a real problem in the third world. Boil your water, use purification tablets, and take a good water filter with you. Iodine is helpful, but not adequate by itself. Hepatitis can also be waterborne, and this is serious business. If you show symptoms of this disease, stop your trek and proceed immediately to a medical center.

In tropical areas, malaria remains a problem, even if you take Chloroquine tablets or other prophylaxis. New strains of malaria are resistant to many of the most common medicines, including Chloroquine. Therefore you should sleep under netting, burn mosquito coils (they really work), and apply insect repellent (preferably DEET) when you are in infested areas.

Windsurfing

Catching air off Maui/SUNSTAR

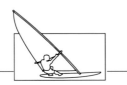

▼

Windsurfing is the water sport of the 1990s. In the hands of experts, the latest boards can go 40 miles an hour, jump waves, even perform loops and other acrobatics. Windsurfing, also called boardsailing, combines the most exciting aspects of skiing, surfing and sailing in what may be the single most challenging and exhilarating solo sport yet invented. And, for the adventurous, the ease of transporting a rig by airplane makes it possible to enjoy the sport throughout the world, wherever one can find wind and water.

In the sections below, we tell you the best places to windsurf both close to home and around the globe. These spots deliver consistent wind, usually in a pleasant, warm-water setting. We've covered all the top destination resorts in a comprehensive comparison chart. We also rank the best tour operators, and provide a run-down on the best equipment to buy if you're looking to get into the sport for the first time.

CHAPTER

26

Aruba--strong winds and flat water equals serious speed/DARRELL JONES

A WINDSURFING VACATION MAY BE THE ULTIMATE ACTION HOLIDAY. YOU can enjoy an exciting, challenging sport at a budget price, typically $500 to $800 for a full week, including lodging, equipment, and in many cases, car rental and airfare. Moreover, since tradewind conditions make for the best sailing, most top resorts are located in the tropics. This means that even when you're not out sailing, you can still enjoy the good life, basking in the sun on pristine beaches.

ARUBA

Speed-sailors' Paradise

Ah, Aruba. Those in the know say Aruba may even top Maui for consistent winds year-round, and it's certainly a superior flatwater destination. The average wind speed, year-round, is over 20 knots. Expect 15-20 knots five days a week in the winter, and 20-30 knots six days a week in the summer. June is historically the windiest month, with steady 25-30 knot trades.

With winds like this Aruba should be an experts-only destination, except for its geography. Situated just 18 miles off the coast of Venezuela, Aruba is long and narrow, with its ends oriented northwest and southeast. The prevailing east/northeast winds blow across the island, affording excellent flat-water sailing on the sheltered lee side. There is also a reef offshore on the lee side that blocks the ocean swell. All this makes for what may be the best speed-sailing destination in the world. And because the flat water is so forgiving, jibing is relatively easy despite the high winds.

Being only 12 degrees above the equator, Aruba offers warm, crystal clear water, which never gets below about 75 degrees. Nobody wears wetsuits in summertime. There isn't a lot of coral to worry about, and most of the sailing is done from white sand beaches. The top sailing areas are at the northwest end of the island, and this is where most of the package tours are based. Fisherman's Huts is probably the top spot, but Palm Beach and Eagle Beach offer good sailing as well. When the wind blows right and a swell's running, there can be terrific wavesailing on the windward side at Boca Grande.

A number of tour operators book windsurfing vacations in Aruba including Vela High Wind Center, Windsurfing Vacations and Sailboard Vacations. (See pages 386-387 for full listings.) This last company is our top pick. Sailboard Vacations (SV) offers week packages, without air or car, for as little as $400 based on double occupancy. SV's equipment is virtually all new, and it is excellent--North and Windwing sails, and Sailboards Aruba customs and BIC production boards. SV's accommodations, private villas, are located quite close to the

Seven Great Windsurfing Vacations

prime sailing spots, so you don't really need to rent a car, although it's awfully convenient to have one. SV even offers wind insurance. For an extra $40 or so, SV guarantees the wind will blow 15 mph or more at least 70 percent of the time during your June, July or August trip, or you get your money back.

Vela High Wind Center also offers a good Aruba program based at the recently completed Holiday Inn hotel. The new sailboard center is probably the best facility on the island, and Vela's equipment comes pre-rigged for your convenience. It's quite a luxury to just grab a rig, tighten the outhaul and downhaul, pop it on a board and go.

While you're in Aruba, don't miss out on all the other attractions. While the official language is Dutch, English is widely spoken. Air temperature averages a balmy 82 degrees, and the humidity rarely gets out of control. There's excellent diving and at night you can squander your hard-earned money at some of the Caribbean's most popular casinos.

CANARY ISLANDS
Sailing Spanish Africa

The Canary Islands are Europe's Maui. Home of World Champion Bjorn Dunkerbeck, these Spanish-ruled islands off Morocco provide outstanding summer sailing for both flatwater fans and ardent wave-sailors. Of the six Canary Islands, the best sailboarding is found on Fuerteventura and Lanzarote, the two westernmost islands in the chain. In winter winds are inconsistent, and the top resorts seem like ghost towns. However, come summer, you'll see the top spots on Fuerteventura crowded with hundreds of European boardsailors. It's easy to understand why. You can count on 15-20 knots five days a week, clear 76-degree water, and miles and miles of golden sand beaches.

Because Lanzarote and Fuerteventura are long and narrow, it is easy to get from one side of these islands to the other, so you can find good sideshore conditions, no matter which way the wind is blowing.

Thus far, few North Americans have visited the Canaries, but that may change once they tire of the same Gorge, Baja, Maui circuit year after year. Most of the serious Europeans bring their own equipment and often stay for a month or more.

It can be expensive to get to the Canaries. The best way to go is to get a charter flight to London, and then book a charter tour to Las Palmas, on Grand Canary Island. From there you can get a local jet to Fuerteventura or Lanzarote for about $90 round trip. Fuerteventura has the most facilities of the two islands, so this should probably be your first stop. Rent a car or hop the bus to Corralejo, at the far northern end of the island. This is where most of the windsurfing resort lodging is situated, and there is great flatwater sailing right off the beach. Expect to pay $40-80 per day for accommodations, and at least $30 per day for a car during peak season.

You can rent production boards from two of the large resort hotels, but the hot set-up is to rent a custom board from Jurgen Hondscheid's shop in Corralejo.

Hondscheid can steer you to the top spots on the North End, many of which are unnamed, or check with the No Work Team surfshop. For the best speed-sailing, head south to Sotavento. There you can rent equipment from the Hotel Gamiones for about $40 per day. It's not up to Maui standards, but is still pretty good. For wavesailing, check out the west side of Fuerteventura, particularly at the ends. Lanzarote also offers a good reef break at La Playa Blanca at the southwest end. In general, Lanzarote may be a little windier than Fuerteventura. It is definitely less crowded in the summer, but you will need a good, rugged vehicle to get to the best spots.

We can recommend the Canaries highly. The speed-sailing, on a good day, is the equal of anything in the world, and it's a refreshing change to experience a culture quite unlike America (remember, this is Spain). English is not widely spoken in the Canaries, outside of the resort areas, so practice your Spanish before you go. During peak season, it is quite possible that all the decent rental equipment will be in use when you arrive. So consider booking a package trip beforehand. Central Tours, (800) 783-9882, offers programs starting at $1,250 including air from New York, lodging, all gear, rental car and instruction at the Dunkerbeck School. TraWell Reisen of Austria offers summer windsurfing packages to Fuerteventura, Lanzarote and Teneriffe starting at $700 per week, including airfare from Vienna. Contact TraWell Reisen, Frankenberggasse 14, A-1040, Vienna, Austria, (011 43) 1 505 0457; FAX: (011 43) 1 505 1224.

MAUI

Boardsailing's Heartland

Sooner or later every boardsailor goes to Maui, the mecca of windsurfing. Once you get there you'll understand why. In the summer, the sideshore trades really do blow 15-25 knots all the time. The water's warm, and in winter, the waves at Ho'okipa are serious. But Maui is not just for experts. It's probably one of the best places to learn to waterstart, because you'll have good instruction, good equipment, but most importantly, the right conditions--strong winds and a sandy beach that drops off quickly so you can't cheat. This isn't to say learning will be easy. It's just that you can count on learning to waterstart in a week in Maui, while the same can't be said of most places in the world. Maui also offers what experts look for--steady, strong winds, and a good selection of sea conditions from flat (Kanaha, Kihei), to big swells (Ho'okipa), or a mixture of both (Sprecklesville).

Unless you've got a buddy with a condo on the windward side, you are wise to book a windsurfing package through one of the well-established shops on the island. If you check our comparison chart you can see that a car, condo, board rental and airfare from LA will run

Aruba/DARRELL JONES

about $800 per person for a week, double occupancy. This will include a top-quality slalom or wave board, with full rig (sail, boom, mast base and roof racks for your car). When booking, find out where your agent is planning to put you. All the action, 90 percent of the time, is on the windward side of the island in the middle, near the airport. If you have a choice, don't stay in Lahaina, or most other places on the leeward side, or you'll be spending a couple of hours a day commuting to and from your sailing spot.

The rental equipment is so new and so good that there's very little reason to bring your own gear, other than personal items such as gloves, booties and harness. The preferred rental board is a 9' to 9'4" slalom, although production boards are available for complete novices, and the latest wave boards can be rented as well. Sail choice is up to the individual, but on a typical Maui day most sailors will be using an RAF slalom in the 4.5-5.1 range. Women can rig one size smaller.

The three top windsurfing shops on the island are Hawaiian Island Windsurfing, Angulo Hawaii and Hi-Tech. All offer pack-

Caught in the act/JAMES W. KAY

to take a day off.

Baja is not blessed with tradewinds, and depends on local thermals or storm winds to generate the power. Therefore, the breezes can be inconsistent. The best season for wind is winter, from late November through mid-February. At other times of year you can get nothing for days on end, though we have sailed San Felipe at the upper end of the Sea of Cortez in June with great results. When the wind is blowing, it often starts in the morning, 10:30 or so, and then blows moderately (10-15) for a few hours. It can then die for a while and come back in much more strongly, 18-25 knots. Although 25-30 is possible, it is unusual. Expect to use a sail one size bigger than you might at Maui most of the time. We would rig a 4.7-5.0 most days. The winds are affected by land masses, so one spot along the coast can be better than another on a given day.

All the top windsurfing resorts are clustered along the southern end of the Baja peninsula near La Paz. Good flatwater spots are Baja Sur, and Bahia de La Ventana. Chop jumpers will prefer Punta Chivato, Palmas de Cortez and Playa Hermosa. You don't need to stick to the resort beaches either. If you've got wheels, load up your rigs and explore.

A word to the wise. Baja may not be the best place for beginning shortboarders. Many of the resorts receive a large swell, or have pretty steep chop that makes it tough to stay under control if you're just making it into the intermediate ranks. If you're just starting on a shortboard, stay at a flatwater location such as Bahia Ventana, or Baja Sur inshore.

With prices under $700 for a full week, double occupancy, there's hardly any reason not to go with a package tour. Most packages offer very similar services--a beachfront hotel with pool, bar and restaurant, high-quality rigs and boards, and instruction packages. In choosing a destination, it's hard to go far wrong. If you're comfortable in swells, Vela is an excellent choice, but the Baja Surf Club, Excursions Extraordinaire and Mr. Bill's are all good, and offer better conditions for novices.

The tough choice is deciding how long to stay. For strong intermediates, a week is about right, however, those learning to sail a shortboard for the first time won't accomplish much in this amount of time. If the winds are strong, experts may want to stay as long as they can. Prices tend to be lower for food and drink than in Maui, and the atmosphere is definitely less intense. Mañana is the watchword. When booking your trip,

age tours, and all provide excellent equipment and service. Because of the low-key atmosphere and outstanding sail selection, Hawaiian Island would be our first choice, followed by Angulo Hawaii (Vela High Wind Centers) a close second. When booking a tour, we recommend spending a little extra to stay at a North Shore guesthouse that has its own beach. This way you won't have to fight the crowds at Kanaha or Sprecklesville. Vela offers nice North Shore cottages with pre-rigged gear. Also, be sure to book a rental car *before* you depart.

BAJA

The Great Winter Escape

Baja is one of our favorite destinations. It's more laid back than Maui, which is too crowded these days, especially on a summer weekend. In Baja, one still has the feeling of being a long way from civilization, and it's much easier to lose track of time, which is the whole point of a vacation anyway. The water is warm, the sun golden, and the setting is interesting enough that you don't feel like you're wasting your time if the wind isn't blowing, or you want

Maui/SUNSTAR

check for special offers on airfare, if it is not included in the package price. Air Mexico seems to have a super special every other month or so--about $350 round-trip from Los Angeles.

OREGON

The Gorge, Heavy Air Haven

The Columbia River Gorge is the mainland's premier windsurfing destination. The Gorge is everything you've heard--tricky, cold and very, very windy. A 3.9 is about the smallest sail you see regularly in Maui, but it's normal at the Gorge. At the peak of summer when the thermals are really pumping up the Columbia, expect a solid 20-30 knots, with some days of 40+.

To sail the Gorge, you had better be pretty good. The chop is tough for intermediates, and you can't count on nice, sandy landing spots. There's enough activity at the Gorge these days to force you to some pretty rocky and miserable put-ins, just to escape the crowds. It's not tropical, but the water conditions aren't quite as bad as you'd think. Most sailors get by with short-sleeved conventional wetsuits. You don't really need a drysuit or gloves in the summer. Water near the river bank is comfortable for swimming and waterstart practice--65-70 degrees. Expect air temperatures in the high 80s to 90s in summer. Daily wind reports can be obtained via MicroForecast's Gorge Wind Line, (800) 695-9703.

There's no shortage of quality board

The new Water Spyder--fast and stable/SUNSTAR

shops in the area. Gorge Windsurfing, 319 E. 2nd, The Dalles, OR 97058, (800) 772-3889, has a great location, good deals on used gear, and bargain rental/training packages. Sailboard Warehouse in Hood River, (503) 386-1699, has equally low prices, and its manager, Bart Vervloet, is a great source for local wind knowledge. Another good full-service shop is Hood River Windsurfing (HRWS), 4 4th Street, Hood River, OR 97031, (503) 386-5787. This outfit has the most complete rental fleet in the Gorge, and some of the best instructors. A complete board and rig cost about $35 per day, but you must post a hefty deposit. HRWS also runs complete vacation packages from $499 per person per week. NOTE: Most of the rental shops sell off their equipment after Labor Day, so if you plan to sail in the late season, bring your own board and rig.

You can also book a great windsurfing week with Joe Field's Heavy Air Gorge, 6005 Rowena River Road, The Dalles, OR 97058, (800) 544-7211, or (503) 298-1513. Field's operation boasts a private launch site near Doug's Beach, the equipment is pre-rigged for you, the accommodations look right out on your sailing site, and there's even a hot tub. Field uses top-quality custom and production boards and Neil Pryde rigs, and Field maintains a Zodiac chase boat for those embarrassing moments. You get all this, plus use of mountain bikes for $550-$750 per week. A good second choice for a complete package is Mr. Bill's Boardsailing Adventures, c/o Cascade Travel Service, 111 Oak Street, Hood River, OR 97031, (800) 533-8452, or (503) 386-7639. You get bed-and-breakfast lodging, and board rental for 5 days for under $600 per person.

Top sailing areas along the Gorge are the stretches from Swell City to the Hatchery for experts, and Rowena to Doug's Beach for all skill levels. The most popular spots on the river, and the best sites for novices, are Bingen and the Hood River Marina. For a good cheap motel near Doug's Beach, your best bet is the Portage Inn--it offers clean, pleasant rooms for under $35 per night. The

The Gorge on a quiet day/DARRELL JONES

newly renovated Lyle Hotel is another good choice in the Doug's Beach area. Those on a tight budget can camp at one of the many private resorts and state parks along the Columbia. The Wind Ranch Campground in Bingen is very convenient, though crowded. Advance reservations are a must for most good camping areas.

CABARETE

The Caribbean Connection

Cabarete, in the Dominican Republic, is the eastern Caribbean's top boardsailing destination. Reliable 20-knot sideshore winds can be expected five days a week from November to April, and June through August. Air temperature is in the high 70s to 80s year-round, and the water temperature is a warm 75 degrees even in winter.

The north shore of the Dominican Republic offers ideal conditions for all levels of boardsailors. An offshore reef keeps the waters close to the beach flat even in high winds, offering a good training ground for intermediates working on their jibes. Experts can also achieve some impressive speeds on the flats inside. Five hundred yards offshore, where the swell and wind-

waves hit the reef, there is prime-time wave-sailing--considered by many to be the best outside of Hawaii.

The Dominican Republic is serviced by major air carriers, so you can bring your equipment without great difficulty, provided your board is under 8'6" (larger boards will be surcharged). For a 160-pound sailor, a 4.7 slalom sail is a good choice for summer, a 5.2 for winter. With good package vacations available, you may want to leave all the gear at home, however. Windsurfing Vacations and Vela High Wind Center offer Cabarete holidays at beachfront condos and resort hotels. Cost per person for a double ranges from about $350 to $600 per week, depending on the season. This includes accommodations and full equipment rental. You won't be disappointed with the gear, which is kept pre-rigged, making life easy. Equipment is high quality, with Neil Pryde, North and Gaastra sails, Excel masts, and a variety of custom and production boards. You won't get the very latest equipment that you might see in Maui, but in general, the rental rigs are quite good, and far superior to the stuff you find in most Club Med-type Caribbean resorts.

Cabarete is becoming increasingly popular, and you can expect prices to go up as more sailors discover Puerto Rico. For now, it offers great wind and water, and relatively uncrowded sailing. Your condos or hotels will be better than you're likely to get in Maui for the same price. We recommend Cabarete as a top windsurfing destination, particularly for East Coasters who can obtain a cheap flight out of Miami.

NEW ZEALAND

Thunder Down Under

New Zealand is a great destination for the resourceful boardsailor. You won't find world-class rental shops or destination resorts a few yards from the beach, but if you're willing to travel around, sampling the wind in various locales, you'll definitely have something to write home about.

The hotbed of Kiwi windsurfing is Wellington, at the south end of the North Island. While Maui may have more days of winds over 15 knots, annually, Wellington averages 173 days a year of winds 30+ knots, and over 40 days of 50+ knot winds. If you like sailing with midget rigs in conditions that make even the Gorge look tame, Wellington is the place. You can sail relatively flat water in Wellington harbor, or jump waves on the South Coast near the airport. The water is miserably cold, even in the summer, so a drysuit is essential. For reliable advice on the best put-ins and wave-sailing spots, contact Wellington's Southcoast Sailboards.

Another great North Island spot is Wanganui, about 150 miles up the west coast from Wellington. There you can rent boards, and enjoy good wave-sailing, with more than 80 days of 30+ knot winds annually. Farther north, along Cape Egmont, there are great secret spots near Oakura and New Plymouth. Here you'll encounter regular 20-knot sideshores, and a strong, well-shaped beach break. If you've gotten the idea that the west coast doesn't offer much flatwater sailing, you're right; the western side of New Zealand gets the swells running across the southern Indian Ocean, and they can really pound when there's a storm. For good flatwater sailing, you'll want a more protected east coast bay.

For pure speed, the inner waters of Auckland harbor on the east coast can be a great spot when it's blowing. When a 20-knot northeasterly is pumping on a week-end, you'll see as many as 100 shortboards in the harbor. The top wave-sailing spot in the Auckland area is Takapuna Beach on the north shore. There's usually a side-shore or side-onshore here when it's windy, but you can't count on it like the trades in Hawaii or the Caribbean.

This points out the biggest problem with Kiwi windsurfing. Winds fluctuate with the constantly changing weather patterns; there is no typical day. The land doesn't heat up enough to create a strong daily sea-breeze as in San Francisco or the Gorge, and there are no tradewinds. Hence, you could spend a couple of weeks Down Under and do very little sailing. On the other hand, you could easily get 30+ knots for a solid week in Wellington or New Plymouth, if you're lucky.

Because the wind isn't guaranteed, you won't find package windsurfing vacations offered to New Zealand. It's also difficult to rent high-quality equipment outside of Auckland. Accordingly, if we were heading Down Under we would probably take a small wave board, and a full rig with us, then rent a slalom board in Auckland. It will cost you about $25 per day for just the board and mast base. Rent yourself a car or small van, (you'll find the best rates at Auckland's Maui Campers--the name is pure coincidence, by the way), and go exploring for a couple of weeks. You may not be able to sail every day, but you'll get a chance to explore a beautiful country and meet some very nice folks on your journey.

Day's end/JOHN KELLY

383

GREAT WINDSURFING RESORTS WORLDWIDE

HERE IS ALL THE INFORMATION YOU NEED TO PLAN A WINDSURFING VACATION AT TOP boardsailing destinations around the world. The package prices in the chart are per person, double occupancy, and include lodging, and complete board and rig rental for one week, except as otherwise indicated. All prices are subject to change. Codes used in the chart are as follows: AC (air conditioning); AIR (includes round-trip airfare); IN (instruction incl.); GO (gear only: board, sail, rig); LS/HS (low/high season); M (meals incl.); PR (pre-rigged sail, mast, boom); SS (sideshore winds); WH (Windsurfing Hawaii); WS (water sports options, e.g. boat sailing, diving); wind speed is in knots per hour; CAR (rental car included). Destination resorts are rated ★ to ★★★★★ for quality, $ and $$ for special value.

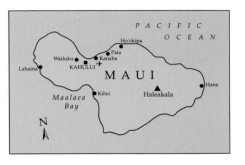

Location/Operator	Contact	Conditions	Boards	Water Temp. (Degrees F)
ANTIGUA				
Windsurfing Vacations	(800) 635-1155	20-25 summer, 5-17 fall, winter. Wind chop	BIC long & short; also custom	76
ARUBA				
Sailboard Vacations	(800) 252-1070	17-30, flat, clear water, some point breaks	BIC, WH, Windsurf, Aruba customs	78
Windsurfing Vacations	(800) 635-1155	Same	Van Der Berg cust. F2, Mistral	78
Vela High Wind Center	(800) 223-5443	Same	Mistral, Seatrend, Sailboard Aruba cust.	78
BAJA				
Excursions Extraordinaire	(800) 678-BAJA	(Punta Chivato)15-30, flat or 6' chop/swell outside	BIC & Shuler custom 12'2"-8'10"	70
Baja Surf Club	(800) 551-8844	(Los Barriles) 15-30, flat bay with wind chop	Fanatic, Cascade and AHD custom	72
Mr. Bill's Boardsailing	(800) 533-8452	(Los Barriles) 15-30, flat bay with chop outside	Seatrend, BIC, F2 production	70
Vela High Wind Center	(800) 223-5443	(Playa Hermosa)18-25, big swell, chop, or waves	Mistral, Seatrend, Naish, ASD custom	72
BARBADOS				
Windsurfing Vacations	(800) 635-1155	15+ Dec-Mar, 20-30 Mar-June, big swell outside	Mistral & custom	75
Vela High Wind Center	(800) 223-5443	15-22 SS; two sites--one wave, one flat	Mistral	74
BONAIRE				
New World Adventures	(407) 647-2170	15-28, flat and waves outside reef	BIC, Aruba, custom 9'-12'	74
CABARETE (Domin. Repub.)				
Vela High Wind Center	(800) 874-4637	15-20 summer, 20-30 winter, SS flat or wave	Mistral, Seatrend, Sailboards Aruba	76
Windsurfing Vacations	(800) 635-1155	Same; best Caribbean wavesailing	BIC, custom	76
CANARY ISLANDS				
Dunkerbeck Windsurf Center	(800) 783-9882	15-25, flat, or wind chop/large swell	F2 and Dunkerbeck custom	75
CANCUN				
Vela High Wind Center	(800) 223-5443	(Playamile)13-22 SS, flat, mild chop	Mistral, Seatrend and custom	76
COLUMBIA RIVER GORGE				
Mr. Bill's Boardsailing	(800) 533-8452	15-40+ SS, steep chop, strong gusts	Tiga and Watson custom	60-70
Joe Field's Heavy Air Gorge	(800) 544-7211	Same	Watson custom 8'2"-9'9", & prod.	60-70
CORPUS CHRISTI, TX				
Mr. Bill's Boardsailing	(800) 533-8452	15-25 SS, flat inside, chop outside	Various custom boards	72
CURACAO				
Windsurfing Vacations	(800) 635-1155	18+ SS, more variable than Aruba, flat inshore	Mistral, BIC, Airtime custom	76
FT. WALTON BEACH, FL				
Rogue Wave Windsurfing	(904) 243-1962	10-18, flat bay good for nov./intm., big shorebreak	Mistral, O'Brien, Fanatic	65-80
GARGANO, ITALY				
TraWell Reisen (Austria)	(01143) 1 650457	12-20, flat bay	Alpha all sizes	75
KAUAI				
Hanalei Sailboards	(808) 826-9000	12-18, flat bay & reef surf	Hi-Tech, Jimmy Lewis custom, BIC	72-78
MAUI				
Hawaiian Island Windsurfing	(800) 782-6105	15-30 SS, flat or wave by choice	Naish cust., Seatrend, AHD, Mistral, BIC	72-80
Maui Windsurfari	(800) 736-6284	Same	Hi-Tech custom & prod., O'Brien	72-80
Vela High Wind Center	(800) 223-5443	Same	Angulo custom, WH, Fanatic, Seatrend	72-80
PORTO POLLO, SARDINIA				
TraWell Reisen (Austria)	(01143) 1 650457	15-25 SS, flat & wind chop	Mistral & custom	66-70
SAN FRANCISCO				
Windsurf Warehouse	(800) 628-4599	15-30, moderate to big chop & tides	Tiga, F2, Seatrend, BIC	55-60
ST. BARTS				
Windsurfing Vacations	(800) 635-1155	14-26, trades, flat, or waves on reef	Tiga, F2, Seatrend, BIC	76
ST. THOMAS, USVI				
Caribbean Boardsailing	(809) 776-3486	14-20, flat. Dec-Jul is best	Mistral, Fanatic, Hi-Fly	72-76
Windsurfing Vacations	(800) 635-1155	Same	Mistral & custom	72-76

COURTESY FANATIC SAILBOARDS

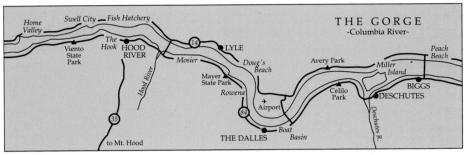

THE GORGE
-Columbia River-

SAILS	ACCOMMODATIONS	% DAYS 15+	COST (ADD'L DAY)	COST/WEEK	SEASON	RANK
UP, Pryde	Beachfront hotel, pool	75%	$85	$650	All	★★★
North, Windwing, PR	Package	82%	$60-100+	$399-699 LS, $599-899 HS	All	★★★★
Hot Sails Maui, WH	Guest cottage, hotels, condos (beach)	82%	$85	$350-800	All	★★★
Mistral, North, Windwing, PR	Beachfrt. hotels, condos, w/pool, AC	82%	$85+	$400-900	All	★★★★
Ultra Profile, WH	38 rooms, AC, pool, restaurant	65%	$100	$795 M, IN	Dec-Feb	★★
Gaastra, Rushwind, ART	45 beachfront rms, pool, rest., ground taxi	60%	$105	$750 M	Nov-Mar	★★★
North, Sailworks	Beachfrt. hotel, AC, rest., dive, mtn. bikes	60%	$95	$600	Nov-Mar	★★
Mistral, North, Waddell, PR	Beachfrt. hotels w/pool, AC, WS & horse opt.	60%	$95	$700 LS, M	Dec-Mar	★★★
Mistral	Luxury hotel, AC, pool	50-80%	$80-$110	$500-700	Nov-July best	★★
Mistral, PR	Beachfrt. hotels, condos with AC, pool	50-70%	$60 Est.	$370-450 LS	Nov-June	★★
North, Pryde	Beachfrt. hotels, condos	50%	Inquire	$400-700	All (Apr-Nov)	★★
Mistral, North, PR	Beachfrt. hotels, condos w/AC, rest., pool	60%	$60	$400 LS, M	All	★★★$
Gaastra, Pryde, BIC, UP	Condos, hotel (beach), pool, rest.	60%	$50-85	$300-650	All	★★★
UP, F2, Mistral, Alpha	Hotel, condos, pool, rest.	70%	$70-95	$1250 incl. AIR from NY	Apr-Oct	★★★
Mistral, North, PR	Beachfrt. hotels, condos w/pool, AC, rest.	65%	$90 Est.	$680 M	Nov-Apr	★★★
North, Pryde	B&B, mtn. bikes; also condos	75%	$85	$450-600	Apr-Sept	★★
Pryde slalom comp. 2.8-6.0 m	Guesthouse w/ hot tub/beach; mtn. bikes	75%	$60-120	$475-750	Apr-Nov	★★★
North, Sailworks	Condos, AC, beachfront, mtn. bikes, rest.	60%	$100	$600	Mar-May	★★
Mistral	Luxury beach resort w/AC, pool, casinos	60%	$105-170	$750-1125	All	★★
Gaastra, Windwing, Mistral	Book separately	30%	$50 GO	NA	All, Feb-May	★★
Alpha, Mistral	Hotel, condos, pool, rest.	70%	Inquire	$500-1,000 LS/HS	Jun-Sep	★★
Pryde, Simmer, WH	Equipment only	75%	$45 GO	$235 GO	All	★★
Gaastra, Simmer, Pryde	Hotels, condos, houses-basic to DLX	75-85%	$45-100	$465; ($830 2 wks); CAR	All	★★★★$
North, Simmer, Pryde	Kihei condos, AC, pool; custom beachfrt.	75-85%	$60-80	$480; ($650 10 days); CAR	All	★★★★$
N. Pryde, ART	Wide range of condos w/AC, some beachfrt.	75-85%	$65-100	$480-750 LS; CAR	All	★★★★
Mistral	Hotels with pool, restaurants	50%	$65+	$400-1,100 LS/HS	Apr-Oct	★★
Pryde, Gaastra, Windwing	Call for recommendation	80%	$40 GO	$200 GO	Apr-Oct	★★★
Gaastra, Pryde, Mistral	Hotel, pool; beachfront cottages	60%	$100-150	$700-1100; airport taxi	Nov-July	★★
Gaastra, Mistral, WH	Various incl. Pt. Pleasant Resort	55%	$25-50 GO	Call for price	All	★★
Mistral	Pt. Pleasant Resort	55%	$130 LS	$1,000-1,300 LS/HS; CAR	Dec-July	★★

385

The Top Windsurfing Tour Operators

Racing the wave/JOHN KELLY

*P*ACKAGE BOARDSAILING VACATIONS ARE MAJOR BARGAINS. HAWAIIAN HOLIDAYS, in particular, offers remarkable value--a week's lodging, board and rig, rental car, and round-trip airfare from the West Coast runs a modest $800 per person on average. With this kind of value, it's crazy not to use a commercial operator for most destinations. Among the windsurfing tour companies we review, the best run their own operations, although some, such as Windsurfing Vacations, merely act as a travel agent for local resorts. In many destinations you will find that local windsurf shops also offer economical lodging and equipment-rental packages.

■ **VELA HIGH WIND CENTERS**
125 University Avenue, #40, Palo Alto, CA 94301, (800) 223-5443, or (415) 322-0613.

Vela is one of the biggest tour operators, with solid programs in Maui, Aruba, Baja, Cancun, Cabarete and Barbados. Vela's Baja package is probably the best for intermediate to advanced sailors, and in Maui, Vela works with Angulo Hawaii, the exclusive rental source for those lovely Angulo wave boards. In most destinations, Vela features pre-rigged equipment and a wide range of accommodations.

Vela's operation is first class; you won't be disappointed. Rating: ★★★★$

■ **HAWAIIAN ISLAND WINDSURFING**
460 Dairy Road, Kahului, Maui, HI 96732, (800) 782-6105, or (808) 572-5601.

Hawaiian Island has friendly service, superb equipment, competitive prices, and the largest rental sail inventory on Maui. Just watch out for the package tour rental cars. During peak season, you can get a real dog. Nonetheless, Hawaiian Island is still our favorite operator in Maui. Rating: ★★★★$

■ **SAILBOARD VACATIONS**
193 Rockland Street, Hanover, MA 02339, (800) 252-1070, or (617) 829-8915.

Sailboard Vacations specializes in Aruba, and has that destination wired. The

Watching the action, Kanaha Beach, Maui/SUNSTAR

that offers both flatwater and wave sailing. The flatwater option makes this a logical choice for Baja beginners. Rating: ★★$

■ Excursions Extraordinaire
P.O. Box 3493, Eugene, OR 97403, (800) 678-2252, or (503) 484-0493.

Excursions Extraordinaire (EE) is one of the smaller operators, but it has a very good location in Baja at Punta Chivato. EE has a new site in Costa Rica (Lake Arenal), and is the only operator on the Oregon coast. EE also operates in Maui, the Gorge, and Corpus Christi each summer. Rating: ★★$

■ Windsurfing Vacations
P.O. Box 1097, Doylestown, PA 18901, (800) 635-1155, or (215) 348-9813; FAX: (215) 348-2341.

Windsurfing Vacations (WV) is a travel agency that books package vacations to a variety of resorts throughout the Caribbean as well as Maui. While the quality of WV's offerings varies, (WV does not operate its own resorts) all the programs offer excellent value, and WV is the only game in town in many parts of the Caribbean. Rating: ★★$

■ TraWell Reisen
Frankenberggasse 14, A-1410 Vienna, Austria. (01143) 1 505-0457; FAX: (01143) 1 505-1224.

If you want to sail in Europe and North Africa, TraWell Reisen is one of your only choices. Destinations include the Canaries, Cuba, Cabarete, Egypt, Greece, Italy, Spain and Turkey. The accommodations tend to be good, though it's crowded during peak season. Boards and rigs (F2s, Mistrals and Alphas) are a cut below what you get in Maui, but still very good. The best way to contact TraWell Reisen is by FAX, but the staff in Vienna also speaks good English if you prefer to call. Rating: ★★

lodgings are well situated, prices are low, and the equipment is excellent. This is our first choice for Aruba. Rating: ★★★$

■ Maui Windsurfari
444 Hana Highway, Ste. G, Kahului, HI 96732, (800) 736-6284, or (808) 871-7766.

Maui Windsurfari features fast Hi-Tech boards, and a fine selection of condo accommodations, as well as North Shore beachfront cottages and rentals. Customers love the equipment, though you can expect to be surcharged for even minor dings. This is a good choice if you're easy on your gear. Rating: ★★★$

■ Baja Surf Club
P.O. Box 8993, Calabasas, CA 93109, (800) 551-8844, or (818) 591-WIND.

The Baja Surf Club has been running package tours out of Baja as long as any-body, and its accommodations are among the best. We wouldn't hesitate to book with them, particularly at the beginning of the season when the equipment is new. Rates are very competitive. Rating: ★★★$

■ Mr. Bill's Boardsailing Adventures
111 Oak St., Hood River, OR 97031, (800) 533-8452, or (503) 386-7639.

Mr. Bill's your man, if sailing the Gorge is at the top of your wish list, although Joe Field's Heavy Air Gorge provides Mr. Bill with stiff competition in Oregon. Mr. Bill's also runs a high-quality Baja resort

INSTRUCTION

It all begins with imagination/SUNSTAR

MASTERING THE BASICS

Longboard Sailing

The sport of windsurfing started decades ago with longboards, plastic 12-footers that weighed 40-50 pounds fully rigged. Though slow to turn, they were reasonably stable, and fun in moderate conditions.

You can learn how to sail a longboard in light to medium winds at any lake or beachfront resort which has a boardsailing shop nearby. Expect to spend 15-20 hours on the board before you have mastered most of the basic techniques. Many shops offer a 2 or 3-day program for $100-$150 including board rental. By all means, try two or three days on longboarding before you book an expensive boardsailing vacation in Aruba, Hawaii or Baja.

The Shortboard Challenge

If you enjoyed the longboard experience, you'll want to move on to shortboards--the speedy but tricky thoroughbreds of the sport. Since a shortboard is very unstable, you cannot simply stand on it and haul the sail up. Instead, it must be waterstarted. Waterstarting requires patience, the right conditions, and a good instructor. While you float upwind of the board, kick the nose downwind so that the wind blows across it. Then haul the mast over the board so that the top end points into the wind, with the boom resting on the back of the board. As the wind starts to fill the sail, place one foot on the board, keeping your body in the water. Grab the mast with your forward hand, the boom with your back hand, and let the wind haul you up on the board. Once you get the hang of it, waterstarting will seem easy, although it is frustrating at first for everyone.

In three to five days you will be able to waterstart well off the beach and tentatively come back in. After a week or so you should have secure two-way waterstarts, and be able to use your footstraps properly. After ten days you'll be able to sail fast in a straight line using your harness and footstraps. After two weeks many sailors are starting to make a few jibes, but this is not always the case.

There is no substitute for time on the water. Learn your skills one at a time, and don't expect to be a pro tomorrow. Two weeks in Maui, Baja or Aruba will teach you enough that you will start having fun, and be able to sail your own shortboard when you return home. Maui is your best warm-water training site, followed by Aruba, the eastern Caribbean and Baja. Package vacations with lessons are available at all these destinations; the leading schools are listed below.

TRAINING CENTERS

MAUI
∎

Hawaiian Sailboarding Techniques with Alan Cadiz, *444 Hana Hwy., Kahului, HI 96732, (808) 871-5423.* A great boardsailor, and a patient, capable instructor, Alan Cadiz may be Maui's best one-on-one

Looking good/SUNSTAR

teacher, and would be our first choice for initial training. Rating: ★★★★

Maui Magic Windsurfing School, *520 Keolani Place, Kahului, Maui, HI 96732, (800) 872-0999, or (808) 877-4816.* Using the latest techniques, including radio communication, Maui Magic guarantees you will waterstart in three days, or you get extra lessons free. Classes can be crowded, but everyone seems to learn. Vela High Wind offers Maui Magic instruction. Rating: ★★★

Windsurfing West, *460 Dairy Road, Kahului, Maui, HI 96732, (808) 871-8733.* Al West has one of the most systematic and successful programs for teaching shortboard technique to beginners. He has probably taught more novices to waterstart than anyone in Maui. All instruction is individualized. Rating: ★★★

ARUBA
∎

Vela High Wind Center offers the most complete instruction programs on Aruba. In addition to regular instruction by certified instructors, Vela hosts special clinics by visiting pros such as Nevin Sayre, Cort Larned and Rhonda Smith. If you're just learning to waterstart, Vela's program may be the best choice, although Sailboard Vacations also offers instruction for boardsailors of all skill levels. Rating: ★★★

BAJA
∎

Go with the **Vela High Wind Center,** or the **Baja Surf Club** for the best organized training programs in Baja. The competition offers good instruction as well, but these two outfits are among the biggest, so you can be assured of having an instructor when you want one. Be aware that conditions in Baja can be tough for beginners. You may want to go to a true flatwater destination such as Aruba, or inshore at Cabarete.

EASTERN CARIBBEAN
∎

Mistral operates windsurfing schools at dozens of major Caribbean resorts: Antigua, Aruba, Bahamas, Barbados, Bermuda, Bonaire, Cayman Islands, Curacao, Dominican Republic, Jamaica, Puerto Rico, St. Lucia, St. Maarten, St. Vincent, Tobago, Trinidad, Turks & Caicos, BVI, St. Thomas, St. Croix, St. John, Belize, Cancun and Cozumel. At each center, Mistral-certified instructors teach both longboard and shortboard techniques to all levels of sailors. Two of the best Mistral programs are the **Bitter End Resort (BVI)**, and **Caribbean Boardsailing** in St. Thomas, USVI. Contact Mistral, Inc., 7222 Parkway Drive, Dorsey, MD 21076, (301) 796-4755. Rating: ★★

Weekend warriors at the Gorge, Oregon/PATRICK McDOWELL

WITH SO MUCH NEW WINDSURFING HARDWARE TO CHOOSE FROM, PICKING the best equipment for the money can be rather daunting, particularly since most gear can't be road-tested before you buy. If you spend a week in Maui, you can try a variety of board designs, and compare different sails, but you still won't be able to sample all the best new equipment available. We've sorted through the stockpile of hardware out there, and selected our favorites, based on performance, value and durability.

BEST SLALOM BOARD
▼

If we could own only one board, it would be a 9' or 9'3" custom slalom board from Jimmy Lewis, Naish or Hi-Tech. These are all very light, very stiff and exceedingly fast. Some boards may jibe a little better in chop, or accelerate faster off a wave, but we can't think of any other brands that will do so many things so well. Look for one at an off-season price of around $900. If ruggedness is a prime concern, we recommend the glass ASD slalom, a highly regarded West Coast board. Its performance is on a par with the best Hawaiian customs, and the manu-facturer offers an unconditional one-year guarantee. The best semi-production board is probably the Seatrend epoxy, at 9' or 9'4". Top-rated production slalom boards are the Mistral Screamer, and F2 Sunset Race. These production models combine superior performance with outstanding durability.

BEST WAVE BOARD
▼

If you're a wave-sailor, go to Maui, sail Ho'okipa, and come home with an Angulo 8'6"-8'10" wave board in your board-bag. Most of the top wave-sailors in Hawaii use an Angulo, or would like to. Angulo boards made in the last couple of years have also retained their value very well on the resale market. Honorable Mentions: Hi-Tech, ASD, Naish, 8'-8'10". For those on a budget, or who tend to sail from rocky beaches, consider the Tiga Wave Production. At $699, it offers durability and top performance at a very economical price.

BEST FLATWATER SAILS
▼

We know this will be controversial, but here goes. The top brand-name flatwater (slalom/speed) sails are Neil Pryde, North and Gaastra, in that order. Neil Pryde sails have a wide wind range, carry their power low, and waterstart well--a big plus for beginners and intermediates. North sails are tough, extremely well made, but a bit less versatile. The Gaastra line seems to work best in the larger slalom sizes. We might give them an edge in speed over Pryde and North in a straight line, but they are somewhat harder to rig and heavier than the competition. (GUN sails are also quite fast in a straight line, and they cost considerably

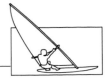

less than the big name brands.)

Excellent flatwater sails are also offered by boutique sailmakers Paia Sails of Maui, and Waddell Sails of Santa Cruz. Paia pioneered the use of fewer battens, for a light, easy to handle speed-sail that is also exceedingly fast. The pick of many of the top sailors on the West Coast, Waddell slalom sails offer very advanced design plus superior craftsmanship and materials.

BEST WAVE SAILS
▼

Simmer Style sails are the standard by which all wave sails are measured. They are tough, extremely well made, and very well balanced--ideal for quick jibes off the lip. However, for small wave and medium wind conditions, we prefer other brands, such as Neil Pryde, that carry more power down low, and can be luffed easier. Maui's Freedom Sails and Paia Sailmakers also build great wave sails, customized for the owner's preferences. The Freedom and Paia wave sails are generally lighter and more versatile than the Simmer models of the same size. Windsurfing Hawaii wave sails have been recently redesigned for increased performance, and are practically bulletproof in use.

BEST MASTS
▼

For traveling, a two-piece mast is essential. Our top pick is the Serfiac Two-in-One. Stiff and light, it offers superior portability because the top section fits within the bottom. A good second choice is the new KC fiber two-piece which combines high performance with very low weight. The alloy Serfiac Gold Sport, the choice of top pros, is the best two-piece mast for racing and speed-sailing. The North metal two-piece is a bit slower, but costs less and is great for big cambered sails. (Use a composite top with smaller rigs.) If you regularly sail in very high winds or heavy surf, use an all-composite mast. The new KC Fiber Maui Power Wave Mast is the best-- very light, strong and durable.

BEST BOOMS
▼

Clamp-on mast fittings are making tie-on booms obsolete, and if you sail more than a few days a year, the extra convenience of clamp-ons is well worth the added cost. Windsurfing Hawaii booms are the industry standard, and the new small-diameter clamp-on model is outstanding, with a well-engineered rotating collar, and comfortable grip. However, if you change sail sizes frequently, we recommend the Fleetwood or Hawaiian Proline booms. Made from high-grade aluminum with over-sized push pins, these are much easier to adjust than the Windsurfing Hawaii booms.

Novices should seriously consider the Pryde and North booms which are sealed and therefore float higher during waterstarting. Probably the best traveling boom is the Primex Hawaiian Snapp Clamp. It can be doubled over on itself, so it takes up half the normal space in your gear bag.

WINDSURFING TRAVELERS' GUIDE

WHAT TO BRING

On a package tour, it's not necessary to bring much of anything except a light wetsuit, and gloves and booties. The equipment you will rent, especially in Hawaii, is likely to be better and newer than what you have at home. If you bring a board, make it an 8' to 8'10" wave board, nothing bigger. Your package will cover rental of a larger 9'-9'8" slalom board for you to use. If we were going to a location where winds can be variable, we might bring sails--a 4.5 and 5.2 are the most versatile for tradewind conditions. You probably won't bother to sail with anything bigger, and if you really need a 3.9 or 4.0, it's easy enough to rent one. Most windsurf rental shops offer a two-sail or one-sail package, which permits you to exchange sizes as needed.

Don't bother to bring a mast, even a two-piece. Do pack a large board-bag; it will come in handy when you're driving around looking for the best wind. If you've got a good harness that fits you well, bring it along, because many rental shops charge extra for this. If you own a decent set of clamp-on booms, definitely bring them if your tour rental source stocks only the older tie-on variety.

GEAR TRANSPORT

Boards under 8'6" can usually be shipped as part of your regular baggage allowance at no extra charge, or for a nominal fee. Larger boards may be subject to a significant surcharge. (And some airlines have a surfboard-only policy, so you may want to remove the footstraps to avoid surcharges.) Use a padded board-bag and cushion the nose, tail and rails with foam tubing. If your board is particularly fragile, bubble-wrap it nose to tail. If you plan to take a mast, which we don't recommend, make sure it's a two-piece. Many airlines refuse to ship a full-length mast, no matter what you pay.

Buy extra insurance for your equipment. The standard insurance offered by most air carriers will not cover the cost of the board alone, much less your whole inventory of sails and gear.

WIND REPORTS

MicroForecasts, (503) 227-7455, offers recorded wind reports for the Gorge, Puget Sound and the Oregon Coast, plus computer weather reports for San Francisco, Chesapeake Bay and New England.

HEALTH & MEDICINE

The three major boardsailing health hazards are sun, staph infections and coral cuts. At a typical windsurfing resort, you'll be spending eight hours a day in intense tropical sun. Be smart. Wear a hat and sunglasses. Use a high-neck lycra skinsuit or shorty top to keep the sun off your shoulders and neck. The best sunblock we've found is AloeGator. It truly lasts for hours, even in the water.

To avoid staph infections, thoroughly clean and disinfect all cuts and abrasions immediately. If the wound is small, use NuSkin (liquid Band-Aid) to keep it sterile and sand-free. For bigger abrasions, use a waterproof dressing covered with duct tape. If you get a coral cut, clean out the wound immediately, using a toothbrush if necessary to get rid of all the coral particles. Contrary to myth, the coral will not grow under your skin, but it will promote bacteria. It is important to treat the cut within the first hour or so, before the bacteria get started. Once the wound is thoroughly cleaned and disinfected, keep it covered for a week. Minor coral cuts should heal within a week or so. If you still notice redness, pain or puffiness, you should see a physician.

Youth Programs

Mankind owes to the child the best it has to give.
-U.N. Declaration

▼

Most of the package adventures listed in this book are designed primarily, if not exclusively, for adults. However, there's no good reason a teenager cannot enjoy trekking in a faraway land, climbing a mountain, or running a whitewater river. In most cases, teens are more than strong enough to do anything an adult can do, and their enthusiasm for adventure typically runs high.

With this in mind, a host of organizations now offer adventure programs designed expressly for the younger set. These programs are tailored for younger minds and bodies, and allow teens to train and socialize among their peers. The result is, predictably, more fun, faster progress, and a greater sense of accomplishment.

To help you select the best program for your teenage son or daughter, we have grouped recommended adventure outfitters by sport or activity, e.g. sailing or mountaineering.

However, many of the best youth adventure programs offer a variety of activities in a single session. Outward Bound, for example, offers popular 2 to 3-week programs which combine mountaineering with hiking and whitewater rafting. Castle Rock Center offers a ter-

COURTESY COLORADO TOURISM BOARD

rific 7-week program that includes some of everything-- from llama trekking to mountain climbing. Be wary of a program that promises too much, however, unless the organization utilizes outside experts for specialized activities.

CHAPTER
27

The Bikers from Hell/MARK GALLUP

WE'VE SELECTED SOME OF THE BEST YOUTH ADVENTURE PROGRAMS BELOW. In most cases these are specialty operations, run by highly trained personnel. From mountaineering to windsurfing, these are the top places for teens to get their first real taste of high adventure. Wherever possible we have included prices in our reviews. However, many organizations can be expected to revise their prices upwards later in the year.

BICYCLE TOURING

Exploring at a Gentle Pace

Bike touring across America or through a foreign country is a great way to broaden one's horizons. Many bicycle tour companies offer programs for teens, led by experienced adult guides. This is a memorable way to discover the world, meet new friends and get fit in the process. Among the better organizations offering youth bike tours are:

■ AMERICAN YOUTH HOSTELS ASSOCIATION (AYHA)
World Adventures Program, P.O. Box 37613, Dept. 811, Washington, D.C. 20013-7613, (202) 783-6161.

AYHA operates 1 to 6-week coed bike tours for teens 15+ in a variety of destinations in North America and Europe. Foreign trips range from $995 to $3,900 in price. Domestic tours organized through the AYHA Cooperative Trip Program are considerably less, ranging from $350 to $1,500. The most popular tours include the Heart of Europe, the East and West Coast routes, Alaska and New Mexico. AYHA keeps its costs down by utilizing the extensive network of international youth hostels. Rating: ★★★

■ STUDENT HOSTELING PROGRAM (SHP)
Box R, Conway, MA 01341, (800) 343-6132, or (413) 369-4275.

SHP has been a youth bike tour specialist for 21 years. It offers coed trips grouped by grade level, 7th to 12th. Two to 9-week trips to a variety of countries worldwide range from $850 to $5,500. Principal desti-

nations are in the US, Canada and Western Europe. Rating: ★★

■ THE BIKING EXPEDITION
P.O. Box 547, 10 Maple Street, Henniker, NH 03242, (800) 245-4649.

This organization has operated bike tours for boys and girls in grades 8-12 since 1973. Four to 6-week trips in North America and Europe range in price from $1,375 to $3,575 (domestic), and $1,900 to $3,000 (foreign). The most popular destinations are coastal Maine and Nova Scotia. Rating: ★★

■ KMB TOURS LTD.
Box 867, Nelson, BC, Canada V1L 6A5, (604) 354-4371.

KMB offers a unique weeklong mountain bike summer camp for youths 9-16, conducted in the heart of British Columbia's beautiful Kootenay Mountains. Along with daily mountain bike forays, kids can canoe, ride horses, and hike from their base at the Hidden Creek Guest Ranch. Cost is approximately $450 for 6 days, all-inclusive. Rating: ★★★

In addition to these programs, many YMCAs and other community organizations offer youth bicycle tours. And, if your child is over 16, he or she can join many of

the commercial bike tours listed in Chapter 5, sometimes at a discount.

HIKING & CAMPING

Growing Up One Step at a Time

Backpacking is an ideal youth adventure activity. It is cheap, challenging and emotionally rewarding. In addition to traditional organizations, such as the Boy Scouts and Girl Scouts, many nonprofit organizations offer backpacking programs for kids. Normally the expense is small and your kids won't have to venture far from home. Wherever there are trails, mountains and forests, good backpacking destinations are to be found.

Many YMCAs offer youth backpack programs, and Outward Bound conducts renowned teen-only backpack trips year-round. (See mountaineering section below.) The National Outdoor Leadership School (NOLS) also offers an excellent monthlong backpacking Adventure Course for boys and girls 14 and 15. The program is conducted in the mountains of Wyoming and Montana and costs about $2,350. Contact: NOLS, P.O. Box AA, Lander, WY 82529, (307) 332-6973. There are also scores of summer camps nationwide that offer backpacking as part of a range of activities. Consult Peterson's *Summer Opportunities for Kids and Teenagers 1991*, 8th Ed., Peterson Press, Princeton, N.J.

By all this we don't mean to suggest that there is anything wrong with joining your kids on a backpack trip. For many families, a trek into the wilderness is a positive experience which brings all family members closer together. The Sierra Club offers dozens of backpack trips designed for the whole family, even small children. Contact your local Sierra Club chapter and consult the annual outing guide, published each January in Sierra magazine. (For further details, contact the Sierra Club Outing Department, 730 Polk Street, San Francisco, CA 94109 and request family

outing information.) Helpful resources for family backpacking include *Family Camping Made Simple*, by Beverly Liston, Globe Pequot Press ($10.95); and *Take 'Em Along: Sharing the Wilderness with Your Children*, by Barbara Euser, Cordillera Press ($7.95).

HORSEBACK RIDING

Riding Academies

There are a host of equestrian academies offering live-in horseback riding programs for teens. Five of the best are:

■ ALLEGHENY RIDING CAMP
Box P, Tyrone, PA 16686, (814) 684-3000.

Located on a 1,000-acre private school site, the Allegheny Riding Camp offers formal equestrian training for girls 8-16. The camp has operated in conjunction with the Greer School for the past 17 years. Hunt, show, jumping and trail-riding instruction is provided by two full-time professionals. Horse care and equine health are also covered. Three, 4 and 7-week programs are available from approximately $1,500 to $3,200. Rating: ★★

■ FOXCROFT SCHOOL
Box 5555, Middleburg, VA 22117, (703) 687-5555.

The Foxcroft School is a leading college-

COURTESY TIROL TOURIST BOARD

preparatory academy for girls 15-18, which offers high-quality training in dressage, hunting, jumping and cross-country riding. Probably the finest full-time academic/riding school on the East Coast, Foxcroft features a 60-stall stable and a full indoor arena. Rating: ★★★

■ FOHLENHOF EQUESTRIAN ACADEMY
Site 7, Comp. 15, R.R. 6, Vernon, BC, Canada V1T 6Y5, (604) 542-4274.

Recognized as BC's best youth riding center, the Fohlenhof Academy is situated in the scenic Okanagan Valley. Your kids probably won't find a more beautiful place to ride in North America. Weekly summer programs on Austrian Haflinger horses are offered in trail-riding, jumping, dressage and carriage riding. While most students have previous riding experience, programs are available for all skill levels, and ages 8 to 21. The Academy boasts outstanding facilities and European professional instructors. Rating: ★★★

■ VERSHIRE RIDING SCHOOL
Vershire, VT 05079, (802) 685-2239.

The Vershire Riding School has been conducting highly rated coed summer programs since 1970. The school's 24-day summer sessions combine strong academics with classic English riding instruction at a cost of around $2,000. Students may attend two consecutive sessions during the summer if they choose. Rating: ★★

■ MORVEN PARK INTERNATIONAL EQUESTRIAN INSTITUTE
Route 4, Box 43, Leesburg, VA, (703) 777-2890.

Located on a 1,300-acre Virginia estate, Morven is, by general consensus, America's finest full-time riding academy. World-class dressage, and combined training instruction is offered on the rider's horse, or on the school's own mounts. In terms of the overall caliber of the teaching staff, horses and facilities, there is probably no comparable program in the United States. Tuition is roughly $550 per week, including accommodations and use of a horse. Rating: ★★★★

To obtain further information on other riding academies in your area, consult the Horseman's Directory, which should be available in your local horse specialty store. If you're looking for a less structured riding

program for your children, consider one of the many Western riding camps that combine wilderness training and horseback adventures for teens. We've listed some of our favorites below.

Western Ranches

■ ELK CREEK RANCH
P.O. Box 1476, Cody, WY 82414, (307) 587-3902. Winter Address: 31 A Academy Street, South Berwick, ME 03908, (207) 384-5361.

Since 1957, the Elk Creek Ranch has conducted outstanding summer adventure programs specializing in equestrian training and trail-riding. Set high in the mountains, Elk Creek Ranch also features backpacking, fishing and glacier skiing. Thirty-day programs for boys and girls 13-18 operate during June and July and cost about $2,200. Rating: ★★

■ ORME SUMMER CAMP AND SCHOOL
Mayer, AZ 86333, (602) 632-7601; FAX: (602) 632-7605.

This is a serious school and a serious ranch, operated continuously since 1929. Respected college preparatory academics are combined with a strong horsemanship and rodeo skills program. Students can enjoy trail-riding and wilderness camping on Orme's 40,000-acre high desert ranch, and participate in organized trips to national parks and scenic backcountry areas. Sessions run from June through August for 2 to 8 weeks at a cost of approximately $1,100 to $3,100. Rating: ★★★

■ CHELEY COLORADO CAMP
P.O. Box 1170, Estes Park, CO 80517.

Set high in the Rocky Mountains, Cheley Camp affords the perfect backdrop for summer trail-riding and mountain skills training. Separate 4-week programs for boys and girls 9-17 are offered from June through August each summer. In addition to horsemanship, mountaineering and wilderness skills are taught by experienced guides. Contact Don and Carole Cheley, Directors, P.O. Box 6525, Denver, CO 80206, (303) 586-4150. Rating: ★★

MOUNTAINEERING

Courage from Challenge

No listing of youth adventure programs would be complete without mention of Outward Bound. Since 1941, Outward Bound has taken both youths and adults into the wilderness to impart physical and mental toughness, respect for the wilderness and self-reliance. These programs can be tough, but for many participants, the Outward Bound experience marks a major turning point in their lives.

■ OUTWARD BOUND NATIONAL OFFICE
384 Field Point Road, Greenwich, CT 06830, (800) 243-8520, or (203) 661-0797.

■ PACIFIC CREST OUTWARD BOUND SCHOOL
0110 SW Bancroft Street, Portland, OR 97201, (800) 547-3312.

With five schools in North America (31 worldwide), Outward Bound offers a host of programs designed specifically for teenagers 14-16. (Seventeen and 18-year-olds are eligible for most regular Outward Bound programs.) The classic course involves 2 weeks of rock-climbing, rafting and backpacking, in Utah's Canyonlands (Colorado Outward Bound--$1,150). In the East, a 3-week combination rock-climbing and canoeing trip is offered just for teens (North Carolina Outward Bound--$1,750).

There are many other specialty programs for young adults, but our favorite is probably the 3-week combined rafting, backpacking and mountain-climbing trek for teens 16+ along the Deschutes River and Central Cascades in Oregon (Pacific Coast Outward Bound--roughly $2,200).

In addition to Outward Bound's regular outdoor adventures for teenagers, Outward Bound conducts unique 3 and 4-week programs for troubled youths 14-17. Offered as the Directive Program on the East Coast, the aim is not to reform tough kids, but to raise self-esteem through canoeing, camping and climbing activities. Cost is roughly $2,200 for 28 days. A similar program, with greater emphasis on mountaineering, is offered on the West Coast in California and Oregon (Ascent Program, 22 days, approx. $2,400). See Chapter 24 for a complete description of Outward Bound's adult programs around the country, and addresses for all five regional schools. Rating: ★★★

■ INNERQUEST, INC.
Route 1, Box 271 C, Purcellville, VA 22132, (703) 478-1078.

Special 1 to 3-week adventure programs for boys and girls 10-18 are conducted by East Coast-based InnerQuest, Inc. The programs feature rock-climbing, caving and multi-day mountain trekking expeditions, along with river programs. Prices range from $350 to $1,000. Because InnerQuest is relatively new, we recommend that you ask for references from recent participants. Rating: ★★

MARK GALLUP

PADDLING

From Thrills to Serenity

Short whitewater raft trips and weekend kayak excursions for teens and young adults are offered by many river outfitters nationwide. Consult our listings in Chapters 6 (Canoeing) and 16 (Rafting). If your child is looking for more than a day or two on the river, however, he or she should consider a specialty paddling center that offers an expedition-type river experience. Here are some of the best.

■ ANDERSON CAMPS' COLORADO RIVER RANCH FOR BOYS
7177 Colorado River Road, Gypsum, CO 81637, (303) 524-7766.

This camp has provided river and wilderness training to boys since 1962. Four and 5-week programs featuring river skills, backpacking, caving and mountaineering are offered each summer in the Rockies along the headwaters of the Colorado River. Rafting is a major focus of the Anderson Camps. This is one of the best locations to learn whitewater, rock-climbing and wilderness skills in an alpine setting. Cost ranges from about $1,600 to $1,900. Rating: ★★

■ KEEWAYDIN CANOE TRIPS
Temagami, ONT, Canada P0H 2H0.

In operation since 1893, the Canadian Keewaydin center offers the most extensive canoeing program of any North American summer camp. Boys 10-18 receive paddling and wilderness skills instruction during 6-week sessions from June through August (3 weeks for ages 10-11). Campers have the opportunity to go on long-distance wilderness canoe trips from a few days to many weeks. Cost is about $1,800 for 6 weeks, while the 3-week session is roughly $950. Contact Daniel Carpenter, Director, 59 Cherry Valley Road, Greenwich, CT 06831, (203) 661-1954. Rating: ★★

■ KEEWAYDIN WILDERNESS CANOE TRIPS
Salisbury, VT 05769, (802) 352-4247.

This organization (not affiliated with Keewaydin Canada) has offered wilderness canoe trips for boys 15-19 since 1963. Keewaydin Vermont's unique program takes teens on challenging 10-day ($1,000) or 4-week ($2,400) journeys along wild, remote rivers in southern Canada. After paddling school in Vermont, the group heads to Quebec to explore such Class II-III rivers as the Mistassini, Nesta Canao and Maicasagi. There is also an advanced Class IV trip to Ungava Bay for experienced paddlers. All trips are lead by Cree Indian guides who teach fishing, shelter-building and other important backwoods skills. Contact Seth Gibson, Trips Director, Box 626, Middlebury, VT 85753, (802) 388-2556. Rating: ★★★

■ VOYAGEUR OUTWARD BOUND SCHOOL
10900 Cedar Lake Road, Minnetonka, MN 55343, (800) 328-2943, or (612) 542-9448.

■ NORTH CAROLINA OUTWARD BOUND SCHOOL
121 N. Sterling Street, Morganton, NC 28655, (707) 437-6112.

These two Outward Bound centers conduct outstanding river expeditions for high-schoolers. The Voyageur school offers 7 to 29-day canoe expeditions on Minnesota and Canadian rivers, or whitewater canoe trips down the Rio Grande. The North Carolina school operates whitewater canoe trips on North Carolina rivers, along with winter canoe trips through the Florida Everglades. Cost is roughly $800 to $2,100 depending on trip length and location. The minimum age is 14. Contact either school for details. Rating: ★★★

Unlocking the Undersea Realm

There are a number of well-established youth scuba diving programs conducted each summer near good dive sites. Most combine a marine sciences curriculum with scuba training, sailing, windsurfing and other ocean sports. All of these offer a challenging and enriching experience along with great diving.

■ ACTIONDIVE

P.O. Box 5507, Sarasota, FL 34277, (813) 924-6789; FAX: (813) 924-6075.

ActionDive conducts 2 to 3-week ocean sports and education programs for teens 15-19 aboard 50' yachts in the British Virgin Islands. The program is designed for previously certified teen divers who will be eligible to receive PADI advanced open water certification and/or specialty certification (night diving, wreck diving) during the program. The ActionDive yachts visit a variety of dive sites and small islands, and sailing, waterskiing and windsurfing complement the dive training. Cost ranges from roughly $1,900 to $2,800. Highly recommended. Rating: ★★★

■ SEACAMP

Box 170, Route 3, Big Pine Key, FL 33043, (305) 872-2331.

Seacamp combines summer academic training in environmental and marine sciences with a scuba certification program for 12 to 17-year-olds. No prior dive expe-

COURTESY FLORIDA AIR ACADEMY

rience is required. Along with the dive training, participants receive instruction in sailing and windsurfing. The 18-day program cost approximately $1,850, plus $350 for scuba in 1991. Rating: ★★

■ CATALINA SEA CAMP

P.O. Box 1360, Claremont, CA 91711, (714) 949-0687.

Catalina Sea Camp has conducted summer ocean training programs for kids 8-17 since 1978. The coed program combines ocean science studies with scuba and skin diving. Windsurfing and on-land recreation are featured in the 1 to 3-week sessions costing $450 to $1,600. With excellent safety facilities and a host of underwater attractions, Catalina Island is one of the best diving destinations in Southern California. Rating: ★★

Good as these programs are, if your child just wants to dive, and he or she is reasonably mature, a much cheaper option is to enroll him or her in a regular dive training class with a reputable dive shop in your area. A typical open water certification course will take 2 to 4 weeks, including both pool training and ocean dives. The experience won't be as exotic as a dive camp in the Caribbean, but the total cost for a basic NAUI, PADI or SSI certification course, including an ocean-diving weekend, will probably be less than $300.

Never Too Young to Start

Believe it or not, summer is prime time for youth ski camps--on glaciers. Mt. Hood is the mecca for summer ski training in North America, with numerous programs to choose from. There are also summer teen ski programs in the European Alps.

■ MT. HOOD SUMMER SKI CAMPS

P.O. Box 317, Government Camp, OR 97028, (503) 337-2230.

The most popular teen ski program in recent years has been the Mt. Hood Summer Ski Camp, now entering its 13th season. The Ski Camp's 11-day programs are designed for intermediate or better young skiers, and cost approximately $600-$725, including dormitory lodging and meals. Instruction is provided by highly qualified pros from Vail, Squaw Valley and other major resorts. The summer ski camps fill up quickly, so book well in advance. Rating: ★★★

DAVID STOECKLEIN

■ DAVE MURRAY SUMMER SKI CAMP

P.O. Box 98, Whistler, BC, Canada V0N 1B0, (604) 932-3141, or (604) 687-1032.

Based at Blackcomb Mountain, this is the longest-running summer ski camp in North America. Junior programs cost about $850 per week including food, lodging, lifts, tennis and mountain biking. Instruction and supervision are excellent. Rating: ★★★

■ AUSTRIAN SUMMER SKI CAMPS

Hintertux Glacier, Austria.

Both Atomic and Blizzard traditionally offer summer glacier skiing programs in Austria. The price, roughly $500 per week, includes ski training, instruction, lift tickets, and room and board. Contact Young Austria (Blizzard), (011 43) 662 257-5821, or David Donahue, Atomic Ski USA, 4 Cote Lane, Bedford, NH 03102, (800) 258-5020, or (603) 668-8980. Rating: ★★★

■ BLIZZARD JUNIOR SKI CAMP

Blizzard, P.O. Box 4186, Malibu, CA 90265, (213) 457-2541. (Winter only)

For kids 8-18, whether they've skied before or not, Blizzard offers supervised ski holidays at Mammoth, plus a Christmas

trip to Utah. There is bus service throughout Southern California. This is a solid program with a 30-year track record. Rating: ★★★

If none of these suggestions fit the bill, you'll find a listing of over 30 summer ski programs in the March or April issue of Powder magazine, Box 1028, Dana Point, CA 92629.

SURFING

Kindling the Flame

Surfing is a great way to tone and strengthen bodies, and to provide youths with the focus and self-esteem they may lack at school. Once a kid gets past the initial learning stage, surfing offers a lifetime of challenge and enjoyment.

■ YMCA CAMP SURF
Imperial Beach, CA 92032, (619) 423-5850, or (619) 292-5942.

The Imperial Beach, California YMCA operates a summer surfing program that may be exactly what your kid has been looking for. The YMCA Summer Surf Camp, one of the few operations of its kind

in the world, is a live-in surfing/ocean activity program for boys and girls 7-17. The Camp's Water Man Program (ages 12-13), costs about $200 per week, which includes food, tent lodging on the beach, and surfing and surf rescue instruction. Kids can enroll for any period from a week to an entire summer.

The Beach Club program (ages 13-17) costs about $400 for 2 weeks, and features diving and sailing along with surfing. The price is all-inclusive, and a teen can stay the full summer if places are available. Participants will go on five California surf trips during each session. A counselor-in-training program is also available.

Both the Water Man and Beach Club programs feature full-time adult supervision, 7 days of surfing a week, and optional Baja surfaris. The 3-day Baja surf trips cost approximately $100, plus transportation fee. The Summer Surf Camp is an outstanding adventure program that has attracted youngsters from around the world. A typical comment: "My son has been twice and wants to go back again." For quality and value, you won't find any better surf program, anywhere. A winter program may be offered next year. Rating: ★★★★$

WINDSURFING

Thrills and Spills

Your kid can learn the fundamentals of longboard windsurfing on virtually any body of water, and most lake-based summer camps now offer windsurfing along with other activities. However, if your kid wants to sail a shortboard, he will need warm water and strong, consistent winds. In the summertime, Maui is the place to go. With its inviting waters and steady tradewinds, Maui offers conditions that enable even total novices to master a shortboard within a few weeks.

■ MAUI MAGIC WINDSURFING SCHOOL
520 Keolani Place, Kahului, Maui, HI 96732, (800) 872-0999, or (808) 877-4816.

Maui Magic is the leading windsurfing training program on Maui. Though not a youth specialty program, its instructors have taught hundreds of young people to waterstart in the warm waters of Kanaha Bay. Custom boards and top-quality rigs come from the island's leading shops. Individualized instruction, using two-way radios, is provided by expert Maui boardsailors. Another reputable windsurf training program is Windsurfing West, 460 Dairy Road, Kahului, Maui, HI 96732, (808) 871-8733. This company employs Jeannie McMurtry, former director of the Maui Windsurfing Youth Clinic. Both schools can book accommodations on Maui, but parents will have to arrange supervision away from the beach. Rating: ★★★

■ FALCON SAILING
13 Hillgate Street, London, England W8 7SP, (011 44) 71 727 0232.

If the kids are dying to windsurf, but you've been planning a European vacation this summer, Falcon offers package windsurfing holidays at 7 resorts in Greece, Turkey and Sardinia. Two-week packages range in price from $500 to $900 per person, including round-trip airfare from London, and Royal Yachting Association (RYA) instruction. A non-sailing option is available at reduced cost for family members who choose not to sail. Teenagers must be accompanied by adults. Rating: ★★

COURTESY MAUI WINDSURFING YOUTH CLINIC

Spinnaker-riding in Tahiti/NEIL RABINOWITZ

YACHTING

Sport for a Lifetime

If you'd like your son or daughter to become a sailor, the best thing to do is contact local yacht clubs in your area. Many offer summer youth programs that are open to the public for a reasonable cost. Most often the boats are provided by the host clubs, and the instructors are consistently good. However, if you live too far from the water and junior's dead set on sailing, there are a number of good residential sailing programs to choose from. Those listed below are premium programs. Local or regional sailing programs tend to be less costly, but equipment may not be the best, and the quality of instruction may be lower.

■ ACTIONSAIL

P.O. Box 5507-A, Sarasota, FL 34277, (813) 924-6789; FAX: (813) 924-6075.

ActionSail offers coed summer sailing programs in the British Virgin Islands and Leeward Islands for teens 12-18. In operation for 17 years, ActionSail teaches sailing and boat handling, celestial navigation and racing techniques aboard 50' yachts. ActionSail can also provide PADI dive training and certification, along with recreational windsurfing. ActionSail's liveaboard programs give the participants a wealth of training, challenge and experience in a 3-week session. This is a strong, well-established program, probably the best of its kind. We can recommend ActionSail highly, if you can afford it. Cost for 3 weeks is about $2,800 per person, including dive certification. A condensed 2-week version of the cruise runs about $1,900. Rating: ★★★★

■ HURRICANE ISLAND OUTWARD BOUND SCHOOL

P.O. Box 429, Rockland, ME 04841, (800) 341-1744, or (207) 594-5548.

This Outward Bound School conducts excellent 2 and 3-week sailing expeditions each summer along the Maine coast. Using 30' sailing dories, high-schoolers learn seamanship, coastal navigation, ocean safety and basic survival skills. As with all Outward Bound programs there is strong emphasis on developing self-sufficiency and improved self-esteem. The program for teens 15-16 runs for 3 weeks in July and costs approximately $1,800. For 16- to 18-year-olds, a number of 2 and 3-week expeditions are offered between May and September at a cost of about $1,600 to $2,200. Rating: ★★$

■ MAN AND HIS LAND EXPEDITIONS

Castle Rock Center for Environmental Adventures, 412 County Road, 6NS, Cody, WY 82414, (800) 356-9965, (307) 587-2076, or (307) 527-7196.

This Wyoming-based outfitter runs a popular sail/dive/windsurf program each summer in the Caribbean. Using large and small boats, windsurfers and scuba equipment, boys and girls 14-18 explore coral reefs and remote islands in the West Indies. Boating and dive instruction are included. The 24-day sessions run in June and July, and cost about $3,000 with all equipment. Rating: ★★

■ OCEAN YOUTH CLUB

South Street, Gosport, Hampshire, England PO12 1EP, (011 44) 705 528421.

For the past 30 years, the Ocean Youth Club has been one of Britain's finest sail training programs for teens and young adults. Employing a fleet of 10 large sailing yachts based in England, Scotland and Ireland, the Ocean Youth Club conducts challenging 1 to 3-week offshore training cruises aboard 50'-70' ocean-going ketches. Both group and individual bookings are available. Cost is roughly $420 per week at peak season, including meals and equipment. Being a nonprofit organization, the Ocean Youth Club can offer prices that are hard to beat, even with airfare to Great Britain. Rating: ★★★$

■ SAIL CARIBBEAN

Michael Liese, 79-A Church Street, Northport, NY 11768, (516) 754-2202.

Sail Caribbean offers a quality liveaboard sailing and ocean sports summer program in the Virgin Islands. Teens age 14-19 can learn to sail 46' yachts to 20 different Caribbean island destinations. Training in seamanship, boat-handling and navigation is provided, and successful students may return home with an American Sailing Association (ASA) bareboat certification by the end of the program. Parents take note: your child's ASA certificate could come in handy on your next charter vacation. Windsurfing, waterskiing and scuba diving are offered as well. Sail Caribbean's 2 to 6-week sessions range in price from $1,850 to $5,500. Rating: ★★

MULTI-SPORT PROGRAMS

The Total Adventure Package

Some youth adventure programs are so diverse by design that it would be unfair to pigeonhole them under one particular activity. Here are some of the best multi-sport programs for teens. These offer everything from llama-packing to mountain biking, all in a single summer holiday.

■ **CANADIAN OUTWARD BOUND WILDERNESS SCHOOL**
P.O. Box 116, Station S, Toronto, ONT, Canada M5M 4L6, (416) 787-1721.

Teens 15 and over can sample a spectrum of adventure activities on 9 to 22-day outings offered by the Canadian Outward Bound School. The summer programs feature canoeing, kayaking, backpacking and mountaineering. Winter courses include dogsledding, skiing and snowcamping. The school's proximity to major rivers makes it ideal for canoe and kayak training. The school operates from May to October, and courses cost approximately $950 to $1,800. Rating: ★★★

■ **MAN AND HIS LAND EXPEDITIONS**
Castle Rock Center for Environmental Adventures, 412 County Road, 6NS, Cody, WY 82414, (800) 533-3066, or (307) 527-6650; FAX: (307) 527-7196.

The Castle Rock Center offers what may be the most complete teen adventure programs in North America. Under the title of "Man and his Land Expeditions," Castle Rock offers three land-based summer programs ranging from 3 to 8 weeks. The 8-week "Full West" trip begins with a 7-day backpack trip in the Rockies, followed by a week in the Grand Canyon. Week 3 is spent rafting the Green River, one of America's most scenic and challenging waterways. Then it's on to Mt. Rainier for a week of mountaineering, crevasse rescue training and ice-climbing.

During weeks 5 and 6, the group tours the Olympic Peninsula, then visits Glacier National Park for fishing and more river running. Then things really get busy. During week 7, the young adventurers sample mountain biking, horsepacking and llama-trekking on three overnight trips in Wyoming's Absaroka Range. Finally, the kids head to the Exum School of Mountaineering for 2 days of rock-climbing instruction and a Teton summit ascent.

Castle Rock's shorter programs are equally remarkable. The 5-week session offers New Mexico backpacking, Green River rafting, horseback riding, llama-trekking, and mountain biking in Wyoming's Absaroka mountains, plus canoeing, fishing and backpacking in Yellowstone, and Teton mountaineering with Exum. Price is about $3,100. Even those on the shortest program won't be disappointed. The 3-week course covers most of the same activities and costs approximately $2,200--not cheap by summer camp standards, but a bargain compared to what adults would pay to do as much.

Participants and parents alike have the highest praise for the "Man and His Land" expeditions. We know of no other summer program which offers a more diverse package of "ultimate adventures" expressly for young adults. Rating: ★★★

■ **JOHN RIDGWAY ADVENTURE SCHOOL**
Ardmore, Rhiconich, By Lairg, Sutherland, Scotland (Great Britain) IV27 4RB, (011 44) 97 182 229.

Since 1969, John Ridgway has directed a multi-sport adventure training center in the Scottish Highlands. Ridgway's Adventure School offers canoeing, rock-climbing, fishing, backpacking, survival training, dinghy sailing, and offshore sailing on a 57' ketch. Separate 2-week programs for 12 to 15-year-olds and 15 to 18-year-olds are available June through August for roughly $775, including board and lodging. This is an excellent program for those who want to sample both land-based and ocean adventures in a short period of time. Participants won't be disappointed with John Ridgway, a true outdoorsman. Rating: ★★★

RESOURCES

Peterson's Summer Opportunities for Kids and Teenagers 1992, (9th Ed.) If you're looking for a summer camp for your kids, start with this comprehensive annual. $10.95 from Peterson's, P.O. Box 2123, Princeton, NJ 08543-2123, (800) 338-3181.

The Teenager's Guide to Study, Travel, and Adventure Abroad. This resource lists over 150 young adult programs worldwide, including bicycle tours, treks and work/study programs. $9.95 from World Wide Books 736-A, Granville St., Vancouver, BC, Canada V6Z 1G3, (604) 687-3320.

Taking the plunge, Lake Oesa, Alberta, Canada/MARK GALLUP

Getting There

Climbing out from the Tasman Glacier, New Zealand/NATHAN BILOW

*The journey of one thousand miles
begins with a single step.*
-Lao-Tse

▼

*I*f you're adventuring outside North America, chances are you'll be getting to your destination by air. If you're only going for a week or two, your airfare may equal, or even exceed, all your other expenses for the trip. However, you can easily reduce air travel costs by 20 to 50 percent, if you take advantage of the airline industry's many bargain programs. In this chapter, we explain how to save big bucks on your flight connections. We cover a host of budget air travel options including charter flights, last-minute programs, standby travel, student discounts and courier flights.

For adventurous travelers headed to the hinterlands, we've included a worldwide travel planner that will help you arrange the cheapest flights to just about anywhere, from the North Pole to the Serengeti. And if you're planning a wilderness adventure, we've listed the leading bushplane and expedition flying services in the Northern and Southern Hemispheres.

CHAPTER

28

747-400 over Mt. McKinley/COURTESY LUFTHANSA

APEX FARES

If you don't know what an APEX fare is by now, you've paid too much. APEX, short for "advance-purchase excursion," designates a discount ticket offered by virtually all major international carriers for those travelers who can book well in advance and return within a particular time limit. You can save as much as 30 percent over standard fares, but you're charged a penalty if you change or cancel your ticket. It's still a good deal, if you know exactly when you're going to travel. Call a travel agent to make reservations, or use the toll-free airline numbers listed at the end of this chapter.

BUCKET SHOPS

Once found only in Europe, bucket shops, or ultra-discount ticket brokers, now thrive in every major US city. The vast majority of their tickets are surplus seats acquired wholesale from major carriers. Good bucket shops offer big savings--you can expect to fly from New York to London

for under $350 one-way, from Los Angeles to Hong Kong for under $800 round-trip, or go around the world with a half-dozen stops for $1,800 or less. What's the catch? You'll get curt, even rude service over the telephone. Don't expect them to book hotels, reserve rental cars, or do the many other things a good travel agency normally would. Tickets often have to be purchased well in advance of your flight, and there can be significant penalties if you need to cancel or change your reservations.

Despite all this, most bucket shops deliver what they promise, and will reward you with outstanding bargains if you shop around and exercise good judgment. You'll still have to pay fairly high prices for certain destinations, notably New Zealand, Australia and Africa, but 20 to 30 percent discounts over "standard" fares are generally the rule. To find a bucket shop in your area, check the newspaper classified advertisements, and also the yellow pages. Be sure to ask which airline will be used. Certain carriers, notably Air India and Egypt Air, are not recommended.

Ask how long the quoted price is guaranteed, and who will provide any refund--the agency, or the airline. Pick up the tickets yourself to avoid delays. Here are some leading discount agencies.

■ **ACCESS INTERNATIONAL LTD.**
101 West 31st Street, New York, NY 10001, (212) 465-0707, or (800) TAKE-OFF; FAX: (212) 594-6711.

■ **EXPRESS DISCOUNT TRAVEL**
5945 Mission Gorge Road #2, San Diego, CA 92120, (800) 228-0513, or (619) 283-6324. Mexico and Hawaii specialist.

■ **P & D TRAVEL**
1545 Wilshire Boulevard, #413, Los Angeles, CA 90017, (213) 483-8539; FAX: (213) 483-7007. Orient and Europe. Very low fares.

■ **PEOPLE'S AIR TOURS, INC.**
2536 West Peterson, Chicago, IL 60659, (800) 635-7184, or (312) 761-7500. Europe, Orient, Pacific, South America specialists.

■ **SUPERTRIP TRAVEL**
3727 W. 6th Street, Ste. 318, Los Angeles, CA 90020, (800) 338-1898, or (213) 382-9688. Orient (incl. China) and Pacific. Very low fares.

CHARTER FLIGHTS

Charter flights, available from most full-service travel agencies, generally offer the lowest confirmed reservation fares to most popular destinations. A New York to London one-way charter fare cost about $285 in 1991. That's hard to beat. The drawbacks are that you usually have to fix your departure and return dates well in advance, and you may have to pay a substantial fee to cancel your ticket or change your flight times. Charter services are generally less well organized than the major airlines, so you'll probably spend more time in line at the airport, and run a greater risk of lost baggage. When dealing with a charter operator, make sure you know which ticket counter they will be using. Often the charter operator will run only one flight per day out of an airport, and there will be no signs telling you where to go when you arrive at the terminal. If the charter's flight number or departure time has been changed, you will be at a complete loss to find your check-in.

Despite all these shortcomings, charters are cheap, millions of passengers use them every year, and their safety and reliability records compare favorably with many large carriers. Remember that it is often possible to book only one leg of a two-way charter. We were able to book the return leg only of a charter from Madrid to the Canary Islands for far less than half of the original charter price. When faced with sending a plane home with empty seats, charter operators are willing to offer deep discounts.

To find a good charter, consult the listings in the Sunday newspapers, ask your regular travel agent, and then contact a specialty charter agent if you haven't found what you need. Before booking, ask the agent about the charter company's reliability. Though American charter companies are bonded with the US government, it can still be a hassle to get your money back if the charter operator defaults. Here are some leading charter operators you can contact directly.

■ COUNCIL CHARTER
205 E. 42nd Street, New York, NY 10017, (800) 800-8222, or (212) 661-1450 in New York. This popular charterer provides flights from the US to destinations worldwide. Book well in advance.

■ DOLLAR STRETCHER
5728 Major Boulevard, Suite 750, Orlando, FL 32819, (800) 669-9985 for reservations, (800) 736-4579 for brochures. This British Airways charter operation flies from the East Coast to Britain, for as little as $450 round-trip.

■ JET VACATIONS, INC.
1775 Broadway, 24th Floor, New York, NY 10019, (800) JET-0999, or (212) 247-0999. Air France subsidiary that runs 747 charters from the East Coast to France, $250 and up each way.

■ MARTINAIR HOLLAND
1165 Northern Boulevard, Manhasset, NY 11030, (800) 366-4655, or (516) 627-8711. Using its own planes, Martinair flies weekly

DAVID STOECKLEIN

charters to Amsterdam from many parts of the US. Round-trip, off-season airfare ranges from $450 (East Coast) to $600 (West Coast).

■ TOURLITE INTERNATIONAL
1 East 42nd Street, New York, NY 10017, (800) 272-7600, or (212) 599-2727. South America and Eastern Mediterranean.

■ TRAVAC INTERNATIONAL
989 Avenue of Americas, New York, NY 10018, (800) 872-8800, or (212) 563-3303; 6151 West Century Boulevard, Suite 728, Los Angeles, CA 90045, (800) 872-8800, or (213) 670-9692. Western Europe specialists.

STANDBY & LAST MINUTE

Standby travel is still alive and well, with most major airlines offering substantial discounts on popular routes, for example $229 for a one-way fare from New York to London. The question you have to ask yourself these days, however, is why bother, when you can get a confirmed reservation for the same price from "last-minute" ticket brokers. Just a few days before flights depart, these agencies obtain surplus seats from charter carriers at fire-sale prices. For the airlines, filling the seat at any price is better than flying empty, and you reap the benefit, if you're able to fly on short notice. In addition to air tickets, big discounts on tours, cruises and accommodations are available as well. Typical discounts are 30 to 50 percent off the regular fare, and your ticket will be confirmed, unlike standby flying.

Most last-minute ticket agencies require that you pay an annual fee ($20-$50). You'll then be informed of travel bargains via newsletters and/or a toll-free travel hotline. You usually book a flight within the last week or so of departure. Most tickets are on unfilled charter flights, although major carriers sometimes will use these distress-sale brokers as well. These are some of the leading last-minute agencies.

■ DISCOUNT TRAVEL INT'L
114 Forest Avenue, Ives Bldg., Suite 205, Narberth, PA 19072, (800) 334-9294. Fee: $45.

■ LAST MINUTE TRAVEL CLUB, INC.
1249 Boylston St., Boston, MA 02215, (800) 527-8646 (LAS-TMIN), or (617) 267-9800. Mostly Boston departures. Specializes in air/hotel packages to the Caribbean and Mexico, and air connections to Western Europe. No fee.

■ MOMENT'S NOTICE, INC.
425 Madison Avenue, New York, NY 10017, (212) 486-0500. Well-established agency; mostly East Coast departures. Offers air/hotel packages to Caribbean and Mexico, cruises, air only to Europe and the West Coast. Fee: $45 (includes traveling companions).

■ WORLDWIDE DISCOUNT TRAVEL CLUB
1674 Meridian Avenue, Miami Beach, FL 33139, (305) 534-2082. Departures from Atlanta, Boston, Chicago, Los Angeles, Miami and New York. Cruises and inclusive tours to all major destinations. Fee: $40 ($50 for family).

COURIER FLIGHTS

If you're willing to give up your baggage allowance and travel with only a carry-on, you can fly to most foreign business centers for less than half the normal fare, and sometimes even free. How? As a courier. By using your baggage allowance for their overnight cargo, courier companies can subsidize your fare and still turn a profit. The main drawback, other than being forced to travel very lightly indeed, is that you may be asked to fly on short notice--though you can give the courier service a general idea of your availability, and they will usually try to accommodate you. Representative courier fares are: New York-London, $175 one-way; New York-Rio, $400 round-trip; Los Angeles-Tokyo, $350 round-trip; Los Angeles-Singapore, $400 round-trip.

Traveling as a courier isn't for everybody, but for those who can cope with the limitations, there's no cheaper way to go. For immediate opportunities, check the travel classifieds in major US cities, including New York, Los Angeles, Miami, Chicago and San Francisco. Look for rock-bottom prices and a reference to "Courier." Or, you can contact the major courier services directly, at the addresses below.

■ NOW VOYAGER
74 Varick Street, Suite 307, New York, NY 10013, (212) 431-1616. London, Paris, Rio, Buenos Aires, Caribbean, Copenhagen, Brussels, Oslo, Caracas, Seoul, Hong Kong, Frankfurt, Amsterdam. Principal booking agency for courier companies flying from New York. $50 registration fee.

■ HALBART EXPRESS
147-05 176th Street, Jamaica, NY 11434, (718) 656-8189, ext. 771. NY to Milan, Amsterdam, Madrid, Mexico City, Frankfurt, Paris, Brussels. Call 6 to 8 weeks in advance.

■ INTERNATIONAL BONDED COURIER
1595 East El Segundo Blvd., El Segundo, CA 90245. Destinations: Los Angeles to Singapore, Hong Kong, Tokyo, Seoul, Taiwan, Bangkok, London, Miami. Call (310) 607-0125 from 11:00-3:00, Monday through Friday.

STUDENT DISCOUNTS

Students, i.e. those under 25, or under 35 within three years of graduation, can obtain dramatic discounts on air travel. We saved over $300 on airfare to the South Pacific, and our student ticket had far fewer restrictions than most APEX or discount fares. Many small foreign carriers deeply discount their airfares for those under 25 with student cards. Air Morocco, for example, provides a 50 percent discount to qualifying students.

The student travel industry leader is STA Student Travel Network. With more than 100 offices worldwide, STA can issue student ID cards on the spot, and can book super cheap flights to just about anywhere--for example, Los Angeles to London for $500 round-trip (low season), or Los Angeles to Tokyo for $589 round-trip (low season). STA discounts are available to enrolled students under 35, and all persons under 26. STA tickets are issued on regularly scheduled flights (not charters), no advance purchase is required, and itineraries or flights may be changed without restriction at STA offices worldwide. The

large network of offices is very useful if you have to change your tickets after you've left the country. Go into an STA office anywhere in the world, and they'll handle your business quickly and efficiently. There are STA offices in many major US cities.

■ STA BOSTON
273 Newbury Street, Boston, MA 02116, (617) 266-6014.

■ STA LOS ANGELES
7204 Melrose Avenue, Los Angeles, CA 90046, (213) 934-8722, or (800) 777-0112.

■ STA NEW YORK
Whole World Travel, 17th E. 45th Street, Suite 805, New York, NY 10017, (212) 986-9470.

■ STA SAN DIEGO
6447 El Cajon Boulevard, San Diego, CA 92115, (619) 286-1322.

■ STA SAN FRANCISCO
166 Geary Street, Suite 702, San Francisco, CA 94108, (415) 391-8407.

PACKAGE TOURS

As you plan your adventure vacation, you'll notice that many tour organizations include air or sea transportation as part of the tour package price. While this makes life easy, it may unnecessarily inflate the cost of your vacation, particularly if you are a student, are prepared to fly as a courier, or are willing to use last-minute ticketing programs. Ask the tour operator if it is able to omit the airfare segment of the trip. This usually can be done with enough advance notice. You may be surprised to see how much you will be paying just to get to your destination. Then, using the tips in this chapter, see if you're able to save some dollars by booking your own flight. Added benefits of this strategy include being able to break up a very long flight, and/or customize your itinerary to add another destination or two.

TOLL-FREE AIRLINE NUMBERS

Aer Lingus (Ireland)	(800) 223-6537
Aerolinas Argentinas	(800) 333-0276
Aero Mexico	(800) 237-6639
Aero Peru	(800) 255-7378
Air Canada	(800) 776-3000
Air France	(800) 237-2747
Air New Zealand	(800) 262-1234
Alaska Airlines	(800) 426-0333
Alitalia	(800) 223-5730
ALM Antilles	(800) 327-7230
America West	(800) 247-5692
American	(800) 433-7300
British Airways	(800) 247-9297
Cathay Pacific	(800) 233-2742
Continental	(800) 525-0280
Delta Airlines	(800) 221-1212
Ecuatoriana Airlines	(800) 328-2367
El Al Israel	(800) 235-3525
Garuda Indonesia	(800) 826-2829
Iberia (Spain)	(800) 772-4642
Icelandair	(800) 223-5500
Japan Air Lines	(800) 525-3663
KLM Royal Dutch	(800) 777-5553
Lufthansa	(800) 645-3880
Mexicana	(800) 531-7921
Northwest	(800) 447-4747
Philippine Airlines	(800) 435-9725
Royal Jordanian	(800) 223-0470
Qantas	(800) 227-4500
Scandinavian Airlines	(800) 221-2350
Singapore Airlines	(800) 742-3333
South Africa Airways	(800) 722-9675
Swissair	(800) 221-4750
TAP (Portugal)	(800) 221-7390
Thai Airways Int'l	(800) 426-5204
Trans World Airlines	(800) 221-2000
UTA French Airlines	(800) 423-7422
United Airlines	(800) 538-2929
US Air	(800) 428-4322
Varig Brazilian Air	(800) 468-2744
Virgin Atlantic	(800) 862-8621

REGIONAL TRAVEL STRATEGIES

Shinakas on Dal Lake, Kashmir, India/CHRIS NOBLE

T O HELP YOU PLAN YOUR MOST EXOTIC VACATIONS, WE PROVIDE A QUICK SUMMARY of the easiest and most economical ways to fly to destinations worldwide, from the heart of the Himalayas to the wilds of Africa. We cover each corner of the world separately, offering tips on little-known carriers, and creative ways to combine flight segments to save both time and money.

AFRICA

■

You'll pay a fortune if you book a round-trip ticket from the West Coast to Africa with a standard travel agent. Africa, including Egypt, is one of the few destinations not greatly affected by the fare wars of recent years. The cheapest way to get to Egypt or East Africa is to find a low fare to London, (e.g. $500-$600 round-trip from New York by charter), and then obtain a round-trip package from London to Nairobi or Cairo. In 1990 a round trip from London to Cairo

could be purchased in London for less than $450. You don't have to be in London to arrange all this either. Get a copy of the **Sunday London Times** at your local library, and write down the numbers of the discount travel agencies which service Africa. Call an agency direct, and have the tickets sent to your home by registered airmail or overnight courier, if you don't have time to pick them up when arriving in Britain. You can also call **London's Air Travel Advisory Board**, *(011 44) 71 636 5000,* for tips on the best deals to European and

African destinations.

Gametrackers International, *1000 E. Broadway, Glendale, CA 91205, (800) 444-BUSH, or (818) 507-8401,* offers some of the lowest fares available to Namibia and South Africa. With a $35 travel club membership, you can save well over 30 percent on normal airfares to the southern regions of Africa. Another option to consider is purchasing an around-the-world ticket. Here's why: Pan Am will charge you about $1,800 to fly New York to Nairobi round-trip, but a good bucket shop will sell you an around-the-world ticket for $1,700 or less. Such a ticket will usually allow numerous stops along the way. Visit Singapore or Hong Kong on the way home to do some shopping, and you may save enough on your purchases to underwrite most of your airfare. A good round-the-world ticket agency is **Air Brokers International,** *323 Geary Street, Ste. 606,*

San Francisco, CA 94102, (415) 397-1383. (Route: LA, Europe, Cairo, Nairobi, Bangkok, Hawaii, LA for roughly $1,700.)

ASIA

∎

Singapore Airlines is the best way to get to Asia if you've got the cash--it boasts new planes, fine food and great service. If you're looking for a bargain, **Northwest** and **TWA** now offer a number of flights at a reasonable cost. Deep discounts are available on all the major Asia runs including Hong Kong, Singapore and Taipei. One major discount ticket broker, **Venton's Overseas Tours,** recently offered LA-Singapore round trips for $730, LA-Hong Kong for only $600. *Call (800) 323-8777 in CA, (800) 222-5292 elsewhere.* If you're visiting more than one Asian city, Circle Pacific fares offer excellent value. **Air Brokers Int'l,** *(415) 397-1383,* gives you most of Asia and the South Pacific (LA, Hong Kong, Bangkok, Singapore, Jakarta, Bali, Sydney, Hawaii, LA) for just $1,499.

Another option is to get a cheap charter to Hawaii, ($150 one-way is possible), and then pick up your ticket to Asia in Honolulu. Prices are often cheaper than on the mainland, especially to Japan. You may also be able to pick up the second half of a charter to Japan that has a few empty seats. Check the Honolulu papers for listings.

For good fares to Japan, contact **Japan Budget Travel,** *9 East 38th Street, Room 203, New York, NY 10016, (800) 722-0797, or (212) 686-8855.* For other Asian destinations, contact **Euro-Asia Express,** *(800) 782-9624 in CA, (800) 782-9625 outside CA;* or consult the travel classifieds in major newspapers. Sample 1991 Euro-Asia Express fares were $600 round-trip to Hong Kong, $650 round-trip to Tokyo.

If you can travel light, Singapore, Hong Kong and Tokyo are some of the hottest courier runs in the world. Check the classifieds in the Los Angeles Times, or San Francisco Chronicle for departures. Typical 1991 courier flight prices were $440 Los Angeles-Hong Kong round-trip, $375 Los Angeles-Tokyo.

CARIBBEAN

∎

Many major US carriers, including **United** and **Delta**, fly to destinations in the Caribbean. This allows you to use airline discount promotions, such as United's Mileage Plus coupons, which can be obtained in most large cities. You can often cut the cost of a Caribbean trip by 30 to 40 percent in this fashion. Just make sure that the coupon you obtain covers the Caribbean flights and is transferable. These coupons are available from flight coupon brokers in most major cities. Check the Sunday classifieds in the New York Times, Los Angeles Times and other big city newspapers.

Most bucket shops can also get you to the Caribbean, although their offerings are sometimes slim. **Pan Express Travel, Inc.,** *25 West 39th Street, New York, NY 10018, (212) 719-9292* is a leading discount ticket broker specializing in very low fares to the Caribbean, and many other destinations.

EUROPE

∎

Among the majors, in 1991 both **American** and **Continental** had special round-trip fares from New York to London starting under $500. Among the small carriers, **Virgin Atlantic,** *(800) 862-8621 or (212) 242-1330,* will fly you from Newark or JFK to London for under $350 one-way, if you purchase within 72 hours of departure. A round-trip London fare was just $525 from New York, or $645 from Los Angeles, subject to the same conditions. **Icelandair,** *(800)*

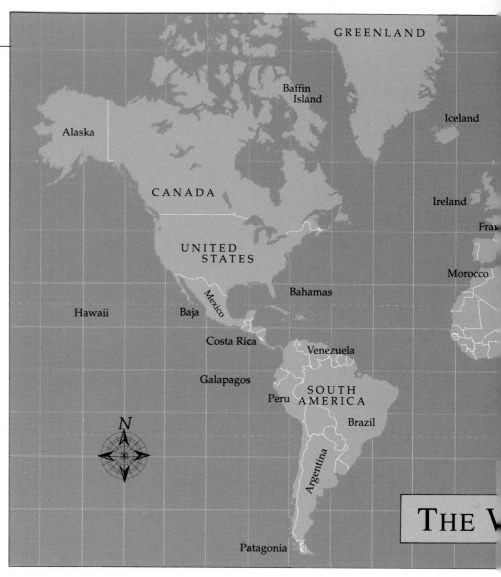

Stingray City, Cayman Islands/STEPHEN FRINK

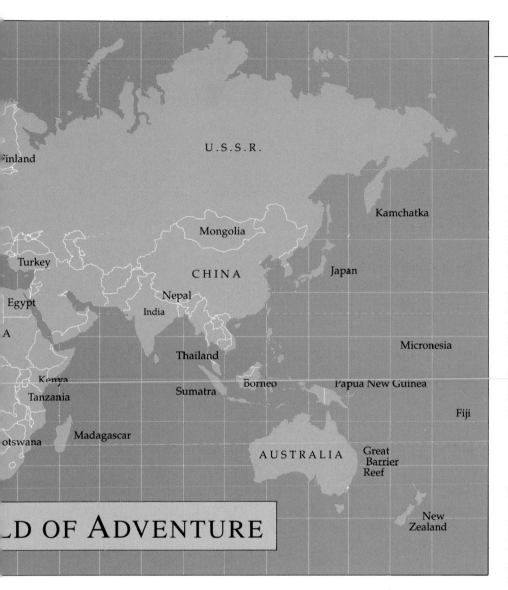

U.S.S.R.

Finland

Turkey

Egypt

Kenya
Tanzania

Madagascar

otswana

Mongolia

CHINA

Nepal

India

Thailand

Sumatra

Borneo

AUSTRALIA

Kamchatka

Japan

Micronesia

Papua New Guinea

Fiji

Great
Barrier
Reef

New
Zealand

LD OF ADVENTURE

SOUTHEAST ASIA

■

Thai International, *(800) 426-5204,* has recently instituted service to the United States. It offers few promotional discounts, but its regular fares are lower than many other carriers to Bangkok. Thai Airways' intra-Asia service is outstanding and cheap. For less than $100, you can fly from Bangkok to Penang. For about $85, you can fly from Chiang Mai to Phuket--otherwise a 22-hour bus ride. The best kept secret in Southeast Asian air travel is **Royal Brunei Airways,** *(800) 228-6588,* or *(213) 386-4888.* The Sultan of Brunei, one of the world's richest men, operates a sparkling fleet of new Boeings, as much for national pride as for profit. Very cheap fares are available from Penang or Singapore to Darwin, Australia and many other Asian destinations. You'll get superb service, arrive on time, and wonder why the plane was so empty.

SOUTH PACIFIC

■

Sure **Air New Zealand,** *(800) 262-1234,* keeps winning all those popularity contests, but is a hot towel and free booze really worth an extra $200? **Continental,** *(800) 231-0856,* or **Qantas,** *(800) 227-4500,* will get you to Auckland cheaper, for around $950 round-trip in low season, $1,250 high season, if a direct flight is all you need. **Air New Zealand** remains the choice if, in addition to New Zealand, you want a stop in Fiji or the Cook Islands. (The Cooks and Fiji's outer islands are beautiful and unspoiled, and the native islanders are among the friendliest people you'll ever meet.) If you're headed to Tahiti, French carrier **UTA,** *(800) 237-2747,* will probably provide the best price.

For passage to Sydney, Brisbane or Perth, check with the bucket shops in major cities. Expect to get substantial discounts in the off-season. A low-season round trip from Los Angeles to Sydney for about $875 is possible if you shop aggressively. High-season round-trips will still probably cost well over $1,100. **Qantas** has the best planes and most departures, but other carriers are the price leaders. Last summer **Northwest,** *(800) 447-4747,* offered an incredible $600 round-trip Australian fare, and it always has attractive prices. Round-trip fares as low as $800 on France's **UTA** were available last year, departing San Francisco, with a stop in Tahiti.

223-5500, offers New York to Luxembourg off-season fares at astonishingly low rates (approximately $450 and up round-trip), if you book within three days of departure, and pay for the ticket at the same time. **Tower Air,** *(800) 221-2500,* operates flights from New York to Oslo, Copenhagen and Stockholm costing $650 round-trip in summer, and less than $550 round-trip in winter.

SOUTH AMERICA

■

Brazil's **Varig Airlines,** *(800) 468-2744,* offers Miami to Rio or Sao Paolo for about $850 round-trip. **VASP Brazilian Airlines,** *(800) 732-8277,* serves the same cities from the West Coast for about $900. Both carriers now offer direct flights to Manaus in the Amazon. **Aerolinas** runs great promotional fares to South America--e.g. $700 to Argentina round-trip; however, there are many restrictions. **American** has among the lowest fares to Ecuador, starting at $500 round-trip. If you're headed for Machu Picchu, consider

Aero Peru, *(800) 255-7378.* You'll get the best deal with a Miami departure--promotional airfares have been quoted as low as $600 round-trip, although a standard high-season fare will exceed $850. For other departure points, consult a major bucket shop.

Tahiti/NEIL RABINOWITZ

SPECIAL FLIGHT SERVICES

Alexander Island, Hampton Glacier, cross-country ski expedition, Antarctica/GORDON WILTSIE

POLAR FLIGHTS

If you're planning an expedition to the Arctic or Antarctic, you'll need the very best logistical support available. These are the leading air services on the top and bottom of the world.

Antarctic

Adventure Network Int'l, Inc., 200-1676 Duranleau Street, Vancouver, BC, Canada V6H 3S5, (604) 683-8033; FAX: (604) 683-6892. ANI has the best planes, and the finest pilots; it is the only logical choice in Antarctica.

Arctic

Aklak Air, Ltd., P.O. Box 1190, Inuvik, NWT, Canada X0E 0T0, (403) 979-3555. Arctic specialists from the Bering Sea to the North Pole. Ice ReCon, Medevac, IFR. Wheels, skis and floats.

Bradley Air Services, Carp Airport, Carp, ONT, Canada K0A 1L0, (800) 267-733 in Canada, (613) 839-3340; FAX: (613) 839-5690. With four Arctic bases and rugged expedition-class aircraft, Bradley is the Arctic's leading carrier.

WILDERNESS AIR TAXIS

Using ski-planes, floatplanes or helicopters, wilderness air taxis will take you to the most far-flung destinations on the globe.

Alaska

Doug Geeting Aviation, P.O. Box 122, Talkeetna, AK 99676, (907) 733-2366. This outfit is legendary in the Alaskan interior.

Rust's Flying Service, Inc., P.O. Box 190325, Anchorage, AK 99519-0325, (907) 243-1595. Alaska's most established flying service. Good pilots and excellent safety record.

Temsco Airlines, Box 8015, Ketchikan, AK 99901, (907) 225-9810, or 225-0555. Both scheduled and charter flights to the far north.

Wright Air Service, Box 60142, Fairbanks, AK 99706, (907) 474-0502.

Canada

Adlair Aviation, Ltd., Box 2946, Yellowknife, NWT X1A 2R3, (403) 873-5161. Solid charter operation with Beaver, Single and Twin Otters; wheels, skis, floats.

Nahanni Air Services, Ltd., Bag Service 2200, Norman Wells, NWT X0E 0V0, (403) 587-2333, or 587-2288 for charters. Strong company with scheduled service to many outposts. Arctic and mountain specialists.

Simpson Air, Ltd., P.O. Box 260, Fort Simpson, NWT X0E 0N0, (403) 695-2505; FAX: (403) 695-2925. Cessnas, floatplanes and Twin Otters. Nahanni Park charter specialists.

Aero Arctic Helicopters, Ltd., Box 1496, Yellowknife, NWT X1A 2P1, (403) 920-2545; FAX: (403) 920-4488.

New Zealand

Alpine Guides (Mt. Cook), P.O. Box 20, Mt. Cook, (011 64) (3) 435-1834. Glacier flights and expedition support.

The Helicopter Line, P.O. Box 4178, Auckland, (011 64) (9) 774-406; FAX: (9) 774-597. Bases: Auckland, Rotorua, Mt. Cook, Franz Josef, Queenstown, Wanaka, Te Anau.

Mt. Cook Line, P.O. Box 4644, Christchurch, (011) (13) 790-690. The most complete wilderness flight service in New Zealand.

SMALL AIR SERVICES

In some areas of the world, such as Fiji and Nepal, your only flying option is a small, local air carrier that may not show up on your travel agent's computers. These listings should help you get off the ground.

South Pacific--Air Polynesie, BP 314, Quai Bir Hakiiem, Papeete, Tahiti, French Polynesia, Phone: 25850; Douglas Airways Pty Ltd., P.O. Box 1179, Boroko, Papua New Guinea, Phone: 253 499; Fiji Air, P.O. Box 1259, 219 Victoria Parade, Suva, Fiji, Phone: 313 666; Friendly Islands Airways, Private Bag, Nuku Alofa, Tonga, Phone: 22566.

Himalayas--Royal Nepal Airlines Corp., Kanti Path, Kathmandu, Nepal, Phone: 214 511.

Africa--Air Botswana, Lobatse Road, P.O. Box 92, Gaborone, Botswana, Phone: 52812; Air Madagascar, 31 Avenue de L'Independance, BP 437, Antananarivo, Madagascar, Phone: 22222; Air Seychelles, Seychelles Int'l Airport, Mahe, Seychelles, Phone: 23603; Kenya Airways, Jomo Kenyatta, P.O. Box 19002, Nairobi, Kenya, Phone: (011 254) 2 822171; Airkenya Aviation, Wilson Airport, P.O. Box 30357, Nairobi, Kenya, Phone: (011 254) 2 501421; Zambia Airways, Ndeka House, Haile Selassie Ave., Box 30272, Lusaka, Zambia, Phone: 213 674.

GETTING THERE

GEAR TRANSPORT

Air Shipping Tips

Let's see, you're headed off to New Zealand, and you want to bring your climbing gear, mountain bike and surfboard with you. Can it be done? Yes. First, heavy articles that you can part with well ahead of time, e.g. your climbing gear, can be shipped by sea to your destination. Allow 5-10 weeks for it to get there. The Postal Service's sea mail is inexpensive for 40 pounds or less. Use commercial shipping services (you'll find them in the yellow pages) for heavier, bulkier items.

The bicycle and the surfboard can both be checked as luggage by most airlines, if the total weight is less than 80 pounds. The bike must be partly disassembled, and placed in a cardboard box or heavy plastic bag supplied by the airline. Pad your derailleur and other vulnerable components. The surfboard can be sent as regular luggage if it is less than 8' in length, and if it is contained in a padded bag. You may have to pay a modest surcharge for the board, perhaps $25-$40.

When transporting valuable sporting gear or camera equipment abroad, carry receipts, insurance inventories, or other written proof that the goods are of US origin. Otherwise customs agents may impose duty on the items when you return.

COPING WITH JET LAG

When it comes to jet lag, the experts seem to agree that an ounce of prevention is worth a pound of cure. While the US military favors a very regimented diet, moderation works for most folks. Avoid overeating before and after the flight. Take extra doses of B and C vitamins, avoid alcohol on the flight, but drink plenty of fluids. Upon your arrival, go right to bed, where practical, and sleep until the local morning. You can get an anti-jet lag diet wallet card from Argonne Nat'l Labs., Public Affairs Office ,9700 S. Cass Ave., Argonne, IL 60439.

If you're hit especially hard by jet lag, you should consult **The Jet Lag Book** by Don Kowet (Crown Pub.), or **Jet Stress** by former airline stewardess Judith Goeltz.

Khumbu, Everest region, Nepal/GORDON WILTSIE

FLIGHT PRECAUTIONS

On international flights, particularly from very busy airports like Heathrow, Chicago, JFK, Sydney and Singapore, really do try to arrive at least two hours before departure. This is absolutely essential where extreme anti-terrorist measures are in effect, as in the Middle East. Make sure your luggage locks work, and that, if you have a backpack, all loose straps and pads are tucked away so as not to catch on baggage handling machines. Attach a strong, plastic identification tag to every piece of luggage, and also leave your name and address on the *inside* of each bag. Always keep your passport with you--never put it in your luggage. Retain all immigration ID cards you receive when you arrive in a foreign country. Without your card you are stuck. (We have seen many Westerners blocked from departing Bali after having lost their cards.)

If your luggage is lost, report this to your airline immediately, and try to find out where it may have gone. Check to see if it actually preceded your arrival. Find out where lost luggage would be stored, and how long the storage area will be open. Leave a local contact number.

RESOURCES & GUIDEBOOKS

Air Courier's Handbook, $8.95 from Big City Books, P.O. Box 19667, Sacramento, CA 95819. Good basic information.

The Airline Passengers' Guerrilla Handbook, by George Albert Brown. This irreverent and fact-filled guide is easily the best resource for getting cheap fares and good service. Buy this book. $9.95 from Blakes Pub. Group, Wash., D.C. 1989.

Condé Nast Traveler. Slick, and targeted at rich folks, this magazine nevertheless offers fine pieces on faraway places, good tips on bargain air travel, and an excellent "Traveler's File" section. Call (800) 777-0700 to subscribe.

Charter Flight Directory, by Jens Jurgen. This annual resource explains how to obtain discount charter flights and package holidays. Available from Travel Information Bureau, P.O. Box 105, Kings Park, NY 11754.

The Complete Handbook for Travelers, by Hal Gieseking. Authored by the editor of the Travel Advisor, this work covers air travel, hotels, vehicle rentals and other travel basics. (Pocket Books, NY)

The New World of Travel, (1991 ed.), by Arthur Frommer, offers a host of money-saving tips for worldwide travel. Though poorly organized, this is still a creative and comprehensive resource. (Prentice Hall)

EXPEDITIONS

How do you get a few tons of climbing equipment to Tibet? Solving logistical questions like this are what Britain's Expedition Advisory Centre (EAC) does best. Founded by the Royal Geographical Society over a century ago, EAC is staffed by experienced researchers and explorers. EAC will consult with expedition leaders and recommend specialty services worldwide. Contact Expedition Advisory Centre, 1 Kensington Gore, London, SW7 2AR, (011 44) 71 581 2057. Specialty publications are available.

Two other organizations that can assist with expedition planning are The Explorers' Club, 40 East 70th, New York, NY 10021, (212) 628-8383, and the South American Explorers' Club, 1510 York Street, #214, Denver, CO 80206.

er

*Let the tourist be cushioned against misadventure,
but your true traveler will not feel that he has had his
money's worth unless he brings back a few scars.*
-Lawrence Durrell

▼

*E*xperienced travelers don't worry about every detail of a trip, or attempt to plan every stop on the itinerary beforehand. On the other hand, seasoned globetrotters pay great attention to the things that are really important--passports and visas, money, health, customs regulations, emergency communications, insurance and language skills. When these things are squared away before you leave, almost everything else can be handled day to day, however your mood suits you. You can get off the plane, confident that you won't be beset by any major disasters, and that you can cope with any serious problem that might arise.

In this chapter we cover the most vital subjects for travelers venturing abroad-- how to obtain your passport and necessary visas, how to select travelers' and health insurance, how to obtain and convert money abroad, what to do in emergencies, and where to go when you need help. While we've given special attention to travel in exotic places, we think you'll find this information valuable for any foreign trip you make, not just an adventure holiday.

CHAPTER
29

Passports & Visas

PASSPORTS

You should carry a passport whenever you travel outside of North America or Mexico. Keep your passport with you at all times, if possible. You can purchase small passport purses that keep your passport and other valuables secured around your neck or hidden beneath your clothing. Keep a separate xerox copy of the identification pages of your passport. It is also wise to carry a certified copy of your birth certificate, or an expired passport, as proof of citizenship. Carry these separate from your other papers, or give them to a traveling companion.

To obtain a passport for the first time, you must apply in person at a Passport Agency listed below, or at one of many post offices and courts authorized to accept passport applications. If you are renewing a passport less than 12 years old, you may apply by mail. Along with the application form, you must provide: 1) proof of US citizenship (birth certificate or old passport); 2) an identification card with your photo and signature, such as a driver's license; 3) two identical, 2" x 2" color, or black and white photos, not more than six months old; and, 4) the fee of $65 for a first-time passport, or $33 for those under 18. To renew an old passport not more than 12 years old, submit your application along with your old passport and the $35 fee ($20 for those under 18).

Both first-time and reissued passports are valid for 10 years. If you renew your passport by mail, allow 2 to 3 weeks for processing. If you apply in person, your passport will often be ready within six working days. In emergencies--where you can prove a need for immediate departure--most agencies will process your application overnight.

Contact the Bureau of Consular Affairs, Public Affairs Staff, Dept. of State #5807, Washington, DC 20520, (202) 647-0518 (24-hour tape). Passports are issued at the following agencies. (If there are multiple phone lines, e.g. 565-3930, and 565-3931, two extra digits appear after the main number.)

Boston Passport Agency, *John F. Kennedy Bldg. Government Center, Boston, MA 02203, (617) 565-3930-33; (617) 353-7155 (tape).*

Chicago Passport Agency, *Suite 380, Klucynski Federal Bldg., 230 S. Dearborn St., Chicago, IL 60604, (312) 353-7155; (312) 353-5426 (tape).*

Honolulu Passport Agency, *Room C-106, New Federal Bldg., 300 Ala Moana Blvd., P.O. Box 50185 Honolulu, HI 96850, (808) 541-1918-20; (808) 541-1919 (tape).*

Houston Passport Agency, *One Allen Center, 500 Dallas St., Houston, TX 77002-4874, (713) 229-3600; (713) 229-3607 (tape).*

Los Angeles Passport Agency, *Room 13100, 11000 Wilshire Blvd., Los Angeles, CA 90024-3614, (213) 575-7075; (213) 575-7070 (tape).*

Miami Passport Agency, *16th Floor, Federal Office Bldg., 51 S.W. First St., Miami, FL 33130-1680, (305) 536-4681-83; (305) 536-5395 (tape).*

New Orleans Passport Agency, *Postal Services Bldg., Room T-12005, 701 Loyola Ave., New Orleans, LA 70013-1931, (504) 589-6161-63; (504) 589-6728-29 (tape).*

New York Passport Agency, *Room 270, Rockefeller Center, 630 Fifth Ave., New York, NY 10111-0031, (212) 541-7710, 7719; (212) 541-7700-09 (tape).*

Philadelphia Passport Agency, *Federal Bldg., Room 4426, 600 Arch St., Philadelphia, PA 19106, (215) 597-7480.*

San Francisco Passport Agency, *Suite 200, 525 Market St., San Francisco, CA 94105-2773, (415) 974-9941-48; (415) 974-7972 (tape).*

Seattle Passport Agency, *Room 992, Federal Office Bldg., 915 Second Ave., Seattle, WA 98174-1091, (206) 442-7945-47; (206) 442-7941-43 (tape).*

Stamford Passport Agency, *One Landmark Square, St. Level, Stamford, CT 06901-2767, (203) 325-3538-39; (203) 325-4401-03 (tape).*

Washington Passport Agency, *1425 K St. N.W., Washington, DC 20524, (202) 783-8170.*

Passport information can be obtained from the **Supt. of Documents, US Government Printing Office,** *Washington, DC 20402.* Ask for Publ. #8969 which contains complete passport requirements and useful tips on foreign travel.

VISA REQUIREMENTS

You will need visas for many countries in Asia, for most African and Middle Eastern countries, and for most remaining socialist nations. Visa requirements vary widely from country to country, so be sure you know what you need before you submit your application. We strongly advise that you contact the embassy or consulate of the country you plan to visit to obtain its current visa policies. Allow three to five working days to obtain a visa if you apply at the foreign embassy or consulate in person. Allow up to three weeks if you submit your visa application by mail.

For roughly $15-$35 per visa, you can make your life easier, by having a visa service do all the leg work. The following agencies can obtain your visas, often in just a few days.

Visa Center, Inc., *507 Fifth Ave., #904, New York, NY 10017, (212) 986-0924.*

Express Visa Service, Inc., *2150 Wisconsin Ave., Suite 20, P.O. Box 32048, Washington, DC 20007, (202) 337-2442.*

Intercontinental Visa Service, *World Trade Center, 350 S. Figueroa St., Ste. 185, Los Angeles, CA 90071, (213) 625-7175.*

Visas Int'l, *3169 Barbara Court, Ste. F, Los Angeles, CA 90068, (213) 850-1192.*

For current visa requirements, consult our listings for guidance, but you should still make direct inquiry with the foreign embassy or consulate, as specifics may have changed since printing. The following list covers most of those countries commonly visited by tourists which require a visa of Americans. Note: this list is not exhaustive. If you are planning to travel outside Western Europe, the United Kingdom and Latin America, double-check to ensure you do not need a visa. An official summary of visa requirements for all countries around the world is available for $.50 from the **US Consumer Information Center,** *Dept. 455W, Pueblo, CO 81009, (719) 948-3334.* Ask for Publication #9517, "Foreign Entry Requirements." Visa information can also be obtained from the **Bureau of Consular Affairs** (address above), by calling (202) 647-1488, or (202) 647-0510 (24-hour information line).

ALGERIA

Visa required. Valid 3 months. 2 photos and 2 applications, $5.25, money order or certified check only. Embassy of the Democratic and Popular Republic of Algeria, 2137 Wyoming Ave. N.W., Washington, DC 20008, (202) 265-2800. (Note: Visa will be denied if passport shows Israeli or South African visas.)

AUSTRALIA

Visa required. Valid 1 year, multiple entries, stays up to 6 months. No charge, 1 photo. Embassy of Australia, 1600 Mass. Ave. N.W., Washington, DC 20036, (800) 826-3179, or (202) 797-3000. Consulates: Los Angeles, San Francisco, Houston, Honolulu, Chicago, New York.

BHUTAN

Visa required. Applicants must be on prepaid tour (at least 2 persons). 2 applications, 2 photos, $20, apply 2 months in advance. Groups contact Bhutan Travel Service, 120 E. 50th St., New York, NY 10022. Individuals write to Bhutan Tourism Office, P.O. Box 159, Thimpu, Bhutan.

BRAZIL

Visa and return ticket required. Obtain visa in advance, 1 photo, $10 by mail, free in person. Embassy of Brazil, 3006 Mass. Ave., N.W., Washington, DC 20008, (202) 745-2828. Consulates: CA, FL, GA, HI, IL, LA, NY, TX.

BRUNEI

Visa and return ticket required. Valid 3 months, single entry. 2 photos, $7.50. Embassy of the State of Brunei Darussalam, Ste. 300, 2600 Virginia Ave., N.W., Washington, DC 20037, (202) 342-0159.

BULGARIA

Visa required. Tourist visa valid for 30 days, $19. Transit visa 30 hours, $12. Send $4.00, plus visa fee, 1 photo and SASE to Embassy of the People's Republic of Bulgaria, 1621 22nd St., N.W., Washington, DC 20008, (202) 483-5885 (mornings). (No personal checks.)

BURMA

Visa required. Organized tours only; 2 applications, 3 photos, $16. Embassy of Myanmar, 2300 S St., N.W., Washington, DC 20008, (202) 332-9044-45. (Note: contact Dept. of State.)

CAMEROON

Visa, vaccination certificate, financial statement and outbound ticket required. Tourist visa valid 3 months. Submit 2 photos, 2 applications, $45 fee. Embassy of the Republic of Cameroon, 2349 Mass. Ave., N.W., Washington, DC 20008, (202) 265-8790-94.

CENTRAL AFRICAN REPUBLIC

Visa, vaccination cert., outbound ticket required. Visa valid 2 months, 2 photos, 2 applic., $20. Embassy of Central African Republic, 1618 22nd St., N.W., Washington, DC 20008, (202) 483-7800-01.

CHAD

Visa and vaccination certificate required. Tourist visa valid 1 month, $12.25. 3 photos, 3 applications, registered or certified SASE. Embassy of the Republic of Chad, 2002 R St., N.W., Washington, DC 20009, (202) 462-4009.

CHINA, PEOPLE'S REPUBLIC

Visa and China International Travel Service (CITS) approval required in advance. $10, 2 photos, and 2 applications. Chinese Embassy, 2300 Connecticut Ave., N.W., Washington, DC 20008, (202) 328-2500. Consulates: Houston (713) 524-0780, New York (212) 868-7752, Los Angeles (213) 380-2508, San Francisco (415) 563-4885, Chicago (312) 346-2087.

LIZ HYMANS

COLOMBIA

Visa or tourist card and outbound ticket required. Tourist card issued free on arrival, valid 90 days. Embassy of Colombia, 1825 Connecticut Ave., N.W., Washington, DC 20009, (202) 332-7476. Consulates: CA, FL, IL, LA, NY, TX.

CONGO

Visa, return ticket, and vaccination certificate required. Submit 3 applications, 3 photos. $15 single entry, $20 multiple, both valid 3 months. Embassy of the Republic of the Congo, 4891 Colorado Avenue, N.W., Washington, DC 20011, (202) 726-5500-01.

CZECHOSLOVAKIA

Visa required. 1 application, 2 photos, certified check. Tourist visa valid 5 months for 30 days, $16

1 entry. Embassy of the Czechoslovak Socialist Republic, 3900 Linnean Ave., N.W., Washington, DC 20008, (202) 363-6315.

EGYPT

Visa required. Available in advance $12, or on arrival $15. 1 photo, cash or money order only. Visa valid 3 months, single or multiple entries. Currency restrictions. Embassy of the Republic of Egypt, 2310 Decatur Pl., N.W., Washington, DC 20008, (202) 234-3903. Consulates: Chicago (312) 443-1190, Houston (713) 961-4915, New York (212) 759-7120, San Francisco (415) 346-9700.

EL SALVADOR

Visa required. Valid 3 months. $10, 1 application, 1 photo, no personal checks. Embassy of El Salvador, 2308 California St., N.W., Washington, DC 20008, (202) 331-4032. Consulates: CA, FL, LA, NY, TX.

ETHIOPIA

Visa and vaccination cert. required. 1 photo, 1 application. Tourist visa valid 30 days, $9.65 + $2 postage. Embassy of Ethiopia, 2134 Kalorama Rd., N.W., Washington, DC 20008, (202) 234-2281-82.

GHANA

Visa, outbound ticket, and vaccination cert. required. For photos, SASE, $30 for 30-day tourist visa. Embassy of Ghana, 352 Int'l Drive, N.W., Washington, DC 20008, (202) 686-4520.

GUATEMALA

Tourist card valid for 30 days given on entry with proof of citizenship and photo ID. Visa valid 5 years, multiple entries, no charge. Embassy of Guatemala, 2220 R St., N.W., Washington, DC 20008, (202) 745-4952-54. Consulates: CA, FL, LA, NY, PR, TX.

GUYANA

Visa required. Single-entry tourist visa valid 3 months. 3 applications, 3 photos, no charge. Embassy of Guyana, 2490 Tracy Pl., N.W., Washington, DC 20008, (202) 265-6900-03.

HONDURAS

Visa and outbound ticket required. Visa valid 30 days, 1 application, no photo, $5. Embassy of Honduras, Suite 100, 3007 Tilden St., N.W., Washington, DC 20008, (202) 966-7702. Consulates: CA, FL, IL, LA, NY, TX.

HUNGARY

Visa required. Entry visa valid for 30 days, within 6 months of issuance; obtain in advance or upon arrival. Single-entry $15, 2 photos, 1 application. Embassy of the Republic of Hungary, 3910 Shoemaker St., N.W., Washington, DC 20008, (202) 362-6730. (Note: call for updates.)

INDIA

Visa and return ticket required. Tourist visa valid 4 months. Send 2 photos, $15, application, and certified SASE. Embassy of India, 2536 Mass. Ave., N.W., Washington, DC 20008, (202) 939-9839. Consulates: San Francisco (415) 668-0683, New York (212) 879-7800, Chicago (312) 781-6280.

JORDAN

Visa required. For current conditions, contact Embassy of the Hashemite Kingdom of Jordan, 3504 Int'l Dr., N.W., Washington, DC 20008, (202) 966-2664. Consulates: CA, FL, MI, TX.

KENYA

Visa required. 1 entry $10, multiple entries $50, both valid for 6 months. 1 application, 2 photos, return ticket, cash or money order only. Embassy of Kenya, 2249 R St., N.W., Washington, DC 20028, (202) 387-6101. Consulates: Los Angeles (213) 274-6635, New York (212) 468-1300.

KOREA (SOUTH)

Visa required for stay in excess of 15 days. 90-day, multiple entry visa, no charge. Republic of Korea, Consular Division, 2600 Virginia Ave., N.W., Suite 200, Washington, DC 20037, (202) 939-5660-63. (10 consulates nationwide.)

LAOS

Visa required. Single-entry, extendable 15-day visa (special approvals required). 3 photos, 3 applications, $15. Embassy of the Lao People's Democratic Republic, 2222 S St., N.W., Washington, DC 20008, (202) 332-6416.

LIBERIA

Visa and vaccination cert. required. Entry visa valid 3 months, no fee, 2 applications, 2 photos. Embassy of Rep. of Liberia, 5303 Colorado Ave., N.W., Washington, DC 20008, (202) 723-0437.

MADAGASCAR

Visa and outbound ticket required. 1 month single entry visa, $22.50, 4 applications, 4 photos. Embassy of the Democratic Republic of Madagascar, 2374 Mass. Ave., N.W., Washington, DC 20008, (202) 265-5525. Consulates: Palo Alto, NYC, Philadelphia.

MALI

Visa and vaccination cert. required. 1 month, extendable, $17. 2 photos, 2 applications, SASE. Embassy of the Republic of Mali, 2130 R St., N.W., Washington, DC 20008, (202) 332-2249.

MAURITANIA

Visa, vaccination cert., and outbound ticket required. Visa valid 3 months, 4 photos, 2 applications, $10, cash or money order. Embassy of the Republic of Mauritania, 2129 Leroy Place, N.W., Washington, DC 20008, (202) 232-5700-01.

MONGOLIA

Visa required. Tourist visa valid 3 months, $14, 1 entry. 1 photo, certified SASE. Embassy of the Mongolian People's Republic, 16th Street, N.W., Suite B 1625, Washington, DC 20010, (202) 483-3176.

MOZAMBIQUE

Visa and vaccination certificate required. Visa valid for 30 days from issuance, 2 applications, 2 photos, $15. Currency restrictions. Embassy of the People's Republic of Mozambique, Suite 570, 1990 M Street, N.W., Washington, DC 20036, (202) 293-7146.

NEPAL

Tourist visa available on arrival at Kathmandu, valid for 15 days, extendable to 3 months. 30-day visa, valid for 3 months, $10, 1 application, 1 photo. Royal Nepalese Embassy, 2131 Leroy Pl., N.W., Washington, DC 20008, (202) 667-4550; or Consulate General in New York, (212) 370-4188.

NICARAGUA

Visa and return ticket required. Visa valid up to 30 days. 1 application, 2 photos, $25, SASE. 1627 New Hampshire Ave., N.W., Washington, DC 20009, (202) 939-6531-34.

NIGER

Visa, vaccination certificate, and outbound ticket required. Single entry valid for 3 months, $24. 3 applications, 3 photos. Embassy of the Republic of Niger, 2204 R St., N.W., Washington, DC 20008, (202) 483-4224-27.

RONNA NELSON

NIGERIA

Visa, return ticket and vaccination certificate required. Visa 3-24 months, no charge, 1 applic., 1 photo, invitation letter. Embassy of Nigeria, 2201 M. St., N.W., Washington, DC 20037, (202) 822-1500. Consulates: CA, GA, NY.

PAKISTAN

Visa and outbound ticket required. Tourist visa valid 3 months, multiple entries, no charge, 1 photo, SASE. Embassy of Pakistan, 2315 Mass. Ave, N.W., Washington, DC 20008, (202) 939-6200, or Pakistan Consulate, 12 East 65th St., New York, NY 10021, (212) 879-5800. Consult with State Department.

PANAMA

Tourist card required. Obtain from airline, $10. Consult with State Department.

POLAND

Visa required for stay over 90 days only. One application, 2 photos. Embassy of Poland, 2640 16th St., N.W., Washington, DC 20009, (202) 234-3800. Consulates: New York (212) 889-8360, Chicago (312) 337-8166, Los Angeles (213) 365-7900.

ROMANIA

Visa required. Single-entry tourist visa for up to 60-day stay, valid 6 months, $16, SASE. No application, no photos. May also be obtained at border. Embassy of Romania, 1607 23rd St., N.W., Washington, DC 20008, (202) 232-4747-49.

RWANDA

Visa and vaccination cert. required. 3-month multiple entry visa, $15, 2 photos, 2 applications with exact date of entry, SASE. Embassy of the Republic of Rwanda, 1714 New Hampshire Ave., N.W., Washington, DC 20009, (202) 232-2882.

SAUDI ARABIA

No tourist visas available at this time.

SENEGAL

Vaccination cert., and return ticket required. Visa required for stay over 90 days, $50.85, cash or money order, 2 applications, 2 photos, SASE. Embassy of Senegal, 2112 Wyoming Ave., N.W., Washington, DC 20008, (202) 234-0540.

SOMALIA

Visa, vaccination cert., and outbound ticket probably required, however, the current political situation is unclear. Contact the State Department, or write to Embassy of the Somali Democratic Republic, Suite 710, 600 New Hampshire Ave., N.W., Washington, DC 20037.

SOUTH AFRICA

Visa, outbound ticket and outbound visa required in advance. No fee, 1 application, certified SASE. Valid 6-12 months, multiple entries. Photo required for visa to be excluded from passport. Embassy of South Africa, Attn: Consular Office, 3051 Mass. Ave., N.W., Washington, DC 20008, (202) 966-1250. Consulates: CA, IL, TX, NY.

SUDAN

Visa required. Single-entry tourist visa valid 3 months, 1 application, 2 photos, $30, cash or money order, SASE, 1 month processing. Visa denied if passport shows Israeli or S. African visas. Embassy of the Republic of the Sudan, 2210 Mass. Ave., N.W., Washington, DC 20008, (202) 338-8565-70, or NY Consulate, (212) 421-2680

SYRIA

Visa required. Single-entry visa valid 3 months, 1 application, 1 photo, SASE. Money order only, approx. $20. Embassy of the Syrian Arab Republic, 2215 Wyoming Ave., N.W., Washington, DC 20008, (202) 232-6313.

TAIWAN

Visa required. Visa valid 5 years, multiple entries, 60 days per stay, no charge, 1 application, 2 photos. Apply to Coordination Council for

North American Affairs (CCNAA), 4201 Wisconsin Ave., N.W., Washington, DC 20016, (202) 662-7562 or 895-1800. Other CCNAA offices in Atlanta, Boston, Chicago, Honolulu, Houston, Kansas City, Los Angeles, Miami, NYC, San Francisco, Seattle.

TANZANIA

Visa and outbound ticket required. Single-entry tourist visa valid for 6 months from issuance, for 30-day stay. 1 photo, 1 application, certified or registered SASE, $10.50, certified check. Travelers with South African passport stamp must request "referred visa." Embassy of the United Republic of Tanzania, 2139 R St., N.W., Washington, DC 20008, (202) 939-6125. Allow 1 month for processing.

THAILAND

Visa may be required. Visa not required for stays up to 15 days, but not extendable. Tourist visa, good for 60 days from issuance, $15, usually extendable in Thailand. 2 photos, 1 application, SASE. Embassy of Thailand, 2300 Kalorama Rd., N.W., Washington, DC 20008, (202) 483-7200. Consulates: Los Angeles (213) 937-1894, Chicago (312) 236-2447, New York (212) 754-1770.

UGANDA

Visa and vaccination certificate required. Visa valid 3 months, 2 applications, 2 photos, $20 (money order). Embassy of the Republic of Uganda, 5909 16th St., N.W., Washington, DC 20011, (202) 726-7100-02.

USSR

Visa probably required. Call or write for current visa regulations. Embassy of the Union of Soviet Socialist Republics, 1825 Phelps Pl., N.W., Washington, DC 20008, (202) 332-1513, or Consulate General in San Francisco, (415) 922-6642.

VENEZUELA

Tourist card or visa required. Tourist card available from airline, 60-day stay.

YUGOSLAVIA

Visa probably required. Valid for 1 year, multiple entries, no charge, no photos, SASE. Embassy of the Republic of Yugoslavia, 2410 California St., N.W., Washington, DC 20008, (202) 462-6566. Consulates: CA (415) 776-4941, IL (312) 332-0169, NY (212) 838-2300, OH (216) 621-2093, PA (412) 471-6191. (Note: check with State Dept.)

ZAIRE

Visa, outbound ticket, and vaccination certificate required. Tourist visa valid 1 month, multiple entries, 3 photos, 3 applic., $20 money order or certified check, SASE. Embassy of the Republic of Zaire, 1800 New Hampshire Ave., N.W., Washington, DC 20009, (202) 234-7690-91.

ZAMBIA

Visa required, vaccination certificate requested. All visas valid 6 months, $15, cash only, 2 photos, 2 applications. Embassy of the Republic of Zambia, 2419 Mass. Ave., N.W., Washington, DC 20008, (202) 265-9717-21. Allow 3 weeks for processing.

OFFICIAL BUSINESS

EMERGENCIES

▼

To avoid emergencies, call (202) 647-5226 for current State Department **Travel Advisories** before you depart. US Embassies and Consulates worldwide will take emergency messages and relay them if they have a reliable address. American Express offices will send and receive important messages, and help cardholders with lost passports, tickets or credit cards. The State Department Citizens' Emergency Center can also send messages and money to US citizens abroad, aid Americans in accidents, disasters or legal trouble, and inform families of injuries or deaths. Contact the Citizens' Emergency Center, Dept. of State, #4811, 2201 C St. N.W., Washington, DC 20520, or call (202) 647-5225. If you obtain coverage before departure, Travel Assistance Int'l will transmit messages, help replace lost passports and visas, provide legal assistance, and arrange emergency evacuation or repatriation. Contact Travel Assistance Int'l, 1133 15th St. N.W., Ste. 400, Washington, DC 20005, (800) 821-2828. The cost ranges from $40 for a week, to $540 for a year.

CUSTOMS

▼

Somewhere on your journey you are likely to encounter a thorough search of all your baggage and personal articles. Don't carry contraband. We've seen Singapore airport police open apparently new, unused film canisters, and Egyptian customs officials open individual prophylactic wrappers. Nothing is sacred. Be smart, travel clean. Also, if you travel with a pack, put good sturdy locks on the compartments. This will protect you, and it seems to reassure airline baggage handlers, as well as customs agents.

A returning US citizen may bring in $400 worth of articles without paying duty. Ten percent duty is imposed on the next $1,000 of goods. If you mail back a parcel exceeding $50 in value the postal service will collect duty and a handling charge. If you're mailing back things you brought from home, avoid duty by writing "American Goods Returned" on the box. To learn more about customs rules and regulations, request the "Know Before You Go" brochure from the US Customs Service, 1301 Constitution Ave., Washington, DC 20229, (202) 566-8195 (message machine).

MAJOR US EMBASSIES

▼

Argentina--4300 Columbia, Buenos Aires.
Australia--Moonah Place, Canberra.
Austria--Blotzmanngasse 16, Vienna.
Belgium--27 Blvd. du Regent, Brussels.
Brazil--Avenida da Nacoes, Brasilia.
Canada--100 Wellington Street, Ottawa.
Chile--1343 Augustinas, Santiago.
China--Guang Hua Lu, No. 17, Beijing.
Costa Rica--Avenida 3 & Calle 1, San Jose.
Denmark--Dag Hammarskjold Alle 24 DK-2100, Copenhagen.
Ecuador--Avenida Patria 12, Quito.
Egypt--Lazougi St., Garden City, Cairo.
Finland--Itainen Puistotie 14A, Helsinki.
France--2 Avenue Gabriel, Paris.
Germany--Deichmanns Ave., Bonn.
Greece--91 Vasilissis Sophias Blvd., Athens.
Hong Kong--26 Garden Road, Hong Kong.
India--Shanti Path Chanakyapuri 21, New Delhi.
Indonesia--Medan Merdeka Selatan 5, Jakarta.
Ireland--42 Elgin Road, Ballsbridge, Dublin.
Israel--71 Hayarkon Street, Tel Aviv.
Italy--Via Veneto 119/A, Rome.
Japan--10-1 Akasaka, Minato-Ku, Tokyo.
Kenya--Moi/Haile Selassie Ave., Nairobi.
Mexico--Paseo de la Reforma 305, Mexico City.
Nepal--Pani Pokhari, Kathmandu.
Netherlands--Museumplein 19, Amsterdam.
New Zealand--29 Fitzherbert Terrace, Thorndon, Wellington.
Norway--Drammensveien 18, Oslo.
Papua New Guinea--Armit Street, Port Moresby.
Peru--Avdas Espana & Incas Garcilaso de la Vega, Lima.
Philippines--1201 Roxas Blvd., Manila.
Portugal--Ave. das Forcas Armadas, Lisbon.
Singapore--30 Hill Street, Singapore.
Spain--Serrano 75, Madrid.
Sweden--Strandvagen 101, Stockholm.
Switzerland--Jubilaeumstrasse 93, Bern.
Thailand--95 Wireless Road, Bangkok.
Tanzania--City Drive, Dar Es Salaam.
United Kingdom--24 Grosvenor Square, London W1.
USSR--Ulitsa Chaykovkogo 19, Moscow.
Yugoslavia--Kneza Milosa 50, Belgrade.

Safeguards

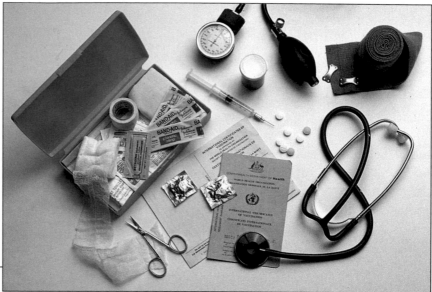

HEALTH & INSURANCE

IMMUNIZATIONS

Your local physician or health clinic can administer the vaccinations you will need for your planned itinerary. For equatorial regions, you will probably have to take typhoid and cholera vaccines. If you travel in Africa south of the Sahara, or in the Amazon, add yellow fever vaccine to the list. Throughout Eastern Africa, equatorial Asia, Latin America and much of the Pacific, you will need to take anti-malarial medication, commencing four weeks before you depart. This will not guarantee that you will not contract malaria, so you should also use insect repellents.

It is a good idea to have a tetanus/diphtheria booster before you leave. A shot of immune serum globulin will also provide about three months protection against Hepatitis A, a very debilitating and potentially fatal disease. However, this immunization is not required, so consult with your physician. Be sure to have all your immunizations entered on an official vaccination certificate, which should also indicate when any further boosters are due.

GENERAL HEALTH

If you're concerned about finding a good physician while you're abroad, contact the International Association for Medical Assistance to Travelers (IAMAT), 417 Center Street, Lewiston, NY 14092, (716) 754-4883, which publishes a global directory of Western-trained, English-speaking doctors. American Express cardholders can get physician referrals and immunization

information from the Global Assist Hotline, (800) 554-AMEX. Two good travel health resources are Dr. Stuart Rose's *1991 Int'l Travel Health Guide*, ($14.95 from Travel Medicine, (413) 584-0381), and Dr. Anthony C. Turner's *Traveler's Health Guide*, ($9.95, or consult your library). The Turner book has very complete coverage of health problems in primitive areas.

A useful physician's desk reference is the 171-page, *Health Information for International Travelers*, available for $5 from the US Government Printing Office, Washington, DC 20402, (202) 275-3648.

MEDICAL INSURANCE

Don't leave home without adequate medical insurance that covers what you plan to do, where you plan to do it. This sounds obvious, but many health policies exclude injuries sustained while scuba diving or parachuting, and many insurers will only cover a few days of emergency care in a foreign health facility. Don't rely on Medicare, which, believe it or not, will not cover foreign medical care at all. Read your health policy carefully. If there are troublesome loopholes, go to a good agent and get additional insurance.

If you're not satisfied with what your own insurer can provide, contact one or more of the following underwriters.

Health Care Abroad, 243 Church Street NW, Suite 100 D, Vienna, VA 22180, (800) 237-6615, or (703) 255-9800, ext. 57. This company offers comprehensive foreign medical care and emergency evacuation coverage, and offers optional accidental

death, trip cancellation and lost baggage protection.

Travel Assistance International (TAI), 1133 15th Street NW, Suite 400, Washington, DC 20005, (800) 821-2828, provides insurance for foreign medical expenses and emergency medical evacuation, and offers a 24-hour travelers' aid service to help with legal problems, lost passports and visas. TAI also offers trip cancellation, baggage, and death and dismemberment coverage.

Mutual of Omaha Insurance Company, Teletrip, 3201 Farnum Street, Omaha, NE 68131, (800) 228-9792. Mutual's Teletrip program offers comprehensive accident insurance for travelers which covers most medical and evacuation costs.

TRAVELERS' INSURANCE

It is easy to obtain good low-cost insurance for the most common accidents and mishaps that occur while vacationing. First of all, your homeowners' insurance may already protect you against theft of tickets and other valuables while you're away from home. Check your policy. If you've got a premium VISA or Mastercard, you probably have substantial accidental death and dismemberment coverage, as well as some protection for lost luggage and trip cancellation. VISA gold cardholders get up to $1 million accident coverage when air or ground transportation is purchased with the card. American Express also provides its cardholders with certain trip accident and lost baggage protection.

Separate trip accident insurance can be purchased from a number of carriers. In addition to those listed above for medical insurance, comprehensive travel insurance packages are offered by **ARM Coverage, Inc.**, P.O. Box 310, Mineola, NY 11501, (800) 645-2424 (ask about the "carefree travel insurance" package); and the **Traveler's Insurance Co.**, 1 Tower Square, Hartford, CT 06183-5040, (800) 243-3144, or (203) 277-2318. ("Travel Insurance Pack" covers trip cancellation, accidents, lost baggage and emergency evacuation.)

AAA's new Trip Assist Worldwide Protection Plan is available to AAA members in many states. This reasonably priced program offers trip cancellation/interruption coverage, emergency medical coverage, and lost baggage protection along with a 24-hour hotline to provide assistance with medical, legal or other travel-related problems. Contact your local AAA office.

DRIVING INSURANCE

Major agencies such as Hertz or Avis provide both liability and property damage insurance when you rent a vehicle overseas. However, deductibles vary dramatically from country to country, and there are many exclusions (e.g. windshields in Australia) which can end up costing you plenty. Unfortunately, paying with a premium credit card (such as VISA gold) does not automatically cover the collision damage waiver overseas, as it does in America.

If you plan to buy a vehicle overseas, or drive for an extended period of time in a number of foreign countries, you should obtain specialized insurance. If your regular carrier will not insure foreign travel, two British firms can provide vehicle coverage just about anywhere in the world, even the Middle East and Africa: **Baggot, Evan & Co. Ltd**, 99 Church Road, London, SE19 2PR, (011 44) 81 771-8844; and **Campbell, Irvine Ltd.**, 48 Earls Court Road, Kensington, London, W8 6EJ, (011 44) 937-9903. Both companies offer complete insurance packages including vehicle, sea transit and personal accident coverage.

You will have trouble renting and insuring a car or motorcycle overseas unless you possess an International Driving Permit. You can get one easily from any AAA office nationwide before you depart. The fee is $5 to $10 and you'll need two passport-sized photos. The permit is good for one year from date of issuance. If you contemplate riding any two-wheeled motorbike, even a moped, be sure to have a motorcycle endorsement.

HEALTH WATCH

BY DR. BOB YOUNG

Travel involves risks to your health that do not exist at home. Serious illnesses can be contracted, particularly in underdeveloped parts of the world where medical care is not readily available, or is of lower quality than in the developed nations. One must accept these facts when engaged in adventure travel.

Take a conservative, preventive medicine approach before you travel to third world areas. Get the immunizations and medications necessary before you leave. Consult with a physician or clinic experienced in travel medicine. Don't rely on travel agents to disclose all the health problems you may encounter at your destination. And remember that foreign countries' stated health "requirements" exist only to prevent the importation of diseases within their borders. What is in *your* best interest, healthwise, is quite another matter.

Water-borne Illnesses

Over half the beds in hospitals worldwide are occupied by victims of water-borne illnesses. If you're going to go into the third world, take the time and trouble to learn about water purification. Boiling your water is the most effective precaution. Alcoholic and carbonated beverages are relatively safe, while bottled water is only as safe as the sanitary conditions where it was bottled. Infectious hepatitis is a serious and frequently encountered illness related to contaminated water. An immune serum globulin injection shortly before departure provides considerable protection.

Insect-borne Diseases and Malaria

The mosquito, as the carrier of many illnesses, has been responsible for more deaths than all the wars in history. Malaria, in particular, remains a serious health risk in many regions, one that kills over two million people annually. It can be effectively prevented by medication (taken before you go) and the use of mosquito netting, coils and repellents. However, some malaria strains are resistant to the most common preventive drugs so you're never 100 percent safe.

Risk Avoidance

Accident-related injuries are the most common health problems suffered by travelers. Don't take risks, such as driving bad roads at night, that you would not take at home. There is something about foreign travel that will induce people to go into parts of towns and involve themselves in situations that they would never do at home. Remember, you can be adventurous without being foolhardy.

If you do have a serious accident or injury in an underdeveloped country, you *will* want to come back to the US. As emergency evacuations can be astronomically expensive--$20,000 and up, you should definitely carry evacuation insurance. (See the preceding page.)

Preventive Medicine

Try to minimize predictable minor problems. Traveler's diarrhea may not be life-threatening, but it can ruin a trip, especially a short one. Take along some basic medications for diarrhea, infection and low-grade pain. Ask the same doctor that handles your immunizations for items that may not be available over-the-counter. As for jet lag, you will find it less severe if you stay awake as much as possible on flights going west, and sleep enroute while traveling east.

Environmental Factors

Americans are often unprepared for the extremes of temperature and altitude they may encounter abroad. If you are headed where it is very cold, bring first-class gear with you. Altitude is an increasingly common cause of health problems to travelers. Unfortunately these can be very serious and occasionally fatal. Being "in shape" has no bearing on susceptibility to altitude problems, nor does a safe prior history at high altitudes. Medication is available that can effectively ward off or treat these problems. See a doctor if you will be traveling in regions above 10,000 feet.

Bob Young, M.D., a California physician with many years of experience in travel medicine, is the author of the book, How to Stay Healthy While Traveling.

Money & Finances

TRAVELERS' CHECKS

American Express travelers' checks are the best. VISA, Thomas Cook and Barclay's are not so close seconds. You're much better off with US currency checks than with anything else, except in Britain. Take a few twenties, but bring mostly $50 and $100 checks--many banks or hotels charge as much as $3 per check as an exchange fee. Always be prepared to show your passport when changing money or cashing travelers' checks. If you have an American Express card, you can write a personal check while abroad to obtain up to $1,000 in American Express Travelers' checks every 21 days. This is the simplest and best way to get more money when you're away from home. American Express offices will also cash cardholders' personal checks for up to $200 in local currency.

Keep records of when and where you spent your travelers' checks and keep a list of your checks' serial numbers separate from the checks themselves. Try to use the checks in numerical order, to simplify your record-keeping. Also write down the number to call in case your checks are lost or stolen. For American Express checks, call (800) 221-7282 in the US and Canada, and consult the nearest AMEX office elsewhere.

CREDIT CARDS

We wouldn't go anywhere without a major credit card (Mastercard, VISA or American Express), preferably a gold or silver model. These cards are recognized worldwide, and you'll find them very useful nearly everywhere there are phones and banks. You can get a cash advance with a Mastercard or VISA at most commercial banks in the world, and these cards can access ATMs in many advanced countries.

Credit cards offer other important advantages to the traveler. Most premium cards now provide free travel accident insurance up to $1 million. The gold cards also cover car rental insurance deductibles up to a specified amount, but this may not apply to foreign rentals. To avoid fraudulent billings, keep your receipts, and write the local exchange rate on the receipt to avoid any confusion. Rarely are exchange rate errors made, but if this does happen, notify your card issuer right away.

Every world traveler should have an American Express card, not just to charge purchases, but also to take advantage of American Express's worldwide travel services. With an American Express card you can cash personal checks, book flights, and get emergency money and assistance if your valuables are lost or stolen. Being able to cash a personal check overseas can be a real lifesaver. And for this, American Express is the only game in town, whether in London or Kathmandu.

CURRENCY EXCHANGE

Before you depart, try to get $50 in the foreign currency of the country you'll be visiting. This will get you through airports and train stations more quickly, with fewer hassles. If the currency you need is not readily available stateside, change $20 to $50 as soon as you get off the plane. Despite what you hear, airport exchange rates are not usually that bad, and in some places such as Austria, the airport rates are identical to what you get in town.

Shop around before exchanging large sums. Most money changers in modern countries post their exchange terms, so it's easy to compare rates. Make sure, however, that you know the *commission* as well as the nominal rate of exchange. You may get a favorable rate only to be socked with a $2 to $5 service charge per check. You will benefit by exchanging at least $100 at a time, using large denomination notes or travelers' checks.

When you receive the foreign currency, count it carefully before you leave the office. Even major banks may short you, or give you torn bills that you won't be able to use. We've also had money changers give us bills that were out of circulation and therefore worthless. Just be careful.

Find out if the country you will visit has currency restrictions. Egypt, for example, in a measure aimed against black marketeers, prohibits tourists from entering or exiting the country with more than a few Egyptian pounds. You can be searched on departure, and your excess currency forfeited. The same can happen in Morocco. In countries like this, save all your currency exchange receipts, and never exchange more than absolutely necessary.

SECURITY

A washable neck or shoulder pouch is the best way to carry your passport and travelers' checks. Keep a separate xerox copy of your passport to assist replacement of lost or stolen travelers' checks. If you have too many checks to carry on your person,

distribute them through your luggage so that a single lost bag doesn't lead to disaster. When checking valuables into a hotel safe, always get a signed receipt, no matter how secure the hotel may appear to be.

AMERICAN EXPRESS

Main Offices Worldwide

Argentina (Buenos Aires)--City Service Travel Agency, Florida 890, 4th Fl., (312) 8416/9.

Australia (Sydney)--AMEX Travel Service, 388 George Street, (2) 239-0666.

Austria (Vienna)--AMEX Europe Ltd. Kaerntnerstrasse 21/23, (222) 51540.

Belgium (Brussels)--AMEX Int'l, 2 Place Louise, (2) 512 7140.

Bermuda (Hamilton)--L.P. Gutteridge Ltd. Harold Hayes Frith Bldg., Bermudiana Road, (809) 29-54545.

Borneo (Bandar Seri Begawan)--Travel Centre Ltd., G6 Tek Guan Place, 56-60, Jalan Sultan, (673) 2-23127.

Botswana (Gaborone)--Manica Travel Ltd., Botsaland House, The Mall, POB 1188, 352021.

Brazil (Rio)--Kontik-Franstur S.A., Avenida Atlantica 2316-A, Copacabana, (21) 235-1396.

British Virgin Islands (Tortola)--Travel Plan Ltd., Waterfront Plaza, (809) 494-6239.

Chile (Santiago)--Turismo Cocha, Augustinas 1173, 698-2164, or 698-3341.

China (Beijing)--China Wrld. Tr. Ctr.,1 Jian Guo Men Wai, 100004, Tel. 5052639, or 5054406.

Costa Rica (San Jose)--Tam Travel, Avenidas Central-Primera, 4th Fl.,POB 1864, 33 00 44.

Denmark (Copenhagen)--AMEX Int'l, Amagertorv 18 (Stroget), 33122301.

Egypt (Cairo)--AMEX of Egypt, six offices, call (2) 750444, (Luxor)--Old Winter Palace Hotel, (95) 82862.

Fiji (Nadi)--The Travel Co. Ltd., Nadi Int'l Airport, POB 9240, 72325.

Finland (Helsinki)--Area Travel, Pohjoisesplanadi 2, SF 00100, Tel.(0) 18551.

France (Paris)--AMEX Travel, 11 Rue Scribe, (1) 47 77 77 07; (Bordeaux)--AMEX V.F., 14 Cours Intendance, (56) 81 70 02.

Germany (Berlin)--AMEX Travel Service, Kurfuerstendamm 11, (30) 882-7575; (Frankfurt/Main)--8 Kaiserstrasse, D-6000, (69) 21050.

Greece (Athens)--AMEX Int'l, 2 Hermou St., Constitution Square, (1) 324 4975.

Hong Kong--AMEX Int'l, New World Tower, 16-18 Queen's Road, Central, (5) 844-8668.

India (New Delhi)--AMEX Int'l Banking Corp., Wenger House, Connaught Place, (11) 332-4119.

Indonesia (Jakarta)--Pacto Ltd., Jalan Surabaya, No. 8, POB 2563, Tel. (21) 34864.

Ireland (Dublin)--AMEX Travel Service, 116 Grafton Street, (1) 772874.

Israel (Tel Aviv)--Meditrad Ltd., 16 Ben Yehuda St., POB 4312, (3) 294654.

Italy (Rome)--AMEX Co. S.P.A., Piazza Di Spagna 38, (6) 676411; (Milan)--Via Brera 3, (2) 85571; Venice--1401 San Moise, (41) 520-0844.

Japan (Tokyo)--AMEX Int'l, Toranomon Mitsui Bldg., 3-8-1 Kasumigaseki, Chiyoda-ku 100, (3) 3508-2400.

Kenya (Nairobi)--Express Kenya Ltd., Bruce House, Standard Street, POB 40433, (2) 334722.

Malaysia (Kuala Lumpur)--Mayflower Acme Tours, Bangunan Angkasa Raya Jalan Ampang, GPOB 10179, (3) 248-6700.

Mexico (Mexico City)--AMEX Travel Service, Paseo de la Reforma 234, (5) 33 03 80; (Cozumel)—Fiesta Cozumel, A. Rafael Melgar 27, (987) 20974.

Morocco (Casablanca)--Voyages Schwartz, S.A., 112 Ave. du Prince Moulay Abdullah, 2731-33 or 2780-54.

Nepal (Kathmandu)--Yeti Travels Pvt. Ltd., Hotel Mayalu, Jamal Tole, POB 76, Tel. 227635.

New Zealand (Auckland)--95 Queen St., POB 2412, (9) 798243; (Christchurch)--Guthrey's Trav., 126 Cashel St., (3) 793560.

Norway (Oslo)--Winge Travel Bureau, Karl Johans Gare 33, Oslo 0121-1, Tel.(2) 412030.

Peru (Lima)--Lima Tours S.A., Belen 1040, POB 4340, Tel. (14) 27 6624.

Philippines (Manila)--AMEX Int'l, Grd. Fl., Philamlife Bldg., Ave Ermita, (2) 509601-02.

Portugal (Lisbon)--Star Travel Service, Avda Sidonio, Pais 4-A, (01) 539871.

Singapore--AMEX Travel Service, UOL Bldg., 96 Somerset Road, Singapore, 235 5788.

Spain (Madrid)--AMEX of Spain, 2 Plaza de Las Cortes, (1) 429-57-75.

Sweden (Stockholm)--AMEX Travel Service, Birger Jarlsgatan 1,`POB 1761, Tel. (8) 143 980.

Switzerland (Geneva)--AMEX Travel Service, 7 Rue Du Mont Blanc, (22) 731-7600.

Tahiti (Papeete)--Tahiti Tours, Rue Jeanne D'Arc, BP 627, Tel. (689) 427870.

Thailand (Bangkok)--Sea Tours Co. Ltd., 965 Rama 1 Road, Siam Center, (2) 251 4862.

Turkey (Istanbul)--Turk Ekspres Travel, Cumhuriyet Caddesi 91, Kat 1, Elmadag, (1) 1301515.

United Kingdom (London)--AMEX Trav. Service, 6 Haymarket, (71) 930-4411; (Edinburgh)--139 Princes St., (31) 225-9179.

USSR (Moscow)--AMEX Travel Service, 21-A Sadavo-Kudringskaya St., (95) 254-2111.

Yugoslavia (Belgrade)--Atlas Yugoslav Travel Agency, Zmaj Jovina 10, (11) 183-062, or `183-160.

EXCHANGE RATES

Here are selected exchange rates for certain major currencies. Use these for rough approximations only. Exchange rates shift daily; you should consult a current business newspaper for the latest figures.

One US dollar ($1.00) equals:

Argentina	9920	*Australs*	**Italy**	1250	*Lira*
Australia	1.25	*Australian Dollars*	**Japan**	128	*Yen*
Austria	11.7	*Shillings*	**Mexico**	3100	*Pesos*
Brazil	620	*New Crusados*	**Nepal**	22	*Nepal Rupees*
Britain	.56	*Pounds Sterling*	**New Zealand**	1.77	*NZ Dollars*
Canada	1.12	*Canadian Dollars*	**Norway**	6.44	*Krones*
Denmark	6.4	*Krones*	**Philippines**	27	*Pesos*
Egypt	3.3	*Egyptian Pounds*	**Peru**	.92	*Inti*
France	5.7	*Francs*	**Portugal**	140	*Escudos*
Germany	1.63	*Deutsche Marks*	**Singapore**	1.68	*Sing. Dollars*
Greece	185	*Drachmas*	**Spain**	104	*Pesetas*
India	26	*Rupees*	**Sweden**	5.97	*Kronas*
Indonesia	1980	*Rupiahs*	**Switzerland**	1.43	*Swiss Francs*
Ireland	.62	*Irish Pounds*	**Thailand**	25.5	*Baht*
Israel	2.35	*Shekels*	**Turkey**	4600	*Turkish Lira*

INTERNATIONAL COMMUNICATIONS

TELEPHONES

You will find it either very easy or very difficult to phone home from foreign countries. There doesn't seem to be any middle ground. Either a country has a modern, direct-dial phone network with English-speaking operators, or things will be hopeless--phones will be hard to find and often out of order, operators will be unskilled, and connections will be poor. You often have to wait in long lines in crowded post offices, or carry buckets of coins.

Do bring an AT&T international calling card. It will be useful in Europe and in large cities in Asia, although more calls can be made with a VISA or Mastercard from airports and hotels. Telephone calls to and from Europe are relatively cheap, if dialed direct. Most Western European phone networks do not impose a flat fee for the first few minutes of overseas calls, so you can place a quick call for very little money. AT&T's USADIRECT service will connect you directly with an American operator when calling home from over 150 countries, including Australia, Austria, Belgium, the British Virgin Islands, Denmark, Finland, France, Germany, Hong Kong, Japan, the Netherlands, Norway, Sweden, and the United Kingdom. Call (800) 874-4000, ext. 375 for a pocket-sized card listing all countries linked to USADIRECT and their applicable access codes. You will be billed at US rates, which saves money from most destinations. AT&T also offers Voice Mark message service, which allows travelers to record and send messages to any telephone worldwide. Call (800) 562-6275.

MAIL & MESSAGES

American embassies will not hold mail or telephone messages for US citizens abroad, except in the case of true emergencies, such as a death in the family. If you have an American Express card, however, American Express offices worldwide will receive and hold mail, telegrams and phone messages. For mail, the sender should mark the envelope "Client Letter Service," print the recipient's last name in block letters and underline it. Call American Express Customer Service at (800) 528-4800 for a worldwide list of participating offices. EurAide also offers a 24-hour telephone answering service for travelers in Europe. Your caller dials a clearinghouse in Europe, which holds messages for the traveler who can call in later over local phone lines. Or the traveler may leave messages for his friends and relatives back home. Cost is $15 to subscribe, plus $15 per week or $40 per month; EurAide operates from May through the first week of October. Contact EurAide, Inc., P.O. Box 2375, Naperville, IL 60567, (708) 420-2343.

INTERNATIONAL COUNTRY CODES

Argentina-213	Ireland-353
Australia-61	Italy-39
Austria-43	Japan-81
Belgium-32	Kenya-254
Bolivia-591	Mexico-52
Brazil-55	Monaco-33
Chile-56	Netherlands-31
China-86	New Zealand-64
Colombia-57	Norway-47
Costa Rica-506	Peru-51
Denmark-45	Portugal-351
Ecuador-593	Singapore-65
El Salvador-503	Spain-34
Fiji-679	Sweden-46
Finland-358	Switzerland-41
France-33	Tanzania-255
Germany-49	Thailand-66
Greece-30	Turkey-90
Hong Kong-852	United Kingdom-44
India-91	Venezuela-58
Indonesia-62	Zaire-243
Israel-972	Zimbabwe-263

To call internationally via AT&T, dial 011, plus the country code, listed above, followed by the area or city code, and the number. The AT&T long-distance operator (dial 00) can obtain foreign area and city codes for most locations worldwide.

In most places in the world, you can receive mail addressed to you care of "Poste Restante" (general delivery). Although the name of the city, province and country will probably be enough, try to supply the sender with the street address of the city's main post office as well. Your name should be printed in block letters and underlined. When receiving Poste Restante mailings, be sure to check under both your first and last names, especially in Asia.

FAX machines have not yet become universal. You will still have to rely on telexes and telegrams in most third world countries. Remember, most telegrams are not instantaneous, but require postal delivery at some point. Thus, allow three to six days for a telegraphic message to reach a party in the United States. You'll find that it is often cheaper to telephone than to send a telegram or telex.

LANGUAGES

English, the official tongue of 426,000,000 people in 40 countries, and the second language of choice in Europe, Asia and the Middle East, is, without question, the most useful language for travelers. You may be surprised at how well you can get by speaking only English in places like Indonesia, Malaysia, Thailand, Egypt, and in most of Africa. We stress this to assure you that you should not put off traveling because of perceived language barriers.

Having said this, however, we also advise that you *should* try to learn some of the language of the countries or regions which you will be visiting. If nothing else, learning numbers through 20 and how to say "please" and "thank you" will win you friends and probably save you money. Also, before you launch into English, ask politely in the local language if the person you're addressing speaks English. Invariably the answer is "a little bit," and your courtesy will be appreciated. Lonely Planet publishes a fine series of *Survival Guides* which include good, basic language primers. Before you head off to a foreign country, get one of these guides, or a Berlitz phrasebook, and practice, practice. The most useful second language for American travelers is Spanish, followed by French.

Serious language training programs for Spanish, French, German and other European languages are available on cassettes from Berlitz, (800) 257-5755, and from International American Schools, 1731 N. Western Avenue, Los Angeles, CA 90027, (213) 469-4488. Language cassettes for all romance languages, as well as Arabic, Japanese, Mandarin, Greek, Russian, Korean, Indonesian, Hindi, Swahili and Thai are available from Audio-Forum, 96 Broad Street, Guilford, CT 06437, (800) 243-1234, or (203) 453-9794.

ORGANIZING YOUR TRIP

ESSENTIAL TRAVEL ITEMS

Here are a dozen easy-to-pack items that every traveler should carry, no matter what the destination or how long the trip.

1) Flashlight, preferably a mini-maglight or other sturdy, waterproof model. Headlamps work great, but make you look like a miner.

2) Small, deluxe folding umbrella--take it with you on the plane, if your destination is anywhere but central Africa.

3) Small, autofocus camera with zoom lens--it's unobtrusive, and will give you great candid shots of locals if you just point and shoot, without raising the camera to your eye. Bring spare batteries.

4) Plastic bottle of iodine--purifies water, and is one of the best antiseptics since you can see where you put it.

5) US $10 Notes--take them wherever you go. American dollars will get you to the airport, and out of trouble, just about everywhere.

6) Medium-sized clear, Tupperware box--use this for your medicines, pills and other easy-to-lose items that should be kept dry. See-through feature appeals to customs agents.

7) Travel clock/calculator--you will use the calculator constantly. Sharp makes a very handy combination alarm clock/calculator that automatically figures exchange rates for two foreign countries.

8) Bic pens and writing paper--if you visit the third world, it'll break your heart to see so many kids with nothing to write with. Take these along as gifts.

9) AloeGator sunblock--it is good for your skin, and is the only waterproof sunscreen that will really stand up to a full day on the river, or in the surf.

10) Cheapo Casio--buy a $15 water-resistant watch as a back-up, set to US time. When you leave, give it away to a local kid.

11) Wide adhesive tape--you will use this to repair your body and gear, and it can also secure valuables out of sight.

12) Sewing kit--Make sure you have some good scissors, safety pins and heavy thread, plus spare buttons.

ADVENTURE INFORMATION

For current information on a variety of outdoor activities, consult **Patagonia's Guideline**, a free service offering tips on where to go and what outfitters to use. Call (800) 523-9597 between 9 AM and 5PM Mountain Time. Listed activities include: rock-climbing, mountaineering, backpacking, whitewater and ocean kayaking, canoeing, rafting, alpine and nordic skiing, fly-fishing and sailing.

The **Official Recreation Guide** (ORG) provides an on-line directory of outdoor activities offered by more than 1,000 outfitters and tour companies. This commercial database can be accessed by anyone with a modem-equipped PC, though it is designed primarily for travel agents. The sheer amount of data can be overwhelming; the system works best if you have a very specific destination in mind. The initial "get-acquainted" session is free. For more information, contact ORG, 100 Second Street East, Whitefish, MT 59937, (800) 826-2135; FAX: (406) 862-6954, or America On-Line (800) 827-6364.

RESOURCES

American Express Traveler's Companion. This invaluable pocket guide covers all the essentials: passports, communications, health, emergency aid, and of course traveler's check refunds. Available free to AMEX cardholders, (800) 528-4800.

Directory of Alternative Travel Resources, One World Family Network, 81868 Lost Valley Lane, Dexter, OR 97431, (503) 937-3351. $7.00. Good listing of cooperative travel groups, working vacations and public interest vacations.

Going Places: The Guide to Travel Guides, is a newly published 772-page resource which reviews more than 3,000 travel guides. You'll also find listings of 75 travel bookshops nationwide. Available for $17.95 from the Harvard Common Press, 535 Albany St., Boston, MA 02118, (617) 423-5803.

The Traveler's Handbook, edited by Melissa Shales, offers useful information on personal security, airline travel, money matters, and other topics of interest to travelers. The essays are dull, but the appendices are invaluable, with listings of visa requirements, mailing regulations, embassies and consulates worldwide, and hundreds of travel publications. Buy this book; every serious traveler should have one. $15.95 from Globe Pequot Press.

World Business Travel Guide is not just for briefcase toters. It includes customs and visa requirements, basic foreign language guides, and maps for 140 cities worldwide. $9.95 at major bookstores.

Lonely Planet Newsletter. This quarterly updates the superb Lonely Planet guidebooks, and contains firsthand tips from travelers in the field. $10 yearly from Lonely Planet Publications, 155 Filbert St., Ste. 251, Oakland, CA 94607, (800) 229-0122.

Great Expeditions, a Canadian magazine, reports on adventure tours and activities worldwide, and offers free classified ads for subscribers--this is a good way to find a travel partner. Contact Great Expeditions, P.O. Box 800-411, Sumas, WA 98295, (604) 852-6170.

Epilogue _____

It is our hope that we have provided you with more than mere references, more than a wish list. We hope that this book, through words and pictures, has served to inspire you to experience all that life has to offer.

Free your mind, and your feet will follow.
-Anonymous

Snowboarding in the Ruth Amphitheater, Alaska Range/CHRIS NOBLE

IMAGES OF ADVENTURE

THE PHOTOGRAPHERS

The vast majority of the images in the book are the creation of professional photographers. Here's a rundown on 38 of the leading shooters who contributed to this edition--those who ran the rivers, climbed the mountains, and flew the skies to capture the world of adventure on film.

ANDY ANDERSON, Fairchild, WA (Fishing). Air Force firefighter Anderson missed the call to Desert Storm, but his fishing images are among America's very best.

RON BEHRMANN, Albuquerque, NM (Ballooning). Behrmann, probably the most prolific balloon photographer in the world, has shot just about every kind of balloon from every angle.

GARY BRETTNACHER, Ketchum, ID (Fishing, Skiing). Brettnacher is one of America's most versatile outdoor photographers, covering everything from heli-skiing to auto racing.

NATHAN BILOW, Crested Butte, CO (Fishing). A versatile, globe-trotting shooter, Bilow photographs a wide variety of sports from snowboarding to fly-fishing.

TIM BROWN, Salida, CO (Kayaking, Rafting). Brown captures the excitement of whitewater sports with colorful, dynamic images.

TOM CAMPBELL, Santa Barbara, CA (Underwater). Campbell, a professional divemaster and dive tour leader, is one of California's leading undersea photographers.

DENNIS COELLO, Salt Lake City, UT (Bicycling). Coello has a vast collection of two-wheeled images from destinations around the globe.

RICH COX, Reseda, CA (Motorcycles). One of the leading motorcycle and aircraft photographers in America, Cox shoots in a studio or on the move with equal skill.

ALAN FORTUNE, Astoria, NY (River-running). Alan specializes in the waterways of the Northeast. His carefully composed shots are ultrasharp, with rich saturated colors.

MARK GALLUP, Calgary, ALB, Canada (Skiing, Youth). A winter sports specialist, Gallup has also supplied many images taken at Canadian summer youth camps.

STEVE GILROY, Bradford, MA (Nature, Rafting, Safaris). Gilroy has utilized his specialty of whitewater photography to explore the most remote regions of Africa, Alaska, South America and the Soviet Union.

DIDIER GIVOIS, St. Béron, France (Hanggliding, Paragliding, Skiing, River Running). An expert skier and hangglider pilot, Givois has produced

Towers of Paine National Park, Chile/GALEN ROWELL

some of the most vivid images in this book.

JOHN HEINEY, San Clemente, CA (Hanggliding, Paragliding). A champion aerobatic pilot, Heiney shoots with remote cameras mounted on the wings and nose of his hangglider.

LIZ HYMANS, Belvedere, CA (Rafting). Ace river guide Hymans has rafted and photographed many of North America's classic rivers.

DARRELL JONES, Miami Lakes, FL (Fishing, Windsurfing). Jones, photo editor of Windrider magazine, shoots all the major water sports.

JAMES KAY, Salt Lake City, UT (Skiing, Windsurfing). Kay covers a wide variety of outdoor sports around the world and has a very impressive New Zealand file.

JOHN KELLY, Telluride, CO (Fishing, Horses, Skiing, Windsurfing). One of the Image Bank's top ten producers, Kelly shoots virtually every outdoor sport from skiing to mountain biking.

ACE KVALE, Verbier, Switzerland, (Skiing, Mountaineering, Paragliding). From New Zealand to the Swiss Alps, Kvale and partner

cal skill with the eye of an artist. We are more than fortunate to be able to use his work here.

KEVIN O'BRIEN, Somerset, PA (River-running). Living only a stone's throw from some of America's best wild rivers, O'Brien specializes in whitewater images.

NEIL RABINOWITZ, Bainbridge Island, WA (Sailing). In heavy demand by magazines and advertisers, Rabinowitz has few peers in the world of boating photography.

RICK RIDGEWAY, Adventure Photo--Ventura, CA (Arctic, Mountaineering, Sailing). Veteran of major summit climbs and Antarctic expeditions, Ridgeway owns and operates the Adventure Photo stock agency.

JOEL ROGERS, Seattle, WA (Mountaineering, Sea Kayaking). Rogers is America's leading ocean kayaking photographer. His latest book, *The Hidden Coast--Kayak Explorations*, was released in the spring of 1991.

GALEN ROWELL, Mountain Light--Albany, CA (Mountaineering, Trekking). You are looking at a Galen Rowell shot of Patagonia. He is considered by many to be the father of adventure photography.

TOM SANDERS, Aerial Focus--Santa Barbara, CA (Paragliding, Skydiving). Sanders uses helmet-mounted cameras while freefalling. He has filmed the skydiving sequences for many major motion pictures.

MARTY SNYDERMAN, San Diego, CA (Underwater). A prolific shooter, Snyderman has captured many unusual sea creatures on film, including whale sharks and giant manta rays.

SCOTT SPIKER, Moscow, ID (Ballooning, Biking, Skiing, Whitewater). A promising new photographer, Spiker already has a great portfolio of skiing, whitewater and ballooning shots.

DAVID STOECKLEIN, Ketchum, ID (Fishing, 4WD, Horses, Skiing, Trekking). Stoecklein has one of the biggest stock files in the business--from fishing in Belize to heli-skiing in the Bugaboos.

ELAN SUNSTAR, Kailua, HI (Hanggliding, Windsurfing). Sunstar's shots are instantly recognizable for their fantastic colors, beautiful bodies and creative camera angles.

GORDON WILTSIE, Bishop, CA (Arctic, Mountaineering). A veteran of polar expeditions and major summit climbs, Wiltsie has captured the frontiers of adventure.

CHUCK WILEY/AMY WALES, Durango, CO (River-running). Two expert river guides, Wiley and Wales have assembled more memorable raft, canoe and kayak images than just about anyone in the business.

ART WOLFE, Seattle, WA (Nature, Trekking). Easily one of the top ten nature/wildlife photographers in the world, Wolfe's work has been featured in many outstanding books including *Alakshak*, and *The Kingdom*.

CHRIS WOODS, Telluride, CO (Soaring). Woods' soaring photos set the standard by which others are judged, and his soaring videos, such as *Running On Empty*, are the best ever made.

JEFFREY ZWART, Santa Ana, CA (Automotive Sport). Zwart's racing images are painterly and impressionistic--the automobile as art.

Mark Shapiro have captured the challenge and drama of alpine sports.

FRANS LANTING, Minden Pictures--Aptos, CA (Nature, Safari). Lanting may be the most traveled wildlife photographer on the planet. From Africa to Antarctica, he has recorded classic images of the natural world.

SCOTT MARKEWITZ, Salt Lake City, UT (Skiing, Rock-climbing, Biking). A true professional, Markewitz's work is always carefully composed and ultra-sharp.

DAVID MUENCH, Santa Barbara, CA (Scenic). Muench is America's preeminent wilderness and landscape photographer.

MICHAEL NICHOLS, VA (Jungle, Nature, Rafting). Nichols has ventured into the jungles of Borneo and the Amazon to capture some of the most haunting images of the primitive world.

CHRIS NOBLE, Salt Lake City, UT (Biking, Mountaineering, Rafting, Skiing). By any measure, Noble is one of the finest outdoor photographers in the world. He combines great techni-

INDEX

THIS INDEX COVERS SIGNIFICANT DESTINATIONS AND ACTIVITIES WORLDWIDE. BE AWARE THAT MANY HUNDREDS OF OTHER LOCATIONS AND TRIPS ARE INCLUDED in this book but could not be indexed due to space limitations. Usually you can find what you want by looking under an activity (such as skiing), and then checking the subheadings within that chapter. Leading outfitters and training centers are indexed on page 432.

OUTFITTER INDEX

Listed below are some of our preferred outfitters or tour companies for the major activities covered in the book. Many have earned a ★★★★ rating or better, and most offer substantial discounts as part of our Adventure Passport program (see page 7.) Consult the topical chapters for comprehensive listings of hundreds of other tour companies, training centers, resorts, and sporting associations.

NOTE: *Discounts are subject to change and may not be available for all itineraries and all seasons. Each outfitter sets its own discount conditions.*